Hatred of America's Presidents

HATRED OF AMERICA'S PRESIDENTS

Personal Attacks on the White House from Washington to Trump

Lori Cox Han, Editor

An Imprint of ABC-CLIO, LLC

Santa Barbara, California • Denver, Colorado

Library of Congress Cataloging-in-Publication Data

Names: Han, Lori Cox, editor.
Title: Hatred of America's presidents : personal attacks on the White House from
    Washington to Trump / Lori Cox Han, editor.
Description: Santa Barbara, California : ABC-CLIO, 2018. | Includes index.
Identifiers: LCCN 2017059986 (print) | LCCN 2017060777 (ebook) |
    ISBN 9781440854378 (ebook) | ISBN 9781440854361 (hard copy : alk. paper)
Subjects: LCSH: Presidents—United States—History. | Presidents—United States—
    Biography. | United States—Politics and government.
Classification: LCC E176.1 (ebook) | LCC E176.1 .H39 2018 (print) | DDC 973.09/9—dc23
LC record available at https://lccn.loc.gov/2017059986

ISBN: 978-1-4408-5436-1 (print)
       978-1-4408-5437-8 (ebook)

22   21   20   19   18   1   2   3   4   5

This book is also available as an eBook.

ABC-CLIO
An Imprint of ABC-CLIO, LLC

ABC-CLIO, LLC
130 Cremona Drive, P.O. Box 1911
Santa Barbara, California 93116-1911
www.abc-clio.com

This book is printed on acid-free paper ∞

Manufactured in the United States of America

CONTENTS

ACKNOWLEDGMENTS

The author, or in this case, editor, of any book that publishes generally has many people to thank for their assistance throughout the process. First and foremost, I am grateful to each of the contributors to this volume for sharing both their time and expertise on the American presidency. It is their knowledge and insight that makes this book a unique contribution to the presidency literature. The guidance and support provided by Kevin Hillstrom and Barbara Patterson at ABC-CLIO were greatly appreciated from start to finish. Two undergraduate research assistants at Chapman University—Jake Kunkel and Brianna Pressey—also provided help with researching the broader topic of presidential hatred, scouring countless databases to see what articles and books existed on this topic. Finally, as always, I am grateful for the support I receive from my family, including my son Davis and my daughter Taylor, and especially my husband, Tom Han, who provides unconditional support for every research project on which I embark. His knowledge of American history and his skill at copyediting my work are invaluable.

Introduction

On May 17, 2017, President Donald J. Trump addressed the graduates at the U.S. Coast Guard Academy. In his address, as is routine for presidents when they speak at a military academy commencement, Trump thanked the cadets and their families for their service to the nation and spoke about policy objectives for his administration. Perhaps not so routine for this type of venue was Trump's partially off-script remarks about his ongoing feud with many in the news media:

> Now, I want to take this opportunity to give you some advice. Over the course of your life, you will find that things are not always fair. You will find that things happen to you that you do not deserve and that are not always warranted. But you have to put your head down and fight, fight, fight. Never, ever, ever give up. Things will work out just fine. Look at the way I've been treated lately—(laughter)—especially by the media. No politician in history—and I say this with great surety—has been treated worse or more unfairly. You can't let them get you down. You can't let the critics and the naysayers get in the way of your dreams.

Whether Trump's assertion is true may depend on not only one's political perspective but also one's historical knowledge of the presidency. Judging to what extent a president has been treated unfairly by or attacked in media coverage is hardly an objective exercise. Supporters of Trump would probably argue that this president, attempting to govern in the volatile and hyperpartisan political environment of 2017, faced unprecedented personal and political attacks and even hatred from opponents in the Democratic Party (for example, the movement to "resist") as well as the Republican Party (the "Never Trump" movement). Those who oppose Trump might argue that the attacks and hatred are justified. Of course, Trump can give as good as he gets when it comes to verbal vitriol; for example, his use of Twitter throughout his campaign and the early months of his presidency included regular attacks against "fake news" and certain members of the press, including this statement on Twitter @realDonaldTrump on February 17, 2017: "The FAKE NEWS media (failing @nytimes, @NBCNews, @ABC, @CBS, @CNN) is not my enemy, it is the enemy of the American People!"

However, hatred of an American president did not originate with Trump, and Trump is certainly not the first president to have enemies who attempt to delegitimize his presidency. Bill Clinton (who was impeached in 1998) and Richard Nixon (who resigned in 1974 over Watergate) certainly come to mind, though they are far from the only presidents who have dealt with political enemies before, during, and after their time in office. Although the hatred and harsh attacks directed at more recent presidents (Clinton, George W. Bush, Barack Obama, and Trump) may seem normal due to influences such as increased partisan polarization and the advent of social media, to name a few, this scorched-earth, blood-sport, smash-mouth style of presidential politics transcends all eras of the American presidency. No president, whether a founding era luminary such as George Washington or Thomas Jefferson, a prominent 19th-century president like Andrew Jackson or Abraham Lincoln, or a notable president of the 20th century like Woodrow Wilson or Franklin D. Roosevelt, has been immune to various personal or political lines of attack. And whether a president is considered great, mediocre, or a dismal failure in the eyes of both presidential scholars and the American public makes little difference when considering the number of attacks and/or scandals each president endured. When considering presidential "greatness" and rankings of former presidents, a topic on which much scholarship has been devoted over the years, those near the top of the list often ranked among the presidents who were subjected to the most widespread and sustained personal attacks.

The most severe form of hatred, of course, has come in the form of assassination, with four presidents dying in office as the result of an assassin's bullet (Abraham Lincoln in 1865, James Garfield in 1881, William McKinley in 1901, and John F. Kennedy in 1963). In addition, serious threats or attempts of assassination have targeted many other presidents (including Andrew Jackson, William Howard Taft, both Roosevelts, Herbert Hoover, Harry Truman, Richard Nixon, Gerald Ford, Jimmy Carter, Ronald Reagan, both Bushes, Bill Clinton, and Barack Obama). Perhaps the most notable was against Reagan in March 1981, when he (along with his press secretary, James Brady, a U.S. Secret Service agent, and a D.C. police officer) was shot outside the Washington Hilton, though all four survived. Since Trump took office, calls for the president's assassination have been frequent. For example, in August 2017, a Democratic state senator from Missouri posted on Facebook her desire for Trump to be assassinated, and during the Women's March in Washington, D.C., on January 21, 2017, Madonna told the crowd that she had "thought an awful lot about blowing up the White House." These types of incidents are investigated by the Secret Service as credible threats to a president's safety and are not protected forms of speech.

The nature of the American political system assumes that a politician at the national level will have enemies—those who do not support their policy agenda or those who just do not like the president personally. Although the type of presidential enemies, lines of attack, and scandals have differed over the years, all presidents have faced hatred, contempt, political attacks, and bad press coverage. The intensity and extent of the hatred, however, has varied in response to a host of factors. This stems from the fact that for all of the institutional similarities that each president encounters while in office, each administration is also unique in many ways—the president's personality (temperament, intellect, governing style, communication strategy), his family (differing roles and public images of the first lady, first children, and other family members), and the political environment in which the president is elected and attempts to govern (electoral coalition, strength of party control in Congress, the economy, world events, and public support). Even the state of the news media as an industry can affect the tone and content of White House coverage, as the competitive nature of news as a consumer-driven product has, at times, provided sensational and biased coverage (such as during the "yellow journalism" era at the turn of the 20th century and the "clickbait" era of online news sources that has become more prominent during the past decade).

DEFINING HATRED

Various definitions of hatred exist, though it can be generally defined as an intense dislike or hostility directed at someone or something. Several synonyms exist as well, such as loathing, aversion, animosity, or ill will, to name a few. When considering hatred that is directed at presidents, the definition can be a bit more specific as some similarities do exist in what drives the hatred. Nearly all presidents were politicians prior to taking office (with George Washington, Dwight Eisenhower, and Donald Trump as notable exceptions), and nearly all willingly sought the office, knowing what the job entailed (those vice presidents who succeeded to the presidency might be exceptions, though they still campaigned for the position of vice president; Gerald Ford might be the only true exception as he was never elected to either office).

Hatred has also existed at different stages in each president's life. Some, like Theodore Roosevelt and Bill Clinton, entered politics at an early age and thus made enemies early in their political career. Roosevelt was just 23 when he was elected to his first political office as a member of the New York State Assembly; Clinton was 30 when he was first elected attorney general of Arkansas, after losing a congressional race two years prior. Some had to contend with family baggage, such as John Quincy Adams and George W. Bush, whose fathers, John Adams and George H. W. Bush, served as president before them; Benjamin Harrison's grandfather, William Henry Harrison, preceded him in the Oval Office (though briefly); and John F.

Kennedy's father, Joseph P. Kennedy, served as a controversial figure as FDR's ambassador to Great Britain during the buildup to World War II. Many, if not all, presidents experienced numerous lines of personal and political attacks during nomination battles and/or the general election when seeking the presidency. Clinton is again a good example, as he survived numerous scandals involving marital infidelity, draft dodging, and even his attempt at smoking marijuana (considered controversial at the time) throughout the 1992 presidential election. Most presidents have experienced intense policy fights while president, especially when attempting to pass major piece of legislations (like Lyndon Johnson with civil rights in 1964, or Barack Obama with health care reform in 2009). Many presidents have also battled negative press coverage, like Richard Nixon, who had a strained relationship with reporters from the time he first entered politics in 1947 until he died in 1994. Many presidents enjoy somewhat of a reprieve from negative press coverage and personal/political attacks when they leave office, though a few, like Nixon and Clinton, had some attacks continue in their post-presidential years.

Another factor that plays into this dynamic can be partly explained by aspects of the study of political psychology, personality, and leadership. Although presidential scholars have long debated the usefulness of analyzing presidents as individuals, leadership style and its connection to a president's personality can be a determining factor in success or failure. Whether it is through what Fred Greenstein calls the "presidential difference" that personality can exert on governing, or James David Barber's assessment of presidential character to determine psychology and personality types, a president's leadership style and public persona reflect not only his attitude about governing but also how he is viewed by other political actors as well as voters. Some presidents (like Clinton) have enormous political skill in dealing with the public aspects of the job, and can therefore withstand attacks and scandals better than others (like Nixon) who are not as adept at communicating and/or playing politics. Both Clinton and Nixon are also good examples of how presidential personalities can be flawed and, as a result, can lead to self-inflicted wounds during their time in office.

The role of media, the expansion of technology, and the growth in the public aspects of the presidency have also played a role in many lines of attack against presidents. The news media have always been among the most influential political actors with which presidents must contend. The presidential–press relationship is often adversarial since the president and reporters have different goals—the president wants positive coverage about the actions and policies of his administration, but "big" stories for the news media (which in turn mean higher ratings and circulations) usually come from negative and scandal-oriented stories about the president and/or his administration. Rarely has a president not complained about the news media, the White House press corps, and the coverage he was receiving. Presidents since the 1930s have also had to grapple with public opinion polling. Whether a president's poll numbers really make a difference in governing is difficult to prove, though the press has often covered the trend line of presidential approval as if the fate of each administration hangs in the balance. In addition to presidential approval, many pollsters also inquire as to whether people "like" the president personally; often, a president has a higher rating for likability than job approval (both Reagan and Obama are good examples of this).

The election of Trump in 2016 has certainly brought the issue of presidential hatred to the forefront, as it raises numerous questions about a president's ability to govern with such intense hatred, and even contempt (which is often defined as anger minus respect) directed at a president. This issue would undoubtedly still be a factor had Hillary Clinton won the 2016 presidential election instead, though for different reasons. Both Trump and Clinton were lightning rods for controversy, scandal, and intense hatred during the campaign, and both experienced high negatives in polling throughout 2016. Poll after poll showed that for each candidate, a majority of those polled disliked and distrusted both candidates—so much so, in fact, that the contest came to be described by many observers as one in which voters felt that they were choosing between "the lesser of two evils."

The legacy of the 2016 presidential campaign, as well as the early months of the Trump presidency, presents an interesting question that only time, and future presidencies, may resolve—does the intense polarization of the current political environment breed presidential hatred, or is it candidate driven? In other words, was the intensity of hatred for both major party candidates in 2016, which carried over into the Trump presidency, a passing phase, or is this the new normal?

PLAN OF THE BOOK

To provide a better understanding of the current state of affairs as related to hatred of presidents, this edited volume provides historical and political context to explain how we got to this point. The following pages offer essays written by both political scientists and historians on each of the 44 men who have held the office of president, beginning with Washington and ending with Trump (though the assessment of Trump's enemies and hatred directed at him only considers his first few months in office, while a more complete analysis is offered of the presidents who preceded him). Although each essay is unique in the story it tells about each individual president, the common theme in each essay focuses on the most prevalent personal and political lines of attack, each president's most prominent enemies, and scandals or controversies that generated significant volumes of vitriol toward the president in question. Perhaps the most important question that is addressed throughout the book is how these issues influenced the president's ability to govern, as well as the impact on the presidency as a political institution. As these essays show, some presidents weathered the storm of hatred better than others; often, the political circumstances at the time (such as the state of the economy, the president's popularity, or whether he was facing reelection) helped to determine if the president was able to effectively combat the attacks, and thus, survive politically.

Further Reading

Barber, James David. *The Presidential Character: Predicting Performance in the White House*, rev. 4th ed. New York: Prentice Hall, 2008.

Cottam, Martha L., Elena Mastors, Thomas Preston, and Beth Dietz. *Introduction to Political Psychology*, 3rd ed. New York: Routledge, 2016.

Cronin, Thomas E., and Michael A. Genovese. *The Paradoxes of the American Presidency*. New York: Oxford University Press, 1998.

Emery, Michael, Edwin Emery, and Nancy L. Roberts. *The Press and America: An Interpretive History of the Mass Media*, 9th ed. Boston: Allyn and Bacon, 2000.

Greenstein, Fred I. *Personality and Politics: Problems of Evidence, Inference, and Conceptualization*. Chicago: Markham Publishing, 1969.

Greenstein, Fred I. *The Presidential Difference: Leadership Style from FDR to Barack Obama*, 3rd ed. Princeton, NJ: Princeton University Press, 2009.

Han, Lori Cox, ed. *New Directions in the American Presidency*, 2nd ed. New York: Routledge, 2018.

Han, Lori Cox, and Diane J. Heith. *Presidents and the American Presidency*, 2nd ed. New York: Oxford University Press, 2018.

Milkis, Sidney M., and Michael Nelson. *The American Presidency: Origins and Development, 1776–2014*, 7th ed. Washington, D.C.: CQ Press, 2016.

Mills, Nicolaus. "Savaging Presidents." *Dissent*, Vol. 48, No. 3 (Summer 2001): 44–48.

Ragsdale, Lyn. *Vital Statistics on the Presidency*, 4th ed. Washington, D.C.: CQ Press, 2014.

1. George Washington

Born: February 22, 1732

Died: December 14, 1799

Time in Office: First President of the United States, April 30, 1789, to March 4, 1797

Election Results: 1789 Election: 69 (100%) Electoral College votes; 1792 Election: 132 (100%) Electoral College votes

Spouse: Martha Dandridge Curtis (m. 1759)

As the first president of the United States, George Washington has always stood apart as the individual who, perhaps more than any other president, defined and shaped the office. After serving as the commander of the Continental forces during the Revolutionary War, Washington was the head of the U.S. executive branch from April 1789 through March 1797. Washington won unanimous victories in both of his presidential elections. In January 1789, the nation's first presidential contest after ratification of the Constitution, Washington won with 69 electoral votes; he tallied 132 in 1792. One of the most important and acclaimed decisions of his career was to choose not to run for a third term, thereby establishing the precedent of a peaceful transfer of power from one president to the next. Washington married widow Martha Dandridge Curtis in 1759, and while Washington never had any children of his own, Martha had two children from her previous marriage, both of whom died before Washington became president. Martha died three years after her husband, in 1802.

It may seem curious to find an essay about George Washington in a volume about criticism and hatred of presidents. Washington was beloved during and after his tenure in public life and remains one of the most venerated public figures in American history, consistently ranking among the top four presidents in virtually all ranking lists. As Joseph Ellis, author of the biography *His Excellency: George Washington*, wrote: "It seemed to me that Benjamin Franklin was wiser than Washington; Alexander Hamilton was more brilliant; John Adams was better read; Thomas Jefferson was more intellectually sophisticated; James Madison was more politically astute. Yet each and all of these prominent figures acknowledged that Washington was their unquestioned superior. Within the gallery of greats so often mythologized and capitalized as Founding Fathers, Washington was recognized as *primus inter pares,* the Foundingest Father of them all."

In the polarized politics of the 21st century, many citizens nostalgically view Washington's administration as a time of unity in politics—a time when real statesmen all worked together for the good of the country. In truth, though, there was a good deal of dissension even in Washington's era. At times these differences prompted the kind of virulent and harsh attacks more typically associated with contemporary politics. Not even Washington escaped unscathed from these clashes. Although Washington remained popular throughout his tenure as president, he faced significant criticism on several fronts, including claims that he was a failure as the commander of the U.S. Army during the American Revolution and that he tried to turn the country into a monarchy, to name just two.

Ultimately, Washington found himself presiding over a nation that was increasingly partisan. Although he aspired to rise above the dissension between the Federalists and Republicans, Washington's policies decidedly favored the Federalists, and not surprisingly this angered the opposition. The harshest criticism came from the most extreme Republicans and appeared in newspapers and pamphlets, but even moderate Republicans expressed a great deal of anger at Washington's policies, even if they were not willing to engage in attacks on his character. By and large, however, Washington retained broad support throughout much of the country. It is somewhat ironic that the president who was so adamantly opposed to factions and political parties was also the first partisan president; however, the dissension during his administration demonstrated the ability of the U.S. political system to accommodate political disagreement without violence and rebellion.

WASHINGTON AND THE PARTISAN PRESS OF THE 18TH CENTURY

Although contemporary presidents likely view the Washington years as a time of relative political comity, without the constant bombardment of the 24-hour news cycle on television and the Internet or the fear that the slightest misstep might be broadcast to millions of people almost instantaneously, 18th-century newspapers served up their fair share of attacks on public figures. Twenty-first-century America is still getting accustomed to a media that is more partisan than it had been for the latter half of the 20th century, but 18th-century newspapers were more partisan yet. This was apparent during the debate over the ratification of the Constitution, and it continued when Washington was president. Due to his popularity, Washington was not typically subject to personal attacks, but after he issued the Neutrality Proclamation in 1793 (which declared that the United States would remain neutral in the war between Great Britain and France), the Republican press editors were willing to directly target him in print. Although he remained civil in the face of such vitriol, he worried that the growing factionalism would undermine the legitimacy of the government. As it turned out, factionalism became the norm in American politics.

During Washington's presidency newspapers were generally subsidized by political parties, and their content reflected the views of that party. *The Gazette of the United States*, edited by John Fenno, supported the Federalists and Washington (although Washington did not regard himself as a Federalist, most political elites perceived his agreement with Alexander Hamilton on most issues to be evidence of his Federalist stripes). *The Gazette* was financially stable due to government printing contracts it obtained through Hamilton, who served as secretary of the treasury. Thomas Jefferson and the Republicans were so angry about the rhetoric of *The Gazette* that Jefferson and James Madison encouraged Philip Freneau to start a Republican newspaper, *The National Gazette*, which benefited from government printing contracts through Jefferson. *The Philadelphia General Advertiser Aurora*, edited by Benjamin Bache, was another prominent anti-Federalist newspaper. Bache, Benjamin Franklin's grandson, was one of Washington's fiercest critics. One piece in *The Aurora*, dated September 11, 1795, erroneously declared that "the name of Washington will descend with his [Alexander Hamilton's] into oblivion."

Although the editor of a given newspaper controlled the content within, it was extremely common during Washington's era for well-known political figures to write pieces under pseudonyms. The famed *Federalist Papers* consisted of individual pieces whose author was listed as "Publius." Just as the authors of the *Federalist Papers* are known to be Madison, Hamilton, and John Jay, the authors of other anonymous pieces were often known. The point is that while most political criticism during that era appeared in newspapers, political criticism did not originate exclusively with journalists. Political figures sometimes used newspapers as the medium through which to communicate their criticism. Jefferson was known to have written some of the articles critical of Washington, for instance.

Given that these newspapers were supported directly by the parties, there was no incentive to be objective and balanced. The readership of newspapers was partisan, and the editors published stories for their audiences. Since Washington was strongly opposed to political parties and factions, he was baffled and frustrated to find himself the target of Republican attacks. Some scholars believe that the relentless criticism he received from those quarters during his second term was a factor in his decision to leave public office. In a letter to Hamilton dated August 26, 1792, Washington expressed concern that newspapers were fomenting an extremism that could result in the dissolution of the country: ". . . I would fain hope, that liberal allowances will be made for the political opinions of each other; and, instead of those wounding suspicions, and irritating charges, with which some of our gazettes are so strongly impregnated, and cannot fail, if persevered in, of pushing matters to extremity, and thereby to tear the machine asunder, that there might be mutual forbearances and temporizing yieldings *on all sides*. Without these, I do not see how the reins of government are to be managed, or how the Union of the States can be much longer preserved." Media critics in the 21st century often complain about the trend toward more partisan news sources and the loss of the "traditional" role of the media as objective arbiter, but in truth, the partisan media of the

21st century is not a new trend, but a return to the type of media found in the 18th and 19th centuries.

REPUBLICAN ATTACKS ON WASHINGTON

Although the disagreements between the Federalists and the Republicans during Washington's administration had existed since the Constitutional Convention and the ratification campaign (when the Republicans were known as Anti-Federalists), Washington's national popularity insulated him from direct criticism throughout his first term. Conflict was most visible in the relationship between Jefferson, the secretary of state in Washington's first term, and Hamilton, secretary of the treasury. Hamilton's vision for the nation involved an energetic federal government that promoted national prosperity through the encouragement of commerce. Jefferson was leery of a large commercial republic and believed that liberty was best promoted by the state and local governments that were most attentive to the circumstances and needs of their citizens. They also differed sharply in their perspective on foreign allies. Jefferson thought the United States' natural ally was France, given its support of the American Revolution and shared democratic ideals. Hamilton was an admirer of the British government and saw in that alliance the prospect of economic and strategic benefits. Although both Jefferson and Hamilton were initially united in their support of Washington even in the face of significant policy differences, as time went on it was increasingly difficult for the two to work together. It was also increasingly clear to Jefferson that Washington favored Hamilton's policies.

The conflict between the Federalists and Republicans did not significantly touch Washington until the passage of the Neutrality Proclamation in 1793. Up until that point any criticism of the administration's perceived pro-British bias was directed at Hamilton. And, indeed, the Republican newspapers frequently criticized Hamilton's policies, both in terms of his preference for Britain as an ally, as well as his economic policies, such as the creation of a national bank.

When France declared war on Great Britain in 1793, the Americans faced a dilemma. On the one hand, many believed that the United States had an obligation to help France. Not only had France given critical aid during the American Revolution, the alliance had been formalized in the Treaty of Alliance of 1778. Siding against France would be a violation of the treaty. On the other hand, the commercial relationship with Britain was more beneficial than that with France. In addition, the prospect of taking a side would inevitably turn the other side into a powerful enemy, which was not a desirable situation for a younger and weaker country. Washington was torn and ultimately decided to simply stay out of the conflict altogether. After consultation with his cabinet, he issued a proclamation which stated that the United States would follow "a conduct friendly and impartial toward the belligerent powers." This statement of neutrality infuriated the Republicans, who felt it was a policy that resulted in consequences that were not neutral at all but rather were injurious to France. Because the neutrality policy was established by Washington himself in a unilateral statement, anger was directed at Washington personally. And once the personal criticism started, it grew far beyond the disgust with the Neutrality Proclamation, expanding to include much of Washington's career. It was almost as though Washington's decision to remain neutral in the French-British conflict was the excuse Republicans needed to attack his entire record.

Most of the criticism directed at Washington came from the Republican newspapers, and one in particular was responsible for the most sustained attacks on Washington—the *Aurora,* edited by Bache. On November 18, 1795, the paper printed a letter to the editor arguing for Washington's impeachment: "The opinion that the President ought to be impeached is gaining proselytes daily, and will soon become general as the subject is more fully understood. . . . The revolution was certainly never designed to benefit the President alone, and if he can exercise unconstitutional and unlawful powers, because he was the commander in chief of the American army, then the revolution was designed alone for his aggrandizement."

Bache was a radical Democrat who had never been a strong supporter of Washington. The editor perceived him to be part of a political elite that was not firmly committed to the democratic ideals of the revolution. Washington's popularity prevented Bache from printing serious criticism before 1793, but the widespread Republican anger against the proclamation created an opportunity for Bache to target Washington directly. The *Aurora* printed stories criticizing Washington on every imaginable front. His manners were considered to be overly formal, smacking of elitism; the fact that he was so well dressed was said to be another indication of elitism and demonstrated that Washington was not a man of the people; his leadership of the Continental Army during the American Revolution was described as weak, and it was alleged that his career was salvaged only because the French came to the colonies' aid; his actions as president were said to enlarge the role of the executive at the expense of elected representatives, leading the nation toward monarchy as demonstrated by his decision to use state militias to forcibly halt protests against taxes on spirits (more commonly known as the Whiskey Rebellion); he was labeled a criminal for his practice of drawing funds from the government that amounted to advances on his salary; and even the public celebration of his birthday was framed as evidence of Washington's intent to turn himself into royalty. In addition to Bache's *Aurora,* Freneau's *National Gazette* also printed sharp criticism of Washington until the newspaper went out of business in late 1793.

The backlash against Washington after the Neutrality Proclamation increased after the ratification of the Jay Treaty in 1795. Treaty negotiations had begun in 1794 when John Jay, chief justice of the United States, was chosen to travel to Britain to negotiate a treaty to establish a firm commercial relationship between the two countries, as well as to resolve some outstanding territory and compensation issues dating back to the Revolutionary War. Reaction to the resulting treaty terms was not positive overall, but Republicans and the South were especially outraged. First, the fact of the matter was that no treaty negotiated by a Federalist would be satisfactory to Republicans and southerners, and the Jay Treaty was no exception. For example, the absence of any provision for compensation to slave owners for the loss of slaves that the British set free during the revolution infuriated them. Throughout the country mass meetings were held to protest the treaty; petitions of opposition were signed, and opponents in the press continued to attack anyone associated with the treaty.

Bache's *Aurora* was at the forefront of the charge against the treaty and Washington, who had signed the treaty into law. The following excerpt of a letter to Bache, dated August 21, 1795, is an example: ". . . we are deemed incapable to judge of our own interests, and too stupid to distinguish truth from falsehood? Or does the President fancy himself the *Grand Lama* of this country that we are to approach him with superstitious reverence or religious regard? His answer to the citizens of Philadelphia bespeaks a contempt of the people, that no other evidence than his own letter would render credible. He has disdained to look down with an eye of complacency from that eminence on which they have placed him . . . We have been guilty of idolatry too long, punishment is pursuing us for it, it is high time that we should no other Gods than one."

The passage from this letter is typical of the Republican criticism of Washington after he signed the Jay Treaty. It demonstrates the personal character of the criticism, accusing Washington of perceiving himself to be above and separate from ordinary citizens, even godlike. Although support for the treaty was lukewarm even on the Federalist side, the Federalist newspapers refrained from significant criticism and defended Washington against the Republican attacks.

In addition to newspapers, several pamphlets were issued with the sole purpose of attacking Washington. The most notable was a piece by Patrick Henry. It was called *Letters to George Washington* and was a long tirade covering much of the same ground found in the *Aurora*. Henry's narrative was more personal, however, because he blamed Washington for refusing to allow him to claim his U.S. citizenship when he was in a French prison. Not coincidentally, Bache published the pamphlet.

WASHINGTON'S RESPONSE TO ATTACKS

Washington struggled in the face of the Republican attacks even though he did not publicly react to them. His difficulties were threefold. First, he truly believed that he was not a partisan, so he thought his critics were simply wrong. He remained convinced that he evaluated policies in terms of the national interest, not the narrow interest of factions. Unlike contemporary presidents who expect partisan criticism, Washington was surprised and hurt at what he perceived to be false claims. As he wrote in a letter to Timothy Pickering, secretary of war, on July 27, 1795: ". . . much indeed to be regretted, party disputes are now carried to such a length, and truth is enveloped in mist and false representation, that it is extremely difficult to know through what channel to seek it. *This difficulty to one, who is of no party, and whose sole wish is to pursue with undeviating steps a path, which would lead this country to respectability, wealth, and happiness, is exceedingly to be lamented*" (emphasis added). Here he describes himself as a man with no party, a characterization with which most Republicans and many Federalists would disagree.

Another facet of his frustration with Republican criticism was that it violated his conception of gentleman-like behavior, which was extremely important to him. From the time of his youth he had felt keenly his lack of a gentleman's classic education and devoted a great deal of effort learning how to live up to those standards. One of the ways Washington educated himself was by following the advice he found in a book called *110 Rules of Civility and Decent Behavior in Company and Conversation*. He copied down all the rules and strived to follow them. Among the rules were those that required a person to "make oneself pleasing to others" and to "detract not from others." For a person who devoted his life to becoming a real gentleman, the discourse coming from the Republican newspapers certainly qualified as speech that detracted from others and did little to appear pleasing to its readers. Washington found it terribly vulgar—exactly the opposite of what was expected in polite society.

The third and final reason that Washington was so disturbed by the personal attacks is that he believed that attacks on him as president were also attacks on the national government. Washington had always been cognizant of the fragility of the new nation, and he calculated virtually all his actions to strengthen not only the country's safety and prosperity, but its national identity. This was true in terms of policies, such as remaining neutral during the war between France and Great Britain, but also his personal comportment. Washington recognized the symbolic importance of the presidency, and his personal behavior (and even appearance) were designed to encourage respect. In his eyes, respect for the president was closely tied to respect for the institution of the presidency and by extension, the national government. By this reasoning, the Republican attacks did not simply offend Washington personally, they undermined the legitimacy of the nation—a new nation that was still trying to form a cohesive union out of a group of independent-minded states. He believed that factional discourse (such as accusations of promoting or enacting unconstitutional measures) made negotiation and consensus virtually impossible. In addition to Washington's substantive objections to hateful rhetoric, Washington personally did not handle criticism well. One of his biographers, William Guthrie Sayen, described him as "thin-skinned," saying, "His internal critic was so fierce that he could not easily tolerate the additional burden of external critics."

Washington was not the only one who found the tone of the criticism disturbing. Jefferson, for example, was not a fan of Washington's policies, and he even wrote anonymous newspaper articles that criticized those policies. But he did not support the level of invective contained in the Republican criticism of Washington. The same was true of other elites. Although Republicans were adamantly opposed to many of Washington's policies, most were unwilling to publicly attack the president's character, and thus those attacks were communicated by newspaper editors or anonymous articles printed in newspapers.

CONCLUSION

It is often said that Washington is more than an important figure in American history; he has become a kind of mythical hero who embodies all the values Americans hold dear. As the myth of Washington gained currency in American political culture, his human failings have been nearly forgotten. It is difficult today to associate the myth of Washington with the harsh criticism he received during his second term. Although it is not uncommon for public memory to "forget" events of the past, it is perhaps more understandable in terms of Washington, for his symbolic authority has always overshadowed his policy decisions and accomplishments. Unlike most of our favorite leaders, whose mistakes and failings diminish the further we move from their time in office, Washington's status as "father of the country" was established even while he was president. Certainly, the partisanship of the era engulfed Washington as it did other political leaders of the time, but the worst criticism came from a few of the most extreme opponents and did not extend to the country at large.

It is difficult to explain entirely the symbolic power that attaches to Washington, but surely it is important that his appearance and behavior were always presidential. Despite his frustration with what he perceived to be unfair criticism, he never responded in kind. Some of his critics argued that his formality was a liability because it made Washington seem less a "man of the people" and more of an elite. Overall, however, Washington was perceptive in understanding the importance of his role in building the new nation. Although his vanity no doubt prompted some of the attention he spent calculating ways to project the right image, he also believed it was his duty to establish precedents that helped solidify the national government. To this end, he was nearly obsessed with making sure that his appearance and actions always projected qualities one would want in a nation: strength, civility, honesty, loyalty, and humility. For all intents and purposes he succeeded. As Americans respected Washington, so were they inclined to respect and support the government he led. According to John Cabot Lodge, "He had imparted to it the dignity of his own great character." Washington was much more of a partisan than he realized, but his decision to resist engaging in partisan attacks of his own helped to establish a level of legitimacy for the government that made peaceful partisan conflict possible.

Karen Hoffman

Further Reading

Ellis, Joseph J. *His Excellency: George Washington.* New York: Alfred A. Knopf, 2004.

Lodge, Henry Cabot. "Washington as Party Man." In *George Washington,* Book 2. New Rochelle, NY: Arlington House, 1970.

McDonald, Forrest. "Treaties and Intrigue, 1795–1796." In *The Presidency of George Washington.* Lawrence, KS: University Press of Kansas, 1974.

Phelps, Glenn A. "George Washington and the Paradox of Party." *Presidential Studies Quarterly,* Vol. 19, No. 4 (Fall 1989): 733–745.

Rosenfeld, Richard N. *American Aurora: A Democratic-Republican Returns.* New York: St. Martin's Griffin, 1997.

Saven, William Guthrie. "George Washington's 'Unmannerly' Behavior: The Clash between Civility and Honor." *The Virginia Magazine of History and Biography,* Vol. 107, No. 1 (Winter 1999): 5–36.

Tagg, James D. "Benjamin Franklin Bache's Attack on George Washington." *The Pennsylvania Magazine of History and Biography,* Vol. 100, No. 2 (April 1976): 191–230.

Tebbel, John, and Sarah Miles Watts. *The Press and the Presidency: From George Washington to Ronald Reagan.* New York: Oxford University Press, 1985.

Viles, Jonas, ed. *George Washington: Letters and Addresses.* New York: Sun Dial Classics, 1909.

2. John Adams

Born: October 30, 1735
Died: July 4, 1826
Time in Office: Second President of the United States, March 4, 1797, to March 4, 1801
Election Results: 1796 Election: 71 (51.4%) Electoral College votes; 1800 Election: 68 (49.3%) Electoral College votes
Spouse: Abigail Smith (m. 1764)
Children: Abigail, John Quincy, Susanna, Charles, Thomas, and Elizabeth

John Adams was born in Braintree, Massachusetts, on October 30, 1735, and died on July 4, 1826, the 50th anniversary of the adoption of the Declaration of Independence and the same day as his longtime friend and political rival, Thomas Jefferson.

Adams's wife, Abigail, was known for being intelligent and articulate about politics; she served as a lifelong adviser to her husband and was influential in her husband's administration. Adams served as the second president of the United States from 1797 to 1801, after serving as vice president to George Washington for two terms. Adams's unprecedented election was the first presidential one involving rival political parties and the only time the president and vice president were elected from opposing party tickets. The presidential election of 1796 was pre-Twelfth Amendment, so the candidate receiving the most Electoral College votes won the presidency, and the candidate with the second highest vote total won the vice presidency. Adams, supported by the Federalists, received the most Electoral College votes (71) and won the presidency. But, Jefferson, supported by the Democratic-Republicans and their campaign efforts, received the second highest number of votes (68) and won the vice presidency. Overall, Adams's presidency and reelection efforts were overshadowed by hatred from members of the rival Democratic-Republican Party and from members of his own party, especially Alexander Hamilton.

INTERPARTY CONFLICTS: DEMOCRATIC-REPUBLICANS AND THE PRINTED PRESS

After serving as vice president for eight years, Adams was hesitant to openly declare his interest in running for president once Washington retired. As he wrote in a letter to his wife, dated February 10, 1796, Adams believed he had the "firmness of Mind enough to bear [the presidency] like a Man, a Hero and a Philosopher." However, in a letter dated January 20, 1796, he also recognized he would become the "Butt of Party Malevolence," as a "vast Body of People Partly Antifederalist, partly desperate Debtors and partly frenchified Tools, will murder all good Men among Us and destroy all the Wisdom and Virtue of the Country." Once Washington made his retirement official, many Federalists showed signs they intended for Adams to succeed Washington. Writing to his wife on March 3, 1796, Adams wrote: "I find the V.P. toasted at most of the Feasts and even Brown has announced Mr. Adams's appearance at the Theatre with Pleasure. And this is as I conjecture Electioneering." Adams welcomed the Federalists' support for his presidential bid. Yet, this presidential election would be different from those preceding it. Previously, there was no question Washington would be elected president, as he won both elections by running unopposed and by a unanimous vote in the Electoral College. Without Washington, there was uncertainty in the choice of president, and rival political parties competed against each other, as Federalists endorsed Adams and Thomas Pinckney and the Democratic-Republicans endorsed Jefferson and Aaron Burr.

Because the election of 1796 was prior to ratification of the Twelfth Amendment, each presidential elector cast their two votes without distinguishing between president and vice president. In other words, without designation, every vote cast was a vote for president. This created an electoral difficulty for both parties because they had to worry about the possibility of an inverted ticket. For example, the Democratic-Republicans could cast one of their votes for a Federalist candidate if they believed their candidates did not have enough support to win both the presidency and vice presidency. Although most Federalists preferred Adams as president, the Democratic-Republicans could vote for Pinckney to elect him as president rather than Adams. Indeed, Pinckney's home state of South Carolina cast all its votes for Jefferson and Pinckney. To prevent the inverted ticket, the Federalists had to ensure Adams received the most votes while diverting just enough votes away from Pinckney to keep him a close second. However, diverting votes away from Pinckney to ensure an Adams victory introduced the possibility of a split ticket. If Pinckney received too few votes, it would allow the Democratic-Republicans to elevate their candidate to the second spot. This is precisely what happened, as Adams received the most Electoral College votes (71) and Jefferson the second most (68); Pinckney came in third (59). This divided executive did not produce conciliation between the parties, and with the rise of partisan newspapers, Adams became the subject of vehement opposition in the press.

Adams faced both domestic and foreign difficulties shortly after taking office. France, enraged by the Jay Treaty, attacked American merchantmen, threatened to seize any ships carrying British goods, and refused to receive Charles Pinckney (older brother of Thomas Pinckney), who was recently appointed as American minister to Paris. Fearing the inevitability of war with France, Adams sent American commissioners to Paris to hopefully resolve the crisis. After arriving, however, talks of negotiation were based on the commissioners paying bribes to French commissioners, and attempts at resolution ultimately failed. This "XYZ Affair" kindled support for war with France, and only staunch Democratic-Republicans stood in opposition. The Democratic-Republicans turned to the printed press, particularly Benjamin Bache's *Philadelphia Aurora*, to express their dissatisfaction with the Adams administration and the Federalists' agenda. Indeed, since its introduction in 1784, the *Aurora* had been used to denounce the Federalist Party, and not even Washington was immune from attacks.

Those opposed to Adams and the Federalist Party used the printed press as a means of attacking both the president's character and his policies. For example, the following appeared in the *Aurora* on April 27, 1798: "The aspect of affairs in America is . . . mysterious and alarming . . . [I]t would be ludicrous to suppose that the querulous and cankered murmurs of blind, bald, crippled, toothless Adams . . . can have any other effect than to afford additional and experimental proof of the folly of trusting such men with power." The *Aurora* was not alone. In the *Richmond Examiner* in 1800, James Thomson Callender described the president as a "strange compound of ignorance and ferocity, of deceit and weakness," a "hideous hermaphroditical character which has neither the force and firmness of a man, nor the gentleness and sensibility of a woman." Therefore, "take your chance between Adams, war, and beggary, and Jefferson, peace and competency." The attacks on his character continued: "That scourge, that scorn, that outcast of America . . . a repulsive pedant, a gross hypocrite, and an unprincipled oppressor [who] . . . in private Life . . . [was] one of the most egregious fools on the continent." Articles often took a sarcastic tone in deriding the president, as did this one in the *Aurora* on June 8, 1798: "TO HIS SERENE HIGHNESS JOHN ADAMS—PRESIDENT OF THE UNITED STATES. The factions and *'unprincipled mercenaries'* who opposed your election compose no part of the American citizens. . . . What, could men who had their country's good at heart have aided in opposition to *you*! To *you*, who are the oracle of all wisdom and the fountain of all patriotism!" Partisan press outlets thus took an active role in framing public opinion against Adams's character.

In addition to attacks on his character, the Democratic-Republicans assailed Adams's policies. The president's appointment of his son, John Quincy Adams, as minister to Prussia and as a commissioner to Sweden drew the opposition's ire in the *Aurora* on March 16, 1798: "[I]t was the duty of every father to provide handsomely for his son, especially when it can be done at public expense. Our hint has been taken, and JOHN Q. ADAMS has been appointed for Stockholm . . . an appointment so repugnant to every idea of propriety." Likewise, the Democratic-Republicans interpreted many of Adams's policy decisions as adverse to democracy and tending toward monarchy. They took every opportunity to remind the public of his alleged preference for monarchy, interpreting the war with France as one that was really being waged against democracy. Indeed, critics wrote in the *Aurora* on March 24, 1798, that he wanted to "reestablish monarchy and thereby maintain that favorite government which Mr. Adams . . . declared 'is the most stupendous fabric of human invention.'" Domestically, in the *Aurora* on March 19, 1798, they warned readers that "JOHN ADAMS . . . would deprive you of a voice in chusing your president and senate, and make both hereditary—this champion for kings, ranks, and titles is to be your president."

In response to these sustained attacks, the Federalists in Congress joined with Adams to pass the controversial Alien and Sedition Acts, which criminalized written, printed, uttered, or published "false, scandalous and malicious . . . writings against the government of the United States . . . or the President . . . to excite against them . . . the hatred of the good people of the United States." Condemning this law as a violation of constitutional rights guaranteed in the First Amendment, the *Aurora* on May 17, 1798, described the gravity of the situation surrounding Adams's reelection: "That there is cause for alarm no one can deny; but that this cause is domestic and not foreign is too palpable to be questioned . . . [W]hile you are [busied] in preparing for an imagined enemy, the real enemy is assaulting the citadel of your dearest privileges . . . and ere long will you be convinced to your sorrow that it was for *independence* and not for *liberty* that the present President of the United States contended." For the Democratic-Republicans, the election of 1800 was more than a choice between Jefferson and Adams; it would decide the very form the U.S. government would take.

INTRAPARTY CONFLICTS: ALEXANDER HAMILTON AND LEADERSHIP OF THE FEDERALIST PARTY

Although antagonism from a rival party was expected, Adams also faced opposition from his own party, specifically Alexander Hamilton. Prior to Adams's presidential campaign, Adams and Hamilton both served in Washington's administration without any apparent animosity between the two statesmen. However, hostilities surfaced during the election of 1796. Although Hamilton supported both Adams and Pinckney, he expressed his preference for the latter and attempted to coordinate electoral votes to elevate Pinckney to the presidency. Hamilton's electioneering was no secret to Adams, and he referred to Hamilton, in a letter to his wife dated January 9, 1797, as a "proud spirited, conceited, aspiring Mortal always pretending to Morality, with as debauched Morals as old Franklin who is more his Model than any one I know. As great an Hypocrite as any on the U.S." Animosity between the two Federalists escalated once Adams took office.

Hamilton was not formally part of Adams's administration. However, he was close with many members of Adams's cabinet members, who corresponded with Hamilton frequently on policy issues. It was clear to Adams that many Federalists in the administration were willing to take their cues from Hamilton rather than from him. Contention heightened when Adams attempted to purge his cabinet of Hamilton's influence. He asked for the resignation of his secretary of war, James McHenry, and his secretary of state, Timothy Pickering, who he suspected were influenced by Hamilton. And in a direct blow to Hamilton, Adams refused to promote him to the lieutenant general and commander in chief of all the armies, a position held by George Washington until his death. Even though Hamilton was the ranking major general, Adams chose to leave the post vacant. In response to Adams's "perverseness and capriciousness" (as expressed in a letter from Hamilton to Rufus King on January 5, 1800), Hamilton began preparations to turn the Federalist Party against Adams and his potential reelection.

In May 1800, a Federalist congressional caucus declared its support for Adams and Pinckney in the upcoming presidential election. By June, Hamilton was actively promoting Pinckney, as he believed Adams was unfit for the presidency. In a letter to Theodore Sedgwick dated May 10, 1800, Hamilton even went so far as to express his preference for the election of Jefferson over Adams, and he threatened to leave the party if the Federalists continued to support such a "weak and perverse man" as Adams. The August prior to the 1800 presidential election, Hamilton penned a critical review of Adams's character, actions, and decisions as president. Despite admonitions from fellow Federalists against publicly denouncing Adams, Hamilton published his *Letter from Alexander Hamilton, Concerning the Public Conduct and Character of John Adams, Esq. President of the United States* in October 1800.

Hamilton made his intentions clear within the opening paragraphs of the *Letter*: While acknowledging that there was no denying Adams's patriotism, integrity, and particular talents, Hamilton asserted that "he does not possess the talents adapted to the *Administration* of Government, and that there are great and intrinsic defects in his character, which unfit him for the office of Chief Magistrate." Based on his observations of Adams's actions prior to his presidency, Hamilton asserted Adams was "a man of an imagination sublimated and eccentric; propitious neither to the regular display of sound judgment, nor to steady perseverance in a systematic plan of conduct; and I begin to perceive what has been since too manifest, that to this defect are added the unfortunate foibles of a vanity without bounds, and a jealousy capable of discoloring every object." Furthermore, Adams displayed a "disgusting egoism, the distempered jealousy, and the ungovernable indiscretion of [his] temper, joined to some doubts of the correctness of his maxims of Administration." In light of his actions as president during his first term, Hamilton concluded that Adams was not worthy of the office: "Occurrences which have either happened or come to light since the election of Mr. Adams to the Presidency, confirming my unfavorable forebodings of his character, have given new and decisive energy, in my mind, to the sentiment of his unfitness for the station." Hamilton concluded his *Letter* with an unconvincing statement of support for the Federalist Party attempting to reelect Adams. Hamilton made it clear he did not support Adams, but he claimed he would not openly attempt to prevent his reelection, as he recognized the "great importance of cultivating harmony" among the Federalists. Deciding to only distribute the pamphlet among Federalists, Hamilton's *Letter* made it clear the type of harmony he sought—a Federalist Party united around someone other than Adams.

CONCLUSION

Newspapers, particularly the partisan press, were an indispensable tool for political parties during the early republic, as papers contributed to organizing partisan efforts, connected voters and activists to a party, and disseminated information to ideologically congruent voters, particularly during elections. Editors of partisan newspapers took active roles in the political process by framing relevant issues for readers (as the *Aurora* did on July 13, 1798): "It is by the dissemination of such salutary truths as are contained in the Aurora and a few other Republican papers that the eyes of the people will be opened." The *Aurora* believed the Federalists passed the Alien and Sedition Acts because they feared the power of the partisan press, and the election of 1800 would determine the nature of scope of the First Amendment and freedom of the press (June 28, 1798): "The people may be gagged by alien and sedition bills; but at elections; they will make their voice heard." Moreover, the *Aurora* believed that it and other members of the partisan press had a hand in preventing Adams's reelection, as it published the following on March 4, 1801, the day of Jefferson's inauguration: ". . . never to trust great power to any man or body of men: never to entrust it long: to preserve to the people the right of recalling at short periods every person placed by them in a political situation; and to preserve inviolate the freedom of the press. The importance of these political maxims were first felt and acted upon in AMERICA. . . . In 1798 and 1799, monarchy openly exulted, and democracy was a term of bitterest reproach. The execrable planners of this dangerous and desperate system, thanks to the freedom of the press, are now fallen; fallen, we sincerely hope, to rise no more."

Regarding Hamilton's *Letter*, it is difficult to measure the impact its publication had on the election. However, historians maintain that it helped prevent Adams's reelection and further fractured the ever-weakening Federalist Party. Hamilton's intention of only distributing the *Letter* to the Federalists was undermined when it was leaked to the Democratic-Republicans, and excerpts appeared in the *Aurora* shortly after Hamilton published it. At the very least, the Democratic-Republicans used the *Letter* to further their opposition efforts against Adams and the Federalists. Indeed, James Madison called it "an important *Denoument* [sic]," a "Thunderbolt," and, in a letter to Jefferson dated November 1–3, 1800, he rejoiced because the *Letter* meant "that Republicanism is likely to be completely triumphant." The Federalist Party lost the election of 1800 and would soon lose their majorities in Congress, never to regain them.

Washington unanimously won the first two presidential elections. His successor, Adams, however, faced an altered political landscape, as political parties produced bitter partisan battles. Adams experienced hatred and defamation from the rival Democratic-Republican Party and many of the Federalists from within his own party. Subsequently, Adams became the first to lose a presidential election as an incumbent (his son, John Quincy Adams, was the second). Adams knew he would not have Democratic-Republicans' support, so he blamed the Federalists' lack of organization and identity in a letter to Benjamin Stoddert dated March 31, 1801: "No party that ever existed knew itself so little, or so vainly overrated its own influence and popularity, as ours." Overall, Adams recognized the difficulty of winning a presidential election without the support of a party, particularly his own.

Robert E. Ross

Further Reading

Adams Family Papers: An Electronic Archive. Massachusetts Historical Society. Available at http://masshist.org/digitaladams.

Brodie, Fawn McKay. *Thomas Jefferson: An Intimate History.* New York: Norton, 1974.

Dunn, Susan. *Jefferson's Second Revolution: The Election Crisis of 1800 and the Triumph of Republicanism.* New York: Houghton Mifflin, 2004.

Elkins, Stanley, and Eric McKitrick. *The Age of Federalism: The Early American Republic, 1788–1800.* New York: Oxford University Press, 1993.

National Archives. *Founders Online.* Available at http://founders.archives.gov.

Pasley, Jeffrey L. "The Two National 'Gazettes': Newspapers and the Embodiment of American Political Parties." *Early American Literature,* Vol. 35, No. 1 (2000): 51–86.

Pasley, Jeffrey L. *The Tyranny of Printers: Newspaper Politics in the Early American Republic.* Charlottesville, VA: University Press of Virginia, 2002.

Rosenfeld, Richard N. *American Aurora: A Democratic-Republican Returns.* New York: St. Martin's Press, 1997.

Watson, Robert P. "The First Lady Reconsidered: Presidential Partner and Political Institution." *Presidential Studies Quarterly,* Vol. 27, No. 4 (Fall 1997): 805–818.

Wilentz, Sean. *The Rise of American Democracy: Jefferson to Lincoln.* New York: W. W. Norton, 2005.

Wood, Gordon. *Empire of Liberty: A History of the Early Republic, 1789–1815.* New York: Oxford University Press, 2009.

3. Thomas Jefferson

Born: April 13, 1743

Died: July 4, 1826

Time in Office: Third President of the United States, March 4, 1801, to March 4, 1809

Election Results: 1800 Election: 73 (52.9%) Electoral College votes; 1804 Election: 162 (92%) Electoral College votes

Spouse: Martha Wayles Skelton (m. 1772)

Children: Martha, Mary, Lucy, Peter, and Jane

Thomas Jefferson was born in his father's home in the Virginia colony on April 13, 1743. He died on the 50th anniversary of the Declaration of Independence, on July 4, 1826. Jefferson was elected president in 1800, but not through a majority of the Electoral College. The election of 1800 included several contestants: Aaron Burr, a senator from New York; John Adams, the incumbent president and Massachusetts native; Charles Pinckney, from South Carolina, who was serving as the minister to France; and Jefferson, sitting vice president under Adams. Jefferson and Burr tied in the Electoral College, with 73 votes each, and as no one candidate secured a majority of the electoral votes, the election went to the House of Representatives for the first time under the new constitutional system. After 35 ballots in the House, Jefferson was ultimately elected on the 36th ballot. Jefferson easily won reelection in 1804 against Charles Pinckney, the first election to follow the ratification of the Twelfth Amendment, which changed the process for candidates running for president and vice president, essentially putting them together, on the same ticket.

In both contests, Jefferson ran as a member of the Democratic-Republican Party. Jefferson concluded his tenure as president in 1809 when he was succeeded by his friend, colleague, and fellow Virginian, James Madison. Jefferson was married to Martha Wayles Skelton, a widow, on January 1, 1772. Martha Jefferson had six children with Thomas Jefferson (including an unnamed son who died within a few weeks of birth), and she died only months after giving birth to her seventh child (she had borne a child to her first husband, and that child also died at a young age). Martha and Thomas Jefferson were married for 10 years before she died. Two Jefferson daughters survived to adulthood, Martha and Mary. Jefferson also had a relationship with one of his slaves, Sally Hemmings. Although there has long been great controversy swirling around this relationship, the Thomas Jefferson Foundation concluded in 2000 that Jefferson and Hemmings sustained a relationship over time, and that Jefferson fathered several children with Hemmings.

Jefferson, as one of the nation's founders and one of its early presidents, has been a somewhat controversial figure throughout U.S. history. His great achievement of writing the Declaration of Independence, a document that gave words to the spirit of independence and desire for liberty among the colonists in 1776, inaugurated him as the poet of American Independence. To a degree, this accomplishment wrapped him in some protective coating when it came to public attitudes toward his political life and presidency. Thus, while he was the subject of many attacks, hatred, and ridicule during his time as president, Jefferson, both as an actual politician and as the embodiment of a certain patriotic ideal, have both been regarded in generally positive terms for more than 200 years.

EARLY ATTACKS

Although Jefferson was generally respected in his early public life, especially for his efforts in the Continental Congress and his authoring of the Declaration of Independence, he was not without his detractors even then. At the time that Jefferson penned the Declaration, he included in the document antislavery language and advocated for abolition. This led to attacks against him from slaveholders—and later prompted criticism from abolitionists who took notice when he did nothing to get rid of slavery. As Virginia abolitionist Moncure Conway stated, "Never did a man achieve more fame for what he did not do."

In the spring and summer of 1781, Virginia came under attack by the British, and one of the British officers, Sir Banastre Tarleton, devised a scheme to undermine the colonial defenses. As the British were making their way through Virginia, which did not have an adequate defense against these incursions, Jefferson was completing his term as governor of the commonwealth. In early June, the British implemented Tarleton's scheme to capture members of the Virginia legislature and Governor Jefferson. Jefferson and several of the legislators who were staying with him at Monticello got word of the coming attack and fled. The legislators left for Staunton, and Jefferson, according to Dumas Malone, sent his family ahead of him first to "Colonel Carter's Belnheim, where he joined them for dinner, and somewhat later to the Coles place, Enniscorthy . . . [ultimately] he took them to his own Poplar Forest in Bedford County." Much was made of this—as letters were written about the events, especially the letters from Eliza Ambler to Mildred Smith noting "the terror and confusion . . . Governor, Council, everybody scampering. . . ." These letters and this narrative became known to John Marshall and others, and became an early line of attack against Jefferson that followed him throughout his public life. The Virginia legislature would later move to investigate Jefferson's conduct during this period, but nothing came of it and he was subsequently thanked for his well-run administration. This incident, which was complicated, in part, because Jefferson's term as governor had expired but the assembly had not had a chance to vote for a successor, followed him and would inevitably be used as a line of attack against him when he ran for subsequent offices. Thus, Jefferson was cast as a coward for having fled in the face of the coming British attack at Monticello and in Albemarle County. Jefferson did not actively respond to these initial attacks, as he had been nominally injured and spent the summer recuperating at Poplar Forest.

ELECTION OF 1796: FEDERALISTS TAKE ON JEFFERSON

When Jefferson was drafted to stand as a candidate for president the first time, in 1796 against John Adams, Charles Pinckney, and Aaron Burr, he came under withering attack, especially from his long-time political nemesis, Alexander Hamilton. Hamilton wrote under an alias, attacking Jefferson on many fronts, including his ownership of slaves. As Washington left office at the end of two terms, he warned against rising partisanship, and the debate and process around the election in 1796 reflected the fears that Washington articulated in his "Farewell Address." Jefferson, as leader of the Democratic-Republican Party, came under frequent attack from the Federalists, who supported Adams.

Malone, one of Jefferson's sympathetic biographers, noted that in 1796, as the Republicans were debating whom to run against Adams, that Jefferson was the most famous of the Democratic-Republicans "owing in no small degree to the advertisement his enemies had given him. No other man did more to build him up and turn him into a symbol than Hamilton did by extreme and unwarranted attacks." Like Jefferson, Hamilton was a member of Washington's cabinet and administration, and he became particularly engaged in the attacks on Jefferson during the 1796 election. Writing under the pseudonym "Phocion," Hamilton published several letters and commentaries about Jefferson. Malone had attributed these letters to an ally of Hamilton's, South Carolina House member William Loughton Smith: "Between October 14 and November 24 [1796], the voluble Phocion published twenty-five installments of election commentary [in the *Gazette of the United States*]." These articles attacked and "denigrated" Jefferson. The attacks on Jefferson in these essays range from calling him again a coward (coming out of the incidents when he was governor of Virginia during the British attack) to his departure from Washington's cabinet as another sign of cowardice, to his relationship with Sally Hemmings. The letters take on all aspects of Jefferson—from lambasting his role as a philosopher and scientist to a full-throated indictment of Jefferson's hypocrisy regarding slavery, his own slaveholding, and his relationship with Hemmings. Biographer Ron Chernow's assessment of this line of attack, particularly the attack on Jefferson as a slave owner who is involved with one of his slaves and has likely fathered children with her, was to "[manipulate] the southern vote." He explains that "Hamilton was trying to have it both ways. As an abolitionist, he wanted to expose Jefferson's disingenuous sympathy for the slaves. As a Federalist, he wanted to frighten slaveholders into thinking that Jefferson might act on that sympathy and emancipate their slaves." This line of attack also echoes the attacks on Jefferson from both the abolitionists and the slaveholders regarding his advocacy within the Declaration of Independence for abolition and then his lack of engagement on the issue followed, ultimately, by his complete change of attitude and support for the institution of slavery.

Jefferson also came under attack during the 1796 election in his home state from vocal Federalists who were not fans of the former secretary of state. Leven Powell and Charles Simms argued against Jefferson, engaging the same issues that Hamilton had pointed out as Phocion. They focused specifically on Jefferson's alleged cowardice as governor of Virginia during the revolution. But they built on this narrative, charging that Jefferson had also left "his post as secretary of state in a time of international crisis." These attacks appeared in several publications, including the *Virginia Gazette & General Advertiser* and the *Maryland Journal* in the fall of 1796. Leven and Simms were Federalist electors, and they argued that Jefferson was not fit for the presidency because of his "lack of firmness and personal fortitude." Distinct from the contemporary process by which presidential electors are designated, the electors in Virginia in 1796 essentially were running for the position to cast their ballots for the presidential nominee. Thus, Leven and Simms were arguing to their constituents in northern Virginia to line up behind them in their support for Adams and against Jefferson. Jefferson did little to combat or respond to the critiques and left it to others, if they chose to do so, to respond. Ultimately,

Jefferson lost the Electoral College battle to Adams in 1796, in part because he lost these few electors. Adams received 71 Electoral College votes, while Jefferson received 68. Thus, the opposing candidates were stuck serving together, as president (Adams) and vice president (Jefferson).

THE ADAMS ADMINISTRATION

Jefferson was not idle during the Adams administration, and various of his stances and actions elicited attacks during this period—especially from Federalists, who anticipated his inclination to stand for the presidency in 1800. The Alien and Sedition Acts, which became law in 1798, made it harder for an immigrant to become a citizen, allowed the president to imprison and deport noncitizens who were deemed dangerous or who were from a hostile nation, and criminalized making false statements that were critical of the federal government. Jefferson and many of his partisans found these laws anathema to their principles, and he and Madison responded with the Kentucky and Virginia Resolutions. The resolutions took direct aim at the Alien and Sedition Acts, arguing that they were unconstitutional and proposing to rectify that unconstitutionality with the powers of the individual states. According to Nancy Verell of the Thomas Jefferson Foundation, "Secrecy was necessary because Jefferson himself, the nation's vice president, might be charged with sedition if he or his closest political ally openly announced that congressional acts were unconstitutional." Controversy surrounded the resolutions, which were denounced by various states. Jefferson himself eluded direct criticism at the time because his authorship was unknown. Jefferson wrote the Kentucky Resolution, while Madison wrote the Virginia Resolution. Of the two, the Kentucky Resolution was more radical and contained more of an argument for state nullification, at least in the early versions of it. Wilson Cary Nicholas notes, in an October 4, 1798, letter about the Kentucky Resolution, that he had disclosed to John Breckenridge, to whom he had passed along the resolution so that it might be submitted for consideration by the Kentucky legislature, that Jefferson had authored the resolution. Nicholas explains that he was trying to keep Jefferson from vilification if his authorship was known: "My chief inducement was to shield you from the invective, that I feared you might be exposed to if I had pursued a different course."

Jefferson was quite busy behind Adams's back during the Adams administration, and the Federalists concluded, according to historian Merrell Peterson, that "the vice presidency . . . was an imposing front behind which the incumbent deviously, secretly, conducted a campaign against the government." He also notes that "Federalist politicos spared no effort to expose the Vice President, to flush him out of his privileged sanctuary, and to arraign him before the public in all the colors of political depravity. Nothing would do so well as Jefferson's own words and deeds."

One such controversy was known as the Mazzei affair. This controversy, which Jefferson brought upon himself in many ways, opened him up to sustained attack from a variety of avenues. Although the letter at the center of this controversy was written and sent in late April 1796, the controversy's impact had long-term implications and followed Jefferson the rest of his life. This letter penned by Jefferson contained a long paragraph that was damning of those in the executive and judiciary branches, as well as all the "officers of the government." Jefferson sent this letter to Philip Mazzei, a former neighbor who was living in Italy at the time. Mazzei shared the letter with at least three others, and Italian and French translations of the letter were soon circulating. The letter was published in French in the Paris *Gazette Nationale ou Le Moniteur Universel* in January 1797. There were several additional paragraphs that centered on American foreign policy that were also included in this French publication of the letter. The letter made it back to the United States, was translated from French to English, and published by Noah Webster in May 1797 in the New York paper *Minerva* (a Federalist publication). This became the basis for extended critiques of Jefferson from Federalists, since in the letter, Jefferson "was portrayed as the leader of a dangerous faction, the head of a French party."

These were not nominal critiques of Jefferson. The Mazzei affair provided substantial fodder for Jefferson's enemies and critics. These comments drew on suspicion of Jefferson's relationship with France while also highlighting Jefferson's own words of criticism against former president George Washington, who remained a popular figure. Although Washington himself never spoke out in response to the Mazzei letter, the letter and the commentary surrounding it dominated many lines of attack at Jefferson in this period when he was serving as vice president. Critiques were made on the floor of the Senate, over which Jefferson was presiding, so he was present for many of these dressings down. Because the details of the letter became so well known, Federalists, the anti-Jefferson press, and others were able to use it to draw not only political but also personal conclusions about Jefferson, and to weave those into their wider attacks on him.

ELECTION OF 1800 AND JEFFERSON'S ADMINISTRATION

As Jefferson prepared for the 1800 election, he weathered a storm of attacks related to the Mazzei affair. The Mazzei letter was frequently cited by political opponents as well as newspapers that opposed Jefferson. Federalists were concerned about what Jefferson would do as president in 1800—asking, according to historian Joseph Ellis, how "could he [Jefferson] take an oath to preserve, protect, and defend the Constitution of the United States . . . if his primary goal as president was to dismantle the federal institutions created by that very document?" The southern Federalists, a group that included John Marshall, chief justice of the Supreme Court and Jefferson's cousin, were quite skeptical of Jefferson as president. Charles Lee, another southern Federalist, sounded an ominous note in a February 11, 1802, letter to Leven Powell: "Mr. Jefferson is well calculated to pull down any political edifice and those will not be disappointed who have feared he would employ himself as industriously and indefatigably in taking to pieces stone by stone the national building as Washington employed himself in putting them together. Even the foundation will be razed in less than four years." According to Henry Adams, a 19th-century historian who took a dim view of Jefferson, "the clergy had always hated Jefferson, and believed him not only to be untruthful, but to be also a demagogue, a backbiter, and a sensualist."

Thus, Jefferson had a variety of enemies as he came into the presidency in 1801. Jefferson's association with Thomas Paine, a founding father who was also a political theorist, and who was anathema to the New England Calvinists and many of the clergy due to his criticisms of organized religion, contributed to their antagonism toward him. Jefferson was fairly convinced that the clergy would have killed him if they could. Adams notes that in the summer of 1802, Jefferson had so riled up the New England clergy (among others) that the months were "marked by an outburst of reciprocal invective and slander such as could not be matched in American history." The charges leveled against Jefferson at this time, that he was a "sensualist" without strong religious beliefs, went back to his earliest days in public life. This also twisted around another approach to discredit Jefferson, again from his time in public office in Virginia—implying that he had become involved with one of his slaves, Sally Hemmings, and had children with her.

It was not just the New England Calvinists and clergy who struck out against Jefferson as he came into office. There was an immediate controversy, the Greene affair, which inaugurated Jefferson's new term as president. The Greene affair was a kind of precursor to the actions that led to the landmark Supreme Court case *Marbury v. Madison* (1803), and certainly stirred early criticism of the new administration. The Greene affair was a result of John Marshall's technical mistake in writing the wrong judicial court in an authorizing commission. Marshall had erroneously indicated that a judge named Ray Greene had been appointed to the circuit court, rather than to the district court to which he had actually been assigned. When Greene sent the commission back to be corrected, however, James Madison, Jefferson's secretary of state, never fixed or returned it. Instead, Jefferson nominated a fellow Republican named David Barnes to fill Greene's spot on the district court. The response to this move, which essentially nullified Adams's appointment and the Senate approval of that appointment, was a blistering attack of Jefferson by the Federalist press, which framed his actions as both lawless and outrageous. The Greene incident laid the foundation for the choices Jefferson and Madison made regarding the undelivered commissions at the end of the Adams administration, which would lead to the suit brought by William Marbury (and the Supreme Court decision in 1803 that formed the basis for judicial review).

Jefferson came under attack during his presidency from numerous judges and justices. Marshall, for example, compelled him to testify in the trial of Aaron Burr after he shot Alexander Hamilton in a duel. Justice Samuel Chase, meanwhile, offered a critique of Jefferson's Republican ideology when he spoke about the likely sinking of the "republican Constitution into a mobocracy" to a Baltimore grand jury. This incident followed the unsuccessful attempt by Jefferson to impeach Judge John Pickering of New Hampshire in 1803. This move to impeach judges also followed on Congress's suspension of the sitting of the Supreme Court, which was not allowed to sit (operate in session) from December 1801 through February 1803. Jefferson tried again—taking on Chase and encouraging Republicans in Congress to impeach Chase, which they did, though for mostly political reasons.

THE CALLENDER AFFAIR

James Callender was an often in-debt newspaper editor and Republican adherent from Scotland who supported Jefferson, his colleagues, and their political views—and who openly criticized Jefferson's political opponents. He wrote several pamphlets in 1796, for example, that were quite critical of Hamilton. At that point in his career, Jefferson thought well of Callender and supported his efforts, especially as they were directed at attacking Hamilton and other Federalists. But Callender later became one of Jefferson's chief antagonists, especially during the early part of Jefferson's administration. Jefferson was known to have subsidized Callender when he was publishing attacks on Hamilton and other Federalists, and Hamilton had an inkling that Jefferson was, according to Chernow, "one of the conspirators behind the Callender expose . . . [but that] Hamilton had threatened Jefferson with public exposure of a shameful episode many years earlier in which Jefferson had repeatedly tried to seduce Betsey Walker, the wife of his friend and Virginia neighbor John Walker." Callender was in the middle of the ongoing/never-ending political and personal dispute between Hamilton and Jefferson, and what is most intriguing about Callender is that he went from being an ally of Jefferson's to being an adversary.

According to Henry Adams, Jefferson had "befriended Callender against his own better judgement, as every party leader befriended party hacks, not because the leaders approve them, but because they were necessary for the press." He had loaned him money on occasion, had helped him get a position at the *Aurora*, the Republican newspaper, and ultimately pardoned him of his libel conviction and arranged for Callender to be reimbursed for the fine he had been forced to pay upon his conviction. But Callender asked for more, and when Jefferson and Madison refused his request for a patronage position as postmaster at Richmond, Callender used his position as editor of a newspaper called *The Recorder* to wage what Adams called "a war of slander" against Jefferson. He essentially attempted to extort or blackmail the president at this point, and Jefferson turned his back on

Callender. But Callender was not done with Jefferson. The Richmond *Recorder* hired Callender, and he set about attacking Jefferson with lots of help from the local Federalists—the same people who had arrested and prosecuted Callender earlier. Callender used his past personal correspondence with Jefferson against the president. These letters, according to Peterson, "mingled money with politics in such a way that it required an act of naiveté to separate them." This was followed by Callender's accusations that Jefferson had kept Sally Hemmings as his concubine, that he had several children with her, and that she served as "housekeeper at Monticello." According to Peterson, Callender's publication of this information "launched the prolific public career of a tale that had titillated Jefferson's enemies in the neighborhood of Monticello for years." Indeed, this rumor had swirled around Jefferson since his earliest days in public life, and continued long after he died—and has been verified, as much as possible, by contemporary historians and experts.

Jefferson never responded to this attack, either at the time or later. Jefferson's friends and defenders did take on this attack, but these responses did little but add to the controversy.

James Callender died not long after this barrage of personal attacks on Jefferson, drowning in the James River while drunk in 1803. In Peterson's estimation, Jefferson thought that these attacks "triggered the revival of accusations of misconduct and cowardice in his governorship of Virginia. . . . By these attacks on his private character the Federalist enemies hoped to deflate his immense popularity with the public."

JEFFERSON AND HAMILTON

Jefferson and Hamilton were famous political adversaries and opponents for many years. Hamilton rarely shrank from leveling critiques of Jefferson in the press, under aliases, with others in conversation or in letters, and in political settings among his fellow Federalists. According to Malone's assessment, "Hamilton expressly said that the trend of his [Jefferson's] tenets was toward disunion, disorder, and discredit. This was the picture of his colleague that he sought from this time forward to impress on the public mind, and he skillfully blended fact and fancy to achieve the desired effect." Hamilton's attacks, leveled under the aliases "Scourge" and "Catullus" during the Washington administration, focused on Jefferson's opinion of the constitutional system and the functioning of the new government, as well as on Jefferson's moral character. The anonymous pamphlet titled *The Politicks and Views of a Certain Party, Displayed* published in 1792 (and suspected, at the time, to be written by Hamilton), pursues many of the same lines of attack against Jefferson as had Hamilton's disguised writings: "A ridiculous affectation of simplicity, stilting himself in the public papers and on invitation cards, plain Thomas, and similar frivolities, a pretended outcry against Monarchy and

Aristocracy may have had a momentary effect with the few ignorant and unsuspecting, but have long ago excited the derision of the many, who know that under the assumed cloak of humility lurks the most ambitious spirit, the most overweening pride and hauteur, and that the *externals* of pure Democracy afford but a flimsy veil to the *internal* evidences of aristocratic splendor, sensuality and Epicureanism." Many of these attacks were responded to by friends and Republican compatriots of Jefferson, but they still took a cumulative toll on Jefferson's reputation.

Hamilton and other Federalists used many of these salacious stories about Jefferson's inappropriate involvement/engagement with either married women (Betsey Walker) or his slaves (Sally Hemmings) as lines of attack on Jefferson, especially during his presidency.

Vice President Aaron Burr proved a particularly intriguing antagonist for Jefferson during the latter's presidency. Henry Adams notes, however, that Jefferson did not take this threat seriously enough: "That he [Jefferson] was afraid of Burr and of the sympathy which Burr's career had excited, was the belief of Burr himself, who responded to Jefferson's caution by a contempt so impudent as to seem even then almost incredible. Believing that the President dared not touch him, Burr never cared to throw even a veil over his treason. He used the President's name and the names of his Cabinet officers as freely as though he were President himself; and no one contradicted or disavowed him." Burr, as Jefferson's vice president, became more and more of a threat to Jefferson (and the Republic) as time went on. Burr, at a Federalist banquet to celebrate Washington's birthday, made a toast to "the union of all honest men." This, according to Henry Adams, apparently was a "dramatic insult . . . flung in the face of the President [Jefferson] and his Virginian friends . . . the Virginians had reason to know that Burr believed himself to have been twice betrayed by them, and that his union of honest men was meant to gibbet them as scoundrels." Burr aligned with the New York Federalists, and ultimately the factions (one led by himself, one led by Hamilton) fought among themselves—at times advocating for separation from the Union. These political factions led to the personal dispute between Hamilton and Burr that climaxed with Burr mortally wounding Hamilton in a duel. During Jefferson's second term, Burr tried to raise an army in New Orleans, and threatened to dismember the Union by organizing the southern states to secede from the Union. Jefferson saw this move as a threat to the country (and himself) and moved against Burr. Burr was captured and Jefferson wanted him brought up on charges of treason, which Marshall and other members of the Supreme Court refused to do.

CONCLUSION

In spite all the personal and political attacks, Jefferson was swept back into office by a landslide in 1804, and his second term continued along many of the same policy areas as had his first term. While he battled with Federalists, especially in the judiciary, other antagonists, like Hamilton and Callender, were no longer around to attack him. His second term was not as robust as his first in many respects because of internal tension between Jeffersonian commitment to republicanism and democracy and the complications of an expanded republic dealing with antagonist foreign powers. As Adams notes, upon the 1804 election, "The White House was filled with an atmosphere of adulation. Flattery, gross as any that man could ask, was poured into the President's ear, but was as nothing compared with the more subtle flattery of the popular vote."

Lilly J. Goren

Further Reading

Ackerman, Bruce. *The Failure of the Founding Fathers: Jefferson, Marshall, and the Rise of Presidential Democracy*. Cambridge, MA: Belknap Press, 2005.

Adams, Henry. *The History of the United States during the Administration of Thomas Jefferson, 1801–1809*. New York: Library of America/Viking Press, 1986.

Beveridge, Albert Jeremiah. *The Life of John Marshall*. New York: Houghton Mifflin, 1916.

Chernow, Ron. *Alexander Hamilton*. New York: Penguin Books, 2004.

Cunningham, Noble E. *The Process of Government under Jefferson*. Princeton, NJ: Princeton University Press, 2015.

Davis, David Brion. *The Problem of Slavery in the Age of Emancipation*. New York: Vintage, 2015.

Ellis, Joseph J. *American Sphinx*. New York: Alfred A. Knopf, 1998.

Goren, Lilly J. *Theory, Practice, Partisanship: An Examination of the Inconsistencies in Thomas Jefferson's Political Thought and Political Life*. Unpublished Manuscript, 1987.

Jefferson, Thomas. *Writings*. New York: Library of America, 1984.

Knott, Stephen F. *Alexander Hamilton and the Persistence of Myth*. Lawrence, KS: University Press of Kansas, 2002.

Malone, Dumas. *Jefferson the Virginian*. Boston: Little, Brown and Company, 1948.

Malone, Dumas. *Jefferson and the Rights of Man*. Boston: Little, Brown and Company, 1951.

Malone, Dumas. *Jefferson and the Ordeal of Liberty*. Boston: Little, Brown and Company, 1962.

McDonald, Forrest. *The Presidency of Thomas Jefferson*. Lawrence, KS: University Press of Kansas, 1976.

Miranda, Lin-Manual. *Hamilton: An American Musical*. Original Broadway Cast Recording.

Peterson, Merrill D. *Thomas Jefferson and the New Nation: A Biography*. New York: Oxford University Press, 1970.

Report of the Research Committee on Thomas Jefferson and Sally Hemmings, January 2000. Available at https://www.monticello.org/sites/default/files/inline-pdfs/jefferson-hemings_report.pdf.

Verell, Nancy. *The Virginia and Kentucky Resolutions.* Thomas Jefferson Foundation. Available at https://www.monticello.org/site/research-and-collections/kentucky-and-virginia-resolutions#footnote18_fm8fad1.

Wiensek, Henry. "The Dark Side of Thomas Jefferson: A New Portrait of the Founding Father Challenges the Long-Held Perception of Thomas Jefferson as a Benevolent Slaveholder." *Smithsonian Magazine*, October 2012. Available at http://www.smithsonianmag.com/history/the-dark-side-of-thomas-jefferson-35976004/?no-ist=&=&=&=&=&preview=&page=1.

4. James Madison

Born: March 16, 1751
Died: June 28, 1836
Time in Office: Fourth President of the United States, March 4, 1809, to March 4, 1817
Election Results: 1808 Election: 122 (69.7%) Electoral College votes; 1812 Election: 128 (58.7%) Electoral College votes
Spouse: Dolley Payne Todd (m. 1794)

Regarded as the father of the Constitution, James Madison has been widely admired as one of the greatest minds this country ever produced. In terms of appearance, he was unimposing. He was a sickly man of unimpressive physical stature, standing less than five-and-a-half feet tall and weighing no more than 100 pounds. Like most of the founding fathers, Madison was raised on a sizable plantation by a family of some means and social influence. After completing his early education at home due to ill health, he enrolled at the College of New Jersey (modern-day Princeton University) and studied classical languages, philosophy, science, and public law. From the late 1770s to the 1780s, Madison was a member of the Continental Congress and the Virginia legislature, among other posts, the most prominent of which was a delegate to the Constitutional Convention in 1787. He entered the newly created House of Representatives in 1789, serving his home state of Virginia for roughly 10 years. In 1794, he married Dolley Payne Todd, whom many have considered a model for the modern first lady. From 1801 to 1809, Madison was secretary of state in Thomas Jefferson's administration, and he became president himself in 1809. In 1812, he led the United States into a war against Great Britain and secured victory in what many have called the "Second American Revolution." In 1817, the Madisons returned to their tobacco plantation in Virginia, where the former president remained politically and socially active. Unfortunately, he lost almost his entire fortune because of falling tobacco prices and financial mismanagement by his stepson. Increasingly confined to his bed, Madison died in 1836, marking a tragic end to a brilliant man.

REPUBLICAN ENEMIES

In 1809, when Madison assumed the presidency, he was confronted by a shifting political landscape beset by factions, political feuds, and personal animosities. The situation required a deft politician who could manage competing agendas and outsize personalities and, at the same time, sell his goals and priorities to a fractious Congress and administration. More often than not, especially during his first term, Madison could do neither. Contrary to expectations, he was not a particularly skilled or compelling politician, and he experienced considerable difficulties translating his vision into actionable policies. A man of ideas accustomed to confronting conceptual dilemmas on a grand scale, Madison approached the nuts-and-bolts world of politics with more than a little hesitation and skepticism. Preferring the genteel intimacy of drawing-room debates over the down-and-dirty world of everyday politics, Madison lacked the natural pragmatism that enabled his enemies to get things done. Too often taking the path of least resistance, he shunned confrontation and sought consensus even on issues that called for a clear and immediate resolution.

From a practical perspective, Madison's critics were correct, but, from a historical one, they missed the point. His limitations as president and lack of effectiveness as a politician were undeniable, but they were as much a product of a dying notion of gentlemanly public service as any political deficiencies on his part. He belonged to a founding generation of Americans that rejected parties, professional politics, and personal ambition as corrupt and illegitimate. In their world, politics was not a career but the preserve of financially independent citizen-statesmen called into temporary public service by their fellow Americans, men whom Thomas Jefferson labeled the "natural aristocracy." Unquestionably loyal to traditional, or Jeffersonian, Republicanism, Madison was greatly troubled by its infighting, competing agendas, and personal rivalries. Once a stable mainstream coalition with a largely unified leadership and purpose, it was splintering into quarreling factions that undermined their shared heritage. By 1809, Jeffersonians were just one of four factions vying for control of the Republican brand. Although the most numerous of the four, they could no longer muster congressional majorities and were forced to rely on support from one or more of their Republican competitors to pass legislation, which frequently thwarted their policy priorities. The demise of the Federalists only made the internal brawling worse, with each faction scrambling to fill the ensuing political vacuum and co-opt remaining Federalists.

Some of the most determined resistance to Jeffersonians, particularly Madison, came from a group of uncompromising conservatives who viewed any sort of constitutional accommodation to evolving circumstances a betrayal of Republican principles. Labeled "Old" Republicans by historians, they were more commonly known as Quids (from *tertium quid*, Latin for "third thing"). They hated Madison because he gradually adapted his thinking about legislative and executive authority to a changing political reality and the practical necessities of governing. Motivated by an outdated agrarian mind-set and an unyielding dedication to states' rights, Quids were strict constructionists wedded to a literal and unbending interpretation of the Constitution. Many of them even saw the Constitution as an agreement among states and not individuals. Their standard-bearers were John Randolph and John Taylor of Caroline, whose conspiratorial outlook made them incapable of working with the president. Randolph was convinced that, with support from other Republicans, Madison would stop at nothing to achieve political and economic domination of the South. Foreshadowing southern fears prior to the Civil War, a few Quids were so obsessed with conspiracies that they perceived a—nonexistent—federal scheme to "enslave" the South, deprive it of its rights, and abolish its economic system. A minority view at the time, it eventually became a majority sentiment in the pre–Civil War South, justifying the secession from the Union.

Of Madison's other adversaries, none were more cunning and manipulative than the "Invisibles" and Clintonites. They were two Republican factions as different from Quids as could be. More alike than unlike and not worried about ideological consistency, they focused on hardening their grip over Republicans and the dying Federalist coalition and building a network of political patronage. The two had some differences, but both displayed a similar dedication to winner-take-all politics, gamesmanship, and unapologetic pandering to their supporters. Their efforts led to the rise of the first real party system in the United States, and they were the core of what would become the Democratic Party. The Clinton, Smith, and Nichols families of New York, Pennsylvania, and Virginia, respectively, led the charge against Madison, using every means at their disposal to limit the president's ability to enact his agenda. Printing articles critical of Madison and his closest advisers was one of their favorite tactics. William Duane, editor of the *Aurora*, never missed an opportunity to paint Madison as a dithering fool incapable of effective leadership and promoting policies out of step with the needs of real Republicans. The *Aurora* greased the wheels of a revolution that overturned the founders' world and inaugurated an enduring era of democratic, populist politics that survives to this day.

FEDERALIST ENEMIES

The president also encountered pushback from Federalists, who had been the Republicans' traditional rivals since the first days of the republic. Among their founders were George Washington and Alexander Hamilton, and they dominated American politics during its first decade but began a steady and quick decline shortly thereafter. Almost a dead letter by the end of Madison's second term, they were a shadow of what they had been at the height of their dominance in the 1790s.

Individual Federalists, such as Charles C. Pinckney and Rufus King, and a shrink-ing faction in the Northeast, could still cause some problems for Madison, but it was nothing he could not handle, provided Invisibles and Clintonites did not inter-fere. Cooperating with Invisibles and Clintonites, who co-opted surviving Feder-alists whenever advantageous, Federalists hoped to revive their fortunes. Despite a Federalist resurgence during Madison's second term, especially in their opposition to the declaration of war against Britain, nothing could prevent their eventual dis-appearance from the political scene.

It was out of this climate of desperation for survival that came a bizarre and poorly organized scheme by Federalists to topple the president and establish politi-cal power over New England. Opposed to war and insisting it would cripple regional commerce and trade with Britain, Federalists assiduously resisted Madi-son's call for war. In both chambers of Congress, they voted against war unani-mously. In the Senate, where Federalists held only six seats, they made trouble for Republicans, hoping to attract as many of the disaffected as possible in order to upend a declaration of war. It was not to be, but it was useful as a warning to the president not to overlook what little power and influence they still held. In addi-tion, it was a glaring reminder to Madison that his enemies were willing to do any-thing to undermine his policies and force him from office. Although Federalist plans ultimately came to naught, the president was constantly looking over his shoulder, which created a political distraction he did not need.

Federalist fears concerning trade and manufacturing, though valid, were over-blown and mostly unfounded. They did indeed take a hit because of the war, but, at the same time, they profited from trade in contraband goods, control of illegal shipping, and diminished but steady manufacturing. Regardless, spotting conspira-cies where none existed and hoping to damage a president most of them despised, the plotters sent delegates from all six New England states to a convention in Hartford in late 1814. Initially, a moderate group headed by Harrison Gray Otis proposed a modest set of proclamations voicing their disapproval of Madison's handling of the war and the continued accumulation of federal influence over the states and New England manufacturing. Frustrated with the moderates' unwillingness to take decisive action and believing reconciliation with Madison was neither viable nor desirable, extremists led by the Essex Junto usurped control of the convention and suggested secession from the Union. Having unsuccessfully demanded the adoption of seven nonsensical amendments to the Constitution and Madison's res-ignation, the Junto saw secession as its only option. Alarmingly, these were some of the most esteemed names in American politics, such as Fisher Ames, Timothy Pickering, and Theophilus Parsons, who came to believe that radicalism offered the most effective way to rid the republic of supposed corruption and abuse of power. In the end, the cabal went nowhere. The conclusion of the war and Madi-son's negotiation of a peace treaty favorable to New Englanders took the wind out of the conspirators' sails, rendering many of their concerns irrelevant and meaningless. After abandonment of the cause by most of the conspirators, all that was left was a handful of ultraconservatives whose support had evaporated.

BANK OF THE UNITED STATES

As Jefferson's secretary of state, Madison relaxed much of his typical opposition to a liberal, or more flexible, interpretation of the Constitution. As president, he realized that strict constructionism and an out-of-hand rejection of greater executive authority straightjacketed presidents and undermined genuine efforts to adjust policies and agendas to evolving political needs. Most Jeffersonian Republicans, despite early opposition to Jefferson's and Madison's policy reforms, were on board by Madison's second term as president. Quids, however, condemned the president and accused him of corruption and selling Republican principles down the river. Their treatment of Madison on this matter was often vicious. Damning what they saw as Madison's unconstitutional seizure of federal powers at the expense of states and landowners, they did their best to attract disaffected Jeffersonians, hoping to drive a wedge between the president and his supporters. Although some Jeffersonians did indeed side with Quids on this issue, the majority of them stuck with the president.

Of the issues that Madison embraced after initial opposition, few, if any, were as inflammatory and polarizing as the Bank of the United States (BUS). George Washington's Treasury Secretary Alexander Hamilton was an avid sponsor of the bank and a dedicated believer in the federal government's implied powers to implement constitutional and legislative provisions. Believing that stable economic growth was a requirement for political stability and progress, which could not be achieved without a national bank, Hamilton worked diligently for its creation. In 1791, Congress obliged. At the time of the bank's founding, Madison was a well- known critic, viewing the BUS as unconstitutional and a blatant example of federal overreach. He was worried that the accrual of so much federal power over the nation's economic and financial resources would lead to corruption and the emergence of a monied class with interests at odds with those of the nation as a whole. Over years, however, Madison abandoned his objections. By the time the bank's charter was due for renewal in 1811, he had become one of its most significant boosters. Unfortunately, Madison's dear friend and political ally Thomas Jefferson did not agree with Madison on this issue. This was a potential challenge for Madison, because it suggested that he could have trouble not only from Quids but also Jeffersonians, on whose support he had been able to rely. As it turned out, help from Invisibles and Clintonites could not be guaranteed either, despite their forward-looking policies and their frequent backing of New England and New York manufacturers.

A majority of traditional Republicans stuck with Madison on this issue but found themselves in a strange and unfamiliar position. Historically, Republicans had been the most vehement critics of the BUS, but, by 1811, traditionalists were its biggest champions. Outraged, Quids labeled Madison a Federalist sympathizer and turncoat. The charge was nonsense, but it got a lot of mileage among his enemies and those who were undecided regarding the bank's future. Madison's efforts were not made any easier by his talented and extremely capable but reviled Treasury Secretary Albert Gallatin, who was the point man for the administration's efforts to secure another BUS charter. Gallatin had Madison's full backing, but John Randolph and his followers rejected everything Gallatin proposed without consideration. Invisibles, with DeWitt Clinton and his uncle George at the helm, were no different, blocking Madison on an issue they may have otherwise supported. Henry Clay of Kentucky, who would reverse himself in 1816, led the attack against Madison and his treasury secretary in the House of Representatives, alleging a pro-northeastern, antiagrarian bias against western states and the support of manufacturing and financial interests at all costs. The fact that Gallatin was a Swiss American born on foreign soil played into the hands of the president's enemies, particularly at a time when anti-immigrant sentiment peaked due to the impending war with Britain.

Unsurprisingly, attempts to renew the bank's charter immediately following its expiration in 1811 were not fruitful. The failure fell squarely on Madison's shoulders and his inability to take charge of the administration's efforts. Madison's flawed penchant for compromise above all and his unwillingness to confront his enemies directly left Gallatin in the wind. Gallatin was an unwelcome messenger at the best of times, but, with such an incendiary issue, leaving him to fight Madison's foes alone was an unmitigated disaster. Had Madison assumed leadership and confronted his opponents assertively and had he actively worked to drum up support for the bank's renewal, the legislation probably would have survived. As it turned out, the focus of antibank efforts was more personal than substantive, and the bank itself never had a fair hearing because of it. The bill died in the Senate, where the vote to approve the charter was a tie, which meant that Madison's vice president, George Clinton, who was also one of Madison's most prominent antagonists, broke the tie with his vote against the bank. His opponents knew that, had the president taken the bull by the horns and actively mustered support for the vote, the bank's defenders probably would have won. They were proven right in 1816, as some of the bank's most vocal opponents switched sides and ensured the renewal of the charter.

CABINET APPOINTMENTS

The situation with Gallatin at Treasury was largely of Madison's own making, and it went back to his first days at the White House. The way Madison handled Gallatin's appointment was part of a troubling pattern of cabinet and Supreme Court nominations that neutered the president's team from the start, thereby allowing Invisibles and Clintonites to place their own personnel in key cabinet posts. Almost immediately upon taking office, Madison tapped Gallatin, who was a holdover from the Jefferson administration, for secretary of state. Gallatin was the incoming secretary of the treasury, but Madison felt it was imperative to have someone he could trust at the state department. Although it was irrelevant in Gallatin's case, the position was a stepping stone to the presidency. Five of the seven presidents after Washington were secretaries of state at some point prior to their election—four of them immediately prior. Given the Invisibles' and Clintonites' political aspirations and their designs on the presidency, they lobbied hard for one of their own to become secretary of state.

Unfortunately for the president, the battle was lost before it began. As always, Madison lacked the guile, fortitude, and political wherewithal to pull it off, and he also underestimated the tenacity and determination of his opponents to install a sympathetic appointee. Unfortunately, he could not have picked a candidate that was more despised by the Invisibles and Clintonites as well as Quids, but for different reasons. Gallatin's most vocal and dogged enemies were from his home state of Pennsylvania, with none more prominent than Senator Samuel Smith and his family. Smith was a kingmaker of sorts in Pennsylvania with political allies in both northeastern and southern states. In Virginia, which was Madison's home state, Smith could rely on Senator William Branch Giles and Wilson Cary Nicholas from the Virginia legislature to stir the pot against the president and organize an effective anti-Gallatin campaign. Ambitious to a fault, Giles eyed the top cabinet post for himself, so derailing the Gallatin nomination was both a personal and political goal.

Marshaling the backing of anti-Gallatin forces in Congress and tying Madison to Gallatin on almost every contentious issue, Giles promised a defeat for the president in the Senate if he refused to withdraw Gallatin from consideration. Madison was wary of capitulating to Giles and alienating his supporters among Jeffersonian Republicans, but he felt he had no choice but to relent and let Giles have his way. Nonetheless, Madison was not about to surrender everything, so he was able to extract a couple of concessions from Giles and his allies as compensation. He retained Gallatin at Treasury with a grudging nod from anti-Gallatin forces, who realized they could not prevent the move anyhow because Gallatin had already been confirmed as Jefferson's treasury secretary. In addition, Madison wanted anyone but Giles as secretary of state, which Invisibles and Clintonites were willing to concede if Madison agreed to nominate Samuel Smith's brother Robert. The president would soon discover that Smith was more inept and a bigger liability than Giles would have been. Smith ignored most of his duties as secretary of state, acting as a mole for his sponsors, while exhibiting no willingness to work with

Madison. After two wasted years and sustained pressure from most quarters, Smith was pushed out. By then, the damage had been done.

SUPREME COURT VACANCY

Nominating a candidate for the state department was a fiasco, but filling the Supreme Court vacancy left by the death of William Cushing in 1810 was just as frustrating. With a barrage from all sides, each one intent on placing a political ally on the bench, Madison hoped to fill the empty seat with a Jeffersonian, who would break the Federalist stranglehold on the Court. Progress was slow, as political posturing wasted an entire year before the nomination process began in earnest. Geographic factors complicated the matter, because, at that time, justices had local responsibilities between Supreme Court terms as magistrates and justices of the peace, which confined them to their own regions. This meant that a replacement for Cushing had to come from New England. Madison chose Levi Lincoln, a former Federalist who migrated to the Republicans and had been attorney general during Jefferson's first term. Surprisingly for a president as opposed to partisanship as Madison was, the choice was purely political. Regardless, Lincoln was not interested because he was losing his eyesight.

Now it was the nontraditionalists' turn. Invisibles and even some who had been Madison's supporters made an even more partisan choice. They settled on Postmaster General Gideon Granger, who was yet another member of the Madison administration doing the bidding of the nontraditionalists. Granger, threatening to disclose dirt he had supposedly dug up on both Madison and Jefferson, was a consummate party hack to whom propriety and norms of political conduct meant nothing. Not wanting to squander their political capital on a deficient candidate with little probability of confirmation, the Invisibles backed off. Madison responded by dismissing the postmaster general as soon as an opportunity arose. Granger declared war and promised to have his revenge on the president. Shaken and irritated by a fight over a clearly unqualified pick pushed by Invisibles, Madison resumed his quest for a Republican who could secure a sufficient number of votes in the Senate.

Madison next turned to a Jeffersonian, Alexander Wolcott, whose actions often made him look like a Quid, especially in his defense of Republican purity. A rare breed, he managed to anger people from every Republican faction, to say nothing of the Federalists. Again, this was a partisan pick by a president customarily at odds with such behavior, but Madison was more concerned with having one of his own on the Court than with political consistency. It seemed that nobody wanted Wolcott except the president; the nomination suffered a quick death. Madison's next selection was John Quincy Adams, a moderate Federalist who actually garnered support across the board. As luck would have it, he was confirmed by the Senate but declined the seat. Finally, Madison turned to the centrist Jeffersonian Joseph

Story, who was confirmed by the Senate and, unlike Adams, accepted the appointment. In the end, the political wrangling during the preceding 18 months had exhausted the president and compelled him to select someone suitable to all sides but whose Federalist leanings he did not like. Story turned out to be one of the longest serving and influential justices ever to sit on the Supreme Court.

PROBLEMS WITH THE MILITARY STAFF

Despite expectations, Story was a success, but the same could hardly be said of Madison's military command. From top to bottom, it was inadequate and woefully unprepared for war. Problems began at the top with William Eustis, a poorly chosen secretary of war lacking relevant experience and knowledge of military affairs. Hoping to avoid political problems with a cabinet member who would have little to do beyond controlling restive Indians on the western frontier, Madison picked Eustis as a sop to his enemies, believing that animosities with Britain would be settled through diplomatic channels. He could not have been more wrong. As war with Britain became more likely, Eustis's shortcomings were increasingly evident. When war finally came, the military was a mess and losses piled up, exposing Eustis as an embarrassingly incapable secretary, while cries for his dismissal grew to a fever pitch. Mercifully, seeing the writing on the wall, Eustis resigned in 1813. He left the military unorganized, inadequately trained, and poorly equipped. Three more secretaries of war followed in quick succession before Madison left office, the first of whom, John Armstrong, was another liability. Lazy, dishonest, and unreliable, his only qualification seemed to be that he was a New Yorker and was expected to have support among some of Madison's enemies. Even so, he was barely confirmed.

Madison hoped to compensate for the misfortunes at the war department by appointing generals he and the rank-and-file could trust. That was not to be, because military appointments were beholden to the same partisan interests and anti-Madison campaigning that derailed his selections for other offices. He was left with a group of generals whose capabilities ranged from impressive to utterly incompetent. Paul Hamilton, Madison's choice for secretary of the navy, appeared to be an example of the former, overseeing a string of naval victories early in the war. From a personal perspective, Hamilton was a disappointment. A man of flawed character who was often drunk and thought nothing of insulting others in public and attacking both friend and foe, Hamilton was not respected by his peers and was reviled by many.

James Wilkinson, governor of the Louisiana Territory and its ranking general, was undeniably an example of incompetence. Ignoring the needs of his soldiers out of negligence and a desire to advance his political ambitions, breaking established norms of political decorum and personal decency, and taking every opportunity to undermine the president, Wilkinson was a fiasco from the start. Except for some military experience early in his career, he was utterly unqualified and ill-suited for the job. As someone without integrity or a sense of right and wrong, he had no compunctions about engaging in illegal or unethical behavior. His biography read more like a rap sheet than the résumé of a military commander. Surprisingly, the Kentuckian still got the job, in part because of Madison's wish to secure backing for the war from western states and silencing the general's political allies.

The president had another, potentially explosive, reason for retaining Wilkinson. Dismissing him could have become a political disaster by inviting scrutiny of a nakedly political and embarrassing decision by Madison's good friend Thomas Jefferson, a decision made while Madison had been secretary of state. Jefferson picked Wilkinson despite knowing that the soon-to-be general had engaged in a treasonous conspiracy with Jefferson's archenemy Aaron Burr to create an independent government on Mexican and American land. Wilkinson "purchased" his appointment by betraying Burr and providing Jefferson with evidence against Burr, whom Jefferson swore to bury at any cost, personal or political. As president, Madison wanted the whole miserable affair to go away. It would have smeared him at the beginning of his presidency and provided his Republican and Federalist enemies, who were already causing the president misery concerning his staffing decisions, with even more ammunition. The fact that he did not want to harm Jefferson or negatively impact his friend's legacy was also a factor. As a final slap in the face, Burr was tried and released on a technicality.

CONCLUSION

Given the abiding contempt among his enemies, it would be easy to conclude that Madison was hated more than admired. Likewise, given his deficiencies as a politician, it would be just as easy to conclude that Madison was an incompetent president. However, when a discussion concentrates on the president's critics and his political failures and largely avoids the other side, such a portrayal is expected. A man of enviable intelligence and knowledge, Madison was actually admired by most of his peers. As father of the Constitution, sponsor of the Bill of Rights, and author of the *Federalist*, Madison's legacy as a giant among American political thinkers was already secure by the time he became president. His legacy as president was mixed, but it never detracted from the other. On balance, by 1817, Madison left the presidency in better shape than it had been in 1809, victorious internationally and poised to lead the nation through emerging industrial change that would underwrite an economic revolution.

Hatred of the president was a product of the times and often had little to do with him directly. Madison took office at a precarious juncture in the history of the early republic, representing a way of life and political outlook that would become irrelevant by the time he died. The shifting political landscape and gradual abandonment of traditional Republicanism and the demise of the Federalists caused an inevitable scramble for power within a splintering Republican coalition. Madison, symbolizing almost everything Invisibles and Clintonites despised and wanted to overturn, drew fire at every turn. Admittedly, Madison did not help himself with a leadership style that was all too often haphazard and ineffective, and his gradual acceptance of expanded federal power frequently alienated him from his traditionalist backers. Still, he never turned his back on the ideals that informed his entire career as a servant of the American people. Madison began his career devoted to Republican governance, the rule of law, and public service, and he left with the same devotion.

Tomislav Han

Further Reading

Cheney, Lynne. *James Madison: A Life Reconsidered*. New York: Penguin Books, 2015.

Hofstadter, Richard. *The Idea of a Party System: The Rise of Legitimate Opposition in the United States, 1780–1840*. Berkeley, CA: University of California Press, 1970.

Ketcham, Ralph. *James Madison: A Biography*. Charlottesville, VA: University of Virginia Press, 1990.

McCoy, Drew R. *The Last of the Fathers: James Madison and the Republican Legacy*. New York: Cambridge University Press, 1991.

Rutland, Robert Allan. *The Presidency of James Madison*. Lawrence, KS: University Press of Kansas, 1990.

Wills, Garry. *James Madison*. New York: Times Books, 2002.

5. James Monroe

Born: April 28, 1758
Died: July 4, 1831
Time in Office: Fifth President of the United States, March 4, 1817, to March 4, 1825
Election Results: 1816 Election: 183 (83.9%) Electoral College votes; 1820 Election: 231 (98.3%) Electoral College votes
Spouse: Elizabeth Kortright (m. 1786)
Children: Eliza, James, and Maria

James Monroe, who was born in Westmoreland County, Virginia, was elected president in 1816 with one of the most impressive résumés of any person to hold the office. A hero of the Revolutionary War who was wounded at the famous Battle of Trenton, Monroe served as a delegate to the Confederation Congress, a senator from Virginia, the American ambassador to France and Great Britain, governor of Virginia, and secretary of state and secretary of war. Monroe was inaugurated as the nation's fifth president on March 4, 1817. Monroe easily won reelection in 1820, and left office on March 4, 1825, when he was succeeded by his secretary of state, John Quincy Adams. Monroe was married to Elizabeth Kortright in 1786, and the couple had three children. Elizabeth Monroe kept a somewhat low profile during her husband's presidency, in part due to frequent illnesses and her penchant for privacy. Fairly or not, she was one of the least popular first ladies in American history.

THE ELECTION OF 1816

Monroe's pursuit of the presidency in 1816 was assisted greatly by a campaign to destroy the opposition Federalist Party that had been underway for more than 20 years. This campaign, organized and directed by Thomas Jefferson, was an unmitigated success and must be seen as one of the most impressive political operations in American history. It was also an effort in which Monroe played a crucial role. As former Colorado senator Gary Hart described it in his brief biography of Monroe, this campaign was "stage manage[d]" by Jefferson, while "Madison was chief theorist, and Monroe was organizer and foot soldier." Jefferson's lieutenants, Monroe in particular, engaged in an intensive effort to destroy the leader of the Federalists, Alexander Hamilton, by leaking revelations of the latter's extramarital affair. They were convinced, mistakenly, that they had discovered a financial scandal involving the treasury secretary. Monroe's effort to destroy Hamilton's reputation was the first instance in American political history of resorting to the politics of personal destruction.

From 1801 to 1817, Jefferson and Madison kept the American government firmly on a Republican tack. Despite presiding over the near-catastrophic War of 1812, Republicans approached the election of 1816 with confidence. One of the architects of that war, Secretary of State James Monroe, secured his party's nomination and easily defeated Senator Rufus King of New York in the Electoral College by 183 votes to 34. King was the consensus choice of the few remaining Federalist members of Congress to be their standard bearer. In keeping with the tenor of the times, both Monroe and King avoided campaigning, with the latter running a particularly passive "campaign." In King's view, the election was settled long before the votes were counted, and he saw no reason to take any pains to "excite the community on the subject." Privately, King's assessment of Monroe as something of a mediocrity can be seen in his postelection assessment that the president-elect "had the zealous support of nobody, and he was exempt from the hostility of everybody."

TEAM OF RIVALS

In his quest for national unity, the incoming president nominated a "team of rivals" for his cabinet positions. His most troublesome appointment was his secretary of treasury, William Crawford, a holdover from the Madison administration. Crawford and the president had a strained relationship throughout Monroe's presidency, as the treasury secretary spent a good part of his tenure positioning himself for the presidency. Two other headstrong members of Monroe's cabinet, Secretary of State John Quincy Adams and Secretary of War John C. Calhoun, also harbored presidential ambitions.

Crawford was the most egregious serial offender of the three when it came to irritating the president. The confrontation between the two men came to a head in 1822, when two of Monroe's nominees for military posts were rejected in a move led by Crawford's political allies in the Senate. Crawford seemed to welcome the prospect of getting fired by Monroe in hopes of improving his chances of securing the presidency himself in the 1824 election. When Monroe did not rise to the bait, Crawford tendered his resignation in July 1822, but the offer was rejected by the president. In 1823, Crawford's Treasury Department was accused of mismanaging federal funds and of covering up this mismanagement. A protracted series of congressional investigations ensued, with Crawford's allies insisting he was innocent and accusing Monroe, Secretary of State Adams, and Secretary of War Calhoun of attempting to undermine the treasury secretary's presidential ambitions.

Crawford's cabinet rival, Secretary of State Adams, noted that the decline of partisan opposition during the so-called "era of good feelings" led to a concurrent rise in personal attacks. Adams observed in his diary in 1820 that "every day is a perpetual struggle in both Houses of Congress to control the executive." He also noted that "as the old line of demarcation between parties has been broken down, personal has taken the place of principled opposition." Adams placed some of the blame for this on Crawford, whose "personal friends," while disavowing any role in this campaign, were constantly undermining the president. According to Adams, "every act and thought of Crawford looks to the next presidency."

PERSONAL ATTACKS AGAINST THE FIRST LADY

One of the primary targets of these personal attacks was the first lady. The Monroe administration may hold a unique place in the history of the American presidency in that the president's wife was subjected to more personal attacks than the president himself. Elizabeth Monroe had a tough act to follow with the popular Dolley Madison; as Louisa Adams, John Quincy Adams's wife, observed, "Dear Dolley was much more popular." Mrs. Monroe's ill-health and reserved manner led her to live a comparatively sheltered life in Washington. Her poor standing in the nation's capital was aggravated by what many viewed as her tendency to put on European or "monarchical" airs. It was said that the first lady had spent $1,500 on an imported dress for a New Year's Day reception celebrating the restoration of the executive mansion, and that she had displayed the audacity to give "a 'royal' nod of the head" to a guest. Her frequent absences from presidential social functions meant that no other women could be invited to dinners at the mansion, causing one male guest to complain that "everyone looked as if the next moment would be his last," while a member of Congress noted that "the President's dinner party was as dull a scene as you can imagine."

To compound matters, the restoration project experienced cost overruns, prompting congressional inquiries and parochial condemnation of the employment of French designers to overhaul the torched mansion. Congress initially appropriated $20,000 to restore the mansion, with the Monroes taking $9,000 as compensation for their donation of furniture, china, and other assorted items the family had brought back from France. The commissioner of public buildings pilfered $10,000 of the appropriation designated for the restoration, forcing Congress to appropriate additional funds and raising more concerns over the first lady's spending habits, which included the purchase of 1,200 bottles of champagne and wine. After a delay in opening the restored mansion to the public, which in all fairness was not complete, Jefferson's granddaughter, Ellen Randolph, wrote, "Mrs. Monroe has made herself very unpopular by taking no pains to conceal her aversion to society, and her unwillingness to be intruded on by visitors."

The first lady stopped the practice of returning social calls in Washington, much to the horror of Ellen Randolph and other leading socialites of the time. Some of the women responded by organizing a boycott. According to one leading lady, "the drawing room of the President was opened last night to a row of beggarly chairs . . . only five women attended." Elizabeth Monroe was known to enforce a strict dress code for events in the executive mansion. Her standards were so high, in fact, that she allegedly turned away a relative who paid a visit on the grounds of improper dress. This alleged "haughtiness," coupled with the distance that the Monroes kept from the Washington community, badly damaged the first lady's reputation both then and now. As Washington insider and noted author Margaret Bayard Smith observed in 1817, at which point the Monroes had lived in Washington for seven years, "both Mr. and Mrs. Monroe are perfect strangers not only to me but all the citizens."

Elizabeth Monroe's appearance also came under fire from her critics in the capital. If she was so sickly, and unable to return social calls, how could she possibly be as attractive as she appeared during her rare public events? The speculation was that she used "rouge on her cheeks" to improve her looks, and this was a practice that only women of "ill-repute," or Europeans, engaged in. To make matters worse, when the Monroe's daughter Maria was married in March 1820, most members of Congress and the entire diplomatic corps were not invited. This "private" wedding generated outrage throughout Washington society, and required the intervention of Secretary of State Adams and others to contain the damage. Much of the criticism was directed at the Monroe's eldest daughter Eliza, who many blamed for limiting the wedding to 42 attendees. Secretary of State Adams seems to have reflected the consensus opinion of Washington insiders when he described Eliza as "an obstinate little firebrand" who had triggered a "senseless war of etiquette." Louisa Adams was even more cutting, condemning Eliza Monroe's "love for scandal" and adding that "no reputation is safe in her hands." She would later observe that Eliza was "so accomplished and ill-bred, so proud and so mean I scarcely ever met such a compound."

REPUBLICAN ENEMIES AND FEDERALIST "FRIENDS"

Monroe's most significant personal and political opposition came from within his own Republican coalition. One of the president's harshest critics was Thomas Ritchie, the editor of the *Richmond Enquirer*. Ritchie was an old-line Republican devoted to states' rights and strict construction (the latter means a literal reading of the Constitution). Ritchie frequently published angry letters condemning Monroe's betrayal of Jeffersonian principles, including one from "Virginius" accusing the president of promoting a nationalist program in order to enhance his popularity. "Virginius" added that Monroe had surrounded himself with sycophants who were deluding him about the public's attitude toward his presidency. Another Republican stalwart, William Branch Giles, charged that the president had abandoned the Constitution in order to enhance his own power.

Monroe's priority as president was to bolster national unity and continue the process of eradicating partisan differences—or more accurately, eradicating any remaining Federalist cells. The president embraced proposals that were anathema to Republicans only a few years earlier, including a national bank, heightened military preparedness, protective tariffs designed to enhance American manufacturing interests, and (qualified) federal support for roads and canals designed to "bind the Union more closely together." This transformation of Republican ideology had the effect of disarming even ardent Federalists like Josiah Quincy of Boston, who noted that Monroe and his fellow Republicans had "out-federalized the federalists." Although Monroe may have embraced certain Federalist principles, he refused to appoint Federalists to positions in his new government. One New Englander urged the president to appoint Federalists instead of the "utterly contemptible" New England Republicans, but Monroe rejected this advice.

Despite drawing the line at hiring Federalists, particularly of the New England variety, the president believed it was important to restore that region's standing in the minds of the American citizenry, which had been badly damaged in the wake of the Hartford Convention of 1814–1815 (a gathering of the New England Federalist Party to discuss grievances concerning the ongoing War of 1812 and the political problems arising from the federal government's increasing power; the convention was seen by some as a gathering of traitors). Following George

Washington's example, the newly elected president decided to travel on an extended tour of New England in 1817. The idea that Monroe would undertake a tour was a bipartisan gesture in itself, harkening back to the days of Washington's Federalist presidency and breaking with Jefferson and Madison's practice of avoiding ceremonies or events with supposedly "regal" overtones.

Monroe's tour captured the attention of the nation's newspapers and went a long way toward further disarming Federalist opposition to the new administration. As historian Robert Pierce Forbes has noted, it was the "arch-Federalist newspaper," Boston's *Columbian Centinel*, "which conferred on Monroe's administration its signature moniker, the 'Era of Good Feelings.'" Despite all the warmth associated with Monroe's visit, the president and his Federalist hosts had two conflicting agendas. Monroe, as historian Sandy Moats has observed, had a vision of a United States liberated from the shackles of partisanship, while his hosts envisioned an era in which Federalists would experience a rebirth by winning appointments in a bipartisan Monroe administration.

In the end, Monroe's visit to New England, and Boston in particular, was something of a failure. The fact that Monroe would deign to travel to the heart of the Federalist empire was not welcomed by Republicans in Congress or in the Republican Party press. The *Virginia Herald* complained that "we had hoped that he [Monroe] would shrink from the glittering 'pomp and circumstance' of courtly parade, and courtier-like attention, which the good people of the North lavish upon him." Monroe's tour became increasingly awkward the closer he got to Boston. In order to escort Monroe to Boston, one greeting committee composed of Federalists met the president in Providence, Rhode Island, while further up the road a second greeting committee composed of Republicans met him in Pawtucket. Neither group was happy because, as one military officer noted, both wanted "to take charge of the President." To further inflame Republican sensibilities, the officer deemed the Federalist delegation as the official presidential escort.

Monroe timed his visit to Boston to coincide with the celebration of the Fourth of July, but even this day of patriotic festivities could not prevent partisan fissures from emerging. Boston's Republicans chose to meet separately with Monroe on that day, ignoring an event hosted by the city's leading Federalists. As Sandy Moats aptly describes it, "overshadowed by its Federalist opponents, Monroe's own party was relegated to the sidelines during his historic visit to Boston."

This was not lost on the president's Republican rivals, including William Crawford, who wrote, "Seriously, I think the President has lost as much as he has gained by this tour." Another fellow Republican, Speaker of the House Henry Clay of Kentucky, condemned the "pomp and ostentatious parade," sardonically adding that if Monroe were successful in converting the New Englanders "he merits the honors of a political saint." Federalists were also disappointed in the aftermath of Monroe's visit after the president opted not to appoint any members of their party to significant positions in his administration. Some Federalists lobbied to have Daniel Webster appointed as the nation's attorney general, a proposal that repulsed both Republicans and Federalists. Many of the latter believed that the party's leaders had dishonored themselves with their over-the-top welcome to Monroe in Boston. As one Federalist Congressman observed, Federalists in New England had "pushed the thing to the very borders of the ridiculous." The position of attorney general was ultimately filled by loyal Republican William Wirt of Virginia. Rufus King, the de facto leader of the disintegrating Federalist Party, noted with chagrin that "our Boston folk have not been honored by an admission to the Cabinet; I allude to the office of Attorney General."

THE ELECTION OF 1820

Monroe ran for reelection in 1820 and did not face an opponent, scoring a victory that was nearly as impressive as George Washington's unanimous win some 30 years earlier. The final tally was 231 electoral votes for Monroe to one for Secretary of State John Quincy Adams. The lone dissenter in the Electoral College was Governor William Plumer of New Hampshire. Legend has it that Plumer did not want to detract from Washington's unanimous election, so he cast his electoral vote for Adams. But in fact Plumer, a Federalist turned Republican, believed that Monroe was profligate in his spending, "had not the weight of character which his office requires," and conducted presidential business "very improperly."

Plumer's son, William Plumer Jr., would write in 1856 that his father "thought that Mr. Monroe's capacity by no means equal to the place. 'We mistake,' he said, 'if we suppose that any but the ablest men are fit for the highest place.' The government of weak men must always be disastrous. 'Woe to thee, O land, where thy king is a child.'" Plumer went on to add that Republicans of the "old school" from the South shared his father's contempt for Monroe. Congressman John Randolph of Roanoke and other hardline Republicans "disliked Monroe, whom they regard as having adopted, chiefly under the influence of Calhoun, some of the worst heresies of the old Federal party." Plumer added that Randolph "said in the House . . . they talk of the unanimity of his [Monroe's] re-election. Yes, sir; but it is the unanimity of indifference, and not of approbation. Four years hence, he will go out, with equal unanimity; and the feeling will be, not indifference, but contempt."

Despite winning one of the most impressive reelections in the history of the United States, Monroe was a lame duck from the day he delivered his second inaugural address on March 5, 1821. Speaker of the House Clay told Secretary of State Adams that Monroe "had not the slightest influence in Congress. His career was considered as closed. There was nothing further to be expected by him or from him." Clay added a remarkably cutting coda to this dire description of Monroe's impotence, noting that there "would not be a man in the United States possessing less personal influence over them [Congress] than the President." These criticisms were echoed by Monroe's old opponent from 1816, Rufus King, who observed that Monroe's "plans and measures . . . are without friends in Congress." Channeling Clay, King added that Monroe, for all practical purposes, might as well be deceased, noting that while the president had not expired, he was "dead as respects direction, or control." Another relic of the disintegrating Federalist Party, Congressman Louis McLane of Delaware, who would later become a close ally of Andrew Jackson, observed that "this poor old President" found himself "woefully beset, deserted by all his old friends."

CONCLUSION

There was one old adversary, or more accurately, a living relative of an old adversary, who rejected the idea that the presidency of James Monroe was an "era of good feelings." At some point in the 1820s, Monroe paid a courtesy call to Elizabeth Schuyler Hamilton, who outlived her husband Alexander by 50 years. Eliza Hamilton had become something of a fixture in the nation's capital, regaling visitors with stories of dancing with George Washington and recounting other tales from the founding era. When Monroe paid a visit, Eliza was in no mood for reconciliation. She refused to offer the president a seat in her parlor and coldly announced that she would accept nothing short of an apology for what Monroe had done to her husband, noting that "no lapse of time, no nearness to the grave, makes any difference."

Eliza Hamilton's contempt for Monroe was perhaps somewhat out of step with the relative comity that existed during his presidency. Monroe's biographer Noble Cunningham has observed that the president "aroused neither the adulation nor the detestation that Jefferson stirred . . . and excited less public controversy and fewer stronger feelings than any of his predecessors." It would, however, be a mistake to assume that the Monroe years were entirely an "era of good feelings."

In the end, James Monroe's vision of eradicating partisanship failed miserably. After the Federalists disappeared they were quickly replaced by the Whigs, while many of the hardline Republicans segued into the Democratic Party of Andrew Jackson, leading to the "second party system." Ironically, in the aftermath of Monroe's effort to eliminate partisan divisions, the kind of personal attacks that launched Monroe's political career escalated dramatically as the nation drifted toward the bloodiest war in its history.

Stephen F. Knott

Further Reading

Ammon, Harry. *James Monroe: The Quest for National Identity.* Charlottesville, VA: University of Virginia Press, 1990.

Cunningham, Noble. *The Presidency of James Monroe*. Lawrence, KS: University Press of Kansas, 1996.

Forbes, Robert Pierce. *The Missouri Compromise and Its Aftermath: Slavery and the Meaning of America*. Chapel Hill, NC: University of North Carolina Press, 2007.

Hart, Gary. *James Monroe*. New York: Times Books, 2005.

Howe, Daniel Walker. *What Hath God Wrought: The Transformation of America, 1815–1848*. New York: Oxford University Press, 2007.

Knott, Stephen F. *Alexander Hamilton and the Persistence of Myth*. Lawrence, KS: University Press of Kansas, 2002.

Leiberger, Stuart, ed. *A Companion to James Madison and James Monroe*. Chichester, UK: Wiley-Blackwell, 2013.

Moats, Sandy. "The Limits of 'Good Feelings': Partisan Healing and Political Futures during James Monroe's Boston Visit of 1817." Worcester, MA: Proceedings of the American Antiquarian Society, 2008.

Schneider, Dorothy, and Carl J. Schneider. *First Ladies: A Biographical Dictionary*. New York: Facts on File, 2010.

Unger, Harlow Giles. *The Last Founding Father: James Monroe and a Nation's Call to Greatness*. Boston: Da Capo Press, 2009.

Waldrup, Carole Chandler. *Wives of the American Presidents*. Jefferson, NC: McFarland & Co., 2006.

Woodward, C. Vann, ed. *Responses of the Presidents to Charges of Misconduct*. New York: Dell Publishing, 1974.

6. John Quincy Adams

Born: July 11, 1767
Died: February 23, 1848
Time in Office: Sixth President of the United States, March 4, 1825, to March 4, 1829
Election Results: 1824 Election: 84 (32.2%) Electoral College votes, 13 (54.2%) House votes; 1828 Election: 43.6% of popular vote, 83 (31.8%) Electoral College votes
Spouse: Louisa Catherine Johnson (m. 1797)

Sixth president of the United States, John Quincy Adams was never much liked. For although he was known as principled and erudite, he was, according to historian Robert Remini, also widely regarded as "demanding, testy, irritable, critical, and fussy." Judgmental even in his self-reflections, Adams once noted: "I am a man of reserved, cold, austere, and forbidding manners; my political adversaries say, a gloomy misanthropist, and my personal enemies, an unsocial savage. With a knowledge of the actual defect in my character, I have not the pliability to reform it." On another occasion, he stated: "I well know that I never was and never shall be what is commonly termed a popular man."

Part of what made him unpopular was his refusal to engage in politics as a partisan. Adams wanted to be seen as a statesman, not a politician. To one friend, he wrote: "My career has attached no party to me precisely because it has been independent of all party . . . the consequence has been that all parties disown me—the Federalists as a deserter, the Democrats as an apostate. I have followed the convictions of my own mind with a single eye to the interests of the whole nation." Given his cheerless temperament and penchant for defying his fellow politicians, it should perhaps be more surprising that Adams ever became president, than that his presidential years were marred by relentless attacks from fevered enthusiasts—attacks that paved the way for Andrew Jackson's celebrated candidacy in 1828.

But prior to becoming president, Adams was genuinely respected for his extensive diplomatic experience, dedication to public service, and keen legalistic mind. During James Madison's presidency, Adams served as the minister plenipotentiary to Russia; led the peace commission that negotiated the Treaty of Ghent, ending the War of 1812; and worked to restore diplomatic relations with the British at the American Embassy in London. Of course, it also helped that his father was former president John Adams. Still, when President James Monroe nominated Adams for secretary of state ("the stepladder to the presidential chair"), only Adams's future presidential rival, Henry Clay, took issue with the choice. Thomas Jefferson, for example, praised Monroe's decision, proclaiming that "They were made for each other . . . Adams has a pointed pen; Monroe has judgment enough for both and firmness enough to have *his* judgment control." In fact, the two men did form a productive partnership, though it was Adams's "judgment" that typically influenced Monroe's decisions and not the other way around. As Remini aptly concluded, "John Quincy Adams is arguably the greatest secretary of state to serve that office . . . responsible for the transformation of the United States into a transcontinental nation . . . [and for] the formulation of one of the most basic and fundamental precepts of U.S. foreign policy, namely the Monroe Doctrine."

Throughout his long political career, Adams maintained that his policy choices were rooted in lofty principles, not self-interest. Even as his wife, Louisa, went to great lengths to court Washington's society on her husband's behalf, Adams eschewed any sort of politicking that involved falsely flattering foes and cultivating favors. (Louisa Adams threw regular parties each Tuesday and hosted several other events, including one for Andrew Jackson.) In early 1823, Adams insisted to a friend: "If I am to be a candidate, it must be by the wishes, ardent and active, of others, and not by mine. . . . If my countrymen prefer others to me, I must not repine at their choice. Indifference at the heart is not to be won by wooing. . . . Merit and just right in this country will be heard. And in any case, if they are not heard 'without my stir' I shall acquiesce in the conclusion that is because they do not exist."

Ultimately, the hatred directed at Adams after he reached the Oval Office did not derive from his lackluster personality, but from suspicions that he had engaged in a "corrupt bargain" with Clay, giving Clay the post of secretary of state in return for the presidency. As such, it was Adams's miscalculations during the 1824 election that inspired the attacks from opponents and impaired his presidential tenure. Although much of what was alleged was both unfair and unfounded, Adams erred in deciding *not* to respond to his partisan critics. Unwilling to accept that the political game had changed around him, Adams was permanently branded by Jackson and his nascent Democratic Party as a corrupt and out-of-touch elitist. The result was that by the time Adams left office in 1829, Clay had become the leader of the National Republicans and Jackson had become the new president.

Importantly, the 1828 "rematch" election between Adams and Jackson marked not only the first time that mass support was channeled into organized political parties, but also the end of the founding generation's elite-centered politics. For while Adams was not technically one of the framers, his father was, and his views reflected that. Adams viewed America as a representative republic, not a democracy. That belief, however, was no longer in vogue. In this sense, his critics were right: he was out of touch. Still, the vitriolic tone and bizarre accusations of moral depravity and public corruption were far removed from what his presidential tenure merited. Prior to detailing the specific attacks on Adams and his administration, it is necessary to review the "corrupt bargain."

THE ELECTION AND HOUSE SELECTION OF 1824

The 1824 election was a riotous affair that began early and ended late. It involved four candidates from the same party, a split electoral vote, and a House decision. All the candidates had impressive résumés and claims to the presidency. Adams, as secretary of state, was positioned as the election's frontrunner, but as was suggested above, House Speaker Clay spent most of Monroe's presidency trying to upset conventional wisdom. Secretary of the Treasury William Crawford of Georgia, the only southerner in the race (after Secretary of War John Calhoun of South Carolina dropped out to pursue the vice presidency instead), had a solid base. In fact, "King Caucus" (a slang term used to describe the perceived "undemocratic" nomination process in 1824) had endorsed Crawford after he had suffered a stroke in 1823, which had, according to Remini, left him "partially paralyzed, speechless, and almost sightless." Jackson, the rugged Tennessean who had become a popular military hero at the Battle of New Orleans, was the only Washington "outsider."

Despite Adams's declarations that he would not actively campaign for the presidency, Remini observed that "he soon discovered . . . that if he really wanted the prize he had to reach for it." In the stealth fashion of that era, Adams penned "anonymous" editorials extolling his virtues and then had sympathetic newspaper editors print them to advance his claims. He also forced himself to attend parties and other social events in Washington at which the young nation's wealthy and politically influential figures often congregated. In the six states with legislative choice and in the 18 states where the popular vote determined the allocation of the electoral votes, Adams's friends worked hard to turn out his supporters. They pursued Crawford's voters in the South and battled Clay in the Midwest. In New York, they offered a deal to Clay's backers in the legislature, but it was declined. (Scholars agree that had Clay been among the top three vote getters whose names went to the House, it is likely that Clay would have engineered his own election to the presidency. In fact, this was his strategy for winning the presidency all along.) Given that he was part of a field of four credible candidates, Adams's strong second-place showings (behind Jackson, but far ahead of Crawford and Clay) in both the popular and electoral vote counts were impressive, especially for such an unpopular Washington insider. The election results were as follows: Jackson earned 151,363 votes (99 electoral votes); Adams garnered 113,142 votes (84 electoral votes); Crawford won 41,032 votes (41 electoral votes); and Clay had 47,545 votes (37 electoral votes). More critically, though, he and his team achieved their larger goal: ensuring that Clay placed fourth, so he would be ineligible for the House election. (The Twelfth Amendment to the Constitution, ratified in 1804, reduced the number of eligible candidates in the event of a House election from five to three).

Then Adams miscalculated. When it became evident that no candidate had received a majority of electoral votes and the House of Representatives would select the president, Adams, rather than retiring home and quietly awaiting the outcome, launched a new campaign. As Clay once remarked: "Kissing was like the presidency. It was not to be sought, and not to be *declined*." He arranged private meetings, sent letters, and attended events around town. He agreed to appoint to the "official printer" posts in Missouri a list of individuals given to him by Missouri's sole U.S. congressman. He gave multiple, vague assurances on patronage issues to key representatives from New York, Maryland, and Massachusetts. Some scholars speculate that Adams may have even engaged in bribery of one or more strategically important lawmakers.

But the coup de grace was the alleged bargain with Clay, who by virtue of his position as speaker and the votes he had earned in the states, was "the kingmaker." Over the course of three meetings with a Clay emissary, Adams, according to Remini, agreed to give Clay "a prominent share in the Administration." Although it was never explicitly stated, it was understood that Adams would offer Clay the secretary of state position. On January 9, 1825, Clay personally met with Adams to learn more about his views on various public issues, though not to discuss the possibility of nomination. After the meeting, Adams was confident Clay would support him despite the fact that the Kentucky legislature was urging Clay to vote for Jackson. When the House voted on February 9, Adams won on the first ballot with the minimum number of states required—13—including Kentucky,

Missouri, Illinois, and New York. (Van Rensselaer, a devoutly religious man, had pledged his vote to Martin Van Buren [for Crawford], but as he went to vote, he spotted a ballot on the floor inscribed with Adams's name and believing it was a sign, he picked it up and "thrust it in the ballot box.") In sum, the optics were all wrong. Adams emerged with the presidency, but also with a reputation for political skullduggery that he would never be able to shake.

THE BACKLASH AND THE BUILDING OF AN OPPOSITION PARTY

Adams was not prepared for what came next: bitter feelings and fierce partisanship. Even before the announcement that Clay would be secretary of state, Jackson's supporters spoke of the House election being a rigged game. Calhoun supporter John Randolph noted that "the cards were stacked." And at a reception given the day after the vote and hosted by President Monroe to honor Adams, a Jackson partisan saw Adams and exclaimed, "There is our 'Clay President' and he will be moulded at that man's will and pleasure as easily as clay in a potter's hands." Robert Hayne further labeled the deal a "monstrous union between Clay & Adams," while Louis McLane exclaimed, "All the waters of the sweet Heavens cannot remove the iota of corruption."

It got worse after Clay accepted the cabinet appointment. According to Remini, the news "struck the Jackson camp like a thunderclap." Jackson ranted in a letter: "So you see, the Judas of the West [Clay] has closed the contract and will receive the thirty pieces of silver. His end will be the same. Was there ever witnessed such a bare faced corruption in any country before?" Recognizing the political opportunity, Jackson then wrote to his friend William Lewis, a former military colleague and political adviser: "Would it not be well that the papers of Nashville and the whole State should speak out with moderate but firm disapprobation of this corruption, to give a proper tone to the people, and to draw their attention to the subject?" The 1828 election had begun—nearly a month before Adams was inaugurated—on March 4, 1825.

Over the next four years, Jackson, his supporters, and a partisan press worked to bring together all who opposed Adams and Clay, including Crawford's former campaign manager, Martin Van Buren, and the newly elected vice president, John Calhoun. Hammering away at the notion that Adams and Clay had engaged in a "corrupt bargain," they erased the legitimacy of the House selection process and Adams's presidential governing authority. Adams's displacement of Jackson, as the first-place finisher and the choice of the people, created two political parties. As historian Mary Hargreaves explained, the Democratic Party formed around "unified opposition to the administration, born of consolidated Southern hostility to Adams on the slavery issue, Western indignation on behalf of Jackson," and the violently anti-Clay forces located in New York and Pennsylvania.

Scholars have noted, however, that even as opposition partisans cried foul, asserting that Adams had "stolen" the election from the people, there was nothing objectively "corrupt" about the alliance of Clay and Adams. The two men knew each other well. They had met in Belgium a decade before, while serving together on the commission that negotiated the Treaty of Ghent. Though their personalities were polar opposite (Clay was a brilliant orator with a sharp wit and a charming politician who reveled in drinking, gambling, and the horses), they held similar visions of an expansive American nationalism and believed in an active, powerful federal government. Aside from their shared ideology, Clay had decided long before any negotiations began that he preferred Adams for the presidency over Crawford, who was ill, and Jackson, who Clay regarded as a "military chieftain."

THE FAILURE OF A PRINCIPLED PRESIDENCY

Adams's gravest mistake was that he chose to combat the corruption charge by dismissing partisanship. He hoped to rise above the scheming and prove himself as a statesman who placed his country above party decision making. Ironically, his nonpartisan stance only served to upset his friends and embolden his critics. It also ended up making him more vulnerable to the allegations, which suggested that he held antidemocratic sentiments and was a corrupt elitist, or a "royalist," as the newspapers claimed.

For instance, Adams naively sought to retain Monroe's cabinet because he was enamored by the idea that the various factions could come together to govern the nation. Since Calhoun was now vice president, he sought to appoint Jackson as his secretary of war. Jackson flatly rejected the offer. Treasury Secretary Crawford also turned down Adams's suggestion to stay on at Treasury. Further embarrassing Adams, 14 of the 41 senators voted against Clay's confirmation to the State Department.

Adams ignored these warnings, believing that his principled leadership would eventually bring around his former foes. In his first annual message to Congress, according to historian Walter McDougall, he proposed "bold federal initiatives," which "nearly blew the dome off the Capitol building." His agenda included sending ministers to a conference of South American nations; building a network of roads, canals, and highways; founding a national university and a naval academy; building an observatory and hiring an astronomer; establishing uniform weights and measures; and creating an executive department focused on the exploration and mapping of the continent. As McDougall explained, Congress was appalled by his wildly ambitious vision: "Who did this man think he was, Louis XIV? Crawford thought Adams' imperious program unconstitutional. Calhoun spied a flank attack on states' rights. Van Buren heard a one-term president talking. All three defected to Jackson."

From then on, Adams's presidency became nearly impossible. The debate over sending delegates to the South American conference was so prolonged that by the time the ministers arrived at the meeting in Panama, it had already adjourned. Adams had also been forced to renegotiate a treaty with the Creeks, specifying the terms of the tribe relocation from land in Georgia, but the Georgia governor was not pleased about the later relocation date (January 1827 rather than September 1826) that had been agreed to. Adams told the governor that he would enforce the federal law; the governor shot back that if he tried, he would be "treated as a public enemy" in his state. The entire episode, as Remini noted, "to protect the Indians under the legal authority of the federal government gained [Adams] nothing but the hatred of all those southerners who lusted after Indian territory and could hardly wait for the next election to replace him in the White House with Andrew Jackson."

Adams also refused to remove "otherwise qualified" appointees who were using their offices to work against him, such as Postmaster General John McLean. He further declined participating in any activities that could be construed as campaign events, such as the 50th anniversary of the Battle of Bunker Hill or a canal opening in Pennsylvania. The obstructionist tactics of the Jacksonian Democrats worked in helping them win seats in Congress during the midterm elections. Democrats won control of the House and extended their majority in the Senate.

By the time the new Congress convened in December 1827, the presidential campaign was nearly in full swing. As a final blow, according to Remini, Jacksonian Democrats "concocted . . . the most lopsided and unequal piece of legislation [on the tariff question] imaginable. Virtually every item in it contained marks of political favoritism." Even though the bill was a mess, Adams backed it because it was the best chance to obtain tariffs for internal improvements. The Congress passed it, believing Adams's support was a bluff and that he would veto it, which would then allow them to argue that in addition to being corrupt, Adams was a hypocrite (i.e., "he said he wanted tariffs, but when we gave him a bill, he sent it back"). When Adams signed the legislation known as the "Tariff of Abominations," he made even more enemies. He not only lost the South, who would now have to live with high tariffs, but many of his friends in New England who wanted tariffs were not protected by the bizarre schedule.

THE SLANDERS OF THE 1828 ELECTION

As the 1828 election approached, the attacks grew louder and more personal. In the spring of 1828, Adams's second son, John, who served as his private secretary, commented that a reporter for a Jacksonian newspaper would not have come to the reception at the White House, if he "had the feelings of a gentleman." Even though the reporter heard John and sought "explanations," none were given. A few weeks later, when John was in the Capitol, the reporter "pulled his nose," a traditional method to proffer a challenge to a duel. When Adams learned of the incident, he sought to squash the conflict by asking Congress to investigate. The investigating committee ultimately agreed that the "assault" reflected poorly on "the dignity of the House"; it also stated that "it was not expedient to take any action." But that was not the end of it. The editor of the *Telegraph*, a friend and supporter of Jackson's named Duff Green, wrote a piece arguing that Adams should not have asked Congress to get involved, and saying, "could not [Adams] have anticipated that the baby, who was considered old enough to . . . bear messages to Congress, would run blubbering to tell his daddy that he had had his nose pulled and his jaws slapped for his impudence." In other words, Green asserted in his editorial that both Adams were spineless cowards.

When it came to partisan politics, Clay rather than Adams did the heavy lifting. He solicited his friends and colleagues to write favorable editorials in pro-administration newspapers, and he coordinated and directed the partisan organizing in the states in advance of any elections. But the problem for the National Republicans was bigger than logistics. As Henry Clay's brother, Porter Clay, wrote in February 1827, "the friends of Jackson are desperat [sic] and clamerous [sic] and consequently active while the friends of the admn. are inactive and luke warm and with out any concert." In essence, Adams was saddled with what today's pollsters refer to as an "enthusiasm gap" between the parties. Adams and Clay were simply ill-prepared and outgunned. Of course, they also had been occupied with the task of governing, while Jackson and Van Buren had been completely focused on "erecting a party machine" and undercutting the Adams administration.

Once the Jacksonians had the county and state committees organized with regular meetings, they worked to knit together their communications by establishing what Remini described as "a chain of newspaper posts from the New England States to Louisiana, and branching off through Lexington and the Western States." As Remini documented, during the six-month period, starting in the summer of 1827, Democrats purchased or started nine papers in North Carolina, 18 in Ohio, and other papers in states across the Northeast and upper Midwest. Duff Green of the *Telegraph*, for example, printed 40,000 weekly copies of his newspaper in 1828. These papers trafficked in all sorts of rumor and innuendo.

One absurd allegation concocted about Adams's past was that he had, in historian Leah Remini's words, "pimped for the czar of Russia," when he had served as a minister to Russia. The story arose out of the fact that the Adams family had a nursemaid who accompanied them to Russia to help care for their young son, Charles. The nursemaid had written a letter about Czar Alexander's reputation for womanizing at court, and when the czar discovered the letter's contents through his post office, he arranged to meet the nursemaid in the presence of both his wife and Charles. After this, the tenor of the election continued to devolve. Adams's political opponents, for example, insinuated that he and Louisa had engaged in premarital sex. Still, the most persistent attack on Adams was that he had bargained with Clay and "stolen" the presidency from Jackson (and the people), which made him personally corrupt as well. Democrats even tallied up his salary for his many years of public service and argued that the amount—$105,000, more than $12,000 annually—had been lifted directly from the pockets of the American people. One claimed to dislike "the kingly pomp and splendor that is displayed by the present incumbent" and another said the election was "a great contest between the *aristocracy* and democracy of America."

CONCLUSION

When the votes were counted in the 1828 election, Jackson won in a landslide, garnering 56% of the popular vote and nearly 100 more electoral votes than Adams (Jackson received 178 electoral votes while Adams could only muster 83). Perhaps unsurprisingly, given how awful and relentless the attacks had been on Adams during his presidency, Adams chose not to attend Jackson's inauguration. He also noted that, "posterity will scarcely believe . . . the combination of parties and of public men against my character and reputation such as I believe never before was exhibited against any man since this Union existed."

Overall, Adams's reaction to accusations that he had been party to a "corrupt bargain"—to stand on principle and adopt a decidedly Washingtonian nonpartisan mien—was worse than the bargain itself. After all, most presidential incumbents, irrespective of the attacks they endure, manage to serve two terms. But in misjudging the public's new demands for democratic posturing and partisanship, Adams made himself vulnerable to his opponents. Still, Jackson had skillfully backed Adams into a tough corner. For if Adams acted like a partisan, it would have been viewed as evidence of his corruptness; if he rose above politics, it would have been viewed as evidence of his arrogance. Out of all this, Clay became his party's leader precisely because while he supported Adams, he had continued to dole out appointments on a partisan basis and play politics. Adams's presidency was undone by his overcompensation to Jackson's charges (not by the negative attacks) and his desire to eradicate the "corrupt bargain" from the electorate's memory.

Lara M. Brown

Further Reading

Adams, Charles Francis. *Memoirs of John Quincy Adams*. Philadelphia: J. B. Lippincott Company, 1875, reprinted 2007.

Brands, H. W. *Andrew Jackson: His Life and Times*. New York: Doubleday/Random House, 2005.

Hargreaves, Mary W. M. *The Presidency of John Quincy Adams.* Lawrence, KS: University of Kansas Press, 1985.

McDougall, Walter. *Freedom Just around the Corner: A New American History, 1585–1828.* New York: HarperCollins, 2004.

Remini, Robert V. *The Election of Andrew Jackson.* Philadelphia: J. B. Lippincott Company, 1963.

Remini, Robert V. *John Quincy Adams.* New York: Times Books, 2002.

Unger, Harlow Giles. *John Quincy Adams.* Boston: Perseus Books, 2012.

7. Andrew Jackson

Born: March 15, 1767

Died: June 8, 1845

Time in Office: Seventh President of the United States, March 4, 1829, to March 4, 1837

Election Results: 1824 Election: 99 (37.9%) Electoral College votes, 7 (29.2%) House votes; 1828 Election: 56.1% of popular vote, 178 (68.2%) Electoral College votes; 1832 Election: 54.2% of popular vote, 219 (76%) Electoral College votes

Spouse: Rachel Donelson (m. 1794)

Andrew Jackson first came to national attention at the end of the War of 1812 as the general who won the Battle of New Orleans. Throughout the war, the British had blockaded the Atlantic coast; toward the end, they sent troops to the Gulf of Mexico to secure their trade along the Mississippi River. When these troops attacked New Orleans in December 1814, they were met by General Jackson, known to his troops as "Old Hickory" because he was so tough in battle. Although the Americans were vastly outnumbered, General Jackson roundly defeated the British in a lopsided battle that saw more than 2,000 British casualties in contrast to fewer than 1,000 on the American side. When the British forces received word that the Treaty of Ghent had ended hostilities on December 24, 1814, they immediately withdrew from the city. Although the Battle of New Orleans had not influenced the peace treaty, the victory played an important symbolic role for the American psyche—the ability to win even when outnumbered fed a vision of potential for the fledgling country. Jackson, the son of poor immigrants and hero of New Orleans, similarly symbolized the great potential of the common man.

Although Jackson's supporters focused on his heroic actions during the Battle of New Orleans, his detractors were more cognizant of his behavior after the battle. When Jackson had initially arrived in New Orleans, residents of the city were in a panic about what they perceived as inevitable defeat. Jackson declared martial law to get control of the situation and gave himself the power to seize property and conscript men. His comment at the time portended his more general attitude about leadership: "Those who are not for us are against us, and will be dealt with accordingly." Although the need for rigid order dissipated following the British withdrawal, Jackson refused to lift martial law, suggesting that enemies lay in wait for the city to let down its guard. Even after the Treaty of Ghent was ratified in February 1815, conscripts were not allowed to return to their businesses. Deserters were imprisoned, and some were even shot. When community leaders criticized Jackson for leaving martial law in place, he dealt with the opposition by arresting the public officials who had voiced it. Only in March, after receiving official word of the treaty's approval through formal channels, did Jackson finally lift martial law.

Jackson's behavior during and after the Battle of New Orleans displayed three attributes that presaged criticism that would later be directed toward him as president. First, the appeal he had to common folk yielded attacks on his less than genteel heritage. Second, he tended to see in black and white, casting others either as friends or enemies, which raised the specter of conspiracies in his perception of his political environment. Third, he often ignored legal niceties when they got in the way of accomplishing what he saw as moral imperatives.

The Jackson era witnessed partisan newspapers loudly advocating either for or against Jackson. Early in Jackson's tenure, three distinct lines of attack were directed at his populist inclinations—what Jackson saw as his love of the common man. The first major attack concerned the inauguration—the presence of tens of thousands of well-wishers fed a narrative that Jackson was encouraging mob rule. The criticism of mob rule intensified when Jackson followed through on his promise to institute rotation in office, connecting him permanently with the spoils system (the practice of political patronage in filling positions within the federal government). Third, when Peggy Eaton, wife of the secretary of war, was ostracized by Washington society for being too common, critics said that Jackson became so preoccupied with the attacks on Eaton that he had a hard time focusing on policy issues.

The fourth line of attack moved from Jackson's defense of the common man to his belief in states' rights. This was exemplified in his vociferous opposition to the National Bank, earning a censure from Congress for his efforts. Finally, his support of tariffs led to the threat of military action during the Nullification Crisis (when some southern states fought against federal authority). In the first three attacks Jackson was portrayed as encouraging mob rule; in the last two, Jackson was called a tyrant and a despot. Through all the attacks, Jackson maintained his image as a tough old hickory tree, inflexible and willing to do anything to win.

POPULAR ELECTION OR MOB RULE?

Democracy came into its own during the Jacksonian era. Jackson initially ran for president in 1824 along with three other candidates who eventually secured votes in the Electoral College. Jackson led the pack, both in the popular vote and in number of electors. But constitutionally, the Electoral College could only choose the president if a majority of electors agreed on the same candidate. With four candidates in the race, that did not happen in 1824. Instead, the top three candidates were placed before the House of Representatives to make the final determination. In what Jackson later described as a "corrupt bargain," Speaker of the House Henry Clay cast his support to John Quincy Adams, giving him the necessary majority. When Adams subsequently named Clay as his secretary of state, Jackson cried foul and immediately began organizing for the election of 1828.

In decrying a system that allowed the most popular candidate to lose the election, Jackson transformed our perception of the presidency. Where previously America's system of government had been praised for its Republican virtues, Jackson advocated for the principle of democracy. Although nominating caucuses had been criticized as elitist even in Thomas Jefferson's 1800 election, Jackson began, with the help of Martin Van Buren, to formulate practical alternatives to caucuses. During the 1828 election, Jackson's campaign organized committees at the local, county, and state levels, encouraging widespread public involvement in the election. At the local level, Hickory Clubs planned barbeques and rallies along with "Hickory Pole" raisings in town centers across the country. This widespread support was enough to assure Jackson a majority in both the popular vote and in the Electoral College.

In the long term, Jackson transformed not only the nominating process, but also America's understanding of the presidency. Jackson advocated for a vision of the president as the only representative of all the people—a vision that is still widely retained. In the short term, his populism endowed Jackson personally as the people's president. This perception was readily apparent at Jackson's inauguration. An estimated 10,000–20,000 supporters flooded Washington, D.C., from around the country. Traditionally, an open house at the White House followed the inauguration, and so the inaugural crowd followed as Jackson rode a white horse from the Capitol up Pennsylvania Avenue. When he arrived at the White House, members of the established Washington society greeted him but, as less refined crowds arrived, the White House proved too small and the refreshments insufficient to satisfy the well-wishers. In the crush of the crowd, Jackson slipped out the back and returned to the hotel where he had been staying. White House staff moved the punch outside to draw the crowd out and minimize damage to the carpet and furniture. Because Washington society harbored fears that President Jackson would initiate some type of mob rule with his focus on democracy, they were quick to describe the open house as a drunken brawl. Accounts of the event still describe the demolition of the furniture in the White House, although the damage was much more limited.

SPOILS SYSTEM

The fear of mob rule focused Washington residents on Jackson's promised institution of rotation in office. In previous administrations, government jobs had been held by well-educated individuals who largely came from elite families. There had been little turnover between administrations, especially during the Era of Good Feelings (a time after the War of 1812 that reflected a sense of national purpose and a desire for unity among Americans). Over time, positions had even been handed down within families. Jackson's campaign rhetoric about the intrigues of Washington had left office holders (and their families) uncertain about their future. From Jackson's perspective, most government positions did not require special merit beyond a good intellect. As a result, he called for frequent rotation in office to uphold his democratic ideal: positions should be open to all who qualified, not the select few.

Knowing of Jackson's determination to replace the Washington "aristocracy," the crowd from the inauguration stayed in town to petition for jobs. Trusting these supporters to reform government and make it answerable to the people, Jackson replaced about one out of every ten federal employees in the first year. The opposition press ballyhooed these dismissals by printing lists of those fired and exaggerating the count to over 20%. Some of the people who were replaced were undoubtedly corrupt—for example, an auditor in the Treasury Department, Tobias Watkins, was tried and found guilty of fraud. But many were replaced without any evidence of either corruption or incompetence, and the opposition newspapers were quick to protest their removal.

Although Jackson maintained that the goal was to reform the system, many saw this as an exercise in consolidating political power. During Jackson's reelection, New York senator William Marcy justified the turnover by the phrase "to the victor belongs the spoils." The war analogy was not lost on Jackson's opponents, who countered that, far from reforming Washington, the turnover increased corruption and incompetence. Such criticisms of Jackson have forever linked his presidency to the "spoils system." This is perhaps best represented by Thomas Nash's 1877 cartoon entitled "In memoriam—our civil service as it was." It depicts Jackson riding a pig wallowing in "fraud," "bribery," "spoils," and "plunder." Jackson's poor choice of appointees resulted in confirmation battles with Congress. Whereas each previous presidential term had suffered only a handful of rejections, 49 of Jackson's nominees were rejected by Congress during his two terms. Although Jackson may not have intended to encourage partisan use of patronage, his widespread replacement of federal employees enabled such manipulation for the foreseeable future.

One early example of this turnover could be seen in the publication of government reports. It was routine at the time for the government to contract out for all its printing needs to businesses with the appropriate machinery—normally, publishers of newspapers. Like the federal bureaucracy, these contracts had been fairly stable. But that changed with Jackson. During Jackson's 1828 campaign, Van Buren had set up a network of newspapers nationwide to share stories promoting Jackson's candidacy for the presidency. Once Jackson was elected, he changed government contracts from the Adams-era printers to his own supporters. From his perspective, the choice of these publishers was more about trust than patronage. After Jackson replaced over two-thirds of the printing contracts, opposition newspapers objected, arguing that this amounted to contempt for freedom of the press.

Not only did Jackson-friendly newspapers gain contracts, but their editors gained political appointments. Those appointed as postmasters or port collectors became powerful figures in their communities. Others became powerful nationally. Jackson brought publisher Francis Preston Blair to run *The Globe* as the administration's newspaper of record. In addition, Blair became a trusted personal adviser to Jackson. Along with several other men who had proved their devotion to him during the election, the president pulled Blair into his inner circle. Members of this "kitchen cabinet" had no formal title, but Jackson trusted them to give him advice on a regular basis. Outsiders looking in criticized the kitchen cabinet as "sinister" and "malign." They charged that since its members had no official authority, it was running the country without the structural checks and balances that attend formal government appointments.

THE EATON AFFAIR

Jackson's reliance on his kitchen cabinet emerged out of discord within the official cabinet early in his administration. The wife of Vice President John Calhoun inadvertently sowed discord within the cabinet when she ostracized Peggy Eaton, the wife of Secretary of War John Eaton, from Washington society. From Floride Calhoun's perspective, Peggy Eaton was uncouth and forward, undeserving of admittance to polite society. These sentiments convinced her to organize the wives of cabinet members and other Washington leaders in rejecting Peggy from social events. They neither called on her nor accepted her calls, and they coordinated her exclusion from formal society events.

This ostracism took on political import because it reminded Jackson of the treatment of his wife during the campaign. Jackson had married Rachel after her first husband had sued her for divorce. But the pair became subject to the attack of bigamy when it was discovered that the divorce had not been finalized. Although they had immediately rectified the situation, 30 years later in 1828 the Adams campaign had attacked Rachel personally as an adulteress. Jackson tried to protect her from the attacks, but they came to Rachel's attention toward the end of the campaign, causing her extreme emotional distress. When she died soon thereafter, Jackson blamed the personal attacks for her death.

Thus, when Jackson heard about the treatment of Peggy Eaton, he took it personally. Still reeling with grief from Rachel's death, Jackson became consumed with anger over Peggy's treatment during his early presidency. His early correspondence dwelt heavily on the issue, reflecting his focus on it at the expense of his public duties. During this period, Jackson failed to take a stand on many issues that came up, allowing them to fester. In addition, this conflict influenced Jackson's relationship with his cabinet members. Because they were unable (or unwilling) to control their wives, he lost his trust in them. Only bachelor Martin Van Buren retained Jackson's trust. Van Buren finally hit upon the solution of replacing the cabinet entirely. He laid the groundwork by resigning as secretary of state so that Jackson could call on all his secretaries to resign. The retirements spawned attacks on the administration as being unstable. One cartoon, titled "The rats leaving a falling house," shows Jackson collapsed in a broken chair, with the faces of the secretaries on rats scurrying away from him. Two pillars toppling to the ground in the cartoon are labeled "Public confidence in the stability of the administration" and "Altar of Reform." When Jackson installed a new cabinet, however, it proved to be more effective than the first at earning Jackson's trust, thus allowing him to turn his attention to his public duties.

BANK WARS AND CENSURE

One of the issues that Jackson had ignored during the Eaton Affair was the National Bank. On the recommendation of Secretary of Treasury Alexander Hamilton, the National Bank had been instituted in 1791 to hold federal deposits and stabilize the economy. But because there was no constitutionally granted power to create a national bank, Jackson, along with many others, balked at its existence. In 1819, the Supreme Court determined that the National Bank was constitutional in *McCullough v. Maryland*. But because the structure of banks encouraged speculation, it caused a financial panic in 1837. Along with many others, Jackson lost the sizable landholdings he had accumulated. As a result, although the bank became much less controversial over time, Jackson spent substantial political energies decrying the whole banking system. For Jackson, the National Bank symbolized the corruption that pervaded Washington and epitomized federal overreach. The bank had been chartered as a private entity for which the federal government had 20% ownership. The 80% of privately owned stock was consolidated in the hands of a few hundred of the richest Americans, as well as around 1,000 Europeans. For Jackson, it was anathema to place the economy in the hands of "opulent citizens" and "foreigners" rather than average Americans.

Consequently, when Congress voted to recharter the bank in July 1832, Jackson vetoed it. It was irrelevant that the Supreme Court had ruled the bank constitutional; from Jackson's perspective, the bank violated the public interest. Jackson's veto caused an uproar because, in the early years of the Union, the veto was viewed as a limited check by the president on Congress. Where today presidents routinely veto bills because of policy objections, in the early 19th century, the norm was that vetoes should only be used to strike down unconstitutional legislation. Jackson's veto became a central issue of the 1832 presidential election. Henry Clay, Jackson's opponent in the election, used it to characterize Jackson as a despot. Jackson countered by typifying the conflict as being between the people and the aristocracy. Apparently, Jackson's argument was the more persuasive, since he won reelection.

But the recharter vote of 1832 had been called early—the bank was still chartered until 1836. With his reelection victory in hand, Jackson decided to press the issue. With Congress out of session in early 1833, Jackson ordered Secretary of Treasury Louis McLane to remove federal funds from the National Bank and deposit them elsewhere. When McLane balked at violating congressional orders and risking the economy, Jackson induced McLane to leave the Treasury Department by offering him the position of secretary of state. Although the next secretary of the treasury, William Duane, shared Jackson's opposition to the bank, he too refused orders to transfer federal deposits. After firing Duane, Jackson finally reassigned Attorney General Roger Taney to become secretary of the treasury. Taney got the funds transferred before Congress came back into session, and Jackson rewarded him with an appointment as chief justice of the Supreme Court.

Once in session, the Senate responded to the deposit of federal funds into what was called "pet" banks by amplifying its characterization of Jackson as a tyrant. These attacks are embodied in a political cartoon entitled "King Andrew the First." In it, Jackson is dressed in royal robes in a pose similar to a playing card king. He holds in his hand a scroll labeled "Veto"; at his feet are tatters of the Constitution and the seal of the National Bank. The cartoon uses the words "Born to Command" to communicate its perception of Jackson acting as a despotic ruler. Sharing this perspective, the Senate began to investigate Jackson's actions. When Jackson refused to provide records documenting his interactions with his cabinet regarding the bank, his nemesis, Clay, called for a censure of Jackson. Although the censure was officially based on Jackson's refusal to provide documents, it was an indirect referendum on his withdrawal of funds and use of the veto to further policy goals.

During the Bank Wars, Jackson was the victim of the first presidential assassination attempt. Because against all odds the assassin had two guns misfire, Jackson subdued him with his cane. Jackson was convinced that the assassin had been hired by the Whig Party because of the Bank Wars. His opponents countered that Jackson had set the attempt up to build public support. But it really had nothing to do with the Bank Wars—the attack was the result of mental illness—and talk of conspiracy dissipated once the man was committed to a mental hospital. In the aftermath of the Bank Wars, Senator Thomas Hart Benton worked for three years to expunge the censure from Senate records. Even so, Jackson saw the censure as a personal affront for the rest of his life. To the nation, though, the censure formalized criticism for Jackson's exertion of power during the Bank Wars.

NULLIFICATION CRISIS

A second issue that Jackson delayed confronting during the Eaton Affair was the Tariff of 1828. Passed under the guidance of President John Quincy Adams, the tariff taxed low-priced imports to protect northern industries. But in the South, it was dubbed the "Tariff of Abominations" because it both increased consumer prices and decreased British imports of southern cotton. Because Jackson was a southerner, many voters in the South who were opposed to the tariff supported him in the election of 1828 on the assumption that once in office he would remove it. Once elected, though, Jackson did not take any action regarding the tariff, and so opponents began to call for a radical response. In particular, they called for state nullification of the tariff, using arguments made anonymously by Jackson's running mate, John Calhoun, in his 1828 "Exposition and Protest." The argument was that because power and sovereignty were granted by the states to the national government, state conventions could meet to determine whether national actions were constitutional. In the event that a convention determined that a law was unconstitutional, it could declare it null and void.

Although Jackson was an adamant states' rights advocate, he did not view the threats of nullification from a southern perspective but rather a national one. He felt that the tariff should continue until he got the national debt under control. Jackson made his opposition to nullification clear in 1830 when he made a toast, "Our federal union: It must be preserved." This created a rift between Jackson and Calhoun and, in 1832, Calhoun stepped down as vice president to take a seat in the Senate—primarily to fight the tariff. The tariff that was passed that year lowered the rates, but not enough to placate southerners. Initially Jackson interpreted South Carolina's continued discussion of nullification as a Calhoun-inspired conspiracy against himself. He described nullification as a transitory "absurdity" that would pass like a "bubble."

But as nullification efforts grew, Jackson's response became more intense. In November, South Carolina sponsored a convention nullifying the Tariffs of 1828 and 1832 and passed enabling legislation to allow merchants to circumvent the payment of the tariff and to provide for the buildup of a militia to protect the state's interest. In December 1832, Jackson responded by changing his language about nullification from "absurdity" to "rebellion" and "treason." Simultaneously he began preparing for war—some thought that he even planned to lead the troops himself. As part of his preparation, he asked Congress for a bill to enforce the collection of revenue by use of the military. Generally called the Force Bill, nullifiers called it the "Bloody Bill." Calhoun led opposition to Jackson in the Senate, simultaneously defending the concept of nullification and describing Jackson's efforts as an attempt to crush South Carolina. Calhoun described Jackson's leadership as nothing less than despotism.

During this escalation, Senator Clay worked for compromise. While passing the Force Bill in February 1833, Congress simultaneously passed a compromise Tariff of 1833, which lowered tariffs to levels acceptable in the South. In March, South Carolina rescinded its nullification of the tariffs but in a claim to independence, it concurrently nullified the Force Bill. Thus, the concept of nullification was left intact to be reintroduced in later conflicts between North and South.

Also related to states' rights during this time period, Jackson signed into law the Indian Removal Act of 1830, which authorized the president to negotiate with Indian tribes in the southeastern states for their removal to federal territory west of the Mississippi River in exchange for their lands. Despite support from southern states, many in New England opposed the plan, as did several Christian missionaries. They decried Jackson's efforts to wrest these lands from Native Americans as avaricious and immoral. The removal, which occurred between 1830 and 1850, included members of the Cherokee, Muscogee, Seminole, Chickasaw, and Choctaw nations. Following Jackson's signing of the bill in 1830, the Cherokee filed several lawsuits against the state of Georgia, with whom it had many ongoing jurisdictional disputes since 1802. In 1832, in *Worcester v. Georgia*, the U.S. Supreme Court ruled against Georgia by ruling that the federal government, through the Supremacy Clause in the Constitution, had sole authority when dealing with the sovereignty of Indian nations. Jackson, however, ignored the Court's ruling and refused to uphold Cherokee claims against Georgia; he reportedly responded to the Court's ruling: "[Chief Justice] John Marshall has made his decision; now let him enforce it!" Jackson chose to continue with Indian removal, though only a small number of Cherokee left voluntarily. The federal government, under President Martin Van Buren, forced the remaining Cherokees west in 1838. Their grim sojourn came to be known in American history books as the "Trail of Tears."

CONCLUSION

The Jackson administration began under a one-party system but, by the time he left office, the Whig Party had united sufficiently to mount an opposition to Martin Van Buren, Jackson's heir apparent. Because the Whigs had no common ideology beyond their opposition to Jackson, they chose not to follow the new tradition of having a national convention to choose a single nominee and to issue a platform advocating a specific set of issues. Instead, Whigs in different parts of the country supported different candidates who reflected the regional interests that Jackson had challenged—the National Bank, states' rights, nullification, and western expansion. The Whigs knew that no one candidate could defeat Van Buren, but they hoped that together they could deprive him of a majority and send the election to the House of Representatives for final determination.

In the end, the Whigs failed to deny Van Buren the necessary majority in the Electoral College, but their strategy in 1836 reflected the conflict that Jackson had sown during his presidency. Jackson was able to gain sufficient support to win each of his battles; but in the process, he left wounded minorities that labeled his actions despotic and tyrannical. Each conflict followed a pattern that began with Jackson's conviction that he needed to support a moral imperative. That conviction supported a determination to use every available means to right the perceived wrong. Jackson routinely labeled as enemies those who dared to oppose him and so was hypervigilant to any possible offense. Throughout his terms in office, Jackson justified his behavior as protecting both the nation and the masses of its citizens. In the process, he instantiated the principle of democracy into the American psyche. He envisioned the president as the defender of the American people and created precedent for future presidents to expand their powers and pursue policies in the public interest without being attacked as a tyrant or a despot.

Theresa Marchant-Shapiro

Further Reading

Brands, H. W. *Andrew Jackson: His Life and Times*. New York: Anchor Books, 2005.

Cole, Donald B. *The Presidency of Andrew Jackson*. Lawrence, KS: University of Kansas Press, 1993.

Meacham, Jon. *American Lion: Andrew Jackson in the White House*. New York: Random House, 2008.

Remini, Robert V. *The Life of Andrew Jackson*. New York: Harper Perennial Modern Classics, 2010.

Schlesinger, Arthur M. *The Age of Jackson*. New York: Little Brown, 1945.

Wilentz, Sean. *Andrew Jackson*. New York: Times Books, 2005.

8. Martin Van Buren

Born: December 5, 1782
Died: July 42, 1862
Time in Office: Eighth President of the United States, March 4, 1837, to March 4, 1841

Election Results: 1836 Election: 50.8% of popular vote, 170 (57.8%) Electoral
College votes; 1840 Election: 46.8% of popular vote, 60 (20.4%) Electoral
College votes
Spouse: Hannah Hoes (m. 1807)
Children: Abraham, John, Martin Jr., Winfield Scott, and Smith Thompson

Born in 1782 in Kinderhook, New York, Martin Van Buren has the distinction of being the first president born after independence and the only one to speak English as his second language, with Dutch being his native tongue. He married his childhood sweetheart Hannah Hoes, a fellow Dutch speaker, in 1807. The couple had five sons and one daughter, but only four of the sons lived to adulthood.

Van Buren became heavily involved in New York politics and eventually transitioned into national politics, becoming the leading organizer of the new Democratic Party constructed around Andrew Jackson in the lead up to the 1828 election. Van Buren was a key supporter of Jackson and was elected vice president for Jackson's second term in 1832. When Jackson declined to seek a third term, Van Buren was his handpicked successor. In the 1836 election, Van Buren faced four regional candidates from the opposition Whig Party who sought to deprive him of a majority in the Electoral College and thus push the election to the House of Representatives. The strategy failed as Van Buren won a majority of the popular vote and 15 out of 26 states in the Electoral College. He thus became the last sitting vice president to be elected directly to the presidency until 1988, when George H. W. Bush made the same transition. Van Buren's tenure in the White House from 1837 to 1841 was turbulent, and he lost his bid for reelection in 1840 to William Henry Harrison, winning only seven states. Yet Van Buren remained politically active and ran for the White House two more times (he made an unsuccessful bid for the Democratic nomination in 1844 and was the nominee of the Free Soil Party in 1848). He died at his estate in Kinderhook in 1862.

There were five general lines of argument seized on by Van Buren's opponents to attack his presidency. First, that Van Buren was a "politician by trade," acting as a calculating opportunist and lacking clear principles. Second, that he was a partisan president who prioritized party interests over national interests. Third, that Van Buren was like Jackson in abusing executive power. Fourth, southern opponents asserted that Van Buren had abolitionist tendencies and would destroy the South if given the opportunity. Finally, Van Buren was accused of living in splendor off the public treasury and at the expense of the common man.

POLITICIAN BY TRADE

The charge that Van Buren was a politician by trade first emerged during the 1836 election and persisted throughout the rest of his presidency. This attack was derived from Van Buren's role as architect of a new party system based on spoils, party organization, and loyalty. His opponents latched on to his history of party organizing and portrayed him as a creature of faction seeking to divide the country. As a foil to Van Buren they even portrayed Jackson favorably, arguing that the old general had been a man of national esteem and character, in contrast to his slippery successor. An essay by anti-Jacksonian congressman—and future hero of the Alamo—Davy Crockett asserted Van Buren was "as opposite to General Jackson as dung to a diamond," as the "little magician"—one of Van Buren's many nicknames—was "secret, sly, selfish, cold, calculating, distrustful, treacherous." These criticisms also appeared in the press, as newspapers like the *New York American* characterized Van Buren as an "illiterate, [a] sycophant, and politically corrupt."

These criticisms were often coupled with accusations that Van Buren was guilty of "noncommitalism,"—an unwillingness to take a stand on any issue. During the campaign, while Van Buren was still vice president—and therefore president of the Senate—the anti-Jacksonian trio of Henry Clay, Daniel Webster, and John C. Calhoun contrived to have Senate votes end in a tie to force Van Buren to cast the deciding vote. Apart from these inner-legislative dealings, Van Buren's critics coined the term "vanburenish" to describe evasive politicians.

Writing in his autobiography, Van Buren did not indicate he was overly troubled by these attacks, but rather that he took a degree of pride in his immense political talents, including his ability to obfuscate. Yet his actions in office suggest he was concerned about being perceived as "noncommital." This is observable in Van Buren's financial programs, particularly his push to remove government funds from state banks—setting up the Treasury as an independent financial entity, completing the work Jackson had begun years earlier—and reaffirming Jackson's executive order that payments to the government be made in gold or silver. Proposing the independent Treasury and remaining committed to Jackson's hard money policies demonstrated his willingness to recommend and push for specific policy measures, as well as commitment to Jacksonian policies. Such moves pushed back on the charges of noncommitalism and the assertion that Van Buren lacked credibility.

PARTISAN PRESIDENT

As one of the builders of the American party system who emphasized party unity and adherence to party philosophy, it is unsurprising that Van Buren came under criticism for being overly partisan. Although these charges were typically voiced by Whigs as early as the 1836 election—Daniel Webster commented that Van Buren put "party above country"—on some issues Van Buren found himself assailed from members of his own party. Conservative Democrats saw Van Buren's idea for an "independent Treasury" as an imposition of party ideology instead of having the national interest in mind. This critique lasted into the 1840 campaign as part of an effort to generate Democratic defections from Van Buren. One essay, published under the pseudonym "A Workingman," argued that Van Buren had subverted the Democratic Party to his own twisted pursuits. In acting "solely and entirely [as] the *head of a party*; and not the impartial chief magistrate of the nation" he had "violate[d] every republican principle which that party sustained." A Workingman even compared Van Buren to a "religious hypocrite, 'stealing the livery of heaven, to serve the devil in.'"

As Van Buren's theory of parties held that if the party sought the national interest, then acting in a partisan manner was necessarily acting in the national interest, it does not seem that the president paid much heed to these criticisms. Yet the charges of excessive partisanship continued to proliferate, particularly as Van Buren made little effort to show that the interests of his party and the nation were aligned. For example, Van Buren inflamed these attacks during a reelection campaign tour in 1839. When he stopped in New York City, Van Buren began his remarks by singling out Democratic listeners in his audience. This evoked enough of a virulent backlash among audience members unaccustomed so such attacks that Van Buren refrained from making further partisan statements, showing that despite his theories, in practice he recognized how charges of partisanship could hurt him politically.

OVERREACHING EXECUTIVE

The Whig Party had been formed largely out of concern about Jackson's extensive use of executive power. It was unsurprising that they would maintain this criticism against Jackson's chosen successor, and the criticisms they leveled against Van Buren were often reminiscent of those Jackson had faced. Van Buren's "independent Treasury" was viewed as an attempt to bring monetary matters under the sole purview of the executive, giving the president, in the words of historian Major Wilson, "unchecked control over the nation's purse." Such control could then lend itself to further actions of executive tyranny when it came to spoils and patronage. The aforementioned "Workingman" charged that Van Buren refused to "let the patronage and power of the federal executive . . . be either lessened, or regulated by law," and that he violated separation of powers by "subvert[ing] the course of legislation, by plotting with his partisans of the Senate."

Democrats who prioritized states' rights also expressed concerns about executive power, seeing the "independent Treasury" as hurting state banks and centralizing national banking policy. From there, they drew similar conclusions as the Whigs, arguing that concentrating bank policy at the national level, particularly in the manner favored by Van Buren, would dangerously increase executive power. The concerns of states' rights proponents correlated with cries of executive despotism as Van Buren attempted to enlarge the army and reform the militia. Enlarging the army already made many uneasy, due to traditional distrust of a large standing army, but the militia plan—which would place the militia more directly under federal control—inflamed fears of too much centralized power, and more specifically, too much executive control. When combined with the "independent Treasury" plan, both Whigs and states' rights Democrats saw Van Buren as attempting to control both the sword and the purse, a certain recipe for presidential despotism.

Against these criticisms Van Buren tried to play both sides. On the one hand, he changed his behavior in the face of attacks on the militia plan, putting it aside and trying to reassert his claim to be a defender of states' rights in a public letter. On the other hand, he remained committed to a Jacksonian notion of a powerful presidency, acting in ways that fueled these criticisms. For example, Van Buren supported Postmaster General Amos Kendall against a monetary settlement demanded by the Senate and later against a writ of mandamus (a court order to do something as required by law) issued from the District of Columbia Circuit Court. When the court found against Kendall, Van Buren attempted to have Congress take away the mandamus power of the Circuit Court, most likely with the intention to keep it from hearing cases concerning the executive's ministerial duties. When considered in conjunction with Van Buren's "independent Treasury," the incident illustrates Van Buren's commitment to executive independence—and by extension executive power—despite relenting in other cases when the political pressure threatened to undermine his coalition, such as with the militia plan.

ACCUSATIONS OF ABOLITIONISM

In building a broad-based coalition, Van Buren recognized and sought to utilize the political power of the South by establishing an alliance between New York and Virginia. As southern political power was bound up with slave owners, the New Yorker adopted a relatively neutral position on slavery, with historian Robert Remini describing him as being "neither its foe nor its friend." This neutrality helped feed into criticisms of noncommitalism. Yet southern Whigs, seeing the precarious geographical arrangement of the Democratic coalition, sought to divide the party by portraying Van Buren as a radical abolitionist.

The charges of abolitionism came from multiple sources, but often drew from Van Buren's political record as a New York legislator, when he had supported Rufus King to be a U.S. senator. To his opponents, this was enough to prove Van Buren was an abolitionist, due to King's long history of opposing the expansion of slavery and the slave trade. Davy Crockett asserted King "was a fanatic" with "[a]ll his prejudices [. . .] enlisted against the South and southern policy." Similarly, they castigated Van Buren's apparent support for a resolution in the New York state Senate, instructing the state's U.S. senators to vote against accepting states into the Union without first banning slavery. More unrealistic attacks, such as the accusation that Van Buren conspired to end slavery by an act of Congress, also emerged. Some partisans, like the editors of the *Richmond Whig*, simply brought up that Van Buren was a northerner from a free state, concluding that "when the test comes, he will support the abolitionists."

These criticisms even extended to Vice President Richard Mentor Johnson. Southerners had opposed Johnson in 1836 for his affairs with a black mistress, so much so that Virginia electors—pledged to the Van Buren–Johnson ticket—voted for Van Buren and not for Johnson. This stand deprived the latter of a majority in the Electoral College, making Johnson the only vice president elected by the Senate. These issues reemerged in 1840, causing such division within the Democratic Party that it did not nominate a vice presidential candidate at all.

Perhaps the most famous attack on Van Buren as a threat to the South was the 1836 novel *The Partisan Leader*, written by Nathan Beverly Tucker. The novel, set in 1849, depicts a United States in which Van Buren has become a dictator armed with a strong central government. Tucker portrays the states south of Virginia seceding due to Van Buren's destructive tariff policies, and the novel's heroes are guerilla fighters seeking to have Virginia join the Southern Confederacy. Although the novel plays on Van Buren's reputation as a shameless and partisan politician—hence the title—its strong sectional component indicates its intended audience were southerners, specifically Virginians, as the novel ends reciting Virginia's motto *Sic Semper Tyrannis*: "Thus Always to Tyrants."

These charges did not go unanswered in the partisan press. Democratic newspapers—primarily the *Globe*, the *Richmond Enquirer*, and the *Argus*—published a series of Van Buren's letters to show the president was not an abolitionist, but rather "a northern man with southern principles," a title the Whig press worked hard to undermine.

Van Buren personally understood the need to keep the South in the Democratic coalition. As a result, any nascent antislavery impulses that he might have had remained suppressed until after he left office. While in office, Van Buren emphasized his opposition to abolitionism. His inaugural address reiterated his campaign promise to oppose congressional efforts to abolish slavery in the District of Columbia and to resist national interference with slavery in the states where it existed. As the 1840 election approached and the issue of admitting Florida as a slave state came to the fore, Van Buren took a more pro-South position, asserting he would veto any restriction Congress tried to place on slave states seeking to enter the Union.

ELITE AND OUT OF TOUCH

The last prevalent line of attack against Van Buren was the accusation of elitism. This criticism was especially potent due to the economic hardship that swept over the country with the Panic of 1837, contributing to the stinging nickname "Martin Van Ruin," and the Whig rhyme "Little Van is a used up man." These harsh economic conditions—which Whigs pinned on Jackson and Van Buren's financial policies—gave a degree of weight to accusations that Van Buren lived in luxury while the common man was hurting. It thereby helped the Whigs undermine and eventually reverse—at least for the 1840 election—the carefully crafted image of the Democrats as the party of the common man and the Whigs as the party of wealthy elites.

During the 1840 campaign, the Whigs, following the lead of newspaper editor Thurlow Weed, began the task of portraying their candidate, William Henry Harrison, as a man of the people. Meanwhile, the Whigs described Van Buren in terms that historian John Niven neatly summarizes as "an effeminate, overindulged fop who led a life of Babylonian splendor." This was, of course, quite ironic considering Harrison had been born into the Virginia aristocracy and was the son of a signer of the Declaration of Independence, while Van Buren was the son of a tavern keeper.

Nevertheless, the Whigs hammered this point, contrasting "the habits, the manners, the reputation of General Harrison" as those befitting "a truly republican candidate" against "the lordly style of Mr. Van Buren." The best example of this assault was a speech made by the obscure Pennsylvania congressman Charles Ogle. For three days, Ogle described "The Regal Splendor of the Presidential Palace" in a speech now known as "The Gold Spoon Oration." In it, Ogle took his listeners on an imaginary tour of the presidential mansion, describing mirrors larger than barn doors, expensive wines, silver and gold utensils, and furnishings in every room "far above any of the salons of Buckingham Palace [. . .] or Windsor castle." Democrats and the partisan press took Ogle to task for his immense exaggerations; the *Washington Globe* called the speech an "omnibus of lies," and Van Buren himself was enraged by the speech. Even Whigs came to Van Buren's defense; Rep. Levi Lincoln of Massachusetts showed that other presidents had spent more on the presidential dwelling than Van Buren. Nonetheless, the charges stuck in the public mind.

That Van Buren possessed an elegant style and enjoyed the finer things did not help counter the argument that he was an extravagant dandy aspiring to aristocratic splendor or inspired camaraderie with the common man. Furthermore, as Wilson has noted, the charge of elitism dovetailed nicely with the Whig cries of executive overreach, making it appear the Whigs were concerned about the common man and defending them against the real threat of monarchy, trumping the Democrats' previous portrayal of the conflict as between the common man and aristocratic elites. When these intertwined attacks were added to the poor economic conditions of the day, Van Buren had little way to inspire the electorate, contributing to his defeat in 1840.

CONCLUSION

Van Buren's most significant contribution to American history perhaps comes from his time as vice president to Andrew Jackson rather than Van Buren's own presidency, for it was during his years as vice president that he helped Jackson form the Democratic Party. However, due to the worsening economic conditions during Van Buren's four years in office, his presidency also helped to create the opposition Whig Party, thus providing the two-party system. The financial crisis that began within months of Van Buren's inauguration in 1837, triggered by many of Jackson's failed economic policies, left little opportunity for Van Buren to chart his own course. After Van Buren's reelection defeat in 1840, his legacy was sealed as an average, one-term president, whose nickname of "Martin Van Ruin" summed up the attitude of voters that he was an elitist and out of touch with average citizens.

Jordan T. Cash

Further Reading

Mushkat, Jerome, and Joseph G. Rayback. *Martin Van Buren: Law, Politics, and the Shaping of Republican Ideology.* DeKalb, IL: Northern Illinois University Press, 1997.

Niven, John. *Martin Van Buren: The Romantic Age of American Politics.* New York: Oxford University Press, 1983.

Remini, Robert V. *Martin Van Buren and the Making of the Democratic Party.* New York: Columbia University Press, 1959.

Silbey, Joel H. *Martin Van Buren and the Emergence of American Popular Politics.* Lanham, MD: Rowman & Littlefield, 2002.

Van Buren, Martin. *Inquiry into the Origin and Course of Political Parties.* New York: Hurd and Houghton, 1867. Available at http://tinyurl.com/h3etctf.

Van Buren, Martin. *The Autobiography of Martin Van Buren.* Ed. John C. Fitzpatrick. New York: De Capo Press, 1973.

Wilson, Major L. *The Presidency of Martin Van Buren.* Lawrence, KS: University Press of Kansas, 1984.

9. William Henry Harrison

Born: February 9, 1773

Died: April 4, 1841

Time in Office: Ninth President of the United States, March 4, 1841, to April 4, 1841

Election Results: 1840 Election: 52.9% of popular vote, 234 (79.6%) Electoral College votes

Spouse: Anna Symmes (m. 1795)

Children: Elizabeth Bassett, John Cleves Symmes, Lucy Singleton, William Henry, John Scott, Benjamin, Mary Symmes, Carter Bassett, Anna Tuthill, and James Findlay

William Henry Harrison, born in 1773, served as president from March 4, 1841, until his death one month later on April 4, 1841. Harrison holds the record for the shortest presidency in American history to date. He defeated incumbent president Martin Van Buren in 1840, 234–60 in the Electoral College, winning 53% of the popular vote. Anna Harrison, the first lady, did not accompany Harrison to Washington, planning to join him later in the year. As a result, she was not in the city when her husband died.

CAMPAIGN OF 1840

Due to Harrison's brief tenure in office, there was not enough time for many personal attacks to develop after he reached the White House. The election that propelled him to power, however, is another story. Harrison first ran for office under the banner of the new Whig Party in 1836. In that effort the party chose to run three regional candidates against Andrew Jackson's vice president, Martin Van Buren, in an attempt to throw the election into the House of Representatives. The strategy failed, but the ensuing Panic of 1837, followed by a severe depression, made Van Buren a significantly weakened incumbent.

The obvious Whig to lead the ticket in 1840 was Henry Clay. Many party leaders, however, were afraid that Clay, already a two-time loser in presidential elections, would cost the party victory in a winnable year. The Jackson campaign model—a military hero who could appeal to the people—appeared to be the better strategy, prompting many national convention delegates to look to Harrison. Although Harrison was hardly a stereotypical "common man"—his father had signed the Declaration of Independence—he did possess a distinguished military record. Harrison's campaign thus focused on his military reputation, particularly his performance in a well-known battle against Shawnee Indians at Tippecanoe Creek (near present-day Lafayette, Indiana) in 1811. When Clay failed to achieve victory on the first ballot in December 1839, the party shifted to Harrison.

The general election campaign of 1840 became the prototype of more modern campaigns, marked by emotional appeals and character attacks. Harrison had been born into an aristocratic Virginia family, and only one wing of his spacious home in North Bend, Ohio, had been a log cabin. Nevertheless, the Whig Party attempted to portray Harrison as someone who came from a humble background, born in poverty in a log cabin, and who understood the world of the farmer and back-woodsman. Democrats ridiculed this image. The *Baltimore Republican,* a newspaper firmly allied with the Democrats, declared, "Give [Harrison] a barrel of hard cider and a pension of two thousand a year, and, our word for it, he will sit the remainder of his days in a log cabin by the side of a 'sea coal' fire and study moral philosophy."

The Whigs took advantage of this slur and transformed it into the main slogan of the campaign. The log cabin and coonskin with a barrel of hard cider became the emblem of the Whig effort. The party published campaign papers such as the *Hard Cider Press* and Horace Greeley's *Log Cabin.* Massive public meetings and rallies featured the construction of log cabins and cider presses, cabins on steam-boats, music, flags, drinking, and stump speakers. E. G. Booz, a distiller from Phil-adelphia, passed out whiskey in log cabin–shaped bottles. Daniel Webster felt compelled to claim that his older siblings had been born in log cabins, and the party used the homespun image against Van Buren, claiming he was the true aris-tocrat who lived in luxury.

Democrats also attacked Harrison's war record, calling him "Granny Harrison, the petticoat general" and charging him with cowardice and incompetence in his military career. Certainly Harrison's record in the War of 1812 was greatly over-shadowed by that of Jackson's. But even his primary claim to fame—the Battle of Tippecanoe—was first reported as a defeat. As with the question of his family wealth, however, Whigs took the battle and made it a campaign slogan, referring to Harrison as "Old Tippecanoe." In this way, the Whigs took the principal attacks against Harrison's elite background and war record and turned them into assets, manufacturing a campaign and candidate image that mirrored Jackson's primary appeal years earlier. Instead of Old Hickory—an affectionate nickname for Jackson among his supporters—Whigs had Old Tip; instead of Hickory Clubs—organizations of Jackson supporters—Whigs created Tippecanoe Clubs.

Finally, Democrats also attacked Harrison's issue positions. They labeled him a Federalist and charged him with being an abolitionist. In fact, Harrison's back-ground saw him taking stands on different sides of several issues over the years, and he tried to portray himself as a friend of slavery to the South and antislavery to the North. The Whig Party had no official platform in 1840, however, and the economic crisis was blamed on Van Buren. The "Log Cabin and Hard Cider" cam-paign of the Whigs easily defeated Democratic insults.

31-DAY PRESIDENCY

The brevity of Harrison's presidency is a story more of potential conflict than actual struggle, but it is not difficult to see what might have been. The Whig victory in 1840 was not limited to the presidency. The party also won unified control of both elective branches of the federal government, the only time in its history the party would enjoy such a position. That political context would seem to suggest that Harrison's principal opposition would come from the ousted Democratic Party. However, Harrison broke precedent by meeting with the outgoing president and other leading Democrats.

Harrison's major source of conflict came from within his own party. Whig leaders looked forward to prosecuting a vigorous policy agenda that promised to roll back Jacksonian accomplishments and realign the nation's policies along Whig lines. There was an expectation that Harrison would be a pliable tool in the hands of other Whig leaders. Henry Clay, who remained bitter over being denied the Whig nomination, expected Harrison to allow him to lead the party from his position in the Senate, serving, in a sense, as prime minister for the new president. Nicholas Biddle, formerly president of the Bank of the United States, told Daniel Webster that "the coming administration will be in fact your administration."

Harrison was not oblivious to these developments, and there is every indication that he intended to push back against Clay's overbearing interference. He had no intention of being treated as a pawn or figurehead. At one point before the inauguration, Clay persisted in urging a particular cabinet appointment on Harrison to the point that Harrison replied, "Mr. Clay, you forget that I am the President." In fact, it was Webster who entered the inner circle surrounding Harrison, not Clay. After the inauguration, Clay pressed Harrison repeatedly to call a special session of Congress to address the economic crisis. At one point Clay even sent a letter to Harrison with a draft proclamation attached. Harrison replied that Clay was "too impetuous" and that he preferred written communication between the two "to a conversation in the presence of others." Clay flew into a rage and left town, two days before Harrison issued a call for the special session.

There is no way to know, of course, how Harrison would have managed the special session, since he died before it began. Certainly Clay would have attempted to push a staunch Whig agenda. If successful, the Whig philosophy of the presidential veto—to be used only rarely, with the president biased in favor of deference to Congress—should have prompted Harrison to accede to a Clay-led policy agenda. But in his inaugural address Harrison made a plea for an end to partisanship, and his generally moderate demeanor suggests he might have pursued a more tempered approach. Whig philosophy also argued in favor of a strong cabinet whose members would have an equal voice with the president in all decisions, but Harrison again indicated that he was not always happy with that arrangement. In a longer presidency it is likely that he would have asserted himself in a manner closer to the precedent set by Jackson.

CONCLUSION

Harrison's election was the first example of modern party marketing, elevating image over issues, and it is there that Harrison experienced the most personal attacks—campaign strategies and attacks that set a standard for elections to come. The locus of those attacks was the opposite party, but the Harrison campaign proved quite skillful at turning insults into assets. In his brief administration, Harrison experienced far more tension with leaders from his own party, primarily due to battles over power, control, and influence as these different leaders fought to direct the party's singular opportunity to set the nation's direction. Harrison's image nurtured during the campaign sent a signal to these leaders that he could be managed. When Harrison took office, however, the inherent constitutional authority of the presidency worked to resist those efforts. There is every indication that Harrison would have asserted his own place in the separation of powers system had he lived.

David A. Crockett

Further Reading

Cleaves, Freeman. *Old Tippecanoe: William Henry Harrison and His Times.* New York: C. Scribner's Sons, 1939.

Peterson, Norma Lois. *The Presidencies of William Henry Harrison and John Tyler.* Lawrence, KS: University Press of Kansas, 1989.

10. John Tyler

Born: March 29, 1790

Died: January 18, 1862

Time in Office: 10th President of the United States, April 4, 1841, to March 4, 1845

Election Results: 1840 Election: Elected vice president; assumed office upon death of William Henry Harrison

Spouse: Letitia Christian (m. 1813), Julia Gardiner (m. 1844)

Children: Mary, Robert, John, Letitia, Elizabeth, Anne, Alice, Tazewell, David, John Alexander, Julia, Lachlan, Lyon, Robert Fitzwalter, and Pearl

John Tyler served as president from the death of William Henry Harrison on April 4, 1841, to the end of the term in 1845. Tyler was the first vice president to succeed to the presidency upon the death of a president. He was part of Harrison's "Tippecanoe and Tyler Too" ticket that defeated incumbent president Martin Van Buren in 1840. The Whig ticket won 53% of the popular vote and defeated Van Buren in the Electoral College 234–60. Tyler was married to Letitia Christian when he entered the White House, but she died of a stroke in September 1842. Tyler married his second wife, Julia Gardiner, in June 1844.

"HIS ACCIDENCY"

Tyler's placement on the Whig ticket was the party's most consequential decision. Tyler was from an elite Virginia family, who started his political career as a Democrat. He twice supported Andrew Jackson for the presidency, in opposition to Henry Clay in 1832. Tyler also opposed the tariff, recharter of the Bank of the United States, and most aspects of Clay's American System. However, Tyler broke with Jackson for what he saw as the president's abuse of executive power, making him available as a Whig running mate in both 1836 and 1840.

Tyler played no role in the construction of Harrison's cabinet, and he was certainly aware of Clay's intention to control the party's agenda from the Senate, serving as a type of prime minister to Harrison's figurehead. Although Harrison pushed back against Clay's impertinence in his brief month in office, his death opened the possibility that Clay could use the Whig majorities in both houses of Congress to prosecute a strong Whig policy agenda.

Tyler's actions assuming the presidency provoked his first opposition. The original Constitution is ambiguous as to the status of the vice president upon a vacancy in the presidency. Harrison's cabinet appears initially to have thought that Tyler should be seen as the "vice president, acting as president"—a perspective not shared by Tyler, who intended to assume the full powers of the presidency. Two days after Harrison's death the cabinet concurred, and Tyler took the oath of office, setting a precedent for all similar circumstances in the future. When Congress met in special session a resolution referring to Tyler as president of the United States prompted some debate in both chambers, as well as some negative votes in the Senate. Although the resolution passed comfortably, some officials persisted in referring to Tyler as "His Accidency." This label called into question his legitimacy and accused him of seizing power for his own ambitions.

"A PRESIDENT WITHOUT A PARTY"

Tyler retained the services of Harrison's cabinet, raising hopes in some circles that he would support the Whig policy agenda. Clay, however, continued to believe he would be the power in what would amount to a regency. These conditions led some observers to fear that Tyler would be "Clay's pliant tool." Indeed, with unified Whig control of Congress and the presidency, all Clay needed to enact his repudiation of the Jacksonian system was Tyler's support.

The first order of business in the Whig program was the reestablishment of a national bank. This measure was the centerpiece of the Whig agenda. But when the bill got to Tyler's desk, he vetoed it on the grounds that it was unconstitutional because it violated states' rights. Daniel Webster, Tyler's secretary of state, helped rally Whig congressional leaders behind a second effort. Tyler's cabinet supported the new bill, and Tyler himself seemed to accept its provisions. When he suggested changes, Webster got them made.

Clay then opened a bitter attack against Tyler on the floor of the Senate. He suggested that Tyler should have resigned if he could not support the will of a majority in Congress, and accusing him of planning to form a third party. Clay also accused Tyler of pride, vanity, and egotism, vices that take on "the character of crimes in the conduct of public affairs. The unfortunate victim of these passions cannot see beyond the little, petty, contemptible circles of his own personal interests." Whig congressman John Minor Botts wrote a letter further attacking Tyler, arguing that he was "making a desperate effort to set himself up with the loco-focos"—basically, aligning himself with the Democrats.

Angered by these attacks from members of his own party, Tyler rejected pleas by Webster to sign the bill. His veto, the second of a Whig bank bill that summer, prompted almost his entire cabinet to resign en masse—only Webster remained. Two days later, the Whig caucus issued a manifesto denouncing Tyler and expelling him from the party. Clay's allies persistently assaulted the president. Botts accused Tyler of perfidy and treachery to his party, comparing him to Benedict Arnold. Whig newspapers bitterly attacked him, he was burned in effigy, and he received hundreds of letters threatening assassination. At one point he was insulted by a mob in front of the White House. Congress even refused to allocate funds to repair the executive mansion. Tyler had become, in Clay's terms, "a president without a party."

CONSTITUTIONAL ATTACKS

In 1842 congressional Whigs twice tried to pass tariff bills that would raise rates in support of the Whig economic agenda. Tyler again vetoed these measures, once again repudiating his own party's core principles. John Quincy Adams chaired a House committee assigned to examine Tyler's use of the veto power. Adams's majority report referred again to Tyler as an "acting president" who was claiming for himself "an inordinate share in the legislative process." Democrats submitted a minority report defending Tyler's use of the veto, but the majority report recommended a constitutional amendment that would allow Congress to override a veto by a majority vote of both houses. That effort failed.

During this same period, Botts introduced a resolution in the House calling for a special committee to investigate the president for possible impeachable offenses—the first time in history that such an effort was taken against a president. Specific charges had to wait until the lame duck session of Congress, but the nine resolutions included such charges as "gross usurpation of power," "wicked and corrupt abuse of the power of appointment to office," and "arbitrary, despotic, and corrupt abuse of the power of the veto power." The House rejected the motion decisively.

Congressional enemies made use of other constitutional tools to attack Tyler. Accusing Tyler of "executive usurpation," Clay engaged in a futile attempt to limit by law the president's control over his cabinet. The Senate rejected four of Tyler's cabinet nominations—one of them three times in one day. He also had four Supreme Court nominees rejected, two of them multiple times, apparently in the hope that Clay would win the 1844 presidential election and make more acceptable choices. Tyler was successful in having most of his vetoes sustained, but on his final day in office he became the first president in history to have a law passed over his veto.

One final area of constitutional battle concerned the annexation of Texas. Both Clay and Martin Van Buren, each party's presumptive presidential candidates, opposed immediate annexation, but Tyler negotiated a treaty with Texas to annex the republic and sent it to the Senate for ratification in April 1844. Tyler's promise of military aid to Texas drew more talk of impeachment from the Whigs. Once again Tyler's own party opposed his actions, and the "abominable treaty" failed. Recasting the treaty as a joint resolution and taking advantage of Polk's victory, Tyler won the final battle as Congress passed a resolution allowing the president to offer statehood, which Tyler did in the waning days of his presidency.

CONCLUSION

Tyler flirted with the idea of running as a third party candidate in 1844, but his desire for Texas statehood—and thus need for Democratic Party victory—prompted him to back away from that effort. Clearly Tyler's primary conflict was with the party that chose him to be Harrison's running mate, and that was due to Tyler's own ambivalent relationship with his adopted party. Had Tyler been a traditional Whig, he likely still would have had to contend with Clay's overwhelming desire to be the agenda-setter of the Whig effort. Assuming he could have managed Clay's ego, his primary area of conflict would have been with the opposition party Democrats. But because Tyler opposed most of the Whig policy agenda, he spent most of his presidency doing battle with his own party—a battle that was exacerbated by the sense of lost opportunity among Whigs, who had won unified control of government only to see their own president foil their plans. Never again would the party enjoy such an opportunity. In the meantime, Tyler demonstrated what a determined president can do who is willing to employ all of the constitutional tools and weapons the document provides. It is difficult to come away from the Tyler presidency not thinking that, in the end, he enjoyed greater success accomplishing his objectives than did his party during his four years in office, despite the consistently bitter and nasty attacks.

David A. Crockett

Further Reading

Morgan, Robert J. *A Whig Embattled: The Presidency under John Tyler.* Lincoln, NE: University of Nebraska Press, 1954.

Peterson, Norma Lois. *The Presidencies of William Henry Harrison and John Tyler.* Lawrence, KS: University Press of Kansas, 1989.

11. James K. Polk

Born: November 2, 1795

Died: June 15, 1849

Time in Office: 11th President of the United States, March 4, 1845, to March 4, 1849

Election Results: 1844 Election: 49.5% of popular vote, 170 (61.8%) Electoral College votes

Spouse: Sarah Childress (m. 1824)

James Knox Polk was born on November 2, 1795, near Pineville, North Carolina, in Mecklenburg County. He died on June 15, 1849, in Nashville, Tennessee. A Jacksonian Democrat, he represented Tennessee in the U.S. House of Representatives from 1825 to 1835, where he served as speaker, and was elected for one term as governor of Tennessee (1839–1841). Polk and his wife, Sarah Childress, had no children. Elected president in 1844, Polk tallied 170 electoral votes of 15 states and 2,698,605 popular votes. Opponents included Whig Party leader Henry Clay, winning 105 electoral votes of 11 states and 1,299,062 popular votes, and Liberty Party nominee James G. Birney with 62,300 popular votes. Polk held office from March 4, 1845, to March 4, 1849.

MANIFEST DESTINY

The election's most intense and popular issue was "Manifest Destiny"—the concept that God was destined to help the United States spread to the Pacific Ocean. Polk was a proponent of the Manifest Destiny ideology and sought all of Oregon, jointly occupied with Great Britain since 1818, and annexation of Texas, a former Mexican province that Mexico still claimed. Annexing Texas meant adding a slave state to the Union and expanding slavery farther west. Polk owned slaves and expected slavery to move westward. Birney was an abolitionist seeking to end slavery anywhere. Although he was a slave owner, Clay nourished vague notions about emancipating slaves or colonizing them overseas. Downplaying Manifest Destiny, Clay hoped that diplomats would resolve Texas annexation. These controversies persisted during Polk's term and into the 1860s.

As president, Polk overcame Whig opposition, pushing Congress to lower the federal tariff and arranging for federal funds to be deposited outside of one central bank. But he made Manifest Destiny his priority throughout his presidency. Gambling with diplomacy, Polk risked war on two fronts if negotiations collapsed with Britain and Mexico. Simultaneous wars were beyond America's military capabilities. First, Polk successfully bargained with Britain to split the Oregon Country (which today includes all of Oregon, Washington, Idaho, parts of Montana and Wyoming, and part of the Canadian province of British Columbia). Some Americans were disappointed that Polk had not demanded all of this territory, but dividing the region at the 49th parallel (with America gaining possession of the land south of that line) was a logical compromise and avoided a war.

Polk, meanwhile, dismissed Mexico's claim to all of Texas. Polk estimated that the Texas Revolution of 1836 resulted in the province becoming an independent republic though Mexico refused to extend recognition of Texas as a sovereign nation. In 1844, Texans and President John Tyler began collaborating on plans for the United States to formally annex Texas. Mexicans warned that annexation was tantamount to declaring war. As these tensions escalated, Polk's determination to stretch America to the Pacific also led him to further complicate matters by offering to buy Mexico's province of California.

Reaching peaceful settlements required delicate diplomacy and compromises. For instance, through British arbitration Mexico *might* have recognized Texas independence *if* America canceled annexation. Unable to find compromise on those thorny disputes, diplomats also disagreed over the Texas boundary. Texans contended that their boundary was the Rio Grande, but Mexicans maintained that the Nueces River was the province's traditional border. Alienating Mexico, Polk arbitrarily insisted on the Rio Grande when his administration completed annexation in 1845. To guarantee that boundary, Polk ordered half of the U.S. Army into Texas—but stopped the troops at the Nueces River, creating a disputed strip of land between the two rivers. Mexico adamantly rejected annexation, refused to sell California, and called for U.S. troops to leave Texas. Aggravating Mexico, Polk confirmed annexation, demanded that Mexico negotiate a price for California, and ordered U.S. soldiers to the Rio Grande. Mexico broke diplomatic relations with America, a signal in the 19th century that nations verged on war. In April 1846, Mexican and U.S. troops skirmished north of the Rio Grande. Polk informed Congress that Mexico "has invaded our territory, and shed American blood upon the American soil." Whigs castigated the president for initiating "Mr. Polk's War," echoing the Federalists' cry in 1812 against "Mr. Madison's War."

WHIG PARTY OPPOSITION

Whigs were Polk's most ardent foes. In Congress, the Senate voted 40 for declaring war against Mexico and 2 opposed—both Massachusetts Whigs, though most Whigs did not oppose Polk on this issue. The House, meanwhile, voted 173 in favor of war, including a few Whigs, and 14 opposed. The "glorious fourteen" were all Whigs, most from New England and Ohio. Whigs radiated their anti-Polk and antiwar rhetoric through congressional speeches, public lectures, books and pamphlets, and periodicals, notably the *New York Herald* and the *National Intelligencer.* Outspoken congressional opponents included former president John Quincy Adams of Massachusetts and Joshua R. Giddings of Ohio. Giddings called the war "aggressive, unholy, and unjust" and asserted that it was fought on behalf of slavery. Senator Thomas Corwin of Ohio accused Polk of "bold usurpation" to make "war on a neighboring republic." Corwin forecast that Polk's actions would immerse "the sister States of this Union into the bottomless gulf of civil strife"—a civil war. Ohio volunteer soldiers reacted by burning Corwin in effigy. Whig statesman Albert Gallatin argued that Polk had "deliberately plunge[d]" North America "into an unjust or unnecessary war."

While many Americans, including most Democrats, supported U.S. territorial expansion, some were doubtful or opposed, and the most vociferous critics condemned Polk for adding "slave" lands by annexing Texas. That Polk owned slaves and approved of slavery's place in the South's economic and social system appeared to give weight to abolitionists' condemnations of his administration's policies. Pressures escalated when David Wilmot, a Pennsylvania Democrat in Congress, introduced a resolution to block slavery from any lands taken from Mexico as a result of the war. Wilmot poured fuel on rhetorical fires when he repeatedly attached his "proviso" to numerous bills in the House.

CRITICS AND POLITICAL ENEMIES

Besides politicians, several public figures opposed the war and detested Polk. These included journalists, authors, and poets, some of whom were also abolitionists. William Lloyd Garrison, editor of the abolitionist newspaper *The Liberator*, condemned Polk's war "of aggression, of invasion, of conquest, and rapine" as a conflict designed to spread slavery. Polk, claimed Garrison, had orchestrated a war "waged for basest goals, by means perfidious, profligate and low." Poet John Greenleaf Whittier wrote a friend that he was "heart-sick with this miserably wicked Mexican War." Other critics included Unitarian clergyman Theodore Parker, essayist Henry David Thoreau, and journalist Horace Greeley of the *New York Tribune*, who labeled Polk "father of lies." Poet James Russell Lowell targeted Polk through satirical fiction in the *Boston Courier*. A clever and acerbic writer, Lowell collected his stories into a book entitled *The Biglow Papers* that framed the war as an obvious effort to add slave states to the Union.

Even when Polk left office, critics pilloried him. William Jay, a New York judge and son of Supreme Court Chief Justice John Jay, blasted out his *Review of the Causes and Consequences of the Mexican War,* asserting, "The conduct of Mr. Polk . . . was all that was false, base, and wicked." Jay concluded that the conflict had been "a war of conquest, so hateful in its objects, so wanton, unjust, and unconstitutional in its origin and character, [it] must be regarded as a war against freedom, against humanity, against justice, [and] against the Union."

Polk seldom answered his opponents. His old Whig rival, Henry Clay, delivered a spiteful antiwar public speech in Kentucky, in November 1847. Clay's address collected several rancorous Whig barbs: Polk had given "improvident and unconstitutional" orders sending the U.S. Army to the Rio Grande, starting an "unnatural war with Mexico" that resulted in America committing "aggression" against its neighbor. Polk restrained himself, in part because Clay's favorite son had been killed in battle eight months earlier. Although some Whigs spread rumors of impeaching him, Polk displayed confidence in himself and his wartime policies. He anticipated and fervently hoped that, like the Federalists who railed against President James Madison, the Whig Party would collapse due to its opposition to his war.

Many of Polk's critics showed no inclination to soften their criticism of Polk even after his death in 1849. At the time of the president's death, Garrison skewered Polk's slave ownership in *The Liberator:* "He probably died an unrepentant man-stealer. His administration has been a curse to the country." Essayist Ralph Waldo Emerson drew the analogy between America's defeat of Mexico and someone "who swallows . . . arsenic." Emerson predicted that by gorging itself with large portions of Mexico's land the United States had ingested poison destined to produce intense debates over expanding slavery into the West and eventually sunder the nation.

CONCLUSION

Two significant Americans crucial to preserving the Union during the Civil War rendered long-lasting negative conclusions about "Mr. Polk's War." Near the war's end in 1848, Whig congressman Abraham Lincoln of Illinois accused Polk of the "sheerest deception" over where the war started. Lincoln demanded that Polk reveal the "exact spot" where the first skirmish took place, expressing doubt that it was on U.S. territory. He argued that the "war with Mexico was unnecessarily and unconstitutionally commenced by the President." In his popular memoirs published in 1885, the former Union general and president Ulysses S. Grant wrote a scathing indictment of Polk and his war. He described the Mexican-American War as "one of the most unjust ever waged by a stronger against a weaker nation" and claimed that "the Southern rebellion was largely an outgrowth of" that conflict. Many historians have concurred with Lincoln's and Grant's views, which remain salient more than a century after they were written.

Joseph G. Dawson III

Further Reading

Bauer, K. Jack. *The Mexican War, 1846–1848*. New York: Macmillan, 1974.

Johannsen, Robert W. *To the Halls of the Montezumas: The Mexican War in the American Imagination*. New York: Oxford University Press, 1985.

Morison, Samuel Eliot, Frederick Merk, and Frank Freidel. *Dissent in Three American Wars*. Cambridge, MA: Harvard University Press, 1970.

Schroeder, John H. *Mr. Polk's War: American Opposition and Dissent, 1846–1848*. Madison, WI: University of Wisconsin Press, 1973.

12. Zachary Taylor

Born: November 24, 1784

Died: July 9, 1850

Time in Office: 12th President of the United States, March 4, 1849, to July 9, 1850

Election Results: 1848 Election: 47.3% of popular vote, 163 (56.2%) Electoral College votes

Spouse: Margaret Smith (m. 1810)

Children: Ann Mackall, Sarah Knox, Octavia Pannell, Margaret Smith, Mary Elizabeth, and Richard Scott

Zachary Taylor, who served as president from March 1849 to July 1850, was a member of the Whig Party. He served in the U.S. Army from 1808 to 1849 and was married to Margaret Smith, with whom he had six children. Taylor's brief political career began with great popularity and ended with his death from a sudden illness. In between, he faced difficulties driven both by regular politics and by broader historical and institutional forces, resulting in sharp criticisms from multiple political parties, Congress, state governors, and the press.

Taylor was once one of the most popular men in the United States. He was a military hero in both the War of 1812 and the Mexican-American War, prevailing in battles against much larger enemy forces. These exploits earned him the nickname "Old Rough and Ready." Because of his great popularity, the Whig Party gave him its nomination for president in 1848, rather than renominate Senator Henry Clay, who had lost the 1844 election. Taylor was an odd choice in some respects, however. He had no political experience and even boasted that he had never voted. Moreover, his status as a war hero did not fit with the Whigs' traditional antiwar stance. Taylor even distanced himself from the Whigs in the campaign, claiming that he was "a Whig, but not an ultra Whig," as he aspired to be a truly national leader, not a mere partisan.

A RESERVED WHIG OR AN ACTIVE LEADER?

In his inaugural address and other remarks, Taylor strongly endorsed the Whig view of a limited presidency that would largely defer to Congress. In some respects, Taylor worked to help his party. For example, he used patronage to reward fellow Whigs, who comprised his entire cabinet. He hired the sympathetic newspaper *The Republic* to publish the government's documents and to promote its politics. And he went on a tour of northeastern states in the summer of 1849 to drum up support. This decision prompted many Democrats to criticize him for electioneering, which was supposedly undignified and unpresidential.

Yet Taylor was often criticized by Whig members of Congress. For example, given the tensions between northern and southern Whigs over the issue of slavery, some Whigs felt they had been slighted in Taylor's use of patronage. According to historian Brainerd Dyer, Rep. Abraham Lincoln of Illinois was disappointed not to receive a political appointment. Congressional Whigs became so divided that "the President and his Cabinet found themselves virtually an Administration without a party." Clay criticized the administration—both the president and his cabinet—for not forging close ties with Congress. Some Whigs in Congress were so disdainful of the administration that they even threatened to purposely be absent from key votes.

STATES' RIGHTS

In August 1849, Taylor issued a proclamation against a "filibuster" force of private American citizens planning to invade Cuba to liberate the island nation from Spain. This led to a naval blockade of the filibuster forces in Round Island, Mississippi, which many locals saw as an unconstitutional infringement on the rights of state residents. The *Mobile Herald and Tribune* questioned the president's authority in "blockading a portion of one of the States and of declaring to men on it that they should have no supplies or provisions, and should leave it only in particular modes of conveyance." Mississippi's governor, meanwhile, declared that "our citizens [were] deprived of the exercise of their rights of freemen, in a time of profound peace, by martial law, and in total disregard of the civil authorities of the State." Mississippi's congressional delegation demanded that Taylor hand over all government documents relating to the matter, and Taylor complied.

SLAVERY AND STATEHOOD

Taylor's greatest political difficulty, and the cause of most of the criticism against him, was the issue of slavery and how it should be dealt with as western territories sought to become new states. Taylor was a slave-owning southerner, but he also wanted to preserve the Union and viewed territorial expansion as a top priority. He opposed what became the Compromise of 1850, which did not restrict slavery in the southwest, and he urged antislavery California and New Mexico to become states, which angered southerners. In February 1850, Taylor met in the White House with three southern Whig members of Congress. They opposed Taylor's plan for the admission of California and sought to talk him out of it, but he stood firm. They then raised the possibility of secession, to which Taylor promised a military response. He called them "damned traitors" and informed them that "if it became necessary, in executing the laws, he would take command of the army himself, and that, if they were taken in rebellion against the Union, he would hang them with less reluctance than he had hung deserters and spies in Mexico!"

SENATOR HENRY CLAY

Some of the sharpest criticism of Taylor came from Senator Henry Clay of Kentucky. Clay was bitter that Taylor had beaten him for the Whig nomination in 1848, and he favored plans for the admission of new states on terms more generous to southern interests. Their strained relationship became even more so in April 1850 when the two men passed on the street in Washington and Clay failed to greet the president. Taylor was angered at the slight, and Clay subsequently apologized.

On May 21, 1850, Clay's criticism of the president became unrestrained. Clay gave a long speech on the floor of the Senate in which he heaped scorn and derision upon Taylor. He specifically criticized the president's plan for California statehood and challenged any of Taylor's allies to defend it. Referring to several related aspects of the slavery question, Clay described "five wounds . . . bleeding, and threatening the well-being, if not the existence of the body politic." He said Taylor's plan was to heal only one of the wounds "and to leave the other four to bleed more profusely than ever." Clay also claimed that Taylor had initiated total war on any compromise measure. Clay's lengthy attack ended only when he became exhausted from his impassioned speech. Clay's harsh criticisms were subsequently echoed by newspapers like the *Union*, which charged that Taylor was stubbornly opposed to any compromise whatsoever and that he seemed not to want to resolve the slavery question.

When administration efforts to encourage Texas to seek statehood led to questions of whether Texas would continue to be governed by Mexico's antislavery laws, and to a dispute about the border with New Mexico, the governor of Mississippi offered to send military forces to protect Texas, and Whig Rep. Alexander Stephens of Georgia threatened to impeach Taylor.

SCANDAL

In April 1850, Taylor's difficulties with Congress over slavery and statehood took a backseat to a scandal within his administration, when it became clear that Secretary of War George Crawford had facilitated government compensation for the Galphin family of Georgia for land that had been seized by the government, after which Crawford was given half of the compensation payment. According to historian Elbert Smith, "Almost everyone, whether Democrat or Whig, who had ever opposed the president for any reason at all attacked the officers involved and the president without mercy." Some in Congress even threatened to censure the president. This criticism diminished Taylor's reputation for honesty, but Taylor resisted firing Crawford because of his friendship for him.

CONCLUSION

Arguably, one of the more lasting controversies about Taylor concerned his death from cholera. Ignoring warnings that an outbreak of cholera in Washington was being spread by tainted food and drink, Taylor consumed several items suspected of being carriers of the disease. The president became ill and died five days later, having served only 16 months in office. (At that time, only William Henry Harrison had served a shorter term.) A rumor spread that Taylor had been poisoned by slavery advocates, but a scientific examination of Taylor's exhumed remains in 1991 indicated that he had died of cholera.

Due to his brief presidency and the difficult circumstances that he faced, Taylor's legacy is limited. His preferred terms for the admission of new states did not survive him, as the Compromise of 1850 passed two months after his death. And the Whig Party died after Taylor's vice president, Millard Fillmore, served the remainder of his term. Taylor faced posthumous criticism for failing to resolve the great sectional divide over slavery and thus failing to prevent the Civil War, though such criticisms also apply to many other presidents. Given Taylor's status as the uneasy head of a divided party ostensibly committed to a weak executive branch, his failure to resolve the divide over slavery is understandable, as is the criticism that it occasioned.

Graham G. Dodds

Further Reading

Bauer, K. Jack. *Zachary Taylor: Soldier, Planter, Statesman of the Old Southwest*. Baton Rouge, LA: Louisiana State University Press, 1993.

de la Cova, Antonio Rafael. "The Taylor Administration versus Mississippi Sovereignty: The Round Island Expedition of 1849." *The Journal of Mississippi History*, Vol. 62, No. 4 (Winter 2000): 295–327.

Dyer, Brainerd. *Zachary Taylor*. Baton Rouge, LA: Louisiana State University Press, 1946.

Ellis, Richard. *The Development of the American Presidency*, 2nd ed. New York: Routledge, 2015.

Holman, Hamilton. *Zachary Taylor: Soldier in the White House*. Indianapolis, IN: Bobbs-Merrill, 1951.

Holt, Michael F. *The Rise and Fall of the American Whig Party*. New York: Oxford University Press, 1999.

Korzi, Michael J. *A Seat of Popular Leadership*. Amherst, MA: University of Massachusetts Press, 2004.

Milkis, Sidney, and Michael Nelson. *The American Presidency, Origins and Development, 1776–2014*, 7th ed. Washington, D.C.: CQ Press, 2016.

Smith, Elbert B. *The Presidencies of Zachary Taylor & Millard Fillmore*. Lawrence, KS: University Press of Kansas, 1988.

Troy, Gil. "How an Outsider President Killed a Party." *Politico*. June 2, 2016. Available at http://www.politico.com/magazine/story/2016/06/history-campaign-politics-zachary-taylor-killed-whigs-political-party-213935.

13. Millard Fillmore

Born: January 7, 1800
Died: March 8, 1874
Time in Office: 13th President of the United States, July 9, 1850, to March 4, 1853
Election Results: 1848 Election: Elected vice president; assumed office upon death of Zachary Taylor
Spouse: Abigail Powers (m. 1826); Caroline McIntosh (m. 1858)
Children: Millard Powers and Mary Abigail

Millard Fillmore was born in a log cabin in the Finger Lakes country of upstate New York in 1800. His childhood was marked by poverty. The second of eight children and the oldest son of Nathaniel and Phoebe (nee Millard) Fillmore, young Millard enjoyed little formal education. During his early years, he apprenticed for a cloth maker and then at a lumber mill. In 1819 he met his future wife, Abigail Powers, a teacher, and became a law clerk. In 1823 Fillmore was admitted to the New York State Bar and opened a practice in East Aurora, New York, thus becoming the town's only lawyer. In 1826 Fillmore married Powers, with whom he had two children, Millard Powers and Mary Abigail. Abigail Fillmore died in 1853, the same year that her husband left the White House. Fillmore married Caroline

Carmichael McIntosh, a wealthy widow, in 1858; she reportedly enjoyed the status that came with being married to a former president, though she required Fillmore to sign a prenuptial agreement. They lived in a mansion in Niagara, New York, until Fillmore's death from a stroke in 1874.

EARLY POLITICAL CAREER

From an early age, Fillmore was interested in politics. He began his political career in 1828 as a member of the Anti-Masonic Party, which supported libertarian principles and was opposed to exclusive groups like the Free Masons. Fillmore served as a delegate to an Anti-Masonic convention in New York that endorsed John Quincy Adams for reelection as president in 1828, in opposition to eventual victor Andrew Jackson. Fillmore also ran for a seat in the New York State Assembly that year, winning three consecutive one-year terms, serving from 1829 to 1831. It was also during this time that Fillmore began a mutual political relationship that would eventually turn into a political rivalry with Thurwood Weed, a political operative and newspaper publisher in New York. Weed helped steer the single-issue Anti-Masonic Party into the Whig Party within a few years; the Anti-Masons had been under attack by southern Democrats on the issue of slavery for years, and merging with the Whig Party only exacerbated the issue.

In 1832, having moved his family to Buffalo, Fillmore won election to the U.S. House of Representatives. He was motivated, in part, by his dislike of President Andrew Jackson (who Fillmore believed was power hungry) and his policy agenda. Fillmore served one term, but he was not renominated by the Anti-Masonic Party in 1834. He returned to Congress again in 1836 as a member of the Whig Party and served three terms. During this time, Weed assumed the leadership of New York Whigs. In doing so, he tried to marginalize Fillmore over the issue of slavery. Weed held a staunch antislavery position and would not support any compromise with the South. Fillmore, however, believed that compromise with the South on the issue of slavery was the key to preserving the Union. Thus, Weed became Fillmore's political enemy. From 1841 to 1843, Fillmore chaired the powerful House Ways and Means Committee. He led the passage of a high tariffs bill to protect imports that was so vehemently opposed by southern states that it made him a hated figure to many southerners in the House.

Despite leaving Congress (he chose not to seek reelection in 1842), Fillmore remained active in politics. Some members of the Whig Party urged Fillmore to run for vice president with Henry Clay in 1844 (supporters included *New York Tribune* editor Horace Greeley), while others encouraged Fillmore to run for governor of New York. Fillmore regarded the vice presidency as the more appealing option, but Weed wanted Fillmore to run for governor. Weed won out by strongly endorsing Fillmore for governor among fellow Whigs and securing the vice presidential nomination for former New Jersey senator Theodore Frelinghuysen. Fillmore understood the true motivation of Weed's support for his gubernatorial campaign: "I am not willing to be treacherously killed by this pretended kindness [and] do not suppose for a minute that I think they desire my nomination for governor." Fillmore ultimately lost the governor's race, as he was perceived by many voters as weak on slavery due to his willingness to seek compromise on slave states and anti-immigrant. Fillmore blamed his enemies, including Weed, New York abolitionists, and Catholic immigrants, for his defeat. In 1847 Fillmore ran for the newly elective office of comptroller in New York. The Whig Party was united behind him, and he won the office by more than 38,000 votes (the largest vote margin ever tallied by a Whig candidate in the state).

FILLMORE AS VICE PRESIDENT

By the late 1840s slavery had become the most incendiary political issue facing the United States. It was polarizing North-South relations and was already threatening to tear the Union apart. No serious presidential candidate could get elected without confronting it in some way, yet most preferred to kick the can down the road so as to avoid further alienating enraged voters. Believing that avoiding the issue would maintain national unity, Whigs preferred to remain silent. However, the choice of slave-owning Mexican War hero Zachary Taylor as their presidential nominee in 1848 spoke volumes, angering antislavery Whigs from northern states. Recognizing the potential political liabilities, they picked Fillmore, an antislavery New Yorker with a more urbane demeanor and ingratiating personality, as Taylor's running mate. Unfortunately, their calculations largely misfired, for Fillmore eventually became an even more reliable friend to proslavery southerners than his president. In addition, Taylor and Fillmore were mismatched in terms of both personality and political views. These differences fueled a mutual dislike that made cooperation in the White House almost impossible.

Taylor and his vice president had not been acquainted prior to the election, underlining an absence of personal ties that exacerbated a fraught professional relationship. The two men could not have been more different and still be members of the same party. Bitter enemies by the beginning of Taylor's presidency, they openly opposed each other regarding the administration's agenda. Not surprisingly, Fillmore was excluded from the Taylor administration and relegated to his duties as the president of the Senate. Whether Taylor did this for political or personal reasons has been the subject of some debate among historians. Most likely, it was a combination of both. One factor that is not in debate is the influence Fillmore's old nemesis Thurlow Weed had over Taylor. Among other things, Weed convinced Taylor to deny Fillmore any patronage appointments from his home state of New York. Granting vice presidents such perks had become customary by then. New York bigwig William Seward, the future secretary of state under Abraham Lincoln, threw his weight behind Weed and enthusiastically stirred trouble for Fillmore whenever the occasion arose.

Both the Taylor and Fillmore administrations became consumed by the question of what to do with the western territories acquired during the Mexican-American War of 1846–1848. With the nation's political map precariously balanced between free and slave states, antislavery and proslavery interests vied for geographic advantage and worked hard to halt the expansion of their opponents' territories. Both sides feared that any expansion would be the beginning of a slippery slope toward their adversaries' complete domination of the federal government and the imposition of a foreign and unwelcome way of life, which would make the disintegration of the Union inevitable. Southern states, where paranoia of political and economic subjugation by the North ran high, felt particularly vulnerable to the spread of antislavery movements in the North. These sentiments were only exacerbated by a slave-owning president who they felt should have been a champion of the southern cause but who instead turned his back on his fellow southerners. They were also infuriated by his references to them as "fire eaters" because of their willingness to destroy the Union over an issue that most Americans opposed and apparently viewed as immoral.

Despite their dislike of Taylor and opposition to his views on slavery, southerners were relieved by the presence of what they believed was a proslavery vice president who seemed to support their territorial objectives and hoped to secure a favorable agreement regarding the disposition of the western territories. Before too long, however, southerners realized that Fillmore was not an outright proponent of slavery but a believer in compromise and the principle of popular sovereignty, which meant that the inhabitants of each new territory would settle the matter for themselves. By the time Fillmore became president and began to deal with the disposition of the western territories himself, southerners were some of his staunchest enemies. John Calhoun of South Carolina, an intellectual giant and unabashed apologist for slavery, had predicted as much and sought to persuade his southern brethren of the futility of compromise with Unionists supposedly bent on the destruction of the South. He died a few months before Fillmore became president but spent his last days warning southerners against cooperation and compromise with northern states dedicated to the abolition of slavery and the dissolution of the South's political and economic institutions.

As it turned out, Taylor had no stomach for a fight over the western territories or the negotiation of a compromise among competing stakeholders. Taylor sat on the sidelines as the "Great Compromiser," Henry Clay of Kentucky, pushed a bill through Congress intended to resolve the dilemma. Taylor, convinced that the prospective law, the Compromise of 1850, was unduly slanted toward proslavery interests, pledged to reject it if it landed on his desk. Fillmore openly opposed him, using his position as president of the Senate to promote it and promising to cast a tie-breaking vote in its favor if the situation required it. With singular animosity toward an administration that he believed had unjustifiably marginalized him, Fillmore pursued Taylor and his cabinet without regard for the consequences. Taylor, for his part, was thrilled to strike a fatal blow against a bill that Fillmore championed and a vice president he hated. Fillmore's support for the bill was noteworthy for its betrayal of administration policies, but, without the backing of the president and the political machinery of the White House, it had no chance. An omnibus package whose scope and length were too much to handle for a Congress that would have had trouble passing something even half the size, the bill was simply too ambitious.

FILLMORE AS PRESIDENT

Turning a political fight over the compromise bill into a personal battle against the president and his cabinet was a mistake on Fillmore's part. Although the bill had little chance of passing anyhow, the vice president's stance undermined what little credibility he may have had with the administration, strengthened Weed's and Seward's resolve against him, and cost him allies who were alienated by Fillmore's overtly personal attacks against Taylor. The real tragedy was that both Fillmore and Taylor had the same objective, which was the preservation of the Union. Together, they could have forged a comparatively broad coalition of northern and southern moderates from both parties. In the end, none of that mattered, because Taylor was dead not too long afterward. After only 16 months as vice president, Fillmore was unexpectedly pushed into the presidency and left to confront the political quagmire in the western territories on his own.

FILLMORE IN THE WHITE HOUSE

Before he could turn his attention to the moribund Compromise of 1850, Fillmore was ensnared by an unnecessary political mess in the White House. Fillmore's disdain for his predecessor's cabinet was well known, so his first order of business was to settle grievances against Taylor's advisers. Not even a full day into his tenure at the White House, Fillmore got rid of the entire cabinet and much of the staff. Whether he actually dismissed Taylor's people directly or forced them to resign is not clear. Regardless, the result and symbolism were clear. Aside from the administrative paralysis such a move caused, especially for someone deemed poorly qualified for the office and needing knowledgeable and skilled people around him, it had reverberations well beyond the White House. The Whigs, who had been splintering into quarreling factions over slavery and sectionalism for some time, descended into chaos. Though he was by no means responsible for the disintegration of the Whigs himself, the new president definitely accelerated the process and made the infighting particularly problematic. Fillmore's selection of a Unionist cabinet willing to compromise with proslavery forces in the South attracted immediate scorn and promises of revenge from northern abolitionist Whigs. In addition, it exacerbated serious personal divisions that had nothing to do with the politics of slavery. Weed, by then an inveterate Fillmore hater, was happily stoking the fire and leading the charge.

Next on Fillmore's agenda was the issue that cost him his relationship with Taylor and many other Whigs, to say nothing of his predecessor's friends and political allies. For all his faults and political failures, Fillmore was genuinely devoted to saving the Union. He believed that this could be achieved only through compromise between antislavery and proslavery forces. He thought that slavery was deeply immoral, which is something his northern foes never understood or wanted to understand, but he feared that unilateral and premature abolition of slavery would devastate the Union. "God knows," he confessed to his Secretary of State Daniel Webster, "I detest slavery, but it is an existing evil, for which we are not responsible, and we must endure it and give it such protections as is guaranteed by the Constitution, till we get rid of it without destroying the last hope of free government" in the United States. Fillmore's political enemies within the Whig Party, however, were convinced that such distinctions were double-talk. They never gave him the benefit of the doubt and consistently spurned any territorial solutions that involved compromise with proslavery legislators.

Unnerved by the deteriorating political situation, Fillmore was anxious to resubmit the compromise bill to Congress as soon as possible, hoping to pass it within a few months. The president leaned hard on Congress to push it through and relied on Clay to shepherd it along. It was not to be, at least not in its original form. As University of Virginia historian Michael Holt put it, "[t]he angry tone of the national debate increased. In Congress, forces for and against slavery fought over every word of the bill. Both sides chipped away at the bill's provisions, and support for it collapsed, much to Fillmore's deep disappointment." Clay, one of the capital's most talented deal makers, was so exhausted and enfeebled by the failed effort that he withdrew from Washington in a fruitless attempt to recuperate. This was a deep blow to the proponents of compromise, and Fillmore was blamed for the result by practically all sides. His enemies, especially northern Whigs and southern Democratic slave owners, welcomed his defeat.

Luckily for Fillmore, a more virile and enthusiastic champion of compromise emerged, armed with a different strategy to secure passage of the embattled legislation. Senator Stephen Douglas (D-IL), who would have otherwise been Fillmore's enemy due to his party affiliation, became an unlikely ally. Douglas's rhetorical skills, as later evidenced by the famous Lincoln-Douglas debates of 1858, were a key aspect of the new effort's eventual success. Realizing that the omnibus bill was unwieldy and promoted widespread opposition from adversaries intent on killing individual parts of the legislation, Douglas divided the omnibus measure into five smaller initiatives, each of which focused on one of the original provisions. For his part, Fillmore believed that the new approach would succeed where previous attempts had failed. He was particularly encouraged by Douglas's views on slavery, which largely overlapped his. Douglas was a supporter not only of compromise among northern and southern political factions but also of popular sovereignty, meaning that new territories and states would decide for themselves through democratic processes whether to become slave or free. This did not endear him to slave-owning Democrats, who increasingly equated such efforts as appeasement of northern interests at the expense of southern objectives. Nevertheless, as Douglas and Fillmore had hoped, the senator's strategy worked. Fillmore was convinced that the passage of the five bills was "a triumph of interparty cooperation that kept the Union intact," in the words of Holt. However, it was anything but a triumph, hardly resounding and extremely close. Douglas and Fillmore had little time to celebrate. Their legislation drew heavy criticism from all sides almost immediately. Deceived by a narrow victory, Fillmore saw "interparty cooperation" where none actually existed. Douglas had managed to cobble together bare coalitions precariously poised between success and failure for the individual bills, but all the bills, according to Holt, included "something for everyone to dislike." The legislation admitted California into the United States as a free state; allowed residents of the New Mexico and Utah territories to decide the fate of slavery for themselves; banned the slave trade in Washington, D.C.; settled border disputes between Texas and the New Mexico territory; and, most controversially, included a new Fugitive Slave Law.

Slave owners railed against the admission of California as a free state and saw popular sovereignty in New Mexico and Utah as a slap in the face. They were convinced that it was nothing more than a thinly veiled attempt to stop the expansion of slavery and, in turn, promote its abolition throughout the Union. The prohibition of the slave trade in the nation's capital was, by southern accounts, further proof of Fillmore's collusion with abolitionists against the South. Turning against a president they once thought would be a political ally, southerners began to entertain radical responses to a situation that offered them few alternatives. Everything from nullification of federal laws to secession was on the table, though at that point only the most extreme of Fillmore's enemies were serious about leaving the Union. Still, the president was not about to leave anything to chance. He dispatched extra troops to federal forts in South Carolina in the hopes that such symbolic measures would dissuade southerners from considering secession and other acts of defiance.

Many northerners, for their part, were convinced that Fillmore was actually colluding with southerners. They characterized the Fugitive Slave Act as a sop to slave owners and the linchpin of a plot to promote the expansion of the dreaded institution above the Mason-Dixon Line. Arguably the most despised part of the Compromise of 1850, the Fugitive Slave Act mandated the return of escaped slaves to their owners, even in free states. Fillmore vowed to enforce the law wherever and whenever circumstances required and declared that it was his constitutional duty to do so. Abolitionists balked, and some antislavery states went so far as to pass legislation that banned enforcement of the law within their boundaries. Fillmore was furious about these acts of defiance and condemned them in the strongest possible terms. Not one to bow to pressure and let his enemies get the best of him, Fillmore decided to make a stand in his home state of New York and use it as an example of federal enforcement powers over the states. He demanded the apprehension and immediate return of escaped slaves to their owners, but New York would not cooperate. When an actual case arose to test the president's mettle, he was bettered by a group of armed abolitionists who snatched the slave in question from federal authorities. Adding insult to injury, prosecution of the offending abolitionists failed.

The New York example, however, was an exception. Proclaiming that "without law there can be no real practical liberty," Fillmore sent federal troops into states and communities that had declared their opposition to the reviled law. Dozens of slaves were captured and returned to their owners. In a Boston case that resembled the failed intervention in New York, Fillmore came out on top, with federal authorities recapturing the fugitive slave and successfully prosecuting the abolitionists involved. In Pennsylvania, the president pursued offending abolitionists with such vigor that he ordered U.S. marshals to charge uncooperative residents with treason. Sadly, Fillmore's almost messianic support for the law, whose enforcement provisions may have been unconstitutional, exposed a man with deep insecurities and an associated need to vanquish all enemies, no matter how big or small, even at the expense of a reputation that had suffered considerably by then.

CONCLUSION

As president, Fillmore had a questionable record at best. Determined to preserve the Union at all costs, he pursued policies that actually had the opposite effect. He inherited a mess from his predecessor but did nothing effective to contain or resolve it. Despite some victories, Fillmore was defeated soundly by his enemies. Many of them survived, though, regrettably, they would accelerate the disintegration of the Union. In the end, it seems that nobody won. As historian Paul Finkelman concluded, "In the end, Fillmore was always on the wrong side of the great moral and political issues of the age: immigration, religious toleration, equality, and, most of all, slavery."

Lori Cox Han and Tomislav Han

Further Reading

Abbott, Philip. *Bad Presidents: Failure in the White House*. New York: Palgrave Macmillan, 2013.

Finkelman, Paul. *Millard Fillmore*. New York: Times Books, 2011.

Gerhardt, Michael J. *The Forgotten Presidents: Their Untold Constitutional Legacy*. New York: Oxford University Press, 2013.

Holt, Michael F. "Millard Fillmore." Miller Center, University of Virginia. Available at https://millercenter.org/president/fillmore.

Rayback, Robert J. *Millard Fillmore: Biography of a President*. Buffalo, NY: Buffalo Historical Society, 1959.

Scarry, Robert J. *Millard Fillmore*. Jefferson, NC: McFarland, 2009.

14. Franklin Pierce

Born: November 23, 1804

Died: October 8, 1869

Time in Office: 14th President of the United States, March 4, 1853, to March 4, 1857

Election Results: 1852 Election: 50.8% of popular vote, 254 (85.8%) Electoral College votes

Spouse: Jane Appleton (m. 1834)

Children: Franklin Jr., Frank Robert, and Benjamin

Few 19th-century political leaders were possessed of more positive advantages than Franklin Pierce. Born in Hillsborough, New Hampshire, on November 23, 1804, Pierce was the son of a Revolutionary War hero who later served as the state's governor in the late 1820s. A graduate of Maine's Bowdoin College, where he roomed with author Nathaniel Hawthorne (who would write Pierce's 1852 campaign biography), and took classes with Henry Wadsworth Longfellow, Pierce parlayed his good looks and academic success into a marriage with Jane Means Appleton, the tee-totaling daughter of Bowdoin's former president.

A successful attorney, Pierce was first elected to New Hampshire's legislature in 1829, serving as its speaker from 1832 to 1833. Elected to the U.S. House of Representatives as a Democrat at age 29, he served for four years, 1833 to 1837, before moving to the U.S. Senate, where he sat from 1837 to 1842. Returning to New Hampshire, he was the state's federal attorney and refused President James K. Polk's offer to be his attorney general. He enlisted during the Mexican-American War (1846–1848) and attained the rank of brigadier general. Rumors persisted that he had fainted and fallen off his horse, an event explained by his defenders as due to a serious war wound. But for Pierce it was slavery and his reaction to it that would define his presidency.

THE SLAVERY ISSUE

Although the 1787 Constitutional Convention compromise rewarded the South by decreeing that slaves would count as three-fifths of a person for both representation and taxation, it also mandated that the American slave trade would end in 1808, 20 years after ratification. However, during the early 1800s, the trans-Atlantic slave trade shriveled as one European nation after another sought to end slavery, both within their national borders and in their colonies. Slave trading ended in Norway and Denmark in 1803, followed by Great Britain in 1807, the Netherlands in 1814, and France in 1818. Although slavery was abolished in Spain and many of its colonies in 1811, it remained in the Spanish colonies of Cuba, Puerto Rico, and Santo Domingo. By the 1820s, most of Latin America's countries had abolished slavery. The United States, however, was the exception to this global trend. With much of the South economically dependent on slavery, it resisted the international emancipation movement and chose only to prohibit slavery north and west of the new state of Missouri in the Missouri Compromise of 1820. The compromise obliged Congress to admit states to the Union as slave state–free state pairs to maintain parity of representation between slave states and nonslave states in the U.S. Senate.

With the 1848 conclusion of the Mexican-American War and the admission of free-state Wisconsin to balance slave-state Texas, eight states had entered the Union under the Missouri Compromise's provisions. This produced a 15–15 North-South Senate equilibrium as intended. However, rapid population growth in the midwestern cities of Cleveland, Cincinnati, Chicago, and Detroit, combined with the waves of Irish and German immigrants in the cities of the Eastern Seaboard, had swelled the population of northern states relative to their southern counterparts by midcentury. The 1850 Census provided a dramatic discrepancy, as the North-South gap of five seats among the original 13 states in the 1789 apportionment (35–30) in the House of Representatives expanded to a northern advantage of 54 seats following the 1853 apportionment (144–90).

It was the 1849 gold rush that led Congress to admit California as a state as soon as possible. However, there was no slave state to pair it with. Outnumbered in the House and fearing that slavery, their "peculiar institution," would be attacked, slavery supporters pushed for congressional protections. The Democratic Party was their vehicle and Pierce's New Hampshire was the most Democratic of the New England states, where pro-abolitionist sentiments were strongest in the entire North. Also, Congress was further troubled by the rise of radical southern "Fire

Eaters," led by South Carolina's Robert Barnwell Rhett. These radicals talked openly of secession unless the international slave trade, which had ended in 1808, was reopened. To forestall the crisis, Congress passed the five acts of the Compromise of 1850, coauthored by Whig senator Henry Clay of Kentucky and Democratic senator Stephen Douglas of Illinois. Its most controversial act was the brutal Fugitive Slave Law, which in effect nationalized slavery by denying runaway slaves any sanctuary within the borders of the United States.

Pierce returned to national politics at the 1852 Democratic National Convention as a quintessential "dark horse" candidate, much as Tennessee's James K. Polk, the last Democratic nominee to own slaves had been at the 1844 convention. The two-thirds rule required by Democrats to select their presidential and vice presidential nominees had given the South a veto over any nominee likely to challenge slavery, but it also presaged a convention deadlock. Although none of the major post–1848 Democratic contenders owned slaves, each feared southern political wrath and committed themselves to defending slavery, thus earning the derisive term "dough-face" in the northern press.

The 1852 convention elicited multiple candidates led by 1848 nominee U.S. senator Lewis Cass of Michigan, a native of New Hampshire and the first of four "doughface" nominees selected by the antebellum Democrats. Other contenders were James Buchanan of Pennsylvania, Polk's secretary of state; William L. Marcy of New York, Polk's secretary of war; and Vermont-born U.S. senator Stephen A. Douglas of Illinois. Buchanan passed Cass on the 20th ballot, and Buchanan was passed by Douglas on the 30th ballot. Cass resumed the lead on the 32nd ballot only to surrender it to Marcy on the 45th ballot. Pierce's name did not even appear until the 35th ballot, but he was the beneficiary of an exhausted convention full of delegates increasingly desperate to find a compromise candidate acceptable to enough voters. Pierce was formally nominated on the 49th ballot with 282 of its 296 votes. It was the only ballot on which he led. Named to run with Pierce was Buchanan ally U.S. senator William Rufus De Vane King of Alabama. King told U.S. representative Cave Johnson of Tennessee "that next to Buchanan he [Pierce] was more agreeable to the South than any other man, for he was a gentleman, a conservative Democrat, and quite respectable for talents and information."

Unlike the Democrats who were united in their commitment to slavery, the Whigs, the ostensible opposition party, were divided between a proslavery faction of "Cotton Whigs" and an antislavery faction of "Conscience Whigs." An article published in *The Primitive Republican* in the summer of 1852 brought up Pierce's proslavery voting record as a House member to dissuade northerners from supporting him. As the paper stated, after conducting a thorough review of Pierce's voting record, it appeared that, "in a word, that he was the unwavering ally and supporter of the Slaveholding Interest." According to historian Leland S. Person, despite "[the] negative campaign against Pierce's character as soon as he accepted the nomination, attacking him for being a gambler, drunk, and coward," Pierce easily won the presidency over the disunited Whigs.

The 1852 deaths of Whig luminaries Henry Clay in June and Daniel Webster in October rendered the Whigs virtually leaderless and their nominee, General Winfield Scott, carried only 4 of 31 states and only 42 of 296 electoral votes. It was the last time the Whig Party fielded a presidential candidate. A mere two years later, wrote historian Corey Brooks, "when Congress passed divisive legislation that could introduce slavery into Kansas, the teetering Whig party came tumbling down. A new coalition that combined most of the Free Soil Party, a majority of northern Whigs, and a substantial number of disgruntled northern Democrats came together to form the Republican party."

In the wake of the Democrats' landslide victory, however, early tragedy befell both men on the ticket. Pierce's Boston victory party turned tragic when a train derailment led to the death of Benjamin, his last surviving son. Pierce's wife Jane, who blamed politics for Benny's fate, lapsed into a depression so severe that there was no Inaugural Ball that year. Vice President King, who sought to better his health during convalescence in Cuba, died barely six weeks after being sworn in. At his 1853 inaugural, Pierce's remarks had echoes of his mourning: "I ought to be, and am truly grateful for the rare manifestation of the nation's confidence; but this, so far from lightening my obligations, only adds to their weight. You have summoned me in my weakness; you must sustain me by your strength."

While New Yorker William Marcy was named secretary of state, three of Pierce's other six cabinet choices came from slave-holding states: Navy Secretary James C. Dobbin of North Carolina, Treasury Secretary James Guthrie of Kentucky, and most importantly, Secretary of War Jefferson Davis of Mississippi. Davis, who had once been a son-in-law of President Zachary Taylor, was sympathetic with the southern "fire eaters." With the free state of California now in the Union, slaveholders saw that the only way that they could counter northern population growth and protect slavery was to extend it beyond the Missouri River into the American West or to purchase Cuba from Spain or seize it if Spain refused. With Pierce compromised by his wife's depression and growing public awareness of his increased dependency on alcohol, the party's stronger personalities pushed him aside.

In 1854, northern Democratic protectors of slavery engaged in a twofold strategy to mollify the South: Stephen Douglas's Kansas-Nebraska Act was introduced early that year, and later that year, Pierce and Marcy instructed James Buchanan, John Mason, and Pierre Soulé, ambassadors to England, France, and Spain, respectively, to further U.S. attempts to acquire Cuba, the largest of the Caribbean slave islands. Meeting in Ostend, Belgium, the ambassadors contended that Cuba was vital to U.S. domestic interests and should be purchased from Spain. However, if Spain would not sell the island, the United States would take it by force. Vehement public opposition to the manifesto erupted in the North and Europe, further undermining Pierce's presidency and confirming that it was wholly subservient to slaveholders. The Ostend Manifesto failed but the Kansas-Nebraska Act passed.

KANSAS-NEBRASKA ACT

The defining legislative event of the Pierce presidency was the May 1854 passage of Douglas's Kansas-Nebraska Act that espoused the doctrine of "popular sovereignty" to permit settlers in the western territories of Kansas and Nebraska to decide whether slavery would be permitted across the Missouri River. Pierce was a strong proponent of the bill. In a letter to L. B. Walker of New Hampshire in March of 1854, the president wrote that "the Nebraska Bill is of course the absorbing question now, as it is in the Country. To my mind it is demonstrably right and patriotic. I sustain it not on the ground, that there is a political necessity in the case, but because the principles it involves command the approbation of my conscience & my judgment."

Northern backlash to the bill was exemplified by John L. Magee's political cartoon, titled "Forcing Slavery Down the Throat of a Free Soiler." It depicts Douglas, Pierce, and proslavery Democrats standing on the "Democratic Platform," on which was written, "Central America," "Cuba," and "Kansas." The Democrats are seen holding down the large head of a "Free Soiler" whose arms are literally tied to the "Democratic Platform" as they shove a slave down his throat. The Free Soiler cries out in agony, shouting "Murder! Help, neighbors help! O my poor wife and children."

In the November 1854 congressional elections, opposition to the Kansas-Nebraska Act and the Ostend Manifesto cost Democrats 75 of their 183 House seats to a collection of anti-Nebraska parties that led to a two-month battle for the speakership won by the Know Nothing American Party candidate Nathaniel P. Banks of Massachusetts. Pierce's presidency had clearly run aground.

BLEEDING KANSAS

Free-state settlers from the northeast moved into Kansas where they were countered by thousands of proslavery "Border Ruffians" from neighboring Missouri eager to elect a proslavery legislature. The Ruffians' sacking of free-state encampment Lawrence, Kansas, on May 21, 1856, and their brutal attacks on northern settlers elsewhere in Kansas provided a frightening foreshadowing of what would come later in the Civil War. Magee's 1856 cartoon, "Liberty, the Fair Maid of Kansas in the Hands of the Border Ruffians," depicted the last three Democratic doughface presidential candidates in an exceedingly negative light: it portrayed Buchanan (the party's 1856 candidate) joining with Secretary of State William Marcy in robbing a corpse; a drunken Pierce (1852) soliciting Liberty, the Fair Maid of Kansas;

and Lewis Cass (1848) staring at her lustfully. In addition, the cartoon depicted another prominent Democratic leader, Stephen Douglas (who would claim the party's presidential nomination in 1860), scalping yet another victim of the ruffians.

A day later on May 22, the most notable attack on abolitionism occurred 1,100 miles to the east in the U.S. Capitol as U.S. senator Charles Sumner of Massachusetts was nearly fatally beaten at his Senate desk by South Carolina U.S. representative Preston Brooks. Contending that Sumner's powerful speech, "The Crime against Kansas," had maligned both his relative Senator Andrew Butler and his own home state, Brooks sought to "teach him a lesson" by beating him like a dog with a heavy gold-headed cane that broke apart in the assault. Days later, John Brown's retaliatory attack on five Kansas slavery supporters at Pottawatomie made it clear that the conflict could not be contained.

The beating kept Sumner out of the Senate for the next three years. The cry of "Bleeding Sumner," combined with abolitionist outrage about events in "Bleeding Kansas," hardened northern opposition to the expansion of slavery and contributed to the political fusion of Free Soilers, Conscience Whigs, and antislavery northern Democrats into the nascent Republican Party.

Congress failed to punish Brooks for the assault, and Pierce remained silent on this attack on a fellow New Englander. Brooks resigned his seat on July 15, 1856, but was reelected two weeks later. Less than six months later on January 27, 1857, Brooks died of croup. Pierce attended the state funeral for Brooks at the Capitol.

Increased public awareness of Pierce's alcoholism, which had escalated during his four years in office, jeopardized his renomination. It is generally contended that the death of Benny, Jane Pierce's melancholic disapproval of her husband's drinking habits, and his political career made her a White House recluse leading to their further estrangement.

In June 1856, the battered Democrats met in Cincinnati, Ohio, for their presidential convention. At this point they were no longer in control of the House and were only barely holding the Senate. All four candidates from 1852—Pierce, Buchanan, Douglas, and Cass—resumed their contest. Eventual nominee James Buchanan took the early lead on the first ballot over Pierce—135.5 to 122.5 with Douglas (33) and Cass (5) trailing badly. It would be Pierce's best showing as he steadily lost delegates on each subsequent ballot until the 16th and penultimate ballot where he won not a single vote. Pierce, once the landslide winner of the 1852 contest, now had the dubious distinction of being the only elected American president to be denied renomination by his own party. As he left office at the end of his term, he was often quoted as stating, "There is nothing left to do but get drunk."

Returning to New Hampshire, Pierce's later years were unhappy as the nation lurched toward civil war and the Union began its dissolution. While New Hampshire provided troops for the Union, Pierce continued to attack the Republican Party and President Abraham Lincoln. His most notable address was in Concord on July 4, 1863, when he told a gathering of 25,000, "True it is, that any of you, that I, may be the next victim of unconstitutional arbitrary, irresponsible power . . . [this] fearful, fruitless, fatal civil war. . . . How futile are all our efforts to maintain the Union by force of arms." That the speech was delivered a day after the Union's victory at Gettysburg led to broadsides accusing Pierce of treason.

On December 2, 1863, Jane Pierce died. Nathaniel Hawthorne, Pierce's most steadfast friend, accompanied him to the gravesite. The following spring, the two men went on a hiking excursion in the White Mountains. On May 19, 1864, while they slept at a hotel on the mountain, Hawthorne died. The pall bearers at Hawthorne's funeral in Concord, Massachusetts, included New England notables Henry Wadsworth Longfellow, Ralph Waldo Emerson, Bronson Alcott, John Greenleaf Whittier, and Oliver Wendell Holmes Sr. Pierce was excluded.

The final indignity occurred in April 1865 following the assassination of President Lincoln. An angry crowd gathered around Pierce's home, demanding that he show an American flag. Pierce confronted the crowd, though, and declared that "It is not necessary for me to show my devotion for the Stars and Stripes by any special exhibition upon the demand of any man or body of men." The crowd eventually dispersed.

CONCLUSION

As Pierce's depression deepened and he succumbed further to alcoholism, he would die on October 8, 1869, from severe cirrhosis of the liver at the age of 64. It was an ignominious end to a life that had once been filled with much early promise. Now lodged close to the bottom of ranked American presidents, the consensus is that Pierce was an honest and decent man who should never have become president.

Garrison Nelson and Erin Hayden

Further Reading

Brooks, Corey. "What Can the Collapse of the Whig Party Tell Us about Today's Politics?" *Smithsonian.com,* April 12, 2016. Available at https://www.smithsonianmag.com/history/what-can-collapse-whig-party-tell-us-about-todays-politics-180958729.

Contradt, Stacy. "The Tragic End to Franklin Pierce's Friendship with Nathaniel Hawthorne." *Mental Floss,* May 23, 2016.

Donald, David. *Charles Sumner and the Coming of the Civil War.* New York: Alfred A. Knopf, 1960.

Gara, Larry. *The Presidency of Franklin Pierce.* Lawrence, KS: University Press of Kansas, 1991.

Hicks, Peter, and John McKivigan, eds. *Encyclopedia of Antislavery and Abolition.* Westport, CT: Greenwood Press, 2007.

Hoffer, Williamjames Hull. *The Caning of Charles Sumner: Honor, Idealism, and the Origins of the Civil War.* Baltimore, MD: Johns Hopkins Press, 2010.

Holt, Michael F. *The Political Crisis of the 1850s*. New York: W. W. Norton, 1978.

Holt, Michael F. *The Fate of the Country: Politicians, Slavery Extension, and the Coming of the Civil War*. New York: Hill and Wang, 2004.

Holt, Michael F. *Franklin Pierce*. New York: Times Books, 2010.

Nichols, Roy F. *Franklin Pierce: Young Hickory of the Granite Hills*, 2nd ed. Philadelphia, PA: University of Pennsylvania Press, 1964.

Person, Leland S. "A Man for the Whole Country: Marketing Masculinity in the Pierce Biography." *Nathaniel Hawthorne Review*, Vol. 35, No. 1 (2009).

"Presidents Behaving Badly: Franklin Pierce's Drinking." *Presidential History Geeks*, March 2016. Available at http://potus-geeks.livejournal.com/695684.html.

Puleo, Stephen. *The Caning: The Assault That Drove America to Civil War*. Yardley, PA: Westholme, 2012.

Webster, Sidney. "Mr. Marcy, the Cuban Question and the Ostend Manifesto." *Political Science Quarterly* (1893): 1–32.

Wellner, Peter A. *Franklin Pierce: New Hampshire's Favorite Son*. Concord, NH: Plaidswede Publishing, 2004.

Wellner, Peter A. *Franklin Pierce: Martyr for the Union*. Concord, NH: Plaidswede Publishing, 2007.

15. James Buchanan

Born: April 23, 1791
Died: June 1, 1868
Time in Office: 15th President of the United States, March 4, 1857, to March 4, 1861
Election Results: 1856 Election: 45.3% of popular vote, 174 (58.8%) Electoral College votes

James Buchanan was president from March 4, 1857, to March 4, 1861, serving as the 15th president of the United States in the time period immediately preceding the Civil War. Buchanan was born in 1791 in Pennsylvania, the only president to hail from that state. He died in 1868 at the age of 77. Buchanan's path to the 1856 presidential nomination for the Democratic Party was paved by controversy within the party and the country as a whole over the slavery question and the recently passed Kansas-Nebraska Act of 1854. As Buchanan had been abroad for several years as the ambassador to the United Kingdom under the Franklin Pierce administration, he had not been directly involved in the battles surrounding the Kansas-Nebraska Act, which allowed territories to determine for themselves whether slavery would be permitted within their borders. In the 1856 presidential election, winning just over 45% of the popular vote and with 174 electoral votes, Buchanan defeated

Republican candidate John C. Fremont and American or Know-Nothing Party candidate Millard Fillmore. Buchanan is the only U.S. president to never marry, and throughout his presidency his niece Harriet Lane acted as his primary hostess at presidential functions.

PERSONAL ATTACKS THROUGHOUT BUCHANAN'S LIFE

In his own time and in later biographies, questions about Buchanan's sexuality abound, no doubt intensified by his status as the only lifelong bachelor ever to occupy the Oval Office. His early romantic experience was marked by tragedy, as his 1819 engagement to a woman named Anne Caroline Coleman who hailed from an influential and wealthy Pennsylvania family ended abruptly. A short time later Coleman died mysteriously, most likely of a drug overdose. In Lancaster, Pennsylvania, where their courtship had taken place, rumors and gossip spread that Buchanan had only been interested in Anne for her money. He was accused of being a cold and inattentive fiancée whose behavior led to her untimely death. One Lancaster lady's letters reveal Anne's friends thought of Buchanan as her murderer, and it was likely that the man himself was aware of and deeply distressed by this indictment of his character.

During Buchanan's political career, politicians who interacted with him, including President Andrew Jackson, reportedly referred to him using nicknames like "Miss Nancy" and "Aunt Fancy," monikers commonly applied to gay men at the time. Attacks were levied against Buchanan for how he looked and sounded, with his enemies mocking his "shrill, feminine voice, and wholly beardless cheeks." For many years prior to becoming president, as a member of Congress, Buchanan lived with another bachelor congressman, William R. King of Alabama. In Washington circles, some derisively deemed King to be Buchanan's "wife," and some accounts indicate that this taunting happened in front of King and Buchanan, not just behind their backs. A recurring theme in political cartoons depicting Buchanan was to draw him as a woman or wearing women's clothing. Using the common nickname "Old Buck" for Buchanan, a former editor of the *Washington Globe* wrote to former president Martin Van Buren in 1860 that the country was cursed with "Hermaphrodites, and of all, Old Buck has proved to be the worst."

Politicians of every political stripe seemed to disparage Buchanan in personal terms throughout his career. His fellow Pennsylvanian congressman Thaddeus Stevens called him a "bloated mass of political putridity," and Iowa senator James Grimes deemed him "a perfect imbecile." President James K. Polk, whom Buchanan served as secretary of state, wrote in his diary that Buchanan was "selfish and all his acts and opinions seem to have been controlled with a view to his own advancement, so much so that I can have no confidence or reliance on any advice he may give upon public questions." Character attacks on Buchanan were prevalent not only by his political opponents, but also by those who presumably should have been his allies. However, despite how many viewed Buchanan, he benefited in the 1856 presidential election from the fact that the Whig Party had collapsed and the newly formed Republican Party was not yet competitive nationally (and especially in the South) against the Democratic Party.

INAPPROPRIATE INFLUENCE OVER THE *DRED SCOTT* RULING

As Buchanan was readying to take office in 1857, the Supreme Court was preparing to make public its ruling in the case of *Dred Scott v. Sanford*. The case concerned a slave named Dred Scott who sued for his freedom because his owner had brought him to free territory for an extended period of time. At his inaugural address, Buchanan said that the issue of how slavery should be regulated in the territories was a "judicial question, which legitimately belongs to the Supreme Court of the United States, before whom it is now pending, and will, it is understood, be speedily and finally settled. To their decision, in common with all good citizens, I shall cheerfully submit, whatever this may be. . . ."

Though the new president appeared to be claiming ignorance of the direction of the Court's impending decision, weeks prior he had contacted Justice Robert C. Grier about the case. Grier hailed from Buchanan's home state of Pennsylvania and likely felt a debt to the president-elect for his seat on the Court (President James Polk had initially nominated Buchanan, but he turned it down; Grier would be confirmed instead in 1846). Buchanan urged Grier to rule against *Scott* and stressed his desire for the Court to issue a broad ruling applicable to all slaves throughout the country. Republicans who attended Buchanan's inauguration saw him whispering with Chief Justice Roger Taney, who was there to swear him into office, and used this as a launching point for attacks that the two were conspiring about the *Scott* decision. The president's critics hated Taney for his staunch proslavery views, and this moment crystallized for them their certainty that Buchanan was intervening behind the scenes on behalf of southern, proslavery interests. These charges would be repeatedly leveled against Buchanan throughout his time in office.

UNFAIRLY PROMOTING SLAVERY INTERESTS IN KANSAS

Following the passage of the Kansas-Nebraska Act of 1854, which authorized territories to decide for themselves under a principle of popular sovereignty whether or not to allow slavery, proslavery and antislavery forces battled in Kansas over the resolution of that question. In 1857, a proslavery document called the Lecompton Constitution was drafted for Kansas. Buchanan tried to persuade some members of Congress to support the document by having members of his cabinet offer them jobs, government contracts, cash, and even (according to the findings of a later

House investigation) prostitutes. Buchanan's position in this matter was particularly egregious for some because in a popular vote the people of Kansas had clearly rejected the Lecompton Constitution. Faithful Republican partisan press outlets like the *Springfield Daily Republican* reviewed Buchanan's message supporting the proslavery constitution as "a disgrace to the man who wrote it and to the nation which he represents before the world," and the *Philadelphia North American* called it "so evidently the work of a mind determinedly defending the wrong, as to destroy all the credit that the President had before possessed."

Buchanan's support at any cost for proslavery interests in Kansas was not only objectionable to Republicans, but also to a significant portion of the Democratic Party aligned with Illinois senator Stephen Douglas. Intraparty criticisms of Buchanan reflected the deepening fractures among Democrats in this era—fractures that could not be smoothed over by the president's efforts to placate various interests. After Buchanan appointed a governor of Kansas deemed to be too cozy with Free Soil ideas (Free Soil states were those that prohibited slavery prior to the Civil War), extremists in the South also turned on Buchanan. One constituent from Georgia wrote his senator to inform him, "If Kansas comes in as a free state, Buchanan will richly deserve death and I hope some patriotic man will inflict it." In a recurring theme for the 15th president, his actions were routinely criticized by actors of all different regions, party affiliations, and political leanings.

CHARGES OF CORRUPTION AS PRESIDENT

In 1860 the House of Representatives authorized a committee to investigate possible malfeasance by the Buchanan administration. It came to be known as the Covode Committee, in recognition of its chair, Representative John Covode of Pennsylvania. The committee trained much of its focus on charges that the administration had engaged in illegal activities to win elections in 1856 and 1858. Specifically, it investigated complaints that the administration had used government funds and lucrative contracts to gain backing for the Democratic Party. Newspapers unfriendly to the Buchanan administration leaked embarrassing pieces of information from the committee's hearings, though the proceedings were supposed to be secret. When the hearings were over, Republican members of the committee signed a public report implicating Buchanan in election fraud, bribery, and corrupt use of patronage, though they stopped short of calling for his impeachment. The hearing transcripts were then printed, bound, and sent all over the country in a massive volume that seemed to imply by its sheer size that there was formidable evidence of corruption throughout the Buchanan administration. With the end of his presidency imminent, Buchanan lacked defenders both within and outside of his party. Both Democrats loyal to Buchanan's rival Douglas as well as

Republicans throughout the country readily believed that Buchanan and his team had plundered the public treasury for political gain.

From the start of the Covode Committee's formation, Buchanan maintained the committee's inquiries into the presidency were unprecedented and unwarranted, declaring "I defy all investigation. Nothing but the basest perjury can sully my good name." He also called the motives of the committee's witnesses into question, deriding them as disgruntled patronage seekers or desperate political parasites, though several had been indisputably quite close to him and were hard to convincingly discredit. Lastly, Buchanan launched vigorous counterattacks against his accusers. He assailed the committee's procedures and motives and asserted he was merely trying to defend the office he held against "the aggrandizement of the legislative at the expense of the executive and judicial departments."

CAST AS A TRAITOR IN THE MIDST OF SECESSION

After Abraham Lincoln's victory in the 1860 presidential election, southern states started to secede from the Union over the winter of 1860–1861. Buchanan's official statement on these events condemned secession while simultaneously indicating it was his belief that the national government lacked power under the Constitution to force the states back into the Union. Furthermore, Buchanan laid blame for the crisis squarely at the feet of abolitionists, charging that "the long-continued and intemperate interference of the Northern people with the question of slavery in the Southern States" had finally produced "its natural effects." The substance of the statement caused many to publicly denounce the president. Buchanan was accused of being a traitor to the country and a supporter of secession, with some of his strongest accusers advocating removing him from office and making him answer for his alleged duplicity. Congressman John Sherman of Ohio proclaimed, "The Constitution provided against every possible vacancy in the office of the President, but did not provide for utter imbecility," and his colleague Charles Francis Adams Sr. of Massachusetts declared, "If there was any way of impeaching him, it would really deserve to be considered. But he may yet be indicted for treason."

The news media environment of the time also proved highly damaging to Buchanan's political standing in the face of the crisis. Newspapers that supported Lincoln cast Buchanan's scapegoating the North for secession as "a 'brazen lie,' and an 'atrocious' perversion of the truth." The *New York Times*, in this era part of the Republican partisan press, lamented on December 5, 1860, that the nation would have "to struggle through three more months of this disgraceful imbecility and disloyalty to the Constitution." The *Chicago Tribune* plastered across its front page its belief that "timidity, imbecility and treason rule in the White House," and the *Times* even published forged letters alleged to have come from Buchanan's pen. This fake correspondence made Buchanan appear paranoid and frantic in the face of the South's challenge. The president was thus seriously impaired by a news landscape where not only were many partisan outlets outright hostile to his administration, but they also operated before standards of professional journalism took hold that might have prevented the publication of such unsubstantiated documents and rumors in their pages.

As Lincoln's inauguration day drew closer, accusations against Buchanan turned even darker, as his detractors implicated him in a plot to prevent Lincoln from assuming office. Many wrote to Lincoln to warn him of Buchanan's alleged plans, calling him "Benedict Arnold," a "cowardly old imbecile and traitor," and urging, "If ever hanging were a proper use to put a man to for his political sins, he really deserves it." The *New York Tribune* even called into question Buchanan's sanity in a December 17, 1860, editorial. Buchanan's buildup of troops in Washington to protect the city from any incursions by the South around this time was read by his critics as "prompted by cowardice, or the spirit of despotism." Such was the misfortune of Buchanan that even where he sought to make what he saw as a show of force to defend the integrity of the Union, it was interpreted by his attackers as precisely the opposite. Fatalistically, Buchanan reported to the press around this time, "If I live until the 4th of March, I will ride to the capitol with Old Abe whether I am assassinated or not."

HISTORY'S UNKIND ASSESSMENT OF BUCHANAN

In the years immediately after Buchanan left office and throughout the Civil War, the former president was treated quite harshly. Editorials and artists' renderings labeled him "Judas" and depicted him with devil horns. Stores featured bank notes with Buchanan pictured in the gallows with a noose around his neck. Abolitionist newspapers printed fabricated stories accusing Buchanan of writing to foreign governments to convince them to recognize the Confederacy, selling Confederate bonds, and throwing his lot in with southern spies. Editors published fake quotes from him, reporting that Buchanan said he hoped the Union Army would "die like rotten sheep" in the South. These unforgiving portrayals were regularly brought to Buchanan's attention, as he himself noted: "If there is anything disagreeable in it, some person will be sure to send it to me." The harassment of the ex-president went further than negative news reports, however: he also received menacing letters and notes threatening to burn his house down from individuals who blamed him personally for the onset of war.

Buchanan appeared to realize that his legacy as president would need defending, but that to launch a full-scale effort to redeem himself during the war would be both inappropriate and fruitless. In 1866, however, Buchanan published *Mr. Buchanan's Administration on the Eve of Rebellion*. He viewed this book as an opportunity to correct the record on his time in office, of which he felt a tremendous amount of unfair and incorrect information had been circulated. He even told his nephew that the book would be "a triumphant vindication of my administration." The work placed blame for the war on everyone but himself and positioned his opponents as enemies of reason itself; unsurprisingly, it was not received well by many at the time. The *New York Herald* countered his take on his last days as president by concluding, "His vindication is at best but a quibbling apology for his lack of earnest patriotism, his lack of moral courage, and his secession proclivities." The *New York Times* called the book's author a "self-apologist for his own imbecile and disastrous administration" and advised that staying silent would have been in better taste and "the best service he possibly could have rendered to his own blighted fame."

Even when Buchanan died in 1868, hostile newspapers felt no need to soften their critiques. An article written around the time of his funeral in the *Cincinnati Daily Gazette* rebuked his administration, noting, "Imbecility—to use no harsher term—was enthroned at the White House . . . and the great mass of the Northern people were alike unable to inspire the Chief Magistrate with patriotism or even with an appearance of energy." The *Chicago Tribune* chimed in, "He never had a guiding principle. During his fifty years of public life there was no policy that he did not both oppose and support. More than half the years of his public life were devoted to intrigue for his elevation to the presidency. The desolate old man has gone to his grave. No son or daughter is doomed to acknowledge an ancestry from him."

The passage of time has not caused his presidency to be looked upon any more charitably. Historian Jean Baker concluded her 2004 work on Buchanan thusly: "He was that most dangerous of chief executives, a stubborn, mistaken ideologue whose principles held no room for compromise. His experience in government had only rendered him too self-confident to consider other views. In his betrayal of the national trust, Buchanan came closer to committing treason than any other president in American history." Modern scholarly rankings of U.S. presidents have piled further insult upon Buchanan, identifying Buchanan as either the worst president in history or as part of a lowest ranking "failure" category.

CONCLUSION

Many of the attacks on Buchanan as president came at a time when the country was coming apart over the issue of slavery, and it was clear that the president was not able to lead the country out of nor successfully navigate through the crisis. With the actions it did take, his administration earned the scorn of North and South, Republicans and Democrats, and proslavery and antislavery interests alike. The attacks wore on Buchanan personally, and meeting with Lincoln on his inauguration day, he told the new president, "My dear sir, if you are as happy in entering the White House as I shall feel on returning to Wheatland, you are a happy man indeed." In a letter a week later, Buchanan sought to minimize the impact of the unraveling of the nation at the end of his presidency on his larger legacy and hoped for a kinder review from history: "The administration has been eminently successful in its foreign and domestic policy unless we may except the sad events which have recently occurred. These no human wisdom could have prevented. Whether I have done all I could consistently with my duty to give them a wise and peaceful direction towards the preservation or reconstruction of the Union, will be for the public and posterity to judge. I feel conscious that I have done my duty in this respect and that I shall at last receive justice."

Buchanan would never receive the political redemption he longed for, in his lifetime or in his later assessment by scholars. However, in the years immediately following his time in office, in the midst of a bloody, devastating civil war, attacks on Buchanan appeared to be a unifying force in the Union, creating a highly visible scapegoat for the onset of the conflict and helping to shore up support for the new Lincoln administration. Whether entirely fair to Buchanan or not, popular representations of the former president as a traitor and a coward were perhaps one way the larger body politic held together in the most difficult time in the nation's history.

Jennifer Rose Hopper

Further Reading

Baker, Jean H. *James Buchanan*. New York: Henry Holt and Company, 2004.

Birkner, Michael J., ed. *James Buchanan and the Political Crisis of the 1850s*. Selinsgrove, PA: Susquehanna University Press, 1996.

Boulard, Garry. *The Worst President: The Story of James Buchanan*. Bloomington, IN: iUniverse, 2015.

Cole, Allen F. "Asserting His Authority: James Buchanan's Failed Vindication." *Pennsylvania History: A Journal of Mid-Atlantic Studies,* Vol. 70 (Winter 2003): 81–97.

Klein, Philip S. *President James Buchanan: A Biography*. Newtown, CT: American Political Biography Press, 1995.

Watson, Robert P. *Affairs of State: The Untold Story of Presidential Love, Sex, and Scandal, 1789–1900*. Lanham, MD: Rowman & Littlefield, 2012.

Weatherman, Donald V. "James Buchanan on Slavery and Secession." *Presidential Studies Quarterly,* Vol. 15 (1985): 796–805.

16. Abraham Lincoln

Born: February 12, 1809

Died: April 15, 1865

Time in Office: 16th President of the United States, March 4, 1861, to April 15, 1865

Election Results: 1860 Election: 39.9% of popular vote, 180 (59.4%) Electoral
   College votes; 1864 Election: 55.1% of popular vote, 212 (90.6%) Electoral
   College votes
Spouse: Mary Todd (m. 1842)
Children: Robert, Edward, Willie, and Tad

After securing the Republican Party's presidential nomination in 1860, Abraham Lincoln won that year's general election with a popular vote plurality of 39.8% and Electoral College majority, securing 180 of 303 electors. Lincoln's first term in office began on March 4, 1861. He was accompanied in Washington by his wife, Mary Todd Lincoln, and his two youngest sons, 10-year-old Willie and 7-year-old Tad. Lincoln's eldest child, Robert, attended Philips Exeter Academy and Harvard College during his father's presidency. In 1864, without the participation of 11 southern states, Lincoln was reelected with a popular vote majority of 55%. He was assassinated shortly after beginning his second term, on April 15, 1865.

Lincoln ranks as one of America's most admired presidents. As a result, many people believe, incorrectly, that Lincoln enjoyed nearly universal support during the Civil War. In reality, Lincoln was an unpopular president who faced vicious and unrelenting criticism for much of his time in the White House. He governed without a reliable base of support. During his tenure, America's political coalitions were heavily fractured, with Democrats divided into Peace, War, and Regular factions, and Republicans identifying as Conservatives, Moderates, or Radicals. None of these groups were loyal to Lincoln.

In Washington, Lincoln faced diverse and unrelenting attacks. His contemporaries questioned whether an "unlettered idiot" with an "unrefined" and "vulgar" appearance was fit for public office. As the Civil War became a more protracted affair, political leaders roundly condemned Lincoln to be a "failure." And no matter how the president proceeded, he faced vigorous opposition. When Lincoln cautiously built support for his war aims, Radical Republicans referred to the president as a "vacillating" and "ignorant" "fool" who was "too undecided and inefficient" to be an effective leader. However, when Lincoln vigorously used his war powers to suppress civil liberties or emancipate slaves, he failed to mollify the Radicals but also inspired heightened abuse from other factions that sought a limited war or a negotiated compromise. Out in the country, Lincoln did not fare much better. On a daily basis, he received hate mail filled with death threats. And, as president, he abstained from reading newspapers because their columns were filled with personal abuse.

LEADER OF THE REPUBLICAN PARTY

Initially, secessionists and their sympathizers hated Lincoln not for his personal qualities, political statements, or expected actions, but, in the words of the

Richmond Enquirer, simply because "the Northern people, by sectional vote, have elected a president for the avowed purpose of aggression on Southern rights." Even though hatred for the president-elect was "impersonal" and based on "sectional stereotype," he began to receive reports of assassination plots. When traveling from Springfield, Illinois, to Washington, D.C., for his inauguration, safety concerns prompted Lincoln to make several revisions to his travel itinerary. Most alarmingly, Allan Pinkerton, William H. Seward, and General Winfield Scott became convinced of a conspiracy to assassinate the president-elect when he changed trains in Baltimore. "To run no risk where no risk was necessary," Lincoln traveled in disguise through Baltimore in the dark of night.

Both friend and foe condemned Lincoln as a weak, fearful coward for sneaking into Washington. After facing such harsh ridicule, Lincoln, from this point forward, refused to acknowledge the danger that he faced on a daily basis, brushing off concerns about his safety by saying, "I guess we won't talk about that now." Throughout his presidency, Lincoln traveled and worked with little security, arguing: "I cannot discharge my duties if I withdraw myself entirely from danger of an assault. I see hundreds of strangers every day, and if anybody has the disposition to kill me he will find opportunity. To be absolutely safe I should lock myself up in a box."

INAUGURATING THE CIVIL WAR

Southerners, border state politicians, and northern Peace Democrats attacked Lincoln for starting an unjust war and provoking secession in the Upper South by, first, refusing to voluntarily surrender Fort Sumter and, second, calling 75,000 militiamen for three months of service. Now, for the first time, hatred of Lincoln became personal as southern newspapers offered cash rewards for Lincoln's "miserable traitorous head."

Lincoln's call for troops to put down "combinations too powerful to be suppressed by the ordinary course of judicial proceedings" was interpreted as a proclamation of war. Initially, border state leaders withheld troops for this "wicked" aggression. In the South, for the remainder of the war, Lincoln the "tyrant" and "murderer" was held responsible for Confederate deaths, the destruction of the South's property and institutions, and the Union blockade that was characterized as a war on innocent civilians, including women and children.

In the North, the Peace Democrats absolved the Confederacy of all blame and, instead, assigned Lincoln responsibility for war. For instance, Brick Pomeroy's *La Crosse Democrat* frequently referred to Lincoln as a "widow maker" and an "orphan maker" with a thirst for blood. And the Dayton, Ohio, *Daily Empire* claimed that Lincoln alone, by "traveling on, on to revolution and despotism," made reunion impossible. Throughout his presidency, Lincoln responded to his detractors by focusing narrowly on policy disagreements. In this case, Lincoln argued that he provisioned Fort Sumter and called the militia into service because secession is unconstitutional without the consent of all other states.

SUPPRESSING CIVIL LIBERTIES

Lincoln was widely condemned as a "dictator" and a "despot" for repressing civil liberties. He came under particular scrutiny for suspending the writ of habeas corpus, which prevents a judicial officer from investigating the reason for a prisoner's detention. When Lincoln first suspended habeas corpus on April 27, 1861, Chief Justice Roger Taney claimed that Lincoln violated his constitutional oath. However, for three reasons, Lincoln's action led to little public outcry. First, habeas corpus was suspended in a limited geographic region of urgent need—specifically, along the route by which troops traveled to the capital. Second, individuals denied the writ of habeas corpus appeared to be engaged in treasonous acts such as rioting and bridge burning. Third, most individuals were released after a few months in prison. In short, suspension seemed justifiable to many northerners as a public safety measure.

On September 24, 1862, however, Lincoln issued a pair of proclamations that formally suspended habeas corpus nationwide and authorized military tribunals for "persons discouraging volunteer enlistments, resisting militia drafts, or guilty of any disloyal practice." This new policy sparked widespread hostility toward Lincoln. First, it was no longer clear that arrested individuals were engaging in treasonous behavior. For example, the military arrested newspaper editors who spoke out against the draft. Second, civilians accused of disloyalty would now stand trial in military courts where they faced, according to William Rehnquist, "stringent penalties for actions that were often not offenses by normal civilian standards" and would be denied ordinary procedural protections such as the right to a jury trial. In the words of the *Illinois State Register*, the Lincoln administration was "seeking to inaugurate a reign of terror in the loyal states by military arrests . . . of citizens, without a trial, to browbeat all opposition by villainous and false charges of disloyalty against whole classes of patriotic citizens, to destroy all constitutional guaranties [sic] of free speech, a free press, and the writ of 'habeas corpus.'"

Lincoln's proclamation of martial law provided military commanders with the ability to use military orders to "browbeat" civilians. This became clear to the public at large in April 1863, when General Ambrose Burnside, head of the Army of the Ohio, issued General Order No. 38, which imposed military arrest on citizens "declaring sympathies for the enemy." General Burnside used this order to arrest a civilian, former Ohio congressman Clement Vallandigham, who, in a series of public speeches, labeled Burnside's order a "base usurpation of arbitrary power" and urged the audience to "hurl King Lincoln from his throne." Vallandigham was seized from his home in the middle of the night, sent to a military prison, tried by a military commission, and sentenced to imprisonment for the duration of the war. This case defined martial law in the popular imagination as "the voice of whichever general was in command."

Democrats and many Republicans censured Lincoln for his "wickedness." For instance, both loyal and opposition newspapers cited the incident as evidence of Lincoln's "high-handed assumption of despotic power" and a portent of "bloody anarchy." Furthermore, this incident sparked calls for Lincoln's assassination.

Throughout the war, Democrats found great success in attacking Lincoln for civil liberties violations. Thus, Lincoln sought to shape public opinion in several ways. First, he argued that the Confederates and their sympathizers used the "cover of 'Liberty of speech' 'Liberty of the press' and *'Habeas corpus'* . . . to keep on foot amongst us a most efficient corps of spies, informers, supplyers, and aiders and abettors of their cause." Second, he claimed that the courts were incapable of managing this threat and, thus, he had to use the powers provided to the president in cases of rebellion. Third, he argued that the punishment was, in fact, necessary for Vallandigham, who through his speech did more than "any other one man" to undermine the effectiveness of the draft. Lincoln asked: "Must I shoot a simple-minded soldier boy who deserts while I must not touch a hair of a wily agitator who induces him to desert?" Fourth, Lincoln minimized the severity of Vallandigham's punishment by changing his sentence from imprisonment to exile. Finally, Lincoln started to monitor how the generals implemented martial law. For instance, when General Burnside suppressed the *Chicago Times*, Lincoln rescinded the order. No longer would martial law simply be the whim of whichever general is in command.

EMANCIPATION

Lincoln was most hated by his contemporaries for emancipation. His policies inspired vitriol from all factions of the Democratic and Republican Parties. Before issuing the Emancipation Proclamation, Radical Republicans attacked Lincoln for being too cautious, timid, and conservative on the slavery issue. Their principal grievance concerned Lincoln's decision in the fall of 1861 to revoke a proclamation by General John C. Fremont that had emancipated slaves of disloyal residents in Missouri. In response, Frederick Douglass proclaimed that Lincoln was "a miserable tool of traitors and rebels" and "a genuine representative of American prejudice and negro hatred." Radical Republican clergymen spoke of Lincoln's inaction as a "crime against humanity and God." Furthermore, Radicals persistently suggested that Lincoln could not be trusted on slavery because of his Kentucky origins.

Lincoln's famous Emancipation Proclamation, announced on September 22, 1862, and issued on January 1, 1863, freed the slaves in the rebellious areas and allowed African Americans to serve in the Union Army and Navy. Public response to the measure threatened Lincoln's ability to lead the Union more than at any other time in his presidency. The proclamation did not go far enough to appease the Radicals, and it threatened to tear apart a fragile Union coalition in the border states and the North. Radical Republicans aside, members of all factional stripes viewed emancipation as a revolutionary step that deviated from the war's original aim of saving the Union. Moreover, among Democrats, a commitment to white supremacy and fears of African American migration and enfranchisement led to bitter denunciation of the president. Opposition to emancipation was strongest in the West and in the border states. In the West, abolition sentiment was weak. Many Republicans in the region had opposed slavery extension primarily to minimize labor competition in the territories. These individuals were cool to the idea of former slaves migrating west.

Of course, the Peace Democrats, who were concentrated in the West, were a bigger problem. Lincoln labeled this group the "fire in the rear" and considered them the primary obstacle to winning the war. Peace Democrats, arguing that Lincoln misrepresented his true aims in fighting the Civil War, justified desertion, discouraged enlistments, and thereby effectively sapped support for and the strength of the Union Army. For instance, in Ohio, according to historian Jennifer Weber, they "asked white men why they were dying for blacks." These sorts of arguments were effective because, according to scholar Robert Churchill, "Democrats believed that citizenship was a privilege of whiteness" and that "conscription alongside black soldiers to fight to abolish slavery would inevitably undermine that racial privilege." To end Lincoln's tyranny, Peace Democrats advocated assassination; they believed that Lincoln's removal would result in peace with Union, despite the fact that all available evidence suggested otherwise.

The border states, which had rebuffed Lincoln's overtures for compensated emancipation, were also hostile. Political leaders and newspaper editors attacked Lincoln for ignoring the Constitution, consolidating power, and changing the aims of the war. Maryland representative John W. Crisfield cited emancipation as just one more piece of evidence for the argument that Lincoln was transforming the presidency into a despotism. More than anything, border state leaders feared the social and racial effects of emancipation including increased free black populations. As a result of the Emancipation Proclamation, the border states saw a severe drop in the number of men serving in the border state troop regiments.

Attacks on Lincoln and his Emancipation Proclamation led to a decline in military enlistments, which, in turn, necessitated conscription and the vast bureaucracy that supported it. As such, Lincoln forcefully advocated for his policy, reiterating that emancipation was a means to victory and, thus, was a legitimate war power. Or, in Lincoln's own words, he considered "slavery to be the right arm of the rebellion, and that it must be lopped off." Given widespread opposition to emancipation, Lincoln was also careful not to crack down too hard on dissent. For instance, when Mayor Fernando Wood publicly attacked Lincoln and his Emancipation Proclamation, the Lincoln administration rejected a request from the local U.S. marshal to imprison the mayor.

CONSCRIPTION AND THE NEW YORK CITY DRAFT RIOTS

In March 1863, Lincoln and a Republican Congress passed the first federal Conscription Act. This law, more than any other federal action, clearly communicated that the Lincoln administration was consolidating power in the federal government. The Conscription Act sent federal government agents into local communities. It created a new bureaucratic apparatus in the War Department, which, in turn, formed enrollment boards in each congressional district tasked with proceeding house-to-house to identify all men aged 20 to 45 and, when necessary, conduct the district's draft lottery. The Conscription Act also empowered local agents of the provost bureau marshal to police disloyalty and "make summary arrest of draft evaders and resisters, deserters and spies." Democrats argued that this was a naked exercise of federal power for partisan purposes as their party had just captured several governorships and statehouses in the 1862 election, which Lincoln and his agents could now bypass.

Unlike emancipation, conscription provided obvious focal points for resistance in local communities—the offices and officers of the local enrollment board along with clear events like the draft lottery. Although draft resistance provoked violence against enrollment officers and property in many states including Indiana, Ohio, Pennsylvania, and Wisconsin, insurrection in New York City resulted in more than 100 deaths, making it the deadliest riot in American history.

New York's Democratic Governor Horatio Seymour encouraged mob action by attacking Lincoln, obstructing the enrollment process, and delivering inflammatory public speeches. In an address to the New York Academy of Music, one week prior to the draft lottery in New York City, Governor Seymour asserted "that the bloody, and treasonable, and revolutionary, doctrine of public necessity can be proclaimed by a mob as well as by a government."

It was the initiation of the draft lottery that sparked the riots in New York City. The action began as a workplace strike. As "employees of the city's railroads, machine shops, and shipyards, iron foundry workers, laborers" proceeded from their place of work to the site of the draft lottery, they advanced from shop to shop to spread information and broaden participation. On their way, protestors denounced Lincoln, destroyed federal property, and defaced and slaughtered both federal officials and local police officers. In response, the draft was postponed and many participants, particularly skilled craftsmen, returned to work.

For the next three days, the violence escalated as the remaining rioters sought "to isolate and remove all manifestations of the Republican social presence." At this stage, the riots made use of existing neighborhood networks to remove Republican, African American, and police elements from the community. This group hindered communication with federal authorities by cutting telegraph lines and removing train tracks, vandalized Republican-owned property (including homes, factories, newspapers), destroyed draft offices and police headquarters, assaulted federal officials, soldiers, and police officers, and articulated hostility against patriotic symbols. Furthermore, this group sought to reduce the African American presence in the city through lynching, the burning of black occupied homes, and the total destruction of African American community institutions. Newspapers helped fan the flames by communicating incendiary rhetoric. For instance, Frank Leslie's *Illustrated Newspaper* justified resistance by proclaiming that, with the Conscription Act, "converts the Republic into one grand military dictatorship."

To gain the support of New York conservatives, deny the rioters further ammunition, and restore order as quickly as possible, Lincoln defied the wishes of Radical Republicans and refused to declare martial law in New York City. The Republican mayor of New York City approved of Lincoln's decision: "Martial law would have exasperated the rioters, increased their numbers, and those in sympathy with them, for the Democratic party were, to a man, opposed to the measure. The probable result would have been the sacking and burning of the city, and the massacre of many [more] of its inhabitants." Furthermore, after the riots, Lincoln chose not to investigate the causes or instigators of the riots because, he argued, that "one rebellion at a time is about as much as we can conveniently handle." These decisions helped cement the legitimacy of the administration in trying times and shows Lincoln's ability to defuse hatred. The draft resumed in New York City the following month without incident.

INTERFERENCE IN ELECTIONS

Hatred spiked when the ballot box failed to provide an effective check on Lincoln's power. In May 1863, midwestern Democrats became convinced that Lincoln sought to monopolize power by establishing a military dictatorship and outlawing democratic elections. In Indiana, the Democratic State Central Committee recommended that individuals carry arms to the ballot box so that force could be used if federal authorities interfere. In the words of Indiana U.S. senator Thomas A. Hendricks, "any attempt by the military to interfere with elections in Indiana, Illinois, and Ohio would trigger civil war" and perhaps secession in the Northwest.

The rhetoric of Indiana's party leaders emboldened the Sons of Liberty, a fraternal organization of rank-and-file Democrats in the Midwest. In advance of the 1864 presidential election, the Sons of Liberty received funds from the Confederacy, procured arms, and devised a plan to liberate rebel prisoners in the event that Lincoln manipulated the electoral outcome. This plot was exposed prior to the election, and its two architects were sentenced to death. Although historians have uncovered convincing evidence of a threat to the federal government, Lincoln disregarded the Sons of Liberty as "a mere political organization, with about as much of malice and as much of puerility as the Knights of the Golden Circle." The idea that Lincoln, the military despot, would put an end to free and fair elections spread beyond Indiana. Among Lincoln's opponents, many agreed with John Wilkes Booth that "*reelection* means *succession.*" Similarly, Brick Pomeroy, in the *La Crosse Democrat*, declared his hope that if the 1864 presidential election failed to remove the "despot," then "some bold hand will pierce his heart with dagger point for the public good."

ASSASSINATION

Confederates and their sympathizers viewed Lincoln "as the major obstacle to the South's achievement of independence" and hatched numerous plots to kidnap or assassinate him. Newspapers advocated and justified assassination. In the South, the *Richmond Dispatch* argued that "assassination in the abstract is a horrid crime . . . but to slay a tyrant is no more assassination than war is murder." In the North, a broad range of Copperhead newspapers agreed. The Greensburg, Pennsylvania, *Argus* argued that Lincoln's "defeat or his death is an indispensable condition to an honorable peace," while the *New York Daily* "wished that Heaven would 'direct its vengeance openly against the man who has drenched this fair land of ours with blood.'"

Lincoln's assassin, John Wilkes Booth of Maryland, viewed himself as a defender of the South and its institutions. Booth thought Lincoln deserved to be assassinated for ignoring the right of southern states to secede, assaulting southern institutions, failing to recognize the constitutional endorsement of slavery and white supremacy, and seeking to install himself as king. By summer 1864, Booth decided that Lincoln, the man who had caused all the country's troubles, must be assassinated: "I would rather have my right arm cut off at the shoulder than see Lincoln made president again." After several false starts, Booth was prompted into action by Lincoln's endorsement on April 11, 1865, of limited black suffrage. Booth proclaimed: "That means nigger citizenship. Now, by God, I'll put him through." On April 14, Booth forged a plan to overthrow the U.S. government by assassinating Lincoln, Secretary of State William H. Seward, Vice President Andrew Johnson, and perhaps others. In the end, Booth's full plan was not realized as Lincoln was the only official assassinated.

Lincoln ignored death threats and, by 1865, so did most of his colleagues. For instance, by 1862, Lincoln's safety helped convince Seward that "assassination is not an American practice or habit." In the end, northerners blamed Lincoln's assassination on the violent rhetoric promulgated by Confederate and Copperhead newspapers. According to the *New York Herald*: "It is as clear as day that the real origin of this dreadful act is to be found in the fiendish and malignant spirit developed and fostered by the rebel press North and South. That press, in the most devilish manner, urged men to the commission of this very deed." Or, in the words of the San Francisco *Daily Dramatic Chronicle*, "The deed of horror and infamy . . . is nothing more than the expression in action, of what secession politicians and journalists have been for years expressing in words. Wilkes Booth has simply carried out what the Copperhead journalists who have denounced the President as a 'tyrant,' a 'despot,' a 'usurper,' hinted at, and virtually recommended. His weapon was the pistol, theirs the pen; and though he surpassed them in ferocity, they equaled him in guilt. . . . Wilkes Booth has but acted out what Copperhead orators and the Copperhead press have been preaching for years."

CONCLUSION

Hatred of Lincoln had a profound impact on the president's ability to successfully prosecute the war, and it left a lasting imprint on American politics. First, Lincoln himself noted that he lacked the support of his party in Congress: "a united constituency; I never have had. If ambition in Congress and jealously in the army could be allayed, and all united in one common purpose, this infernal rebellion would soon be terminated." Republicans of all ideological stripes complained of "grave Executive usurpation," rejecting the premise that the chief executive was responsible for prosecuting the war. This constrained Lincoln and led him to take decisive action during the, approximately, six months of the year in which Congress was adjourned. By proclaiming war, raising troops, and spending money when Congress was out of session, Lincoln created a historical precedent for strong presidential war powers and bestowed the nation with a new interpretation of the Constitution.

Second, Lincoln's fiercest critics were the Peace Democrats of the Midwest. Their relentless attacks against both the war itself and Lincoln's policies undermined support for the president and his wartime policies. They made it more difficult for Lincoln to raise and maintain troops. In addition, the Peace Democrats also transformed the way in which Lincoln prosecuted the war. By manufacturing alarm over Lincoln's exercise of emergency war powers, they likely discouraged the president from leaning on his extra-constitutional powers. After a few deviations in 1861 and 1862, Lincoln largely remained within constitutional bounds, protecting free speech, free press, and democratic elections and by allowing civilian courts to reassert their role in American democracy. Finally, many northerners held the

Peace Democrats responsible for Lincoln's assassination, for they created an atmosphere of bitter hostility toward the president. Consequently, the "smell of treason . . . clung to the garments of the Peace Democrats" and tarnished the reputation and electoral fortunes of the Democratic Party for decades to come.

Darin DeWitt

Further Reading

Bernstein, Ivar. *The New York City Draft Riots: Their Significance for American Society and Politics in the Age of the Civil War*. New York: Oxford University Press, 1989.

Burlingame, Michael. *Abraham Lincoln: A Life*. Baltimore, MD: Johns Hopkins University, 2007.

Churchill, Robert. *To Shake Their Guns in the Tyrant's Face: Libertarian Political Violence and the Origins of the Militia Movement*. Ann Arbor, MI: University of Michigan Press, 2009.

Cook, Adrian. *Armies of the Street: The New York City Draft Riots of 1863*. Lexington, KY: The University Press of Kentucky, 1982.

Cuthbert, Norma B. *Lincoln and the Baltimore Plot, 1861*. San Marino, CA: The Huntington Library, 1949.

Donald, David Herbert. *Lincoln*. New York: Touchstone, 1995.

Fehrenbacher, Don E. "The Anti-Lincoln Tradition." *Journal of the Abraham Lincoln Association*, Vol. 4, No. 1 (1982): 6–28.

Gienapp, William E. *Abraham Lincoln and Civil War America*. New York: Oxford University Press, 2002.

Hanchett, William. *The Lincoln Murder Conspiracies*. Champaign, IL: University of Illinois Press, 1989.

Holzer, Harold. *Dear Mr. Lincoln: Letters to the President*. Carbondale, IL: Southern Illinois University Press, 1993.

Kauffman, Michael W. *American Brutus: John Wilkes Booth and the Lincoln Conspiracies*. New York: Random House, 2004.

Murdock, Eugene C. "Horatio Seymour and the 1863 Draft." *Civil War History*, Vol. 11, No. 2 (1965): 117–141.

Pratt, Fletcher. *Lincoln's Secretary of War*. New York: W. W. Norton, 1953.

Rehnquist, William H. *All the Laws but One: Civil Liberties in Wartime*. New York: Alfred A. Knopf, 1998.

Sandburg, Carl. *Abraham Lincoln: The Prairie Years and the War Years*. New York: Dell Publications, 1959.

Towne, Stephen E. *Surveillance and Spies in the Civil War: Exposing Confederate Conspiracies in America's Heartland*. Athens, OH: Ohio University Press, 2015.

Weber, Jennifer L. *Copperheads: The Rise and Fall of Lincoln's Opponents in the North*. New York: Oxford University Press, 2008.

Weber, Jennifer L. "Lincoln's Critics: The Copperheads." *Journal of the Abraham Lincoln Association*, Vol. 32, No. 1 (2011): 33–47.

17. Andrew Johnson

Born: December 29, 1808

Died: July 31, 1875

Time in Office: 17th President of the United States, April 15, 1865, to March 4, 1869

Election Results: 1864 Election: Elected vice president; assumed office upon death of Abraham Lincoln

Spouse: Eliza McCardle (m. 1827)

Children: Martha, Charles, Mary, Robert, and Andrew Jr.

Andrew Johnson was the 17th president of the United States in chronological terms. In terms of historical ranking, he is arguably near the bottom of most lists generated by presidential scholars. However, historians Lawrence W. Reed and Burton W. Folsom Jr. make a point to exonerate Johnson, the first of only two presidents in American history to be impeached, claiming he "deserves to be remembered more for his ideas, especially his defense of the Constitution in a troubled time." Johnson came to office after the Civil War and found not only large shoes to fill in his predecessor, Abraham Lincoln, but staunch enemies in Congress, dominated by the Radical Republicans.

Johnson was born on December 29, 1808, in Raleigh, North Carolina. Johnson's father died when he was just three years old, leaving the family in poverty and the young man's life on a trajectory for spiting those that were more well-off—a trait that would manifest when dealing with many affluent and socially connected politicians later in life. After Johnson began working as a tailor, the family relocated to Greenville, Tennessee, where he established a new business mending clothing. In 1827 Johnson married a woman in whom he found inspiration and support for the next 50 years, Eliza McCardle.

In 1835 Johnson was elected to the state legislature, and in 1843 he won a seat in the U.S. Congress as the first Democratic representative of Tennessee. For ten years, he served in the House of Representatives, even as divergences in positions regarding slavery and abolition, secessionists and Unionists, began to fester within the Democratic Party. In 1853 Johnson was elected governor of Tennessee, and after deciding not to seek another term as governor, eventually returned to Congress, this time as a senator in 1857.

The Civil War broke out in 1861, and secession of the southern states split the country in two. After Tennessee seceded, Johnson's wife and two daughters were driven out of the state, and the family's property was confiscated by supporters of the Confederacy, many of whom viewed Johnson as a Unionist and an abolitionist, though he originally opposed the emancipation of slaves. His concern lay only with preserving the Constitution and the Union.

In 1862, as a War Democrat in a southern state, Johnson caught the eye of President Abraham Lincoln. Union troops established a limited presence in Tennessee, with the exception of perpetual raids by southern general Nathan Bedford Forrest, and Lincoln appointed Johnson military governor of the state, with a military rank of brigadier general.

Lincoln continued to be impressed with Johnson's work as well as his loyalty, and seeing some political benefit to associating himself with a southern Unionist, he added Johnson to his presidential ticket as he ran for reelection in 1864. Johnson found himself wading into a Republican Party toward the end of the conflict that was less fractured and more radical than the Democrats had been. After Lincoln's reelection, Johnson was accused of being intoxicated at the inauguration in March 1865, an insulting accusation that would emerge more than once. One historian cites an unnamed senator of the day as calling him an "insolent drunken brute in comparison with which Caligula's horse was respectable."

On April 14, 1865, as the American Civil War drew to a close, an assassin's bullet took the life of President Lincoln. This tragedy left a not-yet-unified nation in the charge of a man who to this point had only been vice president for one month. Andrew Johnson was inaugurated in a private White House ceremony the day after his predecessor was shot.

Johnson encountered strict opposition from the Republican-held Congress, fights that began with the expansion of the Freedman's Bureau and then Reconstruction, and ultimately devolved into constrictive policies enacted by the legislature, highlighting the policy differences due to divided government and attempting to trap Johnson into engaging in an impeachable offense. Falling for their enticements, Johnson was the first president to be impeached, though he was narrowly acquitted. He then served out the remaining year of his term, battling with Congress until he lost reelection in 1868. Later, as if his legacy had not entirely been tarnished, Johnson was reelected to the U.S. Senate as a Democrat for Tennessee in 1875, despite the criticism of his presidency, and the only former president to achieve such a feat.

Unfortunately for the former president, this was just months before a stroke took his life on July 31, 1875, in Elizabethton, Tennessee, at the age of 66. Having enjoyed praise and hatred, his was a life and political career of controversy, to be sure, but his legacy will continue to reflect those moments where Johnson, like many chief executives, was showered with disdain.

EXPECTATIONS: THE GOOD, THE BAD, AND THE UGLY

Hatred, as well as praise, for this American president manifested itself in several ways and at varying times. Johnson's administration began due to unusual circumstances and with a positive expectation from some. The South at first found ways to revile the man that would someday soften the Union's stance after the war, and the Radical Republicans that had taken over his newfound party looked to him to be the sword of their retribution, only to find an executive that favored leniency. Expressions of disdain toward Johnson from these forces took the form of news publications and political speeches. However, history may be able to judge lightly in bestowing a ranking on this controversial figure regarding vitriol directed toward him at the time. He was one executive who before, during, and after his presidency found many friends before experiencing the troubles that befell the office and him personally.

As a senator in 1861, Johnson gave a speech canvassing against the secessionists when threats poured in that he "largely indulged in." In response, Johnson let the would-be attackers know that he "did not come there to be shot, but to shoot," and that "if there was to be a fight, he and his friends were ready for it, and that he preferred to finish up the fighting before he made his speech." Afterward, according to a May 17, 1861, article in the *New York Times*, "nineteen-twentieths of the audience were with him." Beyond showing a steadfastness in his positions even before taking on the presidency, this incident showcased his ability to sway the people to his corner.

Johnson took heart in that kind of praise at a time when he was being burned in effigy by southerners. One *New York Times* correspondent, taking a trip to see him speak in Nashville in April 1862, wrote of his newfound feelings toward Johnson, explaining at once that he had been "schooled to oppose" him, now finding him "rather than repulsive, courteous and inviting." The writer went on to say that his "friends in Tennessee are legion." This applied, however, to those across the nation as well, as the Common Council for the City of New York extended an invitation to him, referring to Johnson as "most faithful among the faithless" (as reported in the *New York Times*, August 22, 1861). There was an element of disdain for him, as the first writer had been taught, but the general feeling toward Johnson in the North began on a positive note. That would not last, however, as the political landscape changed drastically, and Johnson found himself in a unique epoch in history.

BECOMING PRESIDENT

Understanding the position of the Radical Republicans as the war dragged on, and Lincoln was reelected at the end of hostilities with Johnson at his side, is paramount to understanding what came next. The Radicals did not share the views on Reconstruction that Lincoln held, and by the election of 1864 that kept the White House in Republican hands, so too did the Congress gain overwhelming power for the party, and the Radicals were at the helm. They felt that Lincoln's postwar policies toward the South were too soft. They wanted retribution, they wanted full rights for the freed slaves, and they did not want to cede any power to seceded states returning to the Union so soon after their attempted secession.

Lincoln was not, as many remember, the only target for assassination on April 15, 1865. Vice President Johnson was also marked for death that night, escaping only as a result of the cowardice of the would-be assassin, George Atzeroth. The third official targeted was Secretary of State William Seward, who was wounded but not killed by conspirator Lewis Powell. The death of the three would have crumbled the Union. Referring to the ambitious plot, the *New York Times* remarked, "While Mr. Johnson lives, its object is unattained." Indeed, this was the sentiment of many after the death of Lincoln and the ascendancy of Johnson, a man whom the South feared and the Radical Republicans anxiously awaited.

An extreme example of this expectation of Johnson's perceived stance on Reconstruction is summed up in a quote from Reverend W. S. Studley of Boston when he said, "In dealing with traitors, Andrew Johnson's little finger will be thicker than Abraham Lincoln's loins." Radicals looked forward to their new leader with "unmitigated delight" according to historian Milton Lomask, and the Republican papers of the time were verbose in their jubilance. The Republican publication the *New York Herald* referred to the ascendancy of Johnson in the footsteps of his predecessor as "Joshua was to Moses." The expectations were high. The result, however, was something quite unexpected and ushered in a tumultuous few years for the party and the Union.

RADICAL REPUBLICANS AND JOHNSON'S VETO POWER

A strict constitutionalist, Johnson also harbored a lack of respect for the "irresponsible central directory" of the government, namely Congress. Though accused by southerners of being a Catholic abolitionist, his feelings on slavery were somewhat of an enigma. His state of Tennessee was the first southern state to end slavery by law, while he later gave no effort in the name of the newly freed slaves while battling Congress as president. An address even caught him uttering words like, "I say, let the Government go on, and slavery get along the best it can," and "before the rebellion, I was for sustaining the Government with slavery," with regard to placing the Union government over any one institution so long as it remained intact.

Perceived changes in Johnson's ideals and his softening of the executive branch's support for Reconstruction ultimately earned him considerable condemnation. No group opposed him more fiercely than the pro-Reconstruction Radical Republicans in Congress. The first major test in the battle over Reconstruction involved a bill to increase the powers of the Freedman's Bureau, an organization under the War Department that sought to furnish freed slaves with economic opportunity, food, and shelter. In February 1866 Johnson vetoed this bill, one of the actions that would show his opposition to Congress on this issue and prove the confusion that would mark his Reconstruction positions. Congress managed to override this veto less than a month later, the first of many overrides that would come to curtail the president's constitutional power. In fact, by the end of the Johnson administration he had issued 19 vetoes, five pocket vetoes, and 16 laws without signature. But Congress held the power, and 15 of the 19 vetoed bills were passed by veto override votes, including the Tenure of Office Act in 1867.

The Tenure of Office Act was specifically designed to protect Secretary of War Edwin Stanton, a holdover from Lincoln's administration and an ally of the Radical Republicans. As the Radicals got a taste of Johnson's Reconstruction designs, and his willingness to go to any length to enact policy, including the firing of dozens of postmasters throughout the country, they felt they needed a safeguard. The Tenure of Office Act, like the Command of Army Act (designed to protect General Ulysses S. Grant), was designed by Congress to "trap" President Johnson into maintaining a federal troop presence in the South for their own Reconstruction policy. Johnson, in the face of this new act passed over his veto, decided to fire Stanton anyway and fall for the trap. What ensued was an event that was arguable in its constitutionality at the time and sent the country into further upheaval.

IMPEACHMENT

On February 24, 1868, the House of Representatives voted to impeach Johnson for "high crimes and misdemeanors." The House issued 11 articles of impeachment, one charging Johnson with the crime of removing Edwin Stanton as secretary of war and one for replacing him, though they continued to include acts such as conspiring with that replacement, Lorenzo Thomas, without advice and consent from the Senate. Other articles were vague and seemingly unnecessary, such as indicting Johnson for a speech given a year and a half prior in which he had denounced Congress. As if passing articles of impeachment were not enough of a show of hatred for a sitting president, the proceedings let the Republicans, who made up 42 of 54 senators in the upper chamber, speak their minds about the "despicable, besotted . . . accidental President." Although Democrats spoke out against the proceedings as an attempt by Republicans to gain sole ownership over the nation, since Johnson was never a true Republican, the vitriol from the Republicans was overwhelming. William D. "Pig Iron" Kelley of Pennsylvania called Johnson the "great criminal whom the American people arraign for thousands of crimes." Others charged that Johnson was a "demagogue" whose actions and policies were not only "degrad[ing] himself, but destroy[ing] the rights of the American people."

Legal scholar Alan Dershowitz referred to the judging body as "anything but impartial jurors . . . [who] had already declared Johnson guilty." When the final vote came down, however, Johnson narrowly escaped removal from office by one vote. Some senators opposed impeachment because of political differences with the

Radical Republicans, while others asserted that their decision showed that they valued the rule of democracy over usurping the executive for political reasons. A total of 35 senators voted for impeachment, while 19 voted against. With a requirement of a two-thirds majority to pass, the vote was lost by one and Johnson remained president.

The Constitution of the United States explicitly lays out the option for impeachment of the president for "high crimes and misdemeanors." Critics of the impeachment campaign, though, assert that Johnson's actions did not match that description. The South attempted to fall away and start its own country; then they tried through force of arms to assimilate the North to adopting its policies. A rift had occurred. But this was an epoch of relatively like-minded people almost completely uprooting democracy itself, undoing the tenets on which the nation was founded, over an argument. As James Brooks of New York, a Senate Democrat, put it, "I solemnly bid them beware . . ." since success of the impeachment would mean that Congress could remove a president "for the hat he wears or for the color of his coat."

CONCLUSION

Despite his impeachment, many historians have retaken stock of Johnson's contribution as an executive, as there were positive aspects and attributes surrounding his political career. From a wide lens, however, it is important to remember the sentiments of the time and how he was received. It cannot be forgotten that this was a president that was threatened with violence, almost assassinated, saw his vetoes repeatedly overridden, and ultimately found himself the first president to be impeached in U.S. history. Since then, historians have offered both positive and negative assessments of Johnson's legacy, but all agree that his time in American politics was nothing if not unique.

Andrew Harman

Further Reading

Dershowitz, Alan M. *America on Trial: Inside the Legal Battles That Transformed Our Nation.* New York: Warner Books, 2004.

Lomask, Milton. *Andrew Johnson: President on Trial.* New York: Farrar, Straus, and Giroux, 1960.

Means, Howard. *The Avenger Takes His Place: Andrew Johnson and the 45 Days That Changed the Nation.* New York: Harcourt, 2006.

Reed, Lawrence W., and Burton W. Folsom Jr. *A Republic—If We Can Keep It.* Atlanta, GA: Foundation for Economic Education, 2012.

Rodriguez, Juan P., ed. *Slavery in the United States: A Social, Political, and Historical Encyclopedia.* Santa Barbara, CA: ABC-CLIO, 2007.

Stewart, David O. *Impeached: The Trial of President Andrew Johnson and the Fight for Lincoln's Legacy.* New York: Simon & Schuster, 2009.

Trefousse, Hans L. *Andrew Johnson: A Biography,* quoted in "Presidents—The Good and the Bad," *Los Angeles Times,* January 18, 2009. Available at http://www.latimes.com /opinion/la-oe-catania18-2009jan18-story.html.

Winston, Robert. *Andrew Johnson: Plebian and Patriot.* New York: Henry Holt, 1928.

18. Ulysses S. Grant

Born: April 27, 1822

Died: July 23, 1885

Time in Office: 18th President of the United States, March 4, 1869, to March 4, 1877

Election Results: 1868 Election: 52.7% of popular vote, 214 (72.8%) Electoral College votes; 1872 Election: 55.6% of popular vote, 286 (81.9%) Electoral College votes

Spouse: Julia Dent (m. 1848)

Children: Frederick, Ulysses Jr., Nellie, and Jesse

Ulysses S. Grant, the triumphant Union general, came to the presidency as arguably the most popular person in the country. He left it as a major world figure and remained extremely popular at home. Future president James A. Garfield "spoke for the nation," said Jean Edward Smith, when he watched Grant depart from the White House and said, "No American has carried greater fame out of the White House than this silent man who leaves it today." Others offered tribute as well. "In him the negro found a protector, the Indian a friend, a vanquished foe a brother, an imperiled nation a savior," thundered the powerful orator and former slave Frederick Douglass; "Mightiest among the mighty dead loom the three great figures of Washington, Lincoln, and Grant," President Theodore Roosevelt asserted. One would be hard-pressed to know of these words of praise, however, if one were limited to learning about Grant from the works of early-20th-century American historians and political scientists.

Hiram Ulysses Grant was born in Point Pleasant, Ohio, to Jesse R. Grant and Hannah Simpson Grant on April 27, 1822. Known as Ulysses, never as Hiram, throughout his childhood, he graduated from the U.S. Military Academy at West Point, where he had excelled in mathematics and horsemanship, in 1843. The academy's records had garbled his name. Thomas Hamer, the congressman who had nominated him to West Point, submitted his name as "Ulysses Simpson Grant," apparently assuming that he bore his mother's maiden name. Ultimately, after becoming frustrated in his efforts at correction, Grant accepted the revision, although only as "Ulysses S. Grant," saying the "S" meant nothing. Inevitably, other cadets who saw him listed as "U.S. Grant" called him "Uncle Sam," so "Sam Grant," he became. Upon graduation Grant fought in the Mexican-American War with courage and skill under General Zachary Taylor. Both Grant and Taylor had reservations about the war, and both exhibited disdain for "spit and polish."

Grant married Julia Dent (1826–1902) on August 22, 1848, and they remained a devoted couple. Julia was remarkable in her own right and was the first president's wife or widow to write an autobiography. It was not published until 1975, nearly three-quarters of a century after her death. The two had four children, Frederick Dent (1850–1912), Ulysses Simpson (1852–1929), Ellen Wrenshall (1855–1922), and Jesse Root (1858–1934).

The Grants were together at his next posting, Sackets Harbor, New York, and then in Detroit. Subsequent orders, though, sent him to the far west, where Julia could not accompany him. Now and then he turned to drink in his loneliness and boredom, and after two years he resigned his commission. The Grants returned together to Missouri and then moved to Illinois. Grant worked hard at a series of jobs, and with the outbreak of the Civil War, rejoined the military. His rise through the Union's military ranks was astronomical, culminating in Abraham Lincoln's decision to make him commander of all Union forces in March 1864. Maximizing his advantages in manpower and resources over his Confederate counterparts, Grant methodically ground the rebel forces down until Confederate general Robert E. Lee surrendered to Grant at Appomattox, Virginia, on April 9, 1865.

After his brilliant military career, Grant served as president of the United States from March 4, 1869, to March 4, 1877. His initial victory in 1868 was substantial, winning nearly 53% of the popular vote, and almost 73% of the electoral vote. His 1872 reelection was a landslide. His popular vote percentage (55.6) was the largest any president received between Andrew Jackson's 56% in 1828 and Theodore Roosevelt's 56.4% in 1904. Moreover, he was the only president between Andrew Jackson (1829–1837) and Woodrow Wilson (1913–1921) to serve two full, consecutive, terms.

Grant's administration introduced the principle of arbitration in international disputes, and worked vigorously on behalf of civil rights for all American citizens. Grant secured creation of the Department of Justice, using it vigorously on behalf of civil rights. He introduced improvements in policies relating to Native Americans, and he appointed the first Native American government official. Although today it is almost entirely unknown, he brought about a needed restructuring of the U.S. judicial system.

To be sure, during Grant's time in office there was corruption. Much of it, however, long predated Grant, affected Congress not the executive, and was prosecuted. Any objective assessment must conclude that Grant's presidency was notable for its accomplishments. His life, similarly, was characterized by heroism—and not only during wartime. During his last months of life he suffered horribly from advanced throat cancer. Terrified that his death would leave Julia destitute—in those harsh days in which the government did nothing to assist former presidents and their families—he wrote furiously to complete his *Memoirs* so that she would have a reliable source of income after his death. He completed this work mere days before his death. Those memoirs have been justly hailed as the finest military memoirs in history, the best of all presidential biographies, and a literary classic. They made Julia wealthy. Death came to Grant at his home in Mt. McGregor, New York, on July 23, 1885. As Josiah Bunting III described it in *Ulysses S. Grant*:

> Grant's conduct as an ex-president (during the presidencies of Rutherford B. Hayes, James A. Garfield, and Chester Alan Arthur) served to make him more popular; he was beloved. His heroic fight against a terrible cancer, the continuing magnanimity of his judgments about men formerly his enemies, his survival with grace through a financial ruin not of his own making—such things commended him to all. His funeral in New York City, in which southern contingents marched proudly near the front of the procession, was an occasion for an overwhelming outpouring of public gratitude, mourning, affection. A giant had left the country, and the nation knew it.

Writing in *The American Commonwealth* in 1914, Lord Bruce classed Grant with Lincoln as presidents belonging "to the history of the world." But while Lincoln's reputation soared in the years after these words were penned, Grant's dwindled. Before long, he came to be derided as among the worst of presidents. Neo-confederate racists mourning the "Lost Cause" condemned his presidency, as did Republican "reformers" who smarted from their inability to secure government positions and were increasingly uncomfortable with black civil rights. Both these were aided in their efforts to undermine him by Grant's own modesty, and by the tendency in popular culture for lurid rumors without foundation, such as that of Grant's heavy drinking, to be accepted as fact without examination. Adding considerably to the noxious mix was a plethora of poor scholarship, leading me to ask in *Maligned Presidents: The Late 19th Century*, "Why have so many written so much for so long that is so wrong?"

DISDAIN FROM "REFORMERS"

Henry Adams, grandson and great-grandson of presidents and a gifted historian, came to Washington determined to effect "reform." During his stay, however, he emerged as one of Grant's most prominent and implacable critics. Soon after his arrival in Washington he was introduced to President Andrew Johnson. The young Adams found Johnson to be enormously impressive. As Garry Wills wrote in *Henry Adams and the Making of America*, Adams had been opposed to slavery, "but not free from racism when it came to black suffrage." He had supported the Thirteenth Amendment abolishing slavery, "but not the Fourteenth and Fifteenth. Henry wrote that the Fourteenth was too punitive to the South," and found that the "Fifteenth Amendment labored under the same difficulties." The Fourteenth, of course, established citizenship for those born here, and the Fifteenth removed race as a criterion for voting. Adams opposed these provisions, and he had a "view of black incapacity that would remain" with him for life.

Grant had been installed in the White House for only a matter of weeks when Adams began condemning the new president and his administration for not showing sufficient zeal for political reform. From that point forward he relentlessly criticized Grant. He proceeded to do his best to boost the careers of other reformers such as Carl Schurz, James Garfield, Samuel Tilden, Lucius Lamar, and Salmon P. Chase and to encourage pro-reform newspapers.

Adams has an honored reputation in historical and literary circles, but he and fellow writers indelibly—and inexcusably—influenced views of subsequent generations with regard to Grant. His oft-repeated quip from *The Education* (1918) that the "progress of evolution from President Washington to President Grant, was alone enough to upset Darwin," for example, was characterized by Grant biographer Jean Edward Smith as a statement that "reflected the bitterness of a self-indulgent and overly genteel young man who had gone to Washington confident of securing a position with the Grant administration and not found one." Adams's portrayal of Grant, Smith continued, "should be read alongside the sketch penned by his older brother, Charles Francis Adams Jr., after the Battle of the Wilderness [during the Civil War]. Both brothers saw the same man, both recognized Grant's force of character, but Charles Francis, a captain in the 1st Massachusetts Cavalry, then on staff duty, saw something more. . . . Henry Adams did not."

VENOM FROM MYTHMAKERS OF "THE LOST CAUSE"

The mythmakers working diligently to exalt the reputation of Robert E. Lee were faced with a monumental task. As Civil War scholar Brooks Simpson described it, "what was most troubling to them about Grant was that he prevailed over Robert E. Lee." The South had been unable to defeat Grant, but "at least one might take solace in denigrating him." It became especially important to the mythmakers to discredit Grant because of his own analyses of the war. "I have had nearly all of the Southern generals in high command in front of me," Grant had said, "and Joe Johnston gave me more anxiety than any of the others." As for the object of their veneration, Grant's dismissive comment, "I was never half so anxious about Lee," must have cut them to the bone.

As the southern states passed their resolutions of secession, they had openly declared that they did so in order to protect and preserve slavery, their "peculiar institution." Following the Civil War, however, southern leaders embarked on a great effort to cleanse and alter the historical record as to their earlier motivations. What they freely admitted and boasted about in 1861, they came increasingly to deny as the century progressed. As Gary Gallagher put it, "the architects of the Lost Cause acted from various motives. They collectively sought to justify their own actions and allow themselves and other former Confederates to find something positive in all-encompassing failure. They also wanted to provide their children and future generations of white Southerners with a 'correct' narrative of the war."

Not everyone was taken in. According to Gallagher, "For example, Frederick Douglass labored throughout the postwar decades to combat what he perceived as Northern complicity in spreading the Lost Cause arguments." A future president, Theodore Roosevelt, whose own southern mother had been sympathetic to the Confederacy, wrote at the very time the "southern vindicators" were distorting history to argue that "virtue and right were completely on the south's side.... As regards the actual act of secession, the actual opening of the Civil War, I think the right was exclusively with the Union people and the wrong exclusively with the secessionists." He followed even more strongly, speaking as an accomplished historian himself, saying: "I do not know of another struggle in history in which the sharp division between right and wrong can be made in quite so clear-cut a manner."

The neo-Confederates (groups who portrayed the actions of Confederate states in a positive light) sought to present a romantic version of valor and victimhood to replace reality, and they succeeded to a remarkable degree. By the early 20th century, Robert E. Lee, who by objective standards could have been branded a traitor, joined the truly magnificent Union figure of Abraham Lincoln as a Civil War figure of truly epic stature. Jefferson Davis did not reflect the personal qualities sought to achieve that status, so he was never in the competition. Grant manifestly did, so it was necessary to destroy his reputation as second only to Lincoln as the Union's savior. Thus, Grant's genius on the battlefield became the subject of derision, as was his strong performance as president. Former Confederate general Jubal Early and his cohorts proceeded vigorously, with a meat axe approach, heedless of surgical precision. They largely succeeded not only in demolishing Grant's reputation, but also in misrepresenting Reconstruction, and even besmirching the entire era between the war and the 20th century. Persisting today, popular culture tends to look askance at Reconstruction, which was perhaps the most progressive period in American history.

Many talented writers in recent decades have studied the deliberate dismantling of Grant's reputation. One of the best and most perceptive results is Joan Waugh's *U.S. Grant: American Hero, American Myth*. She presented two issues: "First, Ulysses S. Grant was a gigantic figure in the nineteenth century, and second, the memory of what he stood for—Union victory—was twisted, diminished, and then largely forgotten." She examines thoroughly, and in an innovative manner, why this figure who had been "equal in stature to George Washington and Abraham Lincoln," had become "eclipsed so completely." Grant sought peace, but "never peace at any price." Nothing less than southern acceptance of the "Union Cause," the preservation of the American republic, and "after 1863, [the] fight for freedom and the destruction of slavery," would do. "To Grant," she wrote, "those were noble ideals worth fighting for, dying for, and remembering in distinctive ways. Thus, his 'version' of sectional harmony rejected, indeed found repugnant, the increasingly popular idea that the Union and Confederate causes were 'separate but equal,' or even worse, that the two were somehow morally equivalent."

The neo-Confederate efforts paid off by dominating histories written in the South, then expanded to the entire country. According to historian Joan Waugh, "Much of the antipathy toward Grant arose from scholars led by William A. Dunning of Columbia University propelled by the 'Lost Cause' ideology that figuratively whitewashed history to portray Reconstruction as the 'tragic era.' Pro-Confederate scholar Claude G. Bowers summed up the argument: 'The Nation had tired of the bludgeoning of the South'. . . . According to Bowers and others, Reconstruction was nothing more than a harsh and corrupt rule imposed on helpless white southerners by a combination of vindictive Radical Republicans, ignorant African Americans, evil carpetbaggers, and turncoat scalawags. Reconstruction led by Grant's Republicans was a dismal failure." Note that Dunning was elected president of the American Historical Association.

ATTACKS FROM THE LEFT

Later scholarship, according to Waugh, "rejected the so-called 'Dunning School' interpretation and recast the story of Reconstruction. One part of the story remained the same. Still deemed a failure, Reconstruction, as shaped by Grant's shortcomings, was now seen as reflecting the deep racism of northern society. William Gillette claimed that northern prejudice was largely responsible for Reconstruction's 'retreat.'" Gillette drew attention to Grant's own racism as well, and that attention was amplified in William McFeely's *Grant: A Biography*, published in 1981, which "damned the president for his inability to secure black civil rights."

McFeely condemns Grant in the first paragraph of his introduction, writing that "no amount of revision is going to change the way men died at Cold Harbor [where thousands of Union soldiers were killed or wounded in 1864], the fact that men in the Whiskey Ring stole money [a tax diversion scandal in 1875], and the broken hopes of black Americans in Clinton, Mississippi, in 1875 [a riot perpetrated by armed white men]." Other scholars, however, have characterized these charges as unfair. Yes, men died at Cold Harbor. It was an error that Grant conceded, and greatly regretted. Men, as a matter of fact, do die in wars, especially one so bloody as America's Civil War. Yes, men of the Whiskey Ring did steal money—and were prosecuted by the Grant administration. Yes, a raging mob had massacred 34 black Americans in Mississippi, and there were numerous such incidents throughout the South. According to historian Frank Scaturro, Grant's new attorney general, a "strict constructionist, used his role as intermediary to narrow in effect Grant's interpretation of the scope of federal authority [regarding Reconstruction]. He conveyed the wrong impression to others by quoting Grant out of context, and he misrepresented the severity of the situation to Grant." Attorney General Pierrepont said Grant had replied to him that the "whole public are tired of these annual, autumnal outbreaks in the South," without adding Grant's following comment from his nomination speech at the Republican convention in 1868: "I heartily wish that peace and good order may be restored without issuing the proclamation. But if it is not, the proclamation must be issued; and if it is, I shall instruct the commander of the forces to have no child's play." Thus, as Scaturro (Grant's most uncompromising defender) points out, "Grant's 'refusal' to send troops, as many accounts represent it, was actually not a refusal at all, but an assurance."

McFeely was awarded a Pulitzer Prize for his biography of Grant, but his book has subsequently been heavily criticized. The distinguished historian James McPherson immediately demonstrated McFeely's "large number of careless errors," and charged that the book reflected a merely superficial "understanding of the nature of Grant's generalship, and the military history of the Civil War in general." Later, Brooks Simpson "refuted point by point much of McFeely's work," and raised so many questions about its veracity that he doubted whether McFeely had even written "true history."

"Grant's low repute among historians has been largely a product of the Dunning school," summarized historian Richard N. Current. "His fame continues to suffer even though the Dunning interpretation as a whole has long been discredited. It is time that revisionist scholars, having already revised practically every other phase of Reconstruction, should reconsider the role of President Grant." Rather than continuing to suffer disdain or condemnation, the record demonstrates that he should be given credit for political sensitivity, and for being "passionately committed" to his goals of Reconstruction and emancipation. He was, Waugh said, the "right man at the right time. No one else in the country possessed his unquestioned status as a symbol of unity and reconciliation." New studies are beginning to depict him as "a thoughtful, intelligent, engaged president, fully aware of the responsibilities, duties, and difficulties inherent in the role of chief executive."

POPULAR CULTURE AND DEMON RUM

Of all the calumnies besmirching Grant's reputation, the one about his drinking is the most lurid, and the most persistent. The tendency of writers, even historians, with regard to Grant and alcohol has been to repeat, rather than to research. Richard Mannion, in his dissertation on Grant's reputation, is an exception. He delves deeply into the question of Grant and drinking. In Mannion's words, "popular culture continued to play havoc with and promote Grant's image as an intemperate lush who could not turn himself away from a stiff drink." The image fit the purposes of the neo-Confederates well, inasmuch as the battle for prohibition portrayed the consumption of alcohol as immoral, and it effectively "fortified the further corrosion of Grant's remembrance and what he stood for." It melded neatly with the Dunning school, which libeled anyone who "supported blacks during Reconstruction" as having "had only political or personal gain at stake." According to Mannion, "Dunning's exasperation with and perceptions of Grant most certainly were driven in large part by his deeply held racist conviction that blacks were indeed inferior to whites and that as an institution, slavery was the proper paradigm for blacks."

Despite overt flaws in his work, Dunning's influence was extraordinary. "Historians and authors competed with each [other] to find adjectives sufficient . . . to define the Reconstruction era in Dunning-esq terms." His racist disciples included Don Seitz, Claude Bowers, Samuel Eagle Foreman, Frederic Paxson, James Albert Woodburn, Thomas Francis Moran, Everson David Fite, William Mace (who argued that "The ex-slaveholder was a better friend to the colored man than either the non-slaveholder or the carpetbagger"), and so on. "It would be difficult to overstate the damage done to Grant's reputation by Dunning's body of work."

During the war, Grant's antagonists, often Democratic partisans of the South, had spread rumors that he was a drunk. In order to reassure himself prior to promoting Grant, Lincoln had Secretary of War Edwin Stanton send a journalist, Charles Dana, "to travel with Grant and report back to both Lincoln and Stanton on Grant's behavior and alleged malfeasance." With the report, all concern vanished. Grant was not only "a great general" according to Dana, but also "a man of great depth, character, and integrity." The rumors of drinking were totally set to rest—even if not for posterity.

Indeed, with regard to more recent descriptions of a three-day bender during the Vicksburg campaign, Mannion dismissed them solely as "lore," and as "undocumented." Its single, original, source was one "Sylvanus Cadwallader, an English journalist for the *Chicago Times* who had been attached to Grant's command." Note that the *Chicago Times* was a Copperhead (Democratic, southern-oriented) newspaper, notorious for its vicious attack on Lincoln's Gettysburg Address, saying, on equality, that the founders had "too much self-respect to declare that negroes were their equals, or were entitled to equal privileges."

Mannion refers both to Brooks Simpson, who described Cadwallader's story as a "tall tale," and to John Y. Simon, who had demonstrated that Cadwallader had not even been with Grant at the time he alleged the incident took place. Mannion documents that "most historians of the early 1950s," and "pop culture" as well, "gave wide play to Grant's intemperance." He notes sadly that "the legend of Grant's drinking is constantly being reinforced in the public memory and it seems to be the one component part of Grant's reputation that can never be rescued, despite evidence to the contrary." Nevertheless, he says, there now is a "profound" body of work demonstrating that the allegations are nonsense, and urges that they continue. Grant's "memory is owed that," wrote Mannion.

CONCLUSION

Throughout the 20th century and into the 21st, Grant's reputation and presidential legacy have shifted as scholars have provided numerous accounts of his successes and failures. Although his presidency ranks below average, due in part to the corruption associated with his administration, his military career generally earns higher marks. Grant provides an excellent case study of a fluid presidential legacy and how critics at the time continue to shape the narrative that is provided by presidency scholars.

Max J. Skidmore

Further Reading

Adams, Henry. *The Education of Henry Adams: An Autobiography*. Boston: Houghton Mifflin, 1918.

Bryce, James. *The American Commonwealth*, 2 vols. [1914]. Indianapolis, IN: The Liberty Fund, 1995.

Bunting, Josiah III. *Ulysses S. Grant*. New York: Times Books, 2004.

Egerton, Douglas R. *The Wars of Reconstruction: The Brief, Violent History of America's Most Progressive Era*. New York: Bloomsbury, 2014.

Foner, Eric. *Reconstruction: America's Unfinished Revolution*. New York: Harper and Row, 1988.

Gallagher, Gary W., and Alan T. Nolan. *The Myth of the Lost Cause and Civil War History*. Bloomington, IN: Indiana University Press, 2000.

Mannion, Richard G. *The Life of a Reputation: The Public Memory of Ulysses S. Grant*. PhD dissertation, Georgia State University; Scholar Works@Georgia State University, 2012.

McFeely, William. *Grant: A Biography*. New York: W.W. Norton, 1981.

Mieczkowski, Yanek. *The Routledge Historical Atlas of Presidential Elections*. New York: Routledge, 2001.

Scaturro, Frank. *Grant Reconsidered*. Lanham, MD: Madison Books, 1999.

Simpson, Brooks D. "Continuous Hammering and Mere Attrition," in *The Myth of the Lost Cause and Civil War History*, ed. Gary W. Gallagher and Alan T. Nolan. Bloomington, IN: Indiana University Press, 2000.

Skidmore, Max J. *Presidential Performance: A Comprehensive Review.* Jefferson, NC: McFarland, 2004.

Skidmore, Max J. *Maligned Presidents: The Late 19th Century.* New York: Palgrave Macmillan, 2014.

Smith, Jean Edward. *Grant.* New York: Simon and Schuster, 2001.

Waugh, Joan. *U. S. Grant: American Hero, American Myth.* Chapel Hill, NC: University of North Carolina Press, 2009.

White, Ronald C. *American Ulysses: A Life of Ulysses S. Grant.* New York: Random House, 2016.

Wills, Garry. *Lincoln at Gettysburg: The Words That Remade America.* New York: Simon and Schuster, 1992.

Wills, Garry. *Henry Adams and the Making of America.* New York: Houghton Mifflin, 2005.

19. Rutherford B. Hayes

Born: October 4, 1822

Died: January 17, 1893

Time in Office: 19th President of the United States, March 4, 1877, to March 4, 1881

Election Results: 1876 Election: 48% of popular vote, 185 (50.1%) Electoral College votes

Spouse: Lucy Webb (m. 1852)

Children: Birchard, Webb, Rutherford, Fanny, Scott, George, Joseph, and Manning

Rutherford B. Hayes, who served a self-imposed single presidential term (1877–1881), was born in Delaware, Ohio. He attended Kenyon College and Harvard Law School, and in 1852 he married Lucy Webb, a teetotaler who would later convince Hayes to ban alcohol from the White House. They raised five children to adulthood: Birchard, Webb, Rutherford, Fanny, and Scott. Three sons—George, Joseph, and Manning—died in infancy. Fanny and Scott came of age in the White House after a bitterly contested election in which, despite losing the popular vote, Hayes defeated Democrat Samuel Tilden by a single electoral vote, 185–184. It was the closest and most uncertain result in American history.

DESERTER EPISODE

Partisan attacks were common during the 1876 election. For example, Hayes supporters charged that Democrats sought to subvert the consolidation of Union and

Confederate troops during and after the Civil War. One Republican member of Congress, Robert Ingersoll (NY), alleged that the cause of the Civil War was solely due to the Democrats. "Every man that tried to destroy this nation was a Democrat," Ingersoll boomed. "Every man that shot Union soldiers was a Democrat. Every scar you have got on your heroic bodies was given to you by a Democrat." Tilden forces fought fire with fire. Their main accusation was that Hayes, while serving as a federal captain during the Civil War, had stolen his own company men's money. Though the charges against Hayes were false, the allegation was based on an actual incident that had been reported by the Democratic *Cincinnati Enquirer.*

Hayes himself countered the accusation in an interview with the Republican-friendly *Cincinnati Commercial.* Hayes explained that in the fall of 1863, a soldier in a Rebel uniform approached a federal picket line claiming that he was a Union man who had been pressed into the Confederate Army. The soldier enlisted in Hayes's regiment, but subsequently deserted with stolen arms and jewelry. On May 9, 1864, the deserter was taken prisoner as a Rebel soldier. Hayes's regiment was assigned guard duty, and the soldiers recognized the deserter. A court martial found him guilty of bounty jumping and ordered his execution, whereupon the man escaped custody. He continued signing up for service, receiving bounties, deserting, and repeating the process. His final sign-up, though, required him to report for federal duty before receiving the bounty. Upon reporting, he was again discovered and again sentenced to a firing squad. He admitted his guilt and surrendered $400 and two stolen watches. Members of the court martial concluded that the money should be used to recruit another soldier to Hayes's regiment.

ELECTORAL CONTROVERSY

Every single electoral vote made a difference in 1876. With such a tight tally, both parties fought desperately for five closely contested states. In Vermont and Oregon— both of which Hayes won—Hayes had appointed a sitting postmaster to be an elector to the Electoral College. Article II, though, bars federal employees from serving in the college. Democrats argued that the electoral vote should either transfer to Tilden or be discounted wholesale.

Vermont settled the matter easily. The partisan Republican governor had no intention of aiding Tilden. More importantly, state law dictated that if an elector could not serve, the winner of the electoral votes could appoint a replacement. Oregon, on the other hand, submitted two sets of electoral results. The Democratic governor certified the election as two votes for Hayes and—because he deemed the third Hayes elector as ineligible—one for Tilden. The secretary of state (also, curiously, a Democrat) of Oregon certified three votes for Hayes. Although institutional rules dominated the Vermont and Oregon disputes, outright corruption reigned in South Carolina, Florida, and Louisiana. On election night, it appeared that Tilden had won all three states; yet, Republican headquarters announced that Hayes had taken them. Both parties claimed fraud.

Democratic complaints centered on events after Election Day—especially in Florida and Louisiana, where partisan canvassing boards ruled in favor of counting Republican votes and tossing Democratic ones. In Louisiana, the chairman of the canvassing board furtively demanded a bribe. Addressing John Sherman (R-OH)—a leader in the Republican Party and soon-to-be secretary of the treasury-elect—Chairman James Madison Wells wrote, "Let me, my esteemed sir, warn you of the danger. Millions have been sent here and will be used in the interest of Tilden, and unless some counter move, it will be impossible for me or any other individual to wrest its [the canvass's] productive results. See our friends and act promptly or results will be disaster. A hint to the wise." Sensing foul play, Democrats in Louisiana and Florida countered the Republican bands of electors with their own Tilden slates. Thus, both states sent multiple delegations to the Electoral College.

Republican complaints focused on Election Day. In some Democratic counties in South Carolina, more votes had been cast than there were registered voters. Furthermore, Republicans rightfully charged local southern leaders with allowing the Ku Klux Klan to intimidate, or vote for Tilden in the place of, black voters. Hayes noted the tragedy: "The Democrats have endeavored to defeat the will of the lawful voters by the perpetration of crimes whose magnitude and atrocity has no parallel in our history. By murder and hellish cruelties, they at many polls drove the colored people away, or forced them to vote the Democratic ticket." A few days later, Hayes, probably correctly, commented, "No doubt a fair election would have carried the state for the Republicans."

SPECIAL COMMISSION

Constitutional questions arose as multiple states sent multiple delegations to the Electoral College. Which results would be counted? And who would decide that question? The Democratic-controlled House concluded that Tilden deserved the electoral votes. The Republican-controlled Senate, meanwhile, determined that Hayes had won.

With conflicting opinions on which delegations were legitimate, who should count the votes, and which man should be president, the House and Senate appointed a special commission made up of five representatives, five senators, and five Supreme Court justices. With seven partisan Democrats and seven partisan Republicans, the relatively independent Justice Joseph Bradley held the swing vote. He decided that each state held the right to determine which candidate deserved that state's electoral votes. In Vermont, state law allowed the winning candidate to replace an illegible elector; this gave it to Hayes. In Oregon, state law left it to the secretary of state to certify the election; he had given it to Hayes. In South Carolina, Democrats and Republicans arranged a quid pro quo: electoral votes for Hayes in exchange for a Democratic governor. In Florida and Louisiana, state election boards had jurisdiction; they both ruled in favor of Hayes. Thus, in every circumstance, Hayes prevailed.

Democrats attacked the ruling, not only for its Republican-favoring outcome, but also the alleged circumstances behind Bradley's drafting of his opinion. The Democratic *New York Sun* ran a series of articles—all of which were read and approved by Tilden before going to print—accusing Bradley of selling his vote the night before the justice announced his opinion. The *Sun* alleged, "During the whole of the night, Judge Bradley's house in Washington was surrounded by the carriages of visitors who came to see him apparently about the decision of the Electoral Commission. . . . These visitors included leading Republicans." The newspaper also reported that Bradley had penned a separate opinion favoring Tilden's ascension and that the justice had read the draft to Justices Stephen Field and Nathan Clifford, both of whom sat on the special commission.

After months of ignoring the charges, Bradley responded in the *Newark Daily Advertiser*. "The whole thing is a falsehood," Bradley said, "Not a single visitor called at my house that evening." He admitted writing "arguments and consideration on both sides" and that, at times, he was inclined to one view or the other. But Bradley asserted that he never read an opinion to Field and Clifford. When asked about it, Field replied, "Justice Bradley *read* no opinion. . . . Beyond that, I think it would be improper for me to say anything. If I should enter upon the subject, I should probably say a great deal more than I wish to say." The implication was that while Bradley never *read* an opinion to Field, Bradley had told Field he would vote for Tilden. The *New York Sun* interpreted Bradley's comments as an obfuscated admission to wrongdoing. The paper called for his impeachment from the Supreme Court. Bradley, meanwhile, began to receive death threats in the mail—to the point where he was assigned federal bodyguards.

Democrats, meanwhile, still held a trump card. At the time, electoral rules stipulated that a state's Electoral College returns could be challenged, whereby the House and Senate would both vote on allowing that state's votes. In a roundabout way, this gave the power of choosing the president to the Democratically controlled House. They could have challenged any of Hayes's Electoral College votes and then voted to bar them in the final tally. Disqualifying Hayes votes did not mean transferring them to Tilden. But it could have ensured that neither candidate received a majority of the electoral votes, thereby throwing the election to the House, where the Democratic majority could have then elected Tilden.

In creating the special commission, both parties had pledged not to raise Electoral College challenges. Nevertheless, with the presidency at stake, northern Democrats prepared to renege on their promise. Moreover, they threatened secession should Tilden be denied office. Just a dozen years after Appomattox, the nation stood at the brink of another secession crisis. Sensing an opportunity—and no doubt, recognizing that secession was not a productive path for the postwar nation—southern Democrats reached out to Hayes. They would vote against Electoral College challenges in exchange for three concessions: (1) ending military reconstruction, (2) suspending the appointments of blacks to southern offices, and (3) placing a southerner in the cabinet. With less than 48 hours before Inauguration Day, Hayes agreed to the deal. And while Hayes might have won the 1876 election, he never escaped its controversy. Republicans disapproved of the backroom deal while Democrats sought his removal from office.

INTRAPARTY ATTACKS FOR ABANDONING RECONSTRUCTION

The election of 1876 was not decided by the special commission, or even the Electoral College, as much as it was by a backroom deal. This would haunt Hayes's administration. Republicans soon turned on Hayes for abandoning reconstruction of the South. Their criticism, however, never included impeachment. In his diary, Hayes noted the intraparty opposition, but saw no "personal hostility" from Republican members of Congress—members whom Hayes sincerely describes as "respectable." The president noted that pacification of the South was a main reason for dissent within the party. But he remained largely unconcerned with Republican dissent because he believed it was not widespread enough to warrant alarm.

A good portion of GOP criticism was relatively mild and probably intended to signal to the president that fellow Republicans expected him to take a firmer stance toward the South. For instance, although Senator Timothy Howe (R-WI) expressed disappointment with the administration for allowing Democrats to take control of the Louisiana state government, he never called for Hayes's ouster. The New York City Republican Central Committee endorsed Howe's speech, but stopped short of calling for impeachment. Even the Republican-friendly *New York Times* became temporarily skeptical of the president. They reprinted a column from the Iowan *Keokuk Gate City* on March 14, 1878 (which *The Times* describes as "a leading Republican paper"), which accused Hayes of seeking reelection above promoting GOP principles. "If he sticks to this motive," the editorial concluded, "the party must make up its mind that no sign or word of leadership is to come from him." In that case, congressional Republicans should not impeach Hayes; they should assume party leadership. The same day, *The Times* reported that former Confederate leaders were "upon more familiar terms with the president than nine-tenths of the Republican Senators." It did not call for impeachment, but it painted a stark picture: "The bottom rail is on top again. . . . The Democracy rules in Washington, and the Democracy is absolutely under the control of men who won distinction by plotting and fighting to destroy their country."

One of the most vocal Republican dissenters was Daniel Henry Chamberlain, the outgoing governor of South Carolina. He asserted that Hayes's plan "consists in the abandonment of Southern Republicans, and especially the colored race, to the control and rule not only of the Democratic Party, but of that class at the South which regarded slavery as a Divine Institution." Party organizer William E. Chandler—who played a significant role in helping Hayes win Louisiana's electoral votes—also voiced intraparty disapproval. In a letter addressed to New Hampshire Republicans, Chandler chided the president: "He should have avoided any yielding or concession to the Democratic Party." Chandler believed that continuing Radical Reconstruction would have consolidated northern Republican gains and helped the GOP make entryway into the South.

Leading abolitionist William Lloyd Garrison publicly announced support for Chandler, lambasting the "fulfillment of a bargain entered into during the presidential count." He charged Hayes with believing that "the best way to protect sheep from being devoured is to give them over to the custody of the wolves, withdrawing both shepherd and watchdog." Garrison concluded that no Republican would have ever voted for Hayes if they had known that it would have led "Southern leaders in the Rebellion again to hold mastery over the nation" (as reported in the *New York Times*, January 24, 1878). Yet, despite Chamberlain's claims of "cowardice and treachery of President Hayes' Southern policy," none of these Republicans called for impeachment.

That, however, did not stop Democratic newspapers from spinning Republican censures—especially Chandler's denunciation—as calls for impeachment. Chandler responded by defending the president. When Chandler's letter was published, he provided an addendum explaining the Democratic attempts to twist his words. Chandler pointed out sections from the original letter that supported Hayes's place in the White House, including the line: "President Hayes should maintain his own rightfulness of title."

IMPEACHMENT ATTEMPT

On May 13, 1878, Representative Clarkson Potter (D-NY) introduced a resolution calling for a committee to investigate the fraudulent votes in Louisiana and Florida. Although congressional Republicans might have opposed some of Hayes's policies, they rallied behind this attempt to oust the president. While taking swipes at the president, the Republican press, too, stood against Potter's resolution. Take the *New York Times* passive-aggressive support on July 1, 1878: "Mediocrity, though a good reason for keeping a man out of the presidency, cannot be assigned as the ground-work of impeachment."

Sensing an opportunity to embarrass Hayes, the Democratic majority rammed Potter's proposal through the House in a highly partisan vote. Speaker of the House Samuel Randall then packed the committee with Hayes's enemies. Potter chaired the committee. Of the 11 members, seven were Democrats. One of the four Republicans was Benjamin Butler (R-MA)—one of only three Republicans (out of 136) who voted to form the committee. Butler was no stranger to impeachment, having led the charge against Andrew Johnson in 1868. His loyalty to the GOP was also in question. In fact, within a few months of joining the committee, Butler would resign from Congress, change his party affiliation, and run for office as a Democrat.

Despite the House of Representatives formally investigating cause for impeachment, Hayes remained calm. He called it "a partisan proceeding for merely partisan ends." In his diary, he noted various reasons why the investigation would fizzle out, making special note that the inquiry was against the interest of the South and the country. Quite prophetically, Hayes predicted, "If the Republicans manage well their side of the controversy, I suspect it will damage its authors."

The most potentially damning witness before the committee was James E. Anderson, who supervised voter registration in Louisiana's East Feliciana Parish. Anderson claimed he had been promised a higher office in exchange for helping swing the election. He also claimed that he had a letter from Senator Sherman saying as much. The story soon unraveled. The original letter mysteriously disappeared, leaving only a copy. Sherman denied the account. Hayes turned over all communiqués with Anderson—none of which indicated misconduct. In fact, after suspecting Anderson of using political office to blackmail others, Hayes considered Anderson's background. The president found him to be "a great scoundrel" and refused to appoint Anderson to any office. Upon investigation, the committee discovered Anderson's copy of the letter had been forged. Only a month after the committee was formed, the House voted 216–21 to uphold the election and take no future action on the issue.

The investigatory committee, however, was not discharged, and soon began investigating Democratic tampering. Just months after the House voted to sustain Hayes's election, the *New York Tribune* published a series of coded letters, along with their cipher, showing that Tilden supporters (including Tilden's own nephew) had tried to bribe election officials in South Carolina, Louisiana, and Florida. The offenders eventually admitted to attempted bribery. Tilden himself was never convicted, but it was odd that he had used ciphers (in the same code, no less) for previous business transactions. Altogether, the ordeal shut the door on a possible 1880 Tilden presidential run. In the end, the Potter Committee came off as partisan and ended up exposing Democratic wrongdoing.

CONCLUSION

The attacks on Hayes had little effect on either the larger body politic or on the administration. The political system did not respond to attacks because the election of Hayes had, in the first place, been a political compromise between competing coalitions. And while Democrats continued to find ways to hammer against Hayes (despite consenting to his election), it should come as no surprise that members of one political party opposed a president from the other party.

The main reason attacks—whether intra- or interparty—never affected the administration is because Hayes simply did not believe in their veracity and/or he placed his trust in the American people over politicians. His diary indicates an unwavering confidence in himself and steadfastness against political opposition. When considered as a nominee for president, Hayes wrote, "I do not feel the least fear that I should fail. This all looks egotistical; but it is sincere." In his first year in office, when Republicans opposed military withdrawal and civil service reform, Hayes commented, "How to meet and overcome this opposition is the question. I am clear that I am right. I believe that a large majority of the best people are in full accord with me." In his second year, with opposition mounting from both parties, Hayes said, "I am not liked as a president by the politicians in office, in the press, or in Congress. But I am content to abide the judgment—the sober second thought—of the people."

Hayes chose not to run for reelection because he believed he had accomplished all his goals. "Nobody ever left the presidency with less regret, less disappointment, fewer heartburnings, or more general content with the result of his term," he reflected. And while friendly and hostile presses constantly chided Hayes, by 1881, the former spoke fondly of the 19th president. The *New York Graphic* asked, "Who since Monroe has gone out both willingly and regretted?" The *New York Times* ran a long recap of Hayes's achievements on March 2, 1881. The paper quoted a friend of Hayes: "He is entirely satisfied with what he believes to be the verdict of the people on his record as president, and . . . he has no uneasiness whatever about the probable verdict of posterity."

Dave Bridge

Acknowledgment: Thanks to Tucker Brackins for research assistantship; and to Kim Kellison and Mike Parrish for feedback.

Further Reading
Bradley, Joseph P. *Miscellaneous Writings of the Late Hon. Joseph P. Bradley*. Newark, NJ: Hardham, 1902.

Hayes, Rutherford B. *The Diary and Letters of Rutherford B. Hayes, Nineteenth President of the United States*. Columbus, OH: Ohio State Archeological and Historical Society, 1922.

Holt, Michael F. *By One Vote: The Disputed Presidential Election of 1876.* Lawrence, KS: University Press of Kansas, 2008.

Rehnquist, William H. *Centennial Crisis: The Disputed Election of 1876.* New York: Vintage Books, 2007.

Samuel J. May Anti-Slavery Collection. Cornell University Library, 2016. Available at Ebooks.library.cornell.edu/m/mayantislavery.

Summers, Mark W. *The Ordeal of Reunion: A New History of Reconstruction.* Chapel Hill, NC: University of North Carolina Press, 2014.

Woodward, C. Vann. *Reunion and Reaction: The Compromise of 1877 and the End of Reconstruction.* Boston: Little, Brown and Company, 1951.

20. James Garfield

Born: November 19, 1831

Died: September 19, 1881

Time in Office: 20th President of the United States, March 4, 1881, to September 19, 1881

Election Results: 1880 Election: 48.3% of popular vote, 214 (58%) Electoral College votes

Spouse: Lucretia Rudolph (m. 1858)

Children: Harry, James, Mary, Irvin, and Abram

Born in the Western Reserve area of Ohio in 1831, James Abram Garfield first entered politics as a state senator just before the outbreak of the Civil War. He rose to regional and national prominence after recruiting and leading Ohio troops early in the Civil War. In 1862, while still fighting in the war, he won election to Congress from Ohio's 19th district. He finally took his seat in Washington in late 1863 after Abraham Lincoln and others told Garfield that they needed every vote in the House of Representatives. After winning a special election to fill a vacant Senate seat in 1880, Garfield did not take the seat because of his nomination and subsequent election to the presidency later that year. Just four months after his March 4, 1881, inauguration, however, Garfield was shot on July 2 by a deranged and disappointed Republican campaign worker who wanted to become an ambassador to France. Garfield died from the wounds on September 19, 1881.

Garfield married Lucretia Rudolph in 1858, shortly before entering the Ohio state senate. They had seven children, five of whom survived past childhood. Two of his sons became prominent government officials: James Rudolph Garfield would become secretary of the interior during Theodore Roosevelt's administration, and Harry Augustus Garfield became president of Williams College, his father's alma mater, and was appointed by Woodrow Wilson as head of the Federal Fuel Administration during World War I.

DREDGING UP SCANDALS IN THE 1880 PRESIDENTIAL CAMPAIGN

At the Republican convention of 1880, the two heavyweight Republican candidates—Ulysses S. Grant and James Blaine—were deadlocked in early voting. Congressman James Garfield, ostensibly the leader of Ohio senator John Sherman's campaign for the nomination, became the compromise nominee after 36 ballots, and he subsequently defeated Democratic nominee Winfield Scott, a Civil War hero, in the general election.

Soon after, Garfield faced attacks in the press and from leaders of the Democratic Party stemming from multiple personal and political scandals. Garfield and his wife Lucretia had both worried that the opposition or the press would dredge up Garfield's extramarital affair with a young reporter in 1864 or other unseemly relationships. In addition, during the 1880 campaign, various rumors swirled about Garfield's behavior away from home, with one tabloid writer for the *New York Independent* noting that his "intellectual acumen" was not matched by his "moral purity." Lucretia herself came under humorous fire from a leading satirical magazine, *Puck*, in July 1880, not for the rumors of marital discord or infidelity, but for the almost mythical status accorded her in campaign literature supporting Garfield. As one column teased, for her "startling and unprecedented achievements," Congress unanimously designated her as both Queen of the May and the Grand Sachem of Tammany Hall.

Due to his prior congressional career, Garfield's involvement in political scandals was both better documented and more damaging to his electoral chances than his lack of "moral purity" regarding his personal conduct. The first and most prominent of these, the Credit Mobilier scandal, occurred while he served as House Appropriations Committee chair. Credit Mobilier, a shell company created by Union Pacific Railroad officials, raked in profits by overcharging for construction of parts of the transcontinental railroad and by soliciting generous federal subsidies. Many members of Congress in turn received shares at undervalued prices or, like Garfield, received questionable dividend payments.

Though Garfield's involvement in the scandal was tangential, the Credit Mobilier investigation coincided with the "salary grab" legislation of 1873, which included a provision that retroactively raised congressional salaries. Garfield still won reelection to the House throughout the 1870s, but the taint of these scandals led to unflattering cartoons and commentaries in the 1880 campaign. And his letter formally accepting the Republican nomination triggered immediate criticism in the press about his connection to Republican bosses in the Senate. His words suggested he would follow the same pattern of prior presidents who said one thing about civil service reform, but, in practice, continued to allow senators to put forward their supporters and cronies for appointments.

This reputation also made him vulnerable to the first "October surprise," a late-breaking story that his Democratic opposition hoped would weaken him ahead of the November election. This surprise was the discovery of an alleged letter on congressional letterhead from Garfield to H. L. Morey of Lynn, Massachusetts. In this letter, known as the "Morey letter" or "Garfield's death warrant" because of its presumptive ruin of his electoral hopes, Garfield supported full Chinese immigration, a controversial position at the time that both candidates, Garfield and Winfield Scott Hancock, strenuously denounced throughout the campaign. Garfield denied that he had written the letter and sent his own handwritten letter to the newspapers, which many published side-by-side with the Morey letter.

Though most experts then and now have deemed it a forgery, the Morey letter put the Garfield campaign on the defensive by highlighting an already existing perception that Garfield was just like all the other corrupt politicians. His opponent, Winfield Scott Hancock, had no trail of political scandal and was still fondly remembered as one of the heroes of Gettysburg, making Garfield seem all the worse by comparison. As Richard Hubbard, the Texas governor, said in seconding Hancock's nomination at the Democratic convention, Hancock's record was "without stain and without reproach, with no credit mobilier [sic] or Degolyer [another contracting scandal loosely linked to Garfield's appropriations committee] frauds around him." The close margin in the popular vote—Garfield won by less than 0.1 percent of the overall popular vote (final estimates range from a margin of about 2,000 to a little over 8,000 votes out of just under 9 million cast)—reflected Hancock's popularity; but the distribution of Hancock's votes, strong in the southern states but weaker in the North and West, left him well short of victory in the Electoral College. Garfield secured 214 electoral votes, compared to 155 for Hancock.

With the election over, Garfield prepared for inauguration in March. Though he sought to balance the competing Republican factions in his cabinet appointments, Garfield drew attacks from both the Half Breeds (Blaine supporters) and Stalwarts (Grant's backers)—and the press. As the *New York Times* editorialized in the Sunday edition on February 20, 1881, Garfield's balancing act revealed "an all-pervading solicitude" to party leaders that would "mean a parceling out of patronage and favors which has in years past been the prolific source of inefficiency and of jobbery more or less flagrant in the public service." From the Stalwart side, Senator Roscoe Conkling of New York criticized Garfield for not being sufficiently receptive to input from Conkling and his senatorial colleagues, bypassing the traditional role of senators in making most appointments. And Garfield's first pick—James Blaine for secretary of state—drew Conkling's considerable ire because of his personal conflict with Blaine.

Yet Garfield still vacillated between completely shutting out the Conkling crew from New York—and ultimately, Ulysses Grant's supporters—to appeasing them with key posts alongside Half Breeds. At one point, he considered putting Conkling himself in the cabinet alongside his mortal enemy Blaine. After the inauguration, Garfield relented to Conkling's demands on important federal positions in New York; immediately, the reform-minded press criticized the president for weakness.

But when challenged by Conkling over the appointment of William Robertson—a Blaine supporter—to be the collector of the port of New York, the president held firm. Conkling and others thought they had a deal with Garfield, but Garfield considered this to be the defining appointment of his presidency and did not back down. And instead of drawing press criticism for indecision or poor administration, Garfield's bypassing of the traditional patronage scheme drew praise. As noted by Mark Wahlgren Summers, Garfield "was far from green when dealing with the press" and had friendships with a few key editors, especially Whitelaw Reid, Horace Greeley's successor as editor of the *New York Tribune*. When Garfield called for an investigation in April of the Star Route scandals involving rural postal routes, these relationships helped his administration remain relatively unscathed in press accounts even as some close allies—Republican National Committee secretary and former senator Stephen Dorsey prominent among them— were implicated.

DISASTROUS CONSEQUENCES OF DEFEATING CONKLING AND WINNING OVER THE PRESS

By defeating Conkling and the Stalwarts in the battle over press coverage and public opinion about appointments, Garfield unwittingly fueled the determination of Charles Guiteau, a disappointed and mentally unstable appointment seeker, to assassinate Garfield. After being personally rebuffed by Garfield and Secretary of State James Blaine for a prominent appointment, Guiteau formulated a plan to kill the president. He claimed, in journal entries written before the attack and statements to police after the shooting, that he was God's instrument in saving both the Republican Party and the country. By killing Garfield, Guiteau wanted to elevate Vice President Chester Arthur, a prominent Stalwart protégé of Conkling and former collector of the Port of New York, to the presidency and avenge Grant's defeat at the 1880 convention. Upon taking the oath of office after Garfield's death in September, Arthur surprised his party, the press, and the public. Instead of shifting administration policy back toward the patronage and machine-dominated politics of Conkling and the Stalwarts that had led to Arthur's own initial political rise, he pushed for and signed major civil service reform legislation—the Pendleton Act—into law in 1883.

CONCLUSION

Lingering sympathy from Garfield's death and Arthur's surprising efforts to fight corruption did not, however, lead to success at the ballot box. Arthur's declining health meant he would not be renominated, and the Republican nominee in 1884, James Blaine, lost to Grover Cleveland, the first Democratic nominee to win the White House after the Civil War. The Republican majority in the House slipped away in the 1884 elections, but they retained the Senate majority.

As the politics of the Gilded Age gave way to the Progressive push for electoral and appointment reform, Garfield's assassination and Arthur's signature on the Pendleton Act spurred further reform legislation aimed at breaking the hold of political machines in both the administrative functions of government and in voting and elections. And another assassination, that of William McKinley two decades after Garfield's, would lead to congressional battles over immigration reform and a mandate to the Secret Service to protect the president. Ultimately, Garfield's presidency did not represent an extraordinary period of rhetorical attacks on a candidate or president. But for Garfield's assassin, it was those critiques that reaffirmed his Stalwart sympathies and served as catalyst for the fateful decision to shoot Garfield on July 2, 1881.

Evan Haglund

Further Reading

Ackerman, Kenneth D. *Dark Horse: The Surprise Election and Political Murder of President James A. Garfield*. New York: Carroll & Graf Publishers, 2003.

Doenecke, Justus D. *The Presidencies of James A. Garfield & Chester A. Arthur*. Lawrence, KS: Regents Press of Kansas, 1981.

Leech, Margaret, and Harry J. Brown. *The Garfield Orbit*. New York: Harper & Row, 1978.

Millard, Candice. *Destiny of the Republic: A Tale of Madness, Medicine and the Murder of a President*. New York: Anchor, 2012.

Peskin, Allan. *Garfield: A Biography*. Kent, OH: Kent State University Press, 1978.

Summers, Mark Wahlgren. *The Press Gang: Newspapers and Politics, 1865–1878*. Chapel Hill, NC: University of North Carolina Press, 1994.

21. Chester A. Arthur

Born: October 5, 1829
Died: November 18, 1886
Time in Office: 21st President of the United States, September 19, 1881, to March 4, 1885
Election Results: 1880 Election: Elected vice president; assumed office upon death of James Garfield

Spouse: Ellen Herndon (m. 1859)
Children: Chester Alan II, Ellen Hansbrough Herndon, and William Lewis
   Herndon

Chester A. Arthur served as the 21st president of the United States from 1881 to 1885. He was born on October 5, 1829, in Fairfield, Vermont. He graduated from Union College in 1848. He married Ellen Herndon in 1859 and had three children (one who died at a young age). Arthur served as a quartermaster general during the Civil War and returned home to practice law. Arthur was a successful lawyer but rose to fame as a political operative in New York working for the Stalwart political machine and its boss, Roscoe Conkling. He was appointed by President Ulysses Grant to be collector of taxes at the New York Custom House (a plum and well-paying party position), a job he held until he was fired by President Rutherford Hayes as part of the latter's efforts to highlight the need for reform of the spoils system. After some backroom negotiation, and as a reward to the Stalwarts, Arthur joined James Garfield on the Republican Party ticket and was elected vice president in 1880. He was sworn in as president on September 20, 1881, after Garfield's death, and served out the rest of Garfield's term. During his time in office his sister acted as his first lady (his wife died in 1880 prior to the presidential campaign), and his children did not live with him in the White House. His achievements as president were limited but included the passage of the Pendleton Act and the controversial Chinese Exclusion Act. He has also been credited with leading the modernization efforts of the U.S. Navy and setting the groundwork for the Panama Canal. Due to an unpublicized illness and destructive attacks by his detractors in both the government and the press, he was unable to gain the popular support needed to win a second term. He was defeated by James Blaine for the Republican Party nomination in 1884 (who then lost the general election to Democrat Grover Cleveland). Arthur suffered from the effects of Bright's disease throughout much of his presidency, and he succumbed to the disease on November 18, 1886, at the age of 57.

Hatred of Arthur came from a variety of different places (Democrats, Garfield's allies, newspapers, cartoonists, and magazines). The attacks on him were often harsh and focused on the circumstances that brought him to the presidency, his long-time association with the political machine and spoils system, his alleged lack of qualifications and experience, and perceptions that he was more of a socialite than a president.

CONSPIRACY THEORIES REGARDING GARFIELD'S DEATH

Arthur was added to the Republican ticket in 1880 (after a long convention fight) as a way of mollifying the Stalwart wing of the Republican Party and ensuring a Garfield nomination. Arthur was a long-time loyal lieutenant to Conkling, which tainted him with the negative reputation of the political machine and the spoils system. It also meant that he came to Washington looking to champion the Stalwarts' opposition to civil service reform. During his first few months as vice president, he sided with his mentor Conkling against the Garfield administration (and even Garfield himself) on some key issues, creating a divide in the administration and sowing the seeds of distrust between the president and the vice president. The impact of this division became evident on July 2, 1881, when Charles Guiteau, a disgruntled job seeker, shot Garfield at a train station in Baltimore. Upon his arrest Guiteau yelled, "I am a Stalwart and Arthur is President now." This declaration sparked immediate and rampant conspiracy theories about the involvement of Arthur and the Stalwarts in the shooting and sent Arthur into seclusion. Garfield did not die immediately but lingered for 79 days before eventually passing away on September 19, 1881. From the time of the shooting until the time of his death, there was a great outpouring of sympathy for Garfield and his family. However, because of the rumors, Arthur was not treated as respectfully. Even though most people eventually realized that Guiteau was suffering from mental illness and no connection between him and Arthur was ever found, Arthur and the Stalwarts continued to be suspected of playing some part in the assassination attempt and were assailed in the press for benefiting from it. Arthur was never able to fully overcome this suspicion, and it remained a black cloud over his administration.

The underlying theme of these attacks on Arthur was a suggestion that he played a role in a potential conspiracy or cover-up. Contemporary newspapers reference the ungracious, cruel, and vitriolic speech used against Arthur, often describing the tone of the stories as brutal and vicious. For example, in one story a reporter wrote, "While Garfield was dying, more and more eyes were turned upon the vice-president and many of these eyes were apprehensive. The unsavory maneuver that had catapulted Arthur to the top was now backfiring with a vengeance." An editorial in the *New York Times* on July 3, 1881, was more direct in its accusations of Arthur: "When James A. Garfield was yesterday reported as being at the point of death, new bitterness was added to the poignancy of public grief by the thought that Chester A. Arthur would be his successor. . . . The man to whom the criminal act of Guiteau ought to bring the gravest reflections is the man who has apparently the most to gain from its fatal issue."

Almost every action taken by Arthur in the years after Garfield's death would be criticized automatically by opponents, many of whom included some sort of snide reminder of the assassination in their remarks. For example, when attacking Arthur's veto of the Chinese Exclusion Act, the *Chicago Tribune* sarcastically referred to his veto (which was overridden by Congress) as "another echo from the bulldog pistol of Charles S. Guiteau." Arthur was never able to get out from under the shadow of the assassination, and it served as a backdrop for almost every action he took as president.

"HIS ACCIDENCY"

After Garfield's death, Arthur faced the challenge of taking over the office of the presidency even though he was not considered qualified or experienced enough for the job. He had not served in any elected capacity and as a party man had always received his political jobs from the spoils system. Many in the government and in the press openly feared that he would allow Conkling and the New York Stalwarts to run his administration because they doubted that he would be able stand up against the machine. The anti-Conkling factions were first to attack Arthur about his lack of qualifications. But Conkling's supporters joined in as well after Arthur broke from Conkling and the machine over civil service reform.

This line of attack focused on his legitimacy and underscored and amplified the doubts that the public had toward Arthur and his ability to do the job. Echoing the critics who had nicknamed Rutherford B. Hayes "His Fraudulency" after the 1876 election, the title of "His Accidency" was assigned to Arthur and used frequently in the press. In an example of how the media raised doubts about Arthur being a legitimate president, a columnist wrote: "President Arthur has less moral backing than any President the United States has ever had. I can tell him from considerable intercourse with people in all directions that he is regarded as the first president whom nobody ever thought of in connection with his high office and has increased unconsciously the dignity of that office by his unworthiness to fill it, and coming to it in the way he did."

Another example comes from Andrew Dickson White, who wrote, "It was common saying of that time among those who knew him best, 'Chet Arthur, President of the United States, Good God!'" A *New York Times* editorial had this to say: "Uncompromising partisans have held before now the office of Vice-President of the United States, but no holder of that office has ever made it as plainly subordinate to his self-interest as a politician and his narrowness as a partisan. While his succession to the presidency depends simply on the issue of a strong man's struggle with death, General Arthur is about the last man who would be considered eligible to that position, did the choice depend on the voice either of the majority of his own party or of a majority of the people of the United States." Stories and editorials like the ones above bombarded the Arthur administration. It is not surprising that Arthur's own confidence level was shaken by these attacks and limited his actions as president.

"A VERITABLE CHESTERFIELD": A PLAYBOY PRESIDENT?

Based on many reports, Arthur was a reluctant president. He never expected to become president and was elevated to the office under tragic circumstances that left him governing a shocked and angry country, suspicious and unwilling to give him the benefit of the doubt. He was not prepared to hold the office, and he was often hesitant to act. Although one might expect a new president to learn on the job, to the press and their readers his indecisiveness was portrayed as laziness and apathy.

Arthur also came to the White House as a single gentleman, sparking curiosity about his love life. His wife had died prior to the 1880 campaign, and his sister acted as his first lady and social secretary. He spent much of his first year renovating the White House and the rest of his term hosting social gatherings in it. By many accounts, Arthur enjoyed the social functions of being president more so than governing. Although the press reported on both the political and social events at the White House, they filled their stories with more gossip than news. All the coverage of the soft news made Arthur appear as someone who was more interested in playing than in working. The amount of gossip in the stories—combined with his own actions, such as buying 20 pairs of pants at once or spending time on designing a presidential flag—also served to minimalize his presidency and confirmed to many Americans that scornful nicknames bestowed on him, such as "Gentleman Boss" or "Elegant Arthur," were accurate. These accounts also made him fodder for further negative stories that consistently questioned his work ethic and his accomplishments.

The stories about Arthur's life and experiences in the White House ranged from humorous to extremely harsh. He was attacked at various times as being "shallow and frivolous" or mocked as a "Grown-Up Playboy." For example, *The New York World* criticized some of the expenditures made at the White House, implying that they were unnecessary and referring to them as "domestics ministering to Arthur's personal comfort and allegedly paid for at public expense rather than out of his private purse or salary." His work ethic was questioned continually and demeaned often, even by his staff. *The Chicago Tribune* wrote, "Mr. Arthur's temperament is sluggish. He is indolent. It requires a great deal for him to get to his desk and begin the disposition of business. Great questions of public policy bore him. No President was ever so much given to procrastination as him." *The Philadelphia Times* also commented, "That Arthurism is to share the same destiny of all the previous Presidential accidencies, no intelligent and unbiased observer of political events can doubt." Arthur did not respond well to these criticisms, which further hampered his ability to gain the respect of the people or overcome his playboy image.

LEADING PROPAGATORS

In considering these attacks, both politicians and media were involved. In terms of political actors, Democrats and Garfield supporters were the leading propagators. Democrats were suspicious of Arthur due to his connection to Conkling and the Stalwarts. Many Garfield supporters, reeling from the assassination and resentful of Arthur, were reluctant to defend the new president, and some worked actively against him. Those leading the attacks on Arthur through the 19th-century media were the daily newspapers (in particular the *New York Times, Cincinnati Enquirer, Chicago Tribune, New York Evening Post*, and *New York Tribune*) and weekly magazines (*Harper's Weekly* and *Puck Magazine*). These organizations spent a lot of time criticizing Arthur in both stories and cartoons. They leveled a constant barrage of negative coverage at the Arthur White House with little positive support.

RESPONSES OF THE PRESIDENT AND HIS ALLIES

Arthur was not someone who enjoyed talking to the press or engaging directly with the public. He granted few interviews and refused to discuss political issues. As president, most of his official communication occurred via written messages. As one newspaper, *The Daily Inter Ocean*, pointed out in September 1881, "His manner is courteous and even cordial but nevertheless somewhat reserved. He speaks but little and seemingly with caution." In fact, he was extremely sensitive to newspaper criticism; according to Thomas Reeves, Arthur was "'touchy about his reputation'. . . . Never forgave the press. . . . Every burning cartoon in *Puck* or biting editorial in the *New York Tribune* only caused him to withdraw further. . . . He felt that he had suffered humiliation and slander at hands of journalists." At one point after reading hurtful gossip about his late wife and his children, he snapped that his private life was "nobody's damn business."

Although Arthur was not a regular communicator with the press, some of his supporters were (including Mark Twain). Stories in friendly papers scolded the papers behind the attacks and praised the character of Arthur in hopes of offsetting the negative stories. They commented about how he had grown in the job and how honorable and productive he was. But their defenses of Arthur were not sufficient to change public perceptions.

In examining these lines of attack one can see why Arthur was distrustful of the press. Immediately after Garfield was shot, Arthur was worried about being too visible to the public while Garfield was lingering between life and death. Although some of his advisers wanted him to become acting president, Arthur declined. He did not want to be seen as being power hungry or disrespectful to Garfield. Based on the vitriol of the news stories, he was also in fear for his life. As Reeves states, "Throughout the months that Garfield lay dying, Arthur lived in total seclusion apparently greatly sobered and stunned by the event. Threats to his life were received regularly and he was afraid to appear in public." Arthur's friends and allies attempted to counteract the conspiracy rumors by showing that Arthur was personally affected by the injury and death of Garfield. They also emphasized that he had not wanted to become president, thereby showing he had nothing to gain by participating in a conspiracy against Garfield. For example, his friends reported that after being formally notified of Garfield's death, Arthur was said to have been found sobbing uncontrollably at his desk. This story and the story of Arthur's refusal to take any power during Garfield's struggle were used by his supporters to try to quell the rumors and present the president in a favorable light.

CONCLUSION

Although short in tenure, the Arthur administration did have some limited success. The passage of the Pendleton Act, which brought much-needed civil service reform and led his Stalwart friends to abandon him, is likely the most significant and memorable action by Arthur. The attacks on his work ethic, his qualifications, and his history as a political boss all served to sink his popularity and seemed to sap his energy. His struggle with Bright's disease also had a debilitating effect on his physical ability to be president. But because he was unwilling to publicly disclose his ailment, the press continued to speculate, criticize, and demean him as lazy and indifferent. He was unwilling to talk to the press or the public no matter if his actions were successful or disastrous. Due to the distractions, he was unable to win a second term, thus making his list of accomplishments small and limiting his legacy.

For some presidents, their legacy seems to grow after they leave office, but that was not the case with Arthur. His experiences in the Oval Office do, however, offer lessons about how a president should deal with the press. Since many of the attacks on him were personal, he was unable to counter them by using the traditional presidential communication forms of the era (memos and speeches). By not responding to the charges and not talking to the public directly, Arthur allowed the attacks to fester. His administration might have been more successful if he had responded. Additionally, the attacks on Arthur left future generations with an important lesson about presidential succession and transition. Arthur would not take on the role of "acting president" during Garfield's incapacity because of concerns of legal precedent. Once he became president he faced questions concerning his legitimacy. What these attacks prove is that a vice president who succeeds to the presidency has to combat the issue of legitimacy immediately and directly. Arthur did not, and it overshadowed his presidency and legacy.

Mary McHugh

Further Reading

Doenecke, Justus. *The Presidencies of James A. Garfield and Chester A. Arthur.* Lawrence, KS: University Press of Kansas, 1981.

Howe, George Frederick. *Chester A. Arthur: A Quarter-Century of Machine Politics.* New York: Frederick Ungar Publishing, 1935.

Reeves, Thomas C. *Gentleman Boss: The Life of Chester Alan Arthur.* New York: Alfred A. Knopf, 1975.

Schwartz, Sybil. "In Defense of Chester Arthur." *The Wilson Quarterly,* Vol. 2, No. 4 (1978).

22. [also 24th]. Grover Cleveland

Born: March 18, 1837

Died: June 24, 1908

Time in Office: 22nd President of the United States, March 4, 1885, to March 4, 1889; 24th President of the United States, March 4, 1893, to March 4, 1897

Election Results: 1884 Election: 48.9% of popular vote, 219 (54.6%) Electoral College votes; 1888 Election: 48.6% of popular vote, 168 (41.9%) Electoral College votes; 1892 Election: 46% of popular vote, 277 (62.4%) Electoral College votes

Spouse: Frances Folsom (m. 1886)

Children: Ruth, Ester, Marion, Richard, and Francis

Little in the first 40 some years of Stephen Grover Cleveland's life indicated that he was destined for the White House. As a successful lawyer in a middling firm and former sheriff of Erie County, New York, Cleveland was not undistinguished; but neither was he particularly eminent. Yet, over the span of four short years the Caldwell, New Jersey, native would become mayor of Buffalo, governor of the Empire State, and emerge as a leading Democratic presidential prospect.

Personal qualities interacting with ripe circumstance account for this rise. Cleveland was a staunch opponent of corruption in a corrupt age. He was not afraid to fight the good fight at a time when there were plenty of opportunities to do so. Indeed, as a reformer affiliated with the "Bourbon" faction (fiscally conservative Democrats who supported laissez-faire capitalism and favored reforms in areas such as civil service to minimize political corruption), he quickly developed a reputation for being willing to take on other politicians in the state capital of Albany, from overbearing state house Republicans to crooked Tammany Hall Democrats. (Tammany Hall refers to the Democratic political machine that controlled New York City and state politics throughout the 19th century.) As General Edward S. Bragg of Wisconsin explained at the Democratic National Convention in 1884, Cleveland became loved in New York "for his character, but . . . also for the enemies he has made!"

Undeniably, Cleveland had backbone. Indeed, as Democratic politician Samuel Tilden once mockingly bellowed, Cleveland has so much backbone, "it makes him stick out in front!" Tilden's statement succinctly—and accurately—describes the nation's 22nd (1885–1889) and 24th president (1893–1897). Cleveland was a large man. In tipping the scales at somewhere around 270 pounds on a 5-foot 11-inch frame, "Big Steve" (as Cleveland was intimately known by old friends) ranks second only to William H. Taft as the heaviest man to serve in the White House.

Cleveland never avoided throwing his weight behind what he took to be the principled position and refusing to budge. Indeed, if there is one theme that the remarkably thin scholarly literature on Cleveland agrees upon it is this: the man's claim to fame rests on his reputation for energy, honesty, and steadfast devotion to duty. It is therefore somewhat ironic that Cleveland's penchant for demonstrating his "backbone" served as a double-edged blade. His stubbornness both caught the national public's attention and catapulted him into his first—mostly successful— term as president. But his inflexibility contributed greatly to the coalitional meltdown and hatred that dominated his second term, when political conditions changed and a subtler leadership approach was called for but not provided.

THE PENALTY OF TREASON IS DEATH!

Cleveland flew into his first presidential term (1885–1889) on the gale force winds of anticorruption sentiment sweeping the nation and busily set to work shaking up Washington politics. Most prominently, he astounded everyone with his willingness to unsheathe his veto pen. By the end of his first term, he had vetoed an unprecedented 414 acts of Congress. (For frame of reference, all the presidents before Cleveland had issued a combined total of only 206 vetoes, 93 of which were issued by Ulysses S. Grant.) By the end of 1887, these vetoes led to the severest threats and insults Cleveland experienced in his first presidency.

The chief targets of Cleveland's veto power were minor congressional pension bills for claimants of Civil War disabilities. These special bills embodied a corrupt system of political patronage in which legislators sought to curry favor with voters in home districts and the powerful lobby of the Grand Army of the Republic (GAR), an organization of Union veterans of the Civil War. Under the highly individualized application system, Congress approved far more pension bills than it could reasonably consider, with the result that it supported many patently spurious claims. Cleveland would have none of it. According to biographer Alyn Brodsky, he spent long, tedious hours fastidiously reviewing pension claims and attached to his vetoes "brief, often sarcastic, at times indignant messages" discrediting sham petitions. Cleveland expected his approach to convert true veterans to his side against the GAR's corrupt leadership, and, according to scholar Robert McElroy, he freely resorted to the veto to protect the "pension list of the republic as a roll of honor."

However, the vetoes left the leadership of the GAR with their own axe to grind. Unsurprisingly, the GAR advocated for pensions that would not be subject to challenge. The views of the GAR frequently shepherded the voting preferences of its members, especially in key northern swing states. These veterans embodied a small but potentially decisive voting bloc during an era of elections decided by thin margins. By provoking veterans' resentment, Cleveland's vetoes imperiled future Democratic electoral fortunes.

In early 1887, the legislative contest over pensions climaxed when Congress attempted to get around Cleveland by passing the comprehensive "Blair Bill." It provided pensions for any veteran of an American war with a minimum of 90 days service. Characteristically, Cleveland blocked the bill despite the potentially grave political costs for his party in the upcoming election. As he once remarked, "What is the use of being elected or reelected, unless you stand for something?"

Although Cleveland's veto of the Blair Bill proved popular among the public at large, and temporarily ended this battle with Congress, the GAR leadership doubled-down as a result of the rebuff. Indeed, they retaliated by reminding the country that Cleveland was "a shirker." That is, one who paid another (in Cleveland's case, a Polish immigrant) to substitute for him in the military during the Civil War. In doing so, this special interest group fervently waved "the bloody shirt" of simmering sectional strife in an attempt to boil northern veterans' growing resentment into outright hostility against Cleveland.

The feud with the GAR came to its final dénouement when Cleveland approved General Richard Drum's recommendation to return captured Confederate battle flags, stored in the War Department since the South's defeat, to their respective states. The return of such potently visible symbols of the rebellion provoked fury from northern leaders and veterans. Lucius Fairchild, the national commander of the GAR, lashed out: "May God palsy the hand that wrote that order! May God Palsy the brain that conceived it, and may God palsy the tongue that dictated it!" After the flag return order, the dislike of Cleveland became so palpable among some Union veterans that they refused to march under a banner honoring the commander in chief. The clamor further crescendoed through a series of public and private letters. They denounced Cleveland as a "viper," "traitor," and "hater of Union veterans."

All of this ultimately led to a final, pitched battle between Cleveland and the GAR in St. Louis. The occasion was the group's 1887 annual encampment, which presidents had previously attended. Here leaders of many of the subunits, or "posts," of the Grand Army passed resolutions condemning the president as a traitor and "Catiline" (the latter references conspirators who sought to overthrow the Roman Republic). The Sam Rice Post of Iowa went so far as to instruct its committee to write resolutions "in burning letters of *red* on blood red paper, to enclose them in a blood red envelope and tie with crimson stained ribbon" to demonstrate that: "'The penalty of treason is death.' It is and shall be made odious. The great Grand Army of the Republic have sworn it." These and many similar resolutions presented Cleveland with a dilemma. He could risk insult and possibly bodily harm if he visited the encampment or incur ignominy as a coward if he did not.

The situation called for a lithe touch, but that was not Cleveland's style. He ignored his advisers' recommendation to wait until growing public concern over his safety reached the point that he could change his plans without suffering political damage. Instead, he boldly attacked the GAR to force the lobby on the defensive. Cleveland did this through a public letter to David R. Francis, mayor of St. Louis, that declared that personal threats did not concern him. Instead, Cleveland indicated in the July 4, 1887, letter that he was shocked by the fact that scores of men in the GAR were threatening the dignity of the presidential office. This, Cleveland informed Francis, was unpatriotic. Furthermore, he declared that he was dutybound to protect the virtue of his office by skirting a confrontation with GAR: "The threat of personal violence and harm, in case I undertake the trip in question, which scores of misguided, unbalanced men under the stimulation of excited feeling have made, are not even considered . . . but I should bear with me there the people's highest office the dignity of which I must protect. . . ."

It was only then, after chastising the GAR for its disrespect and asserting that he was acting on principle by not attending, did Cleveland relent and quietly alter his itinerary to avoid the encampment. He additionally relied on a technicality to rescind his order to return Confederate battle flags to the South. Instead, he asked Congress to take up the issue. In doing all of this, Cleveland both knocked the GAR back on its heels and largely won over public support for himself.

If, however, Cleveland had hoped to win over northern veterans through his tactical thrust and strategic withdrawal, he was wrong. Ultimately, the GAR was able to keep Union Army veterans in a hostile stance against Cleveland. Indeed, it is fair to conclude that the special interest group generated enough hatred of the president to contribute to Cleveland's narrow electoral defeats in the critical states of New York and Indiana during his failed 1888 presidential bid.

"I HATE THE GROUND THAT MAN WALKS ON"

However, Cleveland was not finished. He would return to Washington in 1893 by winning his electoral rematch against incumbent Republican president Benjamin Harrison. This, of course, made Cleveland the 24th president of the United States and the only man in history to serve two nonconsecutive terms.

Cleveland's second term (1893–1897) opened with the bright promise of opportunity. The Populist (People's Party) revolt was in full bloom, and a crisis of confidence in Republican governance was sweeping the country. Indeed, the GOP's electoral losses in the midterm election of 1890 were staggering. Republicans went from holding 169 seats in the House of Representatives (a thin majority) to only 88. With Cleveland's inauguration Democrats additionally won the Senate and attained unified control of government for the first time since before the Civil War.

However, before Cleveland could even get the drapes remeasured for his White House study (known at this time as the "Yellow Oval Room" before later renovations added the West Wing and Oval Office), fate would deal him a cruel hand—in the form of the Panic of 1893. This economic depression struck just as Cleveland was taking office. It hit the nation hard, becoming the worst downturn to rack the United States up to that point in its history. Cleveland's uncompromising leadership in the face of this exogenous shock generated acute antagonisms between him, his party, and the American public. Indeed, Cleveland's penchant for demonstration of backbone engendered so much life-threatening hatred that it led to the advent of Secret Service protection.

Early in the summer of 1893, the president called a special session of Congress to deal with the economic emergency. The president's response menu comprised two objects of potential legislation: stabilizing the value of currency and tariff reform. Cleveland not only mistakenly selected to tackle the highly contentious currency issue first, but he demanded the Democratic Congress repeal the Sherman Silver Purchase Act of 1890—without condition or compromise. Naturally, Cleveland felt he was standing on principle. He was, after all, a probusiness Bourbon Democrat from New York. Within this faction, it was simply believed to be a matter of sound economics to support the Gold Standard when the nation's gold reserves were declining (as they were).

From a purely economic perspective, it is not clear that Cleveland was wrong in thinking this. However, this was not the only issue at hand. Within western and southern Democratic ranks, an inflationary silver-based monetary policy commanded its own influential constituency. Allowing for currency to be redeemed in silver as well as gold was beneficial not only to mining states but to farmers and other debtors. As a result, silver repeal became stalemated in the Senate for three long months while intercoalitional tensions steadily mounted within Cleveland's own party. Nevertheless, Cleveland stuck to script and eschewed compromise. Instead, he used every resource within his arsenal of patronage in a relentless campaign to subdue "Silverite" Democrats' reluctance to support his policy response to the economic crisis.

Still, unconditional repeal of the Silver Act threatened a party split by forcing Democratic representatives from some of the most economically hard-pressed regions to go against their constituents' preferences. As a result, just before the final vote on the measure, Democratic caucus chairman Arthur Gorman of Iowa and other Senate leaders balked. They wrote to Cleveland recommending a compromise plan that would keep some degree of "bimetallism."

Cleveland, however, would have none of this. In fact, he immediately called his cabinet together to let them know of his hostile feelings toward the senators' proposal. He began the meeting by abruptly slamming his fist on the table. Then, he roared: "I will not yield an inch!" And, he did not. Indeed, Cleveland did not budge.

Instead, he stood fast and bent the will of Congress to his liking. They assented to repeal shortly thereafter. However, the fallout proved grave. Not only did the return to the Gold Standard have little immediate impact on the faltering economy, but it was obtained at the cost of provoking intense animosity toward Cleveland within Democratic ranks. Gorman immediately told confidants that he now felt nothing but disgust for Cleveland—a feeling that was mutual. Most famously, Alabama senator John T. Morgan summarized the opinions of many by declaring: "I hate the ground that man walks on."

Cleveland did not have to wait long to suffer the consequences of the discontent he had sown within his own party ranks by forcing silver repeal. Tariff reform was next on Cleveland's agenda. And Gorman was now hell-bent on keeping Cleveland from achieving his potentially transformative reduction plans. As a result, the Senator from Iowa led an insurgency of eight key Democrats to block passage of the version of the tariff bill that carried Cleveland's preferences within it. Instead, Gorman cobbled together another bill comprising a patchwork of compromises and protections for special interests. This bill predictably infuriated Cleveland.

Unsurprisingly, Cleveland did not respond to the Senate's rejection by changing course and seeking intraparty reconciliation. Rather, like in his response to the GAR, Cleveland attempted to explode a mine underneath the feet of his opponents—who just happened to be fellow Democrats. With Cleveland's assent, Representative William L. Wilson read a letter to Congress written by the president inveighing Gorman's bill as a product of "party perfidy and party dishonor." Cleveland's letter fell on deafened ears.

If Cleveland thought he could browbeat a coequal branch of government into submission, like he might a special interest group, he was gravely wrong. Rather than inducing senators in his party to return to the fold, Cleveland's insistence on demonstrating backbone only increased their ire. They felt that norms of respect had been violated and the Constitution's separation of powers scheme undermined. As a result, Gorman launched what Alyn Brodsky described as "the most bellicose attack ever delivered on the Senate floor by a member against the leader of his own party."

The counterattack worked. Cleveland permanently lost the support of many Democratic elites. Perhaps even more importantly, the broader public also turned against Cleveland for the first time in his short political career. For example, scores of hostile letters from members of the public deluged the White House. They were often vitriolic, denouncing Cleveland as "traitor, Judas, and friends of financial bloodsuckers." One suspicious-looking package addressed to Cleveland was even discovered to contain a bomb.

This was not the first time, nor was it the last, someone tried to kill Cleveland and/or hurt members of his family. Economic depression had caused hundreds of banks to close and thousands of farms and shops to go out of business. The percentage of those unemployed skyrocketed into the double digits. And, as is often the case when millions of Americans are hurting and frustrated, the president became the literal target of discontent.

Public resentment boiled into a highly visible threat just barely into the second year of Cleveland's second term. Jacob S. Coxey, a political agitator from Ohio, famously led an "army" of the disgruntled unemployed numbering in the thousands. The movement, which came to be known as Coxey's Army, formed in "divisions" and "regiments" of hundreds throughout the western states. These detachments marched on foot, rafted down rivers, and commandeered trains across the country to converge on the nation's capital. In the process, they unsettled townspeople and local constabularies along their routes. This "petition in boots" embodied a highly visible and potentially violent opposition to Cleveland's staunch policies.

On a tense morning in May 1894, "General" Coxey marched an advance guard of several hundred straight down Pennsylvania Avenue directly in front of the White House and on toward the Capitol steps. On this day, the White House took on the character of a besieged encampment. Special telephone lines stood by to call in any needed police reserves, the largest assemblage of police and bodyguards since the Civil War surrounded Cleveland, and a newly installed guardhouse sheltered officers posted to continuously guard the approach to the White House. The arrest of Coxey (for walking on the Capitol lawn's grass) dissipated this Populist challenge to the president. However, while this highly visible menace subsided, seething public hostility against Cleveland remained palpable. Protecting the president and his family from threats became a growing problem. By January 1894, in response to the swelling number of threats, Cleveland's wife Frances had persuaded him to allow his private secretary, Henry T. Thurber, to increase security of the White House from three to 24 guards. At the time, the Washington metropolitan police provided these guards, but already the steadily growing number and extent of sources of threats drew more agencies into presidential protection.

One such threat had been brewing in Lyons, Colorado. Two Secret Service agents uncovered the plot by gamblers to assassinate the president. Acting quickly, Secret Service Chief William Hazen transferred the agents to Washington with orders to intercept any suspicious characters and especially western dissidents. This expediency sparked the Secret Service's later permanent responsibility for presidential protection. Initially, the agents' vigilance protected the president only in his movements around Washington. But when Frances Cleveland learned of a plot to kidnap their children from their summer home in Massachusetts, the protection was extended.

CONCLUSION

By the end of his second term, Cleveland was not only nearly friendless in his party but felt he was a virtual prisoner to his guards. Such was the final, sad, legacy of a president whose dedication to principle lifted him from obscurity. Yet, it was Cleveland's obstinate penchant for displaying his "backbone" that ultimately contributed to the hatred aimed at the only president to serve two, nonconsecutive terms in the White House.

Curt Nichols and Jeremy Schmuck

Further Reading

Ayton, Mel. *Plotting to Kill the President: Assassination Attempts from Washington to Hoover.* Lincoln, NE: Potomac Books, 2017.

Brodsky, Alyn. *Grover Cleveland: A Study in Character.* New York: St. Martin's Press, 2000.

Cleveland, S. Grover. *Presidential Problems.* Freeport, NY: Books for Libraries Press, 1904.

DeSantis, Vincent P. "Grover Cleveland: Another Look." *Hayes Historical Journal,* Vol. 3, Nos. 1–2 (1980): 41–50.

McElroy, Robert. *Grover Cleveland: The Man and the Statesman,* 2 vols. New York: Harper & Brothers, 1923.

McMurry, Donald L. "The Political Significance of the Pension Question, 1885–1897." *The Mississippi Valley Historical Review,* Vol. 9, No. 1 (June 1922): 19–36.

Melanson, Philip H., and Peter F. Stevens. *Secret Service: The Hidden History of an Enigmatic Agency.* New York: Barnes & Noble Books, 2002.

Merrill, Horace S. *Bourbon Leader: Grover Cleveland and the Democratic Party.* Boston: Little, Brown, and Company, 1957.

Nevins, Allan. *Grover Cleveland: A Study in Courage.* New York: Dodd, Mead & Company, 1932.

Schwantes, Carlos A. *Coxey's Army: An American Odyssey.* Lincoln, NE: University of Nebraska Press, 1985.

Tugwell, Rexford G. *Grover Cleveland.* New York: Macmillan, 1968.

Welch, Richard E., Jr. *The Presidencies of Grover Cleveland.* Lawrence, KS: University Press of Kansas, 1988.

23. Benjamin Harrison

Born: August 20, 1833

Died: March 13, 1901

Time in Office: 23rd President of the United States, March 4, 1889, to March 4, 1893

Election Results: 1888 Election: 47.8% of popular vote, 233 (58.1%) Electoral College votes; 1892 Election: 43% of popular vote, 145 (32.7%) Electoral College votes

Spouse: Caroline Scott (m. 1853), Mary Scott Lord (m. 1896)

Children: Russell, Mary, and Elizabeth

Benjamin Harrison was born in North Bend, Ohio, in 1833. The grandson of William Henry Harrison, the ninth president of the United States, Harrison was born into a politically prominent family. Harrison was a Union general, an elder in the Presbyterian Church, an Indiana gubernatorial nominee, and a senator from Indiana before running for president. He served in the White House from 1889 to 1893, besting Democratic incumbent Grover Cleveland 233–168 in the Electoral College in 1888 despite losing to him by 100,000 popular votes. Harrison and his wife Caroline had a daughter Mary McGee, who along with her two children joined her parents in the White House. Their son, Russell Harrison, his wife May, and their daughter Marthena were also frequent guests at the Executive Mansion. Caroline died tragically near the end of his term of tuberculous. His wife's death and a fractured Republican Party cost him reelection in 1892, when Cleveland became the first (and only) person in U.S. history to be elected to two nonconsecutive terms in the White House. Harrison lost the Electoral College 145–277 and the popular vote 43% to 46% in 1892. The fledging Populist Party took 22 Electoral College votes and 8.5% of the popular vote.

POLITICS OF THE GILDED AGE

Politics of the late 19th century were dominated by questions regarding sectionalism, the tariff, and upheaval wrought by urbanization and industrialization. Though typically thought of as a Republican era, with only two Democrats being elected to the White House between Abraham Lincoln and Herbert Hoover, the country was close to evenly divided in terms of party affiliation during this period. National elections were decided by thin margins and driven in large part by sectional loyalties, forcing presidents of the time to walk a fine line in fulfilling campaign promises and not alienating swing voters for the next election.

The press, though slowly professionalizing and becoming more objective, retained much of its partisan flavor with many newspapers representing one party or the other. In this pre-radio age, the newspaper was the only way to connect with any meaningful segment of the public. Newspaper editors were powerful figures who often weighed in on politics vigorously. Political satire in the form of cartoons was also popular. Fittingly, most criticism that Harrison faced as president emanated from the Democratic press and from his Democratic rivals, though he also faced attacks from within his own party. For the most part, as was the custom of the day, Republican papers supported the president; Democratic ones denounced him; and the independent press was indifferent to a president they saw as insignificant.

The 51st U.S. Congress, swept into power in 1889 with Harrison, represented the first instance of unified Republican rule in more than a decade. This turned out to be both a blessing and a curse for the party. Congress, often acting in concert with Harrison, was one of the most productive in history. It passed several pieces of landmark legislation, including the McKinley Tariff Act, the Sherman Antitrust Act, and the Meat Inspection Act. However, these legislative triumphs opened the Republican Party to various criticisms from members of their own party who opposed such interventionist policies and contributed to historic losses in the 1890 midterm elections. Once Harrison lost his Republican majority in Congress, he found it much harder to accomplish his stated goals.

One of the easiest lines of attacks that newspapers pursued against Harrison included the circumstances under which Harrison had won the presidency. *The Nation* was fond of referring to Harrison as a nominal candidate or the "caretaker of the White House" because of the contentious nature of his nomination (a significant segment of the Republican Party wanted James Blaine as their nominee) and his popular vote loss. Harrison had a generally difficult relationship with the press and thought of them as "cruel, unfair, and discourteous" to both himself and his wife during their time in the White House. Caroline Harrison agreed and frequently commented that she was "being made a circus of" by the press.

HIS GRANDFATHER'S HAT

Criticism of Harrison began before he even became president. Harrison, a gifted speaker, gave campaign speeches from the front porch of his home in Indianapolis. Democrats created a slogan, "His Grandfather's Hat: It's Too Big for Him" and song by a similar name suggesting that Harrison was unable to live up to the legacy of his grandfather, President William Henry Harrison. Republicans attempted to co-opt this criticism by making it their own with the slogan and song, "The Same Old Hat: It Fits Just Right." The magazine *Harper's Weekly* published a cartoon in September 1888 that showed the candidate wearing a hat that was too large. Talk of his grandfather's hat persisted in both the Democratic and Republican press throughout Harrison's presidency. Democratic papers complained that the hat was too large and down around his shoulders while Republicans papers confidently asserted that the hat fit well. Highlighting the ongoing discussions of the "hat" analogy, the *Washington Post* even published a story which reminded readers that Harrison did not literally wear his grandfather's beaver hat but instead made a more contemporary and fashionable choice.

Harrison's appearance was also maligned. He was short at just 5 feet 6 inches, and Democratic papers disparagingly called him "little Ben." Harrison's height led many of his contemporaries to satirize him as a "powerless political pygmy." Some cartoonists combined both images and depicted Harrison as a little man standing in the shadow of his grandfather's large hat.

Lastly, although he was known as a gifted orator, many of Harrison's contemporaries were less than enamored of his prickly personality. This factor, combined with his unwillingness to engage in the politics of patronage, made it difficult for Harrison to curry favor with newspapermen and political bosses.

THE SOUTHERN QUESTION

Perhaps the most significant and difficult question that Harrison faced as president was that of race relations. With Reconstruction ended and African Americans being systematically disenfranchised in many southern states, Harrison and the Republicans had both moral and political incentives to intervene. Harrison and Republican representatives in Congress crafted legislation such as the Blair Bill and the Federal Elections Bill, which would eventually become pejoratively known as the "Force Bill," to address issues of racial injustice. The Force Bill allowed for federal oversight of elections in an attempt to protect newly enfranchised black Americans. The Blair Bill strove to provide federal support for education and was widely seen as being aimed at former slaves in the South. Southern Democrats moved quickly to block these proposals by playing to racial fears and resentments.

Democratic papers reacted passionately to Harrison's support of and attempts to pass a third bill, known as the Lodge Election Bill. Editors accused him of wanting to "colonize" the South with "negro votes." They also accused him of being a con man who used falsehoods to rally support for these proposed laws. As the *St. Paul Daily Globe* wrote on December 11, 1890, "Benjamin Harrison pleads the cause of the force bill with all the fervor and sweltering eloquence of a country shyster in a justice court defending a hog thief."

Many papers criticized Harrison as a sectionalist who did not care about southern concerns. In June 1892, for example, *The State Chronicle* of Raleigh, North Carolina, urged Harrison's defeat in the upcoming presidential election. The paper declared that he would not be fair to the South, that he embodied a hostile southern policy, and that his "high tariffs and money standards are destructive to the liberty of the country. . . ." The paper also asserted that the only peace that the Force Bill would bring to the South "would be the peace that destroyed Roman liberty, blotted out the existence of Poland, extinguished Hungarian freedom and exiled Kossuth its gallant victory. This is the peace to which Harrison and his minions would invite us." Other southern papers agreed with *The State Chronicle*'s assessment of Harrison's "hatred" of the South.

Criticism of the Election's Bill was not limited to the South, however. Big city bosses expressed concerns about how the law would affect their cities, and the growing Farmers Alliance Party in the Midwest questioned whether only Republicans would benefit from federal oversight of elections. Other reformers were concerned about unforeseen consequences of the legislation. The opposition proved fierce, and the Lodge Election Bill never made it past the congressional floor.

As had become the custom of the day, Harrison set out on numerous tours to interact with the public and to address the important political questions of the day. On his southern tour of 1891, Harrison made some efforts to address the topic of racial injustice. Editors of southern newspapers, though, pilloried Harrison whenever he suggested protecting former slaves' right to vote or providing them with adequate educational opportunities. Citizens protested too. During a stop in Texarkana, Texas, the band receiving the president played Dixie and hecklers shouted as he spoke.

At the same time, the African American press criticized Harrison for not doing more for their community on issues of race. Just one month after the inauguration, Frederick Douglass criticized the administration's "lack of vigor and courage in enforcing the law." The *Indianapolis Freeman* revived the campaign criticism of Harrison's appearance and referred to him as "Harrison the short." African American voters were particularly distressed over the defeat of the Federal Elections Bill and criticized Harrison vigorously in the aftermath. These tensions were exacerbated when Douglass announced that he would resign from his position as ambassador to Haiti, and Harrison's cabinet pushed for a white replacement. In the end, Harrison filled the post with a light-skinned black man, John S. Durham.

PATRONAGE

One of the issues that plagued many presidents of this era was patronage. In fact, some scholars argue that Harrison's appointments brought him more negative attention from the media than anything else he did. Pressure was building on presidents during this time to enact some form of civil service reform, and Harrison feared that giving any state-level boss a cabinet-level post might aggrieve reformers. This strategy, however, had significant political consequences for Harrison.

Harrison had trouble on this front from the beginning. Blaine and his supporters expected him to get the secretary of state job, but Harrison was reluctant to make Blaine too powerful so the president-elect dragged the nomination process out for almost two months. In addition to frustrating Blaine, Harrison failed to tap any prominent Republican leaders for any of the other seven cabinet positions. Though Harrison assembled a cabinet he felt comfortable with, his slights of Republican political bosses cost him dearly, not just in his electoral loss in 1892 but more immediately in the battle over patronage.

Members of the party and those that helped the president get elected expected to receive political positions in exchange for their loyalty. Harrison replaced many Cleveland Democrats with Republicans but was unable to please everyone. Appointments that should have allowed Harrison to grow his influence within the

Republican Party instead left many unhappy and disaffected. The *New York Times* published stories about hostility among state Republicans, particularly in Indiana, who were disappointed that they had not received more positions in the new government. The appointments in Indiana, charged the *Times,* did not show "regard for decency and honesty."

A number of strong Republican leaders engaged in disputes with Harrison that began over issues of patronage. Included in this group were powerful figures such as Senator Thomas Platt of New York, Senator Matthew Quay of Pennsylvania, and Speaker of the House Thomas Reed of Maine. These men, along with former First Assistant Postmaster General James S. Clarkson, organized a Grievance Committee against Harrison. The president of Harvard College gave a public speech announcing that he was changing parties because of Harrison's policy positions on civil service reform, among other issues. These public attacks motivated Harrison to run for a second term, something he had not intended to do.

Harrison, a devoted Presbyterian, was even criticized in church. As political cartoonists depicted, Harrison was given a lecture from the pulpit by Episcopal bishop Henry Codman Potter during a service celebrating the centennial of George Washington's birth. Potter addressed Harrison, who was in the congregation, with the following: "The concept of the national government as a huge machine, existing mainly for the purpose of rewarding partisan serve—this was a conception so alien to the character and conduct of Washington and his associates that it seems grotesque even to speak of it. It would be interesting to imagine the first president of the United States confronted with someone who had ventured to approach him upon the basis of what is now commonly called 'practical politics.'"

OTHER CONTROVERSIES

During the summer of 1890, John Wanamaker and other Harrison supporters from Pennsylvania purchased a lot in Cape May. On this land, Wanamaker built a summer home for the Harrisons. This gift became the subject of criticism against the Harrison family. Even after Harrison sent Wanamaker $10,000 to pay for the house, the controversy continued. An opera singer in Chicago even added a verse to one of his songs calling out the president for the house in Cape May.

Harrison was also criticized for the handling of Civil War pensions. The president believed in a liberal interpretation of the law and chose James Tanner, who had similar views, to run the pension bureau. When Tanner proved to be excessively liberal in his dispersal of pensions, however, Democrats pounced, calling Tanner the "personification of Republican recklessness with the people's treasury." Harrison was forced to replace Tanner in September 1889. This appeased some critics but aroused the ire of veterans who felt that Tanner had done right by them. Harrison's second choice, Green B. Raum, was also a veteran but had a more conservative interpretation of the pension system. As a result, the Harrison administration found itself fending off charges that it was being too miserly with deserving military veterans. On October 17, 1892, for example, the *New York Times* criticized Harrison's Pension Bureau for rejecting "thousands of meritorious claims."

THE SILVER QUESTION AND THE TARIFF

The two economic questions that dominated the era surrounded protectionism and the coinage of money. The Republican Party had long championed a protective tariff to help American industry and a reliable currency that allowed greenbacks and silver to be interchanged with gold.

With Harrison's support, Republicans in Congress worked diligently to pass the McKinley Tariff Act. Passed in 1890, this legislation increased protective rates to nearly 50% on many goods. Harrison also lobbied for reciprocity, which let him negotiate rates with foreign governments. The tariff bill soon gained a reputation as being a boon to wealthy industrialists rather than average Americans. The *New York Times*, on September 2, 1892, called out Harrison for his failure "to enact laws providing for the free and unrestricted coinage of silver." Silverites on both parties criticized the president for not supporting the free coinage of silver.

Harrison's position and subsequent legislation on these two issues cost the president important votes in the Midwest. The growing Populist and Farmer's Alliance Parties drew support from aggrieved farmers and workers who had been hurt by these new initiatives. Harrison attempted to staunch losses by touring the Midwest before the 1890 midterm elections, but as noted earlier, the Republicans lost both congressional majorities. Harrison devoted significant time to both issues in his acceptance speech for the nomination in 1892. However, the president was unable to overcome the money question, and his position on silver likely cost him Colorado, Idaho, and Kansas.

CONCLUSION

Harrison endured criticism on a wide range of issues, including his perceived inability to live up to his grandfather's legacy, his support for African American rights, his handling of patronage, the distribution of Civil War pensions, the tariff, and the silver question. This criticism came mostly from Democrats and opposition newspapers. However, Harrison's aversion to doling out political spoils hurt him in his own party as well. Despite having a majority in Congress and passing significant legislation, Harrison was unable to translate legislative success into electoral victory in the midterm election and in his own attempt at winning a second term. This disconnect can be blamed on the close divisions in the electorate and Harrison's inability to unite the Republican Party behind his reelection efforts. Harrison also endured criticism from African American thought leaders and newspapers because of his unwillingness to take a more definitive stand on issues of civil rights. Harrison and his wife, Caroline, were sensitive to criticism and found it difficult to bear at times.

Anne C. Pluta

Further Reading

Calhoun, Charles W. *Benjamin Harrison: The American Presidents Series: The 23rd President, 1889–1893*. New York: Times Books, 2005.

Calhoun, Charles W. *From Bloody Shirt to Full Dinner Pail: The Transformation of Politics and Governance in the Gilded Age*. New York: Hill and Wang, 2011.

Frantz, Edward O. *The Door of Hope: Republican Presidents and the First Southern Strategy, 1877–1933*. Gainesville, FL: University Press of Florida, 2011.

Socolofsky, Homer E., and Allan B. Spence. *The Presidency of Benjamin Harrison*. Lawrence, KS: University Press of Kansas, 1987.

25. William McKinley

Born: January 29, 1843

Died: September 14, 1901

Time in Office: 25th President of the United States, March 4, 1897, to September 14, 1901

Election Results: 1896 Election: 51.1% of popular vote, 271 (61%) Electoral College votes; 1900 Election: 51.7% of popular vote, 292 (65.3%) Electoral College votes

Spouse: Ida Saxton (m. 1871)

Children: Katherine and Ida

Ohio native William McKinley was a veteran of the Union Army, congressman, and governor from Ohio before becoming the 25th president of the United States on March 4, 1897. During his time in Congress, McKinley gained a reputation as an expert on the tariff. The tariff was one of the leading economic issues of the late 19th century. McKinley shepherded through protective legislation bearing his name in 1890. However, his position on the tariff likely cost him reelection to Congress in the same year because the tariff had significantly raised the price of foreign goods. This development was welcomed by American businesses, but consumers, for the most part, hated it. The economic Panic of 1893, however, made McKinley's protectionist position much more palatable by the time of his presidential run.

McKinley's so-called front porch campaign (in which he remained close to home while campaigning, as opposed to traveling around the country) of 1896 propelled him to a victory over famed Democratic orator William Jennings Bryan. McKinley won more than 7 million popular votes, while Bryan won just under 6.5 million. The margin in the Electoral College was 271 to 176. Almost 80% of eligible Americans voted in this hotly contested election. McKinley won a historic reelection in 1900, becoming the first Republican president since Ulysses S. Grant to be reelected. His popularity had soared in the aftermath of the Spanish-American War and because of the return of economic prosperity. The president increased his margin over Bryan, winning the Electoral College 292 to 155 and winning the popular vote by almost 1 million votes. The election of 1900 signaled an end to the razor-thin electoral margins of the post–Civil War era.

Joining McKinley in the White House was his wife, Ida Saxton McKinley. She suffered from phlebitis and epileptic seizures and was for all intents and purposes an invalid. Before becoming seriously ill, Ida McKinley bore two children. However, one died as an infant and the other by the age of five. The public at the time knew little of her illness, but what was known made her and her husband sympathetic figures. The president was often portrayed as a devoted husband to his ailing wife.

McKinley had an affable personality that made him easy to like, even for his opponents. His cordiality led some people to criticize him for being too friendly and not really having any firm convictions. However, historians have found this claim to be without merit and instead see McKinley as a skillful politician who was simply temperamentally cautious and paid close attention to public opinion.

In combination with newly established Republican electoral dominance and America's ascension onto the world stage because of the Spanish-American War, McKinley, for the most part, escaped serious criticism during his time as president. The criticism he did face came from his Democratic opponents, the African American press and community, and those opposed to American expansion in the Philippines.

POLITICS OF THE LATE 19TH CENTURY

Following Grover Cleveland's weak second term and his repudiation at the polls in 1896, the balance of the prior two-and-a-half decades was decisively tipped in the direction of the Republicans. The party of Lincoln benefited from the Cleveland administration's economic missteps and the end of the depression of the mid-1890s.

The tariff question and the economy were top concerns of both voters and elected officials when McKinley entered the White House. McKinley's position of protectionism and the gold standard seemed like prudent choices in the aftermath of the Panic of 1893 and ensuing economic collapse. In addition, industrialization had led to concern about trusts and monopolies and their role in the country's economy.

Despite these pressing economic concerns, foreign policy took center stage during McKinley's presidency with the beginning of the Spanish-American war in 1898. McKinley looked to cultivate a closer and more productive relationship with the press than Cleveland had enjoyed. McKinley was genial and encouraged reporters to set up shop in the White House. This cordial behavior allowed McKinley to cultivate much more favorable coverage than Cleveland had experienced. Moreover, the press was continuing to professionalize and commercialize. At the same time, the partisan press of the 19th century was in decline. A new approach to reporting, called yellow journalism, which relied on sensationalism to drive newspaper sales, grew significantly during McKinley's presidency.

Political cartoons remained an important vehicle used by newspapers to criticize politicians, including presidents. McKinley was the subject of a number of attacks via the political cartoon. Perhaps one of McKinley's most vocal critics in this medium was Memphis-based cartoonist M. B. Trezevant. On January 17, 1900, the *Harlequin* published what it considered a retrospective on Trezevant's best work. Most of these cartoons were critical of McKinley, particularly for his role in expanding the American empire and for his association with big business. A number of these drawings depicted McKinley as a monarch gleefully conquering the world with disastrous consequences. Another theme common in many of the editorial cartoons of this era was the depiction of McKinley genuflecting in the presence of the "Almighty Dollar" or worshiping at the temple of Trusts.

MARK HANNA

The issue on which McKinley probably received the most criticism was his relationship with Ohio industrialist Mark Hanna. The opposition press was fond of portraying McKinley as an "unwitting Stooge to Hanna the money man." This vitriol included a cartoon that depicted McKinley as a ventriloquist's dummy sitting on Hanna's lap. Another drawing showed Hanna alone "as a hulking figure garbed in a loud suit whose pattern was made up of dollar marks." *New York Journal* cartoonist Homer Davenport was especially brutal, drawing one cartoon that depicted McKinley tucked in Hanna's belt with his feet shackled.

Criticism of McKinley's relationship with Hanna became even more focused when Senator John Sherman of Ohio was appointed secretary of state. Many saw Sherman as past his prime physically and mentally, and they viewed his appointment as a way to install Hanna to Sherman's vacated Senate seat. McKinley responded to this line of attack regarding Sherman's appointment by writing a letter to the editor of the *Chicago Tribune*. In this letter, the president wrote that stories about Sherman's mental decline were "without foundation" and the "cheap invention of sensational writers and other evil-disposed or mistaken people." However, McKinley had failed to check on Sherman's condition himself or ask family members about the senator's health. Sherman's diminished capacity became increasingly obvious to McKinley and other cabinet members. By April 1898, the president was forced to secure Sherman's resignation.

RACE RELATIONS

Some of McKinley's most vocal and consistent critics were the editors of African American newspapers. By the close of the 19th century, the Republican Party no longer showed much enthusiasm for protecting the rights of African Americans in the South, where Jim Crow laws and systematic disenfranchisement were taking a heavy toll. In an effort to break the Democrats' hold on elected offices in the South, the Republicans authored a new strategy that included demurring to white southerners on issues of race. McKinley took two tours of the South and both times applied this strategy in both his rhetoric and his actions.

McKinley's southern tour of 1898 took place in the wake of the resounding victory in the Spanish-American War, which had ushered in intense feelings of national pride and unity. Many observers realized that the victory in war presented the country an opportunity to overcome the regional divide that had plagued the United States since the end of the Civil War. As McKinley toured the South, he was greeted by large celebrations of national unity that implied sectional reconciliation. Moreover, McKinley made a number of decisions during his tours, which were seen as signals to white southerners that the administration was ambivalent at best about protecting African Americans. One of the most controversial moments came when McKinley put on a Confederate badge that a veteran of the Civil War presented him in Macon, Georgia. The president tried to quiet the storm by making light of the incident in a letter to the *Cleveland Plain Dealer*. White southern editors were heartened by McKinley's actions on tour, which they perceived as tacit approval for subjugation of African American rights.

At the same time, McKinley and Republicans were silent on episodes of racial violence in the South. Lynching remained a serious threat to African Americans below the Mason-Dixon Line, with almost 100 being murdered by that method in 1898 alone. McKinley's visible inaction on issues of racial violence angered the northern and African American press. After a violent race riot in Wilmington, North Carolina, which left at least eight African Americans dead and hundreds displaced, African American citizens and editors criticized McKinley for not speaking out to support black rights in the South. Citizens wrote the president letters asking for his intervention in bringing the perpetuators in Wilmington to justice. The president made no comment on the event and made no effort to show support for black southerners. Critics in the African American press were further disappointed when McKinley failed to address the riot or any racial issues in his annual message of 1898. McKinley's actions and perhaps more importantly his inactions left members of the African American community and advocates of racial justice feeling abandoned by the president and his party.

WILLIAM RANDOLPH HEARST

McKinley, though generally well liked, had a powerful and vocal enemy in New York publishing giant William Randolph Hearst, publisher of the *New York Journal.* Hearst had inherited a huge sum of money from his mother and spent liberally on the paper. In an effort to drive sales, Hearst and other publishers specialized in what came to be widely known as yellow journalism. This new approach to reporting relied on sensationalism and exaggeration. In the run up to the Spanish-American War, the *New York Journal* and other similar outlets worked hard to build public support for the war. In this effort, Hearst criticized McKinley regularly in print. Famously, Hearst published a letter written by Spanish ambassador Dupuy de Lome that painted McKinley in an extremely unflattering light, calling him "weak" and a "bidder for the admiration of the crown." Some historians viewed these efforts by Hearst and others as important in pushing McKinley into war. However, this view has undergone revision and instead most scholars now feel the president made his own decision. Once the war started, Hearst sensationalized it and was able to build a media empire.

After the war ended, Hearst continued to malign McKinley. On April 10, 1901, Hearst's paper published an editorial that ended with the line: "Institutions, like men, will last until they die and if bad institutions and bad men can be got rid of only by killing, then the killing must be done." In June, Hearst published a suggestion that sometimes assassination was a good thing. When McKinley was killed in September 1901 by Leon Czolgosz, some blamed Hearst and his paper for encouraging the assassin.

THE SPANISH-AMERICAN WAR

The events leading up to the Spanish-American War began in 1895 as Cuba revolted against Spanish rule. During his presidency, Grover Cleveland had encouraged the Spanish to reach a settlement but to no avail. Once president, McKinley increased pressure on Spain to find a way to end the conflict peacefully. The McKinley administration was criticized for proceeding too slowly with Cuba and working with European financial interests to prevent Cuban independence. However, the publication of the Spanish ambassador's letter and the mysterious sinking in a Cuban harbor of the USS *Maine,* an American warship, helped crystalize public opinion in favor of Cuban independence, even if it meant going to war with Spain to secure it. The United States entered the war in April 1898.

The Spanish-American War presented the country with its most serious national crisis since the Civil War. Not surprisingly, the country for the most part rallied around the president. There were a few critics that feared McKinley's association with business and holders of Spanish bonds would lead him to accept a peaceful solution that hurt the Cubans. Another fear was that the president would be "too reluctant or timid to act with firmness towards Spain." However, most of the public and newspaper editors supported expansion, and few spoke out against McKinley.

Instead, critics turned toward Secretary of War Russell A. Alger, who was criticized for the conditions soldiers endured in temporary quarantine camps in which they had been housed upon returning home in order to ensure that any diseases contracted in Cuba did not spread to the general public. Democrats were eager to capitalize on these miscalculations and run on "the woeful failure of the Administration to provide proper food, sanitary conditions, clothing and hospital service from the beginning to the end of the war." A congressional inquiry into the performance of Alger and his department was also undertaken. In an attempt to protect his own image, McKinley toured one of these camps—a facility on Long Island called Camp Wikoff—on September 3, 1898, and invited the press to report on the event. During the peace negotiations, the issue of the Philippines grew increasingly important, as this large group of islands in the western Pacific had come to be regarded by the United States as an important economic and military asset in that region of the world. The Treaty of Paris included the transfer of the Philippines to the United States in exchange for $25 million. McKinley went on a tour in late 1898 to advocate for keeping the Philippines. This tour took place in September after the fighting between U.S. and Spanish forces had ended but before the peace treaty had been signed. On this tour, McKinley encountered large and supportive crowds. The Anti-Imperialist League formed a vocal opposition against McKinley's policy on the Philippines. In conferences across the country, the league adopted resolutions calling for the halt of military activities in the Philippines. As the *New York Times* reported on February 23, 1900, members of the group denounced McKinley's position and called the president a "murderer." At a similar gathering in Cooperstown, New York, speakers blamed the war and conditions in the Philippines squarely on McKinley. Southern Democrats and other Americans objected to the acquisition of the Philippines on the grounds of racial superiority. McKinley tried to neutralize this opposition by sending an outspoken anti-imperialist, Jacob Gould Schurman, president of Cornell University, to inspect the situation on the ground in the Philippines. Schurman reported back that the United States would have to remain on the island for a while. However, this anti-imperialist position represented a minority one. Most newspaper editors supported the taking of the Philippines, and Republicans in particular supported the president's position. The Treaty of Paris was approved by the Senate in February 1899 by a vote of 57 to 27 with some anti-imperialists objecting.

Though more of a fringe group, anarchists also criticized McKinley's plans for the Philippines. These newspapers and leaders of the movement were against American imperial ambitions abroad, and received much more attention in retrospect because of their association with McKinley's eventual assassin, Leon Czolgosz.

CONCLUSION

McKinley won a historic reelection in 1900, largely on the strength of America's triumph in the Spanish-American War. However, his second term was cut short when he was shot in 1901, and he died a month later. During his first term, McKinley faced some criticism for his relationship with Hanna, his inattention to issues of racial injustice, and his imperialist foreign policy. His critics were most often members of the Democratic Party or the opposition press. However, much of this criticism was drowned out by American success in the Spanish-American War. McKinley was further buffeted by the new position of the Republican Party as the majority party in American politics after decades of near balance between the two parties. The American public was supportive of a president who they saw as ushering the United States triumphantly onto the world stage.

Anne C. Pluta

Further Reading

Calhoun, Charles W. *From Bloody Shirt to Full Dinner Pail: The Transformation of Politics and Governance in the Gilded Age.* New York: Hill and Wang, 2011.

Frantz, Edward O. *The Door of Hope: Republican Presidents and the First Southern Strategy, 1877–1933.* Gainesville, FL: University Press of Florida, 2011.

Gould, Lewis L. *The Presidency of William McKinley.* Lawrence, KS: University Press of Kansas, 1980.

Gould, Lewis L. *The Spanish American War and President McKinley.* Lawrence, KS: University Press of Kansas, 1982.

Miller, Scott. *The President and the Assassin: McKinley, Terror, and Empire at the Dawn of the American Century.* New York: Random House, 2011.

Saldin, Robert P. "William McKinley and the Rhetorical Presidency." *Presidential Studies Quarterly*, Vol. 41, No. 1 (March 2011): 119–134.

26. Theodore Roosevelt

Born: October 27, 1858
Died: January 6, 1919
Time in Office: 26th President of the United States, September 14, 1901, to March 4, 1909

Election Results: 1900 Election: Elected vice president, assumed office upon death
   of William McKinley; 1904 Election: 56.4% of popular vote, 336 (70.6%)
   Electoral College votes; 1912 Election: 27.4% of popular vote, 88 (16.6%) Elec-
   toral Votes
Spouse: Alice Hathaway Lee (m. 1880), Edith Kermit Carow (m. 1886)
Children: Alice Lee, Theodore, Kermit, Ethel Carow, Archibald Bulloch, and
   Quentin

Theodore Roosevelt's path to the presidency was brought about through two acts
of hatred. The first act led him to become vice president in the first place, and the
second resulted in Roosevelt becoming president. Even before Roosevelt was governor of New York, Senator Thomas C. Platt, then the boss of New York Republican politics, expressed concern over the potential independence Roosevelt might
exert if elected. After Roosevelt did become governor, the two found themselves
in conflict, including over a prominent franchise tax bill on utilities. Starting in
1899, Platt worked toward getting Roosevelt nominated to be President William
McKinley's vice presidential candidate "to get rid of that bastard," a plan made
more feasible following the death of Vice President Garret Hobart. Platt strove to get
Roosevelt out of New York politics and into a position that Roosevelt himself did
not want initially.

Neither McKinley nor his top political adviser, Senator Mark Hanna, desired to
have Roosevelt on the ticket, with Hanna famously declaring during the Republican National Convention, "Don't you realize that there's only one life between this
madman and the White House?" But Platt's efforts and Roosevelt's popularity
among delegates effectively assured Roosevelt of the nomination. Roosevelt, for his
part, came to accept the position on the ticket, writing to his sister that although
"I should have preferred to stay where there was more work. I would be both
ungrateful and a fool not to be deeply touched by the way in which I was
nominated."

Roosevelt became president on September 14, 1901, following the assassination
of McKinley. Although this ultimate act of political hatred was aimed at McKinley, it resulted in Roosevelt's elevation to the presidency. Many Republican Party
leaders were dismayed at this development due to their continued wariness of Roosevelt. Senator Hanna summed up their view well by proclaiming, "Now, look,
that damned cowboy is President of the United States."

Roosevelt's popularity and political career trajectory had him heading toward
the White House even before Platt's maneuver to get him out of New York. Famed
progressive newspaperman William Allen White contended in April 1899 that
Roosevelt was "more than a presidential possibility in 1904, he is a presidential
probability. He is the coming American of the twentieth century." Whether he had
continued serving as governor of New York or served four full years as McKinley's

vice president, Roosevelt may have maintained such a presence on the national stage as to make White's contention a reality.

HATRED DRIVEN BY ROOSEVELT'S APPROACH TO RACE

Roosevelt's views of blacks were in line with most nonsouthern white Americans of his era. As a race, Roosevelt saw blacks as "altogether inferior to the whites" with any notion of racial equality not likely at the time due to what was viewed as blacks' "natural limitations." Roosevelt did believe that this perceived inferiority could be overcome, both by individuals and eventually in terms of racial equality, but in any event such advancement must "necessarily be painful." To that end, though, Roosevelt would be willing to pursue initiatives or take stances that, for his era, were more progressive and created at least some incremental opportunity for advancement toward racial equality.

Perhaps the most highly charged, racially related event during the Roosevelt presidency started with a request. On October 16, 1901, just over a month into his presidency, Roosevelt invited the African American author and educator Booker T. Washington to dinner at the White House. This event made Washington the first black person to have a personal dinner with any president in the White House. Roosevelt and Washington received praise for their dinner among certain sectors of the populace. Numerous telegrams from blacks, for example, poured into the White House with such plaudits as the dinner being the "greatest step for the race in a generation" and celebrating that "The hour is at hand to make the beginning of a new order." Liberal whites also supported the president for holding the dinner.

In the South, though, the reaction was far from kind. The *Memphis Scimitar* newspaper called the dinner the "most damnable outrage which has ever been perpetrated by any citizen of the United States" and warned that Roosevelt "has not inflamed the anger of the Southern people; he has excited their disgust." Newspapers throughout the South freely hurled racial epithets, including the N-word, at Roosevelt. Such hateful language, however, was not limited to those outside of government. South Carolina senator Benjamin R. Tillman also invoked the N-word in arguing that a thousand blacks "would have to be killed to teach them 'their place again.'" Both Roosevelt and Washington received death threats resulting from the dinner.

Roosevelt's view of the South's reaction to the dinner was "to me literally inexplicable" and "very melancholy that such feeling should exist in such bitter aggravated form in any part of our country." He remained resolute in his actions, however, stating in a private letter, "I would not lose my self-respect by fearing to have a man like Booker T. Washington to dinner if it cost me every political friend I have got." Further evidence of Roosevelt's stance toward the reaction can be seen in a handwritten note by George B. Cortelyou, then White House secretary, on a draft transcript of a statement from John Lowndes McLaurin, South Carolina's other Democratic senator, on which Courtelyou wrote, "Not used. The President said he did not want anyone to make any explanation for him." Humorist and political commentator Finley Peter Dunne may have had the most astute observation about the dinner, noting in the colorful language of a fictional Irish immigrant bartender named Mr. Dooley that "Thousan's iv men who wudden't have voted for [Roosevelt] under anny circumstances has declared that undher no circumstances wud they now vot f'r him."

The Washington dinner was not the only matter in which Roosevelt's approach toward blacks angered the South. For example, his approach to patronage appointments in the South, one of the very issues on which Roosevelt sought Booker Washington's insights, created antagonism among white southerners toward the president. Roosevelt stated that the "prime tests I have applied have been those of character, fitness and ability. . . . I certainly cannot treat mere color as a permanent bar to holding office, any more than I would treat creed or birth place." More finely, though, Roosevelt with Washington's agreement sought "to appoint a very few colored men of high charter—just enough to make it evident that they were not entirely proscribed," or as Roosevelt more succinctly stated to Washington, "though I have rather reduced the quantity I have done my best to raise the quality of the negro appointments." Notwithstanding the limited basis on which Roosevelt saw himself appointing blacks to positions in the South, white southerners were infuriated by this policy.

Roosevelt also angered southerners over the issue of lynching. On Memorial Day 1902 at Arlington National Cemetery, Roosevelt gave a speech regarding the presence of the U.S. military in the Philippines. In an improvised moment, though, where Roosevelt sought to address atrocities committed by U.S. military members, Roosevelt contended that "there occur in our country, to the deep and lasting shame of our people, lynchings carried on under circumstances of inhuman cruelty and barbarity." This speech was the first time any sitting president addressed the issue of lynchings in the United States. Southern response to his remarks was immediate and deeply negative. As one southern senator observed, "I do not think the South will care much for Mr. Roosevelt after this. . . . He is dead so far as my section is concerned."

Rather than retreat in the face of yet even more southern opposition, Roosevelt continually raised the level of his rhetoric in opposition to lynching in general and lynching of blacks in particular. In a letter to the Indiana governor, Roosevelt repeatedly referred to the "lawlessness" of lynching, and concluded that "where we permit the law to be defied or evaded . . . we are by just some much weakening the bonds of our civilization and increasing the chances of its overthrows and of the substitution in its place of a system in which there shall be violent alternations of anarchy and tyranny." Similarly, in an extended passage in Roosevelt's Sixth Annual Message to Congress on December 3, 1906, Roosevelt argued that "the members of the white race on the other hand should understand that every lynching represents by just so much a loosening of the bands of civilization. . . . No man can take part in the torture of a human being without having his own moral nature permanently lowered."

Although Roosevelt's racial views and related policies were progressive for his era, they were not without their limitations and a tinge of practical politics. For example, in his various expositions on lynching, Roosevelt started the discussion with recognition that at times a lynching was in response to a crime committed by a black man, stating that the "greatest cause of lynching is the perpetration, especially by black men, of the hideous crime of rape." Although Roosevelt would typically jump off from this point—for example, citing that "two-thirds of the lynchings are not for rape at all" and that the whites should "let [justice] be justice under the law, and not the wild and crooked savagery of a mob"—Roosevelt's rhetoric was framed around the wrongful actions of a black male committing a crime.

The most notable event for which Roosevelt was criticized by blacks related to the Brownsville controversy, where approximately 20–30 black soldiers allegedly went on a rampage in the town of Brownsville, Texas, in 1906, firing rifles, killing one man and shooting a police lieutenant. Military investigations concluded, based on limited and questionable evidence, that "the raiders were soldiers . . . [which] cannot be doubted." This determination was made even though all the soldiers were accounted for on the base immediately after the shooting in town started. Throughout and following these investigations, no black soldier interviewed would provide any information or name any individual who may have been involved in the Brownsville events.

Well before the Brownsville events, Roosevelt had already articulated a view toward race relations in which "the backward race (i.e., blacks) be trained so that it may enter into the possession of true freedom" and that "the colored man['s] . . . fate must depend far more upon his own effort than upon the efforts of any outside friend." As a component of this view, Roosevelt declared in his Lincoln Dinner Address that "the colored man who fails to condemn crime in another colored man, who fails to co-operate in all lawful ways in bringing colored criminals to justice, is the worse enemy of his own people, as well as an enemy to all the people." Putting this perspective into action, Roosevelt ordered another investigation, this time by new Inspector General Ernest A. Garlington, with the directive that if he could not identify the specific individuals involved, then all members of the three companies who were stationed at Fort Brown at the time would be dishonorably discharged. As in the prior investigations, no soldier broke from the ranks of silence.

A week before the November 6, 1906, congressional elections, Roosevelt summoned Booker T. Washington to the White House to discuss the Brownsville incident. Roosevelt told Washington of his intentions to dishonorably discharge all 167 black soldiers without a trial or being able to face their accusers. Washington believed that blacks would strongly oppose such an action, and following their meeting appealed to Roosevelt to not make any decision until after they could meet again. Roosevelt ignored the request and signed the discharge order; it was dated one day before the congressional elections but not released until after the elections were completed. Roosevelt's delay helped Republican candidates retain black voters, whereas if they would have not voted or voted for the Democratic candidate the outcome of some races may have changed.

Washington's concerns about the reaction to Roosevelt's actions turned out to be well founded, as Roosevelt's popularity with blacks plummeted. Opposition to Roosevelt's handling of the Brownsville matter was not limited to blacks, though. Most notably, Ohio Republican senator Joseph Foraker, with whom Roosevelt had butted heads over railroad regulation and other matters, forced the Senate to further investigate the events down in Brownsville. He also engaged with Roosevelt in what amounted to an extremely heated impromptu debate at the Gridiron Club Dinner in 1907. Roosevelt, in return, actively worked to cause Foraker to be defeated for reelection in 1908. History, however, has treated Roosevelt poorly over the Brownsville matter (in 1972 President Richard Nixon issued honorable discharges for all the soldiers who had been dishonorably discharged by Roosevelt).

INSTITUTIONAL BATTLES WITH CONGRESS

Theodore Roosevelt is often cited as a key actor in expanding the expectations of the presidency and broadening the authority of the office. In doing so, Roosevelt often clashed with members of Congress and Republican Party leaders over matters of public policy, the legislative process, and the roles of the governing institutions. Roosevelt put together whatever legislative coalitions were needed to achieve his policy goals, including at times working with southern Democrats and at odds with fellow Republicans.

Roosevelt's own words from this autobiography may summarize the nature of his conflicts with Congress the best: "The great moral issues [of the 1896, 1898, and 1900 elections] . . . regrettably but perhaps inevitably, tended to throw the [Republican] party into the hands not merely of the conservatives but of the reactionaries. . . . There were many points on which I agreed with [Republican Speaker of the House] Mr. Cannon and [prominent Senate Republican] Mr. Aldrich, and some points on which I agreed with [prominent Senate Republican] Mr. Hale. . . . We succeeded in working together, although with increasing friction, for some years, I pushing forward and they hanging back. Gradually, however, I was forced to abandon the effort to persuade them to come my way, and then I achieved results only by appealing over the heads of the Senate and House leaders to the people, who were the masters of both of us. I continued in this way to get results until almost the close of my term."

The phrase "almost the close of my term" leads to the point where intraparty, institutional, and policy conflicts became consumed by something more akin to hatred of Roosevelt. The 60th U.S. Congress met for its second session in the period between the election of William Howard Taft, Roosevelt's successor, in November 1908, and his inauguration as president in January 1909. On the second day of this session, Roosevelt delivered his Eighth Annual Message. Buried in the second half of a message in a discussion seeking repeal or at least modification of prior legislation limiting the investigative activities of the Secret Service was the sentence, "The chief argument in favor of the provision was that the Congressmen did not themselves wish to be investigated by Secret Service men."

Congress responded with a resolution responding to this line stating, in part, "Whereas the plain meaning of the above words is that the majority of the Congressmen were in fear of being investigated by Secret Service men and that Congress as a whole was actuated by that motive in enacting the provision in question" and "*Be it resolved*, That the President be requested to transmit to the House any evidence upon which he based his statements that the 'chief argument in favor of the provision was that the Congressmen did not themselves wish to be investigated by Secret Service men,' and also to transmit to the House any evidence connecting any Member of the House of Representatives of the Sixtieth Congress with corrupt action in his official capacity, and to inform the House whether he has instituted proceedings for the punishment of any such individual by the courts or has reported any such alleged delinquencies to the House of Representatives." In a Special Message to Congress dated January 4, 1909, Roosevelt interspersed his analysis of the congressional resolution and further explanation of his Annual Message with statements pushing back against Congress such as "This allegation in the resolution, therefore, must certainly be due to an entire failure to understand my message" and that the "issue is simply, Does Congress desire that the Government shall have at its disposal the most efficient instrument for the detection of criminals and the prevention and punishment of crime, or does it not?"

The House of Representatives, still under Republican control, responded to Roosevelt's message four days later by taking the extraordinary step of formally rebuking the president by a vote of 212 yeas, 36 nays, 5 presents, and 135 not voting. No Congress had taken this or any comparable action, tantamount to a congressional censure of a sitting president, since the presidency of Andrew Jackson. Such action set the tone for the rest of the congressional session and Roosevelt's presidency. Congress did not pursue any of Roosevelt's legislative agenda, on one hand, but Roosevelt blocked various congressional initiatives, issuing 6 regular vetoes and rejecting another 17 through a pocket veto. Roosevelt concludes his discussion of these events in his autobiography by noting, "I was not able to push through the legislation I desired during these four months, but I was able to prevent them doing anything I did not desire, or undoing anything that I had already succeeded in getting done."

PROGRESSIVISM AND RELATIONSHIP WITH BUSINESS

Roosevelt also brought a different approach toward the role and authority of the federal government itself. Two chapters in Roosevelt's autobiography and their respective opening sentences—"The Big Stick and the Square Deal," which began "One of the vital questions with which as President I had to deal was the attitude of the Nation toward the great corporation" and "Social and Industrial Justice," which started "[G]overnmental agencies must find their justification . . . in which they are used for the practical betterment of living and working conditions among the mass of the people"—reflect Roosevelt's views on the role of government both generally and with respect to checking certain practices of big business. These views led Roosevelt to use the tools of the federal government in ways that garnered great opposition by those in big business and finance.

Nicknamed "Trust Buster," Roosevelt used the 1904 *Northern Securities Co. v. United States* Supreme Court case not only to dismantle a railroad monopoly, but also, in conjunction with similar cases brought against the American Tobacco Company and the Standard Oil Company, to establish "the entire authority upon which any action must rest that seeks through the exercise of national power to curb monopolistic control." The Roosevelt administration successfully used that authority a total of 44 times to bust monopolies. Roosevelt also used the bully pulpit of his office to mediate a national coal strike in 1902. Legislative successes during his administration included the Elkins Act of 1903, the Hepburn Act of 1906, the establishment of the Department of Commerce and Labor, the Pure Food and Drug Act, and the Meat Inspection Act, not to mention his Square Deal (a domestic program focused on the conservation of natural resources, control of corporations, and consumer protection) and natural resource conservation policies generally.

Roosevelt took on the challenges that he was hurting business or restricting employees' choices, dismissing arguments like these by contending that only dishonest businesses would be hurt by his efforts to protect those who do not have real choices. Underlying his policy positions was a view that a "democracy can be such in fact only if there is some rough approximation in similarity in stature among the men composing it . . . a rich and complex industrial society cannot so exist [as a democracy]; for some individuals, and especially those artificial individuals called corporations, become so very big that the ordinary individual is utterly dwarfed beside them and cannot deal with them on terms of equality." For these reasons, Roosevelt saw the need for the "biggest of all combinations called the Government" to exercise its powers on behalf of those who were not on an equal footing with business interests.

CONCLUSION

Roosevelt approached governing differently than many successors. Trying to create change in politics always is a source of friction with those who oppose the change. Roosevelt, however, seemed impervious to attacks or vitriol hurled his way during his presidency for seeking to do things differently. Through a strong belief in his positions coupled with arrogance and stubbornness, Roosevelt would often simply state that he did not understand the basis of any given attack against him. His response to criticism often amounted to laments that his critics simply did not understand Roosevelt's message or intentions. This approach, however, could also be interpreted at times as a lack of empathy or at least understanding of another person's perspective. For example, Roosevelt countered racial criticisms of his actions in the Brownsville matter by stating that he would have acted the same if the soldiers involved were white. Although this "color-blind" approach may be somewhat progressive for his era, it lacked understanding that the black soldiers may not have been put in the situation they were in if not for racism.

All in all, though, perhaps the thick hide of a Rough Rider is what was needed to push the nation through the governmental changes needed to coincide with the industrial and sociological changes facing the nation during Roosevelt's era. Someone more fragile may have wilted from the scrutiny and attack; instead, Roosevelt would bear down even harder and drive for more successes. His policy and electoral achievements—his 1904 election was the largest popular vote percentage margin of victory since James Monroe's uncontested reelection in 1920—demonstrated that the people of the nation and, at least to some degree, their representatives in Congress were behind Roosevelt and his pursuit of change.

Victoria A. Farrar-Myers

Further Reading

Donald, Aida D. *Lion in the White House: A Life of Theodore Roosevelt*. New York: Basic Books, 2007.

Morris, Edmund. *Theodore Rex*. New York: The Modern Library, 2001.

Roosevelt, Theodore. *The Autobiography of Theodore Roosevelt*. Overland Park, KS: Digireads.com Publishing, 2011.

Theodore Roosevelt Center at Dickinson State University. Available at http://www.theodorerooseveltcenter.org.

27. William Howard Taft

Born: September 15, 1857

Died: March 8, 1930

Time in Office: 27th President of the United States, March 4, 1909, to March 4, 1913

Election Results: 1908 Election: 51.6% of popular vote, 321 (66.5%) Electoral College votes; 1912 Election: 23.2% of popular vote, 8 (1.5%) Electoral Votes

Spouse: Helen Herron Taft (m. 1886)

Children: Robert, Helen, and Charles

History has not been kind to William Howard Taft. Although he served with distinction as governor of the Philippines, secretary of war, president, and chief justice of the Supreme Court, today he is known mainly for his obesity, and, in the words of historian Jonathan Lurie, as "a one-term loser; a conservative of narrow viewpoint; a chief executive lacking initiative, leadership, and popular appeal." This characterization is not entirely inaccurate. Taft's conservative nature, which was far better suited for the judiciary than for national politics, made him resistant to the growth of the American administrative state and to popular proposals to limit the power of corporations. Naturally, Taft thought his positions on many of these issues respected the Constitution's limits on presidential power, but they also left him with few supporters among the Progressive Republicans who originally backed his candidacy.

To a large degree, Taft's reputation as an inept chief executive was shaped by the vicious presidential election of 1912, where he was caught in a battle for the Republican nomination with his former friend and mentor, Theodore Roosevelt. Taft and Roosevelt's long association, as well as the fact that nearly all observers—including Taft himself—agreed that he owed his presidency to Roosevelt, made the fight that much more remorseless and cruel. Numerous lines of attack existed against Taft, and the most prevalent of those shaped his presidency.

THE 1908 CAMPAIGN: RELIGION AND ELITISM

As Roosevelt's chosen successor, Taft enjoyed a relatively easy campaign in 1908 against the fiery populist William Jennings Bryan. Indeed, aside from Roosevelt's own victory in 1904, Taft received more votes than any previous president up to that point. He also embraced a new, personal style of campaigning that required presidential candidates to go on the campaign trail. Taft traveled more than 18,000 miles, delivered 400 speeches, and was the first presidential candidate to have his speeches widely distributed through recordings.

Although Taft was a willing campaigner, his tin ear and frequent inability to read an audience caused him problems. While he was addressing a group of former Union soldiers, for example, he told an uncomplimentary story about Ulysses S. Grant. "In 1854," Taft explained to the veterans, "he resigned from the army because he had to. He had yielded to the weakness for strong drink, and rather than be courtmartialed, he left the army." Although Taft meant this as a tale of redemption, the veterans were furious, and one later suggested that he should "have the grace to go and hang yourself."

Taft's close association with Roosevelt led some critics to accuse him of being little more than a poor imitation of his more charismatic predecessor. Some claimed that T.A.F.T. stood for "Take Advice from Theodore," while another popular joke of the time went like this: "That's a splendid phonograph, old man. It reproduces the sound of Roosevelt's voice better than I ever thought possible. What make? We call it the Taft."

Unlike Roosevelt, Taft also drew criticism for being an elitist. This charge came, in part, from his passion for golf, which was widely considered to be a sport for the elite. One potential supporter from Illinois wrote him that "thousands and thousands of laboring people" considered golf a game for the rich, and suggested that he "cast aside golf and take an ax and cut wood."

One of Taft's chief liabilities was his membership in the Unitarian church, which led some critics to demand to know if the Republican presidential candidate was really a Christian. He had earlier passed up the presidency of Yale because he said he did not believe in the divinity of Christ, and thus he could not in good conscience lead a Congregationalist university. In 1908 an editorial in the *Pentecostal Herald* questioned how a man with such suspect Christian credentials could be a nominee for president. "Think of the United States with a *President* who does not believe that Jesus Christ was the Son of God, but looks upon our immaculate Savior as a . . . low, cunning impostor!" Taft's relative lack of religious conviction caused some moral reformers to doubt his commitment to their causes, too. Carrie Nation, a leader of the temperance movement, pushed him to make a statement about the dangers of alcohol. When Taft refused, she labeled him "a foe of temperance as well as an infidel."

Ironically, after being attacked for a lack of commitment to Christian doctrine, Taft was later accused of being a secret Catholic. These rumors flowed from his time as governor of the Philippines, when he visited the Vatican to negotiate the price of Church-owned lands. According to this line of attack, Taft had overpaid for the lands because of his deep devotion to the Pope. Similar accusations reemerged in the 1912 campaign, and they came to include an outlandish conspiracy theory that Taft's longtime aide, Major Archie Butt, died on the *Titanic* while returning from a secret mission to the Vatican. First Lady Helen Taft was dogged by similar rumors. During the campaign, Christian fundamentalists often questioned her decision to send her daughter to a Catholic school in Manila while Taft was governor, and they criticized her for wearing a veil when she visited the Vatican.

"BIGGER AND MORE TUMBLE-TO-PIECES THAN EVER"

Taft's obesity, combined with his conservative views on the powers of the presidency, made him vulnerable to frequent accusations that he was lazy. The president, always self-conscious about his size, had made a considerable effort to slim down prior to entering the White House. Nevertheless, the pressures of office led him to put on significant weight, exceeding 350 pounds at his heaviest. One rumor that was often repeated in official circles in Washington was that he installed a new bathtub that was the size of a small swimming pool after he became stuck in the previous bath and needed two men to pull him out.

Taft's reputation for sloth was not helped by his habit of falling asleep at the most inopportune times during official functions. As one critic would later write, "The new Administration was on its way somewhere but wither it was going no one—not even the President himself—seemed to know. It was drift, drift, drift—little attempted, nothing done." A 1909 *New York Times* cartoon showed an obese Taft sleeping in a chair, while reporters surrounded him shouting, "Please Mr. President. Do something!" *Life Magazine* chose to criticize him by drawing a comparison to the more vigorous Roosevelt: "Teddy, come home and blow your horn, The sheep's in the meadow, the cow's in the corn. The boy you left to tend the sheep, Is under the haystack fast asleep."

Even his allies drew unkind conclusions about how Taft's obesity affected his mental state. After encountering Taft taking his evening stroll, Henry Adams, the historian and grandson of John Quincy Adams, remarked that he resembled a lumbering hippopotamus. Adams later wrote, "He looks bigger and more tumble-to-pieces than ever, and his manner has become more slovenly than his figure; but what struck me most was the deterioration of his mind and expression. . . . He shows mental enfeeblement all over, and I wanted to offer him a bet that he wouldn't get through his term." Taft's physical appearance, as these examples show, was frequently used as a metaphor for his entire administration, which was disparaged for being slow, ineffectual, and out of touch.

Such criticisms about his lack of vigor, along with those aimed more squarely at his policy decisions, caused Taft considerable concern. He would only take clippings of favorable articles from newspapers, and he stopped reading certain periodicals altogether when their editorial sections became critical of his policies. One longtime aide recalled a conversation between the president and the first lady when she tried to explain his error in ignoring critical papers. "You will never know what the other side is doing if you only read the *Sun* and the *Tribune*," she told her husband. To this sensible piece of advice, Taft responded, "I don't care what the other side is doing."

AN ENEMY OF PROGRESSIVISM

Taft was committed to many of the principles that united the Progressive movement, such as conservation and the regulation of American corporations, but he was unwilling to claim new powers for the presidency to achieve them. This caution led many Progressive Republicans to conclude, unfairly, that he was unsupportive of their goals. Some Progressive outlets, particularly *La Follette's Magazine*, even accused him of betraying Roosevelt's principles.

The most significant rupture with the Progressives—an episode that would contribute to the end of his friendship with Roosevelt—was a clash over natural resource conservation policies. What became known as the "Ballinger-Pinchot" affair eventually ended with Taft's dismissal of the chief forester, Gifford Pinchot, who was a close friend of Roosevelt's. Pinchot's falling-out with Taft came after the president continued to support Secretary of the Interior Richard Ballinger when he was accused of colluding with New York mining and financial interests to gain control of federal lands in Alaska. Pinchot eventually defied Taft's direct order to remain silent on the matter by writing to a Republican senator and denouncing Ballinger as "a foe of conservation." After the letter was read aloud on the Senate floor, Pinchot was promptly dismissed.

There was never any conclusive evidence that Ballinger was guilty of these crimes, but Taft's bungling of this potential scandal generated significant criticism in the press, and it led many Progressives to become openly critical of the president. As the Louisville *Courier-Journal* claimed in one editorial, "For the first time in the history of the country a President of the United States has openly proclaimed himself the friend of thieves and the enemy of honest men. That, and that alone, is the issue precipitated by the executive order of Friday removing Gifford Pinchot from office." Pinchot, who was never close to Taft, concluded that he was an ineffectual coward, once describing him as "a man whose fundamental desire was to keep out of trouble." He later wrote to Roosevelt and accused Taft of abandoning the principles of Progressivism and losing "the confidence of the great mass of the people . . . by aligning himself with the special interests which have always opposed you."

The blowup over Pinchot, along with his clumsy handling of an important tariff bill, left Taft with fewer and fewer allies. *The Nation* summarized his first term in office as an exercise in "monumental and almost incredible blundering," which had left the White House in a "deplorable and mortifying mess."

THE ELECTION OF 1912 AND THE RIFT WITH ROOSEVELT

Taft knew that he was in political trouble well before the presidential election of 1912. His feelings of insecurity only increased once Roosevelt entered the race and Taft realized that he could no longer count on the support of the Progressive Republicans.

Even Helen Taft, who was often a far better political strategist than her beleaguered husband, thought that the situation looked bleak, telling him, "I think you will be renominated, but I don't see any chance for the election."

By this point, Taft also doubted that he would win, but he planned to stay in the race to defeat Roosevelt, who he decided was dangerously radical. He leaned on the Republican political establishment to protect his nomination from Roosevelt and to oppose the former president's push for direct primaries. Yet Taft's reliance on machine politics only opened him up to accusations from Progressives that he was a tool of corrupt political bosses in Pennsylvania and New York. Consequently, Roosevelt condemned him for "receiving stolen goods" and made the dubious claim that "never before has patronage been so shamelessly used in politics."

Taft only inflamed Roosevelt's anger by describing many of Roosevelt's supporters as radicals who "would hurry us into a condition which I would find no parallel except in the French Revolution. . . . Such extremists are not Progressives, they are politically emotionalists or neurotics." Roosevelt, who took this as a personal attack on his mental state, accused Taft of having "yielded to the bosses and to the great privileged interests," which made him "disloyal to every canon of decency and fair play." He described the president himself as a "flubdub," a "floppy-souled creature," a "puzzlewit," a "fathead," and a "man with the brains of about three guinea-pig power."

Taft thought that Roosevelt's violent anger had made him crazed and unstable. "He is to be classed with the leaders of religious cults who promote things over their followers by any sort of physical manipulation and deception," Taft wrote to his wife. "He is seeking to make his followers 'Holy Rollers,' and I hope that the country is beginning to see this." Writing to one supporter during the election, Taft concluded that "[Roosevelt] is really the greatest menace to our institutions that we have had in a long time—indeed I don't remember one in our history so dangerous and so powerful because of his hold upon the less intelligent votes and the discontented." He further branded Roosevelt a "dangerous egoist," concluding that he was a "demagogue" and a "flatterer of the people." Despite his own vicious rhetoric against Roosevelt, Taft was deeply distraught over the battle with his former friend. After one campaign stop, Taft, in tears, confessed to a reporter for the *New York World*, "Roosevelt was my closest friend."

The media took notice of the unusually acrimonious rhetoric of the campaign as well. As *The Nation* reported, "Mr. Roosevelt hits out wildly like a man dazed by the heavy blows he has received . . . there appears the almost insane hatred of Mr. Taft." Democrats were keenly aware of the savage internecine war that Taft and Roosevelt were fighting. William Jennings Bryan, Taft's Democratic opponent in 1908, asked for a ticket to the Republican convention, and he pledged "not to say anything worse about Taft and Roosevelt than they say about each other—a promise I feel sure I can live up to."

The battle between Taft and Roosevelt came to a head at the Republican convention. With Taft and his conservative allies in control of the convention rules committee, most of the disputed delegate seats were awarded to Taft. Roosevelt's supporters viewed this as a corrupt bargain, and they accused Taft of "high treason." At one point, a fistfight erupted on the convention floor after one Roosevelt delegate threatened that if Taft accepted votes from the "stolen" delegates, he "would have forfeited the right to ask the support of any honest man of any party on moral grounds."

In the end, Taft did win the Republican nomination, and Roosevelt and his supporters walked out to start the Bull Moose Party. This resulted in a three-way race in the election of 1912. Taft lost badly, receiving only 8 electoral votes, compared to Roosevelt's 88, which allowed Democratic nominee Woodrow Wilson to win a decisive victory with 435 electoral votes. Nevertheless, many Republican papers blamed Taft's loss on Roosevelt's arrogance. As the *New York Times* later reported, "[H]e did not deserve it. These are the words that are on the lips of multitudes who were opposed to Mr. Taft's election. . . . His defeat under any possible conditions in his own party could hardly have been avoided, but his pitiful showing in the Electoral College is the result of forces that are not to his discredit—quite the contrary. Chief of these is the vindictive and treacherous enmity of Mr. Roosevelt."

CONCLUSION

Taft handled his spectacular loss with surprising equanimity. He never enjoyed being president, and he never became accustomed to the increasingly personal nature of early-20th-century politics. In many ways, the honest and good-natured Taft was an unlikely person to become enmeshed in such a savage campaign. Indeed, even his enemies were willing to concede that Taft was a delightful person and a principled leader. In the end, he was simply caught between an older Republican tradition of patronage politics that embraced a relatively circumscribed role for the president, and the new Progressive politics championed by Roosevelt.

Taft and Roosevelt eventually did make peace, and they remained on cordial terms for the remainder of Roosevelt's life. After a brief period as a professor of law at Yale, Taft was finally appointed to the one position he had always wanted: chief justice of the Supreme Court. He would remain in this position for nine years, where he was no longer subject to the vicious rhetorical attacks he had endured as president.

Colin D. Moore

Further Reading

Anderson, Judith Icke. *William Howard Taft: An Intimate History.* New York: W. W. Norton, 1981.

Anthony, Carl Sferrazza. *Nellie Taft: The Unconventional First Lady of the Ragtime Era.* New York: William Morrow, 2005.

Cashman, Sean Dennis. *American in the Age of the Titans: The Progressive Era and World War I*. New York: New York University Press, 1988.

Chace, James. *1912: Wilson, Roosevelt, Taft and Debs—The Election That Changed the Country*. New York: Simon & Schuster, 2004.

Coletta. Paolo E. *The Presidency of William Howard Taft*. Lawrence, KS: University Press of Kansas, 1973.

Cowan, Geoffrey. *Let the People Rule: Theodore Roosevelt and the Birth of the Presidential Primary*. New York: W. W. Norton, 2016.

Duffy, Herbert S. *William Howard Taft*. New York: Minton, Balch & Company, 1930.

Goodwin, Doris Kearns. *The Bully Pulpit: Theodore Roosevelt, William Howard Taft, and the Golden Age of Journalism*. New York: Simon & Schuster, 2013.

Korzi, Michael J. "William Howard Taft, the 1908 Election, and the Future of the American Presidency." *Congress and the Presidency*, Vol. 43 (May–August 2016): 227–254.

Lurie, Jonathan. *William Howard Taft: The Travails of a Progressive Conservative*. New York: Cambridge University Press, 2012.

Meacham, Jon. *American Gospel: God, the Founding Fathers, and the Making of a Nation*. New York: Random House, 2006.

Morris, Edmund. *Colonel Roosevelt*. New York: Random House, 2010.

Pinchot, Gifford. *Breaking New Ground*. New York: Harcourt, Brace, 1947.

Pringle, Henry F. *The Life and Times of William Howard Taft*, 2 vols. New York: Farrar & Rinehart, 1939.

Taft, Helen Herron. *Recollections of Full Years*. New York: Dodd, Mead & Company, 1915.

28. Woodrow Wilson

Born: December 28, 1856

Died: February 3, 1924

Time in Office: 28th President of the United States, March 4, 1913, to March 4, 1921

Election Results: 1912 Election: 41.8% of popular vote, 435 (81.9%) Electoral College votes; 1916 Election: 49.2% of popular vote, 277 (52.2%) Electoral College votes

Spouse: Ellen Axson (m. 1885), Edith Bolling Galt (m. 1915)

Children: Margaret, Jessie, and Eleanor

Although Woodrow Wilson was born in Staunton, Virginia, he is most closely associated with the state of New Jersey. He received his bachelor's degree from Princeton University, served as president of Princeton, and served as governor of New Jersey prior to gaining the presidency. However, Wilson was born and raised in the South, living in Augusta, Georgia, during the Civil War, and in Columbia, South

Carolina, during Reconstruction. He studied law at the University of Virginia for a year, with further time studying and practicing law before earning a PhD in history and political science from Johns Hopkins University. Wilson held several teaching positions before settling in to a career at his alma mater, Princeton University.

Wilson served as governor of New Jersey for only two years before winning the Democratic nomination and the presidency in 1912. In a four-way contest, Wilson won 435 electoral votes and 41.8% of the popular vote against incumbent Republican William Howard Taft, who came in third with eight electoral votes and 23.2% of the popular vote. Former president Theodore Roosevelt, running as a Progressive Republican, came in second, winning 88 electoral votes and 27.4% of the popular vote, and Socialist Party candidate Eugene V. Debs won 6% of the popular vote, although he failed to win any electoral votes. In a much closer contest in 1916, with only two major candidates, Wilson won reelection with 49.2% of the popular vote and 277 electoral votes, defeating Republican Party nominee Charles E. Hughes, who won 254 electoral votes and 46.1% of the popular vote.

In 1885 Wilson married Ellen Louise Axson, who died in 1914, during Wilson's first term in the White House. They had three daughters, Margaret, Jessie, and Eleanor. Only a year after Ellen's death, before his first term was over, Wilson married Edith Bolling Galt.

WILSON'S POLITICAL ENEMIES

Although Wilson is often considered one of America's greatest presidents, he is also controversial and, for some (particularly modern conservatives), one of America's most hated presidents. Wilson believed in a strong executive branch, and as part of his progressive "New Freedom" platform, his list of accomplishments during his first term included the creation of the Federal Reserve, the lowering of tariff rates, the strengthening of antitrust and fair business competition laws, and implementing a federal income tax. Wilson also took an ambitious and idealistic approach to foreign policy, exemplified by his intervention in the Mexican civil war in 1913–1914 (by demanding that Mexico impose democratic reforms to gain U.S. recognition), and America's entry into World War I in 1917 to "make the world safe for democracy."

However, by engaging in "total war," Wilson relied on extensive emergency powers to govern, and created great controversy in doing so. For example, passage of the Lever Act in 1917 granted the president substantial control over the national economy, while the Espionage Act of 1917 and the Sedition Act of 1918 curtailed various civil liberties and contributed to the first Red Scare (a period of intense public fear about the spread of communism) in 1919–1920. Despite the Allied victory against Germany in World War I, and Wilson's contribution to ending the war with his Fourteen Points (a statement of principles for a peaceful resolution), Wilson's attempt to create a League of Nations failed when he could not get the U.S. Senate to ratify the treaty. Wilson also left a legacy of racist policies while president, including segregating the U.S. Post Office and appointing various cabinet heads who also supported racial segregation.

Throughout his career, first at Princeton, then as governor of New Jersey, and especially while president, Wilson accumulated political enemies who attacked him for both political and personal reasons. While president of Princeton, Wilson incurred the wrath of many alumni and some Princeton administrators with his plan to close down the university's celebrated "eating clubs," as well as the placement of a new graduate school, in an attempt to elevate the academic stature of the university. While governor, Wilson's support for progressive reforms, as well as his decision to run for president in 1912 after such a short tenure in politics, angered both Democrats and Republicans in New Jersey.

Wilson's personal relationships also created controversy. While vacationing in Bermuda without his wife in 1907, Wilson met and began what some historians refer to as a love affair (though the extent of the relationship remains in question) with a woman named Mary Allen Hulbert Peck. Rumors of the relationship would plague Wilson for years, including a potential scandal during the 1912 presidential campaign. A staff member for Theodore Roosevelt's third party campaign came in possession of a love letter from Wilson to Peck. Roosevelt, however, refused to use it against Wilson, saying, "It was hopeless to convince the public that a man who looked like a drugstore clerk was in realty a Romeo." Perhaps the biggest personal scandal of Wilson's career, and thus a recurring line of attack against him, stemmed from his marriage to Edith Bolling Galt, with whom he became engaged less than a year after his wife Ellen's death in August 1914. Prior to their marriage in December 1915, rumors about Wilson's relationship with Edith were extensive, including the suggestion that the two had murdered Ellen. Edith's role as first lady was also controversial following the president's stroke in October 1919, as she became what many called the de facto president, running the executive branch for her incapacitated husband until the end of his second term in March 1921.

Although there are many stories to be told about declarations of hatred for Wilson before, during, and after his presidency, Wilson's response to the women's suffrage movement sparked particularly harsh denunciations. Despite supporting numerous progressive political reforms, Wilson was slow to support granting women the right to vote; the Nineteenth Amendment would not be ratified until August 1920. Prominent leaders of the suffrage movement clashed publicly with Wilson throughout his presidency. The president considered many of the activists, including Alice Paul, to be "unladylike," and he was particularly critical of those who protested outside of the White House. Women's suffrage activists, meanwhile, accused him of being coldhearted and misogynistic. After his death in 1924, Carrie Chapman Catt, another prominent leader of the movement, acknowledged

Wilson's political accomplishments despite not supporting suffrage until well into his second term: "Woodrow Wilson was a great man; history will not deny him that status and no enemy can. It is the fate of the great in political life to be criticized, condemned and hated. It is the mediocre who are popular."

PRESIDENTIAL PREROGATIVE AND WOMEN'S SUFFRAGE: THE ORIGINS OF CONFLICT

From his arrival in Washington, D.C., until the ratification of the Nineteenth Amendment seven years later, Wilson faced relentless attacks by a militant wing of the movement for women's suffrage. The objective of the National Woman's Party (NWP), under the leadership of Alice Paul, was simple: unconditional support for a constitutional amendment to guarantee women's right to vote in federal elections. Whoever was in the White House at that time would have borne the brunt of the attacks by the NWP. The NWP evolved from the National American Woman Suffrage Association's (NAWSA) Congressional Committee, which Paul headed as she organized a famous 1913 women's suffrage parade in Washington, D.C. The NAWSA and NWP would have overlapping memberships during Wilson's first term, with the NWP under Paul taking on an aggressive militancy that confronted Wilson.

Wilson's position on suffrage was somewhat vague, but historians note that he opposed a constitutional amendment for suffrage in favor of one in which individual states would decide the issue for themselves. It was only near the end of the battle for suffrage that he took a strong position in favor of the Nineteenth Amendment. However, neither in word nor deed was Wilson's record on suffrage that simple. Wilson's views on suffrage probably were associated with his upbringing in the South. Trained in the law, and a scholar of history and political science, Wilson noted that with the ending of the Civil War, the *legal* issues confronting the national government had been resolved. The legal issues of the 18th and 19th centuries were replaced at the beginning of the 20th century with social issues, reflecting his progressive Democratic Party agenda. Women were actively a part of that social agenda and by rights should now participate in voting. (Suffrage for women is a complicated tale—as the right for women to vote was dependent on statewide popular referenda in which women did not have a vote, and state governments and Congress in which women did not hold seats. Although a president is given a constitutional role in the passage of legislation, a president has no role in the addition of an amendment to the Constitution, except in how a president chooses to make use of prerogative power.)

A "Woman Suffrage Procession" including troops of women marching from states in the Northeast to Washington, D.C., culminating in a parade and other events in support of women's suffrage, had long been planned for the day before

Wilson was to take the oath of office. The events were organized by the NAWSA and its Congressional Committee, headed by Paul.

On the afternoon of March 3, 1913, while Wilson was en route to Washington from Princeton, New Jersey, the parade got underway to demonstrate nationwide support for a suffrage amendment. Organizers, the police, and reporters estimated that more than 5,000 people participated in the parade. Marchers assembled near the Capitol and headed down Pennsylvania Avenue to the Treasury building. Pennsylvania Avenue, linking the White House to the Capitol, had become the route for inaugural parades, and other parades of major significance; parade organizers had to receive permission to march down that historic avenue. A Pennsylvania Avenue parade became an enticement in recruiting major women leaders in all walks of life, from all around the country, to join in the march. Lines of marchers were well organized, with sections representing different professions, states, alumni from different colleges and universities, women working in government jobs, and countries in which women already had suffrage. Men supportive of the suffrage cause also had their own section.

News organizations featured stories on parade preparation for months in advance of the big day. Not only had information on the event been distributed to all states, but local papers also shared stories on their delegations with the Congressional Committee to be republished in other newspapers. One float in the parade was designated a press float (with embedded journalists). Riding on the float was Helen H. Gardener, a member of the executive board of the Congressional Committee, responsible for the press. She provided material for reporters covering the parade, and as she stated to members of a Senate Committee later investigating the role of the District of Columbia's police force in their difficulties in maintaining crowd control for the parade, her job was "making public opinion."

A key to understanding actions taken by the NWP, and the response of Wilson, is that both sides understood the importance of the role of the press in "making public opinion." There were no polls at that time, but the volume of news stories covering both the actions of the NWP and the Wilson administration's responses suggest that the importance of the press in making their positions known was recognized by both sides. Without the constant demands made by the NWP, it is not clear whether Wilson would have moved forward in taking a leadership role in getting Congress to consider a constitutional amendment to guarantee women's suffrage. There were a number of opportunities for Wilson to take a strong position and push for a constitutional amendment, especially as the nation moved toward war, and then again after the war, as Wilson crusaded to gain support for his League of Nations. But opportunities to take a leadership role were missed.

Wilson was only the second Democrat to win election to the White House since the Civil War (Grover Cleveland had been elected president both in 1884 and 1892). Following the lead taken by Abraham Lincoln, who as a young lawyer in Illinois had written about suffrage for women and as president had acknowledged the work and contributions of women to the Civil War effort, the Republican Party had in 1876 become the first party to allow women to address their national convention. Sixteen years later, it became the first major party to seat women at its national convention. In 1900 the Democratic Party finally allowed women to attend and participate in its convention. The Republican Party platform recognized the role of Republican state legislatures in moving forward on limited equal rights for women, including property rights, and the appointment of women to political offices, as early as 1876. The Democratic Party lagged behind the Republican Party in identifying and supporting rights for women. It is against this backdrop that Wilson came to Washington for his inauguration.

Arriving by train at Union Station on the afternoon of March 3, 1913, with the suffrage parade underway, Wilson took side streets through Washington, D.C., to avoid the parade until he reached his destination, the Shoreham Hotel. This route foreshadowed his subsequent strategy in dealing with the suffragists: avoid confrontation. The coverage of the parade and related preinaugural events had an impact far greater than for coverage of other events associated with the inauguration. The District of Columbia, under the control of Congress, was the subject of a series of hearings to investigate whether the local police force of the district had done its job in maintaining order along the parade route. Testimony from participants and parade watchers noted the hands-off approach of the local police in restraining massive crowds as they pushed into the procession. The women endured heckling from the crowds, as well as more aggressive actions as banners were torn and women grabbed. Mention was even made of the placing of Boy Scouts in strategic locations to prevent a threatened throwing of rats into the procession by local college students.

Hundreds of participants and observers of the parade from many states, and including members of Congress, were interviewed for news articles, and testified before the Senate Committee investigating the actions of the police. Media attention given to the cause of women's suffrage was substantial; at the same time, states were holding referenda questions to advance women's suffrage. But the bar for women to achieve universal suffrage on a state-by-state basis was quite high.

ENGAGING THE PRESS: "MAKING PUBLIC OPINION"

The NWP began publication of *The Suffragist* during Wilson's first year in office. It published on a weekly basis from November 1913 until 1920, when the publication continued on as a monthly for another year. Claiming members from across the country, the NWP both disseminated information to local newspapers on its efforts and collected information from activists at the state level, including episodes of violent behavior aimed at suffrage activists. These reports were often picked up by other newspapers. The publication thus brought nationwide attention to the movement for suffrage, with an impact far larger than suggested by the number of paid subscriptions.

In spite of the constant calls by suffragists to enfranchise women, Wilson seemed oblivious to such efforts. In a July 4th oration at Independence Hall in Philadelphia, just one year into his administration, Wilson noted that in Mexico "eighty-five per cent of the Mexican people have never been allowed to have any genuine participation on their own government." Yet half the population in the United States awaited suffrage. This same pattern was repeated in enough speeches that Sara Bard Field used the phrase "sex blind" when writing about Wilson in *The Suffragist* on September 30, 1916: ". . . the President is sex blind and cannot see women as part of a democracy."

If one looks solely at the speeches of Wilson, he clearly avoids the issue of suffrage, and appears not to take an active role until the amendment is well on its way to approval in the House and Senate. And by the time the amendment is submitted to the states for ratification, women had either achieved or were on their way to achieving suffrage in a number of states. Without an amendment, however, women would not have won suffrage in all the states.

Although Wilson failed to clearly state his support for women's suffrage in public addresses, his position was made known both in private communications and in small-group settings. On October 6, 1915, Wilson announced his engagement to Edith Bolling Galt at the same time he announced he would vote in favor of a referendum in New Jersey calling for women's suffrage. Scholars have noted the opposition within his own Democratic Party to the president remarrying only a year after the death of his first wife. Wilson was determined to go ahead with his marriage as soon as possible, though, and he decided a public announcement endorsing women's suffrage would ward off any concerns. However, his decision to only support an upcoming vote in New Jersey, deferring to each state the decision as to whether women would have the right to vote, was enormously disappointing to suffragists.

Later in the month, on October 15, Wilson alluded to his vote for women's suffrage in the New Jersey referendum in remarks to a gathering of the Daughters of the American Revolution in Washington, D.C. "I know of no body of persons comparable to a body of ladies for creating an atmosphere of opinion!," he stated. "I have myself in part yielded to the influences of that atmosphere, though it took me a long time to determine how I was going to vote in New Jersey."

The suffragists continued to publish photographs and articles of women protesting against Wilson and his failure to support suffrage for all women. While traveling the country in 1916, he was greeted at several locations by organized protesters with signs reading such things as "Wilson he opposes national suffrage," "President Wilson How Long do you want us to wait?" "Vote Against Wilson he opposes national suffrage." In the 1916 election, the NWP adopted a strategy of not endorsing Wilson in any state in which women had not won the right to vote.

After Wilson's reelection, in January 1917, the NWP began protests at the gates of the White House. The group steadily maintained pressure on Wilson to formally endorse a constitutional amendment guaranteeing suffrage for women. The NWP faulted Wilson and prior presidents for the absence of leadership in recommending Congress act on a suffrage amendment. With a Congress only meeting part of a year, the NWP wanted Wilson to call Congress back into session to expedite passage of an amendment.

WILSON RESPONDS: "A BARE COLORLESS CHRONICLE"

Early in 1917, when consideration was being given by the House of Representatives to form a Suffrage Committee, Wilson urged the House rules committee chair to go forward in that action. Each time Congress moved to bring the amendment forward, Wilson responded only after congressional action had been taken.

Wilson took advantage of the news coverage he received as a way of expanding the reach of his messages to the American public. One way in which he did so was to write letters to prominent individuals—letters that subsequently appeared in American newspapers. Just after the United States joined in the fight in World War I, Wilson issued an appeal to Americans to support the war effort, through their labor and service, productivity, and efficiency, both in the United States and in Europe. Wilson urged that his message be widely disseminated. On April 16, 1917, he "beg[ged] that all editors and publishers . . . will give as prominent publication and as wide circulation as possible to this appeal . . . to all advertising agencies . . . give it widespread repetition. . . . And . . . clergymen . . . [Do] not think the theme of it an unworthy or inappropriate subject of comment and homily from their pulpits."

In Wilson's second term, the actions of the NWP became most aggressive. Working patiently for each state to grant women suffrage had become intolerable. In January 1917, the NWP organized picketing at the White House. Signs of the protesters were initially rather tame, from "Mr. President, what will you do for Woman Suffrage" to "How Long must women wait for liberty?" Over the course of seven months, the posters became more aggressive, even as the United States became involved in World War I. Banners posed both question and commentary: "Kaiser Wilson have you forgotten your sympathy with the poor Germans because they were not self-governed? 20,000,000 American women are not self-governed." During the summer the protesters began to be arrested for "obstructing sidewalk traffic." Several thousand women joined in the highly orchestrated picketing, with hundreds arrested, and more than 100 detained or sentenced to prison. The women refused pardons, since publicity was the objective. Several went on hunger strikes in prison and were ultimately force-fed, adding to the news coverage.

In the summer of 1917 the less militant NAWSA tried to stifle press coverage of the protests by the NWP, with assistance sought of Wilson's staff. NAWSA leaders were anxious that the protests were being counterproductive. Wilson himself wrote, "My own suggestion would be that nothing that they do should be featured or put on the front page but that a bare colorless chronicle of what they do should be all that was printed. That constitutes part of the news but it need not be made interesting reading." However, the actions of the NWP made good news copy, and the protests and hunger strikes continued to garner headlines.

As U.S. engagement in World War I deepened, Wilson would often discuss the importance of self-government, but he failed to make the connection between women lacking the vote in the United States, and other governments in which suffrage was denied. The NWP clearly made that connection, however, in publications, on posters held in suffrage parades, and on the banners held by the "sentinels" standing in Lafayette Park across from the White House, and by chaining themselves to the gates of the White House. Wilson remained the primary target of their protests, although opponents of suffrage in Congress also came in for criticism. On January 9, 1918, Wilson finally issued a public statement urging the House to support a constitutional amendment. The work of women in the war effort provided his justification. However, the Armistice bringing an end to World War I came before both houses of Congress acted on a constitutional amendment. Wilson would continue to urge members to vote for the amendment as it moved to the floor in each respective chamber.

Wilson's main emphasis as World War I came to an end was the establishment of a League of Nations. For Wilson, a permanent end to war was an issue of human rights. Guaranteeing the right to vote for all citizens in a new world order was a part of an effort to preserve and expand human rights. Although the NWP's leaders could see the direct link between Wilson's pleas for suffrage in all countries and the legitimacy of their own quest for the vote, Wilson rarely made the connection.

After the Armistice, protests continued while Wilson sought support for his League of Nations. "Watch fires" kept the suffragists warm, as Wilson's speeches helped fuel the flames. Wilson was even burned in effigy in front of the White House gates. Sue White, head of the Tennessee National Woman's Party, was quoted as saying, "We burn not the effigy of a President of a free people, but the leader of an autocratic party organization whose tyrannical power holds millions of women in political slavery."

CONCLUSION

Without the constant public pressure on Wilson it is not clear whether he would have voiced support for a suffrage amendment. For Wilson, suffrage for women was not a legal issue, and therefore not a constitutional question as had been the case for slavery (as addressed in the Fourteenth or Fifteenth Amendments). The NWP had drawn upon the entry of the United States into World War I as a time to extend suffrage to women. How could the United States enter a war on behalf of people in Europe living under authoritarian regimes who lacked a vote, when half of the citizens in the United States lacked a vote?

When the Nineteenth Amendment was finally passed in the House and Senate by a two-thirds vote and submitted to the states for ratification, Wilson was in the midst of a national tour to drum up support for the League of Nations. In an address in California on September 18, 1919, Wilson made a point of emphasizing the importance of fair political representation in the covenant for the League of Nations: "No nation can be a member of that league which is not a self-governing nation. . . . No government which is not controlled by the will and vote of its people. It is a league of free, independent peoples, all over the world." Wilson's principles and the idea of women's suffrage in the United States had finally aligned.

Janet M. Martin

Further Reading

Berg, H. Scott. *Wilson.* New York: G. P. Putnam's Sons, 2013.

Brands, H. W. *Woodrow Wilson.* New York: Times Books, 2003.

Clements, Kendrick A., and Eric A. Cheezum. *Woodrow Wilson.* Washington, D.C.: CQ Press, 2003.

Cooper, John Milton, Jr. *Woodrow Wilson: A Biography.* New York: Alfred A. Knopf, 2009.

Gould, Lewis L. "Edith Bolling (Galt) Wilson," in *American First Ladies: Their Lives and Their Legacy,* ed. Lewis L. Gould. New York: Garland Publishing, 1996.

Graham, Sara Hunter. *Woman Suffrage and the New Democracy.* New Haven, CT: Yale University Press, 1996.

Martin, Janet M. *The Presidency and Women: Promise, Performance, and Illusion.* College Station, TX: Texas A&M University Press, 2003.

Milkis, Sidney M., and Michael Nelson. *The American Presidency: Origins and Development, 1776–2014,* 7th ed. Washington, D.C.: CQ Press, 2016.

Span, Paula. "Woodrow Wilson: How Did the Man Hailed as the Savior of Humanity Suddenly Become America's Most Hated President?" *American History,* August 2011.

29. Warren G. Harding

Born: November 2, 1865

Died: August 2, 1923

Time in Office: 29th President of the United States, March 4, 1921, to August 2, 1923

Election Results: 1920 Election: 60.3% of popular vote, 404 (76.1%) Electoral
   College votes
Spouse: Florence King (m. 1891)
Children: Elizabeth Ann Blaesing (with Nan Britton)

Warren G. Harding was born on November 2, 1865, in Corsica, Ohio (now Blooming
Grove, Ohio). He died of a cerebral hemorrhage or coronary thrombosis on August 2,
1923, in San Francisco, California. Harding was president from March 4, 1921, until
August 2, 1923, when he was succeeded by Calvin Coolidge after Harding's unexpected death. In the 1920 election, the Republican ticket of Warren Harding and Calvin Coolidge beat the Democratic ticket of James Cox and Franklin D. Roosevelt.
Harding won more than 16 million votes compared to Cox's 9 million with an Electoral College split of 404 to 127. Harding carried the majority of the country with the
exception of the southern states. The only southern states he carried were Tennessee
and Oklahoma.

Harding married Florence Mabel Kling on July 8, 1891. She was previously married to Henry Atherton DeWolfe with whom she had a son, Marshall Eugene
DeWolfe in 1880. Marshall died in 1915, and his children Eugenia and George
DeWolfe were Florence's heirs at her death in 1924. During the 1920 presidential
campaign, reporters believed Florence's first marriage ended with her husband's
death and not a divorce. After she assumed the role as first lady, neither her son nor
her previous marriage was commented upon publicly. The Hardings had no
children together, and until 2015, his descendants were only speculative. By several
accounts, Harding had an active love life that did not include his wife. The most well
known and documented of his relationships were with Carrie Fulton Phillips and
Nan Britton. Britton published a book in 1927 entitled *The President's Daughter,*
where she alleged that her daughter, Elizabeth, was the biological daughter of
Harding. Elizabeth never pursued notoriety and refused all interviews throughout
her adult life. After her death in 2015, it was revealed that members of the extended
Harding family contacted Elizabeth's children. DNA testing confirmed they were
genetically related to each other, thus finally confirming Britton's claims that Harding fathered her daughter.

The Harding administration is unusual because almost the entire balance of
scandal and strife emerged following his death. Scholars routinely regard the administration as one of the most plagued and corrupt in American history, but almost all
these critiques did not occur in his lifetime. There were rumors, but they were not
rampant. At his death, Harding was poised to take his place among the most beloved
of American presidents. The lack of active scandal during his presidency almost
certainly stems from his professional background. Harding and his wife both
came from newspaper backgrounds and ran the *Marion Star*; she was more of the
business person and the newspaper thrived under her direction. Harding, by

many accounts, was affable, good-natured, and had a friendly relationship with politicians from both parties in the area. He avoided criticism and never fired an employee his entire career. This character trait carried through into other facets of his life as well. His father once remarked, "Warren, it's a good thing you wasn't born a girl. Because you'd be in the family way all the time. You can't say, No!" Harding's tendency toward loyalty to friends and business allies was a valuable commodity in the newspaper business, but would eventually undermine his political career as he would place faith in others who had less than noble intentions.

Although their marriage may not have been particularly warm, Florence, or Flossie as she was known, persuaded him to pursue a political career. Harding's journalistic skills and cordial relationship with the press undoubtedly helped his ambitions. He was not an especially introspective person and sought the advice of others he deemed better qualified. The 1920 Harding campaign was notable because it wrote press releases and prepackaged stories for national distribution. With their newspaper backgrounds, they took an active hand in shaping public perception by preemptively controlling the flow of information. These were innovative techniques for their time and helped cultivate a positive Harding persona as someone who was in touch with the people. Harding ran for president on a platform of normalcy. It was an appealing message to the average citizen after several years of a devastating world war in Europe.

In June 1923, Harding began a cross-country rail tour. It seemed Harding was priming the country for a 1924 presidential reelection bid. He began complaining of digestion issues in Seattle on July 27, and on August 2 in San Francisco, he went into convulsions and died. The country was shocked and the popular Harding was mourned.

Harding had known a bit about some corruption in his administration, but not the breadth and depth. His careful use of the press, photo opportunities, and carefully cultivated relationships with the media of his day had ensured his reputation was sterling. However, once the flood gates opened, personal and political scandal became widely known. Harding's use of alcohol at the White House during Prohibition hurt his personal reputation as the corruption of his administration started to emerge. As president, he had taken a pledge of abstinence, and when the truth of his ample consumption came to light, people thought he was as corrupt as many of the officials he employed. They began to associate his personal predilections with his professional choices. He was also a voracious poker player, and the public was not amused when it came out he once bet the White House china in a game.

EARLY SCANDAL DURING THE CAMPAIGN

During the 1920 campaign, the most salacious material about Harding emerged from William Estabrook Chancellor, a professor at the College of Wooster. He asserted Harding's great-grandfather and great-grandmother were black and produced notarized affidavits from Ohio residents that backed up the claim. These rumors had circulated throughout Harding's life and were fostered by Harding's naturally tanned complexion. Although ignored by the Republican Party and publicly dismissed by the Democrats, whisper campaigns began to emerge throughout the country about Harding's family tree. Chancellor was unable to get his claims overtly published in any newspaper, likely as a result of Harding's publishing connections. In addition, he was dismissed from the College of Wooster, and the federal government confiscated the copies as well as the plates for his pamphlet, which he had titled *The Right of the American People to Know*. Gossip persisted in the background of Harding's presidency, but nothing was ever published that directly accused or attacked Harding. This rumor was finally resolved in 2015 when it was revealed that based on the genetic testing of Harding's extended family, including descendants of Harding and Nan Britton, with whom he had an extramarital affair, there was less than a 5% chance that Harding had a relative originating in Sub-Saharan Africa.

CABINET MALFEASANCE

As president, Harding largely viewed his job as ceremonial. He expected cabinet officials and staff to do the bulk of the serious work. He nurtured a friendly relationship with the press with biweekly press conferences. He often gave the six-to-eight person press corps unfettered information, with the expectation they would protect his image. Harding built a presidential cabinet with many qualified, well-regarded Republicans, including Herbert Hoover in Commerce and Andrew Mellon in Treasury. However, he also awarded positions to loyal supporters, informally known as the Ohio Gang. Their most prominent members included Attorney General Harry M. Daugherty, Interior Secretary Albert B. Fall, and Navy Secretary Edwin C. Denby. These three men committed acts of cronyism during the Harding administration.

One of the biggest scandals that emerged during the Harding presidency was the situation with the Veterans' Bureau. In June 1921, Harding signed the act creating the General Accounting Office and Bureau of the Budget. They were designed to try to rein in spending and prevent the mishandling of public funds. In July, Congress took up the issue of bonus pay for veterans. Harding was upset because he felt these bonuses would undermine budget reductions overseen by the new Bureau of the Budget. The compromise was the Sweet Act, which created the Veterans' Bureau, and was responsible to the president who had control over their agencies and mission. Harding appointed Charles R. Forbes as the head of this agency. Harding had met Forbes vacationing and gave him the position simply because he liked him and wanted to be a loyal friend. Forbes hired Charles F. Cramer as his general counsel at the Veterans' Bureau. Forbes and Cramer began selling off government surplus for a fraction of its cost. Simultaneously, they started purchasing sites for future hospitals at massively inflated prices based on the amount of kickbacks they received from others. Harding became aware of these activities by early 1923 and called Forbes into a meeting where he lied to the president about the situation. After Harding became aware that Forbes was lying and engaging in illegal activity, he wanted him removed from office. Harding did not want the scandal to break in the press and allowed Forbes to escape to Europe before he accepted his resignation. In March 1923, the Senate began investigating the Veterans' Bureau. Twelve days into the Senate investigation, Cramer committed suicide at his home. Forbes was eventually prosecuted and convicted of his activities.

Another scandal Harding knew about during his lifetime (though it did not emerge until afterward) involved the attorney general's office. Jesse "Jess" Smith was a good friend of Attorney General Daugherty and worked at the Justice Department in a nonofficial appointment. Smith illegally sold the liquor in the government warehouses to bootleggers for large sums of money. Harding became aware of some unusual behavior and told Daugherty right before his rail trip out West in 1923 to remove Smith from Washington, D.C. Harding specifically wanted to make the situation go away rather than prosecute. Smith was found dead at the end of May 1923 of an apparent suicide in Daugherty's apartment in Washington, D.C.

After Harding's death, Calvin Coolidge became president. He kept many of Harding's appointees, but did not shield them from investigation. In early 1924, senators were demanding a full investigation of Daugherty and the Justice Department. Public hearings produced large numbers of witnesses testifying about widespread corruption in the Harding White House. Smith and Daugherty were also implicated in another corruption scandal involving the alien property custodian, Colonel Thomas Miller. The alien property custodian was appointed during World War I to handle property in the United States owned by citizens of enemy nations. Smith illegally transferred a German-owned company to an American-owned company for large sums of money that went to both Smith and Miller. More important, Smith's money was deposited in a joint account owned by Daugherty and Smith. The attorney general used his office to block any requests for information about this bank account, and the potential evidence was destroyed prior to Daugherty's trial for defrauding the government. Ultimately, Miller was convicted, but the charges against Daugherty were dropped under unresolved circumstances with a lack of conclusive evidence.

TEAPOT DOME SCANDAL

The most famous scandal during the Harding administration was Teapot Dome, which permanently associated his administration with corruption. The naval oil reserves in Wyoming at Teapot Dome were transferred from the U.S. Navy to the Department of Interior in May 1921 by executive order. Interior Secretary Albert Fall then gave out no-bid long-term oil leases to his friends with terms not favorable to the national government. The Senate began to investigate in April 1922, but there was a general lack of support in Congress. Senator Thomas J. Walsh from Montana persisted and kept the situation from disappearing from congressional attention. His investigation discovered Fall's financial situation had greatly improved during his tenure at Interior. At one point, Fall explained his windfall in a letter stating the publisher of the *Washington Post*, Edward B. McLean, loaned him a substantial amount of money. Walsh tracked McLean down to Miami where the publisher admitted Fall's story was a lie. It was later proven that Fall received over $400,000 from two oilmen in exchange for favoritism with the leases. Fall was convicted of taking bribes and became the first cabinet level officer to go to prison for his behavior in office.

REPUTATION AFTER DEATH

Harding was a well-regarded and popular president. After his death, though, his reputation soured so significantly that he routinely ranks among the worst of all American presidents. This shift has much to do with Florence Harding and popular culture. Following Warren's death in San Francisco, Florence Harding did not want an autopsy. His body was sent back East for a funeral in Washington, D.C., followed by a burial in Marion, Ohio. Shortly afterward, the Library of Congress contacted her about acquiring the president's papers. She claimed that she had burned them all, honoring her late husband's desire for privacy. As the public became aware of the Senate investigations into Harding's White House, though, her actions were interpreted as a potential cover-up instead of a loving gesture of privacy. When Florence Harding died in November 1924 amid ongoing Senate investigations about her husband's presidency, no close family members were left to defend his rapidly tarnishing reputation. Muckrakers and journalists began to use artistic license to expound on the activities of Harding in the absence of any presidential paper trail. In 1930, *The Strange Death of President Harding* suggested that Florence Harding may have poisoned her husband. The book was based on information from Gaston Means (a member of the so-called "Ohio Gang" of businessmen and politicians who inhabited the Harding orbit, many of whom would be involved in financial and political scandals), who was later discredited. Rumors about Harding that originated with this book still persist today, however. Before that, F. Scott Fitzgerald wrote a play in 1923 entitled *The Vegetable, or From President to Postman* where a thinly veiled Harding seemed hapless and henpecked by his more formidable wife. Muckraker Samuel Hopkins Adams, meanwhile, chose Harding and his administration as the subject of his novel *Revelry* (1926). The novel outlined the Harding scandals in a sensationalized manner that propelled the book into a national best seller.

The book that did the most lasting damage to Harding's reputation, however, was *The President's Daughter* (1927) by Nan Britton, his former mistress. The investigations into the Harding administration scandals were still news when Britton's book was released, and the claims of an illegitimate daughter further undermined his reputation as an upstanding and moral president. It also helped foster another series of negative portrayals of Harding. Frederick Lewis Allen (1931) wrote *Only Yesterday: An Informal History of the Nineteen Twenties,* and Samuel Hopkins Adams (1939) wrote *Incredible Era: The Life and Times of Warren Gamaliel Harding.* By the end of the 1930s, Harding's reputation was in tatters. His most upstanding cabinet member, Herbert Hoover, had a largely disastrous presidency himself, and few people were left to defend his presidency and its record. The Harding administration became synonymous with incompetence, scandal, and ribald corruption.

Fortunately, Florence Harding had been exaggerating when she said Harding's papers had been destroyed. Although not everything survived, a large amount was discovered, catalogued, and microfilmed. These records are available through several sources and help chronicle the activities in the Harding White House. In addition, the love letters between Carrie Phillips and Warren Harding were donated to the Library of Congress and made available to the public online in July 2014.

CONCLUSION

Harding was a man far more popular in life than in death. His relationship and understanding of the press helped his administration create a duality between reality and perception. Harding did not intentionally create a corrupt White House, but made choices that encouraged one. His personal and professional shortcomings undermined his judgment and ultimately, his reputation. By many accounts, he actively avoided confrontation and preferred affable relationships. He allowed loyalty to perceived friends to override any sense of duty to the country. Harding used the press to nurture a friendly presidential image, and also used those connections to help bury unfavorable stories. He allowed men who failed him to abscond instead of confronting them and holding them publicly accountable for their actions. Some members of Harding's cabinet used the executive branch as their path to wealth. Although they were able to succeed for a while, the oversight capacity of the Congress ultimately brought to light several troubling situations. Several investigations resulted in criminal charges with many of the men held accountable.

The afterlife of Harding has been one of foppish hyperbole. He is frequently cast as a person woefully out of his intellectual depth and manipulated by others around him. Between books, Senate investigations, and scandalous rumors, the accomplishments of the Harding administration faded into obscurity. Although he was beloved in life as a president, in death, Harding's reputation was eviscerated by the scandal and never recovered. Instead, the lasting public perception centers on corruption and a best forgotten presidential administration.

Shannon Bow O'Brien

Further Reading

Adams, Samuel Hopkins. *Revelry*. New York: Boni & Liveright, 1926.

Adams, Samuel Hopkins. *The Incredible Era: The Life and Times of Warren Gamaliel Harding*. New York: Capricorn Books, 1939.

Allen, Frederick Lewis. *Only Yesterday: An Informal History of the 1920s*. New York: John Wiley & Sons, 1931.

Britton, Nan. *The President's Daughter*. New York: Elizabeth Ann Guild, 1927.

Dean, John W. *Warren G. Harding*. New York: Times Books, 2004.

Fitzgerald, F. Scott. *The Vegetable, or From President to Postman*. New York: Scribner's, 1923.

McCartney, Laton. *The Teapot Dome Scandal*. New York: Random House, 2008.

Means, Gaston B. *The Strange Death of President Harding: From the Diaries of Gaston Means, as Told to May Dixon Thacker*. New York: New York Guild Publishing Corporation, 1930.

Payne, Phillip G. *Dead Last: The Public Memory of Warren G. Harding's Scandalous Legacy*. Athens, OH: Ohio University Press, 2009.

Sinclair, Andrew. *The Available Man: The Life behind the Masks of Warren G. Harding*. Chicago, IL: Quadrangle Books, 1969.

Transi, Eugene P., and David L. Wilson. *The Presidency of Warren G. Harding*. Lawrence, KS: University Press of Kansas, 1977.

30. Calvin Coolidge

Born: July 4, 1872

Died: January 5, 1933

Time in Office: 30th President of the United States, August 2, 1923, to March 4, 1929

Election Results: 1920 Election: Elected vice president, assumed office upon death of Warren G. Harding; 1924 Election: 54% of popular vote, 382 (71.9%) Electoral College votes

Spouse: Grace Goodhue (m. 1905)

Children: John and Calvin Jr.

Calvin Coolidge was born in Plymouth, Vermont, on July 4, 1872. Beginning in 1921, he served as Warren G. Harding's vice president, becoming president upon Harding's death in office on August 2, 1923. Running in his own right in the 1924 presidential election, Coolidge bested his Democratic opponent John W. Davis and the Progressive Party's candidate Robert La Follette to win with 382 electoral votes and 54% of the popular vote. He married Grace Goodhue in 1905, and the couple had two sons, John and Calvin Jr., the latter of whom died from an infection following an injury at the White House in 1924. Though many backed another Coolidge term, in the lead up to the 1928 election, Coolidge issued the terse statement, "I do not choose to run for president in 1928." Coolidge retired to Massachusetts in 1929 and died of a heart attack on January 5, 1933.

CRITICIZED AS A COLD AND DISTANT PRESIDENT

Accounts of those close to Coolidge reveal he could be a difficult character whose personality made him hard to deal with. He was described as rude and having a short temper, one that could flare up over even minor incidents. Ike Hoover, the White House chief usher from 1909 to 1933, is one source of such less-than-fond memories of the 30th president. Hoover wrote that with Coolidge in the White House, his fellow employees felt perpetual "fear and trembling, lest they lose their jobs" and that the president "kept them in a state of constant anxiety." Some of the president's staff had good reason to worry about being fired. In the summer of 1927 while on vacation in South Dakota, First Lady Grace Coolidge returned later than expected from a hike with her Secret Service agent because they had lost their way. When they arrived at the house, Coolidge was said to be enraged and promptly reassigned and replaced the agent; some speculated that Coolidge feared that Grace was having an affair with him.

The president also reportedly mistreated members of his immediate family. On one fishing trip Coolidge made no effort to help his wife when she accidentally lodged a fishhook into her finger. Instead he merely stared at her before eventually walking away entirely—a response that greatly disturbed Secret Service agents on the scene. After Coolidge's son Calvin Jr. died, President Coolidge became far more critical and tough on their surviving son John. Coolidge made clear to John that he was unhappy with nearly everything he did, including what he wore, his work ethic, and the people he surrounded himself with, leading his son to confess to a friend that going to visit his parents at the White House was "like being in the penitentiary" and that he was always "damn glad" to escape the company of his father.

Hoover also compared Coolidge unfavorably to the other presidents he had served, calling him "the hardest to please and least thought of" chief executive, and "positively unkind." Examples of such "unkindness" also come up in tales of bizarre cruelty involving the president. Coolidge would demand that a Secret Service agent bait his hook for him when out fishing, and on at least one occasion he quickly jerked the line away at the last moment, deliberately trying to embed the hook in the agent's flesh. Political cartoonists liked to depict Coolidge as a dour and disgruntled figure. These portrayals echoed an assessment from Alice Roosevelt Longworth, Theodore Roosevelt's eldest child, that Coolidge looked like he had been "weaned on a pickle." When Coolidge became president after Harding's death, liberal magazine *The Nation* declared, "Now the presidency sinks low indeed. We doubt if ever before it has fallen into the hands of a man so cold, so narrow, so reactionary, so uninspiring, and so unenlightened, or one who has done less to earn it, than Calvin Coolidge."

When he emerged on the national political scene, Coolidge earned the nickname "Silent Cal" for how quiet and withdrawn he was at both public events and in private meetings. Coolidge had never really been known for his eloquence; a common saying when he was lieutenant governor of Massachusetts was that the governor at the time, Samuel W. McCall, could fill any auditorium with his speeches and that Coolidge could empty it. Nor was he praised for his writing. Journalist Heywood Broun called his use of words "one hundred percent wooden" and professed that "he seems to me the least gifted author the White House has known in many generations."

Coolidge's political opponents sought to use his uncommunicative reputation against him. His Democratic rival for the presidency in 1924, John W. Davis, derided Coolidge in a campaign speech, charging that according to his opponent, "If scandals break out in the government, the way to treat them is—silence. If petted industries make exorbitant profits under an extortionate tariff, the answer is—silence. If the League of Nations . . . invites us into conference on questions of worldwide importance, the answer is—silence. If race and religious prejudices threaten our domestic harmony, the answer is—silence." The lasting impression of his taciturnity followed him even in his last years. When news broke in 1933 that Coolidge had died, the writer Dorothy Parker's response was said to be, "How could they tell?"

Coolidge's reticence appeared in part motivated by his desire to avoid conflict and conversations he viewed as a waste of time. Speaking to businessman Bernard Baruch while president, Baruch noted Coolidge was "so different from what people say you are," namely far more talkative and friendly, while "everybody said you never say anything." The president replied, "Well, Baruch, many times I say only 'yes' or 'no' to people. Even that is too much. It winds them up for twenty minutes more." In his bids for public office, Coolidge took a hard line against negative campaigning, declining to even utter the names of those running against him. In response to charges that he was too silent during the 1924 campaign, Coolidge countered, "I don't recall any candidate for president that ever injured himself very much by not talking." Coolidge's autobiography further defended keeping quiet, opining, "The words of the President have an enormous weight and ought not to be used indiscriminately."

Neither did Coolidge seem to care much about what his opponents had to say about him. His vice president, Charles G. Dawes, once asked Coolidge whether he had seen a critical article about him by a widely read columnist, and the president answered, "You mean that one in the magazine with the green cover? I started to read it, but it was against me, so I didn't finish it." Looking back at his career, Coolidge's appraisal was that "I shall always consider it the highest tribute to my administration that the opposition have based so little of their criticism on what I have really said and done. . . . Perhaps one of the reasons I have been a target for so little abuse is because I have tried to refrain from abusing other people."

A "DO NOTHING" PRESIDENT

Coolidge's taciturn personality and conservative belief in limited government, both a marked contrast with some of his fellow 20th-century presidents, contributed to the common complaint, leveled at him both during and after his presidency, that Coolidge was a "do nothing" president. *The New Republic,* for instance, wrote in December 1923 that while Theodore Roosevelt and Woodrow Wilson "cherished visions of a better America . . . Mr. Coolidge has not seen the vision of an America better than the America of which he is president." At times, Coolidge attributed his lack of action to ignorance as well as skepticism of government activism, telling one acquaintance, "The president shouldn't do too much, and he shouldn't *know* too much." As seen in the specific cases below—the floods of 1927, issues of racism and discrimination, and lingering scandals from the Harding administration—Coolidge's inaction was by design.

In 1927 the country faced one of the worst natural disasters in its history when heavy rain caused the Mississippi River to flood portions of ten states, resulting in hundreds of deaths and hundreds of thousands of people displaced or homeless. The floods caused an estimated $1 billion in damage (which represented one-third of the federal budget in 1927). In the contemporary era, presidents typically respond to such crises by visiting the affected areas, publicly surveying the damage, and promising quick and robust federal government relief. Coolidge, though admittedly heading up a government of more limited resources, refused to do any of these things. For many months he ignored calls to ask Congress for aid for the region. Public officials from the affected states begged Coolidge to come visit flooded areas, but he rejected such requests, reasoning that such visits would be an inappropriate aggrandizement of the national government's role in a local matter. When he did finally call for action in a December 1927 message to Congress, the legislation he supported called for most of the costs to be placed on property owners who would be given loans from the government. The negative reaction to this proposal was so great that by February of the following year, Coolidge had thrown his backing behind a $180 million program that included more aid money from the government going to victims. Some of his opponents in Congress supported a more generous bill, but Coolidge argued that such a move would be unprecedented and dangerous. If adopted, Coolidge maintained, "then it becomes a bestowal of favors on certain localities and naturally if one locality is to be favored, all the other localities in the United States think they ought to come in under the same plan and have their floods taken care of."

Unsurprisingly, many of his critics—and especially Americans directly affected by the floods—did not accept Coolidge's framing of his position as a principled stand on limited government. They instead cast his motivations as a product of ignorance or indifference. Local newspapers attacked his blindness to the severity of flood victims' plight. The *Jackson Clarion-Ledger* editorialized, "It has been necessary to school President Coolidge day by day a bit more towards the realization of the immensity of the catastrophe," and the *Paducah News-Democrat* declared that Coolidge was either in possession of "the coldest heart in America or he has the dullest imagination, and we are about ready to believe he has both." Will Rogers quipped that maybe Coolidge was delaying relief legislation in "the hope that those needing relief will perhaps have conveniently died in the meantime." Senator Thaddeus Caraway of Arkansas proposed that perhaps Coolidge would have been more sympathetic had the flooding been in his own hometown, charging, "I venture to say that if a similar disaster had affected New England that the president would have had no hesitation in calling an extra session" of Congress.

When his opponents in the 1924 presidential election spoke out explicitly against the Ku Klux Klan and urged the president to do the same, Coolidge refused to say anything specifically critical and instead talked in generalities about equality and patriotism. Black and Jewish community leaders also appealed to Coolidge to speak out against the violent white supremacist organization, but to no avail. When the KKK held a major march in 1925 down Pennsylvania Avenue in Washington, D.C., charges intensified that Coolidge was essentially condoning the group's activities by refusing to condemn them. The Democratic-leaning newspaper the *Brooklyn Eagle* noted that in contrast to his 1924 presidential opponents Davis and La Follette, "Calvin Coolidge, Puritan of the Puritans, coming of the stock from which the old Know-Nothings were chiefly recruited, seems to imagine that without denouncing the Klan he can avoid loss of votes by saying nice things about the classes that are the victims of the Klan's hostility."

Much of the fallout from the Teapot Dome scandal and other controversies involving Harding's cabinet members took place after the former president's death, under the Coolidge administration. During congressional investigations of the malfeasance, Democrats worked hard to uncover evidence of Coolidge's complicity, but little materialized. Still, Coolidge was attacked for being reluctant to support the investigations and slow to remove tainted officials from his administration. Eventually, Coolidge appointed a bipartisan counsel to investigate the scandal. He insisted that the investigation would rise above petty party considerations. "There will be no politics nor partisanship," he said. "I am a Republican, but I cannot on that account shield anyone because he is a Republican. I am a Republican, but I cannot on that account prosecute anyone because he is a Democrat." Fortunately for the president, some prominent Democratic politicians were found to be involved in the wrongdoing, which undercut the ability of the opposition party to use the events of the Teapot Dome scandal against him. For the president's critics though, Coolidge had still been stained by the scandals. When he left office, *The Nation* observed his presidency "has been distinguished. It has been distinguished, first, by its complacent attitude toward shocking corruption in high office," and later when he died, the same magazine declared "he had been utterly silent in the face of the corruption of the Harding cabinet, in which . . . he sat."

MISUSE OF MEDIA

Even as his detractors lamented Coolidge's inactivity, he was also subject to criticism for the way he used the media as president. Some of these attacks appear to reflect growing pains surrounding changing norms on presidential communication and public leadership and the impact of new and developing technologies. Hostile commentators mocked Coolidge's participation in what modern political observers would recognize as early examples of "photo ops," particularly when he was back on his family farm in Vermont. Writer Sherwin Cook asserted that "no president has ever been willing to submit to such nauseating exhibitions in the news reels as has Coolidge. Cultured Americans wince at the thought of their president putting on a smock frock to pose while pitching hay and milking a bossy." On vacation in South Dakota, the president and his wife wore western-style outfits, and Coolidge received a horse as a present. The progressive outlet *The People's Business* reported of the trip, "The president of the United States has become a pitiful puppet of publicity. The movie pictures' audiences roar with laughter as this bewildered little man teeters down the steps in vaudeville chaps and timidly grasps the reins of the gift horse which he fears to mount."

Coolidge was also rebuked for his close relationships with reporters and efforts to shape coverage—news management strategies that would become routine for presidential administrations of both parties over the next few decades. As quoted in David Greenberg, one correspondent called the president's press conferences "a vicious institution in American life" that was turning newspapers into "propaganda agencies." *The Nation* claimed, "the American people dearly love to be fooled to worship politicians of whom they have created portraits which bear little or no resemblance to the originals," and noted "the Coolidge myth has been created by amazingly skillful propaganda." One editor of this period, also quoted in Greenberg, argued that Coolidge had been sold to the American people "as though he were a new breakfast food or fountain pen."

ACCUSED OF BEING TOO CLOSE TO BUSINESS

Coolidge was also attacked for being overly supportive of industry at the expense of the public good. The president himself perhaps encouraged this view with one of his few well-known quotes, a declaration in a January 17, 1925, speech that "the chief business of the American people is business." This line of criticism came not only from Democrats, but also from within a fractured Republican Party, particularly the progressive wing that nominated Wisconsin senator Robert La Follette to run for president against Coolidge in 1924. Progressive William Allen White compared the president to the literary character of Ebenezer Scrooge, because "he and Coolidge both believe that Commerce is a sacrosanct matter."

Those apparent sympathies with business have also fed accusations of a more serious nature that Coolidge might have prevented the Great Depression or lessened its severity, but chose not to do so. In January 1928, as the stock market continued to rise and the value of brokers' loans skyrocketed at what some believed was an unsustainable and dangerous rate, Coolidge was asked whether he had any qualms about the economy's trajectory. He gave a formal statement to reporters offering assurances he was not worried in the slightest and that these developments were based on a sound and accurate reading of the financial markets. That public encouragement from the president helped shore up what was in reality a tenuous and faulty market. Just days later, in an off-the-record conversation with a financial journal editor, Coolidge indicated that his personal opinion was actually that there was excessive and problematic speculation going on, but that he could not say this because "I regard myself as the representative of the government and not as an individual. When technical matters come up I feel called upon to refer them to the proper department of the government which has some information about them and then, unless there is some good reason, I use this information as a basis for whatever I have to say; but that does not prevent me from thinking what I please as an individual."

This attitude has prompted accusations that Coolidge was either grossly negligent in taking steps to protect the nation in his charge from a looming depression or that the administration purposefully worked to delay the onset of the economic crisis until after he left office. Years later, *The Nation* described that January 1928 statement on the markets as "prostituting the White House as it has never been prostituted before" and "encouraging the maddest, wildest speculation in the world's history." Oswald Garrison Villard wrote of the depression, "The Coolidge policies, so highly praised, were based solely on the crassest materialism and inexorably helped to drive the country into the limitless disaster in which it finds itself today. This disaster spells the end of many things. It is above all the final harvest of the policies of Calvin Coolidge and of those for whom he stood, whose desires he fulfilled, whose faithful servant he was."

Further encouraging this view, numerous accounts of Coolidge's decision not to run for president in 1928 point to remarks made by his wife, both at the time and in her later writings, that her husband could see that a depression was coming, but that he was unwilling to take the actions likely necessary to deal with it, such as increasing federal spending or regulating the private sector. Out of office, in 1932, Coolidge spoke of the "socialistic notions of government" he was witnessing, and he was talking about the actions of the Hoover administration, not Franklin D. Roosevelt and the New Deal. After the depression hit, Coolidge himself indicated he would not have been the right leader to deal with the economic crisis, saying, "We are in a new era to which I do not belong, and it would not be possible for me to adjust to it."

CONCLUSION

Much of the derision and animosity directed toward Coolidge appears to be a product of the time in which he served, a period of significant transition in American politics. Perceptions were dramatically changing about the appropriate role of the president and how powerful the federal government should be, the country was experiencing a booming economy on the verge of collapse, and a modernizing media altered the ways the public could see and hear from the president. Although Coolidge was quite popular during his tenure in the White House, the economic calamity that would soon befall the nation caused many to highlight the darker side of his trademark silence and inaction. Coolidge's administration is often judged based on what came after, and it is perhaps unrealistic and unfair to expect Coolidge to have predicted the Great Depression and acted to prevent it. As detailed above, however, versions of these attacks on Coolidge did exist during his presidency, emphasized by his detractors in the Democratic and Progressive Parties, among rural and minority communities who felt ignored and slighted by the administration, and by journalists and intellectuals frustrated by his constrained view of government authority. Hoover's legacy would ultimately be more directly tied to the United States' worst economic crisis, but the Coolidge years of relative prosperity and calm lost much of their luster in the wake of what was to follow.

Jennifer Rose Hopper

Further Reading

Bates, J. Leonard. "The Teapot Dome Scandal and the Election of 1924." *The American Historical Review,* Vol. 60, No. 2 (January 1955): 303–322.

Coolidge, Calvin. *The Autobiography of Calvin Coolidge.* Honolulu, HI: University Press of the Pacific, 2004.

Ferrell, Robert H. *The Presidency of Calvin Coolidge.* Lawrence, KS: University Press of Kansas, 1998.

Gilbert, Robert E. "Calvin Coolidge's Tragic Presidency: The Political Effects of Bereavement and Depression." *Journal of American Studies,* Vol. 39 (April 2005): 87–109.

Greenberg, David. *Calvin Coolidge.* New York: Henry Holt and Company, 2006.

Hoover, Irwin Hood. *Forty-Two Years in the White House.* Boston: Houghton-Mifflin, 1934.

McCoy, Donald R. *Calvin Coolidge: The Quiet President.* Newtown, CT: American Political Biography Press, 1998.

Shlaes, Amity. *Coolidge.* New York: HarperCollins, 2013.

Silver, Thomas B. "Coolidge and the Historians." *The American Scholar,* Vol. 50 (Autumn 1981): 501–517.

Sobel, Robert. *Coolidge: An American Enigma.* Washington, D.C.: Regnery Publishing, 1998.

31. Herbert Hoover

Born: August 10, 1874

Died: October 20, 1964

Time in Office: 31st President of the United States, March 4, 1929, to March 4, 1933

Election Results: 1928 Election: 58.2% of popular vote, 444 (83.6%) Electoral College votes; 1932 Election: 39.7% of popular vote, 59 (11.1%) Electoral College votes

Spouse: Lou Henry (m. 1899)

Children: Herbert Jr. and Allan

No president ever fell from grace so quickly and from such a height as did Herbert Hoover. Prior to the Great Depression, he seemed not only the embodiment of the American Dream, but the personification of the Noble American. His story was epic. Born in the small hamlet of West Branch, Iowa—itself an example of fabled middle American small towns—Hoover was orphaned at a young age. Nonetheless, he joined the first class at Stanford University and became a mining engineer. By the time he was 30 years old Hoover had become a millionaire, at a time when that designation meant something unimaginable. When World War I broke out, he was first placed in charge of getting Americans out of war zones and back to safety across the Atlantic. He then took on the grim but all-important task of channeling relief efforts, first through warring lines to Belgium and France, then after the war to all of prostrated Europe. The great historian Richard Hofstadter, who at times displayed biting sarcasm in his historical portraits, wrote how, "In a time of havoc and hatred the name Hoover came to mean food for the starving and medicine for the sick. From the ranks of his co-workers a fanatic body of admirers had gathered around him. . . . After five years of war service without salary and without attention to his personal affairs, his fortune had been somewhat scaled down, but he was rich in popularity."

Basking in worldwide adulation, Hoover served as secretary of commerce to successive Republican administrations. An active and highly visible cabinet member, he became one of the great movers and shakers in Washington during the 1920s. In 1928 he capped off his meteoric rise by registering a decisive victory at the polls to become president of the United States. Charles Michelson, the Democratic Party's publicist and Hoover's foremost antagonist, claimed that by 1928 Hoover was "an almost supernatural figure whose wisdom encompassed all branches, whose judgement was never at fault, who knew all the answers to all the questions, and could see in the dark." In sum, Michelson acknowledged, Hoover was regarded by much of the American public as "a miracle man."

THE STOCK MARKET CRASH OF 1929

Despite his widespread popularity, however, qualms about Hoover's presidency were raised from the start. Amazingly, the first elected office Hoover ever held was the highest in the land. In addition, many GOP leaders stayed shy of him because, after his White House predecessor, Calvin Coolidge, he seemed insufficiently conservative. As historian David Lisio put it, "among Republican leaders Hoover was by no means the overwhelming choice for the presidential nomination." Biographer David Burner agreed that "the Republican old guard and a sizeable segment of the business world distrusted him." A Republican senator stated bluntly, "Hoover gives most of us gooseflesh." Nonetheless, Hoover proved too strong for doubters to derail him. As William Allen White, a journalist and Hoover ally, wrote of his candidate in 1928, "never before in a Republican convention has (anyone) . . . beaten into an omelet the hard boiled eggs of the Old Guard."

In the fall of 1929, though, the stock market crash rocked Hoover's young presidency. The convulsions on Wall Street soon triggered the Great Depression, a terrible economic downturn that ushered in an era of mass unemployment, poverty, and economic stagnation. Hoover, ill-prepared to play the role of a public, inspirational leader and bound by ideology to resist government intervention, did not respond well. By late 1930 alone, the national unemployment rate had doubled to 10.7% (it eventually climbed much higher, to 25%). Bank failures climbed to 1,352 in 1930, leaving working people sitting on the steps of closed institutions, crying at the knowledge that their life savings were gone. Hoover bore much of the blame in the eyes of ordinary Americans. Old newspapers stuffed into haggard clothing becoming known as "Hoover blankets," and a "Hoover flag" was a pocket turned inside out.

Hoover was ill-equipped to lead the nation through this trauma. As a young couple, Bert (as his wife Lou called him) wrote in her diary that while at parties she "created her own atmosphere," he "felt like a wet crow." Later, as a public speaker, he was a dismal flop. Burner felt that, "If Hoover's 1928 campaign speeches had seemed dull, his omnibus talks of 1932, crammed with statistics, were even duller and more platitudinous." In many of his public remarks, for example, he employed advanced vocabulary terms, "*Sisyphean, vacuous, supervened, attenuated, palpably*" to describe human hardship, all delivered "in a flat, metallic voice." Furthermore, Burner described Hoover's speeches as "unrelievedly conservative, a defense of the record, not a plan for reconstruction." According to one historian of radio and politics, Hoover compounded these problems by being "slow to heed good political advice" on how to employ the new medium to rally and encourage Americans.

Hoover's declining popularity was closely monitored by the press, which became increasingly critical of the president on matters both large and small. One newspaper editor remarked that "part of Herbert Hoover's loss of popularity might be traced to the circumstance that, in almost all of his photographs, he appeared lumpy, flabby, and ill at ease." Even worse, according to historian Douglas Craig, he alienated the press, and "treated reporters and broadcasters with a combination of contempt and ineptitude"; Michelson felt Hoover was "the thinnest-skinned executive in Washington." Compounding this was the recalcitrance of the president and first lady to even engage the press or the public. As one biographer of Lou Hoover put it, "Neither the president nor his wife ever sought publicity for the sake of publicity." After Lou Hoover flatly told a group of female reporters anxious for a story that "women reporters in Washington all knew she was never quoted," they all left. Hoover was also at times awkward and ham-fisted as he tried to reassure the public that conditions were not as dire as some people thought. In one instance, for example, he declared that "nobody is actually starving. The hoboes are better fed than they have ever been."

DEMOCRATIC ATTACKS ON HOOVER

After their loss in the 1928 election, the Democratic Party underwent a revolution of sorts, shattering a variety of long-standing traditions in American politics. At this time central political committees were weak bodies, only rousing themselves from somnolence every four years to conduct a presidential campaign. In the aftermath of Hoover's 1928 victory, however, they had a new financing source, and a new dynamism. The Democrats' 1928 candidate, Al Smith, had linked up with John

Raskob, one of the richest and most innovative figures in the country, and made him his campaign manager. Raskob stayed on after the election and decided to transform the party, taking over leadership and committing to finance the organization through the 1932 presidential convention. As Michelson explained, the industrialist felt that "the great obstacle to Democratic success was the party's habit of lying dormant for three years and a half and then attempting to effect a political evolution in the brief period between convention and election day." Instead, he would keep the office open and staffed on a regular basis.

Raskob changed American politics by hiring Charles "Charlie" Michelson as his permanent publicity director—the first official at this level to staff either party. Michelson came from an illustrious family: his brother was Albert Abraham Michelson, the first American to win the Nobel Prize in Physics in 1907, for measuring the speed of light. His sister Miriam became a pioneering Jewish feminist author. Charlie was born in Virginia City, Nevada, became a reporter in San Francisco, and from 1917 until he began work for the Democrats, Washington bureau chief for the *New York World*.

Michelson claimed that "Political publicity was a new field for me," but in truth he was an old hand, an established presence in Washington. In a unique, revelatory piece on Michelson in *Scribner's Magazine*, veteran Baltimore journalist Frank Kent wrote that Michelson was "popular among the hundreds of newspaper correspondents in Washington, nearly all of whom are his friends." As a result, he "knows the political game from the inside and knows as many politicians in both parties, in and out of Congress, as any man in Washington. . . ." Michelson was a one-man show, never hiring a research director; Kent described the role he assumed: "He is the publicity director. He is the dynamic force that makes the wheels go around. He is the works. In effect he is the committee." According to Kent, after Raskob and his team "concluded their arrangements with Mr. Michelson, they gave him a free hand and said 'Go to it.' And he went to it like a fireman to a fire, only his idea was not to extinguish the flames but to build them. The goal set for him was to 'smear' Hoover and the Hoover administration. . . . That is his job, and it would be hard to imagine a man with his heart more completely in it." Writing in his memoir, Michelson referred to Kent's piece as "a delightfully written article" but insisted that it's "premise was all wrong." According to Michelson, all he had to do to fulfill his duties was highlight Hoover's actual record.

Michelson started with a shrewd premise. He would write up remarks, then arrange for them to be delivered to the public on Capitol Hill via a senator or representative; thus they were published in the *Congressional Record,* and a newspaper could quote his remarks with an air of authority and no fear of libel. Oliver McKee Jr. described the process thusly in the *North American Review* in 1930: "He thus proceeds to one of his Congressional Democratic friends and says, perhaps to Senator Harrison of Mississippi: 'Pat, here is a good opportunity for a statement.

[Senator] George Moses has gotten off on the wrong foot again. What do you think of this?' He whips out a memorandum, sketching the points to be made, gets Harrison's O.K., and in a few hours, special messenger boys are delivering to the offices of Washington correspondents the Senator's latest blast on the Republican administration. The name on the statement may be Harrison, or Tom Walsh, or Jack Garner, but the wording and phraseology, the kick and the punch, are Michelson's, exhibiting the tricks in the writer's trade. . . ."

Historians agree that Michelson was relentless in his campaign against Hoover and his reputation. James MacGregor Burns described Michelson as "a ghost writer of scores of speeches that . . . slashed and pummeled the Hoover administration." Arthur Schlesinger Jr. wrote that "Michelson turned out an uninterrupted stream of interviews, statements, and speeches in Washington. These releases . . . signed indifferently by leading Democrats in the House and Senate—poured ridicule on the Hoover administration."

The shy Hoover was ill-prepared to deal with this, and he was not well served by his public relations team. David Burner described the president's first press secretary, George Akerson, as "a large, hard-drinking Harvard man . . . well liked by his colleagues. But repeated fumblings in the early . . . years, coupled with some heavy drinking in public" led to his ouster. His replacement, Theodore Joslin, "was defensive, sour, and so obnoxious that even the president found him trying." One reporter, quoting Winston Churchill, described him as "the first known instance of a rat joining a sinking ship." Among his nasty habits, Joslin would read aloud, but not release, printed statements in the press, which frustrated reporters.

Michelson, meanwhile, went to town on Hoover, an easy target as the depression worsened. Michelson described his task: "My work . . . consisted principally of writing speeches, getting out pamphlets, inciting eminent citizens to make statements in our favor, circulating cartoons and editorials. . . ." His articles, wrote Kent, made Democratic arguments "appear not only as sound and original but polished, witty, ironical, studious, and profound. . . . The net result is that they have . . . hit Mr. Hoover with practically everything save the office furniture."

This was based on hard work. Michelson traveled to the Capitol daily to grill Democratic legislators. They fed him ideas for angles of potential attack and shared grievances of their constituents against Hoover and his administration. Armed with this information, Michelson crafted statements for various Democratic lawmakers to deliver. McKee pointed out that, under Michelson, the party's efforts "flood[ed] the country dailies and the weekly press with its printed propaganda." In addition, Michelson occasionally supplied unsigned anti-Hoover editorials to overworked newspaper editors. Of course, the decision to publish rested with the local paper, but, according to McKee, "Any editorial writer can appreciate what a boon it is to receive in the morning mail an editorial contribution, all ready to be sent to the printer. And how much labor is saved thereby, and how much mental and nervous strain!"

The Democrats took special delight in pointing out the stark contrast between Hoover's campaign promises and the economic difficulties into which the country descended during his presidency. During the 1928 campaign, according to Michelson, the candidate "had promised complete, continuous, and progressive prosperity." And who would not, could not believe it? After all, "it was obvious that a country must be fortunate to obtain for its highest officer a universal genius and that is what the American voters elected." But according to Democrats, the Great Depression showed that Hoover's campaign had been based on empty promises. In a radio speech probably written by Michelson, Jouett Shouse, chair of the Democratic Executive Committee, branded Hoover "a monumental failure." Dripping sincerity, he intoned, "I have no unkind personal word to express relative to the President," he stated. "I have pity for him. With all due regard to his unusual abilities, the fact remains that he has proved the most inept, the most ill-suited man who has filled the Presidential chair in fifty years." Shouse argued that "If President Hoover is unpopular it is not due to propaganda from the . . . Democratic National Committee. . . . It is because of the inevitable impression left by the acts of the man himself."

The depression was manna for Michelson and other Democratic critics. Senator Joseph Robinson claimed that "It may be well to trace the beginning of this calamity. . . . The prophets and the high priests of American prosperity, represented by no less . . . than . . . the former Secretary of commerce, now President, contributed by unduly and repeated optimistic statements to the creation of enthusiastic if not frenzied ventures in stocks." Senator Pat Harrison chimed in as well, declaring that "never before has the country witnessed such a lack of leadership and a shifting of responsibility." Shouse himself delivered the premier indictment. He charged that Hoover "came into office heralded as the world's greatest humanitarian and economist. No problem was too vast or too complex for the mind of this master engineer." Yet, instead of delivering, "In so far from being able to stem the tide, we have seen things go from bad to worse, with not even an idea proceeding from the White House as to how conditions could be ameliorated. . . ." In a subsequent address, Shouse proclaimed the "striking fact that he was held up to us from every forum in the land as the man who as none ever preceded him he had his fingers constantly for a period of eight years upon the pulse of business of the country." But upon being "elevated to the White House, [Hoover] found himself, and unfortunately, the American people also found him so utterly incapable of dealing with a situation which meant starvation and degradation throughout this Nation, that not one constructive remedy has to this day came from his sanctified lips."

Michelson came up with all kinds of ways to attack Hoover during the 1932 presidential campaign. Near the end of the presidential campaign Hoover had condemned the Democrats' plan to repeal the Smoot-Hawley Tariff. If that came about, he declared, "the grass will grow in the streets of a hundred cities, a thousand towns; the weeds will overrun the fields of millions of farms." Michelson incorporated this line into various speeches to show how out of touch Hoover was, and during the 1936 presidential campaign, as prosperity returned, Democrats brought out a large harvesting machine proclaiming "it was out to mow the Hoover grass from the streets." Under Michelson the Women's Division of the Democratic Party produced a flier saying one of Hoover's mining ventures had employed workers in conditions resembling slave labor. When Republicans protested, the publicity chief pulled it, although he later claimed, "we found reference to the incident in one of the counter-propaganda books written by a Hoover admirer."

LOSS OF REPUBLICAN SUPPORT AND CONSPIRACY THEORIES

The Great Depression took such a toll on the Hoover White House that even members of Hoover's own party were repudiating him by 1932. Harold Ickes, a progressive Republican, confided in a letter to a colleague that he was "becoming more and more concerned about the present political situation. So far as I am able to judge, not one Republican voter in ten wants President Hoover renominated and hardly anyone believes he can be reelected." Ickes spoke in apocalyptic terms: "The opposition to him comes from people in every walk of life and from every part of the country. He has failed and the people know it."

Hoover's difficulties in the political arena were compounded by a host of conspiracy theorists who created wildly implausible theories about the president. Hoover had been in the public's eye since at least 1914, and hence had attracted some strange commentators, but that universe expanded greatly as he strode toward the presidency. By 1928 there were already claims that he was under the control of British bankers, and that he was a pacifist because of his Quaker religion. After he reached the White House, a slew of books came out containing "proof" that he had run mines filled with slaves, profited from food relief in Europe, and was in fact a British citizen (the latter charge allegedly verified by the appearance of the name "Herbert Hoover" on an English voters' list).

These accounts started with character attacks and then turned to Hoover's record. Robert S. Allen's *Why Hoover Faces Defeat* claimed that "the collapse and failure of Herbert Hoover is the result of basic and fundamental causes—his abysmal incompetence, his pettiness and deviousness in personal relations, his shocking callousness to tragic suffering among millions of his countrymen. . . ."

The leading work in this genre was John Hamill's *The Strange Career of Mr. Hoover under Two Flags* (1931). Hoover appeared in this work, according to the only scholarly article on this literature by Rosanne Sizer, as "secretive, anti-social, woefully ignorant and uncouth, and completely without conscience and moral training." As a mining entrepreneur he had worked, according to Hamill, "with a total disregard for human life and suffering." Hoover cut costs by "skimping on underground support timbers. In all mines under Hoover's control, the workers' death rate rose immeasurably." Hamill proclaimed, "These men were murdered in the lust for gold, sacrificed on the altar of greed." In addition, Hamill argued that Hoover had nothing to do with Belgian relief during World War I, and what little he accomplished was in order to make profits for himself. These spurious attacks continued through the end of his presidency and beyond. As the Hoover family left Washington in 1933 after his defeat at the hands of Democratic nominee Franklin D. Roosevelt in November 1932, rumors abounded that they had purloined a horde of gold from the U.S. Treasury.

The cacophony of attacks enraged Hoover's partisans. Karl Mack, in a letter to the *Washington Post* in 1931, denounced the "ventriloquistic control" of the Democratic Party's publicity director over his "puppets" and insisted the attacks would fail because the Democrats had failed to take into account "that the average intelligence of the electorate in this country is at least more than negligible." In 1947 Eugene Lyons, writing a biography of Hoover, made much stronger charges. In a chapter entitled "The Big Smear," Lyons argued that his subject faced "smear stuff, ugly rumors, verbal tar-and-feathers and high-grade oratorical ectoplasm manufactured by Charlie Michelson and his associated ghosts. . . . It mattered little what went into the Michelson Mills at one end. The genius of its presiding chemists transmuted it into evil-smelling stuff at the other end." He later wrote that the Michelson staff were "Americans and human beings. But one would never guess this from their output."

In 2004 Dale Mayer published a biography of Hoover's wife in which she charged that Michelson had a "total lack of scruples" and that "today's 'negative campaign' techniques are mild in comparison to the intensely personal mud slinging" the Hoovers faced. She even went after Ike Hoover, White House chief usher from 1909 to 1943, who in 1934 published his memoirs about life in the executive branch. Meyer made dubious charges about the usher's book, stating that "the circumstantial evidence suggests that someone had assembled a clever propaganda piece . . . and taken it to the White House where it was submitted for FDR's approval and last minute fine tuning before being unleashed on an unsuspecting public."

Hoover and his family never recovered from these attacks. According to Burner, the "hypersensitive" president nevertheless wrote of his wife, "She was oversensitive," so we can only guess at how much the nasty words affected each of them. Hoover consoled Lou, who was raised an Episcopalian but converted to her husband's Quaker faith, that her birth religion included a "hot hell" for evildoers.

More telling was Hoover's memoirs. In the second volume, published in 1952—20 years after he lost the election to Roosevelt—Hoover devoted 12 chapters and 125 pages just to defenses of his handling of the depression, attempting to rebut old charges that still stung him. He referred to the "campaign of misrepresentation" against him and alleged that the Bonus Army, made up of U.S. veterans, was "organized and promoted by the Communists and included a large number of hoodlums and ex-convicts determined to raise a public disturbance." Still settling old scores, he railed how "old-guard Republican leaders in the Senate and the House, who had been defeated in their presidential ambitions in 1928, certainly did not exert themselves energetically in their traditional duty to counterattack and expose misrepresentations."

CONCLUSION

Many of Hoover's problems were of his own making. These provided an opening, however, for the first modern political attack campaign organized by the parties themselves. In addition, he was the target of paranoid ramblings accusing him of heinous deeds. The shy, circumspect Hoover never recovered from this deluge and bore grudges for the rest of his life.

Robert A. Slayton

Further Reading

Burner, David. *Herbert Hoover.* New York: Alfred A. Knopf, 1979.

Craig, Douglas. *Fireside Politics.* Baltimore, MD: Johns Hopkins University Press, 2000.

Cutlip, Scott. *The Unseen Power.* Hillsdale, NJ: Lawrence Erlbaum Associates, 1994.

"Has Charlie Michelson Lost His Ventriloquism? 'Playing Politics' Has Become a Farce." *Washington Post*, June 6, 1931.

"Herbert Hoover's Service to the Nation Shames Those Who 'Smeared' Him." *Saturday Evening Post,* 232, August 22, 1959, p. 10.

Hofstadter, Richard. *The American Political Tradition and the Men Who Made It.* New York: Vintage Books, 1948.

Hoover, Herbert. *The Memoirs of Herbert Hoover: The Great Depression 1929–1941.* New York: Macmillan, 1952.

Kent, Frank. "Charley Michelson." *Scribner's Magazine,* 88, September 4, 1930.

Kiewe, Amos. *FDR's First Fireside Chat.* College Station, TX: Texas A&M University Press, 2007.

Letter from Harold Ickes to Charles Nagel, March 15, 1932, Papers of Herbert Hoover, Box 287, Herbert Hoover Presidential Library, West Branch, Iowa.

Letter from William A. White to Herbert Hoover, June 18, 1928, Series C, Box 137, William A. White Papers, Library of Congress, Washington, D.C.

Lisio, David. *Hoover, Blacks, & Lily-Whites.* Chapel Hill, NC: University of North Carolina Press, 1985.

Lyons, Eugene. *Herbert Hoover.* Garden City, NY: Doubleday & Company, 1947.

Mayer, Dale. *Lou Henry Hoover.* New York: Nova History Publications, 2004.

McKee, Oliver, Jr. "Publicity Chiefs." *North American Review,* Vol. 230, No. 4 (October 1930).

Michelson, Charles. *The Ghost Talks.* New York: G. P. Putnam's Sons, 1944.

Mintz, Steven, and Susan Kellogg. *Domestic Revolutions*. New York: Free Press, 1988.

Murray, Robert. "Herbert Hoover and the Harding Cabinet," in *Herbert Hoover as Secretary of Commerce*, ed. Ellis Hawley. Iowa City, IA: University of Iowa Press, 1982.

Papers of Theodore Joslin, Box 8, Herbert Hoover Presidential Library, West Branch, Iowa.

"Shouse Declares Hoover 'a Failure.'" *New York Times*, March 4, 1932.

Sizer, Rosanne. "Herbert Hoover and the Smear Books, 1930–1932." *The Annals of Iowa*, Vol. 47, No. 4 (Winter 1984): 343–361.

Speech of Hon. Jouett Shouse, Chairman, Democratic National Committee, April 13, 1931, Papers of Herbert Hoover, Box 130, Herbert Hoover Presidential Library, West Branch, Iowa.

Walker, Stanley. *City Editor*. Baltimore, MD: Johns Hopkins University Press, 1999.

Young, Nancy. *Lou Henry Hoover*. Lawrence, KS: University Press of Kansas, 2004.

32. Franklin D. Roosevelt

Born: January 30, 1882

Died: April 12, 1945

Time in Office: 32nd President of the United States, March 4, 1933, to April 12, 1945

Election Results: 1932 Election: 57.4% of popular vote, 472 (88.9%) Electoral College votes; 1936 Election: 60.8% of popular vote, 523 (98.5%) Electoral College votes; 1940 Election: 54.7% of popular vote, 449 (84.6%) Electoral College votes; 1944 Election: 53.4% of popular vote, 432 (81.4%) Electoral College votes

Spouse: Eleanor Roosevelt (m. 1905)

Children: Anna Eleanor, James, Franklin, Elliott, Franklin Delano Jr., and John Aspinwall

Franklin Delano Roosevelt was born on January 30, 1882, in Hyde Park, New York. He married Eleanor Roosevelt (his fifth cousin, once removed) in 1905 and had six children, one of whom died in infancy. On April 12, 1945, at the age of 63, Roosevelt died of a massive cerebral hemorrhage while in Warm Springs, Georgia. On November 8, 1932, Roosevelt (also commonly known by his initials of FDR) was elected as the 32nd president of the United States, defeating the incumbent president, Herbert Hoover. In the 1932 election, Roosevelt won 472 electoral votes (57.4% of the popular vote) and carried all but six states. He would win reelection as president three more times. In 1936, he defeated Alf Landon decisively by winning 523 electoral votes, 60.8% of the popular vote, and all but two states. Roosevelt broke the two-term precedent in 1940 by defeating Republican nominee Wendell Wilkie, 57.4% to 44.8%. Although the popular vote was narrower that year than in his 1936 triumph, he comfortably won the Electoral College, 449–82, and carried all but ten states. Roosevelt's final presidential campaign came in 1944, when he defeated Thomas Dewey by a slightly smaller margin than from four years previously, 53.4% to 45.9%. He won easily in the Electoral College, however, claiming 432 votes to Dewey's 99 and carrying all but 12 states.

A CONSEQUENTIAL PRESIDENCY

Many Americans harbored passionate feelings about Roosevelt and his presidency—both positive and negative—because of the unparalleled length of his time in the Oval Office and because his policies made significant changes in how the United States addressed important matters of both domestic and foreign policy. The strongest base of opposition was probably among conservative southern Democrats, who saw Roosevelt's progressive "New Deal" program as a short-term response to the Great Depression (with a return to the status quo once the crisis passed). Some of the more conservative senators like Harry Byrd and Carter Glass of Virginia, Cotton Ed Smith (South Carolina), and Millard Tydings (Maryland) soon realized, however, that Roosevelt's plans would fundamentally change the country and their party in ways that they deeply opposed.

Following significant policy defeats in 1937 and 1938, conservative Democrats were joined by Republicans who opposed much of Roosevelt's domestic program. Some conservative critics even charged that under Roosevelt, communists were infiltrating all aspects of American life. This paranoia reached the point that the House of Representatives created the Committee on Un-American Activities in 1938 specifically to investigate the threat of communism in America. This committee was initially placed under the leadership of conservative representative Martin Dies (D-TX). Under his supervision, the committee eventually evolved into a weapon for conservatives to wield against the New Deal, which was depicted as making America more susceptible to communism. As the 1930s drew to a close, concerns about America's role in the world provided another policy issue that would drive hatred of Roosevelt. Specifically, the nation struggled to reconcile its desire to help Europe resist fascism with the pull of isolationism. Underlying both of these broad lines of attack on Roosevelt was anti-Semitism, for many of Roosevelt's critics believed that Jews exercised undue influence on the administration. Despite the hatred of some political elites, however, Roosevelt remained a generally popular political figure.

HUEY LONG

Democratic senator Huey Long of Louisiana was one of Roosevelt's earliest and most formidable political enemies. In 1932 Long helped Roosevelt capture the Democratic nomination, but the alliance did not last long. Long came to feel that

Roosevelt's policy proposals to combat the depression were too timid and too protective of business interests that monopolized wealth and access to culture. In addition, Long craved national political power and believed that the president was an impediment to his ambitions. Rather than following political niceties, Long frequently insulted the president's advisers and showed little deference to the president in their personal interactions.

In 1934 Long founded a national political organization that came to be known by the slogan "Share Our Wealth." The group was founded on the idea of confiscating large personal fortunes and employing steeply progressive income taxes and limits on estate sizes so that wealth would no longer be concentrated among the fortunate few. Some of the core elements of the program included giving every family enough money to buy a home, an automobile, and a radio; public pensions for the elderly; and sending worthy boys to college. In addition to the family benefits, Long proposed public works programs, a shorter workweek, a national minimum wage, and paying bonuses due to soldiers. According to historian William Leuchtenberg, Long's political organization had more than 27,000 clubs in 1935 with more than 7.5 million supporters. The majority of these supporters were in neighboring southern states, but his appeal also began to spread to other parts of the country.

Long's growing popularity among working-class Americans raised real concerns for Democratic leaders about Long's future plans, such as a presidential race in 1936. Trying to blunt Long's appeal, the administration gave control over federal patronage to Long's opponents, and federal prosecutors aggressively investigated tax fraud among Long's supporters. The White House was so concerned about Long that it commissioned a poll to evaluate his political support, and the results indicated that Long had broad national popularity and could win as many as 6 million votes. Roosevelt subsequently co-opted some of Long's ideas into his Second New Deal, such as Social Security, the Works Progress Administration, and the establishment of the National Labor Relations Board.

The political threat Long posed to Roosevelt disappeared when Carl Weiss shot Long on September 8, 1935. The "Kingfish" (as Long was known) died two days later. After Long's death, the Share the Wealth movement dissipated, and its members largely returned to the fold of the Democratic Party.

FATHER COUGHLIN, THE RADIO PRIEST

Reverend Charles Coughlin, who boasted a weekly radio audience of 30–45 million people, emerged during the 1930s as another powerful critic of Roosevelt and his New Deal policies. Initially supportive of the New Deal, Coughlin was critical of Secretary of Agriculture Henry Wallace, and he was disappointed that Roosevelt did not do more to promote inflation through the monetization of silver.

Coughlin was anti-Semitic as well, and the presence of Bernard Baruch and Henry Morgenthau Jr. in Roosevelt's cabinet led Coughlin to speculate whether one set of "money-changers" (in the Hoover administration) had simply been exchanged for another.

Convinced that capitalism was finished, Coughlin formed the National Union for Social Justice that served as a vehicle for promoting social justice that bore a striking resemblance to Italian corporatism (which is a sociopolitical organization by groups within a society, like business, agriculture, labor, etc.). In addition to dispensing with the capitalist system, Coughlin argued that the party system needed to be purged. His National Union for Social Justice included a 16-point platform, and the overall goal was to create an organization of middle- and lower-class voters who were resentful of their current plight regardless of their regional, ethnic, and religious differences. The Roosevelt administration regarded Coughlin's criticisms as a serious problem, for his message appealed to a key Democratic voting bloc: lower-middle-class, old immigrant Catholics in the urban Northeast.

DR. FRANCIS TOWNSEND

Dr. Francis Townsend was a California physician who created an economic assistance plan that, according to him, would both put the nation on the road to recovery and provide assistance to the elderly. His plan was to pay each pensioner $200 a month. In return, recipients would promise to spend the money in the United States as well as retire from all gainful work. Townsend proposed that a 2% tax on business transactions would provide the necessary funding. By September 1934, there were some 1,200 Townsend clubs, primarily in the West. There was a great deal of criticism regarding the financing for the plan, but its appeal was that ordinary Americans could support each other without having to rely on the perceived paternalism of the New Deal. Supporters also believed that it would get young people working so they would have less time to devote to sexual promiscuity and drinking. In a bigger picture, Townsend mobilized a large, new constituency in American politics: the elderly. Numerous politicians on the West Coast were fearful of electoral consequences if they did not support Townsend's plans.

AMERICAN LIBERTY LEAGUE

The relationship between Al Smith and Roosevelt, a pair of New York Democrats, was convoluted at best. Smith had long viewed Roosevelt as his protégé and saw the latter's 1928 triumph in the governor's race as vindication. But relations between the two men became strained after Roosevelt orchestrated the passage of a statewide bond issue over Smith's objections in 1931. Smith and financier John Jacob Raskob grew increasingly concerned that Roosevelt might beat Smith out for the Democratic presidential nomination in 1932. As the 1932 campaign began, Roosevelt found a base of support among southern and western members of the party while Smith demonstrated his strength in the larger cities. It was during this period that the ideological differences between the two men appeared. After Roosevelt delivered a speech advocating for government assistance to the "Forgotten Man," Smith responded at a Jefferson Day dinner in Washington with an argument that Roosevelt was engaging in demagoguery by not confronting the protests by radicals. At the Democratic Convention, Smith fell short in his bid to claim the party's nomination. On the fourth ballot, Roosevelt reached a deal with the Texas delegation to name John Nance Garner as his running mate. This put Roosevelt over the top and left Smith with no choice but to endorse the ticket if he wanted to keep his place as a party leader.

By 1934, though, Smith and some other Democrats grew increasingly concerned about the direction of the country. Smith, Raskob, and John Davis (Democratic presidential nominee in 1924), with support from business interests like General Motors, Sun Oil, and Montgomery Ward, formed the American Liberty League in 1934. The founders of the American Liberty League charged that Roosevelt's policies undermined the principles of laissez-faire economics in favor of greater government regulation. They asserted that legislation like the Securities and Exchange Act, National Industrial Recovery Act, and Agricultural Adjustment Act undermined property rights and that government should encourage private enterprise. Their overriding goal was returning the Democratic Party to a more probusiness set of policies.

At the beginning of the 1936 campaign, Roosevelt gave a pair of speeches attacking entrenched business interests as a serious threat to the nation's economic recovery. Shortly thereafter, at the American Liberty League's annual dinner, Smith attacked the New Deal for more than an hour, comparing Roosevelt's plans to communism and suggesting that his administration was un-American. Most of the leading figures in the Liberty League had decided to leave the Democratic Party if Roosevelt was renominated, so Smith and others threw their support behind the Republican nominee, Alf Landon.

Smith's speech wound up backfiring politically, however, because it provided Roosevelt with another opportunity to identify the Republican leadership with the economic royalists who had brought the Great Depression to the United States. The Republican platform supported much of the New Deal in 1936, and leading Republican figures, including Landon, tried to create as much distance as they could between themselves and the Liberty League. Beyond the electoral numbers, the bigger effect from the 1936 election was the birth of the New Deal coalition that included the urban state party organizations and city political machines, white southerners, African Americans, Jews, and Irish Catholics. Organized labor replaced the pro-business Democrats that were typified by the membership of the American Liberty League.

THE UNION PARTY

Although there was little chance that Roosevelt would lose the 1936 election, Coughlin had been so encouraged by the success of candidates backed by his National Union for Social Justice in primaries early in the year that he decided to create his own party, the Union Party. Coughlin orchestrated the selection of North Dakota representative William Lemke (nonpartisan) as the party's presidential candidate. In Coughlin's eyes, the New Deal was a communist plot and needed to be eliminated from the United States. When Lemke's campaign foundered, Coughlin lashed out against Roosevelt, branding him a liar, a double-crosser, and a communist. He also leveled ugly attacks against Roosevelt's Jewish advisers. There was one brief moment of concern in the Roosevelt White House when Coughlin appeared to explore an alliance with Francis Townsend and Gerald L. K. Smith, but they were never able to effectively coordinate their activities and the real threat passed. In September 1936, Coughlin suggested that assassination was an acceptable alternative when ballots were useless. The Vatican sharply criticized Coughlin and sent the papal secretary of state, Cardinal Eugenio Pacelli (later Pope Pius XII), to visit the United States and remain in the country for the duration of the election. Roosevelt closed the 1936 campaign with a rally at Madison Square Garden in which he uttered one of his famous lines about his political enemies: "They are unanimous in their hate for me—and I welcome their hatred." After Roosevelt's landslide reelection victory, Coughlin briefly left the airwaves. That silence, however, would not last. Coughlin later resumed his radio program, where he emerged as a strong proponent of supporting the fascist powers in Europe and maintaining America's isolationist stance.

ROOSEVELT'S COURT-PACKING PLAN

Roosevelt had a contentious relationship with the U.S. Supreme Court, which was controlled by conservatives through his first years in the White House. One of the earliest pieces of legislation passed during the New Deal was the National Industrial Recovery Act of 1933. In 1935, though, the Court struck it down, ruling that it was an improper delegation of power from the legislative to the executive branch and that it interfered with intrastate commerce. The following year the Supreme Court struck down the Agricultural Adjustment Act because of its tax provisions. Roosevelt became increasingly concerned that the Court might strike down additional pieces of legislation that served as the foundation for the New Deal.

Addressing the nation on radio, Roosevelt claimed that "the Courts . . . have cast doubts on the ability of the elected Congress to protect us against catastrophe by meeting squarely our modern social and economic conditions." Later in his address, Roosevelt suggested that the Supreme Court had exceeded its constitutional powers.

More specifically, he said, "In the last four years the sound rule of giving statutes the benefit of all reasonable doubt has been cast aside. The Court has been acting not as a judicial body, but as a policy-making body."

Increasingly convinced that the Supreme Court was acting as a super-legislature by vetoing legislation without any regard for the will of the majority, Roosevelt proposed expanding the number of justices on the Supreme Court from 9 to 15. This proposal would have allowed him to appoint as many as six new justices in 1937 and thus make the Court much less likely to take issue with his New Deal laws and programs.

However, Roosevelt committed a major political misstep: he failed to consult with his allies in Congress, and this provided the energy to throw congressional conservatives across both parties together and would continue to block liberal policy proposals long after FDR left the White House. Vice President Garner, who was not supportive of the New Deal, expressed opposition to the bill by holding his nose and turning his thumb down. Conservatives in Congress attacked the proposed legislation, but were also joined by more liberal members as well as Senator Burton Wheeler (D-MT) who argued that FDR's plan was not liberal and Senator Hiram Johnson (R-CA) who suggested the bill would make the Supreme Court subservient to the president. Senator Carter Glass (D-VA) expressed fear that a more liberal Court might undo racial segregation in the South. Senator Josiah Bailey (D-NC) argued, "If the court bill was passed, the road to an American dictatorship will be cleared of all obstacles."

The chairman of the House Judiciary Committee, Representative Hatton Sumners (D-TX), refused to bring the bill up in committee, which meant that the Senate would be forced to work on the bill first. Senator Burton Wheeler (D-MT) led much of the opposition in the Senate while Republicans and southern conservatives largely avoided the fray, content to allow liberals to take the lead in criticizing Roosevelt's court-packing plan. Besides the internal opposition, the nation's bar associations were against the plan, senators were receiving massive amounts of mail from constituents expressing opposition, and most of the press, including the friendly William Allen White, roundly condemned Roosevelt's plan.

After the hearings started in the Senate, Wheeler met with Chief Justice Charles Evans Hughes, who indicated that the proposed bill would destroy the Court as an institution. He also contended that the reason for the administration's legal failures was poor work by the attorney general rather than a Court seeking to block Roosevelt's initiatives. The following week the Court defused much of the impetus for Roosevelt's court-packing scheme when it issued rulings favorable to his administration. It upheld a minimum wage law in Washington that struck down the precedents that had limited government regulation of wages and hours. As a result, the Senate Judiciary Committee voted 10–8 to report Roosevelt's bill unfavorably while Justice Willis Van Devanter announced his retirement on the same day.

Roosevelt huddled with House allies trying to organize a discharge petition to force the bill out of committee, but they refused. The Senate majority leader, Joseph Robinson (D-AR), was unable to prevent more senators from announcing their opposition to the bill. The politics of the bill took its toll on Robinson, and he died of a heart attack. In an episode replete with errors, Roosevelt made one more: he refused to attend Robinson's funeral in Arkansas because he blamed Robinson for the bill's failure. Any remaining support Roosevelt had in the Senate rapidly disappeared, and Garner delivered the news to the president that he did not have the votes for the bill. The whole affair thus had mixed results for Roosevelt. On the one hand, the Supreme Court did not strike down another major piece of New Deal legislation, but he also burned valuable political capital in his unsuccessful quest to increase the size of the Court.

THE ROLE OF THE EXECUTIVE

In 1937 Roosevelt sought approval for legislation that would reorganize the executive branch. Louis Brownlow chaired a commission of reformers and political scientists, and they recommended expanding the White House staff, adding new cabinet departments, and introducing a merit system for federal employees. Roosevelt characterized the bill as one that would promote greater government efficiency by reducing clutter and improving coordination among executive branch departments and included support from former presidents William Howard Taft and Herbert Hoover. Given the political circumstances of dictatorships rising across Europe, Senator Edward Burke (D-NE) expressed the opposition best, "I am not willing in the search for efficient government to establish one-man rule in this country!" The same forces that objected to Roosevelt's plan to change the Supreme Court viewed the attempts at executive branch reorganization as another attempt to undermine the democratic institutions of the United States.

In April 1938, protesters marched up Pennsylvania Avenue opposing the program, and Coughlin continued to use his radio program to encourage listeners to resist what he believed was the growing tyranny of Roosevelt's administration. In fact, the public was so roused that Congress received more than 330,000 telegrams opposing the bill. As Congress considered the legislation some opponents, including Senator Arthur Vandenberg (R-MI), concluded the symbolism of the proposal was even more sinister than its actual elements. The symbolism of Nazism was a powerful framework for rallying opponents, but there were also concerns about greater transfers of power from Congress to the executive branch.

Roosevelt was also condemned on the home front by fascists who loathed the president and his political beliefs. For example, Coughlin had abandoned his arguments about social justice and replaced it with Jew baiting. Some groups referred to the New Deal as the "Jew Deal" while a chapter of the Christian Front in New

York, an anti-Semitic group, used a likeness of Roosevelt for target practice. Members of the Christian Front often sought to provoke fights in Jewish neighborhoods, and the leader of the New York faction, John F. Cassidy, stated that members would respond to the communist threat with firearms. The FBI raided the Christian Front in January 1940 and arrested 17 leaders on charges that they intended to kill members of Congress, seize the Customs House, and major armories.

Although there was opposition to Roosevelt among conservative political elites and far-right activists and organizations, the American public was broadly supportive of the president. As a result, Roosevelt's reorganization bill passed in the Senate 48–42 despite opposition from some of the president's most strident critics. Despite wielding an overwhelming Democratic majority in the House, however, Speaker William Bankhead (Alabama) struggled to move the bill forward. The chairman of the Rules Committee, Representative John O'Connor (New York) was determined to block the bill from a vote because he believed Roosevelt was trying to become a dictator. Once floor debate concluded, the House voted on a motion to recommit the bill to the Rules Committee, which would effectively kill the bill, and the motion carried through a bipartisan coalition of all Republicans and more than 100 Democrats. In the aftermath, supporters of the bill, including Brownlow, lamented that opposition was not based on substance, but simple hatred for the president.

THE PURGE

By the late 1930s Roosevelt had grown increasingly angry with some fellow Democrats who were attempting to destroy parts of his New Deal agenda even as they tried to associate themselves with him during their election campaigns. At the same time, Roosevelt generally avoided supporting anti-poll tax or anti-lynching legislation in order to maintain the support of southern Democrats. Nonetheless, southern Democrats sought greater control over their party during the late 1930s. By virtue of seniority, many southern Democrats held valuable institutional positions that would disappear if they joined the Republicans, and it is worth noting that Roosevelt remained quite popular politically in their states. One final consideration may have also played a role: leaving the Democratic Party could lead to a political realignment that would empower African Americans, and real political competition could endanger the careers of these conservative Democrats.

Southern Democrats increasingly adopted a stance of preventing any new liberal social or economic legislation from passing and then forcing Roosevelt and fellow New Dealers out in 1940. Among this group was Vice President Garner, who was alienated by Roosevelt's refusal to support balanced budgets and his refusal to take a stronger stand against sit-down strikes. In late December 1937, this group of Democratic senators developed a set of conservative principles that they believed would help spark an economic recovery. As historian Susan Dunn noted, this manifesto did not contain any legislative proposals other than tax cuts and a call for a balanced budget.

Roosevelt saw the actions of southern Democrats who pretended to be liberal not only as a personal betrayal, but a betrayal of the nation. In June 1938, a small inner circle of Roosevelt confidants recommended that he attempt to defeat some of the obstructionist Democrats during the midterm elections of 1938. Although Roosevelt might not win every battle, perhaps the threat of future action might scare some of the others from undermining his policies in the future.

There was a certain irony in Roosevelt's position change because during his first term he had worked to build an inclusive Democratic Party and had shied away from challenging the idea of white supremacy. For example, Senator Carter Glass (D-VA) was a consistent foe of the New Deal and even compared its ideas to Hitlerism. Glass had voted against the National Industrial Recovery Act and the Social Security Act, two of Roosevelt's greatest triumphs. Yet the president endorsed him for reelection in 1936.

One of the first steps in Roosevelt's plan to neutralize the conservative southern wing of his party was releasing the *Report on Economic Conditions of the South,* a document that painted a devastating picture of the economic challenges facing the American South. Many white southerners vigorously objected to the report, and it failed to do much in terms of persuading southerners to vote against Roosevelt's political opponents. Senators Walter George and Cotton Ed Smith, for example, easily won their primary elections in 1938. But Roosevelt exulted over the defeat of Representative John O'Connor, saying, "Harvard lost the schedule but won the Yale game."

On the whole, the midterm elections in 1938 were bad for Roosevelt, as Democratic majorities in the House and Senate shrank significantly. Republicans were emboldened by their gains and had less interest in forming a coalition with conservative Democrats, effectively quashing any hopes of a party realignment along liberal/conservative lines. Not surprisingly, the attempted purge did little to heal relations between Roosevelt and southern Democrats, but they remained supportive of the president so long as policies focused on solving economic concerns rather than trying to reshape racial relations in the South.

ROOSEVELT'S RELATIONSHIP WITH ORGANIZED LABOR

Although organized labor eventually emerged as a stalwart supporter of Roosevelt, he had his share of enemies in the labor movement. Given his pro-business leanings as governor of New York, he was not a clear friend to labor at the beginning of his administration. The National Industrial Recovery Act (NIRA) guaranteed the right of collective bargaining, but did not ban company unions or the open shop, and the goal was promoting planning and cooperation that would ease the economic crisis facing the nation. Early on, workers were broadly supportive of the NIRA, but by 1935, labor leaders were threatening that the entire movement would oppose Roosevelt especially as his NIRA administrator, S. Clay Williams, was an opponent of labor rights.

John L. Lewis, the leader of the United Mine Workers (UMW), quickly embraced the NIRA despite his laissez-faire beliefs. Seizing on the passage of the NIRA, Lewis sent organizers into the mining communities to sign up members and rapidly increased the membership of the UMW. Using that leverage, as well as support from Roosevelt himself, Lewis negotiated a much better code under the NIRA than existed for other industries.

Passage of the Wagner Act allowed workers to join unions, and there were a rash of sit-down strikes in early 1937. One of the most devastating was at the General Motors plant in Flint, Michigan, because it had the only set of dies for every model that GM manufactured. Roosevelt refused to order federal forces to eject the striking workers. In fact, the president was flummoxed that leaders at GM would not sit down and negotiate with the workers. The governor of Michigan, Frank Murphy, shared Roosevelt's antipathy to sending in troops because there would be too much bloodshed. Due in part to the stances taken by Roosevelt and Murphy, General Motors would eventually recognize the United Auto Workers, and the United States Steel Corporation would soon make a similar decision by recognizing the steelworkers' union.

However, the smaller steel companies staunchly resisted Lewis's organizers and did not follow U.S. Steel. This resulted in a series of violent clashes between union organizers and law enforcement that helped shift public opinion against organized labor. When Roosevelt criticized both sides in this dispute, Lewis renounced support for Roosevelt's New Deal policies. However, Roosevelt's public position may have been reassuring to a public that was growing increasingly concerned about class warfare in the United States. Although there was tension in the relationship, Lewis and Roosevelt continued to work together, but they would completely break by early 1939. This break has been attributed both to personal distaste for one another and to Lewis's unhappiness when Roosevelt attempted to change U.S. foreign policy in response to the outbreak of war in Europe. During the 1940 campaign, Lewis, an isolationist, upped the stakes by promising to resign if Roosevelt won reelection (which he did after Roosevelt's victory).

REPUBLICAN OPPOSITION TO ROOSEVELT

Although Roosevelt faced a great deal of resistance from within his own party, particularly southern Democrats, he certainly had his share of enemies within the Republican Party. One of his most notable foes was Senator Robert A. Taft of Ohio, who was first elected in 1938. Taft was a proponent of balanced budgets and criticized the expansion of federal power at the expense of state and local governments. At times, Taft suggested that the real danger to democracy in the United States was the White House rather than Nazi Germany.

On matters of foreign policy, Taft was an isolationist who believed that Europe's troubles were not the business of the United States, but his positions were a bit more complicated. Shortly after his election to the Senate, Taft began campaigning for president in 1940 and moved sharply into the isolationist camp. He argued that supporting the Allies with only money was immoral because an unwillingness to back that up with men was cowardice. In fact, Taft wrote a letter to a friend expressing his support for the America First Committee. Taft even went so far as to accuse Roosevelt of fear-mongering and using the possibility of war in Europe to divert attention from the alleged failures of the New Deal. Taft proclaimed that rather than getting involved in Europe's concerns, America would be better off solving her problems at home.

Republican senator Arthur Vandenberg of Michigan was another reliable vote against New Deal policies. He consistently attacked the New Deal for its spending despite supporting some of its progressive impulses. Vandenberg even went so far as to suggest in a 1940 magazine article that the New Deal could be salvaged if Republicans had control of the government. Unlike Taft, Vandenberg was a consistent voice on matters of foreign policy although he, too, tried to draw some important distinctions. For example, while Taft had voted to repeal the arms embargo in 1939, Vandenberg voted against it. He believed that the Atlantic and Pacific oceans would protect the United States as long as the country minded its own business. Although not a supporter of Hitler, he believed the United States should continue its policy of non-involvement and neutrality. Rather than fully endorsing the isolationist brand, Vandenberg was an advocate for "insulation" where the United States would build up defenses so that it would discourage the possibility of Nazi attack.

AMERICA FIRST

In the late 1930s, America engaged in one of the most spirited debates in history over whether to intervene in a rapidly expanding war in Europe. Roosevelt was a voice for intervention and pushed the country in that direction through small, discrete policy changes, but he faced an isolationist movement that represented a broad cross-section of American society. The movement spanned the country (although it was strongest in the Midwest), included members of all political parties, and ran the gamut of economic class.

In Congress, Roosevelt faced opposition from both parties, but it was Republicans who were the strongest supporters of isolationism. For example, Representative

Hamilton Fish (New York) scorned those who wanted to spend American blood and treasure to police the world. Even more progressive Republicans expressed opposition. Senator Gerald Nye of North Dakota argued that there was nothing in Europe worth the sacrifice of a single American. Senator Hiram Johnson (California), meanwhile, dismissed the idea that Hitler could conquer Europe.

The isolationist movement extended beyond Congress to include prominent public intellectuals and newspaper editors who routinely scorned and attacked Roosevelt over his European policies. Charles Beard wrote a series of books in the late 1930s including *America in Midpassage* and *A Foreign Policy for America* arguing that the responsibility of the United States was making its own civilization better by solving the social and economic crises at home. Lawrence Dennis was another intellectual who attacked Roosevelt for alienating fascists and believed that democracy and capitalism were spent forces. Instead, America would need to develop its own version of Hitler. William Randolph Hearst, Robert McCormick, and Oswald Garrison Villard also published newspapers and magazines that routinely supported isolationism and criticized Roosevelt's interventionist instincts.

College students were especially active in the isolationist movement, and Yale University was the epicenter. In early 1940 R. Douglas Stuart Jr., with two fellow students, future president Gerald Ford, and future Supreme Court justice Potter Stewart, drafted a petition demanding the United States refrain from war even if England was facing defeat. They further argued that negotiation was the solution to any international crisis. Stuart dropped out of Yale to promote isolationism and found support from prominent individuals. The former chairman of Sears, Roebuck & Company, Robert Wood, agreed to serve as temporary chairman of the isolationist movement and would soon attract interest from a wider range of political actors including Robert McCormick, Hugh Johnson (who Roosevelt had previously fired as head of the National Recovery Administration), Representative Bruce Barton (R-NY), and Jay Hormel.

The America First Committee was established in July 1940 and served as the organizing point for isolationism in the United States. On its face, America First was nonpartisan, but the reality is that the organization consisted largely of Republicans and Democrats hostile to the New Deal. Although isolationist, America First was not pacifist because the group favored making sure the United States possessed a military with the capacity to win wars in both the Atlantic and Pacific. The committee started running newspaper advertisements by October 1940. In 1941 famed aviator Charles Lindbergh joined the organization, and he quickly became its chief spokesman and most attractive speaker at rallies. One problem that America First did face was charges of anti-Semitism, in part because of prejudiced remarks from Lindbergh and other prominent members of the organization

Republicans nominated Wendell Wilkie as their presidential candidate in 1940. He initially refused to challenge Roosevelt's foreign policies, but later in the campaign he promised never to send American troops overseas. In 1941, Senator Gerald Nye stated at an America First Committee meeting that he believed that there had been a conspiracy at the Republican National Convention to deny the American people a real choice on the question of international affairs because isolationism was a popular policy and Wilkie was too much of an interventionist. Both Nye and John Lewis accused Roosevelt of manipulating the country into war in a manner not unlike what Woodrow Wilson had done during World War I. Lewis gave speeches during the campaign in which he claimed that Roosevelt's internationalism would end social reforms in the United States. He argued that it would be the poor and working class who would pay the steepest price for American involvement overseas. By the end of the campaign Lewis was openly suggesting that if the nation reelected Roosevelt they would be giving a blank check to a warmonger.

CHARLES LINDBERGH

Although best known for his part in the isolationist movement, Lindbergh first challenged Roosevelt in 1934. The root of the issue was Roosevelt's decision, after deciding that private airlines were overcharging the government on air-mail contracts and consulting with the Senate, the cabinet, and the Army, to give the task to the Army Air Corps. Lindbergh argued that Roosevelt was abusing his power with such a sweeping decision, that the change would harm the private sector, and that the pilots in the Army Air Corps were ill-equipped to the task. After a rash of accidents and deaths of pilots, Roosevelt was forced to retreat on his policy, but the incident left Lindbergh convinced that the president had the potential to become a demagogue.

Lindbergh visited Germany in 1936 and quickly embraced Nazism, believing that it could be a force for good and a bulwark against the threat of communism in Russia. After war broke out in Europe, Lindbergh delivered a series of radio speeches and articles in *Reader's Digest* and *Atlantic Monthly* describing his position on how the United States should respond. Lindbergh argued that Germany should rightfully dominate Europe since it was Germany that was holding back the threat of communism. The United States should have taken stronger steps to bring the countries of Europe together in such a way to defend the interests of white people and preserve the existing world order. If the United States could not do anything to end the war in Europe, the only response was complete neutrality. The problem Lindbergh faced in his position was Hitler's behavior: signing the nonaggression pact with the Soviet Union and allying with Japan—hardly the mark of a country defending the white race.

As the war in Europe raged, Congress considered the Lend-Lease Bill that would allow the Allies to lease supplies from America. Lindbergh testified against the bill. Roosevelt grew concerned about Lindbergh after he joined the America First

Committee in 1941, and Lindbergh marked that decision by giving a series of speeches attacking the administration of leading the country into war and focusing on the wrong enemy. Roosevelt decided it was time to bring Lindbergh down and questioned his patriotism at a news conference. Lindbergh responded by resigning his Army commission. After Hitler invaded the Soviet Union, Roosevelt extended the Lend-Lease program to Russia. Lindbergh and other isolationists believed that this was proof of everything that he had been saying: Roosevelt was un-American.

The administration continued poking at Lindbergh as Secretary of the Interior Harold Ickes raised the issue of the medal Hermann Göring had given Lindbergh in 1936. The action provoked responses from Lindbergh that would inevitably lead to political mistakes and his address in Des Moines, Iowa on September 11, 1941, was the final straw. In that speech, Lindbergh attacked the administration, Britain, and most notably, Jews. Lindbergh implied that Jews exercised control over the media and movies to influence public thought and that they were to blame for dragging the United States into war.

CONCLUSION

Roosevelt attracted plenty of enemies as the longest-serving president in American history. Rather than shrinking from the challenge of his enemies, he and allies seemed to embrace them and often delighted in responding. The fact that political opposition emerged and hatred developed should not have been much of a surprise given how much the administration challenged and transformed the foundations of the modern state. He presided over massive changes in both domestic and foreign policy and earned the ire of Republicans and Democrats alike.

Craig Goodman

Further Reading

Dunn, Susan. *Roosevelt's Purge: How FDR Fought to Change the Democratic Party.* Cambridge, MA: Harvard University Press, 2010.

Dunn, Susan. *1940: FDR, Wilkie, Lindbergh, Hitler: The Election amid the Storm.* New Haven, CT: Yale University Press, 2013.

Fried, Albert. *FDR and His Enemies.* New York: St. Martin's Press, 1999.

Leuchtenberg, William E. *Franklin D. Roosevelt and the New Deal, 1932–1940.* New York: Harper, 1963.

Patterson, James T. *Congressional Conservatism and the New Deal: The Growth of the Conservative Coalition in Congress.* Lexington, KY: University of Kentucky Press, 1967.

Skowronek, Stephen. *The Politics Presidents Make: Leadership from John Adams to Bill Clinton.* Cambridge, MA: Harvard University Press, 1993.

Smith, Jean Edward. *FDR.* New York: Random House, 2007.

33. Harry S. Truman

Born: May 8, 1884
Died: December 26, 1972
Time in Office: 33rd President of the United States, April 12, 1945, to January 20, 1953
Election Results: 1944 Election: Elected vice President, assumed office upon death of Franklin D. Roosevelt; 1948 Election: 49.5% of popular vote, 303 (57.1%) Electoral College votes
Spouse: Bess Wallace (m. 1919)
Children: Margaret

Harry S. Truman served as the 33rd president of the United States. A U.S. senator from Missouri, Truman was picked by Franklin D. Roosevelt to be his running mate in the 1944 presidential election. The Roosevelt-Truman ticket defeated the Republican nominees Thomas E. Dewey and John Bricker in a popular vote (53.4% to 45.9%) and Electoral College (432–99) landslide. On April 12, 1945, Roosevelt died of a cerebral hemorrhage and Truman became president. In 1948 he survived doubts about whether he would even be nominated again, and faced what most considered to be a hopeless quest for reelection against Dewey, who had been renominated by the Republican Party. But in one of the great upsets in presidential electoral history, Truman defeated Dewey by more than 4% in the popular vote. He also secured a relatively easy victory in the Electoral College, winning 303 to Dewey's 189. Strom Thurmond, the candidate of the Dixiecrats, a southern-based offshoot of the Democratic Party, won 39 electoral votes. Truman declined to run again in 1952. In total, he served just shy of two terms. Truman married Bess Wallace in 1919, and they had one daughter, Margaret.

The story of Truman and the "hatred" meted out at him and his administration takes two broad forms. The first surrounds his perceived inability and unpreparedness to take over and fill Roosevelt's giant shoes. Although Truman soon won many skeptics over, he constantly had to push back against those who believed that the pressures of the presidency would soon see him crumble. His stunning reelection in 1948 went a long way to dispel those doubts. Second, whatever respect he could garner in the wake of large policy achievements, such as his decisive move to drop the atomic bomb and bring World War II to a close, his controversial decision to desegregate the military, and his reelection, the ceaseless trickle of bad news of scandal and corruption by his subordinates fed a vision of Truman as a crony politician. He remained decisive on any number of unpopular decisions, such as the firing of the popular General Douglas MacArthur for insubordination, but these led Truman to become increasingly defensive in the waning days of his administration. He left office with only a 32% approval rating according to one poll, and he was widely considered at the time to be a failed president. However, that assessment has undergone a profound change in the decades since he left the Oval Office.

PRE-PRESIDENCY TROUBLE

After trying and failing at many business ventures, Truman served in a variety of political offices, attaining some of them with the assistance of Tom Pendergast, a Kansas City businessman who was tremendously influential in Missouri politics in the first half of the 20th century. After Truman was selected by Pendergast to run for the U.S. Senate, virtually guaranteeing his election, he was often derisively referred to as the "Senator from Pendergast." For the most part, Truman ignored these assaults, though the perceptions of cronyism and political favoritism followed him into the White House.

AGENDA-SETTING AND NEGATIVITY

Prior to Truman, presidents did not often send out specific agenda requests to Congress. Five months into his presidency, however, in September 1945, Truman did so. Though this was something of a landmark in presidential history, the proposed agenda, while extensive, did not have much of a legislative impact.

Truman's presentation to Congress was a lengthy and rambling 21-point message that attempted to set the postwar political and economic agenda for the country. It is worth noting that such presidential insinuations into the legislative process had been generally considered impertinent until toward the end of Roosevelt's presidency, when the practice became grudgingly tolerated. According to political scientist Andrew Rudalevige, under Truman "the 'president's program' truly took hold . . . the struggling Truman administration realized that, if the Republican 'do nothing' Congress was to be made a successful electoral foil in 1948, the president needed an affirmative and comprehensive marker of his own. Special legislative messages were . . . packaged for congressional consideration nearly weekly." Truman called for new public works programs, legislation guaranteeing "full employment," a higher minimum wage, extension of the Fair Employment Practices Committee (or FEPC, a war-time agency that monitored discrimination against African Americans in hiring practices of government agencies and defense industries), a larger Social Security system, and a national health insurance system.

One of the key areas was the Employment Act of 1946. The act was more symbolic than substantive, placing responsibility for the health of the economy squarely on the president's shoulders, though with little with which to accomplish that monumental task save for the creation of a Council of Economic Advisers, an in-house political apparatus that the president could cultivate. Taken together, these requests demonstrated an interest in maintaining and building on the New Deal. When companies began reverting back to peacetime operations, Truman pushed for quick demobilization of the military—a political necessity as the troops and their families clamored for a hasty return to civilian life—and the temporary extension of governmental economic controls.

Truman's program went nowhere. Although he won passage of a "full employment" bill—the Employment Act of 1946—the measure had no teeth. Republicans and conservative southern Democrats in Congress were dead-set against many of the other proposed reforms, including an extension of FEPC, national health insurance, and a higher minimum wage. The public, moreover, remained divided over the prospects of an enlarged social welfare state and continued government intervention in the economy. Liberal Democrats and key constituents of the Democratic Party supported such measures, but many other Americans did not. Although not a lot of "hatred" was spewed at Truman, the question of competence and being in over his head began to cement and would set the backdrop for the rest of his administration, despite his decisiveness in approving the dropping of atomic bombs on Japan—an action that brought World War II to a close.

TRUMAN AND ANTICOMMUNISM

Anticommunist crusader Joseph McCarthy (R-WI) sought to make a name for himself in the Senate and settled on an anticommunist crusade to ferret out suspected sympathizers in the federal government. He accused the Truman administration of coddling State Department communists even though he was unable to provide any evidence to support his accusations. Indeed, the number of supposed communists in the State Department changed almost as often as he made the claim. Nonetheless, McCarthy was a constant thorn and source of frustration if not embarrassment for the administration. Truman stated that the charges were baseless, but "McCarthyism" continued to pick up steam.

Truman had to deal with Democrats as well, but it was McCarthy who most irritated the president. McCarthy sent Truman a telegram that demanded Truman turn over any and all evidence he had of security clearances that had been violated because of communist affiliations. McCarthy closed with a provocative observation: "Failure on your part will label the Democratic party as being the bed-fellow of international communism." That day, February 11, 1950, Truman fired back in a letter that he did not send, a habit he developed when he was angry as a method of cooling off. The letter he penned to McCarthy says, in its entirety:

My dear Senator: I read your telegram of February eleventh from Reno, Nevada with a great deal of interest and this is the first time in my experience, and I was ten years in the Senate, that I had ever heard a Senator trying to disgrace his own Government before the world. You know that isn't done by honest public officials. Your telegram is not only not true and an insolent solution that should have been worked out between man and man but it shows conclusively that you are not even fit to have a hand in the operation of the Government of the United States. I am sure that the people of Wisconsin are extremely sorry that they are represented by a person who has as little sense of responsibility as you have. Sincerely yours, HST.

McCarthy remained on the offensive, delivering an angry and pointed speech on the Senate floor later that month criticizing Truman and mocking Secretary of State Dean Acheson, who had also staunchly defended the Truman administration as well as the State Department. McCarthy described Acheson as a "pompous diplomat in striped pants, with a phony British accent." Truman defended his secretary of state, and fired a parting shot at McCarthy: "I think the greatest asset the Kremlin has is Senator McCarthy."

ELECTIONS, CORRUPTION, AND TROUBLE WITH DEMOCRATS

Accusations of corruption hound any politician that comes up through a political machine, and Truman was no exception. There is no evidence that Truman ever engaged in dishonesty, but many historians contend that he seemed to abide corruption by loyally defending associates and officials who were so accused.

Some of Truman's harshest critics in this area were fellow Democrats. Some Democrats never became comfortable with the plainspoken failed haberdasher from Missouri who had assumed the mantle of the presidency after the death of the great FDR. After initially high approval ratings that ranged from the mid-60s to mid-80s in the first six months of his presidency in the aftermath of World War II, Truman's political standing began to sink.

On the eve of the 1946 midterm elections, Truman's approval hovered at around 30%, and the Democrats lost badly. Republicans gained control of both houses of Congress for the first time since 1933. Senate Republicans went from 38 seats in the 79th U.S. Congress to 51 in the 80th, and their House counterparts increased from 190 to 246. As Democrats retreated to lick their wounds, many of them determined that Truman ranked high on their list of political liabilities. Even though, historically, presidents' parties tend to lose seats in the midterm, the Democrats had taken a larger hit than normal, and many placed the blame squarely on Truman. Looking ahead and fearing a loss of the presidency as well as Congress, conversations started to swirl about what to do about their seemingly hapless man in the White House. In one remarkable proposal, a young Democratic senator from Arkansas, J. William Fulbright, suggested that Truman appoint Republican senator Arthur Vandenberg of Michigan as his secretary of state. At that time, that cabinet position was third in line for the presidency. Then, Fulbright argued, Truman could resign and the country would be less likely to remain mired in a partisan stalemate. This of course did not sit well with Truman, who allegedly referred to Fulbright ever after as "Senator Halfbright." The feud with Fulbright would extend into the second term as well, and the stress of near constant criticism from the public contributed to increasing combativeness of the president. Truman, who had never been known to mince words in private or in his diary, became increasingly outspoken in public as well.

Toward the end of his presidency, the Truman White House was caught up in a variety of minor scandals, none of which implicated the president directly, though he did often go to great lengths to protect the underlings who were mixed up in them. For example, his old nemesis Fulbright, acting as chair of a subcommittee of the Banking and Currency Committee, produced a report on the Reconstruction Finance Corporation (RFC), which was responsible for various lending programs. The RFC had been the subject of some controversy over influence peddling from various Democratic operatives, including some in the White House. Indeed, a mink coat became a symbol of that corruption when it was discovered that one was given to a businessman and former employee of the RFC, purportedly for favors done while at the RFC. The controversy intensified when reports emerged that the recipient of the coat subsequently gave it to his wife, who worked in the White House.

Fulbright's subcommittee investigated this and other accusations of influence peddling. In one instance, Truman shocked Fulbright and another committee member when, after they discussed their concerns over two former directors, one a Democrat and the other a Republican, were under suspicion, Truman immediately reappointed both to their positions after their terms expired. Robert Donovan, author of a two-volume account of the Truman administration, argued that Truman was not an "incessantly combative president," but was a "counter puncher" when he felt put upon. And by February 1951, he felt supremely put upon and acted and reacted with a chip on his shoulder.

Truman was likely never going to establish a productive working relationship with Fulbright anyway. Fulbright, a Rhodes Scholar who was educated at Oxford and had already served as the president of the University of Arkansas, was the antithesis of Truman. Truman was undeniably smart and well versed in history, but did not have the same level of formal education and likely felt a bit insecure about it. As Donovan recounts, the RFC report produced by Fulbright's committee angered Truman so much that he referred to the senator as an "overeducated s.o.b." and even called the report "asinine" in the press, which took many, including his wife Bess, by surprise.

It is likely Truman could have defused this situation if he had fired some whose influence peddling embarrassed the administration. But Truman, either out of a sense of loyalty or defiance in the face of the incessant criticism (and probably a combination of both), flat out refused to do so. He did fire individuals from time to time, but only when there was no other possible way out. For example, after a series of scandals crippled his old friend Bill Boyle, who was chair of the Democratic National Committee, Truman reluctantly demanded his resignation. The scandals took their toll on the president. The tough exterior Truman maintained masked a vulnerability he showed to few. As he wrote a friend late in his second term, Truman admitted, "I suppose it is necessary to put up with these things, but it hurts sometimes."

Even after Truman stunned the political world in 1948 by winning an upset victory over New York governor Thomas Dewey, the political environment did not get better. The impending conflicts in Korea and China overwhelmed the administration. Truman blasted his political opponents, albeit in his diary. He perceived hatred with every word printed in newspapers. As one of his biographers, Donald McCoy, put it, "much in public print set him off." Truman was always a fighter, but he hurt easily and in his diary, which he had to know would be published someday, he pulled no punches and did not discriminate. News outlets including the Associated Press, big papers such as the *New York Times*, and even his "hometown" papers, the *St. Louis Post-Dispatch* and the *Kansas City Star*, failed to escape his wrath. He rejected print journalism and lamented that he hoped that television would be the saving grace of the free press, ". . . provided we do not let these same liars and black mailers control that means of communication too." In December 1952, just over a month before he prepared to leave the White House, he confided in his diary, referring to the press: "To hell with them. When history is written they will be the sons of bitches—not I."

TRUMAN AND CIVIL RIGHTS

By late 1947, Truman foresaw that advancing the cause of civil rights was a moral imperative but carried great political risk. In the 1940s, the Democrats were composed of a fragile coalition that included southern party members determined to preserve segregationist "Jim Crow" laws and culture in the region. As historian Alonso Hamby points out, Truman entered the presidential election year of 1948 outflanked on civil rights from both Henry Wallace, running as a Democrat, and Dewey, the Republican, both of whom touted their relatively extensive civil rights bona fides. Truman tried to hold the fragile coalition together, and if he managed to win the election, he needed southern Democrats in Congress to achieve almost anything he wanted. However, Truman forged ahead in the face of these political risks.

Truman directed the Justice Department to file an amicus curiae brief that reinforced the pro–civil rights position in *Shelley v. Kraemer*, a case that dealt with African American access to fair housing. In early 1948, he sent Congress a laundry list of proposed civil rights measures, including proposals to desegregate the military and deal with discrimination in the federal bureaucracy. The result, according to Hamby, was "little short of politically disastrous." Truman's already downward sloping approval ratings plummeted dramatically, especially in the South, and his disapproval ratings skyrocketed. Truman knew going in that this would be a challenge to his electoral strategy, but he deserves credit for following his instincts and pursuing what he felt was right and long overdue, especially given that the odds of an electoral victory in November were long, and the political downside was likely to be swift, harsh, and threaten to splinter the Democratic coalition.

THE 1948 PRESIDENTIAL CAMPAIGN

If Truman felt disrespected and underestimated early in his presidency, he was deeply beleaguered by the time the 1948 campaign commenced. Ironically, Truman did not have to field much direct criticism from Dewey, his Republican opponent. Much of the vitriol aimed at him came from Democrats, some of whom were determined to see their party represented by another nominee in the upcoming election.

Truman entered the nomination phase behind many other potential nominees, including Dewey, his eventual opponent, and General Douglas MacArthur. Even the enormously popular Dwight D. Eisenhower, supreme allied commander during World War II, was considered a potential Democratic nominee as he had not yet declared a political party affiliation. Understandably, Truman was nervous. Eventually Eisenhower let it be known that he would not be a candidate for either party in 1948. Truman relaxed and eventually, his path to renomination was secured.

The next order of business was to find someone who would agree to be Truman's running mate, not an insubstantial task given the dismal prospects for his reelection. Truman felt particularly fraught given the sheer amount of high-profile Democrats who came out against him. Truman really wanted Supreme Court Associate Justice William O. Douglas to run with him, given Douglas's appeal to young voters and the left. Douglas, however, turned down the offer. Truman took the rejection personally and quietly held bitter feelings toward Douglas for several years. Soon, though, he was able to secure Senator Alben Barkley of Kentucky.

After Barkley joined the ticket, Truman began to take aim at Republicans in the general election. Over the course of the campaign and the famous whistle-stop tour (during which he traveled the country by train), he focused less on Dewey and more on the Republican-controlled "Do-Nothing" 80th U.S. Congress that had stymied him throughout his first years in the Oval Office. He also labored mightily to counter the impression that his campaign was doomed. For example, Truman formally accepted his nomination at the Democratic convention with a speech of feisty optimism, "Senator Barkley and I will win this election and make these Republicans like it." The method with which he leveled his criticism was so pointed that it gave rise to his signature campaign battle cry, which would follow him long after he was reelected and even after he left the White House: "Give 'em hell, Harry!"

ASSASSINATION ATTEMPT

Almost all presidents receive death threats, but only 15 have endured actual attempts on their life. Four presidents died as a direct result of assassination (Abraham Lincoln, James Garfield, William McKinley, and John F. Kennedy), and Ronald Reagan was shot but survived. Truman was the target of at least one, and possibly two, assassination attempts.

The first was in 1947, about the time the United States was in the process of recognizing the state of Israel. Although it has not been fully corroborated, the story alleges that Truman was targeted by the Stern Gang, a Zionist group that may have sent bombs to various world leaders, including Truman. On October 30, a widespread uprising in support of a Puerto Rican independence movement occurred. Truman called the uprising "an incident between Puerto Ricans," seemingly dismissing it. Two nationalists, Oscar Collazo and Griselio Torresola, hatched a plan to assassinate Truman to call attention to the movement and perhaps as retribution for Truman's seeming dismissal of the cause. On November 1, the two would-be assassins approached Blair House, just across from the White House on Pennsylvania Avenue. Truman and his family stayed in Blair House from 1948 to 1952 while the White House was being renovated. Torresola and Collazo raced toward Blair House and began firing. A White House police officer named Leslie Coffelt returned fire and killed Torresola instantly. Coffelt, injured in the attack, was taken to a local hospital and died a few hours later.

For his part, Truman almost missed the entire event. He was upstairs in Blair House taking a nap when awoken by the commotion. He looked out the bedroom window and saw the wounded Collazo, but ducked down after being yelled at by the Secret Service to get away from the window. Truman's reputation in life was one of a man nearly unflappable, and his reaction to the attempt on his life bears this out. On November 2, just one day after the shooting, Truman responded to his friend and Secretary of State Dean Acheson, who had written the president a longhand note of concern. His text, written in Truman's matter-of-fact style, is worth quoting: "It was a most unnecessary happening over there at the Blair House and the people who really got hurt were wonderful men. The two men who did the job were just as stupid as they could be. I know I could organize a better program than the one they put on. They came nowhere near their objective—one of them faces the gallows and the other one is dead, although they did injure two good Guards and kill another one all unnecessarily." Collazo was indeed sentenced to die in the electric chair, but Truman commuted his sentence to life in prison a week before the execution was to take place.

FIRING GENERAL MACARTHUR

While engaged in Korea, General Douglas MacArthur, a popular political and military figure, saw his role in formulating the direction of military action in the Far East increase, a fact that did not sit well with prominent Republicans in Congress. For example, Republican leader Joseph Martin argued that Truman should clear the way for Chiang Kai-shek, the former president of the Republic of China, to attack mainland China to propel the United States to victory in Korea. Martin went so far as to claim that if Truman failed to do so, he would be guilty of murdering American soldiers on the peninsula. Truman responded to these pointed allegations by asserting his wish for a united front to bring both China and Korea to the negotiating table. To be sure, Truman had good reason to worry. A pact between the Soviet Union and China held that an attack on one of these powers would be interpreted as an attack on both and require a retaliatory response. Attacking China in any way could lead to World War III.

European leaders as well as many in the United States felt that MacArthur was the primary architect of American foreign policy as it related to the Far East. European leaders worried that MacArthur would pull American policy away from Europe and toward Asia. Martin asked MacArthur to comment on China. Counter to Truman's stated policy positions, MacArthur basically concurred with Martin and sent him a letter to that effect. Martin, emboldened by near unanimous support from Republicans and even by some Democrats who broke with the president, released the letter, making MacArthur's insubordination public (by defying the policy stated by Truman as commander in chief). Other cables showed that MacArthur had engaged in clandestine communications with Japan where he informed them that he planned to redirect the war into a full-scale confrontation with communist China, a direction clearly at odds with Truman's prosecution of the conflict.

After consulting with several of his top advisers, including the Chairman of the Joint Chiefs of Staff Omar Bradley, Secretary of State Dean Acheson, Secretary of Defense George Marshall, and others, all of whom concurred with sanctions short of formally proposing MacArthur's ouster, Truman fired MacArthur. On April 11, 1951, Truman released the following statement:

> With deep regret I have concluded that General of the Army Douglas MacArthur is unable to give his wholehearted support to the policies of the United States Government and of the United Nations in matters pertaining to his official duties. . . . I have decided that I must make a change of command in the Far East. I have, therefore, relieved General MacArthur of his commands and have designated Lt. Gen. Matthew B. Ridgway as his successor. Full and vigorous debate on matters of national policy is a vital element in the constitutional system of our free democracy. It is fundamental, however, that

military commanders must be governed by the policies and directives issued to them in the manner provided by our laws and Constitution. In time of crisis, this consideration is particularly compelling.

The consequences for Truman, public and political, were swift and harsh. His approval rating fell to 22%, lower even than Richard Nixon's during the Watergate scandal. MacArthur enjoyed the support of the public and much of the media, and calls opposing his dismissal rang out across the entire country. Even so, Truman instructed his staff not to publicly criticize MacArthur. Truman did not immediately respond, though he was quoted in the 1960s as having said that "I fired him because he wouldn't respect the authority of the President. I didn't fire him because he was a dumb son of a bitch, although he was, but that's not against the law for generals. If it was, half to three-quarters of them would be in jail."

PRESSURES ON THE TRUMAN FAMILY

Truman grew up on a family farm in Missouri and his family, and most particularly his mother, his wife Bess, and their daughter Margaret, were the center of his life. Most presidential families are subject to scrutiny, insults, or even expressions of hatred, and Truman's family was no exception. Truman largely took insults and epithets directed his way with public grace, though he stewed in private. However, as the pressures toward the end of his term grew, he was more prone to publicly let his anger fly in a raw, sometimes unhinged way—especially when family members were targeted. Indeed, it could be argued that he saved his most bitter epithets for those whom he felt crossed the line. Truman was prime to "erupt" when he felt his wife or daughter were insulted.

Probably the most famous incident involved Truman's daughter Margaret, an aspiring singer. Margaret had a good voice, and even had a reasonably successful career as a singer, but the limits on her voice were likely to keep her from entering the upper echelons of stardom. Still, Truman, always the protective father, supported her career and cheered her on even when many in his inner circle, including Bess, were skeptical of how far her talent would carry her.

In December 1950, the pressures of being president, the constant low approval, the conflicts in Korea and China, and the death of Secretary Charlie Ross, an old friend and confidante, all weighed heavily on the president. Seeking a distraction, Truman went to watch Margaret perform a concert in Washington, where the audience generally received her well. However, the next morning Truman read harsh criticism of her performance in Paul Hume's column in the *Washington Post*. As noted above, Truman was often prone to let off steam by writing a diatribe in the form of a letter he never intended to send, or in his diary. Not this time. Truman wrote a letter to Hume, and he did not hold back:

Mr. Hume: I've just read your lousy review of Margaret's concert. I've come to the conclusion that you are an "eight ulcer man on four ulcer pay." It seems to me that you are a frustrated old man who wishes he could have been successful. When you write such poppy-cock as was in the back section of the paper you work for it shows conclusively that you're off the beam and at least four of your ulcers are at work. Someday I hope to meet you. When that happens you'll need a new nose, a lot of beefsteak for black eyes, and perhaps a supporter below! [Columnist Westbrook] Pegler, a gutter snipe, is a gentleman alongside you. I hope you'll accept that statement as a worse insult than a reflection on your ancestry. H.S.T.

Truman's letter leaked out to the public. For his part, Hume later expressed regret that its contents became common knowledge. He also acknowledged that Truman was under tremendous strain when he wrote the note and should be afforded understanding. Still, most letters that were received by the White House condemned Truman's public attack. Margaret, embarrassed by the letter, said that Hume had every right to say what he thought. The uproar faded, and is generally now considered one of the defining moments in the character of Truman as a no-nonsense, tell-it-like-it-is politician. The bad feelings were short-lived, and when Truman and Hume met in Independence seven years later, Hamby notes that their encounter was "utterly friendly."

CONCLUSION

Even though he left office "hated" with a 32% approval rating and a 56% disapproval rating, most historical rankings of presidents now include Truman in the "near great" category, clearly below the likes of George Washington and Abraham Lincoln, but often ranking in the top 10 presidents and drawing high marks from liberal and conservative scholars alike. Indeed, in the 2017 C-SPAN poll of presidential scholars, Truman ranked sixth, situated between Dwight Eisenhower (fifth) and Thomas Jefferson (seventh). Truman scored particularly high, within the top 5, in the categories of Crisis Leadership (4), International Relations (5), Pursuit of Equal Justice for All (4), and Performance within Context of Times (5).

Daniel E. Ponder

Further Reading

Donovan, Robert J. *Conflict and Crisis: The Presidency of Harry S. Truman, 1945–1948.* New York: W. W. Norton, 1977.

Donovan, Robert J. *Tumultuous Years: The Presidency of Harry S. Truman, 1949–1953.* New York: W. W. Norton, 1982.

Hamby, Alonzo L. *Man of the People: A Life of Harry S. Truman.* New York: Oxford University Press, 1995.

McCoy, Donald R. *The Presidency of Harry S. Truman.* Lawrence, KS: University Press of Kansas, 1984.

McCullough, David G. *Truman.* New York: Simon and Schuster, 1992.

Neal, Steven. *Harry and Ike: The Partnership That Remade America.* New York: Touchstone, 2001.

Rudalevige, Andrew. *The New Imperial Presidency: Renewing Presidential Power after Watergate.* Ann Arbor, MI: University of Michigan Press, 2005.

Truman, Harry S. *Memoirs.* Garden City, NY: Doubleday, 1955.

34. Dwight D. Eisenhower

Born: October 14, 1890

Died: March 28, 1969

Time in Office: 34th President of the United States, January 20, 1953, to January 20, 1961

Election Results: 1952 Election: 54.9% of popular vote, 442 (83.2%) Electoral College votes; 1956 Election: 57.4% of popular vote, 457 (86.1%) Electoral College votes

Spouse: Mamie Doud (m. 1916)

Children: Doud and John

Dwight David Eisenhower entered the White House in 1953 with some unique advantages and conversely some distinctive disadvantages. What was different about Eisenhower than many other presidents before or after is that he was aware of both these strengths and liabilities, and had some fairly distinct, well-developed ideas on how to maximize his assets and minimize his liabilities. Every president enters office with strengths and weaknesses, political supporters and opponents, but Eisenhower's were more unique than most other chief executives. Much of his career involved issues of risk management, and this experience served him well during the eight years he worked in the Oval Office.

EISENHOWER AS GENERAL

One of Eisenhower's main strengths—that only a few other presidents have enjoyed—was that he was a war hero. A five-star U.S. Army general who served as supreme commander of the allied expeditionary forces of Europe during World War II, he had played an important role in helping the United States and its Allies win an unambiguous victory over both Nazi Germany and the Empire of Japan. No one in American politics in the 1950s was willing to question that achievement. That popularity transcended partisan and ideological divisions.

Another advantage enjoyed by Eisenhower was that he came into office with what was for all practical purposes a clean slate. He had not been involved in politics for years as a senator, representative, or governor and had no record that had alienated others, having spent the bulk of his adult life in the U.S. Army. Although the Army had factions within it and Eisenhower had made decisions that people had objections over, most of these issues were technical or professional in nature and did not translate into difficulty in the world of civilian politics. To give one example, Eisenhower and his friend George S. Patton Jr. had been early advocates of mechanization, and developing the tank as a weapon. Both faced opposition from the established infantry and cavalry branches, and eventually returned to the traditional career paths for officers in those branches. When war did come in the 1930s and 1940s, the United States was woefully unprepared in organizational and technological resources to fight armored warfare. In many ways, the United States never made good this shortcoming during the war, but that was hardly the fault of Eisenhower or Patton. Nor was it an argument that could be used to win votes, or at least cost Eisenhower support.

In matters of command, Eisenhower's decisions and expertise were open to more criticism. Several critics questioned his decision making during World War II. Ralph Ingersoll, the founding editor of *PM*—a New York city daily—wrote a book in 1946 in which he argued that the British were directing strategy and manipulating Eisenhower with a "British dominated" staff. He also argued that Eisenhower was indecisive and did not have a staff designed to run a battle, and that these two factors cost the Allies a chance to end the war in 1944. Ingersoll had served on U.S. Army General Omar Bradley's staff, and if one reads the general's memoirs carefully, it is possible to see that he had similar views. Those criticisms were muted though, and Bradley was largely respectful of Eisenhower in his account. In 1952, Chester Wilmont, an Australian reporter, offered a critique of "Ike"—a popular nickname for Eisenhower since his childhood—that was almost a 180-degree opposite of Ingersoll. Wilmont argued that American decisions had delayed the end of the war, helped accelerate the decline of the United Kingdom as a world power, and wrote off Eastern Europe to Soviet domination. As presented, though, this argument took the personal onus off Eisenhower and put it on the United States in general, and the U.S. Army in particular.

A bigger criticism of Eisenhower concerned the partition of Berlin after World War II. During Eisenhower's first year in the White House, the final volume in Winston Churchill's memoirs appeared. Churchill was careful to avoid criticizing Eisenhower directly—he even offered the president the opportunity to read early drafts. There was no profit in antagonizing Eisenhower, as the United Kingdom and the United States faced a common Cold War threat in the form of the Soviet Union. The final Churchill volume stressed issues of strategy and policy. He complained much about the decision to forego a move on the German city, claiming it complicated postwar issues. This criticism of Eisenhower and the decision to give up Berlin would grow, but not until the 1960s after he had left office. In the late 1950s two British field marshals, Lord Alanbrooke and Lord Montgomery, published memoirs designed to correct what they saw as Churchill's self-serving account of history. During this literary firefight, they hit Eisenhower. Alanbrooke allowed Sir Arthur Bryant to publish portions of his diaries in two volumes. His motivations were economic and honor. In the first case, since he was a field marshal, Lord Alanbrooke was still on active duty and was receiving half pay instead of the more generous pension that was awarded to retirees. In the second case, he believed—with good reason—that Churchill's memoirs had slighted the contributions of himself and the other members of the British Chiefs of Staff Committee in making strategy, and he was trying to correct the historical record. Publishing his journals may not have been the best way to advance the cause of the chiefs. His diary entries were often an emotional release from dealing with the brilliant but frustrating prime minister. Alanbrooke's criticisms of Eisenhower were minor compared to those about Churchill, whose expertise the field marshal savaged with biting criticisms. Alanbrooke's tepid observations about Eisenhower focused on his aptitude for planning and his distribution of supplies. Montgomery's book came out in between the two Alanbrooke/Bryant volumes. He believed Eisenhower had misled his readers with his wartime memoirs, and Montgomery believed it was his duty to offer the truth to his readers. His account was about his entire military career, but in the sections about Europe he stressed command issues. At the end, though, he discussed matters of strategy. He argued the failure to seize Vienna, Prague, and Berlin squandered the political victory that the Allied armies had earned.

Montgomery's comments infuriated Eisenhower in a profound and personal manner. He considered organizing a conference to refute Montgomery's arguments. After he left office, he commissioned *The Papers of Dwight David Eisenhower* project with Johns Hopkins University Press in part to refute Montgomery's assessment. In a more immediate sense, these criticisms had almost no impact on Eisenhower's popularity with the American people. In the United States, reviewers and critics tended to focus on the remarks about Eisenhower and presented these criticisms as an us (American) versus them (British) feud. This interpretation was widely off the mark—Montgomery was extremely unpopular within the Royal Air Force and the Royal Navy for failing to understand the advantages that air and sea power offered—but a presentation that made this debate one of the American view versus the British view—with the underlying assumption to an American audience that Eisenhower was right—translated into no political advantage for Eisenhower's partisan and ideological opponents.

Eisenhower was far more vulnerable on the issue of logistics. During the war, he allowed Lt. Gen. John C. H. Lee to set up a wasteful system of supply. Despite repeated recommendations to get rid of Lee, Eisenhower refused. After D-Day, the U.S. Army began to face significant supply issues that limited its ability to pursue German units as they collapsed and fell back in northern France. There were shortages in both ammunition and manpower. The training system for replacements was set up to train individual infantrymen, not artillery gunners or tank crews. Many of these problems were systematic to the organizational structure of the U.S. Army and beyond Eisenhower's control, but he tolerated the wasteful Lee who had no ability to right the situation. Supply, though, is a complicated and less than engaging issue that is of interest more to specialists than the lay public, and these legitimate criticisms never bothered Eisenhower during his years in the Oval Office.

Eisenhower's handling of personnel was an issue that could have done him more damage. During the war, he dismissed several officers. The best-known incident was the removal of Maj. Gen. Lloyd Fredendall from his position as commanding general of II Corps after the German Army defeated it at the Battle of Kasserine Pass. Fredendall and his staff believed he had been wronged and spent much of their postwar years trying to redeem his historical reputation. The fact that Eisenhower replaced Fredendall with Patton, who won several clear victories with the corps really limited that removal as an issue of contention. Patton was a hero and a winner. Fredendall was not and there was little political gain to be made serving as his champion.

Patton, who was a true friend of Eisenhower's in full meaning of that word, turned out to be a bigger threat to him. Eisenhower had relieved Patton of his command of Third U.S. Army over a dispute about de-Nazification efforts in Bavaria and comments Patton had made to reporters about this issue. The incident did not show Eisenhower at his best. He ignored Patton's plausible defense and allowed critics of the Third Army's commander to attend the meeting where the two confronted one another, and offer detailed critiques for which Patton had no advanced warning. Patton and Eisenhower never saw one another again. Patton's family published an edited version of his diary in 1947 as *War as I Knew It*. The book was critical of Eisenhower—Patton had used it as a release mechanism to deal with the stress of the war—but there was speculation there was much more in the unpublished portions that could hurt Eisenhower. Publishers approached Beatrice Patton, the general's widow, about publishing the diary in its entirety. Beatrice Patton was no supporter of Eisenhower in 1952, but also believed—with good reason—that the media had treated her husband unfairly. She simply did not want to revisit those issues, and refused.

RELATIONSHIP WITH KAY SUMMERSBY

The diary contained both legitimate and petty criticisms of Eisenhower, but it also discussed what was probably the biggest threat to Eisenhower from his military career: his relationship with his driver, Kay Summersby. There was a good deal of gossip at the time that he was having an affair with her. Such a revelation at any time during Eisenhower's political career could have been devastating, given social attitudes in America at the time. Eisenhower's actions during the war fueled some of these rumors. "I was interested to see that Kay, his chauffeur, had been promoted to hostess," Alanbrooke noted after the war. "In so doing Ike produced a lot of undesirable gossip that did him no good." The whispers got back to Mamie Eisenhower, and she complained to her husband. He dismissed the talk as just that. He had a war to win.

After the war, Eisenhower had little contact with Summersby. She is briefly mentioned in his memoirs. For her part, Summersby moved on with her life. She wrote a book about her work on Eisenhower's staff, immigrated to the United States, and married. With no substantiation to the gossip and without Summersby trying to do anything to build on the loose talk, the issue simply faded away.

Yet, the issue exploded in 1974 when journalist Merle Miller's book *Plain Speaking: An Oral Biography of Harry S. Truman* appeared in print. The book is a series of interviews with Truman. Miller claims Truman said Eisenhower requested permission from George C. Marshall to get a divorce so he could marry Kay Summersby. The problem with this assertion is that there is no evidence to substantiate it. Many people have even questioned if Truman made these comments. Miller spent the rest of his life trying to find evidence in support of Truman's claim. In 1988, he published a biography of Eisenhower, *Ike the Soldier: As They Knew Him*, which he finished two weeks before he died. "One of Miller's motives for writing the book centered on his desire to find some substance for rumors Eisenhower had an affair with his Irish driver, Kay Summersby," D. K. R. Crosswell, Miller's research assistant, noted, "I never found any evidence of Eisenhower's infidelity." Crosswell dismissed Truman's comment as "an old man's active imagination and too much bourbon."

Summersby was still alive at the time Miller's Truman biography appeared in print, and was soon getting offers to write a book of her own. "I'm short of money," she admitted to a reporter, "and the temptation is great." In another interview that was not made public until after her death she stated, "To tell you the truth, there wasn't that much between me and Ike." She added: "If I write anything about Ike and me, it's only because I need the money."

In the end, financial need won out. Summersby soon became ill with cancer and had large medical bills that she needed to pay. Simon & Schuster gave her a $50,000 advance, but she died before the book was finished. Wanting to recoup its investment, the publishing house relied on the ghostwriter that Summersby had hired to finish the project. Simon & Schuster made its money back with *Past Forgetting: My Love Affair with Dwight D. Eisenhower* in which Summersby and/ or her ghostwriter claim there was indeed an affair, although the two tried but failed to sexually consummate their relationship. The ABC television network even turned the book into a miniseries in 1979 starring Robert Duvall as Eisenhower and Lee Remick as Summersby.

BATTLES WITH DEMOCRATS AND REPUBLICANS

Although his military career was more advantage than disadvantage, Eisenhower entered politics with real political liabilities. The biggest was that he was a political minority in the late 1940s, a Republican at a time when the Democrats were the party of the majority. Part of his election in 1952 was due to Truman fatigue, rather than a genuine turning away from the policies of the New Deal and the Fair Deal. At first, though, Eisenhower looked to be in a strong political position. The Republicans retook control of both the House and the Senate in 1952. Republican leadership in both chambers was strong: Joseph W. Martin would be serving as speaker of the House of Representatives for a second time, and the majority leader in the Senate, Robert A. Taft, had been in the upper chamber for 14 years.

Events did not transpire as smoothly as Eisenhower hoped when he took office in January 1953, however. Taft, a conservative, had been Eisenhower's main rival for the Republican nomination. The conservatives dominated the Republican caucus in the Senate, but Taft was in control of this group and he was willing to work with Eisenhower, who was more moderate, in a constructive manner. His health, however, collapsed quite suddenly. Diagnosed with cancer, he died six months after Eisenhower took office. William Knowland of California took over as majority leader. He had less influence over his caucus than Taft, and Eisenhower did not like him personally. Martin had been a Taft supporter, but was willing to work with the administration. At first, both got along well, but Eisenhower soon began to believe, to paraphrase the words of his press secretary, that Martin did not have the sense to come in out of the rain. For his part, the speaker thought that Eisenhower had a staff with little political experience, and often advanced dumb ideas.

As these tensions heightened, relations between the executive and legislative branch suffered. Eisenhower had personalized staff and command relationships during his military career, avoiding individuals he did not like. He did the same as a politician. He came to dislike Knowland and Martin and limited his contact with both.

THE "HIDDEN HAND" PRESIDENCY

In 1954 things got worse. The Democrats retook control of both the House and Senate, and would retain a majority in both for the rest of Eisenhower's time in office. The new Democratic majority brought Sam Rayburn and Lyndon Johnson—both of Texas—to power as speaker and majority leader, respectively. Unlike Martin and

Knowland, Eisenhower enjoyed working with the two Texans, and relations between the Oval Office and Congress were cordial.

Nonetheless, Eisenhower now faced a political opposition that had grown in power and was now in the majority. Even though his poll numbers were high, he could expect more attacks on both partisan and policy matters. Eisenhower's response was to use what political scientist Fred I. Greenstein has called the "hidden hand presidency." He had used a similar approach as the supreme commander of the allied expeditionary forces. Eisenhower was aware of his personal popularity and that the public looked to the presidency to serve as a unifying symbol. He was also aware that he was a partisan leader, and would increase opposition when he tried to implement policies that ran counter to the views of the other side. His solution was to use a series of subordinates as lightning rods on partisan and policy matters. Eisenhower, meanwhile, took a detached stance of being above the fray.

Vice President Richard Nixon was Eisenhower's main weapon when he wanted to deliver partisan, political attacks. Nixon played this role well and gave many speeches during the midterm elections. As a result, he collected several political debts, which helped him secure the Republican nomination in 1960 when Eisenhower faced the constitutional two-term limit. On foreign policy, Secretary of State John Foster Dulles, the grandson and nephew of two previous secretaries of state, gave tough, anticommunist speeches, interviews, and congressional testimony that were often laced with religious righteousness. On civil rights, Herbert Brownell Jr. took the public lead advancing policy ideas that were not popular with many people who had voted for Eisenhower. In conjunction with these lightning rods, Eisenhower responded to questions during press conferences with long, syntactically complex answers that he designed to be—and often were—confusing.

Eisenhower knew that with the Democrats in power in Congress he had to work with them in a bipartisan manner. He, however, often found indirect ways to apply pressure to legislators. Behind the scenes, he would approach the well-known and wealthy campaign supporters of various congressmen and senators and ask them to lobby on his behalf.

This approach had mixed results for Eisenhower. Lyndon Johnson and Sam Rayburn were willing to work with the president, particularly on foreign affairs and defense matters. On some matters, though, it was clear that they were responding to political pressure coming from supporters at home that Eisenhower had arranged.

More significant were splits within the Republican Party along lines of ideology and the executive-legislative branches. Many senior Republican senators and congressmen had chaffed during the New Deal and Fair Deal years and were determined to reverse the policies of the previous two Democratic administrations. During the Truman years, Republicans proposed an amendment to the

Constitution to limit the chief executive to two four-year terms, a clear response to Franklin D. Roosevelt's four presidential election victories. This type of action continued even after the 1952 presidential election. Knowland was more than willing to challenge Eisenhower's foreign policies in East Asia. "The more I see of Knowland, the more I wonder whether he is a Republican leader or not," Eisenhower observed. Senator Joseph McCarthy of Wisconsin kept up his investigations of civil servants that he had started when Truman was in office. Senator John Bricker of Ohio proposed another constitutional amendment limiting the authority of executive agreements. In both of these later cases, these Republican senators were seeking to attack or limit the power of the executive branch even though Eisenhower was a Republican.

Eisenhower refused to take on McCarthy publicly, believing it would only elevate the Wisconsin Republican, but he was livid when the senator began attacking the U.S. Army for harboring communists. McCarthy was focused on the fact that an Army dentist who refused to take a loyalty oath had been promoted. This led to abusive treatment of a general appearing in front of his committee to the point that Secretary of the Army Robert T. Stevens ordered him to stop testifying. Eisenhower worked to put pressure on senators to reign in McCarthy. This approach generally worked, and the Senate held hearings to see if one of McCarthy's aides had tried to use the influence of the senator's office to help limit the military service of another aide. These hearings led the U.S. Senate as a whole—in a strong, bipartisan vote—to censure McCarthy. This repudiation broke McCarthy's political power in Washington. Knowland, however, was one of the few senators to vote against the censure. Eisenhower expressed exasperation with the California senator's vote, declaring that "in his case, there seems to be no final answer to the question, 'How stupid can you get?'"

Another problem with Eisenhower's behind-the-scenes approach is that it led critics to assert that he lacked leadership skills and political courage. Many leading newspaper columnists and reporters were dismayed at his seemingly weak response to McCarthy. Some of his leading critics on this issue included syndicated columnists Joseph Alsop and Walter Lippmann and *Washington Post* editorial cartoonist Herbert Block (better known as Herblock). Convinced that these and other leading journalists in Washington leaned toward the left, Eisenhower limited the social contact he had with reporters. He also encouraged television coverage of his press conferences so that he could circumvent print news media and take his message directly to the American public.

EISENHOWER AND NIXON

Eisenhower used Vice President Nixon to make partisan attacks when they were necessary. Nixon was smart and well informed on policy matters, but he was also more than willing to throw sharp elbows in the political arena. He had earned a reputation as a nasty mudslinger in his House and Senate campaigns. Eisenhower had complicated, ambiguous, love-hate feelings toward Nixon. He was disappointed by Nixon's willingness to go negative, and yet it was Eisenhower who gave Nixon these assignments. In the 1956 presidential election, former Minnesota governor Harold Stassen, who was working on the White House staff at the time, announced that he had lost faith in Nixon and would campaign to have him dropped from the ticket. Although this decision technically belongs to the party, the convention normally nominates whoever the presidential nominee wants. Eisenhower's response to Stassen's effort was that the former governor was free to take a leave of absence and support—or not support—anyone he wanted.

This response was hardly an endorsement of Nixon, the man that Eisenhower said should be president should he die in office. It also seemed to offer an opening for Democrats in the general election. Democratic nominee Adlai Stevenson attempted to exploit this issue. He tried to use Eisenhower's subordinates against him, saying, "'Trust Ike and ask no questions' really means something else." It meant trusting Dulles, Nixon, Brownell, and others. This approach did not work. Eisenhower was too popular, and whatever American voters thought of other members of his administration, they were comfortable having the former general in the White House. He was reelected in strong fashion.

EISENHOWER AS LAME DUCK PRESIDENT

Criticism of Eisenhower intensified during his second term. Several U.S. Army officers, many of them prominent veterans of World War II, expressed misgivings about the Eisenhower administration's national security strategy, dubbed the "New Look." This approach relied heavily on nuclear weapons and "massive retaliation." This strategic approach favored the U.S. Air Force over the other services, since it was the branch of the armed service most capable of delivering nuclear munitions at the time. Eisenhower relied on nuclear weapons, because they were cost-effective. The problem was that they limited his discretion. This strategy limited the U.S. response to any number of problems in world affairs. Many issues did not require the blunt force of a nuclear response, or the threat of that type of devastation. Eisenhower, however, feared the strain on the budget of having a large, conventional military. After he retired, General Maxwell Taylor, the chief of staff of the U.S. Army in the late 1950s, wrote a book critical of Eisenhower's defense policies. He also went on to join the presidential campaign of Senator John F. Kennedy, who adopted many of Taylor's positions as his own. Taylor returned to active duty under Kennedy, eventually becoming chairman of the Joint Chiefs of Staff.

At the same time that Eisenhower absorbed criticism of his defense policies from what was basically his right flank, Eisenhower also took criticisms from his left flank. In 1956 the Soviet Union successfully put the first artificial satellite in orbit around the Earth. This achievement convinced many Americans that the United States was falling behind scientifically. It also convinced many that there was a frightening "missile gap"—a disparity in the nuclear arsenals—between the Soviet Union and the United States. Soviet premier Nikita Khrushchev did much to promote this position with a series of bombastic speeches. The result was a craze of bomb shelter construction across the United States in the second half of the 1950s, as many Americans tried to prepare themselves for the coming of World War III. Eisenhower knew there was no missile gap. The Central Intelligence Agency had accurate data that made it clear the United States had significantly more military resources in this area than the Soviet Union. Eisenhower tolerated Khrushchev's speeches because he knew the harsh rhetoric was a cover for Soviet military inferiority. The bold talk was a concession in many ways to U.S. dominance and kept the Soviets from challenging the United States in the mediums of air and space. The problem Eisenhower faced was that domestic critics were using this charge against his administration in effective fashion. He could not release data to prove that these accusations were false, because it would undercut his efforts to give Khrushchev the hollow rhetorical victory.

Political attacks also continued from both the right and the left on domestic affairs. Many liberals believed that he was the captive of his political subordinates. Many critics—particularly those without military experience of their own—tended to see him as a simple-minded general who was out of his depth when it came to the sophisticated, high-level political ways of Washington. Press conferences in which he seemed surprised at the policies of his own administration seemed to confirm this point of view. Jokes abounded about his lack of intelligence.

Conservatives were also unhappy with Eisenhower. Their complaints involved matters of both foreign and domestic policies. They charged that Eisenhower had not gone for a win in the Korean War, that he had appointed judges that favored racial desegregation, that his administration had continued Truman's containment policies, and that he had made no effort to dismantle the New and Fair Deals erected by the Roosevelt and Truman administrations. The John Birch Society, an arch-conservative organization founded in 1958, even accused Eisenhower of being a tool of a communist conspiracy.

CONCLUSION

Many of these criticisms helped the Democrats in the 1960 presidential election. Although they did not campaign against Eisenhower himself, they did criticize the policies of the Republican administration. On the other hand, these criticisms failed to hurt Eisenhower personally. He left office with both his health and reputation intact. Indeed, public opinion polling data from that era indicate that Eisenhower was even more popular when he left office than when he first took up occupancy in the Oval Office.

Nicholas Evan Sarantakes

Further Reading

Ambrose, Stephen E. *Eisenhower: Soldier and President.* New York: Simon & Schuster, 1990.

Greenstein, Fred I. *The Hidden-Hand Presidency: Eisenhower as Leader.* Baltimore, MD: Johns Hopkins University Press, 1994.

Johnson, Paul. *Eisenhower: A Life.* New York: Penguin Books, 2014.

Morgan, Kay Summersby. *Past Forgetting: My Love Affair with Dwight D. Eisenhower.* New York: Simon & Schuster, 1977.

Smith, Jean Edward. *Eisenhower in War and Peace.* New York: Random House, 2012.

35. John F. Kennedy

Born: May 29, 1917

Died: November 22, 1963

Time in Office: 35th President of the United States, January 20, 1961, to November 22, 1963

Election Results: 1960 Election: 49.7% of popular vote, 303 (56.4%) Electoral College votes

Spouse: Jacqueline Bouvier (m. 1953)

Children: Caroline, John Jr., and Patrick

John F. "Jack" Kennedy was on the receiving end of enormous levels of hatred during the years he served as president, and he is a unique case in the study of presidential hatred. Although he was one of America's most popular presidents, he was also killed by assassination—the most extreme expression of political hatred possible.

Many scholars believe that Kennedy's death in office was, among all presidential deaths, perhaps the most grieved by the American public, due in part to the extensive television coverage of the assassination and events that followed in the days after.

Historians note that in terms of sheer numbers, Kennedy had a lower percentage of people who disliked or disapproved of him than most other presidents. His 70% average approval rating remains among the highest of any president, and his ratings have only improved over time. During Ronald Reagan's first term (1981–1985), for example, 30% of Americans said they wished Kennedy were president, and in 1985, one survey found that Kennedy was rated highest among the nine previous presidents in the areas of confidence, personality, trust, ability to get things done, domestic affairs, and the setting of high moral standards. But Kennedy was not the only member of his large family that some hated. His father, patriarch Joseph P. Kennedy, and his brothers Robert and Ted, were also hated for a wide variety of reasons.

THE 1960 PRESIDENTIAL CAMPAIGN

"I sincerely fear for my country if Jack Kennedy should be elected president," said conservative Republican senator Barry Goldwater in 1960. "The fellow has absolutely no principles. Money and gall are all the Kennedys have." The sentiments behind Goldwater's biting comment were widely shared by critics of Kennedy and his powerful, politically connected family. Kennedy's critics called him a shallow celebrity. They routinely criticized his lifestyle—the tan, the sailing, the trips to his family's luxurious properties, such as Hyannis Port, Massachusetts, and Palm Beach, Florida, and viewed him as a lightweight playboy, and even falsely charged that he had been married once before. In 1960, when divorce was regarded as enormously controversial if not scandalous, the discovery of another marriage would have spelled doom for Kennedy's political aspirations. (As of 2018, Ronald Reagan and Donald Trump are the only presidents to have been divorced—Reagan once, and Trump twice.)

Kennedy's elite education at private New England schools followed by his undergraduate degree from Harvard was also a source of anger to some and gave rise to accusations that he was an elitist and a snob. His enemies also spoke of Kennedy's poor health, the extent of which was not as widely known then as it is today, but nevertheless was broadly acknowledged at the time, especially among his congressional colleagues, the press, and his political rivals.

Other sources of anger among Kennedy's political enemies included his scant record of legislative achievement and poor attendance record as a U.S. senator. Critics also charged that Kennedy was a political opportunist who had no fixed ideology. They accused him of being just another scheming politician who was ever-changing and politically malleable. Though he had extensive military experience, having served heroically in World War II, and though he had 14 years of duty in the U.S. Congress before his election to the presidency, Kennedy's youth was another source of resentment for his opponents (including for both his predecessor, Dwight D. Eisenhower, and Kennedy's vice president, Lyndon B. Johnson). Kennedy's detractors have also focused on such issues as his personal recklessness regarding his private life, but these issues were not common knowledge during his presidency, and were not covered by the press, and thus were not a source of hatred at the time. There was also tremendous anger directed at the Kennedy family. Once elected, some feared that the family planned to occupy the White House for

24 consecutive years: two terms for Kennedy, two for his brother Robert, and then two for his youngest brother, Ted. Political dynasties have always existed—the Adams, Roosevelts, Bushes, and Clintons—but the potential for a Kennedy dynasty seemed at the time greater, as all three brothers served in the U.S. government at the same time, as Robert was Kennedy's attorney general and Ted was elected senator from Massachusetts in 1962.

THE KENNEDY PRESIDENCY

Much of the hatred toward Kennedy during the early 1960s was an extension and lingering of earlier hatreds and resentments: Al Smith's 1928 presidential campaign (as the first Catholic nominated by a major party for president); the "socialism" of FDR's New Deal; the 1945 "sellout" at Yalta; the "losing" of China in 1949; the "stalemate" of Korea; and two landmark decisions by the Supreme Court during the Warren years (the 1954 *Brown v. Board of Education* decision that desegregated public schools, and the 1962 *Engel v. Vitale* decision outlawing school prayer in public schools).

Kennedy's political opponents' list of grievances and resentments cast a wide net. Some held bigoted views of Catholics and their mostly urban adherents, predominantly of Irish and Italian ancestry, whom they considered mindless people controlled by Rome. Some also were deeply suspicious of the East Coast and the so-called northeastern establishment who were blamed for everything from the introduction of fluorinated water (seen by some as an overreach by government officials) to U.S. membership in the United Nations. Kennedy was specifically accused of promoting a United Nations–backed world socialist government.

Another unusual feature about political hatred during the Kennedy years is that some of those angry at Kennedy were also angry at Eisenhower, his Republican predecessor. One does not see such continuity of hate across party lines that much anymore in American politics. However, it is important to recall that the movement that smeared Kennedy as a communist sympathizer was an extension of the movement that tarnished Eisenhower with many of the same charges during his two terms. For example, Robert Welch, founder of the far-right John Birch Society, called Eisenhower a "conscious, dedicated agent of the Communist Conspiracy." Conservatives routinely charged that many members of the press were controlled by communists, and that Walter Lippmann, Edward Murrow, Eleanor Roosevelt, and Harry S. Truman were also communists. The far right also saw no distinction between Eisenhower/Nixon and Kennedy/Johnson, arguing that neither was tough enough against the communist menace.

One rather unique element of the discord during the early 1960s was that the hate extended to Kennedy's administration and cabinet. For example, in separate incidents in Dallas, angry mobs spat in the faces of Johnson, his wife Lady Bird, and Adlai Stevenson, Kennedy's ambassador to the U.N. Far-right Texas congressman Bruce Alger publicly called Johnson a "socialist and a traitor." Presidential aide Arthur Schlesinger Jr. was accused of wanting to make America socialist, and Robert Kennedy was hated almost as much as the president.

THE TURBULENT 1960s

For most Americans, the 1960 election that lifted Kennedy to the White House did not represent a dramatic break with the past, despite the many differences between Eisenhower and Kennedy in terms of party, age, background, region, religion, experience, and, most glaringly, their perspectives on the role the federal government should play in the life of the citizenry. But the early 1960s were a time of violence, hate, and deeply felt divisions in which numerous powerful and well-organized and financed hate groups operated. These included George Lincoln Rockwell, the American founder of the American Nazi Party, and the Minutemen, a military group that had its origins in the John Birch Society. The National States Rights Party, founded in 1958, spewed racism and anti-Semitism. Several assassination plots were foiled as early as the fall of 1960. Burning crosses were common sights in the South, and white mob violence exploded at the University of Mississippi and elsewhere over desegregation and the civil rights movement. On the world stage, meanwhile, concerns grew that tensions in geopolitical hotspots like Berlin and Cuba might trigger nuclear war. The public remembers the early 1960s as the calm before the storm to follow, as the second half of the decade would include other political assassinations in addition to the one that claimed President Kennedy's life (Malcolm X in 1965, Martin Luther King Jr. and Robert Kennedy in 1968), urban unrest in numerous cities, the rise of a drug-fueled counterculture, and escalating public protests (particularly on college campuses) over the Vietnam War. But nostalgia for the so-called "peace" of the Kennedy years ignores the level of hatred that existed at the time. Also, some do not remember all the hatred during the Kennedy years due to the chaos that followed his death. The years following the tragedy in Dallas were perhaps the most turbulent in American history, making the Kennedy years seem calm in comparison.

KENNEDY'S CRITICS ON THE RIGHT

The main policy areas that generated the most vitriol toward Kennedy concerned four main topics: Kennedy's Catholicism, his stance on civil rights for African Americans, charges that he was a socialist, and charges that he was also too accommodating with communism and the Soviet Union.

Kennedy's quest to become the nation's first Roman Catholic president incited much religious-based hatred. The Texas reverend W. A. Criswel said before the

1960 election that Roman Catholicism "is not only a religion, it is a political tyranny" that "threatens those basic freedoms and those constitutional rights for which our forefathers died." Oil baron H. L. Hunt would circulate nearly 200,000 copies of the sermon. Kennedy felt the need to address his religion in a well-received speech in September 1960 to the Greater Houston Ministerial Association, in which he offered assurances that there would be a wall of separation between the White House and the Vatican.

Regarding civil rights, Kennedy was hounded by the John Birch Society, among whose many causes was the movement to impeach Earl Warren over his liberal decisions, especially school integration. Many right-wing activists at the time equated racial integration with communism, and they insisted that Kennedy's sympathy for the civil rights movement was weakening America both at home and abroad. One of Kennedy's harshest critics was retired general and far-right activist Edwin Walker, who called Kennedy "a liability to the free world." Kennedy had earlier relieved General Walker of his command post in Germany for insubordination. Kennedy's foreign policy detractors wanted a rollback of communism around the world, not containment. Kennedy was accused of acting weakly in Berlin and allowing the Berlin Wall to go up. Kennedy's right-wing critics charged that the United States was losing the Cold War to the communists in Asia, Africa, Eastern Europe, the Caribbean, and the Middle East. Cuba was a source of particularly intense frustration among right-wing foreign policy "hawks" (those who favored war or hardline military postures over more diplomatic approaches). Kennedy was blamed for the failed 1961 Bay of Pigs invasion, and was especially criticized for not providing adequate air cover to the invaders. Eighteen months later, the right was disgusted with Kennedy's pledge after the Cuban Missile Crisis to never again invade or attack Cuba. Kennedy and his administration were also charged with failing to prevent Laos and the Congo from becoming solidified communist states, as well as pushing for disarmament and eroding American military strength. "The Kennedy-Johnson Administration based nearly every foreign policy decision—in Laos, Cuba, Africa, Geneva, Berlin—on the assumption that Communists have 'mellowed,' despite all evidence to the contrary," wrote right-wing activist John A. Stormer in 1964. "If American leaders persist in refusing to pursue a victory while Communists base their actions on the premise that either capitalism or socialism must triumph, then surely America will lose."

KENNEDY'S CRITICS ON THE LEFT

Interestingly, many of the issues that generated hatred of Kennedy from the right also generated disproval of the president from the left. The left had always been suspicious of Kennedy. Most liberals fervently supported Adlai Stevenson or Hubert Humphrey in 1960 (the latter was viewed as the quintessential liberal at the time), and the left had also long been distrustful of the Kennedy family. Ambassador Joseph Kennedy's policy of appeasement provoked scorn among the left in the 1930s, as did Robert Kennedy's open friendship with and support of fellow Catholic Joe McCarthy in the early 1950s. Only late in the 1960 campaign did Eleanor Roosevelt, an iconic hero of progressives, come around to endorsing Senator Kennedy. Furthermore, Kennedy campaigned to the right of Nixon in 1960 on the issue of foreign affairs, complaining repeatedly that Eisenhower and his vice president (Nixon) had allowed the Soviet Union to open a deadly "missile gap" advantage over the United States (in reality, this missile gap did not exist). As president, he also appointed five Republicans to his cabinet: Robert McNamara as secretary of defense; C. Douglas Dillon as secretary of the treasury; John McCone as director of Central Intelligence; McGeorge Bundy as national security adviser; and Christian Herter as U.S. trade representative.

Regarding civil rights, many liberals argued that Kennedy was moving too slowly. Whereas many southerners despised Kennedy for interfering in what they considered local matters, liberals believed that Kennedy treaded cautiously on issues pertaining to African Americans because he was afraid of alienating southern Democrats. After all, Kennedy had only won the presidency because he had managed to win the 79 Electoral College votes of Texas, Louisiana, Arkansas, Georgia, South Carolina, and North Carolina, as well as 5 of the 11 Electoral College votes of Alabama. (In Alabama that year, voters chose electors individually instead of as a slate. As a result, only five electors were pledged to Kennedy, and the remaining six were unpledged and ultimately voted for Senator Harry F. Byrd of Virginia.)

Many on the left also accused Kennedy of being too accommodating with big business. These critics distrusted the Kennedys' vast wealth, and were especially critical of the business background of Kennedy's father, whom they viewed as a crook. The same sentiments applied to the charge that Kennedy was too accommodating with the Soviet Union. Many progressives were urging Kennedy to reach out to the Soviets long before his June 1963 American University address, which was known for Kennedy's foreign policy statements and was interpreted by some as his hinting at pulling troops out of Vietnam. In addition, some progressives believed that Kennedy was too aggressive against Cuban leader Fidel Castro, particularly following the failed Bay of Pigs invasion in early 1961.

In general, Kennedy was fully aware of the nation's toxic political climate, and he even addressed many of these issues head on. On November 18, 1961, in an address to the Democratic Party of California in Los Angeles, he said:

Now we are face to face once again with a period of heightened peril. The risks are great, the burdens heavy, the problems incapable of swift or lasting solution. And under the strains and frustrations imposed by constant tension and harassment, the discordant voices of extremism are heard once again in the land. Men who are unwilling to face up to the danger from without are convinced that the real danger comes from within. They look suspiciously at their neighbors and their leaders. They call for a man on horseback because they do not trust the people. They find treason in our finest churches, in our highest court, and even in the treatment of our water. They equate the Democratic Party with the welfare state, the welfare state with socialism, and socialism with communism. They object quite rightly to politics' intruding on the military—but they are anxious for the military to engage in politics. But you and I and most Americans take a different view of our peril. We know that it comes from without, not within. It must be met by quiet preparedness, not provocative speeches. And the steps taken this year to bolster our defenses—to increase our missile forces, to put more planes on alert, to provide more airlift and sealift and ready divisions—to make more certain than ever before that this nation has all the power it will need to deter any attack of any kind—those steps constitute the most effective answer that can be made to those who would sow the seeds of doubt and hate. So let us not heed these counsels of fear and suspicion.

ASSASSINATED IN DALLAS

Due to the many tensions in Dallas in November 1963, Kennedy's aides urged him not to go, as did many of the city's leading civic figures. On November 22, a handbill featuring two mug-shot style photographs of Kennedy was widely distributed in the city. The text of the handbill stated:

Wanted For Treason

THIS MAN is wanted for treasonous activities against the United States:

1. Betraying the Constitution (which he swore to uphold):
   He is turning the sovereignty of the U.S. over to the communist controlled United Nations.
   He is betraying our friends (Cuba, Katanga, Portugal) and befriended our enemies (Russia, Yugoslavia, Poland).
2. He has been WRONG on innumerable issues affecting the security of the U.S. (United Nations—Berlin wall—Missile removal—Cuba—Wheat deals—Test Ban Treaty, etc.)
3. He has been lax in enforcing Communist Registration laws.
4. He has given support and encouragement to the Communist inspired racial riots.
5. He has illegally invaded a sovereign state with federal troops.

6. He has consistently appointed anti-Christian to Federal office: Upholds the Supreme Court in its Anti-Christian rulings. Aliens and known Communists abound in Federal offices.

7. He has been caught in fantastic LIES to the American people (including personal ones like his previous marriage and divorce).

Signs at the Dallas airport greeting JFK the day he was shot included: YANKEE GO HOME AND TAKE YOUR EQUALS WITH YOU; HELP JFK STAMP OUT DEMOCRACY; LET'S BARRY [sic] KING JOHN; YOUR [sic] A TRAITOR. Along the parade route, one sign read: I HOLD YOU JFK AND YOUR BLIND SOCIALISM IN COMPLETE CONTEMPT.

POST-PRESIDENCY HATRED

There exist several strands of post-Kennedy hatred, and they come from both the political left and the political right. Much of this hatred is focused on what each group feels is the false myth of the Kennedy years. It must be emphasized, though, that each of these groups is a small minority, and that neither the level of their vitriol nor their raw numbers compare to those who strenuously opposed Kennedy during his years in office.

Some people believe that had Kennedy lived, the United States never would have gotten mired so deeply in Vietnam. Indeed, that was the impetus for Oliver Stone's 1992 film *JFK*. Some liberals, however, insist that Kennedy bears just as much responsibility for America's ruinous intervention in Vietnam as Johnson. This group feels frustrated by the so-called Kennedy legend. (They also point out that Kennedy's closest adviser, his brother Robert, fully supported the Vietnam War while his brother was president; Robert Kennedy did not denounce the war until his 1968 presidential run, which he began after Eugene McCarthy, running on an antiwar platform, almost won the New Hampshire primary over President Johnson.)

A second group of Kennedy detractors focus on the seemingly never-ending revelations of the late president's womanizing, both before and during his presidency. The disclosures regarding Kennedy's numerous affairs first surfaced in the 1970s, and have continued ever since. Recent years have even seen the publication of "tell-all" books by Kennedy's various mistresses. Though each new revelation does nothing to alter the views of Kennedy's most ardent supporters, it nevertheless does constitute a major thread of current-day Kennedy haters.

Though it is impossible to accurately quantify, speculation might suggest that the largest group of current Kennedy haters are focused on the belief that Kennedy is simply the most overrated figure in American history. Interestingly, this school

6lvv

of Kennedy skeptics has its foot in both the left and the right. To some on the left, Kennedy gets too much credit for liberal programs and policies that Johnson signed into law. The largest group, by far, of current Kennedy haters are those who believe that the late president was nothing but style over substance. These critics complain that Democrats have benefited these past 50-plus years from the adulation of the slain president. Others argue that Kennedy was a Cold War hawk who would be a Republican today, as he favored tax cuts for the rich and was strong on defense.

Anger at Kennedy among prominent conservatives continues to this day. According to Brent Bozell III, founder of the conservative Media Research Center, the nation's largest media watchdog organization, "Tell me what JFK's legacy is? Substance? Camelot? What the hell does Camelot mean? ... [I]f Jack Kennedy hadn't been assassinated, he would have a legacy like Jimmy Carter's: nothing" (author interview, June 3, 2004). Similarly, Curt Smith, a speechwriter for President George H. W. Bush, called Kennedy "unbelievably shallow and superficial." Kennedy's accomplishments as president "are almost none. ... Camelot has nothing to do with substance, nothing to do with character." Smith also complained about the fact that Kennedy is remembered by the left as a liberal icon. Kennedy "was a very moderate president, of course," he said. "He had to be pushed and kicked, screaming, into doing anything regarding civil rights" (author interview, May 7, 2004). Historian Robert Dallek, one of Kennedy's more recent biographers, noted: "In 1988, 75 historians and journalists described JFK as 'the most overrated public figure in American history.'"

Perhaps the single central irony to the study of hatred toward Kennedy is that most of the scholarship on the topic has focused on hatred coming from the radical right, but it was a member of the radical left, Lee Harvey Oswald—a member of the organization Fair Play for Cuba who railed against capitalist exploitation and who narrowly missed killing Edwin Walker in Dallas earlier in November 1963—who killed him.

CONCLUSION

Despite President Kennedy's record-level approval ratings, both during and after his presidency, he was still subject to enormous levels of hatred and expressions of vitriol during his presidency. Many of the issues that caused such hatred remain with us today: race, the appropriate role of the federal government in American life, America's leadership on the world stage, and the threat of enemies, both foreign and domestic. Above all, the Kennedy years remind us that the anger on both the right and left that surfaced during the 2016 presidential contest was not a new phenomenon in American politics.

Bernard von Bothmer

Further Reading

Bugliosi, Vincent. *Reclaiming History: The Assassination of President John F. Kennedy*. New York: W. W. Norton, 2007.

Chomsky, Noam. *Rethinking Camelot: JFK, the Vietnam War, and U.S. Political Culture*. Boston: South End Press, 1993.

Dallek, Robert. *An Unfinished Life: John F. Kennedy, 1917–1963*. Boston: Little, Brown and Company, 2003.

DeGregorio, William A. *The Complete Book of U.S. Presidents*. New York: Barricade Books, 1993.

Hamilton, Nigel. *JFK: Reckless Youth*. New York: Random House, 1992.

Hersh, Seymour M. *The Dark Side of Camelot*. Boston: Little, Brown and Company, 1997.

Lasky, Victor. *JFK: The Man and the Myth*. New Rochelle, NY: Arlington House, 1993.

Minutaglio, Bill, and Stephen L. Mavis. *Dallas 1963*. New York: Twelve/Hachette Book Group, 2013.

Perret, Geoffrey. *Jack: A Life Like No Other*. New York: Random House Trade Publishers, 2002.

Reeves, Thomas C. *A Question of Character: A Life of John F. Kennedy*. New York: Free Press, 1991.

Stone, Oliver, and Zachary Sklar. *JFK: The Book of the Film*. New York: Applause Books, 1992.

Stormer, John A. *None Dare Call It Treason . . . 25 Years Later*. Florissant, MO: Liberty Bell Press, 1990.

Talbot, David. *Brothers: The Hidden History of the Kennedy Years*. New York: Free Press, 2007.

von Bothmer, Bernard. *Framing the Sixties: The Use and Abuse of a Decade from Ronald Reagan to George W. Bush*. Amherst, MA: University of Massachusetts Press, 2010.

Waldron, Lamar, and Thom Hartmann. *Ultimate Sacrifice: John and Robert Kennedy, the Plan for a Coup in Cuba, and the Murder of JFK*. New York: Carroll and Graf, 2005.

White, Theodore H. *The Making of the President 1960*. New York: Atheneum, 1961.

Wills, Garry. *The Kennedy Imprisonment: A Meditation on Power*. Boston: Little, Brown and Company, 1981.

36. Lyndon B. Johnson

Born: August 27, 1908

Died: January 22, 1973

Time in Office: 36th President of the United States, November 22, 1963, to January 20, 1969

Election Results: 1960 Election: Elected vice president, assumed office upon death
of John F. Kennedy; 1964 Election: 61.1% of popular vote, 486 (90.3%) Electoral
College votes
Spouse: Claudia Alto "Lady Bird" Taylor (m. 1934)
Children: Lynda Bird and Lucy Baines

Accidental presidents are vice presidents who assume the presidency on the death
or resignation of the president. In the 20th century, Lyndon Baines Johnson was
the fourth vice president to become president following the death of his predecessor, and the circumstances of his ascension to the Oval Office were perhaps the
most tragic. Although John F. Kennedy was elected in one of the closest presidential elections in history (about 100,000 popular votes), his public approval rating
was strong, averaging just over 70% during his short time in office, and climbed as
high as 83% at one point early in his administration. In the wake of his assassination his presidency came to be described as "Camelot." In fact, it was his wife, Jacqueline, who first made the comparison to the Broadway musical of the same
name in a *Life* magazine interview penned by author Theodore White shortly after
Kennedy's death. One might say that Kennedy's presidency was a tough act for
Johnson to follow.

Johnson had a storied political career even before Kennedy asked whether he
would be willing to serve as vice president. Elected to the House of Representatives
in 1936 on the New Deal platform, Johnson ran for the Senate in 1948 and in a
highly controversial primary election defeated a popular former governor, Coke
Stevenson, by 87 votes out of just under 1 million votes cast. His election to the Senate alienated much of the conservative crowd across Texas who mockingly referred
to him as "Landslide Lyndon." He rose quickly through the ranks of the Senate by
turning the position of majority leader of the Democratic Party into the most
important post in the Senate, and he directed the passage of the major legislative
initiatives of the 1950s. Johnson's colleagues did not find his persuasive tactics
endearing, but they produced results. Journalists Rowland Evans and Robert Novak
described the "Johnson Treatment" as follows:

The Treatment could last ten minutes or four hours. It came, enveloping
its target, at the Johnson Ranch swimming pool, in one of Johnson's offices,
in the Senate cloakroom, on the floor of the Senate itself—wherever Johnson
might find a fellow Senator within his reach. Its tone could be supplication,
accusation, cajolery, exuberance, scorn, tears, complaint, the hint of threat. It
was all these together. It ran the gamut of human emotions. Its velocity was
breathtaking, and it was all in one direction. Interjections from the target
were rare. Johnson anticipated them before they could be spoken. He moved

in close, his face a scant millimeter from his target, his eyes widening and narrowing, his eyebrows rising and falling. From his pockets poured clippings, memos, statistics. Mimicry, humor, and the genius of analogy made The Treatment an almost hypnotic experience and rendered the target stunned and helpless.

Johnson decided rather late to run for the Democratic presidential nomination in 1960 and finished a disappointing second to Kennedy when—to Johnson's surprise—Kennedy wrapped up the party's nomination on the first ballot. Johnson was a master of counting votes, but not this time. Most political observers were surprised when Kennedy asked Johnson to be his running mate, and Kennedy himself was reportedly surprised when Johnson accepted. With the prospect of a close general election looming, however, Johnson was obviously crucial in helping the junior senator from Massachusetts win the South and especially Texas.

Johnson may have been an accidental president, but he understood presidential-congressional relations better than anyone. Shortly following Kennedy's assassination, Johnson spoke to a joint session of Congress and directly challenged his former colleagues: "Today in this moment of new resolve, I would say to all my fellow Americans, let us continue. This is our challenge—not to hesitate, not to pause, not to turn about and linger over this evil moment, but to continue on our course so that we may fulfill the destiny that history has set for us." He claimed that the immediate tasks were for Congress to first honor the fallen president by passing the civil rights bill that the Kennedy administration had introduced the previous summer and then pass Kennedy's tax bill, which had lingered in Congress even longer. Both were passed in relatively short order, and Johnson followed up these with other successes in the spring and summer of 1964. In the fall of that year Johnson was reelected overwhelmingly, defeating Republican senator Barry Goldwater of Arizona with over 60% of the popular vote and winning 44 states plus the District of Columbia. His presidency started with a flourish of activity, but ended in a quagmire with the country divided along lines of race, party, and support for the Vietnam War. Beleaguered on all sides—and especially by criticisms of America's military involvement in Vietnam—Johnson decided not to run for reelection in 1968.

THE FEUD WITH ROBERT KENNEDY

A bitter feud between Johnson and Robert Kennedy, John F. Kennedy's younger brother, was part of the backdrop of much of Johnson's vice presidential and presidential years, involved many loyalists from both sides, and was well known and well documented. The relationship between the two was much more complicated than it seemed on the surface and the enmity ran deep.

Johnson and Kennedy first met in the Senate cafeteria in 1953, but Kennedy's animosity for Johnson predated that meeting. Johnson spoke freely and with contempt for Kennedy's affluent father, Joseph Kennedy, and the politician, Senator Joseph McCarthy (R-WI), for whom Kennedy served as an aide during the early 1950s. As McCarthy and his aides respectfully rose from their breakfast to shake hands with Johnson, Kennedy refused to even look at him. Johnson responded by approaching Kennedy with hand outstretched, a clear effort to embarrass the young staffer in front of McCarthy and his peers by cajoling him into shaking hands.

A few years later, as John Kennedy considered whether to run for president in 1960, he dispatched his brother Robert to visit Johnson at his ranch in Texas. Even though Robert was still relatively young (36), he was his brother's campaign manager, and they needed to gauge Johnson's interest in running for president. Johnson still viewed the younger Kennedy as the green Senate staffer he had met years earlier and not at all his equal. Kennedy understood that, but he had a mission and he came away from the meeting with three conclusions. First, Johnson was not planning to run for president. Second, Johnson would not help or hurt his brother's campaign. And third, Johnson was planning to actively work to deny Adlai Stevenson a third Democratic party nomination for the presidency (he lost both the 1952 and 1956 elections by a wide margin). Kennedy believed Johnson's promises, even though he eventually broke all three.

Whereas Johnson's style was determined and controlling, John Kennedy was quiet and calculating. Kennedy thought that he needed a skillful southern Democrat to help him with the South, and Johnson was clearly the most influential option available. As a result, on the morning of July 13, 1960, the new Democratic presidential nominee offered the vice presidency to Johnson. Kennedy reported to his brother Robert that as he suggested the idea to Johnson, he suddenly seized the opportunity and accepted. Johnson expected that if elected Kennedy might serve two terms, and at 52 his prospects seemed uncertain given that his own father had only lived until the age of 60. When Robert Kennedy heard Johnson had accepted he reportedly objected, "Oh my God. Now what do we do?" He quickly went to Johnson's hotel suite in protest and implored him to withdraw, but to no avail. Kennedy later told a journalist and friend, "Yesterday [when my brother won the nomination] was the best day of my life, and today [when Johnson joined him] is the worst day of my life." The result was that many of the Kennedy loyalists also resented Johnson and in turn he resented them, which created a dreadful climate for Johnson during the Kennedy presidency.

That discord not only set the context of Johnson's relationship with the Kennedys for the three years of the Kennedy presidency, but also colored Johnson's five years in the Oval Office. Although Johnson and Robert Kennedy shared generally similar views on public policy, the mutual contempt between the two, according to

Jeff Shesol, was "so acute, their bitterness so intense and abiding, they could scarcely speak in each other's presence." This animosity carried over to many of the Kennedy's young, Ivy League–educated aides. In his memoirs, then-congressman Tip O'Neill of Massachusetts recalled that those close to the Kennedys "had a disdain for Johnson that they didn't even try to hide. . . . They actually took pride in snubbing him." As a result, when Johnson attended policy meetings he said little or nothing unless specifically asked for his comment. Rather than becoming part of Kennedy's inner circle, Johnson was given minor duties such as chairmanship of the National Aeronautics and Space Council and the Committee on Equal Employment Opportunity (later the Equal Employment Opportunity Commission). Kennedy also sent Johnson on "goodwill" tours throughout the world just to give him something to do. The lack of usefulness took a toll on Johnson. At one point, he lamented to House Speaker Sam Rayburn, a fellow Texan, that "being vice president is like being a cut dog."

Of course, all of that changed in an instant when Kennedy was assassinated on November 22, 1963, in Dallas, Texas, where he and Johnson had traveled to soothe discord between the liberal and conservative elements of the state Democratic Party. Shortly after Kennedy died, Johnson was sworn in on Air Force One as the 36th president of the United States. Prior to being sworn in, Johnson called Robert Kennedy, not to offer his condolences, but to ask the attorney general the procedure for his swearing in. Kennedy resented Johnson and later bitterly attacked Johnson for his impatience and insistence that Jackie Kennedy appear by his side as he was sworn in on Air Force One. When the plane landed in Washington, a clearly miffed Robert Kennedy entered the plane and departed with Mrs. Kennedy and the body of his brother without ever speaking to the new president.

Johnson concluded that he should maintain the general direction of Kennedy's presidency by taking up his highest priorities before moving on to enact his own programs. When he asked a joint session of Congress to "let us continue" with Kennedy's legislative priorities on November 27, 1963, he effectively invoked the words of his predecessor who in his inaugural address told the country "let us begin" to undertake pressing national work, even though it would not be finished "in the first thousand days, nor in the life of this administration, nor even perhaps in our lifetime on this planet." Johnson's rhetoric, however, did not appease the Kennedys nor mitigate the years-long rivalry between Johnson and Robert Kennedy. Although Johnson retained most of Kennedy's cabinet and many of them for the full term of his presidency, Robert Kennedy and several staff loyal to the family served for only a short time in the early days of the Johnson administration in order to facilitate a smooth transition of power.

With the vice presidency vacant there was a "draft Robert Kennedy" movement at the 1964 Democratic National Convention. To prevent that from being successful, Johnson issued a statement that ruled out all his cabinet officials because he found them to be invaluable in their current positions. This was an unpopular move with the Kennedy supporters, but Robert Kennedy announced two days prior to the convention that he was leaving the position of attorney general to run for the U.S. Senate seat held by Republican Kenneth Keating in New York. Eager to pick up a seat in the Senate for his Democratic Party, Johnson set aside his personal animosity toward Kennedy and supported his campaign. Kennedy defeated Keating by a 53% to 43% margin.

The rivalry between Johnson and Kennedy and his supporters subsided somewhat until March 16, 1968, when Kennedy picked up the mantel of his elder brother and announced that he would challenge Johnson for the Democratic nomination. At the time, it was widely expected Johnson would "officially" declare his intent to run, but earlier in the week he had only narrowly defeated Senator Eugene McCarthy of Minnesota in the New Hampshire primary. Ultimately, Johnson decided against running for reelection, and there seemed to be a reconciliation of sorts with Kennedy. On April 3, 1968, after Kennedy had entered the presidential race and Johnson had dropped out, the two, along with several aides, met in the White House. Regarding Vietnam Johnson told Kennedy he would be happy to take suggestions on ending the war stating, "I feel no bitterness or vindictiveness. I want everybody to get together to find a way to stop the killing." Johnson assured Kennedy that "he had never viewed him with contempt," and that the "difficulties" between them had been exaggerated. Johnson wanted Kennedy to know that he did not hate him, and did not even dislike him. A little over two months later, on the night of the California primary, Kennedy was assassinated. Historian Garry Wills points out that if the two were working together and not fighting, so much more could have been accomplished. But, that was not to be. He goes on to describe the long-lasting feud as "like watching two very powerful railroad trains racing at top speed toward each other along a single set of tracks."

JOHNSON'S SUPPORT OF CIVIL RIGHTS AND THE ENEMIES IT GENERATED

In many parts of the country, particularly the South, race relations were terrible in the 1950s and 1960s. The South was still segregated and demonstrations, protests, riots, and other forms of violence were becoming increasingly common. Things were so bad that one Gallup survey in 1963 found that 78% of respondents would move if a black family moved into their neighborhood. Johnson came from Texas, which was one of 11 states that seceded during the Civil War to form the Confederacy. During the first two decades of Johnson's congressional career he not only voted with the South against civil rights at every opportunity, but he was aligned closely with the team of leaders that actively plotted to defeat civil rights legislation. Among those leaders was Senator Richard Russell of Georgia. Russell was an avowed segregationist and served as Johnson's mentor when he came to the Senate. In fact, Russell spent a considerable amount of time at the Johnson home (he had never married) and was even known to the Johnson daughters as "Uncle Dick."

It turned out, however, that Johnson was a "man of his times." As a member of the House of Representatives, Johnson voted against legislation to end discriminatory measures such as the poll tax, segregation in the armed forces, and even lynching. During his first eight years in the Senate he voted consistently against civil rights legislation as well. In 1957, however, the man who had opposed civil rights his entire congressional career suddenly changed. Johnson not only voted in favor of federal civil rights legislation in 1957 and 1960, but he navigated each bill through the Senate. Given Johnson's track record on civil rights, his leadership did not suddenly endear him to those who expressed solidarity with the cause. On the other hand, it sowed the seeds of discontent with his old allies in Congress from the South. Indeed, many critics asserted that Johnson changed his stance on civil rights only because he thought it would advance his political fortunes.

That discontent quickly solidified when Johnson assumed the presidency. As mentioned earlier, in his first national address Johnson had urged the Congress to pass what became the Civil Rights Act of 1964 as a tribute to Kennedy. In his appeal Johnson said, ". . . no memorial oration or eulogy could more eloquently honor President Kennedy's memory than the earliest possible passage of the civil rights bill for which he fought so long. We have talked long enough in this country about equal rights. We have talked for one hundred years or more. It is time now to write the next chapter, and to write it in the books of law." The purpose of the legislation was to end segregation and racial discrimination in public accommodations, public education, and other federally assisted programs. Senator Russell led a bloc of southern Democrats in the Senate to filibuster the bill. He vowed to fight "with our boots on, to the last ditch." It was a bitter pill for Russell as he faced the fact that "he had raised to power a man who was committing himself to the destruction of the way of life he treasured." Johnson, however, pressed his former colleagues hard. In particular, Johnson convinced Senator Everett Dirksen of Illinois, the Republican leader, to concede the bill was an idea whose time had come. Dirksen was instrumental in getting additional Republican support, which was necessary for the legislation to pass. By the time Johnson signed the legislation into law, he had convinced numerous friends, among them many prominent African Americans and northern liberals, that he believed in the cause of racial justice. On the other hand, his reputation did not fare so well in the South. Senator Herman Talmadge of Georgia, a lifelong segregationist, was asked how he felt about Johnson signing the Civil Rights Act. He replied, "sick." Johnson understood the price that he and the Democrats would pay politically. He reportedly told one of his top aides, "the Democratic Party just lost the South for a generation."

Johnson's standing with conservative white southerners further eroded when he fought for and signed additional civil rights legislation including the Voting Rights Act of 1965 and the Fair Housing Act of 1968. In 1965, Johnson signed Executive Order 11246 to enforce affirmative action to remedy discrimination in hiring and employment, and in 1967 the Senate confirmed his appointment of the first African American, Thurgood Marshall, to the Supreme Court. In 1965, Congress approved and the states ratified the Twenty-Fourth Amendment, which made poll taxes unconstitutional. Johnson may have lost the South for the Democratic Party for a generation or more, but many historians assert that his administration also did more to advance federal civil rights than any since Abraham Lincoln. When asked by a reporter how he reconciled his new interest in civil rights with his voting record on civil rights while in Congress, the president replied, "I did not have the responsibility then that I have now, and I did not feel its importance as I now do. But I am going to do everything I can to right the wrongs of the past, no matter how many mistakes I may once have made."

REPUBLICAN MISCHIEF

During his first State of the Union address in January 1964, Johnson proposed a national program he called the "War on Poverty" to address the national poverty rate, which hovered at around 19%. The War on Poverty was part of his broader Great Society agenda that also included programs such as Head Start and Upward Bound to confront issues in education, Medicare and Medicaid to tackle issues in health care, and other reforms and programs in such areas as consumer protection, the environment, housing, and transportation. In terms of both complexity and scope, the country had not seen a domestic agenda of this nature since Franklin D. Roosevelt's New Deal. Johnson's supporters, many of his detractors, and the Washington press were astonished at his success in getting many of these initiatives passed.

Much of Johnson's success, however, was due to the overwhelming majority that Johnson's party enjoyed in Congress following the 1964 elections. The Democrats held 295 of 435 seats in the House of Representatives and 68 of 100 seats in the Senate. The Republicans managed to pick up 47 seats in the House and three votes in the Senate in the 1966 midterm elections, but that was far from sufficient to block Johnson's policy agenda in many areas. Thus, the Republicans found few opportunities for legislative victories outside the area of civil rights where they were able to at least slow legislation by joining with southern Democrats who were in many cases representing pro-segregationist white constituencies.

Since the Republicans did not have the votes to stop Johnson's legislative agenda, they turned to making mischief for his administration by linking individuals with questionable backgrounds to Johnson. In late 1963 and early 1964 Republicans on the Senate Rules Committee pushed for an investigation into Bobby Baker, who had been one of Johnson's political advisers when he was majority leader in the Senate. Baker had allegedly arranged sexual favors and bribes in exchange for special treatment. Baker quickly resigned when these accusations became public, and following Kennedy's assassination the investigation was delayed, and when it was resumed any role that Johnson may have played was dropped. Second, in 1964 one of Johnson's top aides was forced to resign after a sex scandal just a few weeks before the presidential election. Walter Jenkins was arrested along with another man on charges of disorderly conduct in a YMCA restroom. Although many newspapers refused to run the story, Republican Party operatives encouraged the press to print the story to embarrass the president. Third, Johnson nominated sitting associate justice and his former legal and political advisor, Abe Fortas, to become chief justice when Earl Warren retired in 1968. Unhappy with the direction of the Warren Court and determined to embarrass Johnson, conservatives registered their disenchantment by aggressively questioning Fortas about his relationship with Johnson and threatening to filibuster his nomination. In the end, Fortas received a majority of votes in the Senate, but not the supermajority needed to end the filibuster, so Johnson was forced to withdraw the Fortas nomination.

VIETNAM AND THE ANTIWAR MOVEMENT

The U.S. first sent military advisers to Vietnam in the early 1950s, but escalated involvement throughout the Kennedy administration. When Johnson became president in late 1963, he did not feel that he could simply withdraw U.S. troops from South Vietnam and allow the communists to advance in Southeast Asia. He knew that his political opponents would place the blame for such a development squarely on his doorstep. Johnson's first goal regarding Vietnam, upon which he based his decisions almost exclusively, was his desire to keep it from becoming a major political issue. Early on this meant the goal was to keep Vietnam from complicating his election-year strategy. By 1966 he told Senator Eugene McCarthy, "I know we oughtn't to be there, but I can't get out. I just can't be the architect of surrender." Although Johnson was mostly successful in doing that, the war soon came to haunt him, and would ultimately end his presidency.

In early August 1964, the destroyer USS *Maddox*, which was on an intelligence patrol in the Gulf of Tonkin, came under attack by North Vietnamese torpedo boats. Two nights later, the *Maddox* and USS *Turner Joy* reported that they were receiving radar signals indicating they were under attack again. Johnson quickly authorized retaliatory strikes against torpedo boat bases and an oil storage facility in North Vietnam. Three days later Congress passed a resolution providing the president with a blanket authorization for the use of force in Vietnam. Senator

Wayne Morse (D-OR), one of only two senators that voted against the resolution, said at the time, "I believe this resolution to be an historic mistake." By the end of 1967 the United States was spending $25 billion per year on the war, troop strength reached almost 500,000, and more than 15,000 American soldiers had been killed with another 110,000 wounded.

In the early days of the war most Americans were generally supportive of the Johnson administration, but the polls showed that by early 1968 a majority of Americans thought that sending troops to Vietnam had been a mistake. Protests against U.S. involvement in Vietnam started in 1965, primarily on college campuses among left-leaning artists, intellectuals, peace activists, and young people who rejected authority. Many of Johnson's former colleagues from the Senate came to oppose the war including Republican senator George Aiken of Vermont, and prominent Democrats like Senator and Chairman of the Foreign Relations Committee William Fulbright of Arkansas, Senator Eugene McCarthy of Minnesota, and Senator George McGovern of South Dakota, among others. In fact, Fulbright held a series of televised hearings on the war in Vietnam in 1966 and later in the year published a book entitled *The Arrogance of Power*, which criticized the reasons behind the war. McCarthy ran against Johnson in the New Hampshire primary in 1968 as an antiwar candidate and garnered 42% of the vote behind Johnson's 49%.

As the United States escalated bombing of North Vietnam and other military actions in Vietnam, however, domestic opposition to the war—and support for the protest movement—steadily grew. Protests reached a peak in early 1968 following the Tet Offensive. On the Tet holiday, which is the Vietnamese New Year, the North Vietnamese launched a series of surprise attacks against military and civilian targets throughout South Vietnam. The attacks were intense, and the South Vietnamese temporarily lost control of several cities. The South Vietnamese eventually regrouped and defeated the insurgency, but the cost was high in terms of casualties, resources, and support for the war among American voters who had been repeatedly assured that the United States was nearing victory in Vietnam.

The resolve that the North Vietnamese demonstrated during the Tet Offensive surprised the Johnson administration and shocked most Americans. Up until that time the Johnson administration's assessments of the war were lean on details, but high in optimism. The Tet Offensive, though, opened up a perceived "credibility gap" between the optimistic reports of the administration and the U.S. military and the actual conditions in Vietnam. As public support for the war collapsed and the number of casualties grew alarmingly, Johnson's job approval ratings dropped to just 35% in August, and protest and civil unrest grew.

These circumstances, coupled with the advent of television, meant that the protest movement of the late 1960s was arguably one of the most effective in history. The anti-Vietnam movement became a pervasive presence in newspapers, on radio, and on television. Popular musical acts like Country Joe and the Fish, Bob Dylan, Joan Baez, and many others epitomized the opposition to the war in Vietnam and the hatred for Johnson. Antiwar protesters gathered daily at the White House and chanted, "Hey, Hey LBJ, how many kids did you kill today?"

Throughout all his years in politics, liberals had always annoyed Johnson. They never trusted him and he never trusted them. Johnson once said, "The difference between liberals and cannibals is that cannibals eat only their enemies." Vietnam, however, burdened Johnson deeply and in a personal way. He painstakingly agonized with decisions related to the war, he was troubled over his son-in-law who served in the Marines in Vietnam, and it was commonly known among those close to him that he wept when signing letters of condolence to the survivors of those killed in action.

CONCLUSION

A president's job approval ratings typically exhibit what is referred to as a "decay curve" during their presidency. This simply means that for almost all presidents their job approval ratings trend downward over time. For most presidents, this indicates that making public policy will become more challenging. For other presidents, it means that it becomes downright impossible as opposition to their administration grows. The latter was the case with Johnson. Even though he felt confident that he could win in 1968, the "race" between Kennedy and Johnson lasted only 15 days. On March 31, 1968, in a speech to the country from the White House, Johnson said: "With American sons in the fields far away, with America's future under challenge right here at home, with our hopes and the world's hopes for peace in the balance every day, I do not believe that I should devote an hour, or a day, of my time to any personal partisan causes. Or to any duties other than the awesome duties of this office—the Presidency of your country. Accordingly, I shall not seek, and I will not accept, the nomination of my party for another term as your President."

Historians credit Johnson with major advances in bolstering civil rights and in fighting poverty in the United States. However, his presidency also resulted in the marginalization of Congress, the press, and the public in foreign policy decisions. His successor, Richard Nixon, did much the same thing. As a result, Congress revoked the Gulf of Tonkin Resolution in 1971 and passed the War Powers Resolution in 1973 over the veto of Nixon. By 1974, Arthur Schlesinger Jr. coined the phrase "imperial presidency" and wrote a widely read book of the same name that was highly critical of the capacity for Johnson and other presidents to make policy unilaterally.

Randall E. Adkins and Paul Landow

Further Reading

Califano, Joseph. *The Triumph and Tragedy of Lyndon Johnson: The White House Years.* New York: Simon and Schuster, 2015.

Caro, Robert A. *The Years of Lyndon Johnson: Means of Ascent.* New York: Alfred A. Knopf, 1990.

Caro, Robert A. *The Years of Lyndon Johnson: The Passage of Power.* New York: Alfred A. Knopf, 2012.

Dallek, Robert. *Flawed Giant: Lyndon Johnson and His Times, 1961–1973.* New York: Oxford University Press, 1998.

Evans, Rowland, and Robert Novak. *Lyndon B. Johnson: The Exercise of Power.* New York: New American Library, 1966.

Fulbright, William. *The Arrogance of Power.* New York: Random House, 1966.

Johnson, Robert David. *All the Way with LBJ: The 1964 Presidential Election.* New York: Cambridge University Press, 2009.

Schlesinger, Arthur M., Jr. *The Imperial Presidency.* New York: Houghton Mifflin, 1973.

Shesol, Jeff. *Mutual Contempt: Lyndon Johnson, Robert Kennedy, and the Feud That Defined a Decade.* New York: W. W. Norton, 1998.

37. Richard M. Nixon

Born: January 9, 1913

Died: April 22, 1994

Time in Office: 37th President of the United States, January 20, 1969, to August 9, 1974

Election Results: 1960 Election: 49.5% of popular vote, 219 (40.8%) Electoral College votes; 1968 Election: 43.4% of popular vote, 301 (55.9%) Electoral College votes; 1972 Election: 60.7% of popular vote, 520 (96.7%) Electoral College votes

Spouse: Thelma Catherine "Pat" Ryan (m. 1940)

Children: Patricia and Julie

Few figures in American life have aroused such strong negative feelings as Richard M. Nixon. Despite his enormous political successes, including one of the largest electoral landslides in the history of presidential elections in 1972, Nixon remained throughout his career the target of public ridicule and animus. Many have sought to account for this curious capacity to mobilize winning popular majorities while simultaneously producing such negative responses. Some point to his psychology, others to his character, and others to lapses in public morality. His supporters maintain that Nixon was opposed, even hated, by liberal elites because he defeated their agenda and represented the voice of the forgotten middle America rather than vocal liberal constituencies such as racial minorities and left-wing activists. But whatever the source for this unique combination of political success and strong political backlash, Nixon became iconic as the corrupt, power-hungry, and ultimately tragically flawed American political leader. As the only president to have ever resigned the office as a result of Watergate, arguably the worst political scandal in modern American history, Nixon was the recipient of a tremendous storm of criticism of sometimes vitriolic intensity. However, Nixon's acute sense of the animosity directed against him originated well before the Watergate scandal began to be reported in the pages of the *Washington Post* by Bob Woodward and Carl Bernstein. Indeed, Nixon's belief that he was not merely facing political opposition, but rather enemies, provoked reactions by Nixon and his aides that only served to further deepen the hostility levied at him and his presidency. Due to this downward cycle, Nixon may have been the most hated president since the Civil War.

Biographers have long noted that Nixon developed this sense of being an outsider early in his life, and that this fueled his drive to achieve, animated his political campaigns, and deeply shaped his presidency. Indeed, Nixon rose to power rapidly, and did so through a natural succession from the House of Representatives (1947–1951), to the Senate (1951–1953), to the vice presidency (1953—1961), and then—after two trying electoral losses, one for the presidency in 1960 and one for California governor in 1962—the penultimate rise to the presidency in 1968, repeated in the landslide election of 1972. But there were always critiques levied at him and his public persona. Nixon was sensitive to these attacks, which mounted over the years of his presidency, and seemed to simply confirm and deepen his sense of being on the outside, of being the victim of unfair criticism, and of facing enemies arrayed against him. During the Senate Select Committee on Watergate's blockbuster televised hearings, a major revelation was that Nixon had his closest aides produce a list of such enemies, one that ultimately grew to well over 200 names of individuals and organizations. This more or less formal list was but a manifestation of Nixon's persistent sense that the protesters, the intelligentsia, the establishment, and the news media, as well as his formal political adversaries—the Democrats, the Congress, and the courts—were "out to get him."

WINNING THE PRESIDENCY IN 1968

Because of his infamous red-baiting campaigns as a successful candidate for the House of Representatives (1946); the U.S. Senate, from California (1950); and as Dwight Eisenhower's vice president, Nixon faced a suspicious, and often an outright antagonistic news media, along with a host of other strong critics when he launched his first bid for the presidency in 1960. Always having opposed what he regarded as the privileged liberal establishment, Nixon ran against the epitome of the liberal elite, John F. Kennedy, and came up short by less than 1% of the popular vote. This loss hammered home for Nixon the uphill battle he was waging against the establishment, and highlighted a new and important theme for him in identifying his enemies—the hostility of the press. Nixon was particularly bitter over the televised national presidential debates between himself and Kennedy—the first in American history. Those who watched the debates, the common wisdom says, favored Kennedy while those who listened on the radio favored Nixon. There is no evidence to support this claim, but Kennedy had an intuitive sense for how to make the most of his television persona, while Nixon had yet to master the medium.

In 1962, Nixon ran for governor of California and lost. At his most vulnerable following his second electoral loss in two years, Nixon openly revealed his strong belief that the news media bore a special hostility toward him. He concluded his loss in the 1962 gubernatorial election with a swipe at the media that would taint his public image for years: "I leave you gentlemen now and you will write it. You will interpret it. That's your right. But as I leave you I want you to know—just think of how much you're going to be missing. You won't have Nixon to kick around anymore, because, gentlemen, this is my last press conference."

From 1962 to 1968, Nixon sought to be both outside and inside of national politics. After Kennedy's assassination in 1963 and the 1964 landslide loss of Republican nominee Barry Goldwater to Lyndon Johnson, Nixon became the Republican Party's national leader by fund-raising and campaigning for Republicans in the 1966 midterm elections. By mid-1966, Nixon was the clear front-runner for the 1968 Republican nomination. Nixon represented a middle-road mainstream, according to historian David Greenberg, "the businessmen and housewives, realtors and shopkeepers, bankers and doctors." Providing a new kind of conservative agenda that targeted big government and the liberal establishment elites that governed, he sought to galvanize the broad middle class to his side.

The 1960s were also a time of great cultural change, and Nixon represented himself as the vanguard of resistance to the antiwar, civil rights, and counterculture movements of the period. Nixon criticized media coverage of antiwar protests that seemed overly sympathetic, and criticized radical students and professors who were most vocal in opposing the Vietnam War, such as members of Students for a Democratic Society (SDS) and the Berkeley Free Speech Movement (FSM). He claimed to represent the "silent center": the "millions of people in the middle of the American political spectrum who do not demonstrate, who do not picket or protest loudly," but who "work hard, carry a mortgage, pay their taxes and who do their best to send their children to college." These nonelite outsiders, who Nixon had associated himself with throughout his career, included several key constituencies of the Democratic Party's national electoral majority: blue-collar workers, Catholics, and white southerners. This was a new way of channeling a politics of resentment, and it served to provoke sharper lines in the nation's politics and produced growing hostility to Nixon's candidacy, and ultimately his presidency, from liberal professors, student antiwar activists, civil rights and black power advocates, and champions of the counterculture movement that had become a real force by the 1968 election.

But it also produced a victory for Nixon in the 1968 election, which was one of the closest in history. Although he won by a margin of less than 1% of the popular vote, he had significant electoral success in every region of the country. Despite a strong showing in the Deep South for segregationist Alabama governor George Wallace, a third party candidate, Nixon still won that region over Vice President Hubert Humphrey, the Democratic Party's nominee. He also won the Midwest and Mountain West, losing only in the Northeast. Although his Electoral College vote margin was substantial—301 to Humphrey's 191—Nixon won the popular vote by less than 1%, with 43.4% of the vote versus 42.7% for Humphrey.

In his victory speech and inaugural address, Nixon signaled a message of unity to the nation, promising to "bring us together." But Nixon entered the presidency with the nation deeply divided, and with deep anger already aimed at him from the antiwar advocates, civil rights leaders, and the liberal leaders that he had attacked on his way to victory. In addition, the new president would face not only a nation in turmoil over Vietnam and civil rights, but he encountered an executive branch run by liberal Democrats (with many career holdovers from the Kennedy and Johnson years throughout the bureaucracy), a Congress firmly in the hands of the Democratic Party, and a news media that Nixon felt was compounding the nation's divisiveness and undermining his authority.

THE CIVIL RIGHTS AND ANTIWAR MOVEMENTS

During the 1968 campaign, the Democratic Party was weakened by two issues that were highly divisive for its long-standing New Deal coalition (which included labor unions; blue-collar workers; racial, ethnic, and religious minorities; farmers; white southerners; people on relief; Democratic state party organizations; city machines; and intellectuals), civil rights and Vietnam. Major protest movements erupted in response to developments in both of these volatile political arenas, and Democrats—who had controlled the White House from 1961 until Nixon's January 1969 inauguration—struggled mightily on both of these fronts.

In 1964, Lyndon B. Johnson signed the landmark Civil Rights Act, outlawing racial segregation, and in 1965 he followed suit by signing the historic Voting Rights Act. The historic legislation, combined with massive nonviolent civil disobedience throughout the South, transformed the nation's race relations and politics. In the late 1960s, the civil rights movement increasingly focused their attention on the North, and on de facto (in practice), rather than de jure (in law), segregation. As controversy over this ensued, protests became more heated, and the civil rights movement splintered as more militant groups emerged to challenge racial discrimi-nation in the North with more aggressive, provocative tactics and rhetoric. Racial violence plagued cities throughout the nation—especially in nonsouthern cities—every summer from 1964 through 1967. Nixon ran for office in 1968 with Wallace on his right, pushing for a return to racial segregation, and Humphrey on his left, representing the Democratic Party's aggressive legislative embrace of civil rights. He therefore took a middle path, embracing calls for "law and order" before more progress on racial equality, offering support for civil rights but opposing aggressive efforts to promote racial integration.

In pursuing the presidency, Nixon became well known for his so-called "southern strategy": seeking the support of white southern voters by slowing down, or even outright opposition, to the civil rights agenda. During his 1968 campaign, Nixon pursued support from southern leaders, obtaining a key endorsement from Republican South Carolina senator Strom Thurmond, an ardent segregationist. In return for the support from Thurmond, Nixon promised a slowdown on federal civil rights enforcement. He delivered on this promise from the start of his presidency, as both the Department of Health, Education, and Welfare (HEW) and the Department of Justice (DOJ) ordered slowdowns in court-ordered desegregation early in his administration. In early 1970 Nixon fired Leon Panetta, the director for HEW's Office of Civil Rights, because Panetta was too aggressive in pursuing school desegregation. In his first year in office, moreover, Nixon nominated two southern conservatives to the Supreme Court, Clement F. Haynsworth and G. Harrold Carswell. Nixon's efforts were opposed by the Senate, which rejected his Supreme Court nominees because of their positions opposing desegregation. The Supreme Court, meanwhile, issued several rulings requiring the president to move ahead with the enforcement of civil rights.

Civil rights leaders were deeply suspicious of Nixon when he assumed office in January 1969. One of Nixon's strategies in dealing with civil rights was to quietly ignore pressures to pursue more aggressive desegregation. A leaked memorandum from his Urban Affairs Council secretary, Daniel P. Moynihan, who had also served Kennedy and Johnson, encouraged the president to pull back from the issue, to tamp down rising violence and disruption over race: "The time may have come when the issue of race could benefit from a period of 'benign neglect,'" Moynihan contended. "We may need a period in which Negro progress continues and racial rhetoric fades." "I agree," Nixon jotted. The leaked memo only served to escalate distrust between the civil rights community and the new president.

Therefore, despite the fact that Nixon had developed a positive relationship with Martin Luther King Jr. while vice president by virtue of his expressions of support for the 1957 Civil Rights Bill, Nixon soon found himself deeply opposed by King and other black leaders. National civil rights leaders such as Roy Wilkins and Clarence Mitchell from the National Association for the Advancement of Colored People (NAACP) and Ralph Abernathy from the Southern Christian Leadership Conference (SCLC) openly opposed Nixon's "go-slow" policy on school desegregation. After meeting with the new president, Abernathy denounced the meeting as "fruitless" and "disappointing." This upset Nixon and his aides: "Abernathy went out and stabbed us on TV," Haldeman wrote. "Proved again there's no use dealing honestly with these people. They obviously want confrontation, not solutions." "The problem as I see it," Nixon told Moynihan, "is that [blacks] don't think that I care. We must demonstrate to them we do care by our actions and not just by our words."

In Nixon's second term, he proposed a constitutional amendment banning the use of bussing to achieve racial integration. Nixon had vocally opposed bussing from the beginning of his 1968 presidential campaign, and his proposed amendment further solidified his reputation as an enemy of the civil rights movement in the opinion of black leaders. The NAACP national chairman, Bishop Stephen G. Spottswood, declared that the NAACP considered itself "in a state of war against President Nixon." Beyond the mainstream civil rights organizations, Nixon felt that young black power advocates such as Eldridge Cleaver and the Black Panthers, a provocative black power group based on the West Coast, were destructive and likely to fan the flames of violence. He continued Johnson's surveillance and harassment of the Black Panthers.

In the end, Nixon's overarching political strategy recognized African Americans as Democratic Party voters and therefore saw little of political value in pursuing bold civil rights policies. At the same time, he recognized that outright defiance of civil rights gains, such as espoused by politicians like Wallace, would lose him the presidency. Nixon therefore did what the courts and the Congress required on civil rights, while vocally opposing strong enforcement of desegregation through the unpopular bussing remedies that courts were mandating. This helped him both divide Democratic white southern voters from African American voters and to appeal to the "silent majority" who were increasingly upset about racial violence, disruptive protests, and rapid social change in the arena of race. These were largely northern white ethnic voters—Irish, Italian, Slavic, Polish—who had traditionally voted Democratic, but Nixon hoped they would move to the Republican Party in increasingly larger numbers because of their opposition to the destabilizing social and cultural changes of the 1960s, including the Democratic Party's aggressive civil rights agenda.

In addition, opposition to the Vietnam antiwar movement was central to Nixon's political strategy of building a "silent majority." The Vietnam War was a critical component in Nixon's 1968 victory: Johnson had become so unpopular because of the war that he declined to run for reelection. But Humphrey, who had managed to secure the Democratic Party's 1968 nomination despite serving as Johnson's vice president, was saddled with defending Johnson's increasingly unpopular Vietnam policies. Nixon, meanwhile, campaigned on a vague promise to end the war. Humphrey's nominating convention in Chicago was marred by police violence against antiwar demonstrators, and the television footage was used by Nixon in television commercials that contrasted the rising civil disorder under the Democrats with promises that he would restore "law and order" to the country.

Even before Nixon won the 1968 election, he sought to sabotage peace talks that Johnson was engaged in, fearing that a successful peace arrangement prior to the election would help Humphrey win the election. Johnson learned that Nixon had dispatched Anna Chennault to let South Vietnam president Nguyen Van Thieu know that he could get a "better" deal if he waited until Nixon became president. "This is treason," said LBJ. "They're contacting a foreign power in the middle of a war." Johnson decided not to make this public, as he obtained the information through a National Security Agency (NSA) wiretap of Nixon that he did not want to make public.

Nixon's inauguration was marred by protests and violence, centered on opposition to the Vietnam War. The "counter-inaugural" was organized by the umbrella antiwar organization—The National Mobilization Committee to End the War in Vietnam (also known as "the Mobe")—which planned protests for the entire inaugural weekend. Thousands of protesters filled Washington, and Nixon's motorcade was assaulted with sticks, stones, bottles, cans, forks and spoons, tinfoil balls, and smoke bombs.

Although the antiwar movement began on university campuses, and SDS was at the forefront of the movement, by the time Nixon assumed the presidency protests against the Vietnam War embraced students, parents, celebrities, civil rights activists, and more. The antiwar protests, which began during the Johnson years, reached their peak during Nixon's presidency.

Shortly after assuming the presidency, Nixon began the secret bombing of Cambodia, a country adjacent to Vietnam that had been infiltrated by North Vietnamese forces. At the same time, there were widespread demonstrations against the war. On October 15, 1969, "Moratorium Day," there were 20,000 protesters in Washington, and hundreds of thousands more demonstrated in cities across the nation. Coretta Scott King, Martin Luther King Jr.'s widow, spoke in Washington; Senators Eugene McCarthy and Charles Goodell and movie stars Shirley MacLaine and Woody Allen spoke in New York City; and the television networks ran major prime-time specials featuring moratorium leaders Sam Brown and David Hawk. CBS news anchor Walter Cronkite said that the protests were "[h]istoric in its scope. Never before had so many demonstrated their hope for peace." Nixon was increasingly upset by these media reactions. As antiwar protests continued, he sought to reduce the impact of the antiwar movement by tracking it, withdrawing U.S. troops from Vietnam, instituting a draft lottery, and eventually ending draft calls.

On November 3, 1969, Nixon responded to the escalating protests against the Vietnam War. He sought to persuade the country that his administration had been deeply involved in seeking to end the war, but that they would only do so on terms favorable to the United States. Most importantly, he spoke to Americans who were disturbed by the protests and accompanying violence: "And so tonight—to you, the great silent majority of Americans—I ask for your support." The televised audience was large—70 million—and the message was a powerful one. Nixon identified the protesters as noisy and disruptive, and the great majority of Americans as silent, hard-working, and patriotic. Polls showed that the speech was enormously effective; the president's approval ratings climbed from 52% before the moratorium to 68% following his speech. Congress passed resolutions by large majorities supporting the president's Vietnam policy.

But when the secret bombing of Cambodia became public knowledge in the spring of 1970, new protests erupted across the country. At Kent State University, one such antiwar protest turned tragic as four protesters were killed by members of the Ohio National Guard that had been called in to control the demonstration. Nixon was terribly upset: "Is this because of me, of Cambodia? . . . How do we turn this stuff off?" The photographs of the Kent State student protest and resulting violence were striking, and they appeared on the front pages of nearly every newspaper in the United States. A student strike at more than 500 universities, in response to the Kent State shootings, was joined by protests all over the nation, and Senators Frank Church (D-ID) and John Sherman Cooper (R-KY) introduced legislation to end the funding of ground troops in Cambodia. By April 1971, 500,000 people participated in another antiwar protest in Washington, thousands were arrested, and Daniel Ellsberg passed the Defense Department's classified history of U.S. involvement in Vietnam, known as the Pentagon Papers, to the *New York Times*. There were also counterdemonstrations. The most famous of these took place in New York City in May 1970, where hard-hat construction workers violently attacked an antiwar demonstration in the Wall Street area, injuring many of the demonstrators. Nixon was encouraged by this, but at the same time was worried about the escalating protests.

In many ways the Vietnam protests, and the targeting of Nixon by the leaders of the antiwar movement, became the context from which the Watergate crisis emerged. H. R. Haldeman, Nixon's powerful chief of staff and closest adviser, said: "Without the Vietnam War, there would have been no Watergate." Haldeman understood that the war, and particularly the antiwar movement, provoked Nixon perhaps more than any other crisis he confronted. As the Ellsberg case involving the Pentagon Papers demonstrates, Nixon and his top advisers were willing to engage in illegal activity to suppress antiwar activity, including surveillance of leaders of the movement and breaking into offices. They even considered firebombing organizations like the Brookings Institution that were opposed to the president. Carl Bernstein, who broke the Watergate story with his *Washington Post* colleague Bob Woodward, wrote that "Vietnam and Watergate are inextricably linked in the Nixon presidency."

THE PRESS IS THE ENEMY

On one of Nixon's infamous tapes, from December 14, 1972, the president is heard saying: "Never forget, the press is the enemy. The establishment is the enemy. The professors are the enemy. Professors are the enemy. Write that on a blackboard 100 times and never forget it." In the 1960 and 1968 presidential elections, nearly 80% of newspapers endorsing a candidate supported Nixon over his opponents. Still, Nixon harbored a strong resentment of the news media. He felt that many of the nation's leading correspondents were openly hostile to him and his administration. He often turned this into an attack on the "liberal" news media as part of his broad antiestablishment campaigns. But was the press truly his enemy?

At the start of his presidency, with his first news conference of January 27, 1969, Nixon was received with strong approval from Helen Thomas of the United Press International (UPI) wire service, and from Mary McGrory, a *Washington Star* columnist who was known as a strong critic of Nixon. McGrory told Nixon's director of communications, Herbert Klein, that she had been impressed with the new president's performance, and that perhaps Nixon was "different now that he's president." The double-edged compliment reflected the suspicious approach that many in the Washington press corps took toward Nixon.

Nixon, for his part, was also suspicious of the press. This antagonism went back to criticism by liberal journalists of his campaign for the House in 1946, when his critics in the press saw his campaign as a "new beginning in the commercialization and packaging of political candidates" and Nixon himself as "manipulative, exploitive, opportunistic, even deceptive and dishonest." This divide in perceptions continued with his successful run for the Senate in 1950, when he received heavy criticism in some media for his reliance on negative campaigning. But it was the way the news media broke the story about his campaign finances in the 1952 presidential campaign that crystallized Nixon's belief that the press was his enemy. The muckraking liberal journalists Drew Pearson and Jack Anderson ran a column about Nixon's "secret fund," financed from corporate interests. This story, based in part on information they received from a friend of Nixon's named William Rogers, nearly led Eisenhower to replace Nixon on the Republican ticket. Nixon managed to keep his place as the GOP vice presidential nominee on the strength of his memorable and nationally televised "Checkers" speech, in which he portrayed himself and his family as simple and humble Americans. Nixon never forgot Anderson's leading role in the episode, however, and it began a two-decade long conflict between Nixon and Anderson. That conflict became so intense that Nixon, while president, reportedly ordered CIA surveillance of Anderson and his family. White House operatives Gordon Liddy and Howard Hunt, who would later become infamous through their involvement in the Watergate affair, even considered assassinating the journalist. The plot was called off when Charles Colson, who was one of Nixon's most important political advisers, told Liddy and Hunt to back off Anderson and instead focus on breaking into the Democratic National Committee's headquarters in the Watergate Hotel.

Perhaps no journalist antagonized Nixon more, however, than the cartoonist Herbert Block of *The Washington Post*. Known under the pen name of Herblock, he drew negative images of Nixon that became indelibly linked to the president. For example, during the 1966 midterm election campaign, as Nixon crisscrossed the nation to campaign for Republican members of the House and Senate, Herblock drew a memorable image of Nixon emerging out of a manhole in a city street, connecting with what Democratic Party's national chairman Stephen Mitchell had called Nixon's "gutter campaign."

In his successful 1968 presidential campaign, Nixon became more guarded and careful with his statements and appearances, avoiding conflicts with the press. Reporters began to resent his distance, and some took to characterizing him as an artificial individual seeking to win political office with a campaign lacking in substance, focused only on innuendo and imagery. Nixon responded by developing a deep suspicion of the news media in general, and of liberal journalists, even though he enjoyed more positive press coverage throughout the 1968 campaign due to the campaign's attempts to limit access to the candidate and an extended honeymoon lasting through most of his first year in the presidency. William Safire, who was one of his chief speechwriters, wrote that Nixon often told him that "the press is the enemy . . . to be hated and beaten." Another of his speechwriters, Ray Price, wrote that he could "appreciate [the news media's] resentment," since the White House communications aides "did often lie, mislead, deceive, try to use the press, and to con them."

It is worth noting that the nature of the presidency's relationship with the news media had shifted during the 1960s to an increasingly adversarial, perhaps even cynical regard for official power, particularly from the presidency. After their experience with Johnson's often willful misleading of the news media over Vietnam, which contributed mightily to Johnson's downward spiral in public approval, news journalists were increasingly poised for mistrust of the presidency. That the next president was Nixon, who had a history of conflict with news journalists, just escalated the tensions in the presidency-press relationship. Tom Wicker, who covered Nixon during his presidency, wrote a sympathetic political biography of Nixon in which he observed: "It was . . . Nixon's primary misfortune not to suffer some wholesale, vaguely 'liberal' press instinct to do him in, but to come to office at a time when the president and the White House no longer were held in the respect that once had been palpable among Washington journalists."

Six years after his California gubernatorial election loss and his famous "last press conference," Nixon had become president. At some level, the negative end to his former political career helped produce a honeymoon in Nixon's first year: "California served a purpose," he said. "The press had a guilt complex about their inaccuracy. Since then they've been generally accurate, and far more respectful." Several formerly critical liberal opinion makers reversed their previously negative views about Nixon. Walter Lippmann, a leading public intellectual, found Nixon to be a more "mature and mellower man, who is no longer clawing his way to the top." Norman Mailer, the well-known novelist who had hated Nixon for years, professed that Nixon had now earned his respect. And Robert Semple Jr., the *New York Times* journalist, wrote a glowing feature on Nixon for the newspaper's magazine, claiming that the "McCarthy-era" Nixon had "vanished" and that "in his place stands a walking monument to reason, civility, frankness."

But by 1971 national tensions over Vietnam and other political issues had taken their toll. Nixon became increasingly secretive, holding few press conferences, forgoing interviews, and generally keeping the media at arm's length. Several journalists began to wonder if they had gone too easy on the new president. John Osborne began writing a regular column for *The New Republic* that he entitled "The Nixon Watch." He wrote that journalists as a group "share a sense that Richard Nixon ought to be faulted for a fundamental lack of political honor, for what he is doing to the political process with his tactics of concealment and pseudo-disclosure."

The biggest source of conflict between Nixon and the news profession prior to Watergate were the June 1971 lawsuits to stop the *New York Times* and the *Washington Post* from publishing the Pentagon Papers. Ellsberg, a former National Security Council agent with links to the CIA, had given a 7,000-page classified document commissioned by Robert McNamara, who served as secretary of defense in both the Kennedy and Johnson administrations, to the *New York Times*. The report was based on nonclassified documents, and it provided a self-critical history of America's involvement in Vietnam. Many Nixon staffers thought that the publication of the report should not concern the Nixon administration, as it cast a negative light on Kennedy and Johnson. Charles Colson even asked Howard Hunt to find information in the report that they could use against leading Democrats.

However, Nixon and his national security advisor, Henry Kissinger, believed that the publication would set a precedent that could harm their own efforts to stop leaks and maintain secrecy. Moreover, Nixon saw Ellsberg as a liberal antiwar intellectual who had leaked national security secrets. He instructed Attorney General John Mitchell to sue the *New York Times* to stop it from being published. Although a federal district court provided the White House with an injunction to prevent the publication of the report by the *New York Times*, the Supreme Court ultimately rejected the administration's argument, ruling that the First Amendment protected the right to publish the materials without any prior restraint.

The Pentagon Papers case had a major impact on Nixon's relationship with the press. It escalated the news media's sense that the Nixon administration was threatening them. The National Press Club's Board of Governors commissioned an investigation of the administration's relationship with the news media, and the committee in charge, including Dan Rather from CBS, severely criticized the Nixon administration.

The publication of the Pentagon Papers also led to the creation of the White House "Plumbers," and therefore to the Watergate scandal itself. Nixon wanted the FBI to be far more aggressive in investigating Ellsberg, and to pursue other leakers of government information as well. Realizing that Director J. Edgar Hoover was unwilling to use the FBI to "plug leaks" from the White House, Nixon wanted it done "in-house." "If we can't get anyone in this damn government to do something about the problem . . . then, by God, we'll do it ourselves," said Nixon. The result was the establishment of the Plumbers, a group of operatives charged with secretly tracking down potential leaks and using any means—including illegal means—to stop them. Working under John Ehrlichman, Egil Krogh and David Young were charged with running the overall operations of the Plumbers, which included E. Howard Hunt from the CIA and G. Gordon Liddy from the FBI. Ellsberg became their primary target early on. Colson wanted to link Ellsberg to their political opposition—"the enemy camp." Since the FBI had already interviewed Ellsberg's psychiatrist, Dr. Lewis Fielding, the Plumbers decided to break into Fielding's office to obtain his notes on Ellsberg. They hoped that the files on Ellsberg might include material that could be used to publicly discredit him as mentally unstable. Although the operation yielded nothing, it was in many ways the beginning of Watergate. Indeed, it was internally labeled as "Hunt/Liddy Special Project #1," and it is hard not to see the connection between Hunt and Liddy's involvement later in the burglary of the Watergate complex's Democratic Party's national headquarters that June.

WATERGATE: A CANCER GROWING ON THE PRESIDENCY

The news media's relationship with the Nixon administration turned significantly worse as the Watergate scandal unraveled, but in the initial stages of the reporting after the June 1972 burglary of the DNC headquarters most Washington press corps journalists were unwilling to see it as a major concern. The *Washington Post*'s Stephen Isaacs said that he and his peers were "over compensating" so that their readers would not see them as being "in the tank for [George] McGovern," the Democratic Party's presidential nominee for the 1972 election. In addition, the administration was intent on directly intimidating news organizations to prevent them from further investigating their illegal activities. These efforts included threats to discontinue television licenses through the Federal Communications Commission; the shutting down of reporters' access to top White House officials; and investigations of journalist Daniel Schorr, *Newsday*, and others. The CBS Network was a particular target for the Nixon administration, as Rather and Schorr pursued the Watergate story seriously, and Walter Cronkite agreed to air two in-depth investigations of Watergate on the nightly news. After the first one aired, however, Nixon was so upset that he had Colson call the chairman of CBS, William Paley, and express their frustration in an obscenity-laden rant, saying that the show illustrated the network's clear pro-McGovern bias. Paley responded by asking the producer of the in-depth Watergate investigations to significantly shorten the planned second broadcast.

After the burglary of the Watergate's Democratic Party headquarters, the *Washington Post* referred the story to two new reporters on their police desk, Woodward and Bernstein. Their dogged pursuit of the story, through laborious pursuit of information by phone calls and knocking on potential informants' doors, eventually persuaded the nation's leading journalists to pursue the story more seriously. By 1973, as the connections between the burglary at the DNC headquarters and top Nixon officials began to become increasingly apparent, Senator Sam Ervin (R-NC) led his subcommittee to hold nationally televised hearings on Watergate. Nixon was increasingly sure that the news media "were out to get him" during this period, in part because journalists that had previously held back on criticizing the Nixon administration began covering the Nixon White House much more aggressively.

In June 1973, Nixon's White House counsel, John Dean, testified before Ervin's Senate Committee on Watergate. Dean's testimony was devastating to the president, implicating him directly in the cover-up of the burglary. Nixon vehemently denied his involvement, famously insisting that "I am not a crook."

But it was the release of the Watergate tapes transcripts on April 30, 1974, that really turned the news media against Nixon. For example, Helen Thomas, who had been relatively restrained in her criticism of the Nixon White House, stated that she had believed that Nixon was a liar ever since his 1946 campaign for the House of Representatives. Negative press on the Nixon administration became pervasive: between April 1973 and August 1974 *Newsweek* had 35 covers featuring Watergate and *Time* ran more than 30. Meanwhile, Nixon was involved in illegal behind-the-scenes activities that would ultimately become public, and which would bring down his entire presidency: suborning perjury; authorizing payments of hush money; offering clemency to defendants; and asking the Internal Revenue Service (IRS) to pursue audits against his "enemies." The enmity between the president and the news media escalated all the way to August 1974, when Nixon announced his unprecedented resignation from the presidency.

WATERGATE AND THE ENEMIES LIST

Watergate resulted ultimately from Nixon's deep fears of being surrounded by enemies. These fears led Nixon and his aides to counter the hatred he perceived as directed against his presidency, and against himself personally. There was indeed a great deal of animosity directed at Nixon, from the antiwar movement, the civil rights leadership, and the news media itself. But Nixon exacerbated this hostility through the actions he took in response to his belief that it ran deeper than simple political opposition, that he was opposed by enemies.

Much of the antiwar and civil rights protesting of the 1960s was about a resistance not just to policies, but to an overall political system. When Nixon was elected, it seemed to many new-left radicals that he embodied the worst of that system. For example, the politically radical investigative journalist I. F. Stone called Nixon a "moral monster," with no remorse over the countless deaths in Vietnam. Robert Kennedy, who was the leading antiwar candidate for the Democratic presidential nomination in 1968 until his assassination, said that Nixon "represents the dark side of the American spirit." Radical antiwar groups such as Students for a Democratic Society (SDS) taunted Nixon at rallies, cheering for the North Vietnamese. There were ugly threats against Nixon as well, including assassination attempts. Given the killings of King and Kennedy in 1968 and the attempted assassination of George Wallace in 1972, the Secret Service had dramatically increased its protective presence around Nixon. The consensus in the Secret Service, however, was that Nixon was reckless about his own safety. At a moratorium protest in the fall of 1969, Black Panther leader David Hilliard threatened, "We will kill Richard Nixon," and was subsequently arrested. Hilliard insisted he was not serious, but that he was "talking the language of Nixon and Mitchell," whom he called "Hitler's helpers." But Nixon seemed oblivious to the danger. For example, after the shootings at Kent State, antiwar protesters surrounded the White House. The Secret Service told Nixon it was too dangerous for him to leave. However, in the middle of the night the president went to the Lincoln Memorial to talk to students, and the Secret Service had to quickly scramble to catch up.

Threatening behavior at the White House was common during the Nixon presidency. More than 100 people each year were detained by Secret Service agents and White House guards. The Secret Service was on guard for plots by militant black activist groups, including the Black Panthers. One allegation that a disgraced former New Orleans police officer, Edwin Guadet, had threatened to kill Nixon when he visited the city in the summer of 1973 led to a nationwide manhunt. Perhaps the most serious threat came from Arthur Bremer, who planned to assassinate either Nixon or Wallace. After several failed plots to kill Nixon, Bremer shot Wallace at a campaign rally in Laurel, Maryland, in May 1972. Although Wallace survived, he was paralyzed from the waist down, and Bremer spent 35 years in prison for his crime. In 1974 Samuel Byck tried to hijack a commercial airliner and crash it into the White House to kill Nixon. Byck killed a guard at Baltimore Washington International Airport, then shot the pilot and copilot before killing himself.

This environment contributed to Nixon's enthusiasm for plans to target his political enemies.

In August 1971, Dean wrote a memo that argued for the creation and maintenance of a list of White House "enemies." According to Dean, the purpose of the memo was to "maximize the fact of our incumbency in dealing with persons known to be more active in their opposition to our Administration." This meant the use of government agencies, like the IRS, to "screw our political enemies." Along with Colson, Dean sought to develop the "enemies list" and then provide it to a "project coordinator" who could determine how the White House "can best screw them." Within a month, Colson had an eclectic list of 20 names, including leading politicians and their aides, leaders of major liberal advocacy groups, nationally known entertainers, and professional journalists. The list soon grew to more than 200 names, as others in the administration added to it. Included on the expanded list were obvious political opponents like Senators Ted Kennedy, Edmund Muskie, and Walter Mondale, but also the presidents of major universities and foundations, leading newspaper columnists and television newsmen; even football star Joe Namath made the list.

Dean proposed that the enemies list be used as "targets" for harassment, including IRS audits. Nixon supported this, and wanted the IRS to focus on Democratic National Committee chair Larry O'Brien. Although the new IRS commissioner, Johnnie M. Walters, moved cautiously ahead with an audit of O'Brien's taxes, he also sought to resist the broader push to use the IRS to target the White House's political enemies. In the end, Secretary of Treasury George P. Shultz refused to cooperate with the "political enemies" plan, and defended Walters's refusal to participate in it as well. Although few IRS audits were performed to harass Nixon's enemies, the impetus behind this push speaks volumes about the way that Nixon perceived his political opposition—as enemies to be opposed using whatever means that he had at his disposal.

CONCLUSION

From the heights of a historic landslide presidential election victory in the fall of 1972, Nixon rapidly fell to the lowest imaginable political depths with the Watergate scandal and his subsequent resignation in the summer of 1974. Although Watergate occurred more than 40 years ago, it continues as the primary icon of political ambition pursued beyond the limits of the law and the Constitution. Nixon's Icarus-like fall is often attributed in part to Nixon's abiding sense that he was opposed by enemies who were untrustworthy and who would do whatever they could to bring him down. There is no doubt that in Nixon's long political career that he engendered political enmity as he proceeded to the heights of power. Moreover, as president, Nixon faced indeed strong hostility, from antiwar and civil rights protesters, and from the national news media as well. But the intensity of the opposition increased as Nixon sought to retaliate against his enemies. In light of the deep partisan polarization of the late 20th and early 21st centuries in American politics, Nixon's debilitating and deepening obsession with his political enemies should be understood as having laid the groundwork for a politics of resentment that would both carry him and his party to victory, but which would also leave the nation perpetually in a state of political warfare. Always perceiving enemies surrounding him, Nixon resorted to unscrupulous political strategies and tactics that ultimately produced his political—and personal—downfall.

Scott J. Spitzer

Further Reading

Ayton, Mel. *Hunting the President: Threats, Plots, and Assassination Attempts from FDR to Obama.* Washington, D.C.: Regnery History, 2014.

Barber, James. *The Presidential Character: Predicting Performance in the White House,* 4th ed. New York: Pearson Longman, 2009.

Brodie, Fawn. *Richard Nixon: The Shaping of His Character.* New York: W. W. Norton, 1981.

Carmines, Edward G., and James A. Stimson. *Issue Evolution: Race and the Transformation of American Politics.* Princeton, NJ: Princeton University Press, 1989.

Feldstein, Mark. *Poisoning the Press: Richard Nixon, Jack Anderson, and the Rise of Washington's Scandal Culture.* New York: Farrar, Straus and Giroux, 2010.

Flamm, Michael. *Law and Order: Street Crime, Civil Unrest, and the Crisis of Liberalism in the 1960s.* New York: Columbia University Press, 2005.

Graham, Hugh Davis. "Richard Nixon and Civil Rights: Explaining an Enigma." *Presidential Studies Quarterly,* Vol. 26 (1996): 93–106.

Greenberg, David. *Nixon's Shadow: The History of an Image.* New York: W. W. Norton, 2003.

Harris, Richard. "The Presidency and the Press." *The New Yorker,* October 1, 1973.

Kaiser, Robert G. "The Disaster of Richard Nixon." *The New York Review of Books,* April 21, 2016.

Koncewicz, Michael. *They Said No to Nixon: Republicans Who Stood Up to the President's Abuses of Power.* Oakland, CA: University of California Press, 2018.

Kotlowski, Dean. *Nixon's Civil Rights: Politics, Principle, and Policy.* Cambridge, MA: Harvard University Press, 2001.

Kutler, Stanley. *The Wars of Watergate: The Last Crisis of Richard Nixon.* New York: W. W. Norton, 1992.

Maltese, John Anthony. *Spin Control: The White House Office of Communications and the Management of Presidential News.* Chapel Hill, NC: University of North Carolina Press, 1992.

Nelson, Michael. *Resilient America: Electing Nixon in 1968. Channeling Dissent, and Dividing Government*. Lawrence, KS: University Press of Kansas, 2014.

Perlstein, Rick. *Nixonland: The Rise of a President and the Fracturing of America*. New York: Scribner, 2008.

Phillips, Kevin. *The Emerging Republican Majority*. New Rochelle, NY: Arlington House, 1969.

Reeves, Richard. *President Nixon: Alone in the White House*. New York: Simon & Schuster, 2001.

Volkan, Vamik D., Norman Itzkowitz, and Andrew W. Dod. *Richard Nixon: A Psychobiography*. New York: Columbia University Press, 1997.

Weiner, Tim. *One Man against the World: The Tragedy of Richard Nixon*. New York: Henry Holt and Company, 2015.

Wicker, Tom. *One of Us: Richard Nixon and the American Dream*. New York: Random House, 1995.

Woodward, Bob, and Carl Bernstein. *All the President's Men*. New York: Simon & Schuster, 1974.

38. Gerald R. Ford

Born: July 14, 1913

Died: December 26, 2006

Time in Office: 38th President of the United States, August 9, 1974, to January 20, 1977. Became vice president December 6, 1973, following resignation of Spiro Agnew; assumed presidency on August 9, 1974, upon resignation of Richard Nixon

Election Results: 1976 Election: 48% of popular vote, 240 (44.6%) Electoral College votes; lost to Democratic nominee Jimmy Carter

Spouse: Elisabeth "Betty" Bloomer Warren (m. 1948)

Children: Michael, Jack, Steven, and Susan

Gerald Rudolph Ford was born Leslie Lynch King, on July 14, 1913, in Omaha, Nebraska, to Dorothy Gardener and Leslie King. Dorothy met King in college, but it was not until after they were married that King became physically abusive and began to drink heavily. Days after Leslie was born, King went after Dorothy and her newborn with a butcher knife. King was arrested, and although divorce was rare in the early 20th century, Dorothy divorced King and retained full custody of Leslie after an Omaha court found King guilty of extreme cruelty. Soon after, Dorothy met Gerald R. Ford, a painter; they married a year later. Dorothy and Gerald Sr. then referred to Leslie as Gerald R. Ford Jr., and Gerald grew up believing that Gerald Sr. was his father. Ford officially changed his name to Gerald R. Ford Jr. in 1935.

After high school, Ford attended the University of Michigan from 1931 to 1935, where he was a center on the celebrated football team. When he completed his college degree he turned down opportunities to play professional football to attend Yale Law School, where he graduated in the top third of his class. He then started a law firm in Grand Rapids, Michigan, which he temporarily abandoned to serve in the Navy during World War II. After the war he returned to his law firm and married Elizabeth Bloomer Warren, known to her friends as Betty. In that same year, Ford ran for and was elected to the House of Representatives in 1948 from the state of Michigan as a Republican. He served in Congress until he was called upon by Richard Nixon to serve as vice president in late 1973, following the resignation of Spiro Agnew.

Ford's assent to the presidency is one of the most unique in presidential history. He was never elected to the vice presidency, or the presidency. Ford came to the presidency by way of one of the biggest presidential scandals in American history, leading to the country's first and only resignation by a president. After Agnew resigned due to bribery charges, Ford was appointed and confirmed as vice president. Eight months later, Nixon resigned, and Ford assumed the presidency. It is in these shocking, unprecedented, tumultuous circumstances that Ford came to power.

It comes as no surprise that the rancor around Nixon's resignation, and the perceived less legitimate means by which Ford assumed the most powerful position in the world, came to color Ford's short time as America's unelected president. He faced considerable criticism from a galvanized and hostile media, pressure from Nixon loyalists, and indignation from congressional Democrats bitter about his decision to pardon Nixon. Despite his acclaimed speech after being sworn in as president, wherein he tried to heal the country and restore trust in the presidency, Ford could not quite move past Nixon's indiscretions, and he left Washington having never been elected to the office of president in his own right.

GOVERNMENT DISTRUST AND THE ADVERSARIAL PRESS

After the long, drawn out, unpopular Vietnam War, and following the Nixon resignation, public trust in government was at an all-time low. In 1964, according to Pew Research, 77% said they could trust the federal government to do the right thing nearly always or most of the time; by the time Ford assumed office ten years later that number had dropped to around 35%. Low levels of trust in government increased the news media's desire for investigative reporting and public support for a sincere watchdog role for the political press. These trends had substantial consequences for Ford.

Following Nixon's resignation, the members of the Washington press corps were emboldened, due to their primary role in the events surrounding his departure. In brief, the Watergate scandal involved the wiretapping of the Democratic National Committee (DNC) headquarters at the Watergate office complex in Washington D.C. by the Nixon White House. Evidence showed that the White House attempted to cover up their involvement and obstruct the FBI investigation of the break-in. Reporters Bob Woodward and Carl Bernstein of the *Washington Post* relentlessly pursued leads around rumors of White House involvement, following the arrest of five men charged with breaking into the DNC headquarters at Watergate, on June 17, 1972. They helped uncover the connection between the break-in and the Nixon White House with help from their anonymous source, "Deep Throat," revealed in 2005 to be W. Mark Felt, deputy director of the FBI. The role of the media in Watergate has come to define the meaning of watchdog reporting, exemplifying effective adversarial journalism. In fact, in 1974, *Time* reported that applications to journalism schools surged in the midst of the Watergate scandal.

Running high following this investigative reporting victory, the media was increasingly critical of Ford, and did not hold back. As detailed by Yanek Mieczkowski in his book *Gerald Ford and Challenges of the 1970s*: "The post-Vietnam, post-Watergate suspicion was highly visible in the media. After covering the Vietnam War and Watergate, and trapping the president in lies during both events, the press would not let presidential statements go unexamined. Reporters, hunting for fame, fortune, and Pulitzer Prizes, engaged in 'investigative journalism' both in print and on television. (CBS's news magazine, *60 Minutes,* became a top-rated program during the 1970s and spawned imitations such as ABC's *20/20*). Ford became the subject of the more aggressive and cynical journalistic code."

This ire was intensified when, after a month in office, Ford chose to pardon Nixon of any criminal prosecution. Any goodwill that Ford had accumulated after assuming office was lost, once he pardoned Nixon. The most prominent lines of attack that Ford faced were that he was an accidental president, and that he was accident-prone and intellectually unfit for the job.

THE ACCIDENTAL PRESIDENT

The circumstances surrounding Ford's assent to the presidency are one of the most unique in American history. Although Nixon had just won his reelection campaign for president by one of the widest margins in American history—Nixon beat Democrat George McGovern by 18 million votes, and secured all electoral votes but those belonging to Massachusetts and the District of Columbia—he would not finish out his term; Ford would come to assume the office after many months of unprecedented political turmoil.

When Nixon and Agnew were elected to a second term in November 1972, Ford had just won his reelection contest as a representative of the state of Michigan for the 13th time. However, soon after the Nixon/Agnew victory, evidence surfaced that Agnew had accepted more than $100,000 in bribes when he was governor of Maryland, and on October 10, 1973, Agnew resigned. Resignation seemed reasonable, given the political fallout surrounding the allegations. However, in his memoir, *Go Quietly . . . or Else,* Agnew implied that Nixon used his bribery charges to divert attention away from Watergate, and suggested that Nixon would have had him assassinated had he not resigned.

Agnew's resignation initiated the first use of the Twenty-Fifth Amendment, which states that when there is a vacancy in the office of the vice president, the president will nominate a replacement that must be confirmed by a majority vote in both chambers of Congress. However, in 1973 Democrats controlled both chambers, and thus any replacement Nixon announced would need support from Democrats. With few bargaining chips, given the scandal that had just rocked his administration, Nixon invited Democratic leaders from the House and Senate to consult with him on a confirmable replacement. It was under these circumstances that Ford was nominated and confirmed to the vice presidency. A Democratically controlled House and Senate that fully anticipated that he would take over from Nixon, who was also facing indictment, and presumed to be on his way out, confirmed Ford. Their presumption was right; eight months after being confirmed to the vice presidency, Ford was sworn in as president.

Although Ford entered office with 70% public approval, the "honeymoon period"—the name given to the early part of a president's term, when the public, press, and Congress are willing to give him the benefit of the doubt and be supportive of his legislative agenda—did not last. Ford's honeymoon ended abruptly when he made the decision to pardon Nixon a little over a month after being sworn in.

The decision to pardon Nixon came as a surprise to members of Congress, the public, and the media, all of whom reacted negatively. The strongest criticisms attacked Ford's legitimacy; many speculated that Ford had pardoned Nixon as the result of a bargain struck between Nixon and Ford. The theory was that Nixon had said he would resign in exchange for his full pardoning by Ford, thereby giving Ford the presidency. However, no evidence of this claim ever emerged. There was evidence that Nixon loyalists who stayed on during the Ford transition lobbied Ford to pardon their old boss, warning Ford that Nixon's health was deteriorating due to the stress. But Ford denied predetermining he would ever pardon Nixon. His decision to do so came after he was assumed the office, and as an effort to bring his administration out of Watergate's shadow. In his announcement of the pardon, Ford stated: "There are no historic or legal precedents to which I can turn in this matter, none that precisely fit the circumstances of a private citizen who has resigned the presidency of the United States. . . . Many months and perhaps more years will have to pass before Richard Nixon could hope to obtain a fair trial by jury. . . . But it is not the ultimate fate of Richard Nixon that most concerns me . . . but the immediate future of this great country. . . . It can go on and on, or some-one must write 'The End' to it. I have concluded that only I can do that. And if I can, I must."

The response to the Nixon pardon from congressional Democrats was swift, and critical. The September 16, 1974, issue of *Time* magazine quoted California Democrat Don Edward as saying, "That's the end of the honeymoon." *Time* went on to say "that curt comment may prove to be as good a summary as any of the political consequences of President Ford's complete pardon of Richard Nixon." Democratic senators Robert Byrd and George McGovern also spoke out against the pardon, asserting that it "sets a double standard—one standard for the former president of the United States and another standard for everybody else." Other Democrats were more sympathetic to pardoning Nixon, but saw fault with the timing. This same article quoted liberal Democrat Walter Mondale who said, "No one wished the former President to go to jail, but to grant a pardon for unspecified crimes and acts is unprecedented in American history." Mondale's criticism was echoed by scholars like James MacGregor Burns and Arthur M. Schlesinger Jr. By pardoning Nixon before any charges had been made, Ford put forward the notion that there is no crime above the president. In a September 21, 1974, article, *Nation* editor Carey McWilliams wrote, "[Ford] created the impression that he would have pardoned Nixon no matter what criminal charges might have been lodged against him or what evidence might have been presented to support them. In effect, the President said that no crimes that Nixon might have committed would preclude a pardon." And to summarize the week's events, *Time* magazine concluded: "The real question is whether justice—and the country—have been served by giving Nixon a pardon. The American people deserve to know the entire story of Watergate. . . . The Sabbath pardon eased the plight of the man who received it, but gravely complicated the future of the man who granted it, Gerald R. Ford."

Outside the White House, picketers held up a large bed sheet that read, "PROMISE ME A PARDON AND I'LL MAKE YOU PRESIDENT." Inside the White House, Jerry terHorst, Ford's press secretary and childhood friend, resigned, in protest of the pardon. As Ford's press secretary, terHorst had spent the first month of his tenure reiterating that Ford would not pardon Nixon, which in effect Ford had promised at his vice presidency hearings. Eventually, Congress responded by creating a committee to investigate the decision to grant the pardon. In October, a month after the pardon, Ford sat down in front of this committee, where he was barraged with questions from members of Congress putting him in a subordinate position. Thus, the entire ordeal brought into question Ford's legitimacy, and his credibility, at a time when he had little legitimacy to spare, and the credibility of the Office of the President was already weakened.

THE ACCIDENT-PRONE PRESIDENT

Gerald Ford's intellect was also a major focus of derision for his critics. Ford was dubbed the Klutz-in-Chief, after being caught on camera tripping or falling several times. For example, he slipped on the steps coming out of Air Force One when he arrived in Austria for a diplomatic visit. Several times when he was playing golf, he hit the ball into the gallery of spectators—once hitting a lady on the head. While playing doubles in tennis, he hit his own partner with the ball.

Critics seized on these displays of clumsiness as visual evidence that Ford lacked the competence and leadership capacity to be president. Again, the press was his biggest critic. An example of the press drawing into question Ford's competency occurred in early 1975, when Tom Brokaw, then a young NBC White House correspondent, asked Ford if he was "intellectually up to the job of being president." This line of questioning led to calls to see Ford's college transcripts. Many believe this questioning was a result both of Ford's unprecedented path to the Oval Office as well as the emboldened media attitude following Watergate.

Late night television also piled on. On November 8, 1975, just over a year after Ford's swearing in, Chevy Chase debuted his impersonation of Ford on NBC's new sketch comedy show, *Saturday Night Live*. Although presidents are now routinely parodied on this show, Ford had the unique misfortune of being the first. *Saturday Night Live* debuted in October 1975, and after a month, they finally took on the White House and Ford. In their first sketch parodying the president, Chase walks out to address the press, running into the American flag before he takes the podium. The sketch shows him repeating himself multiple times, clearly unable to read from a script, reinforcing the narrative that Ford was not smart. As Ford, Chase then pours himself a glass of water, but drinks from the empty cup, hits his head on the podium, and then slips and falls down several times; all of this took place in under a minute. The caricature continued the following week, when Chase depicted Ford as being unable to count, and answering his full glass of water as if it were a telephone, before tripping over his own charts, and toppling over his desk onto the ground. Weekend after weekend, the American public tuned in to see their president ridiculed.

CONCLUSION

The effects of the attacks on Ford's presidency as illegitimate, and his character as lacking credibility and competence, had a direct impact on his ability to pass his legislative agenda. Congressional Democrats were unwilling to work with Ford and ended up attempting to pass their own aggressive agenda. Ford vetoed 66 bills in his short time as president—12 of those vetoes were overridden. These attacks also colored his presidential campaign against Jimmy Carter in 1976; given the circumstances, Ford had only served as president for several months before he had to start campaigning, and these salient criticisms were too much to overcome. He lost the election to Carter by about 2 million votes. Although he assumed office ready to sow trust and pardoned Nixon to get out of the shadow of Watergate, the way in which the pardon was carried out smelled of more scandal, and American voters decided that the only possible way forward was without Ford.

The broader impact of the attacks on Ford was on the fundamental concern about the size and scope of presidential power, and that legitimate or not, and competent or not, the presidency elevates and empowers whomever occupies the oval office. In light of this, those in academic circles began to reconsider their celebration of the enlarged presidency, where those who studied presidential power saw the growth of the executive as indicative of American power, and necessary to its maintenance, and not a threat to democracy. Ford's pardon, seen as an unsavory misuse of authority, sustained calls for renewed attention to presidential abuses of power following the Nixon scandal and resignation, and arguments emerged that perhaps more effort needed to be made to reign in presidential power—heavily influenced by the perception that Nixon had violated it, yet was absolved from any consequences because of Ford's actions.

Meredith Conroy

Further Reading

Baughman, James L. "There Were Two Gerald Fords: John Hersey and Richard Reeves Profile a President." *American Literary History,* Vol. 24, No. 3 (2012): 444–467.

Cannon, James. *Gerald R. Ford: An Honorable Life.* Ann Arbor, MI: University of Michigan Press, 2013.

Kalman, Laura. "Gerald Ford, the Nixon Pardon, and the Rise of the Right." *Cleveland State Law Review,* Vol. 58, No. 2 (2010): 349–366.

Leibovich, Mark. "Chevy Chase as the Klutz in Chief, and a President Who Was in on the Joke." *The New York Times,* December 29, 2006.

Werth, Barry. *31 Days: The Crisis That Gave Us the Government We Have Today.* New York: Nan A. Talese, 2006.

39. Jimmy Carter

Born: October 1, 1929
Time in Office: 39th President of the United States, January 20, 1977, to January 20, 1981
Election Results: 1976 Election: 50.1% of popular vote, 297 (55.2%) Electoral College votes; 1980 Election: 41% of popular vote, 49 (9.1%) Electoral College votes

Spouse: Rosalyn Smith (m. 1946)
Children: John William, Donnel, James, and Amy

Born in Plains, Georgia, in 1929, James Earl "Jimmy" Carter served as the 39th president of the United States. The son of a successful small businessman and farmer, Carter attended the U.S. Naval Academy, graduating in 1948. In 1953, following a brief stint in the Navy, he returned home to Georgia to take over the family peanut farm. He entered state politics in the early 1960s, winning elections for state senate in 1962 and governor in 1970 (following an unsuccessful gubernatorial bid in 1966).

Although generally popular in his own state, Carter barely registered in national polls when he entered the race for the 1976 Democratic presidential nomination. He was, however, a skilled retail politician, and his reputation for honesty and piety—he was a devout southern Baptist—resonated with an electorate still reeling from the Watergate scandal. By April Carter had locked up the Democratic nomination; he would go on to defeat the incumbent, Republican president Gerald Ford, in a closely contested general election, winning 50% of the popular vote to Ford's 48%. Joining the new president in the White House were his wife of 30 years, Rosalynn, and a nine-year-old daughter, Amy (the Carters' three adult sons no longer resided with their parents).

From an early point in his presidency, Carter was the target of vicious attacks from activists and lawmakers on both sides of the political spectrum. Why did a man elected on the strength of his sunny disposition and reputation for truthfulness engender such strong reactions? The answer can be traced in part to the unfortunate timing of Carter's presidency. By the late 1970s, many of the pillars of the postwar political order were beginning to crumble. The nation's disastrous military intervention in Vietnam had split the foreign policy establishment into competing camps of hawks and doves; movements for women's rights and gay and lesbian rights were opening new fault lines in the electorate; and the Democratic Party's core constituencies—union workers, African Americans, white southerners, and socially liberal activists—were increasingly at each other's throats. Carter, who had studied to become a nuclear engineer, tended to view governing as an exercise in practical problem solving. Yet the emerging divisions in the Democratic Party—and American society more broadly—proved beyond his capacity to resolve. Carter would serve only a single term in the White House, losing decisively to Ronald Reagan in 1980.

THE FOREIGN POLICY HAWKS

Shortly after taking office, Carter used a commencement address at the University of Notre Dame to sketch a bold new vision for American foreign policy. Sensing that Americans were wary of foreign entanglements, he pledged to replace the hard-line anticommunism that had led the United States into Vietnam with a foreign policy based on international collaboration and respect for human rights. Carter's first attempt to make good on the promise involved the long-simmering dispute over control of the Panama Canal. For years, Latin American leaders had denounced U.S. control of the canal as an affront to the region's independence, and by 1977 many in the Washington foreign policy establishment had concluded that formal control of the canal was no longer essential to U.S. security. Within six months of taking office, the new administration had negotiated a pair of treaties that transferred legal title over the Canal Zone to the government of Panama while authorizing the United States to defend the canal in the event of a foreign military threat.

The administration touted the agreement as a major foreign policy triumph, and mainstream business groups were inclined to agree. Yet the treaties encountered fierce opposition from an array of conservative organizations whose foreign policy views owed more to the staunch anticommunism of Barry Goldwater and Ronald Reagan than the moderate internationalism of the U.S. Chamber of Commerce. Among the groups that actively opposed ratification were the American Conservative Union, the Conservative Caucus, the Committee for the Survival of a Free Congress, the American Security Council, the National Conservative Political Action Committee, Eagle Forum, and the Young Americans for Freedom. Coordinating the opposition forces were two hastily formed umbrella groups, the Committee to Save the Panama Canal and the Emergency Coalition to Save the Panama Canal.

Instead of focusing their efforts on traditional face-to-face lobbying of the senators who would be tasked with ratifying or rejecting the treaties, the opposition groups pursued a grassroots strategy that cast the president as a dupe of the Soviets. Because Panama's leaders harbored communist sympathies, or so the argument went, the president was effectively handing the Kremlin a critical strategic asset. As the conservative activist Phyllis Schlafly explained in a 1977 newsletter, Panamanian president Omar Torrijos was "part of a Marxist military junta operating in close collaboration with Communist Cuba and the Soviet Union. . . . The real issue here is U.S. control versus Communist control!"

To get out the message, treaty opponents relied on direct mail, television "documentaries," and a traveling "Truth Squad" featuring prominent Republican politicians and retired military officers. The American Conservative Union alone spent $1.4 million opposing the treaty, an amount that paid for 2.4 million pieces of mail, a barrage of print advertisements, and a 30-minute video that was broadcast on 150 television stations and seen by more than 10 million viewers. In the end, the Panama treaties squeaked through the Senate—but not without forcing the administration to expend an enormous amount of political capital. Carter's second major foreign policy initiative, the SALT II arms reduction treaty, would not fare so well.

Carter inherited a delicate situation in the area of arms control. In 1972, the Nixon administration had secured Senate ratification of a major anti-ballistic missile treaty known as SALT I. In 1974, Ford and Soviet leader Leonid Brezhnev, meeting in Vladivostok, agreed on a framework for further arms reductions. By this point, however, the mood in Washington had shifted. The fall of South Vietnam, coupled with mounting evidence of Soviet meddling in Africa and elsewhere, suggested that the global balance of power had shifted toward Moscow, and by the time Carter settled into the Oval Office the Vladivostok framework was already coming under attack from a number of well-funded advocacy groups. Yet in keeping with his principled commitment to peace through diplomacy, Carter pressed ahead, eventually finalizing a new agreement (SALT II) that promised significant cuts to both countries' nuclear arsenals.

Perhaps not surprisingly, conservative think tanks described the agreement as dangerously favorable to the Soviets. Even before the terms of the treaty were announced, the recently formed Committee on the Present Danger (CPD), a group composed of hawkish foreign policy luminaries, spent $750,000 on mobilizing public opposition. The American Security Council (ASC) and a hastily formed offshoot known as the Coalition for Peace through Strength were perhaps even more influential. In addition to funding countless direct mail attacks, the groups produced a film, *The SALT Syndrome*, which featured prominent former military leaders warning that Carter had gifted the Soviets a permanent advantage in the arms race. The film, which aired more than 600 times on local television stations, was so influential that the administration deemed it necessary to issue a formal rebuttal.

The Soviet invasion of Afghanistan in December 1979 sealed the fate of SALT II. By this point the treaty had become so toxic that Carter himself withdrew it from Senate consideration. Nonetheless, the controversy took a heavy toll on the president's approval ratings. By mid-1979, polls indicated that only about a third of Americans approved of Carter's handling of foreign policy. The White House's internal polls reached similar conclusions, finding that 62% of Americans now felt that America's position in the world was "becoming weaker." Writing in *Human Events*, conservative commentator Bentley T. Elliot summarized the critics' case against the president, observing that Carter had "tried so hard in so many ways to convince the world of his desire for peace—at almost any price—that many people now believe he is a pacifist."

Other administration initiatives added fuel to the fire. The extension of formal diplomatic recognition to the People's Republic of China (PRC), for example, was attacked in the conservative press as aiding the communist cause. Notwithstanding the fact that Carter's China policy was largely consistent with that of his Republican predecessors, Charles Johnson argued in *Commentary* that the president, "instead of firmly insisting on American policy," had passively assented to the "blunt terms" of the Chinese. *National Review* editor William F. Buckley agreed that the president had been "pushed around" by his communist interlocutors.

The final year of Carter's presidency was consumed by efforts to negotiate the release of 52 Americans held by student revolutionaries in Iran. After diplomacy failed, the president reluctantly authorized a military rescue attempt, which ended in disaster when a pair of American helicopters collided in the Iranian desert. Although the hostages were safely returned to the United States on January 20, 1981—the day Carter left office—the conservative press roundly panned the president's response to the crisis. Writing in *Human Events*, retired admiral Thomas Moorer argued that the Iranian Revolution was the natural culmination of Carter's efforts to improve relations with America's adversaries. When one considered that the president had given away the Panama Canal and "betrayed" Taiwan, it was hardly surprising that "one little country after another was thumbing its nose at the U.S." "Right now," Moorer wrote, "we're the biggest patsy in town."

THE BIRTH OF THE RELIGIOUS RIGHT

The hot-button issues that are today associated with religiously motivated voting were largely absent from the 1976 campaign. The candidates' views on abortion were roughly identical; both men claimed to be personally opposed to the practice but neither expressed much enthusiasm for new federal restrictions. Nor was there much debate on the subject of gay rights. By the midpoint of Carter's presidency, however, it was apparent that both abortion and homosexuality would feature prominently in his 1980 reelection bid.

Abortion emerged as a major political issue in 1978 when pro-life Senate candidates, backed by grassroots religious activists, defeated pro-life incumbents in both Iowa and New Hampshire. In 1979, a popular film produced by the evangelical activist Francis Schaeffer, *Whatever Happened to the Human Race?*, implored evangelicals to rise up against their "pro-abortion government" and halt "the slaughter of the innocents." In this changed environment, the president's personal professions of faith became increasingly irrelevant. Christian Voice was but one of many groups that used direct mail to mock the openly devout president for his inaction on abortion. In the fall of 1980 the group distributed 500,000 mailers asking voters to ponder why, if the president believed abortion was a sin, he had refused to "do anything to end" the practice.

The issue of gay and lesbian rights burst onto the national scene in 1977 when local officials in Dade County, Florida, enacted an ordinance prohibiting discrimination on the basis of sexual orientation. Outraged evangelicals, including Miss America runner-up Anita Bryant and televangelist Jerry Falwell, denounced the law as an affront to biblical values and a grave threat to the nation's children, and they ultimately secured its repeal in a popular referendum. Evangelicals were further enraged when leaders of the National Gay Task Force secured a meeting with Carter's assistant for public liaison, Margaret "Midge" Costanza. If the president was going to welcome "practicing homosexuals" into the White House, Falwell asked rhetorically, why not invite "murderers and bank robbers" and other moral deviants to join the administration?

Carter's efforts on behalf of the Equal Rights Amendment (ERA) further eroded his support among evangelical voters. At the time of his inauguration, 34 states out of the required 38 had ratified the amendment, which declared that "[e]quality of rights under the law shall not be denied or abridged by the United States or by any State on account of sex." Carter took several steps to promote the ERA, including dispatching Vice President Walter Mondale to lobby for passage of a resolution extending the ratification deadline and holding a public signing ceremony when the extension passed (though his signature was not required by the Constitution). In addition, the first lady traveled to several state capitals to lobby wavering lawmakers.

But by this point the ERA had become a political lighting rod. Schlafly, in particular, had succeeded in stoking fears that the measure would mandate unisex bathrooms and require women to register for the draft. In November 1977, when delegates to the administration-supported International Year of the Woman (IYW) conference came out in favor of ratification (as well as women's reproductive rights and gay and lesbian rights), Schlafly and other conservative activists denounced the president as an ally of "radical" feminists. The administration had played into the hands of the "women's libbers," Schlafly claimed, allowing them to use "taxpayer money to lobby for the ERA . . . and to promote [their] narrow radical view of women."

Arguably the most important cause of the rift between Carter and his fellow evangelicals, however, was the Internal Revenue Service's decision to revoke the tax-exempt status of private religious schools that discriminated on the basis of race. As early as 1970, the IRS had announced its intent to deny tax-exempt status to segregated private schools. It was not until 1976, however, when the agency stripped Bob Jones University, a prominent fundamentalist school, of its tax-exempt status, that the issue began to draw national attention. Two years later, in an effort to address the problem of private academies formed for the purpose of avoiding court-ordered integration decrees, the IRS issued new regulations requiring that religious schools demonstrate "good faith" efforts to enroll minority students.

Concerned that the new regulations represented the first step in a larger plot to bring religious institutions under federal control, evangelicals lashed out at the federal government, sending more than 400,000 letters of protest to Congress and more than 125,000 to IRS headquarters. A *Conservative Digest* poll conducted in August 1979 found that evangelicals viewed the IRS regulations as the single most important issue facing the country. The significance of this finding was not lost on Republicans, who included a plank in their 1980 platform pledging to "halt the unconstitutional regulatory vendetta launched by Mr. Carter's IRS commissioner against independent schools." To drive home the point, the party's 1980 nominee, Ronald Reagan, made a campaign stop at Bob Jones University, where he spoke before 6,000 cheering students and faculty.

By early 1980, a number of deep-pocketed religious interest groups were lining up to oppose the president's reelection. The most celebrated group, the Moral Majority, was formed in 1979 by the televangelist Falwell and the veteran conservative strategists Howard Phillips, Richard Viguerie, and Paul Weyrich. But the same years witnessed the formation of other influential religious advocacy groups—including Focus on the Family (1977), Christian Voice (1978), the Religious Roundtable (1979), and Concerned Women of America (1979)—all of which were highly critical of the Democrats' stance on social issues.

The irony, of course, was that Carter was not only a devout southern Baptist, but also relatively conventional (for the time) in his views on abortion, homosexuality, and other issues of concern to evangelicals. Carter attempted to stake out the middle ground in the culture wars, only to be relentlessly attacked from the right for spinelessly acquiescing in policies favored by atheists, feminists, gay rights activists, and other real or purported foes of organized religion.

ATTACKS FROM THE LEFT

Aware of Carter's religious background, many feminists were from the outset skeptical of the new president's commitment to reproductive rights. But it was Carter's support for renewal of the Hyde Amendment—banning the use of federal funds to pay for abortions—that sparked the first full-fledged confrontation. When Carter defended the amendment in an interview, a group of 40 female Carter appointees, led by Midge Costanza, met and drafted a letter informing the president that he had "underestimated the deep feelings of women across the country on the [abortion] issue." When news of the insurgency leaked, Carter was indignant, calling the secret meeting "inappropriate" and expressing "resentment" at the effort's organizers. In the end, Costanza abandoned the idea of a joint letter but encouraged pro-choice staffers to write the president individually. Several did so, and their letters pulled no punches. The Equal Employment Opportunity Commission's (EEOC) Eleanor Holmes Norton, for example, accused the president of callous indifference to the plight of "poor blacks," who were more likely than others to suffer the effects of the Hyde Amendment.

Women's rights activists were further aggrieved by Carter's tepid support for the policy proposals of his own National Advisory Committee for Women, a group cochaired by Bella Abzug and Carmen Delgado Votaw. Never one to shrink from a fight, Abzug was from the outset critical of administration policies that she deemed harmful to women. In early 1979, after Carter made known his dislike of Abzug's "confrontational style," the former congresswoman met with members of the press to air her grievances. Carter responded by requesting her resignation—a move that turned into a public relations disaster when fully half of the committee resigned in protest. Although Carter continued to press ahead with some of the committee's recommendations—including ERA ratification—Abzug and several other leading feminists campaigned against him during the 1980 Democratic primaries. As Abzug told an audience of college students, when Carter fired her "it was though every woman in this country was fired." As a result, women were now "on the fringes of democracy looking in."

The president fared little better with another core Democratic constituency: organized labor. With Democrats enjoying unified control of government, many union leaders were initially hopeful that a Carter presidency would see progress on long-stalled labor priorities, from revising the hated Taft-Hartley Act, to enacting national health insurance, to raising the minimum wage. But while Carter sympathized with many of labor's aims, he was reluctant to pursue policies that seemed likely to add to the deficit or discourage economic growth. By 1978, it was clear that the president would not invest political capital in ambitious projects like health care reform or a large stimulus package. As a result, his relationship with labor quickly soured. George Meany, head of the powerful AFL-CIO, gave Carter a grade of "C–" for his first year in office.

One initial bright spot in Carter's relationship with labor was the Humphrey-Hawkins Act, an ambitious piece of legislation, strongly favored by leading unions and civil rights groups, which promised coordinated economic planning with respect to prices and wages, as well as a legally enforceable right to employment. In September 1976, under pressure from labor leaders, Carter had given the bill his "complete endorsement." When Humphrey-Hawkins was reintroduced in 1977, however, the president and his economic team began to temporize. Fearing that the measure would bust the budget and exacerbate the nation's deepening inflation problem, Carter's team worked with congressional leaders to weaken the bill, replacing many of its specific spending provisions with vaguely worded goals and priorities. A New York Times editorial summed up the reaction of the bill's supporters, writing that Carter had "play[ed] a cruel hoax on the hard-core unemployed, holding before them the hope—but not the reality—of a job." William "Wimpy" Winpisinger, the colorful head of the million-member International Association of Machinists, was even more blunt, calling Carter "The best Republican President since Herbert Hoover."

Carter's liberal critics soon found a champion in Massachusetts senator Edward M. "Ted" Kennedy. Never particularly close to the president, Kennedy broke with Carter for good in July 1978 when it became clear that the White House would not give its full support to Kennedy's national health insurance bill. A few months later, in December 1978, Kennedy delivered a harshly critical speech designed to lay the groundwork for a primary challenge. Calling "decent quality health care" a "right, not [a] privilege," Kennedy launched a not-so-subtle broadside against Carter's fixation with balanced budgets. "Sometimes a party must sail against the wind," he declared. "We cannot afford to drift, or lie at anchor. We cannot heed the call of those who say it is time to furl the sail."

Although Carter outlasted Kennedy in the battle for the 1980 nomination, Kennedy, who had the full-throated backing of organized labor and many civil rights activists, seriously damaged the incumbent's chances of winning reelection. Most importantly, he succeeded in cementing the image of Carter as a soulless technocrat whose centrist leanings on issues ranging from abortion to social spending were out of synch with the base of his own party. So long as Carter occupied the White House, Kennedy declared in a January 1979 speech, women, minorities, and the handicapped would continue to "suffer from injustice," the ERA would remain stalled in the states, and "the state of a person's health" would continue to be "determined by the amount of a person's wealth."

CONCLUSION

Carter and his defenders viewed these charges as grossly unfair. Faced with a sputtering, inflation-ridden economy and spiraling budget deficits, Carter had little choice but to "furl the sail" of American liberalism. Still, Kennedy's litany of complaints provides a good sense of the impossible dilemmas Carter faced as a result of having assumed office at a transformative moment in American political history—a moment when the nation's postwar economic boom was sputtering to a halt; when new ideological fault lines were opening around issues such as abortion and women's rights; when new technologies, such as direct mail, made it possible for interest groups to appeal directly to voters; and when the Democratic coalition was itself increasingly fragile and internally divided. With the benefit of hindsight, it was perhaps an ominous sign that a president so committed to holding the middle ground on the divisive issues of his day became, for so many Americans, an easy man to hate.

John W. Compton

Further Reading

Balmer, Randall. *Redeemer: The Life of Jimmy Carter.* New York: Basic Books, 2014.

Buckley, William F. "China and Panama: The Connection." *National Review,* Vol. 36 (1977): 1072.

Clymer, Adam. *Edward M. Kennedy: A Biography.* New York: William Morrow, 1999.

Cowie, Jefferson. *Stayin' Alive: The 1970s and the Last Days of the Working Class.* New York: New Press, 2010.

Crespino, Joseph. "Civil Rights and the New Religious Right," in *Rightward Bound: Making America Conservative in the 1970s*, ed. Bruce J. Shulman and Julian E. Zelizer. Cambridge, MA: Harvard University Press, 2008.

Critchlow, Donald T. *Phyllis Schlafly and Grassroots Conservatism: A Woman's Crusade.* Princeton, NJ: Princeton University Press, 2005.

Diamond, Sara. *Roads to Dominion: Right-Wing Movements and Political Power in the United States.* New York: Guilford Press, 1995.

Elliot, Bentley T. "Jimmy Carter: Four Years of Failure." *Human Events*, Vol. 40 (1980): 641–648.

"Enfeebled U.S. Stance Encourages Foreign Outrages." *Human Events*, Vol. 39 (1979): 987–988.

Flippen, J. Brooks. *Jimmy Carter, the Politics of Family and the Rise of the Religious Right.* Athens, GA: University of Georgia Press, 2011.

Johnson, Chalmers. "Carter in Asia: McGovernism without McGovern." *Commentary*, Vol. 65 (1978): 36–39.

Self, Robert O. *All in the Family: The Realignment of American Democracy since the 1960s.* New York: Hill and Wang, 2012.

Skidmore, David. *Reversing Course: Carter's Foreign Policy, Domestic Politics, and the Failure of Reform.* Nashville, TN: Vanderbilt University Press, 1996.

Skowronek, Stephen. *The Politics Presidents Make: Presidential Leadership from John Adams to George Bush.* Cambridge, MA: Belknap Press, 1993.

40. Ronald Reagan

Born: February 6, 1911

Died: June 5, 2004

Time in Office: 40th President of the United States, January 20, 1981, to January 20, 1989

Election Results: 1980 Election: 50.7% of popular vote, 489 (90.0%) Electoral College votes; 1984 Election: 58.8% of popular vote, 525 (97.6%) Electoral College votes

Spouse: Jane Wyman (m. 1940), Nancy Davis (m. 1952)

Children: Maureen, Christine, Michael, Patricia, and Ronald Jr.

Perhaps no other president in the post–World War II era remains as revered to a generation of conservatives as Ronald Reagan. Dubbed the "Great Communicator," Reagan left office more popular than when he entered the White House. Trust in government rose during his two terms, despite the fact that the "Gipper" weathered blistering scandals (such as the Iran-Contra affair) and economic tumult with relative equanimity. In fact, he earned the sobriquet "the Teflon president" because few controversies seemed to "stick" to him with the public, and because most political foes were wary to attack him personally lest their own popularity suffer. His communication style, honed during his years as an actor spokesman for General Electric, was marked by folksy charm and self-deprecating humor.

Reagan was nonetheless harshly criticized by many progressive members of the media and Democrats during his political career, and some of these condemnations seemed based on genuine alarm about his political beliefs and actions. By the time he ran for the presidency (unsuccessfully in 1976 and successfully in 1980), Reagan was a prominent and outspoken conservative. He gained the national spotlight for his advocacy of Barry Goldwater in the 1964 presidential election with his stirring anticommunist speech "A Time for Choosing." He had come to the conclusion a decade earlier, as president of the Screen Actors Guild, that many actors and Hollywood groups were fronts for pro-Soviet interests. He later earned notoriety for his turbulent two terms as California's governor (1967–1975) as the state faced imminent bankruptcy and the nation struggled with its response to the civil rights movement, rioting in inner-city communities over economic and social issues, protests against the Vietnam War, and domestic economic insecurity.

Many of the most enduring personal attacks against Reagan were first leveled against him during his two terms as governor of the Golden State. The invectives leveled against Reagan in Sacramento—that he was an extremist, a racist, anti-intellectual in his governing approach, and a hypocrite who turned a blind eye to the poor—were variably duplicated on the domestic front during the 1980 presidential campaign, with concomitant portrayals of him as a belligerent, dangerous leader on the foreign policy front. But such tactics, employed by his political foes in California, by President Jimmy Carter's campaign in the 1980 presidential election, and later by Democratic nominee Walter Mondale and his proxies in 1984 to paint him as a dangerous extremist and as an incompetent buffoon, arguably backfired.

Empirical evidence, insofar as public opinion polls and Reagan's landslide presidential election victories in 1980 and 1984 are concerned, suggests that the nation's 40th president was rather successful in casting off the negative portrayals levied by his political rivals. Reagan's deft posturing and communication style tended to limit the ability of his adversaries to utilize the politics of personal destruction to undermine his electoral victories, leadership, or legacy. Nonetheless, negative portrayals of Reagan and his wife, Nancy, were commonplace in popular culture during his years in the public eye, and he was the target of death threats and a 1981 assassination attempt.

PERSONAL ATTACKS ON GOVERNOR REAGAN

Several interconnected lines of personal attacks are notable in criticisms of Reagan as governor of California from 1967 to 1975. First, he was portrayed as an extremist with ties to right-wing, reactionary groups. Edmund G. (Pat) Brown, Reagan's Democratic rival in the gubernatorial election of 1966, began his campaign by suggesting that Reagan was a "front man" for extremists. Indeed, many critics charged that Reagan had links to the John Birch Society and that, as the *Chicago Defender* claimed in 1966, "He commands the loyalty of a group of fanatics that will stop at nothing to put him over as governor now, and President later." One prominent state labor leader, frightened by Reagan's support of business interests, suggested in the *Wall Street Journal* that same year the existence of a "'conspiratorial alliance' directed at 'an extremist takeover in California this year, and an extremist drive for the Presidency two years from now.'" Finally, as reported in the *New York Times* in 1971, Reagan's efforts to trim the state budget were called "inhumane" by critics who asserted that this "budget of his goes back to all that Birch Society stuff" of rhetoric targeting government spending during his first gubernatorial campaign in 1966.

Second, Reagan was typecast by his political opponents in Sacramento as an anti-intellectual fraud who owed his political rise to his mediocre acting talents. He was frequently derided for his career in Hollywood and characterized as an actor who lacked credibility for public service. In 1966 the *Washington Post* compared Reagan to Efrem Zimbalist Jr., who played Inspector Erskine in the television series *The FBI*. The newspaper suggested that "If Ronald Reagan, surely a less talented thespian, can aspire to the Governorship of California, why can't the FBI someday be headed by J. Edgar Zimbalist Jr.?" Reagan was frequently portrayed by critics as an obtuse television performer void of substance and uninterested in intellectual analysis. As one example, the *Sun Reporter* in 1972 contended that "the governor is a man who has refrained from any type of reading outside of the scripts which were handed to him . . . during the period when he was a Hollywood performer."

Few issues galvanized personal attacks on Reagan as an anti-intellectual extremist in the governor's mansion more than his education budget cuts and response to turmoil on university campuses. As the Vietnam War fueled student protests and African Americans demanded political and social equality, Reagan not only took quick actions to restore order at the protest-wracked campus of the University of California–Berkeley by dispatching law enforcement in 1967 but also cut public education budgets significantly—a move that many in the academic community viewed as punitive and disciplinary. The *Sacramento Observer* contended in January 1974 that "The general consensus among California's academic leadership is that the Reagan Administration has been the greatest destructive force and greatest enemy public education has faced in 50 years." Moreover, Reagan's support of the Regents of the University of California for the firing of Angela Davis, a black philosophy professor who was a member of the Communist Party and made fiery speeches outside the classroom, was regarded by critics as an "unconscionable" political vendetta. "Reagan and his regents," a critical editorial in the *Sun Reporter* in 1970 surmised, "continue to demonstrate their know-nothingism. . . . The firing of Angela Davis was an evil deed by an insensitive and frightened few." The Regent's sacking several years earlier of Dr. Clark Kerr, president of the University of California, Los Angeles— with Reagan's blessing—for alleged lenience toward student demonstrations and strikes had been met with similar resentment by faculty, students, and the press.

Finally, Reagan was depicted as a racist. Portrayed as drawing his support from "Goldwater disciples" and "dangerous reactionaries of the John Birch Society" opposed to civil rights, Reagan was castigated for his support of the repeal of the Rumford Act of 1963. The state law forbade racial discrimination in the realm of housing, but was overturned by voters a year later. The U.S. Supreme Court then invalidated the revocation of the law in *Reitman v. Mulkey* (1967). Reagan vowed to continue working toward the repeal of the Rumford Act, which he believed interfered with private property rights on principle. His stance drew blistering assaults from critics including the black-owned *Chicago Defender*, which in 1967 charged that the governor was "taking the people for fools [by denying] that his position implicitly supported racial discrimination."

On the campaign trail in 1966, Reagan's references to "crime in the streets" and his tough stance on law and order were viewed by many blacks, as reported in the *New York Times*, as a "kind of code for anti-Negro sentiment." As governor, charges of racism were intricately linked to his support for economic policies that putatively advantaged the wealthy over the poor and minority communities. Critics condemned Reagan as a hypocrite for finding loopholes to avoid paying state income tax in 1970 even as he lambasted welfare recipients for seizing on rules that enabled them to benefit from social programs. Reagan contended that "we're caught up with a legal kind of cheating" on welfare programs. In 1970, as Reagan's administration prepared to release a report that purported to document the highest rate of welfare fraud in the state's history, his detractors discerned bigotry. The governor was accused of lowering taxes to "stick it" to the poor and defenseless. "This method of pandering to a racist majority often comes in the form of accusations of welfare fraud," claimed the *Sun Reporter,* and amounted to little more than a deplorable plot to scapegoat the poor. In the most extreme example, Reagan was vilified as an "evil man" who callously cut benefits to the most vulnerable in society "while unswervingly serving his god, the homeowning taxpayer."

Reagan remained steadfast in his governing principles, forging state budgets that brought California into the black. He also framed his deployment of the National Guard in response to the Berkeley protests as fulfillment of a 1966 campaign promise to address disorder on college campuses where, he claimed, "many leftist campus movements had transcended legitimate protest" through the actions of "beatniks, radicals and filthy speech advocates" that were bent on anarchy rather than academic freedom. Though try as his critics did to portray him as rigid and obdurate, Reagan nonetheless, according to the *Washington Post* in 1974, ". . . demonstrated an impressive capacity to adjust to the shifting currents of the period over which he presided" while never budging from his "pristine faith in unfettered free enterprise and his suspicion of government."

The governor's astute communication style blunted the personal attacks by his detractors. As one observer noted in the *Chicago Tribune* following Reagan's successful gubernatorial reelection bid in 1970, "Even Reagan's worst enemies concede he probably is the most effective political speaker on the stump in either party today. . . . Political one-liners and quickly delivered jokes are the true Reagan trademark and also help get his philosophy across." Moreover, Reagan utilized the medium of television as a significant equalizer against efforts to villainize him in the press. As Pat Brown acknowledged in the *Washington Post,* "he is not aloof from the people; he stares earnestly toward them at eye-level . . . Reagan is not likely to change, because a majority of people in those homes—according to most of the polls—favor what they see him doing and what they hear him saying. Nothing fortifies or justifies a politician's habits as success in the opinion polls." Others affirmed that Reagan adroitly used direct communication with voters to galvanize support among the "Great Silent Majority." As one Republican suggested in the *New York Times*: "He puts the voter on the couch and says soothingly, 'you're great. Why don't they appreciate you?' He's like a medicine man with his little bottle of elixir that will make everything go away—those fuzzy wuzzy blacks staring at you on the 11 o'clock news and those professors who keep saying how smart they are and how dumb you are."

These skills would prove similarly indispensable to Reagan on the presidential campaign trail and in the Oval Office. His most ardent political opponents for the White House—Jimmy Carter in 1980 and Walter Mondale in 1984—would become largely flummoxed over the inefficacy of personal attacks on the "Great Communicator" and were forced to exchange assaults on Reagan's personal character for substantive policy disagreements. The failure of these rhetorical assaults was not lost on Reagan's foes in Congress or in the press, who were generally rather circumspect in leveling personal attacks during his two terms in office (1981–1989).

REAGAN DEPICTED AS RACIST AND WARMONGER
ON 1980 CAMPAIGN TRAIL

Charges of racism against Reagan reemerged during and after the 1980 presidential campaign, first from the Carter team and later across Reagan's two presidential terms from progressive intellectuals. Carter was quick to seize on Reagan's support of the Tenth Amendment and states' rights and link those positions to implicit racism. On the campaign trail in September 1980, Carter told a gathering of blacks at the Ebenezer Baptist Church in Atlanta that "You've seen in the campaign the stirrings of hate and the rebirth of code words like 'states rights' in a speech [delivered by Reagan] in Mississippi. . . . Hatred has no place in this country. Racism has no place in this country." In a clear gaffe he later regretted, Reagan had criticized Carter for launching his campaign in Atlanta, the birthplace of the Ku Klux Klan (KKK)—and was thoroughly chastised by the incumbent president. However, earlier in the campaign season Carter's Secretary of Health and Human Services, Patricia Harris, asserted that Reagan's candidacy "raised the specter of white sheets." The KKK had endorsed Reagan and his platform, an endorsement the campaign immediately and unequivocally repudiated. Nevertheless, at the same event in Atlanta, Representative Parren Mitchell (D-MD) told the audience that "I'm going to talk about a man (Reagan) who has embraced a platform that some men known as the Ku Klux Klan said couldn't be better if they'd written it themselves . . . who seeks the Presidency of the United States with the endorsement of the Ku Klux Klan." Carter later remarked, however, that he did not believe Reagan held racist beliefs. The Reagan campaign's response to charges of racism was that Carter was in such a weak position for reelection that his words could be turned against him. In Pensacola, Florida, Reagan told an audience about his stance on racial issues, "You know, I recognize that there are some charges that have been made against them and I'd like to talk for a moment about those." He made it a point to turn toward a sign that read 'Black Americans for Reagan' and said, "God bless you, and God bless those who brought that sign and, by golly, it shows that you can't fool all of the people all of the time."

Reagan's defenders in the press posited that Carter's allegations of racism were specious. Some emphasized Reagan's outreach to blacks and support for his economic policies from leading conservative African American scholars including Thomas Sowell and Walter Williams. Others accentuated a perceived pattern of personal attacks characteristic of Carter's past campaigns, including the smearing of incumbent Georgia governor Carl Sanders, who Carter said lacked integrity and used "political influence to get rich" without substantive evidence. Carter's gubernatorial campaign also distributed a leaflet in segregationist counties showing Sanders with a black athlete.

The Carter campaign also indefatigably attempted to paint Reagan as a warmonger and make "him" the issue in foreign policy. Carter employed "coded" words such as "dangerous" and "disturbing" in describing Reagan's stance toward the Soviet Union. Carter charged that Reagan would be too hasty in decisions to deploy troops abroad, and his campaign seized on a comment by Judy Bratteson, a New York Republican, that Reagan was ". . . a little too military. He might jump the gun" amid the continuing war between Iran and Iraq. For his part, Reagan called Carter's tactics, which relied on a compilation of "hawkish" statements the Republican candidate had made, "below decency." Reagan declared that "I think it is inconceivable that anyone, particularly a President of the United States, would imply . . . that anyone, any person in this country, would want war. And that's what he's charging, and I think it is unforgiveable."

In the end, the Carter campaign's personal attacks proved ineffective. In the closing month of the campaign, as the polls began to shift to Reagan, Carter asserted in an interview with ABC News that personal attacks on Reagan had been "excessive" and a mistake. His press secretary, Jody Powell, said the campaign would instead shift its focus to "the very real differences between the candidates and the substantive nature of those differences." The Carter campaign's decision was clearly driven by polling data that showed 40% of respondents positing that he had run a mean-spirited campaign. As a result, Steve Neal of the *Chicago Tribune* noted that "Reagan's aides . . . urged him to ignore Carter's attacks, arguing that his mild, statesmanlike style has made him appear more presidential than Carter."

Carter's turnabout reflected a fundamental dilemma. How could he hedge against Reagan's candidacy in light of a poor economy, allegations of a weak and indecisive foreign policy that gained currency in light of the Soviet invasion of Afghanistan and the ongoing Iranian hostage crisis, and draw distinctions between his approach and that of Reagan? Personal attacks seemed befitting. Yet, as political scientist Stephen Wayne asserted to the *Christian Science Monitor*, Carter wrestled with the best way to make such distinctions from his very acceptance speech as the Democrats' nominee in 1980: the president ". . . strained to make out a precise difference between a Democratic or Republican victory. He strained to portray Reagan as a potential horror. He barely mentioned the difficulties of his own record. He strained with his voice to generate enthusiasm." On balance, Reagan may well have been able to make the case that his gubernatorial record in California was the "second toughest job in America" provided a reassuring political command at a time when scholars were discussing the "twilight of the presidency." Carter's pledge at the 1980 Democratic Convention to make "the radical, perhaps dangerous, nature of Ronald Reagan's character" the centerpiece of his campaign had failed. Douglas Hallett of the *Wall Street Journal* saw the writing on the wall before the general campaign went into full operation. He presciently noted that "Mr. Carter should examine the landslide defeats his two fellow Democrats Edmund G. 'Pat' Brown and Jesse Unruh suffered against Mr. Reagan in California before using the same bogus issue."

REAGAN ATTACKED AS INDOLENT BUT WELL-INTENTIONED IN 1984 CAMPAIGN

If Reagan's prospective reelection effort seemed in peril with the economic recession of 1982–1983 and the military build-up and growing rhetorical war with the

Soviet Union, by 1984 it was "Morning Again in America." The economy had rebounded and Reagan took an early and commanding lead in the polls against Democratic nominee (and former vice president in the Carter administration) Walter Mondale, who struggled to galvanize enthusiasm for his candidacy as Election Day approached. Mondale straddled a fine line between attacking Reagan personally and in policy terms, but ultimately personal assaults on the president gained little traction. In this regard, Mondale's rhetoric against Reagan focused largely on the arms race and intersected with questions about the incumbent's competence in office.

The leitmotif of Mondale's personal attacks on Reagan was a sharp critique of the president as "out of touch" and lazy. Mondale's vice presidential running mate, Geraldine Ferraro, suggested that Reagan's foreign policy had failed due to "ignorance" and a "lack of personal involvement." On arms control, Ferraro argued Reagan's performance was substandard due to a lack of mastery on the subject and "fundamental misconceptions." Mondale opined that Reagan had "a naive and primitive notion of national strength." The Mondale team's tactic was to question Reagan's leadership by depicting him as well intentioned but uninformed about complex issues.

Reagan's age played an implicit role in attacks on his competence. In 1984 he was the oldest president to have served in the Oval Office as he turned 73 in February that year. Senator John Glenn (D-OH), in a bid to revive Mondale's troubled campaign, told a crowd in his home state that "We've got the President worried now. He's had some sleepless *afternoons*." Mondale insinuated that the Reagan campaign was "a Hollywood, celluloid campaign that's running away from the facts."

The Mondale campaign's frustration that Reagan appeared immune from personal attacks *or* critiques of the president's policies reflected the uneasy balance in the ultimately elusive search for a successful campaign strategy. Howell Raines of the *New York Times* placed the dilemma in sharp relief: "'Get tough' with President Reagan, the Democratic elders have told their nominee. Then, in the next breath comes the solemn warning that, of course, Mr. Reagan is so popular that it would be a deadly political mistake for anyone to attack him 'personally.'"

As for the president, he largely refused to engage in personal attacks against Mondale. Vice President George Bush framed this decision as one rooted in Reagan's belief that "campaigns should be fought and won on the issues, and he is not going to defend to the level of the low-road personal attacks that have been leveled against him." Perhaps Reagan's most decisive counterattack came against Mondale on October 7, 1984, when he used humor to address the Mondale campaign's insinuations that he was getting too old for the rigors of the Oval Office. Reagan gleefully stated that "I will not make age an issue of this campaign. I am not going to exploit, for political purposes, my opponent's youth and inexperience."

One of Mondale's surrogates, Representative Tony Coelho (D-CA), contended that Reagan looked and acted "old" at the debate. But when pressed on whether Reagan should take a senility test, Mondale recoiled immediately, stating "I don't have any advice on that." The debate may not have changed public opinion in any substantive fashion, but Reagan's performance appeared to dispel allegations that he was too elderly or out of touch for a second term.

REAGAN ACCUSED OF RACISM IN THE OVAL OFFICE

Reagan faced fewer sustained personal attacks in the Oval Office compared to the campaign trail. His widespread popularity and solid victories in 1980 and 1984 made political opponents wary of criticizing his character, particularly in the midterm elections of 1982 and 1986, though Democratic opponents felt he was vulnerable on policy matters. One great exception, however, was the African American community. Black intellectuals, in particular though not solely, accentuated his lack of popularity in African American households, where there existed a broad perception that his policies of budget cutting and entitlement reform had racist undertones. Many of the critiques were similar to those leveled against Reagan during his time as governor of California, though the timbre was generally more muted.

Though they were generally careful not to label the president an outright racist, critics nonetheless emphasized Reagan's past opposition to civil rights legislation, his economic policies, and symbolic actions that, in their view, were at odds with a commitment to address blacks' concerns. William Raspberry of the *Washington Post*, citing polling data that showed 87% of African Americans disapproved of Reagan, suggested that his "nice guy" image was insufficient to surmount blacks' antipathy: "He seems not to understand that the attitude of blacks toward his administration is not primarily a matter of 'perception.' Blacks—particularly low-income blacks—see his programs and policies as inimical to their interests because they are." Civil rights leader Jesse Jackson went much further and provided a succinct summary of blacks' frustration with Reagan: "President Reagan and his Administration have combined regressive economics with race conscious behavior. Mr. Reagan has never met with the Congressional Black Caucus or with the national civil rights leadership. He has suggested that it is still open as to whether Dr. (Martin Luther) King was a Communist. . . . Representative Charles Rangel, an expert on drug policy was excluded from a meeting on that subject in the White House because there was 'no chair.' The White House is more segregated than Howard Beach [the site of a racially charged incident in Queens, New York in 1986]. From his earlier language that drew the Ku Klux Klan to his 1980 campaign opener in Philadelphia, Mississippi where in 1963 two Jews and a black had been killed in the civil rights struggle; to the Presidential trip to Bitburg, West

Germany, where so many Jews died; to the veto of sanctions against South Africa; to the nomination of a Chief Justice whose house deed prevented Jews from buying, Mr. Reagan has sent a consistent series of signals across the land."

Reagan's steadfast opposition to new civil rights legislation and his ultimately failed nomination of Robert Bork to the Supreme Court were seized on by critics to suggest that if Reagan the man was not racist, his stances sustained racist undercurrents. Richard Cohen of the *Washington Post* seized on Bork's opposition to such laws as the Civil Rights Act of 1964 and abolition of the poll tax, and Reagan's quip that even bigots "have certain constitutional rights" to argue that the president "has persisted in extolling equality while the government does little to enforce it . . . In other ways—affirmative action, busing, open housing—the Reagan administration has shown blacks that the government to which they had always looked for help is now looking away."

Several other cases illustrated blacks' frustration with Reagan's policies. In the realm of education, Reagan sought to reverse a long-standing federal policy against taxpayer subsidies of schools practicing racial segregation or discrimination that emanated from the Supreme Court decision in *Brown v. Board of Education* (1954). Connected to the issue was a lawsuit filed by Bob Jones University, which had its eligibility for taxpayer subsidies revoked in 1970 due to a ban on interracial marriage and dating based on religious views. Reagan argued that the revocation of subsidies gave the Internal Revenue Service too much bureaucratic power to classify schools as "charitable" or "religious." Although Reagan eventually reversed course after a significant backlash, black journalist William Raspberry contended that "the impression here is that Reagan is not a racist in the manner in some of his anti-black, segregationist, turn-back-the-clock supporters, but that he simply does not give much of a damn one way or the other. In practical effect, it amounts to the same thing."

Finally, Reagan's tepid support for a national holiday to celebrate the legacy of slain civil rights leader Martin Luther King Jr. raised further doubts among blacks about his commitment to equality. As Roger Wilkins in the *Los Angeles Times* suggested, once legislation passed in Congress, "Even this holiday itself, the one the President is now celebrating with such energy, was an event he originally contemplated with singular lack of enthusiasm. He first opposed it on the grounds that the establishment of a new national holiday would be too expensive. Then, responding to a news-conference question about what secret FBI tapes might reveal about King's connections with communism, Reagan said, 'We'll know in about 35 years won't we,' referring to the time when FBI records would be unsealed." Embarrassed by his public commentary, Reagan ultimately called King's widow, Coretta Scott King, to apologize. He suggested that he made a "flippant response to a flippant question." Still, the perception of Reagan bowing to racist tendencies persisted when it was revealed that he had phoned New Hampshire governor Meldrim

Thompson, who in 1977 had visited South Africa and praised the all-white regime for the policy of apartheid, and said that public views of King were "based on image, not reality." "In assailing King," Earl Hutchinson of the *Louisiana Weekly* contended, "Reagan followed the age-old ultra-conservative and racist script that King was a radical and racial agitator."

For his part, Reagan told the American Bar Association that he had an "unshakable commitment to eliminate discrimination against blacks, women, and other minorities." As president-elect in 1980 he met with leaders of national black organizations and professed that he would defend the rights of minorities "even at the end of a bayonet." He also attempted to portray his cabinet selections and judicial appointments as diverse. Still, as one observer noted as Reagan departed the Oval Office, "a large number of blacks look back with anger at policies they believe contribute to racial tensions now and will taint race relations later."

NANCY REAGAN AND ASTROLOGY IN THE WHITE HOUSE

The singular personal attack, if considered as such, made on First Lady Nancy Reagan came in 1988 with the publication of Donald T. Regan's memoir *For the Record: From Wall Street to Washington*. Regan had served as the president's secretary of the treasury from 1981 to 1985 and chief of staff from 1985 to 1987. In his book, Regan revealed that the first lady had relied on the advice of astrologist Joan Quigley to help determine the timing of her husband's speeches and travel. Nancy Reagan's use of astrology in connection with the president's calendar was putatively prompted by the 1981 assassination attempt against him. The backlash took on subtle tones of ridicule in the media and disbelief in the religious community, though direct personal attacks on the first lady's character were not prominent. Larger questions about the impact of astrological advice on the president's activities took center stage.

The repercussions were particularly notable among Christian leaders who supported Reagan. One evangelist who backed him in the 1980 campaign said the president did not have "a good grasp of biblical truth." Another religious leader had 40,000 Christians sign petitions urging the first lady and the president to reject astrology. Without a public denunciation by the White House, the Reagans would "legitimize astrology and the occult and set our nation on a collision course with God." Commentator Paul Hirst added that "Far from being amusing, Ronald and Nancy Reagan's infatuation with astrology is chilling. Astrology is pernicious because it treats human affairs as if they were determined by nonhuman causes."

If Nancy Reagan remained subdued during the firestorm, the president sought to defend his wife publicly. For her part, the first lady told an adviser that she was "taken aback by the vengefulness of the attack . . . it comes through that Donald Regan doesn't really like me." The president condemned Regan's memoir, stating he had no use for "kiss and tell" books. He reiterated publicly that "No policy or decision, in my mind, has been influenced by astrology."

The president and first lady weathered the storm largely because the story appeared to many to be the product of vindictiveness on the part of a disgruntled, former adviser with an axe to grind with his boss. As Godfrey Sperling of the *Christian Science Monitor* suggested, "The negative effect of the disclosure is widespread, the shock deep." However, he went on to note that polling did not suggest that the public was "very aroused over this development" as many Americans apparently consulted astrological forecasts casually.

PERSONAL ATTACKS IN POPULAR MUSIC CULTURE

Vitriol against Reagan was widespread in 1980s popular culture, and was most prominent in songwriters' and singers' portrayals of the president as timeworn, out of touch, and dangerous. Though too many to recount in detail, several examples suffice—and suggest how musical artists of the day memorialized Reagan through personal attacks on his character. A common feature of popular songs was to depict Reagan as "old" and "scary" as well as corrupt. The British group Simply Red criticized Reagan's economic philosophy in "Money's Too Tight to Mention." John Fogerty's 1984 track "The Old Man Down the Road" is also putatively a reference to Reagan as a decrepit, sinister figure who lives in isolation. In 1986 the Violent Femmes released "Old Mother Reagan" with lyrics that described the subject of the song as "dumb" and "dangerous." Finally, many listeners interpreted Don Henley's 1989 hit song "End of the Innocence" as a commentary on corruption in the Reagan presidency, notably the Iran-Contra scandal.

Perhaps the most scorching musical attack on Reagan, if indirectly, is found in Bob Dylan's 1983 song "Jokerman," which allegedly characterizes the president as an anti-Christ type figure without moral conscience bent on social, economic, and geopolitical turmoil.

Finally, Reagan's foreign policy was caricatured as reckless and at times inhumane by a number of groups and singers. Don Henley's 1984 song "All She Wants to Do Is Dance" protests American indifference to the Reagan administration's funding of the Nicaraguan Contras, while U2's 1987 song "Bullet in the Blue Sky" castigates the death of innocents in Central America via U.S. arms deals. The British group Def Leppard's 1987 track "Gods of War" features sound-overs of Reagan's speech on the bombing of Tripoli to the background of exploding bombs.

There is precious little that presidents can say or do about negative portrayals of them in popular media in a free society. Their best strategy is to remain silent, or laugh it off (or fume) in private. There is no evidence that Reagan himself was overly concerned. The frustration of his advisers, however, might well be summed up in columnist (and unofficial Reagan campaign adviser) George Will's attempt to arrogate Bruce Springsteen's 1984 hit "Born in the USA" for the president's reelection campaign. When Springsteen publicly stated he opposed many of Reagan's policies, Reagan campaign officials dropped the song from rally events and replaced it with Lee Greenwood's "God Bless the USA."

DEATH THREATS AND ASSASSINATION ATTEMPTS

Four presidents have been assassinated in the history of the Republic. Several others, including Andrew Jackson, Theodore Roosevelt, and Ronald Reagan, were fired upon by would-be assassins. On March 30, 1981, Reagan was shot outside the Washington Hilton by John Hinckley Jr., a mentally ill man who attacked Reagan in a bizarre attempt to impress actress Jodie Foster. Hinckley also shot Press Secretary James Brady, who suffered brain damage as a result, and two others. For his part, Reagan handled the assassination attempt with a superlative equanimity. After being rushed to the hospital, he told the first lady, "Honey, I forgot to duck," and joked to doctors "I hope you're all Republicans." After recovering from his injuries, Reagan appeared before Congress to a standing ovation to pitch his legislative agenda.

Less prominent was reporting of a number of other death threats to which Reagan and the White House took a largely subdued tact. In 1981 Edward Richardson of Pennsylvania penned a death threat letter prompted allegedly by a "prophetic dream" in which John Hinckley Jr. ordered him to kill Reagan. In 1982, James Lewis, who had written an extortion letter to the drugmaker Tylenol, was charged with writing a death threat to Reagan. In 1983 a Springfield, Virginia, man, Michael Charters, was indicted after telling officials he had attempted to buy a gun to kill Reagan as well as actress Raquel Welch and actor Clint Eastwood. Charters had made a threat to kill Reagan a year earlier. In 1984 the FBI sought a suspect who fired two shots from a taxi cab at a Republican campaign worker and shouted "Reagan is next." In 1985, as Reagan was leaving the Bethesda Naval Hospital in suburban Maryland, a disgruntled ex-Marine, Robert Hummel, was taken into custody by the Secret Service for verbal threats against the president made at a bar. Hummel blamed Reagan for the deaths of servicemen in Beirut.

CONCLUSION

Reagan was regularly subjected to personal attacks during his many years in politics. Yet on balance the nation's 40th president was able to fend off the most vicious personal attacks through a combination of direct communication with voters, disarming humor, and high personal popularity that deflected the most vitriolic personal or policy criticisms outside the election arena. The exception may well be his legacy among African Americans, who continue to perceive Reagan administration policies and actions to be tinged with racism. As the nation drifts further away from the Reagan years, it remains an open question whether the personal attacks of yesteryear and their fleeting effects at the time provide a basis for Reagan's historical redemption, if required—or demand revisionist interpretations of his character and legacy.

Richard S. Conley

Further Reading

Abrams, Herbert L. *The President Has Been Shot: Confusion, Disability, and the 25th Amendment in the Aftermath of the Attempted Assassination of Ronald Reagan.* New York: W. W. Norton, 1992.

Amaker, Norman C. *Civil Rights and the Reagan Administration.* Washington, D.C.: Urban Institute Press, 1988.

Bates, Toby Glenn. *The Reagan Rhetoric: History and Memory in 1980s America.* DeKalb, IL: Northern Illinois University Press, 2011.

Benze, James G. *Nancy Reagan: On the White House Stage.* Lawrence, KS: University Press of Kansas, 2005.

Berman, Larry, ed. *Looking Back on the Reagan Presidency.* Baltimore, MD: Johns Hopkins University Press, 1990.

Brands, H.W. *Reagan: The Life.* New York: Anchor Books, 2016.

Cannon, Lou. *President Reagan: The Role of a Lifetime.* New York: Simon and Schuster, 1991.

Cannon, Lou. *Governor Reagan: His Rise to Power.* New York: Public Affairs, 2003.

Collins, M. Robert. *Transforming America: Politics and Culture during the Reagan Years.* New York: Columbia University Press, 2009.

Dallek, Robert. *The Right Moment: Ronald Reagan's First Victory and the Decisive Turning Point in American Politics.* New York: Oxford University Press, 2004.

Germond, Jack W., and Jules Whitcover. *Blue Smoke and Mirrors: How Reagan Won and Why Carter Lost the Election of 1980.* New York: Viking, 1981.

Hannaford, Peter, ed. *The Quotable Reagan.* Washington, D.C.: Regnery, 1998.

Hanska, Jan. *Reagan's Mythical America: Storytelling as Political Leadership.* New York: Palgrave Macmillan, 2012.

Johnson, Haynes. *Sleepwalking through History: America in the Reagan Years.* New York: Anchor Books, 1992.

Noonan, Peggy. *What I Saw at the Revolution: A Political Life in the Reagan Era.* New York: Random House, 1990.

Pemberton, William E. *Exit with Honor: The Life and Presidency of Ronald Reagan.* New York: Routledge, 2015.

Piven, Frances Fox, and Richard A. Cloward. *The New Class War: Reagan's Attack on the Welfare State and Its Consequences.* New York: Pantheon Books, 1982.

Raphael, Timothy. *The President Electric: Ronald Reagan and the Politics of Performance.* Ann Arbor, MI: University of Michigan Press, 2009.

Schmertz, Eric J., Natalie Datlof, and Alexej Ugrinsky, eds. *President Reagan and the World*. Westport, CT: Greenwood Press, 1997.

Shimko, Keith L. *Images and Arms Control: Perceptions of the Soviet Union in the Reagan Administration*. Ann Arbor, MI: University of Michigan Press, 1991.

Shull, Steven A. *A Kinder, Gentler Racism? The Reagan–Bush Civil Rights Legacy*. Armonk, NY: M. E. Sharpe, 1993.

Stuckey, Mary E. *Getting into the Game: The Pre-Presidential Rhetoric of Ronald Reagan*. New York: Praeger, 1989.

Stuckey, Mary E. *Playing the Game: The Presidential Rhetoric of Ronald Reagan*. New York: Praeger, 1990.

Troxler, L. William, ed. *Along Wit's Trail: The Humor and Wisdom of Ronald Reagan*. New York: Holt, Rinehart, and Winston, 1984.

Troy, Gil. *Morning in America: How Ronald Reagan Invented the 1980's*. Princeton, NJ: Princeton University Press, 2013.

Vaughn, Stephen, et al. *Ronald Reagan in Hollywood: Movies and Politics*. New York: Cambridge University Press, 1994.

News Articles Cited

Aarons, Leroy. "Ripping up Reagan: Reagan and Reality." *Washington Post*, September, 17, 1970, p. C8.

Aarons, Leroy. "The Reagan Regime in Retrospect: Champion of Conservatism Learns Art of Political Compromise." *Washington Post*, December 23, 1974, p. A2.

Allen, Ira. "Democrats Attack Administration for 'Worshipping Greed.'" *Washington Post*, March 29, 1984, p. A14.

Anderson, Bill. "Reagan's Victory over Image Actor." *Chicago Tribune*, November 19, 1974, p. A2.

Cattani, Richard J. "Carter and the Eroding Presidency." *Christian Science Monitor*, August 18, 1980, p. 1.

Chandler, Russell. "Petitions from Conservative Christians Urge the Reagans to Reject Astrology." *Los Angeles Times*, June 21, 1988, p. 21.

Chicago Defender. "Extremist Reagan." September 3, 1966, p. 10.

Chicago Defender. "Reagan, the Racist." October 3, 1967, p. 13.

Chicago Tribune. "Reagan 'Expects Worse' from Carter in Campaign." July 26, 1980, p. W3.

Clymer, Adam. "War and Debate Marked a Week of Lost Changes for Presidential Candidates." *New York Times*, September 29, 1980, p. D13.

Cohen, Richard. "The Civil Rights Thing." *Washington Post*, October 9, 1987, p. A27.

Coleman, Milton. "Reagan and Mondale Exchange Salvos on Defense." *Washington Post*, October 11, 1984, p. A1.

Denton, Herbert H. "Reagan Assures Blacks He'll Defend Civil Rights: Reagan Tells Blacks He Would Defend Rights Forcibly." *Washington Post*, December 12, 1980, p. A1.

Fay, Joyce S. "Mondale's Attacks Take on a Personal Tone." *New York Times*, September 19, 1984, p. B8.

Gailey, Phil. "Reagan and Mondale Polish Debate Strategies." *New York Times*, October 4, 1984, p. B16.

Gilder Lehman Institute. N.D. "Ronald Reagan on the Unrest on College Campuses, 1967." Available at https://www.gilderlehrman.org/history-by-era/sixties/resources/ronald-reagan-unrest-college-campuses-1967.

Greenfield, Meg. "Welfare Cheaters and the Rest of Us." *Washington Post*, March 12, 1972, p. C1.

Hallett, Douglas. "Reagan as 'Extremist' Isn't Likely to Sell." *Wall Street Journal*, August 19, 1980, p. 28.

Hawkins, Augustus P. "California Needs Sane Leadership." *Sacramento Observer*, January 14, 1974, p. A4.

Hirst, P. "Reagan's Look to the Stars Signals the Defeat of Reason." *New Statesman*, May 13, 1988, p. 9.

Hutchinson, Earl Ofari. "Ronald Reagan Was No Friend to Blacks." *The Louisiana Weekly*, January 31, 2011, p. 5.

Human Events. "Carter's Politics of Hate." September 27, 1980, pp. 1–2.

Jackson, Jesse. "Atonement for Racist Episodes Isn't Enough." *New York Times*, January 28, 1987, p. A27.

Lama, George. "Reagan Says Age of Aquarius Doesn't Rule Him." *Chicago Tribune*, May 4, 1988, p. 1.

Lee, May. "See Heavy Losses and Few Gains Blacks Look Back With Anger at Reagan Years." *Los Angeles Times*, January 20, 1989, p. 1.

Lewis, Anthony. "Abroad at Home: A Nice Guy Contest?" *New York Times*, September 21, 1980, p. A27.

Lewis, Anthony. "Abroad at Home: Reagan Sheds Reagan." *New York Times*, August 7, 1983, p. A21.

Lindsey, Robert. "What the Record Says about Reagan." *New York Times*, June 29, 1980, p. SM3.

Los Angeles Times. "A Bad Sign? Some Protestants Chagrined over Reagan Astrology Story." May 14, 1988, p. 6.

McAllister, Bill, and Donnie Radcliffe. "White House Condemns Regan Book." *Washington Post*, May 10, 1988, p. A1.

Neal, Steve. "Reagan Calls War Innuendo 'Unforgiveable.'" *Chicago Tribune*, September 24, 1980, p. 2.

Neal, Steve. "The Fine Art of Mud-slinging." *Chicago Tribune*, October 26, 1980, p. A1.

Neal, Steve. "Mondale Says Reagan Lacks Facts." *Chicago Tribune*, October, 2, 1984, p. 5.

New York Times. "An Uneasy Undertone." November 6, 1966, p. 130.

Oakland Post. "President Denies Injecting Racism Into Campaign." September 21, 1980, p. 2.

Perlez, Jane. "Bush Says Democrats Are Making 'Kamikaze' Attacks on President." *New York Times*, September 20, 1984, p. B21.

Quinn, Matthew C. "An Exuberant and Confident Walter Mondale Today Belittled President." *United Press International*, October 11, 1984.

Raines, Howell. "Reagan Presses 'High Road' Response." *New York Times*, September 23, 1980, p. A26.

Raines, Howell. "Wedding Mondale to a Poor Strategy." *New York Times*, September 11, 1984, p. A27.

Raspberry, William. "A Bow to Racism . . ." *Washington Post*, January 15, 1982, p. A15.

Raspberry, William. "Reagan's Problem with Blacks." *Washington Post*, February 22, 1982, p. A11.

Roberts, Steven V. "Ronald Reagan Is Giving 'Em Heck." *New York Times*, October 25, 1970, p. SM22.

Roberts, Steven V. "Reagan: Critics Call His Budget 'Political' and 'Inhumane.'" *New York Times*, February 21, 1971, p. E3.

Roberts, Steven V. "Many Who See Failure in His Policies Don't Blame Their Affable President." *New York Times*, March 2, 1984, A14.

Saad, Lydia. N.D. "Presidential Debates Rarely Game-Changers." *Gallup Poll*. Available at http://www.gallup.com/poll/110674/presidential-debates-rarely-gamechangers.aspx.

Sacramento Observer. "Reagan's 'No Tax' Welfare for the Rich." May 20, 1971.

Sacramento Observer. "Reagan May Be President?" July 1, 1974, p. B-2.

Safire, William. "'There You Go Again.'" *New York Times*, October 30, 1980, p. A27.

Sawyer, Kathy. "Ferraro Attacks Reagan on Arms Control." *Washington Post*, September 19, 1984, p. A7.

Schellhardt, Thomas. "Carter Mutes Personal Attacks on Reagan." *Wall Street Journal*, October 10, 1980, p. 12.

Schram, Martin. "Carter Says Reagan Injects Racism: President Says Reagan Has Injected Hatred and Racism into Campaign." *Washington Post*, September 17, 1980, p. A1.

Smith, Hedrick. "Few Democrats Attacking President." *New York Times*, September 23, 1982, p. B27.

Sperling, Godfrey. "Superstition and the Reagans." *Christian Science Monitor*, May 17, 1988, p. 11.

Sun Reporter. "The Firing of Angela Davis." September 27, 1969.

Sun Reporter. "Robbing the Poor?" January 3, 1970.

Sun Reporter. "Angela Davis' Firing: An Evil Act." June 27, 1970.

Sun Reporter. "Reagan: An Evil Man." August 1, 1970.

Sun Reporter. "Evil in the Name of Law and Order." March 4, 1972.

Taylor, Paul. "Mondale: Reagan Naïve." *Washington Post*, October 17, 1984, p. A6.

Tolchin, Martin. "O'Neill Leading Party Offensive against Reagan." *New York Times*, June 10, 1983, p. A18.

Walsh, Edward. "Carter Says Attacks on Reagan a Mistake, Blames Frustration." *Washington Post*, October 9, 1980, p. A1.

Washington Post. "Method Actor." November 5, 1966, p. A12.

Weinraub, Bernard. "Reagan Is Accused of Lax Presidency." *New York Times*, February 10, 1984, p. A18.

Wilkins, Roger. "A Dream Still Denied an Equality Irony: Reagan Becomes Chief Celebrant of King's Birthday." *Los Angeles Times*, January 19, 1986, p. 1.

Will, George. "The Smear." *Washington Post*, September 21, 1980, p. D7.

Williams, Juan. "Reagan Calls Mrs. King to Explain." *Washington Post*, October 22, 1983, p. A1.

41. George H. W. Bush

Born: June 24, 1924

Time in Office: 41st President of the United States, January 20, 1989, to January 20, 1993

Election Results: 1988 Election: 53.4% of popular vote, 426 (79.2%) Electoral College votes; 1992 Election: 37.4% of popular vote, 168 (31.2%) Electoral College votes

Spouse: Barbara Pierce (m. 1945)

Children: George Walker, Robin, John Ellis "Jeb," Neil, Marvin, and Dorothy

George Herbert Walker Bush was born in Milton, Massachusetts, on June 24, 1924. The future president was part of a prominent family that had roots tracing back to the American colonial era. His mother was Dorothy Walker, and his father was Prescott Bush, a World War I veteran, businessman, and Republican senator from Connecticut. George's grandfather, Samuel P. Bush, was also a successful businessman who held a minor position in President Herbert Hoover's administration. The family was based in New England for many years, and includes five generations of alumni of Yale University, where George was also a member of the secret society of Skull and Bones.

World War II intervened, however, and Bush deferred his enrollment at Yale to enlist in the U.S. Navy after the Japanese attack on Pearl Harbor. Although he was one of the youngest (for a time *the* youngest) naval aviators, Bush excelled and earned the rank of lieutenant junior grade in August 1944. His combat experience included 58 missions, including one in which he was shot down near Chichi Jima and subsequently rescued by a U.S. submarine. Bush was decorated with the Distinguished Flying Cross. As of 2018, he is the last president to have military combat experience.

In June 1945, Bush married Barbara Pierce, who was distantly related to former president Franklin Pierce. The two met at a country club dance while both were still attending prep school. The Bushes had six children: George Walker (b. 1946), the future governor of Texas and 43rd president of the United States; John Ellis (b. 1953) or "Jeb," the future governor of Florida; Neil (b. 1955); Marvin (b. 1956); and Dorothy (b. 1959). The Bush's second child, Robin (1949–1953), died at less than four years of age due to leukemia.

Before following his father's footsteps into public service, Bush worked in the Texas oil industry, ultimately starting his own successful business. As a Republican in a then heavily Democratic state, Bush was badly defeated in his first run for public office in 1964. Bush ran for a seat in the U.S. Senate against Senator Ralph Yarborough, the Democratic incumbent, and lost by double digits in an especially bad year for Republicans across the nation. Two years later, however, Bush was elected to the House of Representatives from a Houston-area district. While Bush compiled a mostly conservative voting record during his two terms, he did encounter considerable criticism for voting for the Fair Housing Act of 1968. Although Bush had opposed the 1964 Civil Rights Act during his first Senate campaign, he became convinced that racial discrimination in housing was unacceptable. At an angry town hall meeting back in the district, Bush was chastised for supporting the bill, but earned the audience's respect for standing by his convictions.

In 1970, Bush gave up his House seat to make another run for the Senate. Once again, he was defeated, this time by Democrat Lloyd Bentsen, who would run on the national Democratic ticket against Bush 18 years later as the vice presidential running mate of presidential nominee Michael Dukakis. President Richard Nixon then installed Bush as U.S. ambassador to the United Nations. In the middle of the Watergate scandal, Bush moved from that post to the chairmanship of the Republican National Committee. After months of loyally defending Nixon, Bush finally joined leading Republicans in calling for the president's resignation in August 1974. President Gerald Ford, Nixon's successor, appointed Bush U.S. envoy to China and then director of the Central Intelligence Agency. His extensive experience seemed to make Bush a promising presidential candidate in 1980.

In that year's Republican primary season, Bush was understood as a moderate in the mold of Ford, Nixon, and Dwight Eisenhower. The party, however, moved sharply to the political right with the nomination of Ronald Reagan. Indeed, Bush only won a handful of state contests. Seeking to balance the GOP ticket with a moderate and someone with foreign policy experience, Reagan chose Bush as his running mate. To placate party conservatives, Bush reversed himself on the abortion issue, espousing a pro-life stance. He also declared his support for Reagan's supply-side economic policies, which he had once denounced as "voo-doo" economics. For the rest of his political career, Bush's critics would seize upon these flip-flops as evidence of his lack of convictions. Meanwhile, doctrinaire social and economic conservatives would never fully trust Bush as one of their own.

As vice president, Bush served in close capacity to Reagan during the latter's two terms in office. As a result, the former's role in the Iran-Contra scandal came under scrutiny during the 1988 presidential campaign, in which Bush sought to secure the Republican nomination and keep the Republican's White House winning streak alive. The Iran-Contra affair was a complex scheme involving secret arms sales to Iran, a nation that the United States had designated as a state sponsor of terrorism. Iran also had ties to terrorist groups holding Americans hostage in the Middle East, and the Reagan administration wanted to bring them home. The profits from the arms sales were then covertly sent to the Nicaraguan Contra rebels, who were seeking the overthrow of the pro-Soviet Sandinista regime of their country. Congress had previously outlawed Contra aid over the objections of the administration. Though Reagan's own involvement was limited at most, the more hands-on Bush was accused by Democrats of complicity with— or even masterminding—the entire Iran-Contra scheme. "Where was George?!" Democrats chanted from the floor of their 1988 party convention.

For the most part, Bush was successful at reassembling the electoral coalition that gave Reagan two landslide victories. He won 426 electoral votes, 40 states, and over 53% of the popular vote in the November 1980 election. Bush's opponent, Massachusetts governor Michael Dukakis, took 111 electoral votes, 10 states, and less than 46% of the popular vote. For several months in the campaign, Dukakis was leading in the polls, but the Bush campaign began a sharp counteroffensive in August, lambasting Dukakis as a stereotypical Massachusetts liberal who favored more taxes, more spending, weak national defense, and soft-on-crime policies. One television advertisement against Dukakis proved particularly effective, although it aroused critics of Bush to accuse him of using racist tactics. The ad used dramatic imagery of a black convicted criminal, Willie Horton, to assert that Dukakis was weak on crime. Long after the campaign, Bush's critics charged that his campaign had blatantly sought to tap into white suburban angst about crime by stoking racial anxieties.

THE BUSH PRESIDENCY

Upon becoming president, Bush faced a heavily Democratic Congress. This reality complicated his ability to maintain and expand the policies of the Reagan adminis-tration. He was elected as an heir apparent to Reagan, famously pledging to protect his predecessor's historic tax cuts from congressional Democrats seeking to close large budget deficits. "Read my lips! No new taxes!" Bush asserted at his convention nominating speech in August 1988. That campaign promise lasted about a year and a half, as Bush declared that he would sign off on tax revenue increases in what became the 1990 budget deal. The budget was approved in October 1990 with most congressional Republicans voting against the package. Representative Newt Gingrich (R-GA) began his national political rise by leading the Republican oppo-sition to the budget. Conservative Republicans were aghast, as their suspicions that Bush was never a committed believer in Reagan's economic policies seemed to be confirmed.

On many policy matters, Bush found success on Democratic terms. He won bipartisan support for a stronger Clear Air Act, immigration reform, more funding to fight AIDS, and the Americans with Disabilities Act. He vetoed a civil rights bill, but later signed a watered-down version of this legislation. One particularly politically damaging Bush veto was of a bill that called for unpaid leave for workers who experience family or medical emergencies. Democrats charged that this action contradicted the "family values" platform he embraced in his 1992 reelection campaign.

In foreign affairs, Bush found more success. Communist regimes in Eastern Europe and the Soviet Union disintegrated between 1989 and 1991, effectively ending the Cold War, and demanding that the administration carefully manage the transition. Bush faced criticism for not gloating and more openly celebrating the American triumph. Conservatives and even some Democrats chastised Bush for not using these events to claim vindication of American foreign policy. Spiking the football, however, was out of character for Bush. When China violently cracked down on pro-democracy demonstrators in June 1989, Bush was again criticized for a muted response. Indeed, Bush continued to pursue free trade policies with that country over the objections and criticisms of human rights activists and hard-line anticommunist Republicans.

THE 1992 PRESIDENTIAL CAMPAIGN

Bush enjoyed record high job approval ratings after a successful U.S.-led campaign to remove Iraqi forces from Kuwait in early 1991. The Persian Gulf War commanded widespread bipartisan support, and American casualties were low. Bush's popularity during and immediately after the war convinced a lot of leading Democrats to take a pass at running for president in 1992, as conventional wisdom appeared to suggest that the president would be a shoo-in for reelection. After the war, however, Bush was attacked across the political spectrum for not pursuing the overthrow of Iraqi leader Saddam Hussein and not responding to the dictator's violent reprisals on his own people. In addition, the American economy became sluggish through 1990 and 1991. But dramatic events overseas attracted far more of Bush's attention than domestic affairs—or at least that's what Bush's political opponents claimed. Indeed, Democrats began to attack Bush for lackadaisical leadership in domestic policy and traveling abroad too much. A popular T-shirt marketed by Democrats commemorated a "George Bush: The Anywhere but America" tour, which the president found especially aggravating. Arkansas governor Bill Clinton, the Democratic frontrunner for 1992, centered his campaign on Bush's allegedly poor handling of the economy.

First, however, Bush had to deal with an emerging threat on his right flank. Patrick J. Buchanan, a speechwriter, commentator, and staffer for presidents Nixon and Reagan, challenged Bush for the 1992 Republican nomination. Buchanan was a combative social conservative and isolationist who criticized Bush's economic policies with the same furor as the Democrats, albeit from a right-wing perspective. Lambasting Bush as "King George," he attacked the president for the tax increase, denounced the president's free trade policies, and accused the administration of allowing the National Endowment for the Arts to fund pornographic work. Although Buchanan did not win a single primary or caucus, he drew noticeable percentages of the vote in several states, and forced the sluggish Bush campaign to work harder on unifying the GOP party base and developing a coherent message for reelection.

After Buchanan had been vanquished, Bush faced another challenger for the general election in Texas billionaire H. Ross Perot. Running as a centrist reformer, the independent Perot campaign continued Buchanan's protectionist campaign against Bush and attacked Bush for high budget deficits. The Perot candidacy gave anti-Bush voters a sort of off-ramp if they felt unable to vote for Clinton, whose candidacy was ensnared in many personal scandals. Final election exit polls revealed, however, that Perot voters were evenly split between Bush and Clinton as a second choice. There is little evidence to substantiate the claim of many Bush supporters that Perot swung the election to Clinton. The final outcome was a stinging defeat for the incumbent president: 370 electoral votes, 32 states, and 43% of the popular vote for Clinton, while Bush took 168 electoral votes, 18 states, and over 37% of the popular vote. Perot took 19% of the popular vote but carried no states. Bush had been the first incumbent vice president to be elected to the presidency since Martin Van Buren 152 years earlier. Like Van Buren, Bush also met his same one-term fate.

LINES OF ATTACK AGAINST GEORGE BUSH

Throughout his political career, Bush endured numerous criticisms and lines of attack from opponents and enemies. Some were directed at his personal background and family, while others were more political in nature.

Although Bush had a long record of service and sacrifice, his patrician background became a target for critics. Future Texas governor Ann Richards mocked him from the podium of the 1988 Democratic National Convention, famously saying that, "he was born with a silver foot in his mouth." More seriously, as the nation descended into recession, Bush was accused of indifference and lacking empathy with financially struggling Americans. Bush regarded the recession as minor and cyclical and did not share the view that major corrective actions needed to be taken, though under political pressure he released a package of dormant economic proposals in early 1992. Other photo ops and public appearances only seemed to make matters worse. At a supermarket check stand, Bush appeared bewildered by an electronic scanner; during the 1991 Christmas shopping season Bush bought $28 worth of gifts as a way to express confidence in the economy;

when he finally began campaigning for reelection in New Hampshire his slogan was the bland "Message: I care."

Similarly, there is a long history of American distrust of secretive organizations of powerful people. Skull and Bones, a Yale University secret society, has been the subject of conspiracy theories for well over 100 years. Some of America's most elite families have Skull and Bones members. Prescott Bush, the elder George Bush, and his son George W., who would eventually become America's 43rd president, were all "Bonesmen." Bush rarely spoke of his membership in Skull and Bones, but many of his policy choices, as well as his background in the CIA, spawned conspiracy theories about his motives and his loyalties.

Bush and his eldest son, George W., also had roots in the Texas oil industry. The Persian Gulf War was politically popular in America, but there was still a domestic antiwar movement. Critics charged that Bush was pursuing a "blood for oil" policy to protect petroleum interests in Kuwait and Saudi Arabia. When antiwar hecklers shouted this line of criticism at him in a speech, Bush responded that the war was not about oil, but about stopping Saddam Hussein's "naked aggression." Bush did not always follow the oil industry's preferred policies, as he instituted a moratorium on offshore drilling for the West Coast.

Although Bush was known as a president who had in-depth knowledge of policy issues, the public aspects of his time in office often did not receive high marks. For example, while Reagan was a committed ideological conservative who had a clear sense of where he wanted to take the country, Bush was more of a pragmatist. He dismissed "the vision thing" as unimportant, but in 1992, Clinton and the Democrats criticized him for this as indicative of his lethargic leadership skills. In addition, Bush's proclamations of himself as the "education president" and the "environmental president" were ridiculed by Democrats as vapid and lacking in substance.

In addition, successive presidents faced accusations that they were not doing enough to account for American prisoners of war and missing in action personnel from the Vietnam War. While speaking before National League of Families of American Prisoners and Missing in Southeast Asia on July 24, 1992, Bush was heckled by POW-MIA families. After enduring their treatment for several minutes, Bush finally lost his cool and exclaimed, "Would you please shut up and sit down?" The episode came at a time when Bush was already enduring a losing reelection campaign.

Other lines of attack came from his time as Reagan's vice president. Bush was implicated in a conspiracy theory asserting that the 1980 Reagan-Bush campaign sought to delay Iran's release of American hostages in exchange for policy concessions from the new administration. Bush was accused of being a liaison to the Iranians in the scheme. A subsequent congressional investigation could not substantiate the allegations. Then, as president, Bush found himself in the thankless position of having to mop up the financial mess left over from the Reagan administration's disastrous deregulation of the savings and loan industry. Depositors had to be bailed out, and criminal investigations were conducted on many reckless leaders in the S&L industry. The bailout took several years and cost taxpayers hundreds of billions of dollars. New regulatory legislation had to be enacted. Several S&L chiefs were prosecuted and sent to jail. Bush's son Neil served on the board of directors of a failed institution called Silverado Savings and Loan. Government regulators criticized Neil Bush's actions but deemed them noncriminal. Nonetheless, Bush faced the inevitable accusations of favoritism.

For many years, Bush held a low opinion of his 1992 rival, Bill Clinton. Bush regarded him as dishonest and lacking in character. Yet, when agents of Saddam Hussein plotted an ultimately failed effort to assassinate Bush when he made a post-presidential visit to Kuwait (the plotters were caught before they could make an attempt on Bush's life), the Clinton administration retaliated with a cruise missile strike on Baghdad, Iraq, in June 1993. By the mid-2000s, when both Bush and Clinton were former presidents, the two became friends as they partnered to raise funds for the Indian Ocean tsunami relief in 2004, and then for Hurricane Katrina relief in 2005. The two men have reportedly remained close since then. News outlets reported that Bush cast his 2016 presidential ballot for Clinton's wife, Hillary; the Bush family neither confirmed nor denied the report.

THE BUSH DYNASTY

In 1994, two years after his father was defeated for reelection, George W. Bush was elected governor of Texas over incumbent Ann Richards, who had so famously mocked the elder Bush on prime-time television in 1988. Jeb Bush's 1994 campaign for governor of Florida fell short, but he was elected in 1998 and reelected in 2002. George P. Bush, who was Jeb's son and the elder Bush's grandson, was elected Texas land commissioner in 2014. George W. Bush enjoyed strong popularity during his governorship. After his landslide reelection as governor of Texas in 1998, George W. Bush began preparing for a presidential run in 2000. The elder Bush was vocal in his support for his son, both during the campaign and the bruising recount that followed. Democrats accused Governor Jeb Bush of covert meddling in the Florida recount to give his older brother an advantage. Jeb Bush mounted a presidential campaign that quickly fizzled out during the 2016 Republican primaries. Future president Donald Trump and other Republicans hinted that Bush was seeking to continue a Bush dynasty. Trump also mocked Jeb Bush as "low energy."

CONCLUSION

As heir apparent to the namesake of the Reagan Revolution, Bush was tasked with preserving, protecting, and defending his predecessor's achievements. At the same time, Bush had to rectify the unforeseen consequences of Reagan administration policies that were either no longer working or had become outdated due to changing circumstances. Boxed in by a Democratic Congress, Bush's ability to be a conservative revolutionary like Reagan was further limited. His penchant for moderation and compromise only served to anger conservative activists who became further convinced that Bush was not a believer in their causes. Democrats gave Bush little credit for the policy concessions that he made. By the 1990s and beyond, being an outsider was an advantage in American politics. As a consummate Washington insider, it would be impossible for Bush to co-opt the language of outsider candidates like Perot and Clinton. By the end of his presidency, he faced attacks from across the political spectrum that choked off just about any course of action he might have chosen. Although Bush got high marks from the American people when it came to personal character and integrity, Bush left the presidency as a man whose country had moved on without him.

Donald A. Zinman

Further Reading

Greene, John Robert. *The Presidency of George H. W. Bush*, 2nd ed., revised and expanded. Lawrence, KS: University Press of Kansas, 2015.

Han, Lori Cox. *A Presidency Upstaged: The Public Leadership of George H. W. Bush*. College Station, TX: Texas A&M University Press, 2011.

Kelley, Kitty. *The Family: The Real Story of the Bush Dynasty*. New York: Doubleday, 2004.

Meacham, Jon. *Destiny and Power: The American Odyssey of George Herbert Walker Bush*. New York: Random House, 2015.

Naftali, Timothy. *George H. W. Bush*. New York: Times Books, 2007.

Zinman, Donald. *The Heir Apparent Presidency*. Lawrence, KS: University Press of Kansas, 2016.

42. William J. Clinton

Born: August 19, 1946

Time in Office: 42nd President of the United States, January 20, 1993, to January 20, 2001

Election Results: 1992 Election: 43% of popular vote, 370 (68.8%) Electoral College votes; 1996 Election: 49.2% of popular vote, 379 (70.4%) Electoral College votes

Spouse: Hillary Rodham (m. 1975)

Children: Chelsea.

Surrounded by controversy for much of his political career, Bill Clinton was the 42nd president of the United States. Born William Jefferson Blythe on August 19,

1946, in Hope, Arkansas, he never knew his father, who died three months before Clinton's birth. Eventually adopting the last name of his stepfather Roger Clinton, an alcoholic and abusive husband who was also by all accounts an inadequate step-parent, Bill did not have a happy or stable childhood. Whatever stability the young Clinton had was thanks to his maternal grandparents, who cared for him during his mother's absences. An ambitious and extremely intelligent student, Clinton attended Hot Springs High School and worked as an intern for Arkansas senator William Fulbright. Upon graduation, he enrolled at Georgetown University to study international relations. After attending Oxford University on a Rhodes Scholarship, he entered Yale Law School and then obtained a teaching position at the University of Arkansas. During his studies at Yale he met Hillary Rodham, whom he married in 1975.

Armed with political aspirations from an early age, Clinton made an unsuccessful run for the Arkansas House of Representatives in 1974. Just two years later, he was elected Arkansas attorney general, which he followed with a successful bid for governor in 1978. Lacking experience and political discipline, he was not reelected in 1980. Two years later, however, he reclaimed the office. Reelected three times, Clinton honed his political skills and styled himself a "New" Democrat. His centrist, pragmatic approach to politics won him fans from both sides of the aisle but alienated others who criticized him as an opportunist. After declining to make a run for the White House in 1988, Clinton threw himself into the 1992 race. He only managed 43% of the popular vote, but it was enough to defeat the incumbent, Republican George H. W. Bush, and independent business executive Ross Perot. During his two terms in office (he cruised to reelection over Republican nominee Robert Dole in 1996) he presided over a booming economy and fulfilled a number of campaign promises. He also governed as a centrist and often worked with Republican lawmakers. Unfortunately, political controversies and personal scandals overshadowed his accomplishments, and the latter even led to his impeachment by the GOP-controlled House of Representatives in 1998. Nonetheless, Clinton left the White House with respectable approval ratings. Following his two terms in the White House, he devoted himself to the Clinton Foundation, an international nonprofit philanthropic organization. Ethical and legal problems dogged the foundation, but Clinton and his defenders asserted that these criticisms stemmed from long-standing political animosities. In addition, his wife's two failed presidential runs were immense disappointments to him.

A MATTER OF CHARACTER

Attacks against Clinton's character from political opponents emerged early, even before his years as Arkansas governor. By the time he assumed the presidency, Clinton had already attracted a long list of Republican enemies. Accompanied by a staff that had no shortage of confidence but lacked familiarity with Washington and knowledge of how to get things done, the president did nothing to hide his contempt for political insiders. He had been in the White House barely 18 months before his enemies were denouncing him as unfit for office. On some issues, such as the Religious Freedom Restoration Act, the North American Free Trade Agreement (NAFTA), and, later, welfare reform, Republicans set aside their growing dislike of the president long enough to work on issues that mattered to both sides. Clinton, though, held grudges against uncooperative Republicans and often undermined future collaboration as a result. At the same time, Republicans and their allies in conservative media found considerable political advantage in leveling accusations that Clinton was a dishonest and deeply flawed president.

Clinton's election coincided with the rise of an especially aggressive team of anti-Clintonites led by Republican House members Newt Gingrich and Dick Armey. Renouncing customary niceties, they were true enemies, openly displaying a lack of respect for the president and taking aim at his administration with a conservative policy agenda that they promised would more effectively address America's problems. Leveraging the hate and disgust that conservatives across the country felt toward Clinton, they got the chance to do just that when Gingrich, Armey, and other Republicans eager for confrontation took control of Congress during the 1994 election. They took the reins of Congress armed with the Contract with America, a conservative legislative agenda authored by Gingrich and Armey. It included demands for a balanced budget, tougher anticrime laws, welfare reform, tax credits, consolidation of U.S. international military power, reduction of capital-gains taxes, and other provisions intended to stymie Clinton administration proposals. This was a radical and ambitious experiment that ultimately failed to secure most of its objectives but nonetheless put Clinton on notice that his more progressive policies would continue to face stiff opposition.

For Republicans, the Contract with America and the defeat of the president's policy agenda were undeniable priorities, but proving him a liar became as much of a priority as any policy objective. For example, they seized on Clinton's grand-jury testimony about his affair with White House intern Monica Lewinsky. Asked by independent counsel Kenneth Starr whether he was having an affair with Lewinsky, the president responded that "it depends on what the meaning of 'is' is." Parsing his words and taking great care not to be unnecessarily specific or to volunteer facts not in evidence, Clinton acted with all the skill of a defense attorney, utilizing every rhetorical trick at his disposal to confuse or mislead Starr. Another example was his reply during the 1992 campaign to a question about using marijuana. Clinton asserted that although he had tried it once, he did not inhale. Republicans returned to such statements again and again to paint Bill Clinton as "Slick Willie"— essentially a silver-tongued con man.

Republicans reveled in publicly denouncing Clinton, which played well with constituents in rural, conservative states in the South and West where he was deeply unpopular. Conservative legislators gave the folks back home exactly what they wanted. Referring to Clinton's reputation for concealing the truth, Republican representative J. C. Watts of Oklahoma stated that Congress "must draw a line between right and wrong . . . with the big fat lead of a No. 2 pencil" so that "every kid in America can see it" and "truth can prevail." Republican senator Robert Dole from Kansas, sardonic as always, quipped during the 1996 presidential campaign, "if something happened along the route and you had to leave your children with Bob Dole or Bill Clinton, I think you would probably leave them with Bob Dole."

MEDIA ONSLAUGHT

As Republicans in Congress inflamed opposition to Clinton, the news media fueled the fire. The *Arkansas Democrat-Gazette*, which emerged as a vocal critic of Clinton during his years in Arkansas, printed stories of alleged infidelities, collusion with state troopers, and cover-ups of personal and political misbehavior. The newspaper's coverage eventually led Clinton to refer to it as his "chief tormentor." Prominent right-of-center newspapers such as the *Wall Street Journal* and conservative news magazines such as the *National Review* did their part, digging consistently to uncover the next scandal. Worryingly for Clinton, he was regularly targeted by mainstream news sources as well for alleged personal foibles and shortcomings. *New York Times* columnist Maureen Dowd, for example, was a constant irritant to both of the Clintons, dwelling at length on their missteps and personality flaws. Left-wing media outlets like *Mother Jones* candidly expressed their disappointment with the president whenever he failed to adhere to the progressivist cause. Liberal activists and organizations were not much different in that regard.

Traditional print media, though, were giving way to cable news during the Clinton years. The 24-hour news cycle, driving the emergence of cable-television news channels at the expense of the three broadcast television networks, stimulated competition and a hunger for scandal and sensation. Fox News, founded in 1996 by Clinton nemesis Rupert Murdoch, soared in popularity on programming that focused heavily on criticizing Clinton on both policy and personality grounds. It was a beacon of conservatism, offering a platform for some of Clinton's most ardent enemies and propelling personalities like Bill O'Reilly and Sean Hannity to stardom within a few years.

The media revolution also affected radio programming, turning commentators and talk-show hosts into celebrities. Rush Limbaugh was arguably the most famous personality in this new age of right-wing radio. His bull-in-the-china shop approach and excoriations of political corruption and political correctness resonated with blue-collar conservatives. He rose to fame bashing the Clintons for their supposed anti-Americanism and skewered them (and Democrats in general) on a daily basis.

Each in their own way, the news media, especially conservative outlets, ratcheted up the pressure on an administration that sputtered so much during its first months that Clinton looked doomed to be a one-term president. Clinton ultimately managed to improve his standing with the American public, largely due to perceptions that his administration deserved credit for a thriving U.S. economy, but the relentless barrage of questions, doubts, criticisms, and accusations leveled against him by his political and ideological foes necessitated almost constant damage control by the Clinton team. The effort to blunt criticism and minimize its impact sapped needed energy from the implementation of the administration's agenda.

THE BABY BOOMER

William F. Buckley, founder of the *National Review* and widely considered one of the greatest conservative minds of the 20th century, raised serious and disturbing questions about the baby-boom generation. He spoke for older Americans who felt their accomplishments were under siege by an irreverent group of leftist students and intellectuals. Buckley also authored some of the most eloquent and biting criticisms of the president, his administration, and what Buckley felt was the free-love, anti-American culture from which the Clintons emerged. Describing baby boomers as entitled, lazy, and disrespectful brats from privileged backgrounds, he held them responsible for fomenting what he described as gratuitous political chaos and senseless rioting during the 1960s and 1970s. These sentiments resonated with many Americans who had matured during the Great Depression and World War II. This "Greatest Generation," to use the term famously coined by journalist Tom Brokaw, embraced hard work, dedication to family, sacrifice, and public service. Though it may sound naïve to those who came of age decades after the war, they promoted peace, the spread of democratic governance, and American political, diplomatic, and military leadership.

News of Clinton's efforts to evade the Vietnam draft and his subsequent participation in antiwar demonstrations did not help his standing among veterans and conservatives. They viewed these elements of Clinton's past as further proof of his disrespect for the military and soldiers who fought and died defending their country. As a result, Clinton never gained the complete trust or respect of the military's top brass and much of the rank-and-file. Conservative commentators pounded the draft issue and questioned Clinton's qualifications as commander in chief and his dedication to defending America's national interests.

THE LIMITATIONS OF CLINTON HATING

Clinton's ultramarital sexual liaisons and reputation for dissembling and half-truths cost him on both a personal and political level. Efforts by Republicans to discredit the president and undermine his agenda were frequently effective. But, despite the endless scandals, personal transgressions, and some notorious policy failures, staffers and Democratic constituents—and the majority of American voters—were willing to look past the problems.

Much to the frustration and confusion of Clinton's Republican enemies, he had an uncanny ability to beat the odds, often enjoying high approval ratings during the most trying times. Clinton supporters and friends, though frequently turned off in the short term, ultimately did not waver in their support. His conservative adversaries never quite understood Clinton's resilience and ability to energize voters, and they failed to appreciate that many Americans placed greater importance on Clinton's economic and social policies than on any personal shortcomings. And, when he left office, even a good number of those who had been hurt by him recalled the former president fondly and remained impressed by his political skill. But, no matter how appealing he may have been to his Democratic followers, conservatives did not let go of the issues they believed would bring him down. Democrats may have forgiven the president, but Republicans never forgave or forgot.

ATTACKS ON THE FIRST LADY

The first lady was a lightning rod for anti-Clinton criticism throughout Bill Clinton's two terms in the White House. Though described by many as brilliant and more intellectually disciplined than her husband, Hillary Clinton was not always likable or ingratiating. Those close to her husband complained that she was abrasive, intolerant, and even more arrogant and condescending than her political enemies. Like her husband, she was also paranoid and unusually thin-skinned, which made for an awkward dynamic in the White House. However, while her husband could turn on a natural charm and charisma that stirred affection among those around him, the first lady had no such skills and never felt the need to cultivate a softer and more sympathetic image. Even some of the president's most vehement opponents could not help but be impressed by his ability to work a crowd to his advantage.

Chicago-born Hillary Rodham earned a political science degree from Wellesley College, an institution framed by some conservatives as a kind of finishing school for privileged feminists. She then enrolled in Yale Law School, where she met fellow classmate and future husband Bill Clinton. In 1974, she moved to Arkansas to help him with his congressional campaign, but she quickly attracted fire from her husband's political foes. They accused her of being a condescending and intolerant outsider who did not understand or respect Arkansans or their lifestyle. Despite these relentless criticisms, however, Clinton was gradually able to enhance her appeal among the state's residents to the point that some observers even came to see her as an asset to her husband's political career.

Despite his extramarital affairs and the marital problems that ensued as a result, Bill Clinton was his wife's biggest fan and most ardent defender. He trusted her completely and valued her input tremendously, relying on her advice and counsel before all others. Consequently, she wielded considerable power and influence as both adviser and first lady. Some critics, however, have suggested that the first lady's position of influence during Bill Clinton's two terms in office was partial compensation for his betrayals and indiscretions. Others even insinuated that Hillary Clinton's prominence stemmed from the leverage she had over her husband, that is, she knew "where the bodies were buried."

According to many Republican and/or conservative narratives of Bill Clinton's political ascendancy, Hillary played a pivotal role in shaping his winning presidential campaign in 1992. They claim that she personally banished most of the advisers from his Arkansas days—despite her husband's objections—and helped organize a campaign team of eager and comparatively young and motivated staffers. Most of them had no past connection to Clinton but were united by an abiding desire to promote a passionate man who promised nothing less than to transform American politics. His zeal was infectious and his agenda to improve the lot of the poor, blue-collar workers, and the middle class, while encouraging markets and economic expansion, was formidable.

Republicans recognized Clinton's political gifts but saw his wife as a potential weak link. They established a drumbeat of criticism against her, charging that she was not liked but feared by everyone in the Clintons' orbit and that she continually interfered in affairs that should not have been her business in the first place.

Bill Clinton's promise during the campaign that Americans were getting "two for the price of one"—a suggestion that his spouse would have an expansive role in the White House and his administration—also proved controversial. Most feminists were thrilled at the prospect of having an active—and activist—first lady, but the issue divided women in a way neither of the Clintons had foreseen. Despite large numbers of women who hailed Hillary Clinton's ascent and looked on her as a role model, others with more conservative and "traditional" social views viewed her as an opportunist who prostituted herself to a serial adulterer simply to gain power and political clout. They perceived her rise as a setback for women because it perpetuated harmful stereotypes and validated the notion that women could get ahead only by hitching their wagons to a man.

One interview early in the 1992 campaign was particularly problematic for Hillary Clinton and her image with homemakers and full-time moms. Confronting allegations that her husband had engaged in an affair with a woman named Gennifer

Flowers, Clinton declared that "I'm not sitting here, some little woman standing by my man like Tammy Wynette." Conservatives seized on these words to frame her as an arrogant and condescending woman who did not deserve to be first lady. Clinton refused to back down, however, adding on another occasion, "I suppose I could have stayed home, baked cookies, and had teas" instead of pursuing a career and fighting alongside her husband.

President Clinton's enemies also found traction with arguments that his decision to select his wife to spearhead an ambitious health care reform effort was nepotism pure and simple. Giving the first lady so much power and latitude was not a smart move, because it simply encouraged adversaries that had already caused the future president enough harm. Armies of Hillary haters across the country expressed fears that the first lady would have unrestricted discretion to do things official aids and advisers could not by evading institutional rules and political norms, and maybe even constitutional restrictions. More than anything else, they were livid at the thought that an unelected presidential spouse would wield so much influence over the nation's health care system. For them, "two for the price of one" was a nightmare, and they were determined to undermine the first lady's power and influence in the White House.

HILLARYCARE

Bill Clinton thought that health care reform would be his crowning achievement. In 1992, candidate Clinton spoke passionately and poignantly about the more than 20 million Americans without health insurance and the additional 30 million or so who were underinsured, promising to address what was perhaps the most urgent and significant domestic-policy issue in a generation. He had not been in office even a week when he announced the creation of the Task Force on National Health Care Reform. It was launched by the president with enthusiasm and fanfare, initially attracting the support of working-class and poor Americans across the country.

He appointed the first lady to head the task force and then tapped Ira Magaziner, a management consultant with no background inside the beltway, as its director. With all the opposition to the president's "two for the price of one" pledge, Washington's resistance to the first lady's involvement, let alone her role as the point person on the task force, was swift and considerable. Republicans, rife with anti-Hillary sentiment, viewed Magaziner's appointment as a transparent and misleading effort to blunt anti-Hillary skepticism by making it appear that Magaziner was her superior. Within a day of Clinton's announcement, an ABC News poll indicated that almost half of all Americans were against the first lady's appointment and were concerned about her relative lack of experience with health care. A *Boston Globe* editorial complained that the first lady and Magaziner "elbowed aside some of the most experienced economists in the world" to reform the "health-care system by themselves."

Clinton recruited a group of industry experts who were intimately familiar with the technical aspects of the health care industry but according to Republican critics knew next to nothing about translating their ideas and calculations into legislation. Conservatives on Capitol Hill and on the nation's airwaves insisted that these steps showed that she was intent on micromanaging the entire task force. They also charged that she made matters worse by keeping the task force's work secret, excluding Congress, most of the White House staff, relevant cabinet departments, and health care executives from the proceedings and inquiries. The final product was dense and difficult to understand, coming in at almost 1,400 pages. The sheer size of the act alone made it ripe for mockery from Republicans and media and industry allies who attacked it as a classic example of "big government" overreach. The Clinton health care plan encountered strong opposition immediately upon its release, galvanizing Republicans and health care industry executives into action against it. Predictably, Republicans charged that the legislation ceded too much power to the government over a vital sector of the economy. They labeled the plan a socialist scam. Libertarians, like conservatives, were turned off by the amount of power and influence the federal government would have over the health care industry and the market instability this could cause, to say nothing of the fiscal deficits it could generate. Democrats and many health care activists, by contrast, were strongly supportive of the Health Security Act through the summer and early fall of 1993. They argued that the legislation reflected a concern with making health care both better and more affordable, that its size was inevitable given the complexity of health care, and that the task force had been wise to sidestep Congress because politicians had been unable to craft meaningful health care reforms for decades. Democratic lawmakers began backing away from the legislation in early 1994, however, after Clinton's approval ratings sagged in response to a flurry of political setbacks and controversies, including exhausting budget battles with the GOP and an ill-fated U.S. military incursion in Somalia, among others.

The health care bill was officially killed by Senate Majority Leader George Mitchell in September 1994, when he pulled the legislation from the chamber's schedule.

A STAR-STRUCK PRESIDENT

Another angle of attack that Republicans pursued against Bill Clinton was to accuse him of being excessively cozy with Hollywood's biggest stars and studio bigwigs. He often invited them to the White House, especially those who had donated large sums to Democratic campaigns. They stayed in the Lincoln Bedroom, a guest suite in the residential wing of the White House that American presidents had used as an office from 1825 to 1945. Republican critics cried foul, accusing the president and first lady of selling access to one of the most revered and sacred spaces in Washington so they could channel money to Democratic political action committees. In all, over 800 people, from actors, directors, and producers to CEOs, investment bankers, and media moguls spent nights in the Lincoln Bedroom. Producer Steven Spielberg gave more than $300,000 for the privilege, while Hollywood titan Lew Wasserman gave in excess of $200,000 for his visits. Republican critics also asserted that Marc Rich, an international financier convicted of tax evasion and tax fraud, in effect bought his presidential pardon with a large contribution to the Clinton Library in Little Rock, Arkansas.

Conservatives pounced on and fed perceptions that Clinton was a star-struck president with a revolving door policy for Hollywood's rich and famous. Eventually, Clinton's friends and staffers, reacting to Republican attacks, advised him that his coziness with Hollywood was an additional liability he did not need. Clinton, however, continued to maintain relationships with many show business figures and personalities.

Despite his apparent obsession with Hollywood, Clinton did not treat all of its denizens equally. Some paid a hefty price for their allegiance to him and the first lady. Producers Harry Thomason and spouse Linda Bloodworth-Thomason, who had been Clinton's public relations gurus since his Arkansas days, were part of this group. Despite wide-ranging access to the president and his staff, they did not enjoy his undivided respect or attention. The president leaned on the Thomasons only as needed, embracing them now, ignoring them later. When prevailing winds blew the wrong way, the Thomasons faced media scrutiny and accusations for things the president had done. They were held responsible for the president's unnaturally close relationship with Hollywood and accused, for instance, of arranging the president's haircut aboard Air Force One by Hollywood stylist Christophe as the presidential plane held up traffic at Los Angeles International Airport.

THE CLINTONS AND THE MEDIA

The first couple reserved some of their most pointed scorn for the news media. Blaming newspapers and television outlets for hounding him mercilessly and diminishing his achievements, Clinton lamented that the media "scandal machine had taken a lot of joy out of being president," according to Taylor Branch in the *Clinton Tapes*. In a 1998 *Today Show* interview, the first lady blamed the media and Republican lawmakers for pursuing her husband with unsubstantiated rumors and allegations. She decried the existence of a "vast right-wing conspiracy" whose purpose was to discredit the president and undermine his policy agenda and charged that CNN, the *Washington Post*, the *New York Times*, and other mainstream media outlets were being manipulated by Clinton's political opponents. In a *Huffington Post* article written a few years after Clinton's departure from the White House, Marcus Baram wrote that Clinton had "accus[ed] CNN of succumbing to scandal fever" and becoming a "convergence of cash-paying tabloids and mainstream outlets," which undermined its professionalism and reputation. The Clintons claimed that the network had a vendetta against them because the future first lady had moved her 1992 Gennifer Flowers interview from CNN to CBS. As previously indicated, it did not take long for Maureen Dowd of the *New York Times* to become a Clinton enemy due to her unflattering columns about Clinton and his wife. President Clinton told Branch that Dowd "must live in mortal fear that there's somebody in the world living a healthy and productive life." The *Washington Post* drew the Clintons' fury over Bob Woodward's account of possible Clinton campaign ties to secret donors in the Chinese government. *Rolling Stone*, too, became a Clinton enemy. Its offense, according to Baram, was an apparently innocuous question about the "economic impact of NAFTA on America's working class." Incensed, Clinton let loose on William Greider, the author of the *Rolling Stone* article, accusing him of being a "faulty citizen," who "only worr[ied] about being doctrinaire and proud." Paradoxically for a Democratic president, he called Greider a "bitchy and cynical liberal."

CLINTON AND GORE

Al Gore, Clinton's vice president and the Democratic nominee in the 2000 election, did not have an especially close friendship, but their relationship was originally based on trust and a certain degree of admiration. Gore did not delude himself about the reasons Clinton selected him as his running mate in 1992. Like most such decisions, it was a function of pure political calculus. Some political observers have speculated that the Clintons never considered Gore their intellectual equal. Even if true, however, Clinton relied extensively on Gore and delegated considerable responsibility to him. These responsibilities ranged from policy areas that Clinton regarded as uninteresting and low profile or those areas, such as environmental policy and bureaucratic reform, that Gore himself viewed as falling within his expertise. Above all, Gore was loyal and dedicated, suppressing his anger and disappointment over the president's personal scandals and standing by his boss through thick and thin, despite media charges of guilt by association. During Gore's 2000 presidential campaign, Clinton was initially supportive, offering his help in any way Gore deemed necessary and most useful. But when the Gore campaign took steps to distance their candidate from the scandal-tainted Clinton, the relationship between the two men cooled considerably.

TOO MANY SCANDALS

During the more than 20 years Bill Clinton spent in public office, scandals would come and go, but allegations of marital infidelities did not subside. "Bimbo eruptions," a term coined by long-time Clinton friend and political adviser Betsey Wright, colored both his gubernatorial and presidential legacies. Some observers believe that Clinton never quite understood the media's fascination or his enemies' obsession with what he thought was a private matter. He was convinced that, if he could just get them to listen, his ideas would win them over. Republicans were in no mood to listen to a scandal-ridden president. Clinton grew increasingly frustrated and angry over his opponents' concerns with extramarital dalliances. On more than one occasion, he demanded that Republicans focus on his policy proposals instead of malicious rumormongering. However, Clinton made it easy for his Republican enemies.

The first major flare-up over Clinton's alleged infidelities occurred in January 1992, just as the Democratic presidential primaries were getting underway. At that time a woman named Gennifer Flowers revealed an alleged 12-year affair with then Governor Clinton. Clinton's enemies and the news media picked up the story and ran with it, in the process almost derailing the candidate's presidential hopes. Setting a pattern for future damage-control efforts, the Clintons responded with a full-court press of denial and character assassination against Flowers. On the other hand, conservatives, realizing they had an issue that could fatally damage Clinton's candidacy, assumed full attack mode. However, despite the questions raised by his opponents concerning dishonesty and marital infidelity, Clinton survived the allegations, appearing none the worse for wear to both supporters and his frustrated enemies.

Although the Flowers affair did not, in the end, derail Clinton's presidential aspirations, doubts about his character and philandering would persist among his enemies and eventually boil over. Over the years, as increasing numbers of women came forward with accusations against Clinton of affairs, inappropriate behavior, and even sexual assault, Republicans assailed the president again and again early on, Clinton withstood these accusations without too much political fallout. As his presidency unfolded, however, the barrage of allegations and accusations from reputed victims took a cumulative toll. Dolly Kyle Browning, Elizabeth Ward Green, and Myra Belle Miller all pointed to affairs with then Governor Clinton. Juanita Broadrrick even accused the president of raping her in 1978. White House aide Kathleen Willey stated that the president had groped her in 1993.

Without a doubt, the two most prominent sex scandals concerned Paula Jones and Monica Lewinsky. Paula Jones was a public employee in Arkansas who claimed that, in 1991, then-Governor Clinton invited her to his hotel room and subsequently exposed himself and propositioned her. In a 1994 article in the *American Spectator*, David

Brock revealed details of the incident, causing Jones to go public with her account. She filed a sexual harassment suit against the president just a few days after the story broke. Her attorney aired Jones's allegations on more than a dozen talk shows, slamming Clinton as a liar and philanderer and claiming that she "does not respect a man who cheats on his wife, and exposes his" genitals to someone he does not know.

This was catnip to the president's Republican enemies. Here was proof, they believed, of his deficient character, disrespect for women, and disregard for the law. Like Jones's attorney, they made their rounds on various news programs, taking the president to task and even calling for his resignation. Despite what the president's critics described as damning evidence, however, feminists again stood by Clinton. Meanwhile, Clinton and his attorneys denied the charges and launched an unrelenting attack against Jones to undermine her story and show her to be depraved and a liar. Much to the chagrin of the Clinton team, the Supreme Court validated the opposing attorney's action to permit a civil lawsuit against a sitting president to proceed. After a blizzard of disclosures, depositions, motions, and countermotions, Clinton ultimately settled with Jones, paying her $850,000 in damages but not admitting any guilt in the matter.

The import of the Jones case was its connection to Lewinsky and, in turn, the president's impeachment in late December 1998. Lewinsky, originally an unpaid intern in Chief of Staff Leon Panetta's office but later a paid employee in the Pentagon, began an affair with Clinton in 1995. Almost 30 years his junior, Lewinsky saw Clinton on and off for about two-and-a-half years, during which they had sexual relations in the Oval Office. In January 1998, the *Drudge Report* revealed news of the affair. A few days later, the *Washington Post* issued an expose of the president's affair with Lewinsky. Dozens of stories from numerous sources followed. Clinton offered an emphatic denial of the affair, declaring that "I did not have sexual relations with that woman, Miss Lewinsky." He continued to lie about the affair until news of Lewinsky's testimony to Starr surfaced in August 1998. He was forced to confirm the affair and admit he had been lying about it.

Clinton, however, had previously testified in a deposition for the Jones suit and a grand jury convened by Starr that he had not engaged in sexual relations with Lewinsky. As a result of Lewinsky's testimony and Clinton's admission in August, Starr recommended that perjury and obstruction of justice charges be filed against the president by the House Judiciary Committee. Questions also arose about the extent of Clinton's involvement in a possible cover-up, as Starr was privy to information that the president may have exerted undo pressure on Lewinsky to hide details of their relationship from prosecutors and Jones's attorneys. Also, Clinton associates suggested that he had asked Vernon Jordan, a Democratic kingmaker of sorts inside the beltway, to secure employment for Lewinsky somewhere in Washington in exchange for Lewinsky's silence. These allegations were never proven or included as part of the impeachment indictment.

THE WHITEWATER SCANDAL

The most lethal political scandal not related to marital infidelity to cast a cloud over the Clinton White House was one the Clintons imported to Washington from Arkansas. It was known as Whitewater, which referred to the Whitewater Development Corp., a failed real-estate investment venture that the Clintons had undertaken with Arkansas friends James and Susan McDougal. The McDougals funneled money they borrowed from the Small Business Administration to Madison Guaranty Savings and Loan, which they owned, through Whitewater. As federal investigators closed in, Hillary Clinton took James McDougal as a client to defend him against various fraud charges. McDougal also involved former Arkansas judge David Hale and Governor Jim Guy Tucker in a scheme to move funds through dummy corporations and mislead the government. The McDougals, Hale, and Tucker were all eventually convicted of federal crimes, but the Clintons were untouched.

Early in Clinton's first term as president, as news of Whitewater surfaced, Republicans demanded the appointment of a special prosecutor to investigate the Clintons and determine their role in the venture. The Clintons' enemies were convinced that they had gotten away with fraud and embezzlement—and that if such charges were proven they could force the impeachment or even the resignation of the president. Attorney General Janet Reno, after appointing a special prosecutor, asked a three-judge panel created under an independent-counsel law to replace him with Kenneth Starr, who was given wide-ranging authority to conduct his investigation. Within a few years, Starr was also granted authority to look into the Jones matter, and, through it, the Lewinsky affair. After discovering that the president had lied under oath about his affair with Lewinsky and tried to mislead prosecutors and congressional investigators, Starr recommended that perjury and obstruction of justice charges, among others, be filed against Clinton.

Democrats harshly criticized Starr as a political partisan who was conducting a fishing expedition to bring down Clinton. They characterized the charges preferred by the House as flimsy and unsubstantiated and accused Starr of having a vendetta against the Clintons. Alarmed by an investigation that cost almost $80 million and lasted over four years, Democrats dismissed what they believed was a Republican conspiracy. Not unexpectedly, the Clinton White House also framed the Starr investigation as a partisan witch hunt. Armed with the results of Starr's investigation, the GOP-controlled House of Representatives made Clinton the second president in U.S. history to be impeached. The Republican-led Senate, however, acquitted Clinton of both perjury and obstruction of justice charges. A two-thirds majority (67 votes) were required for conviction, and neither charge received a majority of votes. All 45 Democratic Senators voted "not guilty" on both charges, and they were joined by five Republicans on the obstruction charge and ten Republicans on the perjury charge.

CONCLUSION

With unmatched intelligence, an enviable command of facts and issues, and plenty of down-home charisma, Clinton connected with voters in a way few had before him. Unfortunately, his deficiencies were just as prominent and conspicuous, clouding his achievements and compromising his political career. Seemingly endless personal and political scandals sapped energy and momentum from an administration with an ambitious agenda.

Tomislav Han

Further Reading

Branch, Taylor. *The Clinton Tapes: Conversations with a President, 1993–2001*. New York: Simon and Schuster, 2010.

Campbell, Colin, and Bert A. Rockman, eds. *The Clinton Legacy*. New York: Chatham House, 2000.

Denton, Robert E., Jr., and Rachel L. Holloway, eds. *Images, Scandal, and Communication Strategies of the Clinton Presidency*. New York: Praeger, 2003.

Isikoff, Michael. *Uncovering Clinton: A Reporter's Story*. New York: Crown, 1999.

Klein, Joe. *The Natural: The Misunderstood Presidency of Bill Clinton*. New York: Doubleday, 2002.

Rozell, Mark J., and Clyde Wilcox, eds. *The Clinton Scandal and the Future of American Government*. Washington, D.C.: Georgetown University Press, 2000.

Stewart, James B. *Blood Sport: The Truth behind the Scandals in the Clinton White House*. New York: Simon and Schuster, 2012.

Toobin, Jeffrey. *A Vast Conspiracy: The Real Story of the Sex Scandal That Nearly Brought Down a President*. New York: Touchstone, 2000.

Woodward, Bob. *The Agenda: Inside the Clinton White House*. New York: Simon and Schuster, 1994.

43. George W. Bush

Born: July 6, 1946

Time in Office: 43rd President of the United States, January 20, 2001, to January 20, 2009

Election Results: 2000 Election: 47.9% of popular vote, 271 (50.4%) Electoral College votes; 2004 Election: 50.7% of popular vote, 286 (53.2%) Electoral College votes

Spouse: Laura Welch (m. 1977)

Children: Barbara and Jenna

George W. Bush was born July 6, 1946, and served as the 43rd president from January 20, 2001, to January 20, 2009. Born in New Haven, Connecticut, Bush spent most of his childhood in Texas. He is the oldest child of George Herbert Walker Bush, the 41st president of the United States, and Barbara Bush. Bush is the second presidential son to follow his father into the White House (the first being John Quincy Adams, the sixth president, son of John Adams, the second president). The Bush family, with roots that trace back to the American colonial era, includes other prominent politicians as well. Bush's grandfather, Prescott Bush, served as a U.S. senator from Connecticut (1952–1963), and his brother, John Ellis "Jeb" Bush, served two terms as governor of Florida (1999–2007). Bush earned a bachelor's degree from Yale University, where he was also a member of the secret society known as "Skull and Bones." He would later earn an MBA from Harvard University. He first entered politics in 1978 in an unsuccessful bid for a congressional seat in Texas. He would go on to be a part owner of the Texas Rangers baseball team, and was elected governor of Texas, defeating incumbent Democrat Ann Richards in 1994. He won reelection to that office in 1998 with a record-breaking 69% of the vote, and resigned the office upon his election as president.

Bush's election in 2000 had a relatively low 51% turnout and was one of the most controversial elections in history. Even though Bush lost the popular vote to Democratic nominee Albert Gore by just over 500,000 votes (Bush received 47.9% compared to Gore's 48.5%), Bush won the Electoral College with 271 electoral votes to Gore's 266 (one of the electors from the District of Columbia did not cast a vote as a protest). Bush won 30 states while Gore carried 20 in addition to the District of Columbia. In the 2004 presidential election, turnout increased to nearly 57%, and Bush earned 286 electoral votes to Democratic nominee John Kerry's 251. Bush also increased his share of the popular vote to 50.7%, while Kerry earned 48.3%, though the 2004 election outcome was still considered close.

Bush married Laura Welch on November 5, 1977; she accepted his marriage proposal after a brief three-month courtship. Bush credits his wife with bringing stability to his personal life; numerous reports have chronicled issues with alcohol in his earlier adult life, including a drunk driving arrest in Maine in 1976. Bush has stated publicly that he stopped drinking the day after his 40th birthday in 1986, and has abstained from alcohol ever since. Bush also left the Episcopal Church to join the United Methodist Church with his wife. They have twin daughters, Barbara Bush and Jenna Bush Hager. Jenna is married to Henry Hager. The Hagers have given Bush two granddaughters, Margaret Laura Hager and Poppy Louise Hager. Since leaving the White House, Bush has maintained a fairly low public profile for a former president. His presidential library is located on the Southern Methodist University campus in Dallas, Texas. He published his memoirs, *Decision Points*, in 2010, and he also took up painting as a hobby.

ELECTION LEGITIMACY

A major line of attack throughout Bush's administration was that his elections were so close and controversial. The 2000 election was considered controversial because it was the first time since 1888 (when incumbent Grover Cleveland won the popular vote, but lost in the Electoral College 233–168 to Benjamin Harrison) that the winner of the popular vote lost the Electoral College vote. It was made more controversial due to what happened in Florida, where his brother, Jeb, was governor. On election eve all major television networks called the state of Florida for Gore based on early exit polling from the Voter News Service. However, the turnout in the panhandle portion of the state, which is in a later time zone, was smaller than expected, which skewed the exit polling results. Later in the evening, the networks called the state for Bush, which presumably gave him the presidency. However, the networks would later reverse that decision and return Florida to the category "too close to call," leaving the election result undecided and the nation in a state of intense political anxiety.

According to the initial tally, Bush won Florida by a mere 537 votes (the closest state result in any presidential campaign), which required a mandatory recount. This resulted in an examination of Florida's election practices that revealed a number of controversial issues. Among these was Palm Beach County's use of the so-called "butterfly ballot," on which the presentation of presidential candidates was confusing; it is assumed that thousands of voters who thought they were voting for Gore instead voted for Reform Party candidate Patrick J. Buchanan. There were also issues raised about the governing practices of counting overseas ballots. The mandatory statewide recount ended in the same result, giving Bush the electoral votes of Florida (the 25 electoral votes gave Bush a total of 271, just barely a simple majority). Following the result of the mandatory recount, Gore requested a manual recount in Miami-Dade, Broward, Palm Beach, and Volusia counties because state law allowed candidates to challenge at least three precincts. Some of these counties began and news throughout the nation focused on the recount in Florida with images of poll workers examining punch card ballots to see the intent of the voter; "hanging," "dimpled," and "pregnant" chads were a frequent topic of news coverage during this time, and Florida's secretary of state Katherine Harris became a household name. Litigation also began with Bush working to halt the manual recount in those counties. This culminated in the Supreme Court case *Bush v. Gore* (2000), in which the Court handed down its decision on December 12, 2000, stating that the recount in Florida should end and that the previous vote certification should stand. In addition, the Court ruled that the method approved by the Florida Supreme Court for recounting ballots was unconstitutional in that the different standards violated the equal protection clause. Thus, Bush won the state of Florida, and ultimately, the presidency, with Gore conceding defeat on December 13, 2000.

Whether or not the Supreme Court should have accepted the case on appeal from the Florida State Supreme Court remains controversial. The decision was also controversial, in part, because the justices in both the majority and the minority relied on unprecedented constitutional arguments mostly out of line with their own judicial philosophies. The more conservative justices in the majority had argued against states' rights to end the recount, which gave Bush the victory, while the more liberal justices in the minority had argued on behalf of states' rights to have Florida continue the recount.

The 2004 election was also close, although the focus of Bush's second election shifted to Ohio. In January 2005, U.S. senator Barbara Boxer (D-CA) and House Representative Stephanie Tubbs Jones (D-OH) filed a congressional objection to the certification of Ohio's Electoral College votes. There were issues with voting machines throughout Ohio. The Senate voted it down 74 to 1, and the House voted it down 267 to 31. This was the second time in history when there was a congressional objection to a state's certification of an Electoral College vote. Afterward, a number of books were published questioning whether Bush actually won the 2004 election. House Speaker Dennis Hastert (R-IL) said at the time that only the "loony left" would think he had not. These questions of legitimacy would hound Bush throughout his presidency.

WAR ON TERROR

Perhaps the most defining feature of the Bush administration was the nation's response to September 11, 2001, and the subsequent War on Terror. This resulted in a record high approval rating for the president in the immediate aftermath, but then followed by many lines of attack directed at his response to terrorism. In August 2006, *The Economist* referred to the totality of the Bush administration response as "a litany of abuse." Generally, the president's response to any lines of criticism about the War on Terror and subsequent wars in Iraq and Afghanistan was to suggest people were "emboldened only by hindsight."

Documentary filmmaker Michael Moore was a prominent critic of Bush and his decisions regarding the War on Terror. Moore produced a documentary, *Farenheit 9/11*, presenting Bush as a "lazy, duplicitous leader, blinded by his family's financial ties to Arab moneymen and the Saudi Arabian royal family." In the film, he depicts Bush's calm demeanor, which Moore frames as an inappropriate response, in the minutes after being told that planes have crashed into the World Trade Center. The 2004 film also includes a later encounter between Bush and Moore in which Bush told the filmmaker, "behave yourself, will ya? Go find real work." Disney ordered Miramax to not release the film because "it would harm the company's negotiations for favorable treatment for its Florida theme parks from that state's governor," which at the time was Bush's brother, Jeb (though it was still released). Political action committee Citizens United filed a complaint about the movie, stating that ads for the film constituted political advertising and could not be aired 60 days before an election or 30 days before a party convention, though the Federal Election Commission unanimously dismissed the claim. Years later, in 2016, the Bush Presidential Library released photographs of Bush from September 11 to counter Moore's claims that the president's response was lacking when he first learned of the terrorist attacks.

Bush took significant criticism for his administration's "enhanced interrogation techniques" that were used to get information from terrorism suspects. Although Bush said, "this government does not torture people," the enhanced techniques that his administration sanctioned included sleep deprivation, slapping, subjection to cold, subjection to waterboarding (which is simulated drowning that can result in brain damage), broken bones, and psychological damage. These techniques were used at extraordinary rendition sites around the world. The U.S. Senate Intelligence Committee concluded that use of the techniques "was not an effective means of acquiring intelligence or gaining cooperation from detainees." In 2008, Congress passed the Intelligence Authorization Act that banned the use of the techniques. Bush vetoed this act. Senator John McCain (R-AZ), a decorated Vietnam veteran who had spent years in captivity as a prisoner or war, said the techniques were torture. There was also some question of when people knew, and what they knew, about the techniques. Bush claimed that he had spoken with Central Intelligence Agency director George Tenet about the techniques as early as 2002, but the CIA had no evidence of a conversation until 2006. In a March 2008 radio address, Bush claimed that "the CIA program had a proven track record and that the CIA obtained critical intelligence as a result of the CIA's enhanced interrogation techniques." Vice President Dick Cheney responded to the Senate report saying that he would "do it again in a minute" and Attorney General Michael Mukasey said that the Senate report selectively chose evidence to "demoralize the CIA." When Barack Obama became president in 2009, he halted the enhanced interrogation techniques, saying that the measures "amounted to torture" and that he believed "waterboarding was torture and, whatever legal rationales were used, it was a mistake."

Additionally, Bush was criticized for his language about the War on Terror on several occasions. For example, in his 2002 State of the Union address, Bush used the term "axis of evil" to describe Iran, Iraq, and North Korea—three nations he said were sponsoring terrorism and seeking weapons of mass destruction: "States like these and their terrorist allies constitute an axis of evil, arming to threaten the peace of the world." Critics responded that grouping the three nations together oversimplified the unique danger that each nation posed to world peace. Another example came during a May 19, 2006, press conference, when Bush was asked about progress in the War on Terror. He replied, "the conditions are such that they can attack us there, my answer is: bring 'em on." He took a significant amount of heat and a week later in a joint news conference with British prime minister Tony Blair, Bush said he regretted his choice of language.

2004 CONTROVERSY OVER MILITARY SERVICE

The military record of Bush, which had been a minor issue of controversy during the 2000 presidential election, became newly relevant during the 2004 presidential campaign. When Kerry, a highly decorated Vietnam War veteran, decided to run on the campaign slogan that he was ready to serve, he was targeted by conservative supporters of Bush and the Republican Party in general for his record of service in Vietnam. The 527 group (which is a tax-exempt political organization) Swift Boat Veterans for Truth launched an ad attacking Kerry's service in Vietnam, particularly his involvement in the anti–Vietnam War efforts upon his return to the United States, calling Kerry's criticisms of the war a "betrayal of trust." This led to counterattacks from Kerry supporters against Bush for his lack of military service in Vietnam. Bush had volunteered to serve in the Texas Air National Guard in 1968. Once Vietnam was introduced into the campaign, another story from Bush's past rose to the surface. On September 8, 2004, *CBS Evening News* anchor Dan Rather reported that he had a source from the Texas House of Representatives, Ben Barnes, who claimed he helped Bush avoid the draft in 1968. Barnes was a Democrat who was working for the Kerry campaign. Then, the CBS news program *60 Minutes* found documents in the private papers of Colonel Jerry Killian indicating that Bush had asked how he could get out of reporting for duty. As Killian had died in 1984, there was no way to confirm the authenticity of the documents. Dan Bartlett, counselor to Bush while president, said that Kerry was attacking Bush for political reasons. Bush responded directly to the attack, which had expanded to include accusations that his father had helped him avoid military service, saying "any allegation that my dad asked for special favors is simply not true and the former president of the United States has said that he in no way, shape or form helped me get into the National Guard. I didn't ask anyone to help me get into the Guard either." A 2004 *National Review* article reviewed Bush's military service and demonstrated that he had met his requirements. Within two weeks of the initial report, CBS confirmed it could not authenticate the documents. As a result of Rather's part in telling the story, he was asked to step down from the anchor desk; he left the *CBS Evening News* in March 2005 and left CBS altogether in 2006 after more than 40 years with the network.

HURRICANE KATRINA

On August 29, 2005, Hurricane Katrina, one of the deadliest storms in U.S. history, hit the Gulf Coast resulting in $100 billion in damages and more than 1,000 people dead. Bush's handling of the disaster became a prominent line of attack from many angles. One such angle dealt with the issues of race and poverty, as 67% of the residents of New Orleans were African American and 30% of the residents lived below the poverty line. One voice that drew much media attention was that of rapper Kanye West, who called Bush a racist because of his administration's slow and inadequate response. Bush responded that "[he] called me a racist . . . I resent it. It's not true." When the hurricane hit, the president was in Texas on vacation and, on the advice from his staff, he stayed there. This undermined his reputation for being an effective crisis manager and undercut his claims of being a decisive leader. When he was told about the damage, he flew to the nation's capital to make plans for handling the crisis. While en route to Washington, D.C., Air Force One flew over New Orleans and Bush was photographed looking out the window. He was criticized for being too distant from what was happening. Bush also praised FEMA director Michael Brown (who would be fired soon after) for his efforts and was criticized for being out of touch as much of the criticism of the handling of the hurricane was directed at Brown. In his autobiography, Bush argued, "That photo of me hovering over the damage suggested I was detached from the suffering on the ground. That was not how I felt. But once that impression formed, I couldn't change it."

DOMESTIC POLICY

When Bush ran for office, he intended to have a strong position on domestic policy. His key piece of legislation early on was the No Child Left Behind Act, a bipartisan effort that had significant influence on education policy throughout the nation through standards-based reform. In addition, in 2001, Bush also banned the use of federal funds for stem cell research from human embryos. Both domestic policy actions were considered controversial and generated much criticism from Bush's political opponents. Although the 9/11 attacks resulted in a dramatic shift toward foreign policy and contingency wars, other domestic policy positions throughout his time in office would cause conflict.

For example, Bush was attacked for rolling back environmental progress. Within his first 100 days of office, the Bush administration relaxed some clean air regulations, reversed Clinton administration initiatives on drinking water, and promoted oil exploration. One of his first acts as president was to withdraw from the Kyoto Protocol, an international treaty to reduce greenhouse gas emissions that the United States had joined in 1997. Bush announced his decision on March 28, 2001, citing his reasons as "the incomplete state of scientific knowledge of the causes of, and solutions to, global climate change" and the energy crisis in the United States. During a March 2001 press conference, Bush said that he would "not accept a plan that will harm our economy and hurt American workers." In May 2001, a report by the conservative Heritage Foundation defended the president's environmental record, arguing that the decision was not a "drastic reversal of U.S. policy." Critics on the left, however, did not relent. The Union of Concerned Scientists and other environmental and scientific organizations accused Bush of failing to acknowledge basic science on environmental issues. In a May 2007 *Vanity Fair* article, Robert F. Kennedy Jr. argued that Bush put lobbyists from industry into positions of power in important agencies. In 2008, Senate Democrats attacked Bush for doing "great damage to our environment."

Another line of attack regarded Bush's economic policy. Social conservatives praised Bush's stance on issues such as his opposition to same-sex marriage and abortion; fiscal conservatives expressed dismay at the increasing federal spending and rising national debt that occurred during the Bush years. For example, Chris Edwards of the Cato Institute called Bush the "mother of all big spenders," arguing, "the Bush Administration has consistently sacrificed sound policy to the god of political expediency." The chair of the Federal Reserve, Alan Greenspan, argued that Bush "swapped principle for power" and that "little value was placed on rigorous economic policy debate or the weighing of long-term consequences." In each of the first three years of his presidency, Bush signed tax cuts into law. Bush defended his actions with regard to the economy saying, "Ensuring that Americans have more to spend, to save and to invest, this legislation is adding fuel to an economic recovery." In September 2008, as Bush prepared to leave office amid an economic collapse, he said "there will be ample opportunity to debate the origins of this problem, now is the time to solve it." Many people argued that the Bush administration had been lax in regulating the financial industry, leading to the collapse of major economic sectors such as housing and banking. In addition, 2008 Republican presidential nominee John McCain said that the Bush administration allowed the Securities and Exchange Commission to be less active in regulatory behavior, which also lead to the economic collapse. The Bush White House defended the policy moves, saying that reforms were proposed but that Democrats had blocked them.

PERSONAL ATTACKS

Bush won top villain of the year in 2006 in an Associated Press-AOL poll. He was also considered a top hero in the same survey; 25% of people surveyed said he was the villain while 13% said he was a hero. Bush had no official response to the poll. This dichotomy was indicative of the polarization among voters regarding Bush throughout his two terms in office.

In 2008, Oliver Stone released a film, *W*, which was intended as a critical chronicle of Bush's life. The movie did relatively well, making $25.5 million at the box office. Reviews of the movie indicated that it "[succeeded] in making George W.

Bush more likable." Reviewers argued that Stone and writer Stanley Weiser made people hate the other major characters, including political adviser Karl Rove, Vice President Cheney, and Condoleezza Rice (who served as both national security advisor and then secretary of state) so much that Bush, as portrayed in the movie, was seen more favorably. The president's brother, Jeb Bush, responded in the *Washington Times* in 2008 that the "Oedipal rivalry is high-grade, unadulterated hooey." Neither Bush nor his presidential library has ever responded officially to the Stone film.

Another line of attack against Bush was making fun of the way that he spoke and the words he would pronounce incorrectly. Jacob Weisberg in a January 2009 *Slate* article listed more than 500 "Bushisms." *Saturday Night Live*'s Will Ferrell performed a Bush impersonation that became famous. Bush's response to this line of attack was claiming that he had a good sense of humor. Bush told Jimmy Kimmel on March 3, 2017, that he laughed at Ferrell's SNL impersonation. Bush said, "I love humor, and the best humor is when you make fun of yourself." Perhaps one of the most prevalent criticisms of Bush focused on his intelligence, or to his harshest critics, his lack thereof. For example, to many critics, Cheney held the real power in the White House, with Bush as simply a figurehead who did not have the knowledge to govern. In addition, presidential adviser Karl Rove was often described by Bush detractors as the brains behind Bush's presidency; a 2003 book on the subject by James Moore and Wayne Slater, titled *Bush's Brain: How Karl Rove Made George W. Bush Presidential*, gave Rove credit for Bush's political successes in both Texas and on the national level. Although generally recognized as not having the highest IQ among the nation's presidents, Bush was nonetheless viewed as someone with strong interpersonal communication skills and emotional intelligence. *New York Times* columnist David Brooks, in a 2012 interview with *Playboy* magazine, said that Bush was "60 IQ points smarter in private than he was in public. He doesn't want anybody to think he's smarter than they are, so puts on a Texas act. It becomes so deep, it's part of him now. I've rarely seen a person whose off-the-record manner is so different from his on-the-record manner."

SPOUSE AND CHILDREN

Unlike her husband, whose approval ratings sagged badly in the final years of his presidency, First Lady Laura Bush left the White House with a 76% approval rating according to Gallup. Her rating ranged between 63% and 80% throughout the eight years of the Bush presidency. She was not controversial and did not generate any lines of attack against the president. His daughters, however, did become the subjects of some criticism. Bush's daughters, Jenna and Barbara, who were in college and 19 years old during the first year of his administration, were both charged with underage alcohol offenses in Texas. In June 2002, *Fox News* reported that the Bush twins were "at it again," drinking and smoking with no visible security. Throughout the daughters' time in college, Bush officially had no comment on the matter. However, his mother, former first lady Barbara Bush, said of the incident that "what goes around comes around" and that "he is getting back some of his own," referring to her son's own misdeeds in his younger years. The White House asked the media to not pursue stories about the daughters' drinking. Bush has never responded to this line of attack. Generally, the American people were not too concerned with the Bush daughters. In June 2001, 79% of Americans said they felt the Bush daughters were acting about the same as their peers.

CONCLUSION

Bush averaged a 49% approval throughout his eight years in office, according to Gallup, but his popularity waned considerably during his time in the Oval Office. After September 11, 2001, Bush achieved his approval high point at 90%, measured by Gallup during September 21–22, 2001. He hit a low of 25% three different times, with the last measured October 31–November 2, 2008—just before the 2008 election that made Democratic nominee Barack Obama his successor. His last measure as president in 2009 had him at 61% disapproval and 34% approval.

The president preceding Bush and the presidents since have all encountered extreme ideological polarization in the Congress they work with, whether in a situation of unified or divided government. As a result, the body politic has been living in a near constant state of negative attacks from all sides against all sides. As the Pew Research Center reported in 2015, there has been a growing divide among Republicans and Democrats into "ideologically uniform silos," and the nation is experiencing increasingly rigid sorting of conservatives into the Republican Party and liberals into the Democratic Party. There is not as much overlap politically as there once was. Although the negativity toward his presidency was likely a result of this polarizing trend, so too did his presidency contribute to the hyperpartisan political environment that persists at the national level.

Leah A. Murray

Further Reading

Baker, Peter. *Days of Fire: Bush and Cheney in the White House.* New York: Doubleday, 2013.

Bush, George W. *Decision Points.* New York: Crown, 2010.

Edwards, George C., III, and King, Desmond. *The Polarized Presidency of George W. Bush.* New York: Oxford University Press, 2007.

Minutaglio, Bill. *First Son: George W. Bush and the Bush Family Dynasty.* New York: Random House, 2001.

Smith, Jean Edward. *Bush*. New York: Simon & Schuster, 2016.

Toobin, Jeffery. *Too Close to Call: The Thirty-Six-Day Battle to Decide the 2000 Election*. New York: Random House, 2001.

44. Barack Obama

Born: August 4, 1961

Time in Office: 44th President of the United States, January 20, 2009, to January 20, 2017

Election Results: 2008 Election: 52.9% of popular vote, 365 (67.8%) Electoral College votes; 2012 Election: 51.1% of popular vote, 332 (61.7%) Electoral College votes

Spouse: Michelle Robinson (m. 1992)

Children: Malia and Sasha

Barack Hussein Obama II served as the 44th president of the United States from January 20, 2009, to January 20, 2017. He was born in Honolulu, Hawaii, on August 4, 1961, and was one of the youngest presidents to ever serve. Obama won his first election over John McCain with 52.9% of the popular vote and 365 votes in the Electoral College. He won his reelection bid over Mitt Romney in 2012 with 51.1% of the popular vote and 332 votes in the Electoral College. Obama was joined in the White House by his wife, Michelle, and their two daughters. Malia and Sasha were 10 and 7, respectively, when the first family moved into the official presidential residence.

Obama's parents were Kenyan-born economist Barack Obama Sr. and Stanley "Ann" Dunham, an anthropologist born in Wichita, Kansas. They divorced when Obama was still a toddler, and his mother married Obama's stepfather, Lolo Soetoro, a geography graduate student from Indonesia. Young Obama spent most of his childhood in Hawaii, but lived for two years in Indonesia with his stepfather and mother. He returned to the states to live with his maternal grandparents in Hawaii. After graduating from Punahou High School in 1979, Obama attended Occidental College in Los Angeles where he became politicized through campus activism in the South African divestment movement. He transferred to Columbia University where he studied political science, and went on to earn a law degree from Harvard.

Prior to entering politics, Obama worked as a law professor and community organizer in Chicago. In 1989, he met Michelle LaVaughn Robinson, a fellow Harvard Law School graduate, at a law firm in Chicago where Michelle worked as Barack's supervisor. Barack proposed two years later at a restaurant in Chicago, and the Obamas married on October 3, 1992. Obama taught constitutional law at the University of Chicago Law School from 1992 to 2004, and was elected to the

Illinois state senate from 1997 to 2004. He served as a U.S. senator representing the state of Illinois from 2005 until his election to the presidency in 2008.

Obama was the first African American president. He was also the first president to be called a "liar" while giving an address to a joint session of Congress (by Republican representative Joe Wilson of South Carolina in September 2009), and the first president to be sued by members of Congress from the opposite party (by Republicans over the Affordable Care Act) in 2015. He was also hung in effigy in public on numerous occasions in different parts of the country, and faced more death threats than other presidents in modern history.

Obama experienced a greater volume and intensity of hatred than perhaps any other president, but certainly more than any president in the modern media age. A quick online perusal turns up hundreds of racist T-shirts, bumper stickers, hats, and coffee mugs such as "Somewhere in Kenya a Village Is Missing Its Idiot"; "Islam's Trojan Horse"; and "I'm Not a Racist: I Hate His White Half Too." While other presidents faced hatred in response to political circumstances or their policies and actions (e.g., Abraham Lincoln, Andrew Johnson, Herbert Hoover, Richard Nixon, Donald J. Trump), Obama faced a steady stream of hatred from political thought leaders and the public based on his identity.

During his presidency, remarkably coherent themes of Obama hatred emerged from political leaders, right-wing media, and the public. Obama was the first presidential candidate to run in the social media age that emerged with the advent of Facebook (2004) and Twitter (2006). He was also the first president to govern in the social media age, and as such, he faced a more hostile public discourse environment than previous presidents. People are more likely to express bigoted opinions on social media because they can do so anonymously, or with a selective group of "friends." The Obama campaign's skillful use of social media has sometimes been cited as a factor in Obama's presidential victories, but social media also ensured that biases and bigotry would be front and center in his campaign and presidency.

THE RACIALIZED PRESIDENCY

According to political scientist Rogers Smith, the U.S. presidency holds singular importance as the office of the symbolic leader of the "free world," and as such, presidents are supposed to represent the ideal "true American." When Obama took the oath of office, however, people who had long associated "true Americans" with white skin (either consciously or subconsciously) faced a new reality. This racial bias in who is considered a true American has origins in our nation's history. Black people were enslaved and not considered full citizens at the founding. Even after the abolition of slavery and the formal extension of voting rights in 1870, most black people were barred from electoral participation until passage of the Voting

Rights Act of 1965. Today, black Americans continue to experience racist microaggressions, stereotypes, and institutional racial biases in many areas of American life.

An unspoken conflation of whiteness and being a "true American" posed a problem for an African American president. Prior to Obama, the "true American" in the White House had always been white. Americans of all races are more likely to think of white people as ideal citizens. Social psychologists Thierry Devos and Mahzarin Banaji note that "to be American is implicitly synonymous with being White." Obama's blackness in the White House directly challenged the idea that a "true American" is a white American, and some Americans responded by casting doubt on—or outright rejection of—the legitimacy of his presidency. Most of the Obama hatred involved "othering," which is a process of excluding those perceived to be "outsiders." He was framed as a foreigner, as less than human, and as a dire threat to American values.

CRITICISM OF OBAMA AS UN-AMERICAN

Some Obama hatred is measurable because it was public, but with the advent of e-mail communication and social media technology, it is impossible to track and measure the entire volume of his hatred. The examples presented here thus represent the tip of the iceberg of Obama hatred.

The first theme of Obama hatred framed him as foreign and un-American. Many of these criticisms were disguised using "dog whistle" politics—messages that use coded language that has meaning to a targeted segment of society that is not apparent to a broader audience. For example, Obama was targeted in the conservative press and viral e-mails with a fabricated story about his unwillingness to wear a flag pin or put hand over heart during the national anthem and the Pledge of Allegiance. None of the major candidates in the 2008 race regularly sported flag pins on the campaign trail, but Obama was the only candidate singled out by right-wing and mainstream media for this "flap." The un-American framing was also prominent during the 2012 campaign when Republican presidential nominee Mitt Romney's top surrogate, John Sununu, suggested that Obama needs to "learn how to be an American."

One way Obama was framed as "foreign" or "un-American" was through propagation of a myth that he is Muslim, a follower of Islam. Obama's father was Muslim, but Obama is a practicing Christian who prays on a daily basis and frequently consulted with Christian leaders during his time in office. The origin of the Muslim myth can be traced to an anonymous article published by the blog InsightMag.com in January 2007 claiming that candidate Obama studied at a Madrassa (Muslim seminary) in Indonesia for four years. This fictional claim inspired a wave of commentary from right-wing talk radio and cable television news that solidified this myth in the minds of millions of Americans. According to a CNN-ORC International Poll in September 2015, nearly 30% of Americans thought Obama was a Muslim, and 43% of Republicans believed this claim—a number that has increased since Obama was first elected.

Another way Obama was painted as un-American was through false assertions that he had not even been born in the United States. The seeds of this so-called "birther movement" were sown almost as soon as he announced his candidacy. Stories that questioned Obama's legal citizenship status immediately began circulating among conservative media outlets, Republican political operatives, and conservative American voters. Multiple conspiracies gained immediate traction in the right-wing press, including the idea that Obama's birth certificate was a forgery, that he was born in Kenya and not Hawaii, and that he transferred his citizenship to Indonesia when he was a child. Birtherism was started by fringe Illinois political candidate Andy Martin in 2004 who put out a campaign mailer claiming Obama was a closet Muslim. Birtherism was advanced by Orly Taitz, a conservative activist from Orange County, California, who brought a lawsuit disputing the legitimacy of Obama's birth certificate in 2008. Joseph Farah of the right-wing website WorldNetDaily ran frequent birther stories and funded billboards in California and Louisiana calling on Obama to release his "real" birth certificate.

In June 2008, birtherism moved to the mainstream when the *National Review*, a prominent conservative publication, called on Obama to release his birth certificate in order to dispel the growing chorus of rumors. The birther movement resonated with millions of Americans because it channeled their fear and anxiety about a nonwhite president into a concrete call for action. Obama responded to birthers by releasing his short-form birth certificate in 2008, but the pressure only intensified, and he released the long-form version in April 2011. Prior to the long-form release, a Gallup poll in 2011 found that 62% of Americans were not sure whether the president was born in the United States, a number that dropped to 53% postrelease.

The Obama White House hoped that the presentation of birth certificates would put the politically motivated charges of noncitizenship to rest. But people determined to undermine Obama's presidency simply ignored or discounted the evidence. After the release of both birth certificates, reality television star Donald Trump revived the birther movement with frequent appearances on *Fox News* and *Fox Business News* in which he questioned Obama's birthplace. He was joined by Hollywood martial artist Chuck Norris and Fox News host Lou Dobbs in promoting the birther myth. Some Republican elected officials also fanned the flames throughout the controversy, including Republican representatives Roy Blunt (Missouri), John Sullivan (Oklahoma), and Bill Posey (Florida). Alabama senator Richard Shelby once told the press, "Well his father was Kenyan and they said he was born in Hawaii, but I haven't seen any birth certificate. You have to be born in America to be a president."

The birther movement was effective in convincing many Americans that Obama was un-American. In 2015, according to polling reported in *USA Today*, one in five Americans still believed that Obama was born in another country. Political scientist Philip Klinker finds that people who believe the birther myth have significantly higher levels of racial resentment than other Americans. Sociologist Matthew Hughley examined reader comments in online articles from the *New York Times* and the *Wall Street Journal* about Obama's birthplace and found that they "reveal the sustained conflation of citizenship with an ideal or 'hegemonic' form of White racial identity." The racist overtones of the birther movement are apparent when one considers the relatively scant attention paid to the fact that Senator McCain, Obama's opponent in 2008, was actually born outside the United States (in the Panama Canal Zone).

UGLY COMPARISONS OF OBAMA TO A PRIMATE

Another common theme of Obama hatred was to portray him and his wife Michelle as primates. Such images draw upon a century-long history of the so-called "coon caricature" of African Americans in cartoons, postcards, advertisements, and film. These dehumanizing caricatures imply that black people are more simian than human. Photo-shopping Obama as a primate was especially popular. A Google search of "Obama" and "monkey" nets over 12 million hits of images of both Barack and Michelle Obama as primates. In one viral e-mail, Obama is depicted in a family photo as a baby monkey, sitting with two monkey parents, with the caption "Now you know why no birth certificate." This photo made international news when it was leaked to the press in 2011. The sender was Marilyn Davenport, a prominent member of the Orange County Republican Party in southern California.

During both the 2008 and 2012 elections, numerous photos of yard signs were circulated that presented Obama as a primate, and similar images were sold on T-shirts and even baby onesies. Association of Obama with primates was not isolated to social media. In 2010, popular cable news host Glenn Beck compared Obama's America to the "damn planet of the apes" in response to the president's support for labor unions. Beck's words were amplified through social media's sharing of his controversial video.

Perhaps the most controversial representation of Obama as a primate appeared on the cover of the *New York Post* on February 18, 2009. It merged two contemporary political events—the mauling of a woman by a neighbor's pet chimpanzee and the passage of a hotly contested economic stimulus package championed by the Obama administration. The cartoon shows two police officers standing near the body of a chimpanzee they just shot to death, remarking that "they'll have to find someone else to write the next stimulus bill." This cartoon drew widespread criticism for its use of an old racial stereotype of depicting African American people as primates who are less than human.

The primate theme was especially public during the 2016 election season, even though Obama was not a candidate. In 2016, Dan Johnson, a Republican state legislative candidate in Kentucky, posted several images on Facebook depicting both Barack and Michelle Obama as monkeys, including a picture of a baby chimpanzee captioned with "Obama's baby picture." He also posted a photo of Ronald Reagan feeding a primate with the caption "Rare photos of Ronald Reagan babysitting Barack Obama in early 1962."

In 2016, Beverly Whaling, the mayor of a small town in West Virginia, resigned after she commented approvingly on a friend's post that described the first lady as an "ape in heels." Pamela Ramsey Taylor, the woman who made the original post, was later fired from her job as the director of the nonprofit Clay County Development Corporation.

The Obamas-as-primates theme was popular beyond elected officials as well. In 2016, Michelle Herren, a pediatric anesthesiologist, was fired from the Denver Health Medical Center after calling Michelle Obama "monkey face" on Facebook. That same year, an Arkansas high school science teacher Trent Bennett resigned from his job after referring to Michelle Obama as "America's First Chimp" and the president as "her spider monkey hubby" on Twitter. Bennett also made numerous claims that Obama was born in Kenya. Progressive journalist Brian Beutler attributed this measurable increase in public acts of racism during the 2016 election season to the campaign of Republican presidential nominee Donald Trump, which was heavily criticized for allegedly engaging in racially charged messaging. Beutler and some other observers believed that the tenor of Trump's campaign emboldened racists who had previously been more hesitant about sharing their beliefs in public.

EQUATING OBAMA WITH HITLER

Another theme of Obama hatred was to equate him with Adolf Hitler. Journalist Chris Osterndorf writes that "Obama isn't the first U.S. president or world leader to be compared to Hitler, and he won't be the last. But the persistence of the Obama/Hitler comparison, the way it permeates the bottom rungs of political discussion, is unique." Legal scholar Cynthia Bond posits that the Obama-Hitler frenzy right after Obama took office was an "attempt to 're-other' Obama now that he has entered the office that most visibly represents the United States as a nation" against the backdrop of "racial anxieties, and even outright panic, about a 'non-White' president." The Obama-is-Hitler theme was first publicized a few days before Obama took office by popular conservative columnist Thomas Sowell, who wrote in *Slate* that "[M]any 20th-century leaders with inspiring rhetoric and great self-confidence led their followers or their countries into utter disasters. These ranged from Jim Jones who led hundreds to their deaths in Jonestown to Hitler and Mao who led millions to their deaths."

Within weeks of Obama taking office, cable news host Glenn Beck compared him to the leader of the Nazi Party. Right-wing radio host Rush Limbaugh stated that: "Adolf Hitler, like Barack Obama, also ruled by dictate." Dr. Ben Carson, a 2016 presidential candidate, said the United States under Obama is "very much like Nazi Germany. . . . You had the government using its tools to intimidate the population."

Hundreds of memes circulated during the early years of Obama's presidency claiming that Obama's policies were similar to those of Hitler. The normal practices of a president promoting public policy, like the bailout of the auto industry and passage of the Affordable Care Act in the case of the Obama administration, were characterized by his political and ideological opponents as such extreme abuses of presidential power that they warranted Hitler comparisons. The North Iowa Tea Party paid for billboards with images of Obama and Hitler, and a Republican organization in Maryland penned a letter stating that "Obama and Hitler have a great deal in common." Arizona state representative Brenda Barton defended a Facebook post comparing Obama with Hitler: "It's not just the death camps. [Hitler] started in the communities, with national health care and gun control. You better read your history. Germany started with national health care and gun control before any of that other stuff happened. And Hitler was elected by a majority of people." The Obama-as-Hitler framing persuaded millions of Americans. According to a 2010 Harris Poll, 20% of Americans and 38% of Republicans agreed that Obama is "doing many of the things that Hitler did."

Obama-Hitler comparisons intensified in 2015 when Texas Republican Randy Weber tweeted, "Even Adolph [*sic*] Hitler thought it more important than Obama to get to Paris. (For all of the wrong reasons). Obama couldn't do it for right reasons," in reference to Obama missing a march to honor the victims of the *Charlie Hedbo* attack. Later that year, after Obama reached an agreement with Iran to limit that nation's nuclear program, Fox News host Mike Huckabee declared that Obama was taking Jews "to the door of the oven." Other right-wing media outlets echoed this Hitler comparison, including other Fox News hosts, *Breitbart*, *The Washington Examiner*, and even the *Washington Post* (in a column by conservative pundit Marc Theissen).

DEATH THREATS AGAINST OBAMA

Obama hatred also came in the form of death threats. According to legal scholars Gregory Park and Danielle Heard, Obama faced the most death threats of any president in the modern age. He also was the first candidate to receive Secret Service protection while running for the office—18 months before the election date—due to threatening discussions about him on White supremacy websites. These fears were founded as multiple arrests were made during the 2008 campaign.

When authorities arrested Raymond Hunter Geisel in Miami in April 2008 for threatening to kill Obama, they found a handgun, armor-piercing ammunition, body armor, a machete, and knives. Later in the campaign, federal authorities foiled a plot by three white supremacists to use rifles to assassinate Obama during his address at the Democratic National Convention in Denver. In September 2008 law enforcement arrested Omhari Sengstacke, who was wearing body armor and in possession of a gun near the Obama family home in Chicago. A month later, two white supremacists, Daniel Cowart and Paul Schlesselman, were arrested in Tennessee when a source reported that they planned to go on a killing spree targeting African Americans, ending with Obama.

Serious death threats continued after the 2008 election. For example, in December 2008, federal agents arrested Mark M. Miyashiro for threatening to kill the president-elect when he was on vacation in Hawaii. They found two high-powered guns and ammunition. In 2017, Colorado man Michael Francis Clapper was sentenced to nearly four years in prison for writing letters threatening to blow up the White House and kill Obama.

Death threats were remarkably common in public forums during Obama's presidency. A few days after the election, for example, people rallied in Maine in front of African American figures hung by nooses in trees. At a university in North Carolina, someone spray-painted "shoot Obama" and "kill that nigger" in a space set aside for free speech on campus. A football player at the University of Texas in Austin was kicked off the team for posting "All the hunters gather up, we have a nigger in the White House" on Facebook. In January 2017, Lawrence Mulqueen was arrested for a Facebook post stating that he "will kill" President Obama.

IMPLICATIONS FOR THE COUNTRY

The historic hatred aimed at Obama has implications for both the country and the office of the presidency. Racist appeals stoked existing racial biases and created more bias. Obama hatred also reinforced a limited notion of who can legitimately serve as president.

Obama hatred both reflected and reinforced deep-seated racial bias in the country. His presidency polarized the electorate, increased different forms of racism in the population, and facilitated the election of Donald J. Trump. But first, it is necessary to know how Obama presented his presidency versus how it was framed in order to parse out the effects of Obama hatred.

Obama employed what came to be called a "postracial" strategy on the campaign trail and in the White House. He avoided racially charged language and proclaimed that "there's not a Black America and White America and Latino America and Asian America; there's the United States of America." Obama's postracial approach was prominent in the Philadelphia speech where he condemned the racialized remarks of his former pastor, Reverend Jeremiah Wright. He also used race-neutral language in criticizing the Bush administration's response to Hurricane Katrina on the campaign trail. In contrast to previous African American presidential candidates such as Shirley Chisholm, Jesse Jackson, and Al Sharpton, Obama did not openly advocate for civil rights. Once elected, Obama sustained his postrace strategy with a race-neutral policy agenda, only occasionally taking tepid positions on race, such as his response to the racial profiling of Harvard professor Henry Louis Gates Jr. ("the Cambridge police acted stupidly in arresting somebody when there was already proof that they were in their own home") and George Zimmerman's shooting of Trayvon Martin ("If I had a son, he'd look like Trayvon").

Obama also invoked a postracial approach with his self-presentation style. Legal scholar Frank Rudy Cooper points out that Obama skillfully avoided the "threatening Bad Black Man" stereotype, choosing to employ a more "comforting Good Black Man" presentation to appeal to white voters. Obama's Good Black Man presentation was characterized by remarkable emotional restraint and observable kinship with whites, a common navigational strategy for black men seeking positions of power. Legal scholar Ian Haney López argues that Obama's postracial pitch was a strategic imperative for winning the White House. As sociologist Tamari Kitossa points out, "Black people do not rise to positions of power and influence in the White world without conceding the necessity of sustaining hegemonic White supremacy."

In the last two years of his presidency, however, Obama visibly shifted away from a postracial approach. In June 2015, in an appearance on Marc Maron's radio show, Obama told the nation: "Do not say that nothing's changed when it comes to race in America—unless you've lived through being a Black man in the 1950s, or '60s, or '70s. It is incontrovertible that race relations have improved significantly during my lifetime and yours, and that opportunities have opened up, and that attitudes have changed. That is a fact. What is also true is that the legacy of slavery, Jim Crow, discrimination in almost every institution of our lives—you know, that casts a long shadow. And that's still part of our DNA that's passed on. Racism, we're not cured of it."

Obama faced harsh criticism from right-wing media outlets and in social media for acknowledging lingering racism.

REALIGNMENT OF RACISM AND PARTISANSHIP

The first effect of the racialized hatred aimed at Obama was a more polarized electorate than any other point in modern U.S. history, and according to many progressives, a corresponding realignment of Jim Crow racism with the Republican Party. This was a setback since the nation had made measurable progress on race since the civil rights movement of the 1960s. White opinions had steadily become more racially tolerant, and by the mid-1990s, a vast majority of whites had come to support the integration of public transportation and schools and equal access to employment. Whites exhibited lower levels of support for interracial marriage and housing equality, suggesting that "the greatest shifts in Whites' racial attitudes occurred with respect to the most public, impersonal domains of society." Overt prejudice against an African American president had also declined, from 3 in 5 white people saying they would not vote for a black president in 1958, compared to 1 in 10 whites in a more recent polling.

But the story of racial progress in America is more complicated. When Obama was elected, three-quarters of white Americans still held negative stereotypes about Latinos and blacks, and whites and blacks were as divided on policy issues in 2008 as they were in 1988, the last time a black presidential candidate ran. Furthermore, Jim Crow racism had gone into hiding rather than disappearing altogether. Sociologist Eduardo Bonilla-Silva writes that overt racism of the Jim Crow era has been replaced by more covert color-blind racism that enables white people to ignore the unearned privileges of their whiteness, and reinforces an invisible white norm. With the color-blind approach, "Whites have learned how to talk the talk, without walking the walk."

Although Obama ran a postracial campaign tailored to appeal to white voters, a majority of white voters did not vote for him in 2008 and 2012. Only 43% of whites voted for Obama in 2008, and this number fell to 39% in 2012. It is important to note that Democratic presidential candidates have lost the white vote since 1976, but Obama's share was significantly lower than expected given the state of the economy and other factors that predict presidential vote choice. Political scientist Michael Lewis-Beck and his colleagues find that racial resentment cost Obama what otherwise would have been a landslide in 2008 based on standard election models. Political scientist Chris Parker and his colleagues analyze electoral returns and find that "Although Obama ultimately won, we cannot reject that race—and racism in particular—played a significant role in the outcome." Political scientist David Redlawsk and his colleagues find that 30% of white Americans were "troubled" by the idea of Obama as the first black president. Furthermore, indifference to black suffering was positively correlated with opposition to Obama in the 2008 election, and antiblack stereotypes significantly eroded white support for Obama in that election. Antiblack sentiment cost Obama an estimated 4% of votes in the 2012 election.

Another effect of the hatred aimed at Obama was his historic drop in public favorability. Obama swept into office on a wave of Democratic enthusiasm and the most positive media coverage of any U.S. president since the advent of mass communication. His 68% starting approval rating was second only to John Kennedy's at 72%, but it plummeted to 47% within a year—the largest drop on record. Obama joined Ronald Reagan as the only other president with approval lower than 50% at the one-year mark, but Reagan fell 2 points while Obama plunged more than 20 points.

Another implication of hatred aimed at Obama was the polarization of the country along partisan lines. Obama holds the record for the most politically polarized job approval ratings of any president in his first year. In January 2010, Obama had a 65-point gap between job approval ratings from Republicans (23%) and Democrats (88%), far larger than Bill Clinton's 52% partisan gap in approval early in his first term. Additionally, overall levels of racial resentment increased significantly during Obama's time in office. By 2012, both implicit and explicit racism were on the rise with 51% of Americans harboring explicit antiblack attitudes compared to 48% in 2008. Implicit antiblack attitudes jumped from 49% to 56% over the same period. Additionally, Jim Crow racism, which had ceased to be related to partisanship in the post–civil rights era, became realigned with party. According to polling, people harboring overt racist beliefs became significantly more likely to vote Republican. Racial resentment also drove some Americans to switch from the Democratic Party to the Republican Party.

Another implication of the hatred aimed at Obama is the election of Donald Trump in 2016. For some, it is no coincidence that nearly 63 million people voted for the most prominent mouthpiece of the birther movement to succeed the first black president. Trump built his political credentials through media appearances in which he attacked Obama using the birther myth that played on racialized fear of the "other." According to religion scholar Eddie Glaude, a political environment marked by "racial anxiety and anguish" led to Trump's victory. The 2016 election outcome was framed as a response to economic anxiety, but data does not support this. The typical Trump voter was better off than the typical American—earning a median household income of $72,000 compared to the national median of $62,000. During the primary, Trump voters had higher incomes than those who voted for Ted Cruz, Bernie Sanders, or Hillary Clinton. Political scientist Philip Klinker compared economic anxiety and racial anxiety among voters in the 2016 election and found that economic concerns did not explain support for Trump, but racial anxiety did. Specifically, Trump supporters have higher levels of resentment toward African Americans, are more likely to think that Obama is a Muslim, and are more likely to describe Muslims as "violent" than other voters. Some scholars argue that the 2016 election was a reaction to eight years of dog whistle and overt racism aimed at Obama. Indeed, Michael Tester finds that racial attitudes were an even bigger factor in determining vote choice in the 2016 election than in 2012 or 2008.

IMPLICATIONS FOR THE PRESIDENCY

The election of an African American man to the presidency is a sign that the republic is becoming more inclusive in choosing our leaders, but the volume and intensity of hating Obama reveals the limits of this progress. Americans are fond of telling their children that every child can grow up to be president, and Obama's experience both reinforces and challenges this idea. He was treated as an illegitimate occupant of the White House by right-wing media and many Americans, and as such, his presidency reinforced narrow ideas of who can *legitimately* be president. As noted in the introduction, the president embodies notions of a "true American." For some, Obama's blackness meant he could not be a "true American," and his presence in the White House was seen as a threat to both the institution and the existing social order. Eric Hehman and his colleagues find that, for white Americans, Obama's low performance ratings were linked to "how American" he was perceived to be, while Vice President Joe Biden's ratings were not linked to perceptions of his "Americaness."

What does it mean that Obama faced more hatred and death threats than any other president in the modern age? What does it mean that, in order to win, the first black president, according to sociologists Eduardo Bonilla-Silva and Victor Ray, "had distanced himself from most leaders of the civil rights movement, from his own reverend, from his own church, and from anything or anyone who makes him 'too Black' or 'too political?'" For a country that prides itself on these democratic principles, we are surprisingly complacent about nonmeritorious race and gender restrictions on the presidency. The identity of the person leading the country matters because policy action varies by sex, race, class, and their intersections. For example, female leaders are more likely to put issues involving women, children, and the family on the agenda. African American legislators promote more liberal policies than white legislators and are more likely to participate in oversight hearings on racism. The identity of the president also matters in terms of being a role model. African Americans displayed higher political interest, efficacy, and a sense of racial identity in the 2008 election, and they turned out to vote at unprecedented rates.

CONCLUSION

Who gets to be president matters, and how presidents are treated when they get there also matters. In November 2014, after fanning the flames of racist birtherism for years, Trump Tweeted, "Sadly, because president Obama has done such a poor job as president, you won't see another Black president for generations!" It may be many years before we elect another African American president, but some observers believe that if that proves to be the case, it will have more to do with the unrelenting racialized hatred aimed at Obama than his job performance in the White House.

Caroline Heldman

Further Reading

Bobo, Lawrence D. "Obama and the Burden of Race." *Focus Magazine,* Vol. 37, No. 4 (2009): 16–17.

Bobo, Lawrence D., and Camille Z. Charles. "Race in the American Mind: From the Moynihan Report to the Obama Candidacy." *Annals of the American Academy of Political and Social Science*, Vol. 621 (January 2009): 243–259.

Bogle, Donald. *Toms, Coons, Mulattoes, Mammies, and Bucks: An Interpretive History of Blacks in American Films.* New York: Continuum International Publishing Group, 2001.

Bonilla-Silva, Eduardo. *White Supremacy and Racism in the Post–Civil Rights Era.* Boulder, CO: Lynne Rienner Publishers, 2001.

Bonilla-Silva, Eduardo. *Racism without Racists: Color-Blind Racism and the Persistence of Racial Inequality in the United States.* New York: Rowman & Littlefield, 2010.

Bonilla-Silva, Eduardo, and Victor Ray. "When Whites Love a Black Leader: Race Matters in Obamerica." *Journal of African American Studies*, Vol. 13, No. 2 (2009): 176–183.

Bouie, Jamelle. "You Know Who Else Said That?" *Slate.* January 13, 2015. Available at http://www.slate.com/articles/news_and_politics/politics/2015/01/republicans_comparing _barack_obama_to_hitler_my_favorite_examples_of_the.html.

Childs, Sarah, and Mona Lena Krook. "Analyzing Women's Substantive Representation: From Critical Mass to Critical Actors." *Government and Opposition*, Vol. 44, No. 2 (2009): 125–145.

Cooper, Frank R. "Our First Unisex President? Black Masculinity and Obama's Feminine Side." *University Law School Faculty Publications,* Paper 52 (2009).

Devos, Thierry, and Mahzarin R. Banaji. "American = White?" *Journal of Personality and Social Psychology*, Vol. 88, No. 3 (2005): 447–466.

Gamble, Katrina L. "Black Voice: Deliberation in the United States Congress." *Polity*, Vol. 43, No. 3 (2011): 291–312.

Garland, Jon, and Neil Chakraborti. "'Race', Space and Place Examining Identity and Cultures of Exclusion in Rural England." *Ethnicities*, Vol. 6, No. 2 (2006): 159–177.

Haney-López, Ian F. "Post-Racial Racism: Racial Stratification and Mass Incarceration in the Age of Obama." *California Law Review*, Vol. 98, No. 3 (2010): 1023–1074.

Hehman, Eric, Samuel L. Gaertner, and John F. Dovidio. "Evaluations of Presidential Performance: Race, Prejudice, and Perceptions of Americanism." *Journal of Experimental Social Psychology*, Vol. 47, No. 2 (2011): 430–435.

Hill, Rickey. "The Race Problematic, the Narrative of Martin Luther King Jr., and the Election of Barack Obama." *Souls*, Vol. 11, No. 1 (2009): 60–78.

Howell, Jaclyn. "Not Just Crazy: An Explanation for the Resonance of the Birther Narrative." *Communication Monographs*, Vol. 79, No. 4 (2012): 428–447.

Hughey, Matthew W. "Show Me Your Papers! Obama's Birth and the Whiteness of Belonging." *Qualitative Sociology*, Vol. 35, No. 2 (2012): 1–19.

Hutchings, Vincent L. "Change or More of the Same? Evaluating Racial Attitudes in the Obama Era." *The Public Opinion Quarterly*, Vol. 73, No. 5 (2009): 917–942.

Kitossa, Tamari. "Obama Deception? Empire, 'Postracism' and White Supremacy in the Campaign and Election of Barack Obama." *Journal of Critical Race Inquiry*, Vol. 1, No. 2 (2011): 1–56.

Klinker, Philip. "The Causes and Consequences of 'Birtherism.'" A paper presented at the annual meeting of the Western Political Science Association, Seattle, WA, April 17–19, 2014. Available at https://wpsa.research.pdx.edu/papers/docs/Birthers.pdf.

Klinker, Philip. "The Easiest Way to Guess If Someone Supports Trump? Ask If Obama Is a Muslim." *Vox*, June 2, 2016. Available at http://www.vox.com/2016/6/2/11833548/donald-trump-support-race-religion-economy.

Lewis-Beck, Michael S., Charles Tien, and Richard Nadeau. "Obama's Missed Landslide: A Racial Cost?" *PS: Political Science and Politics*, Vol. 43, No. 1 (2010): 69–76.

Manuel, Tiffany. "Envisioning the Possibilities for a Good Life: Exploring the Public Policy Implications of Intersectionality Theory." *Journal of Women, Politics & Policy*, Vol. 28, Nos. 3–4 (2007): 173–203.

Minta, Michael D. "Legislative Oversight and the Substantive Representation of Black and Latino Interests in Congress." *Legislative Studies Quarterly*, Vol. 34, No. 2 (2009): 193–218.

Park, Gregory S., and Danielle C. Heard. "'Assassinate the Nigger Ape!' Obama, Implicit Imagery, and the Dire Consequences of Racist Jokes." Cornell Law Faculty Working Papers, August 14, 2009. Available at http://scholarship.law.cornell.edu/cgi/viewcontent.cgi?article=1063&context=clsops_papers.

Parker, Christopher S., Mark Q. Sawyer, and Christopher Towler. "A Black Man in the White House?" *Du Bois Review: Social Science Research on Race*, Vol. 6, No. 1 (2009): 193–217.

Peacock, Thomas. "I Share a Dream: How Can We Eliminate Racism?" *Tribal College Journal of American Indian Higher Education*, Vol. 23, No. 1 (2011).

Philpot, Tasha S., Daron R. Shaw, and Ernest B. McGowen. "Winning the Race: Black Voter Turnout in the 2008 Presidential Election." *Public Opinion Quarterly*, Vol. 73, No. 5 (2009): 995–1022.

Piston, Spencer. "How Explicit Racial Prejudice Hurt Obama in the 2008 Election." *Political Behavior*, Vol. 32, No. 4 (2010): 431–451.

Redlawsk, David P., Caroline J. Tolbert, and William Franko. "Voters, Emotions, and Race in 2008: Obama as the First Black President." *Political Research Quarterly*, Vol. 63, No. 4 (2010): 875–889.

Santana, Arthur D. "Virtuous or Vitriolic: The Effect of Anonymity on Civility in Online Newspaper Reader Comment Boards." *Journalism Practice*, Vol. 8, No. 1 (2013): 18–33.

Silver, Nate. "The Mythology of Trump's 'Working Class' Support." *FiveThirtyEight*, May 3, 2016. Available at https://fivethirtyeight.com/features/the-mythology-of-trumps-working-class-support/.

Smith, Rogers M. *Civic Ideals: Conflicting Visions of Citizenship in U.S. History*. New Haven, CT: Yale University Press, 1999.

Smith, Stephen C. "Anyone Can Grow Up to Be President! (And Other Myths of the American Presidential Election Process)." *New Political Science*, Vol. 15, Nos. 1–2 (1994): 7–29.

Tesler, Michael. "The Spillover of Racialization into Health Care: How President Obama Polarized Public Opinion by Racial Attitudes and Race." *American Journal of Political Science*, Vol. 56, No. 3 (2010): 690–704.

Tesler, Michael, and David O. Sears. *Obama's Race: The 2008 Election and the Dream of a Post-Racial America*. Chicago, IL: University of Chicago Press, 2010.

Wilkins, Amy. "'Not Out to Start a Revolution': Race, Gender, and Emotional Restraint among Black University Men." *Journal of Contemporary Ethnography*, Vol. 41, No. 1 (2012): 34–65.

45. Donald J. Trump

Born: June 14, 1946
Time in Office: 45th President of the United States, January 20, 2017, to Present
Election Results: 2016 Election: 46.2% of popular vote, 304 (56.5%) Electoral College votes
Spouses: Ivana Zelnickova (m. 1977); Marla Maples (m. 1993); Melania Knauss (m. 2005)
Children: Donald Jr., Ivanka, Eric, Tiffany, and Barron

On November 8, 2016, Donald J. Trump shocked the political world with his upset victory over Democratic nominee Hillary Clinton in what many called the most negative presidential campaign in history. As the first president ever elected with no prior political or military experience, Trump's populist economic views and politically incorrect rhetoric resonated with American voters who agreed with Trump's promises to "Make America Great Again" and "Drain the Swamp" in Washington, D.C. At the age of 70, Trump, a former businessman and television personality, became the oldest person ever elected to the presidency.

Born in 1946 to Fred and Mary Anne (nee MacLeod) Trump, and raised in Queens, New York, Trump was the fourth of five children. He joined the family real-estate business after graduating with an economics degree from the Wharton School of the University of Pennsylvania in 1968. He served as chairman and president of The Trump Organization from 1971 until January 2017, at which time he turned the management of his business interests over to his two oldest sons. Trump's real-estate development business focused primarily on building office towers, hotels, golf courses, and casinos. Various products have been produced and sold under the Trump name over the years, and he is also well known for his 1987 book *The Art of the Deal*, a *New York Times* bestseller; for producing and starring in *The Apprentice*, a reality television show that ran for 12 years on NBC; and for owning and producing the Miss Universe Pageants from 1996 until 2015.

Throughout his business career, Trump remained in the public spotlight as one of the richest men in the United States. He regularly made news for business successes (such as the completion of Trump Tower in Manhattan in 1983 and the renovation of Wollman Rink in Central Park in the mid-1980s) and failures (such as various bankruptcies for his casino properties during the 1990s and 2000s). Trump has also been a staple of celebrity news and gossip columns, due in part to his three marriages. He married his first wife, Ivana Zelnickova, a model from Czechoslovakia, in 1977, with whom he had three children: Donald Jr. (born in 1977), Ivanka (born in 1981), and Eric (born in 1984). Ivana would play a significant role in The Trump Organization during their marriage, particularly with major hotel renovations. They divorced in 1992 after Trump's affair with actress and model Marla Maples. Trump would marry Maples in 1993, two months after the birth of their daughter Tiffany; the couple would divorce in 1999. Trump married his third and current wife, Melania Knauss, a Slovenian model, in 2005. They have one son, Barron, born in 2006. Trump's daughter Ivanka, along with her husband, businessman Jared Kushner, both serve as advisers in the Trump White House.

2016 PRESIDENTIAL CAMPAIGN

Prior to his presidential campaign in 2016, Trump had often talked publicly about entering politics. He considered running for president in 1988, 2000, 2004, and 2012, and for governor of New York in 2006 and 2014. In 1999, Trump formed an exploratory committee to seek the presidential nomination of the Reform Party, and would win the Reform Party primaries in California and Michigan despite dropping out of the race. In 2011, Trump again publicly speculated about running for president, and early polling showed him as competitive in Republican primaries. He spoke at that year's Conservative Political Action Conference (CPAC) and became a prominent voice within the so-called "birther" movement that questioned whether Barack Obama had been born in the United States (therefore calling into question the legitimacy of Obama's presidency due to the constitutional requirement that presidents must be natural born citizens). In April 2011, Trump would take credit for Obama publicly releasing his long-form birth certificate from the state of Hawaii.

A few days later, Trump attended the White House Correspondents' Association dinner as a guest of the *Washington Post*, and was the subject of jokes by both Obama and guest comedian Seth Meyers. Obama spent five minutes addressing Trump:

Now, I know that he's taken some flak lately, but no one is happier, no one is prouder to put this birth certificate matter to rest than the Donald. And that's because he can finally get back to focusing on the issues that matter—like, did we fake the moon landing? What really happened in Roswell? And where are Biggie and Tupac? But all kidding aside, obviously, we all know about your credentials and breadth of experience. For example—no, seriously, just recently, in an episode of Celebrity Apprentice—at the steakhouse, the men's cooking team did not impress the judges from Omaha Steaks. And there was a lot of blame to go around. But you, Mr. Trump, recognized that the real problem was a lack of leadership. And so ultimately, you didn't blame Lil' Jon or Meatloaf. You fired Gary Busey. And these are the kind of decisions that would keep me up at night. Well handled, sir. Well handled.

Meyers went after Trump as well, saying "Donald Trump has been saying that he will run for president as a Republican, which is surprising, since I just assumed he was running as a joke." Many pundits would later speculate that Trump made up his mind to seek the presidency that night, though he had considered running for years prior.

Trump officially announced his campaign for president at Trump Tower on June 16, 2015. He revealed his campaign slogan, "Make America Great Again," which centered around issues such as illegal immigration, bringing jobs back to the United States, and the fight against terrorism. A total of 17 candidates sought the Republican presidential nomination, including several current and former governors and U.S. senators. Employing politically incorrect and hyperbolic campaign rhetoric right from the start, Trump garnered tremendous news media coverage, especially on cable news. He led state and national polling among the crowded field of candidates throughout the prenomination period, and his raucous campaign rallies, where Trump often spoke off-script, became a mainstay of his campaign. Trump would participate in all but one of the Republican primary debates (skipping a debate right before the Iowa caucuses to hold an event to benefit military veterans), where he honed his antiestablishment message while attacking and insulting the other politicians on the stage. Throughout the Republican nomination process, Trump marketed himself as the alternative to the Republican establishment, which gained him support among many voters who had been disaffected by "politics as usual" in Washington.

Many lines of attack emerged against Trump during the nomination phase of the campaign, and many centered on the controversial comments he made during interviews or campaign rallies. Charges of racism and bigotry became a predominant line of attack from Trump's enemies. Trump had made controversial comments about illegal immigration in his campaign announcement speech, saying that those crossing the southern border from Mexico were "bringing drugs.

They're bringing crime. They're rapists." In what Trump considered strong language in discussing the threat of terrorism, his critics labeled him xenophobic when discussing immigration of Muslims, as when Trump said that he was "calling for a complete and total shutdown of Muslims entering the United States until our country's representatives can figure out what the hell is going on." In addition, Trump began his attacks against what he called the "fake news," though his campaign continually benefited from free media coverage that dwarfed that of any of his competitors.

After losing the Iowa caucuses to Senator Ted Cruz of Texas, Trump would win the New Hampshire and South Carolina primaries, as well as a majority of the remaining contests, never giving up the mantle of "front runner." He secured enough delegates to win the nomination in early May when his only two remaining opponents, Cruz and Ohio governor John Kasich, dropped out. However, the fear that Trump might win the nomination caused great consternation within the Republican Party, as numerous critics emerged among political and opinion leaders on the right, due in part to Trump's many populist views (for example, opposing free trade and military interventionism) that did not align with traditional conservatism. Prominent politicians such as Speaker of the House Paul Ryan often waffled on his support for Trump as the Republican nominee, and 2012 Republican nominee Mitt Romney gave a highly critical, anti-Trump speech in March 2016 stating that Trump was a "fraud," his promises "worthless," and that Trump was "playing the American public for suckers: he gets a free ride to the White House and all we get is a lousy hat." Several delegates who were opposed to Trump would try to deny him the nomination at the Republican National Convention. In addition, Cruz refused to endorse Trump when he spoke to the delegates, and Kasich refused to even attend the convention despite it being held in his home state (in Cleveland). The Never Trump movement (also known as the Stop Trump or anti-Trump movement) would include hundreds of prominent Republicans and/or conservatives, including current and former politicians, who openly opposed Trump's candidacy throughout 2016. Well-known conservative pundits who opposed Trump included Bill Kristol, George Will, Glenn Beck, Charles Krauthammer, and Erick Erickson. *National Review,* an influential conservative magazine, published an entire anti-Trump issue in January 2016, and would continue to argue against a Trump presidency throughout the campaign. Even former presidents George H. W. Bush and George W. Bush would not endorse Trump, and some prominent party members would endorse or vote for Hillary Clinton in the general election. Trump's selection of Indiana governor Mike Pence, well liked and respected among his fellow conservatives, was an attempt by Trump to assuage the resistance to his candidacy within the Republican Party.

Numerous lines of attack would emerge against Trump during the general election campaign, and most from the nomination battle would continue as well.

Two of the most prominent stories that emerged in the fall dealt with Trump's treatment of women. In early October, the *Washington Post* released video and audio of Trump making an appearance on the television show *Access Hollywood* from 2005, in which he made vulgar comments about women. Amid the fallout from this story, about a dozen women also publicly accused Trump of sexual assault and/or inappropriate conduct. Trump denied all accusations. Another prominent story that dogged Trump throughout the campaign dealt with his refusal to release his tax returns; critics demanded to know how much he had paid in taxes, and some also claimed that Trump was lying about his net worth.

The personal animosity between Trump and his Democratic rival, Hillary Clinton, was intense throughout the campaign. The three debates between the two in September and October were the most watched of any previous presidential campaign, and they featured extremely contentious personal and political attacks. Trump had for months been calling his rival "Crooked Hillary" out on the campaign trail, and those who attended his rallies regularly chanted "lock her up" over the ongoing story of Clinton's controversial use of a private e-mail server while secretary of state. Clinton had also attacked many of Trump's supporters, stating in early September: "You know, just to be grossly generalistic, you could put half of Trump's supporters into what I call the basket of deplorables. They're racist, sexist, homophobic, xenophobic, Islamaphobic—you name it." Clinton later walked back part of her comment (she expressed regret at using the word "half"), but she continued to blame Trump for "hateful views and voices" that she said contributed to violence at some of his campaign rallies and encouraged racism across the country. In the end, thanks in part to a strong antiestablishment mood among the electorate, and miscalculations by the Clinton campaign (including taking for granted that several so-called "rust belt" states would remain in the Democratic column), Trump won the election, securing a solid Electoral College victory despite losing the popular vote to Clinton by nearly 3 million votes.

TRUMP AS PRESIDENT

Within 24 hours of Trump winning the election, protests erupted in major cities across the country. Massive demonstrations also took place in many parts of the country on the day of Trump's inauguration. The sense of shock and outrage among the protesters was fueled, in part, by the fact that most major media outlets had incorrectly predicted a Clinton victory on Election Night. "Not my president" became a popular chant during the protests, and #notmypresident quickly trended on Twitter. Green Party candidate Jill Stein, who had received roughly 1% of the popular vote, challenged the results in the states of Wisconsin, Michigan, and Pennsylvania, the three blue states that Trump had turned red to secure his

Electoral College victory. The Clinton campaign joined the recount effort in Wisconsin, though the legal challenges did nothing to change the election results. Efforts were also launched to lobby various state electors to switch their Electoral College votes from Clinton to Trump. The final Electoral College tally was Trump's 304 to Clinton's 227, with seven "faithless" electors who voted for other candidates, though this also did not change the election results and in fact, took only two votes away from Trump while taking five away from Clinton. In Hawaii, Senator Bernie Sanders (I-VT) received one electoral vote. In Texas, Governor John Kasich (R-OH) received one electoral vote, and former representative Ron Paul (R-TX) received one electoral vote. In Washington, former secretary of state Colin Powell received three electoral votes and Faith Spotted Eagle (a Native American activist) received one electoral vote.

On January 20, 2017, Trump took the oath of office as the 45th president of the United States. He entered office with the lowest approval rating (45%, according to Gallup) of any president since the advent of public opinion polling in the 1930s, and his approval rating has gone lower since. Since then, the so-called "resistance" movement against Trump has continued, as have protests against Trump and/or his administration's policies, including the Women's March in Washington, D.C., on January 21, a Day Without Immigrants on February 16, a Day Without a Woman on March 8, the March for Science on April 22, an Impeachment March on July 2, as well as several protests at various Trump properties. There were numerous lines of attack against Trump and his administration during his first several months in office, with many of Trump's actions considered controversial and/or unconventional. A prominent story line in the news media has been about alleged Russia "collusion" with the Trump campaign during the 2016 election. In early January, intelligence agencies concluded that the Russian government interfered in the election to influence the outcome in favor of Trump—often by planting fake stories to denigrate Clinton. Numerous investigations were launched by the FBI and in intelligence committees in the House and Senate. Trump called many of these efforts a "hoax" and "fake news"; his firing of FBI director James Comey in May 2017 would lead to the appointment of a special prosecutor, former FBI director Robert Mueller, to investigate these allegations.

Politically, Trump and his agenda have been met with nearly unanimous opposition from Democrats in Congress, and Trump continues to battle with various members of his own party as well (ranging from Senate Majority Leader Mitch McConnell of Kentucky to prominent members of the Senate like John McCain of Arizona). Many of Trump's policy decisions have been called controversial by his critics, including a travel ban for several majority Muslim countries (initially blocked by some lower federal courts, though the Supreme Court reinstated key provisions in June 2017); his withdrawal of the United States from the 2015 Paris Climate Accord; and attempts to repeal and replace Obamacare, among others.

Trump continued to rail against various members of the news media, labeling many stories "fake news" during rallies, interviews, and on social media. He also refused to attend the White House Correspondents' Association dinner in April. His administration has seen various staff shake-ups within the first several months (including changes in key positions such as chief of staff, press secretary, national security adviser, and others), and the presence of his daughter and son-in-law as policy advisers has contributed to various "palace intrigue" stories in the press about in-fighting and factions within the administration. Trump's comments following a violent protest in Charlottesville, Virginia, in July, in which he did not immediately condemn by name the white supremacist groups who organized the rally, brought extensive criticism from across the political spectrum.

CONCLUSION

Trump is like no other president who has held the office, and everything that he does and says seems to generate controversy among various individuals and groups. Unfairly or not, many of his harshest critics continue to judge him based on a standard set by those presidents who preceded Trump, yet Trump is not only vastly different in his experience and approach to the job, but he does not seem to care if he conforms to expectations. Many of Trump's opponents talk of impeachment, yet Trump's fiercest supporters continue to rally behind him. The paradox for Trump's presidency lies in the fact that the antiestablishment fervor that helped him win the White House has not been as helpful in governing, which often means working and cooperating to get things done within the Washington establishment. Hatred, enemies, and lines of attack may not be Trump's only legacy as president, but they will surely play a prominent role.

Lori Cox Han

Further Reading

Allen, Jonathan, and Amie Parnes. *Shattered: Inside Hillary Clinton's Doomed Campaign.* New York: Crown, 2017.

Gingrich, Newt. *Understanding Trump.* New York: Hachette, 2017.

Han, Lori Cox, and Diane J. Heith. *Presidents and the American Presidency,* 2nd ed. New York: Oxford University Press, 2018.

Pollak, Joel, and Larry Schweikart. *How Trump Won: The Inside Story of a Revolution.* Washington, D.C.: Regnery, 2017.

ABOUT THE EDITOR AND CONTRIBUTORS

EDITOR

Lori Cox Han is professor of political science at Chapman University. With research and teaching interests in the presidency, media and politics, and women and politics, she is the author of several books, including *Presidents and the American Presidency*, 2nd ed. (coauthor Diane J. Heith); *Women, Power, and Politics: The Fight for Gender Equality in the United States* (coauthor Caroline Heldman); *In It to Win: Electing Madam President*; *A Presidency Upstaged: The Public Leadership of George H. W. Bush*; and *Governing from Center Stage: White House Communication Strategies during the Television Age of Politics*. She is also editor of *New Directions in the American Presidency*, 2nd ed.; and coeditor of *Rethinking Madam President: Are We Ready for a Woman in the White House?*; *The Presidency and the Challenge of Democracy*; and *In the Public Domain: Presidents and the Challenge of Public Leadership*. She is past president of the Presidency Research Group, an organized section of the American Political Science Association devoted to the study of the presidency. She received her PhD in political science from the University of Southern California.

CONTRIBUTORS

Randall E. Adkins is professor of political science and associate dean of the College of Arts & Sciences at the University of Nebraska at Omaha, where he teaches courses on the presidency, Congress, political parties, and campaigns and elections. He received his PhD from Miami University, and he is a former American Political Science Association Congressional Fellow.

Dave Bridge is associate professor of political science at Baylor University, where he specializes in Supreme Court politics within American political development.

His recent publications can be found in *Polity, Law & Social Inquiry;* and *Journal of Church & State.* He received his PhD from the University of Southern California.

Lara M. Brown is associate professor and director of the Graduate School of Political Management (GSPM) at the George Washington University. She is the author of *Jockeying for the American Presidency: The Political Opportunism of Aspirants.* She received her PhD from the University of California, Los Angeles.

Jordan T. Cash is a doctoral student in the Department of Political Science at Baylor University. His research focuses on American institutions, constitutional law, and American political thought. He earned his bachelor's degree in history and political science from the University of Nebraska at Omaha and his master's degree in political science from Baylor University.

John W. Compton is associate professor of political science at Chapman University. His most recent book is *The Evangelical Origins of the Living Constitution.* He received his PhD from the University of California, Los Angeles.

Richard S. Conley is associate professor of political science at the University of Florida. His research interests include the presidency, presidential-congressional relations, comparative executives, and Native American politics. His recent books include *The Historical Dictionary of the Reagan-Bush Era, Presidential-Congressional Relations,* and *The Historical Dictionary of the U.S. Constitution.* His received his PhD from the University of Maryland.

Meredith Conroy is assistant professor of political science at California State University, San Bernardino. She is the author of *Masculinity, Media, and the American Presidency.* She received her PhD from the University of California, Santa Barbara.

David A. Crockett is professor and chair of the Department of Political Science at Trinity University. Often asked if he is related to the famous Davy Crockett, he says that he is not a direct descendant, but a first cousin five times removed. He is the author of *The Opposition Presidency: Leadership and the Constraints of History* and *Running against the Grain: How Opposition Presidents Win the White House,* as well as numerous articles on presidential politics. He received his PhD from the University of Texas at Austin.

Joseph G. Dawson III is professor of history at Texas A&M University. His publications include *Commanders in Chief: Presidential Leadership in Modern Wars,* and articles in the *Journal of Military History* and the *Journal of Strategic Studies*. He earned his PhD in history from Louisiana State University.

Darin DeWitt is assistant professor in the Department of Political Science at California State University, Long Beach. His research and teaching interests include American institutions, political parties, and state politics. He received his PhD in political science from the University of California, Los Angeles.

Graham G. Dodds is associate professor of political science at Concordia University in Montreal, Canada. His research focuses on American political development and the U.S. president's use of unilateral directives. He is the author of *Take Up Your Pen: Unilateral Presidential Directives in American Politics*. He earned his PhD from the University of Pennsylvania and has worked as a research fellow at the Brookings Institution and as a legislative assistant for a member of the U.S. House of Representatives.

Victoria A. Farrar-Myers is a senior fellow at the John Goodwin Tower Center for Political Studies at Southern Methodist University. Among her many publications, she is the author of *Scripted for Change: The Institutionalization of the American Presidency*. She has served as the 2014 Fulbright distinguished chair in American politics in Australia and as an APSA congressional fellow. She received her PhD from the University of Albany, SUNY.

Craig Goodman is assistant professor of political science at the University of Houston–Victoria. He teaches classes on Congress, the presidency, and Texas politics. He received his PhD from the University of Houston.

Lilly J. Goren is professor of political science and global studies at Carroll University. Her teaching and research interests include American government, the presidency, public policy, politics and culture, and political theory. Her books include *Mad Men and Politics: Nostalgia and the Remaking of Modern America*; *Women and the White House: Gender, Popular Culture, and Presidential Politics* (winner of both the 2014 Susan Koppelman Book Award and the 2014 Peter C. Rollins Book Award); *You've Come a Long Way, Baby: Women, Politics, and Popular Culture*; and *Not in My District: The Politics of Military Base Closures*.

Evan Haglund is assistant professor of public policy at the U.S. Coast Guard Academy. Prior to completing his PhD in political science at Vanderbilt University, he was a foreign service officer, with assignments at U.S. embassies in Ljubljana, Slovenia, and Accra, Ghana. He worked as a legislative analyst for a D.C. lobbying firm after receiving his bachelor's degree in public policy studies from the University of

Chicago. His research focuses on presidential appointments and executive branch performance.

Tomislav Han is an independent scholar with research expertise in U.S. constitutional and intellectual history. He is the author of *The Transformation of Aristotelian Political Epistemology in Eighteenth-Century American Constitutional Discourse* and coauthor of *Handbook to American Democracy*. He received his PhD in history from the University of Southern California.

Andrew Harman is a foreign affairs scholar and student of the history of conflict. He earned an MA in war and society at Chapman University and has published articles discussing African American civil rights as well as World War II.

Erin Hayden is a 2017 graduate of the University of Vermont and is currently in the Masters of Public Policy Program at American University.

Caroline Heldman is associate professor of politics at Occidental College in Los Angeles and the research director for the Geena Davis Institute for Gender in Media. Her research specializes in media, the presidency, and systems of power (race, class, gender). She received her PhD from Rutgers University. She is the author of *Protest Politics in the Marketplace: Consumer Activism in the Corporate Age*; *The New Campus Anti-Rape Movement: Internet Activism and Social Justice*; and *Women, Power, and Politics: The Fight for Gender Equality in the United States* (with Lori Cox Han); and coeditor of *Rethinking Madam President: Are We Ready for a Woman in the White House?*

Karen Hoffman is visiting assistant professor of political science and associate director of the Les Aspin Center for Government at Marquette University. Her research interests include political communication and political institutions, including presidential rhetoric and media studies. She is the author of *Popular Leadership in the Presidency: Origins and Practice*. She received her PhD from the University of Chicago.

Jennifer Rose Hopper is assistant professor of political science at Southern Connecticut State University, where she specializes in the American presidency, mass media, and political communication. She is the author of *Presidential Framing in the 21st Century News Media: The Politics of the Affordable Care Act*.

Stephen F. Knott is professor of National Security Affairs at the United States Naval War College, and the Thomas and Mabel Guy professor of history and government at the Ashbrook Center at Ashland University. He is the author of *Alexander Hamilton and the Persistence of Myth* and *Rush to Judgment: George W. Bush, the War on Terror, and His Critics.*

Paul Landow is assistant professor of political science at University of Nebraska at Omaha. He received his PhD from the University of Nebraska and concentrates his teaching and research on the politics of Omaha and Nebraska.

Theresa Marchant-Shapiro is associate professor of political science at Southern Connecticut State University. Her most recent book is *Professional Pathways to the Presidency*, which examines how well prior professional experiences prepare presidents for greatness once in office. She earned her BA from Brigham Young University and her MA and PhD from the University of Chicago. Her research interests are connected to decision theory—in terms both of mass political behavior and of public leadership.

Janet M. Martin is professor of government and legal studies at Bowdoin College. Her research and teaching interests center on the U.S. presidency and Congress. Her most recent book, coedited with MaryAnne Borrelli, is *The Gendered Executive: A Comparative Analysis of Presidents, Prime Ministers, and Chief Executives.* She is also the author of *The Presidency and Women: Promise, Performance, and Illusion*, which won the Richard Neustadt prize in 2004.

Mary McHugh is executive director of the Stevens Service Learning Center and adjunct faculty member in the Political Science Department at Merrimack College in North Andover, Massachusetts, where she teaches a variety of classes in U.S. politics and American political institutions. She earned an MA in political science from Boston College, a BA in government and history from Colby College, and is currently working on her dissertation. Her research interests include civic engagement, political humor, the presidency, and Congress.

Colin D. Moore is associate professor of political science and director of the Public Policy Center at the University of Hawaii. He is the author of *American Imperialism and the State, 1893–1921.*

Leah A. Murray is professor of political science and philosophy at Weber State University. Her teaching and research interests include the American presidency, the U.S. Congress, political parties, and campaigns and elections. She received her PhD in political science from the University of Albany, SUNY.

Garrison Nelson is the Elliott A. Brown professor of law, politics, and political behavior at the University of Vermont. He received his AB from Boston University and an MA and PhD from the University of Iowa. He is the author of more than 150 articles and professional papers on national politics focusing on the U.S. Congress and elections in Vermont. He is an editor of the seven-volume *Committees in the U.S. Congress, 1789–2010*; coauthor of the *Austin-Boston Connection: Five Decades of House Democratic Leadership, 1937–1989*; and author of *Pathways to the U.S. Supreme Court: From the Arena to the Monastery*. His most recent book is *John William McCormack: A Political Profile*.

Curt Nichols is associate professor at Baylor University. He specializes in the study of the presidency, American political development, and public law. His latest project, a book tentatively entitled *A Tide in the Affairs of Presidents*, traces the source of cyclical dynamics in American politics to new mainsprings. This work further explores how presidents have periodically led efforts to overcome complicated iterations of the "crisis of governing legitimacy," which is now placed at the crest of the recurrent, wave-like flow of political time.

Shannon Bow O'Brien is a lecturer in the Government Department at the University of Texas at Austin. She received her PhD from the University of Florida. Her primary areas of research are the American presidency and American political development. She has a forthcoming book entitled *Why Presidential Speech Locations Matter*.

Anne C. Pluta is assistant professor of political science at Rowan University. Her research interests include presidential communication and the media. Her work has appeared in *Presidential Studies Quarterly* and *Congress & the Presidency*. She received her PhD from the University of California, Santa Barbara.

Daniel E. Ponder is L. E. Meador professor of political science at Drury University. A specialist in American politics and political institutions, he is the author of *Good Advice: Information and Policy Making in the White House*, as well as numerous articles, essays, and book chapters. His most recent book is *Presidential Leverage: Approval, Trust, and the American State*. He received his PhD in political science at Vanderbilt University.

Robert E. Ross is assistant professor in the Department of Political Science at Utah State University. His research interests include American political development, constitutional theory, and the development of representative institutions in American politics. He has published in *Publius: The Journal of Federalism* and *Polity*.

Nicholas Evan Sarantakes is associate professor of strategy and policy at the U.S. Naval War College in Newport, Rhode Island. He earned a BA from the University of Texas, an MA from the University of Kentucky, and a PhD in history from the University of Southern California. He is the author of five books, including his most recent, *Making Patton: A Classic War Film's Epic Journey to the Silver Screen*. His current research interests include urban warfare and the World War II home front. He has won five writing awards for his articles.

Jeremy Schmuck is a graduate student at Baylor University studying international relations and American government. His current research interests include presidential leadership and the relationship of the U.S. Supreme Court to Congress and the presidency.

Max J. Skidmore is University of Missouri curators' distinguished professor of political science, and teaches at the University of Missouri–Kansas City. His recent books include *Presidents, Pandemics, and Politics*; *Poverty in America*; *Maligned Presidents: The Late 19th Century*; and *Bulwarks against Poverty*. He is editor of the international peer-reviewed quarterly journal, *Poverty and Public Policy*. His PhD is from the University of Minnesota.

Robert A. Slayton is the Henry Salvatori professor of American values and traditions in the Department of History at Chapman University. He is the author of eight books, including *Beauty in the City: The Ashcan School* and *Empire Statesman: The Rise and Redemption of Al Smith*. He received his PhD in history from Northwestern University.

Scott J. Spitzer is associate professor of political science at California State University, Fullerton. His research focuses on the U.S. presidency, racial politics, and social welfare policy making, particularly in the 1960s and 1970s. His work has been published in *Presidential Studies Quarterly* and *The Sixties: A Journal of History, Politics and Culture*. He received his PhD from Columbia University.

Bernard von Bothmer teaches American history at the University of San Francisco, where he received USF's 2010 Distinguished Lecturer Award for Excellence in Teaching and USF's 2016 Distinguished Adjunct Teaching Award, and also teaches at Dominican University of California. He received a BA with honors from Brown University, an MA from Stanford University, and a PhD from Indiana University. He is the author of *Framing the Sixties: The Use and Abuse of a Decade from Ronald Reagan to George W. Bush*.

Donald A. Zinman is associate professor of political science at Grand Valley State University. His research relies on an American political development approach to study political parties, the presidency, and elections. He is the author of *The Heir Apparent Presidency*. He received his PhD in political science from the University of Texas–Austin.

INDEX

Note: Page numbers in **bold** indicate the corresponding chapter for each president.